FROMMER'S

SPAIN & MOROCCO ON $25 A DAY

by Darwin Porter

1983-1984 Edition

Published by Frommer/Pasmantier Publishers
A Simon & Schuster Division of
Gulf & Western Corporation
1230 Avenue of the Americas
New York, NY 10020

ISBN 0–671–44792–0

Manufactured in the United States of America

*Although every effort was made to ensure the accuracy
of price information appearing in this book,
it should be kept in mind that prices
can and do fluctuate in the course of time.*

CONTENTS

Introduction   **SPAIN ON $25 A DAY**   1

    1. How to Save Money on All
      Your Travels—The $15-A-Day
      Travel Club   2

Chapter I   **GETTING THERE**   5

    1. Plane Economics   5
    2. Traveling Within Spain   7

Chapter II   **THE SCENE IN SPAIN**

    From Bullfights to Hotels to
      Sangría   10

Chapter III   **MADRID**   23

    1. The ABCs of Madrid   26
    2. Hotels in Madrid   35
    3. The Restaurants of Madrid   46
    4. The Top Sights   59
    5. The Sporting Life   73
    6. Shopping in Madrid   74
    7. Madrid After Dark   78

Chapter IV   **RING AROUND MADRID**   86

    1. Toledo   87
    2. Aranjuez   96
    3. El Escorial and the Valley of
      the Fallen   98
    4. Segovia and La Granja   102
    5. Alcalá de Henares and El Pardo   107
    6. Ávila   110
    7. Guadalupe   114
    8. Mérida   115
    9. Zafra   116
    10. Badajoz   117

Chapter V	CITIES OF THE HEARTLAND	119
	1. Salamanca	120
	2. Zamora	124
	3. León	125
	4. Valladolid	128
	5. Burgos	130
	6. Cuenca	134
Chapter VI	ANDALUSIA	137
	1. Jaén, Baeza, and Úbeda	138
	2. Córdoba	141
	3. Seville	148
	4. Jerez and Cádiz	159
	5. The Huelva District	165
	6. Ronda	166
	7. Granada	169
Chapter VII	THE COSTA DEL SOL	179
	1. Algeciras	180
	2. Tarifa	181
	3. Estepona	182
	4. Puerto Banús	184
	5. San Pedro de Alcantara	185
	6. Marbella	186
	7. Fuengirola and Los Boliches	192
	8. Mijas	194
	9. Torremolinos	196
	10. Málaga	206
	11. Nerja	211
	12. Almería	213
Chapter VIII	VALENCIA AND THE COSTA BLANCA	215
	1. Valencia	215
	2. Benidorm	223
	3. Alicante	227
	4. Elche	231
	5. Murcia	232
Chapter IX	SETTLING INTO BARCELONA	234
	1. Finding a Room	235
	2. The Catalán Cuisine	240
	3. The Top Sights	245
	4. The City After Dark	250

Chapter X	**BRANCHING OUT FROM BARCELONA**	**253**
	1. Montserrat	253
	2. Tarragona	255
	3. Sitges	257
	4. Andorra	261
	5. Lloret de Mar	264
	6. Tossá de Mar	266
	7. Cadaqués	269
	8. Figueras	270
	9. Cardona	272
	10. Gerona	272
Chapter XI	**ZARAGOZA AND PAMPLONA**	**274**
	1. Zaragoza	274
	2. Pamplona	279
Chapter XII	**ALONG THE ATLANTIC**	**282**
	1. San Sebastián	283
	2. Guernica	289
	3. Santander	290
	4. Santillana del Mar and the Caves of Altamira	292
	5. Oviedo	295
	6. La Coruña	296
	7. Santiago de Compostela	297
	8. Pontevedra	300
	9. Vigo	301
	10. Tuy	302
Chapter XIII	**THE BALEARIC ISLANDS**	**304**
	1. Finding a Room in Majorca	306
	2. Sampling the Cuisine	311
	3. Island Attractions	314
	4. Ciudad de Ibiza	321
	5. San Antonio Abad	325
	6. Santa Eulalia del Rio	327
	7. Minorca	328
Chapter XIV	**GIBRALTAR**	**334**
	1. Where to Stay	335
	2. Where to Eat	338
	3. What to See and Do	342
	4. The Rock After Dark	347

Chapter XV **THE CANARY ISLANDS** **349**

   1. Gran Canaria (Las Palmas) **352**
   2. Tenerife **367**
   3. Lanzarote **389**
   4. Fuerteventura **405**

Chapter XVI **MOROCCO ON $25 A DAY** **407**

   1. The ABCs of Morocco **408**
   2. Tangier **423**
   3. Ceuta **433**
   4. Tetuan **434**
   5. Chaouen **435**
   6. Rabat **436**
   7. Meknes **441**
   8. Fez **445**
   9. Marrakesh **452**
   10. The Edge of the Sahara **462**
   11. Casablanca **466**
   12. Essaouira **471**
   13. Agadir **472**
   14. The Anti-Atlas **475**

Appendix **THE FOOD AND THE LANGUAGE**

   1. Menu Translations **478**
   2. Capsule Vocabulary **481**

MAPS

Spain 11
Central Madrid 25
Madrid 60
One-Day Tours from Madrid 87
Western Spain 126
Seville 149
Granada 168
Valencia 216
Barcelona 236
Central Barcelona 246
Eastern Spain 278
Mallorca (Majorca) 305
Canary Islands 351
Morocco 409

The author gratefully acknowledges the contributions of Pierre Français for his field work in researching this guide, as well as Margaret Foresman, longtime newspaper editor of Key West, Florida, for her editorial assistance. I am also appreciative of the research efforts of Mr. and Mrs. Peter J. E. Barnes of London, England.

Inflation Alert!!!

Spain, once one of the cheapest countries in the Western world, has witnessed some of the worst inflation in Europe. Prices in Madrid have been compared with those of Frankfurt, Germany. Morocco also has experienced dramatic rises in prices, although nothing comparable to Spain.

Although the budget hotel and restaurant shopper will still find many bargains, know that some overeager hoteliers, in their leap forward, have been known to increase prices more than 100% within a one-to two-year period. Of course, they are the exception rather than the rule.

Without exception, it can be predicted that every hotel and restaurant listed in this guide will raise their tariffs during the lifetime of this edition—perhaps by no more than 20% to 30%, but that is painful enough. When using this guide in planning your budget for a trip, it is wise to take into account the probable increases.

The author of this book has spent laborious hours of field research trying to ensure the accuracy of prices that appear here. As we go to press, we believe we have obtained the most reliable data possible—but we cannot predict in these uncertain times just how long these tariffs will hold.

SPAIN ON $25 A DAY

SPAIN IS EUROPE'S lady of mystery. Dressed in jet-black velvet, she softens her austerity with a red rose.

By the millions, suitors cross her courtyard. Some stay forever; others retreat at the sight of something brutal in her cold dark eyes; still others return again and again, as if by chance—on some off moment—they will seduce her.

She is the eternal enchantress, a cloak-and-dagger queen who has never embraced today—much less tomorrow. She reaches out and takes the inventions of Western man and uses them for her convenience. But she never makes them her own.

For her glory she looks not to washing machines and television sets. Rather, she casts her eye on a more golden day when her star was in ascendancy. A day when her soldiers of fortune sailed throughout the world—Columbus to America, Balboa to the Pacific, Pizarro to launch the conquest of Peru, Cortés to begin his march through Mexico. On their heavily laden galleons, gold and silver were shipped back to her treasure chest.

She used this booty unwisely. Fortune turned against her. But in her deepest despair she never hid behind her fan, preferring to face the sight and sound of death. She remained—and is to this day—regal and proud, always the queen.

By all means, pay this lady of Spain a visit.

THE SPECTACLE OF SPAIN: Spain is a land of golden-brown plains, snow-capped mountains, valleys with terraces of grapevines, olive groves, unspoiled fishing villages, snug harbors, sandy beaches, ancient walled cities, great art treasures, romantic castles, Gothic cathedrals, cave dwellings, flower gardens, scrub grass, and palaces left over from the Golden Age.

Picture yourself as part of the life of this striking, dramatic country.

—You're in a flower-filled Moorish courtyard drinking cool sangría and listening to the splashing sounds of the same fountain that harem girls heard centuries ago.

—You're in the Plaza de Toros watching a savage, thick-necked black bull lift a horse and its rider off the ground and hurl them into the air.

—You're lying on the beach in Marbella watching as a bikini-clad French movie star emerges from the water.

—You're looking at a lantern that goes on at sundown, casting a faint glow against a background of the plains of La Mancha; and, in the distance, on the ridge of a hill, you think you see that lanky scarecrow, Don Quixote, on his weary Rozinante, trailed by his faithful, donkey-riding squire.

My aim is to aid you in a discovery of some of the beauty and mystery of a land that is often violent, always passionate, and forever intriguing.

THE QUESTION OF PRICE: Spain is a mecca for the traveler who craves beauty, a colorful and rich culture, comfort, and bountiful food.

In days gone by, the proud caballero was the world's greatest tourist, calling on the Incas or the American Indian. Now the tide has turned. The world is coming to Spain in armadas that would have dwarfed Philip's, making it the most popular tourist attraction in Europe. But the miles and miles of white-skinned northerners lining the beaches from the Costa Brava to the Costa de la Luz were bound to alter the price structure of Spain.

Unlike the always-plentiful bargains in the Spain of the past, today's values must be sought out; they won't come looking for you. Part of the purpose of this book is to help you find them quickly. Regrettably, the price structure of Spain has now caught up with continental Europe. I still don't find it as expensive as Frankfurt and Paris, as do some columnists.

However, Madrid and the Costa del Sol are expensive, and you must proceed through them with caution.

In the less visited places, especially those not trampled by tourists, you'll find plenty of low-priced budget establishments.

THE $25-A-DAY BUDGET: The budget that I have allocated—$25 per day per person—covers the basic living costs of three meals a day and the price of a room. Naturally, the costs of sightseeing, transportation, shopping, laundry, and entertainment are *extra,* although I'll show you how to keep those expenses trimmed to a minimum.

Travel in Spain and Morocco offers several bonuses for $25 a day. For example, more often than not you will be given a private bath with your well-appointed bedroom. Similarly, for the price of the menu of the day (a fixed-price meal of the day), you'll always get three courses, plus the regional wine. Even the tip is included in the bill, although it's customary to leave something extra if the service has been good.

The $25-a-day budget roughly breaks down this way—$15 per person (based on double occupancy) for a room and a continental breakfast, $4 for lunch, and $6 for dinner.

Of course, for those who can afford more, I've included a lot of splurges, both hotels and restaurants that offer good value in the more medium-priced travel range.

1. How to Save Money on All Your Travels—The $15-A-Day Travel Club

In just a few paragraphs, you'll begin your exploration of Spain, Morocco, and the Canary Islands. But before you do, you may want to learn how to save money on all your trips: by joining the widely known $15-A-Day Travel Club, which has gone into its 20th successful year of operation.

The Club was formed at the urging of readers of the $$$-A-Day and Dollarwise Guides, who felt that such an organization could bring continuing travel information and a sense of community to economy-minded travelers in all parts of the world. And so it does!

In keeping with the budget concept, the membership fee is low and is immediately exceeded by the value of your benefits. Upon receipt of U.S. $14 (U.S. residents), or $16 (Canadian, Mexican, and other foreign residents), to cover one year's membership, we will send all new members by return mail (book rate) the following items:

(1) The latest edition of any *two* of the following books (please designate in your letter which two books you wish to receive).

Europe on \$20 a Day
Australia on \$20 a Day
England and Scotland on \$25 a Day
Greece on \$20 a Day
Hawaii on \$25 a Day
Ireland on \$25 a Day
Israel on \$25 & \$30 a Day
Mexico on \$20 a Day
New Zealand on \$20 & \$25 a Day
Scandinavia on \$25 a Day
South America on \$25 a Day
Spain and Morocco (plus the Canary Is.) on \$25 a Day
Washington, D.C. on \$25 a Day

Dollarwise Guide to the Caribbean (including Bermuda and the Bahamas)
Dollarwise Guide to Canada
Dollarwise Guide to Egypt
Dollarwise Guide to England and Scotland
Dollarwise Guide to France
Dollarwise Guide to Germany
Dollarwise Guide to Italy
Dollarwise Guide to Portugal (plus Madeira and the Azores)
Dollarwise Guide to California and Las Vegas
Dollarwise Guide to Florida
Dollarwise Guide to New England
Dollarwise Guide to the Southeast and New Orleans
(Dollarwise Guides discuss accommodations and facilities in all price ranges with emphasis on the medium-priced.)

The Adventure Book
(From the Alps to the Arctic, from the Sahara to the Southwest, this stunning four-color showcase features over 200 of the world's finest adventure travel trips.)

How to Beat the High Cost of Travel
(This practical guide details how to save money on absolutely all travel items—accommodations, transportation, dining, sightseeing, shopping, taxes, and more. Includes special budget information for seniors, students, singles, and families.)

The New York Athlete
(The ultimate guide to all the sports facilities in New York City for jocks and novices.)

Museums in New York
(A complete guide to all the museums, historic houses, gardens, zoos, and more in the five boroughs. Illustrated with over 200 photographs.)

The Speak Easy Phrase Book
(The four most useful languages—French, German, Spanish, and Italian —all in one convenient, easy-to-use phrase guide.)

Where to Stay USA
(By the Council on International Educational Exchange, this extraordinary guide is the first to list accommodations in all 50 states that cost anywhere from $3 to $25 per night.)

(2) A one-year subscription to the quarterly eight-page tabloid newspaper—**The Wonderful World of Budget Travel**—which keeps you up to date on fast-breaking developments in low-cost travel in all parts of the world bringing you the latest money-saving information—the kind of information you'd have to pay $25 a year to obtain elsewhere. This consumer-conscious publication also provides special services to readers: **The Traveler's Directory** (a list of members all over the world who are willing to provide hospitality to other members as they pass through their home cities); **Share-a-Trip** (offers and requests from members for travel companions who can share costs and help avoid the burdensome single supplement); and **Readers Ask . . . Readers Reply** (travel questions from members to which other members reply with authentic firsthand information).

(3) A copy of **Arthur Frommer's Guide to New York,** a newly revised pocket-size guide to hotels, restaurants, nightspots, and sightseeing attractions in all price ranges throughout the New York area.

(4) Your personal membership card which, once received, entitles you to purchase through the Club all Arthur Frommer publications for a third to a half off their regular retail prices during the term of your membership.

So why not join this hardy band of international budgeteers and participate in its exchange of travel information and hospitality? Simply send your name and address, together with your membership fee of $14 (U. S. residents) or $16 (Canadian, Mexican, and other foreign residents), in U. S. currency to: $15-A-Day Travel Club, Inc., Frommer/Pasmantier Publishers, 1230 Avenue of the Americas, New York, NY 10020. And please remember to specify which *two* of the books in section (1) above you wish to receive in your initial package of members' benefits. Or, if you prefer, use the last page of this book, simply checking off the two books you want and enclosing $14 or $16 in U. S. currency.

THE FUTURE OF THIS BOOK: Spain, let us remember, is a volatile country: today's undiscovered fishing village may be tomorrow's chicly fashionable beach resort. Therefore I'd like to encourage you to share your reactions to places already recommended—Has the service deteriorated? Have the prices gone up?—as well as any new finds you may have discovered. Have you stumbled upon an unheralded inexpensive restaurant? A pension that is colorful, clean and comfortable? A village fiesta unique and impressive?

All of us have one common goal: to travel far and wide as comfortably and inexpensively as we can. Your assistance can be helpful in achieving that aim. Like its sister books, *Spain and Morocco on $25 a Day* has sections devoted to readers' suggestions. If yours is included in the next edition—and that goes for the supplements on Morocco and the Canary Islands as well—you will not only get a free copy of the new book, but you'll have the pleasure of sharing a special treasure with others:

Please send your comments, discoveries or criticisms to Darwin Porter, Frommer/Pasmantier Publishers, 1230 Avenue of the Americas, New York, NY 10020.

Chapter 1

GETTING THERE

1. Plane Economics
2. Traveling Within Spain

IN RELATION TO the other Western European countries, Spain sometimes seems a bit remote, perched as it is on the seemingly isolated Iberian peninsula. But in terms of its distance from North America, Spain is one of the closest of all Western European countries. I'll first discuss the basic structure of air fares to Spain, then deal with methods of traveling within Spain once you arrive.

1. Plane Economics

In what follows I'll try to unravel the current options available by classifying fares according to their basic function. Remember, however, to check the airlines to find the most up-to-date fares and those that most suit your travel plans and needs. And note that all the fares presented in these pages, while accurate as of this writing (autumn, 1982), could be out of date at the blink of an eye.

APEX: The most heavily used fare to Madrid is the round-trip APEX, which is valid for a stay abroad from 7 to 180 days. This Advance Purchase Ticket must be bought at least 21 days in advance of an outbound flight to Madrid.

In general (subject to variations among the airlines) the seasons are: basic —the winter months; shoulder—generally the months of May and September eastbound; June westbound; and peak—June, July, and August, eastbound; July, August, and part of September, westbound. The costs round trip from New York to Madrid are currently $572 basic, $594 shoulder, and peak $647.

The cheapest fare is the Midweek APEX which leaves New York for Madrid only on Tuesday and Wednesday. The round-trip cost is $480 in basic, $498 in shoulder, and $543 in peak. Tickets must be purchased at least 14 days in advance of travel, and the stay abroad must be a minimum of 7 days, but not more than 180 days.

REGULAR FARES: If for some reason you cannot meet the requirements of the APEX ticket, you may need to purchase a regular ticket. However, the cost is substantially more, and there is no shoulder season. The low-season fare is $974 per person round trip between New York and Madrid, the price rising in peak to $1234 round trip. On this type of ticket, you can fly at your discretion, without restrictions on the days spent on land.

Air Services to Madrid

Iberia has daily flights which go directly from New York to Madrid. It also flies directly from Miami to Madrid on Tuesday, Thursday, Saturday, and Sunday. Twice a week an Iberia flight originates in Washington, D.C., stopping first in New York before proceeding to Madrid. There are also Iberia flights from Montréal to Madrid on Monday, Wednesday, Thursday, Saturday, and Sunday.

In addition, **TWA** has direct flights from New York to Madrid and other flights which leave New York but stop over in Lisbon before flying on to Madrid.

Charter Flights

Transatlantic air fares climb steadily, but cheap charter flights from New York to Madrid can be arranged through **Nueva York Hispaño,** 261 West 70th St., New York, NY 10023 (tel. 212/595-2400). This office uses both Iberia, the national airline, and Spantax, a private Spanish charter firm.

Prices vary according to season: April 1 to April 30, round trip is $439; one way, $255. May 1 to June 14 and August 15 to October 30, round trip is $439; one way, $255. June 15 to August 15 (the high season), round trip costs $489; one way, $285.

Flights to Morocco

Royal Air Maroc has direct flights from New York to Casablanca, operating four times a week during the peak season. During off-season months, such as November, flights may be curtailed to just two times a week (check with the airline or your travel agency).

The bargain fare is the APEX. In shoulder season (that is, from mid-August to November and from April 1 to mid-June), the round-trip, New York-Casablanca fare is $570. In basic season (November through March), the fare is $523 and rises to $621 in peak season (mid-June to mid-August). The APEX ticket is valid for a stay abroad of from 7 to 180 days, and it must be purchased at least 21 days in advance of an outbound flight to Casablanca.

By the time you read this, these APEX fares will have been raised, although to how much wasn't known at press time. However, they'll be slightly more expensive than the fare below.

The cheapest way to fly from New York to Casablanca round trip is on Royal Air Maroc's "Magical Kingdom Fare." Tickets must be purchased at least 7 days in advance, and on this low-cost fare you must stay abroad a minimum of 7 days, but not more than 60 days. In off-season, November to March 31, the round-trip fare is $545 per person. In shoulder—that is, from April 1 to June 14 and from August 15 to October 31—the fare rises to $570. It peaks at $599, the high-season tariff in effect from June 15 to August 14.

The regular fares from New York to Casablanca are $974 round trip in basic season, going up to $1234 in peak. With these more expensive fares, you can fly as you please during the validity of the ticket. You're also allowed unlimited stopovers to the cities serviced by Royal Air Maroc in Morocco.

A Final Note: As new and cheaper tickets are constantly being offered by the airlines, always check with them or your travel agent for the up-to-the-minute ways of saving money on transportation.

2. Traveling Within Spain

With the exception of its government-owned airlines, **Iberia** and **Aviaco**, Spain's transportation facilities are, in general, a bit less developed and up-to-date than those of other Western European countries—but they make up for their relative dowdiness by the moderate cost of their fares.

THE TRAINS: The **Spanish State Railways (RENFE)** provide the most economic means of discovering the second-largest country in Europe. On peninsular routes, the main long-distance connections are normally served with night express trains with first- and second-class seats and with beds and bunks. There are also fast daytime trains of the Talgo, Ter, Corail, or Electrotrain types, which have a high standard of comfort and high commercial speeds. There is a general fare for these trains, with supplements for bunks, beds, and certain superior-quality trains. Nevertheless, the Spanish railway is one of the most economical in Europe, a fact which makes this mode of transport the most advantageous in the majority of cases.

Direct trains connect Madrid with Paris and Lisbon; Barcelona with Paris and Geneva; and, on the frontiers, at Valencia de Alcantara-Marvão (Portugal), Irun-Hendaye, and Port Bou-Cerbère (France), international connections are easily made. There is also an express from Algeciras to Hendaye with direct coaches.

In general, however, travel by rail in Spain is incredibly slow and difficult, and you must plan well in advance. Sometimes it takes a full day to travel to your destination. For example, count on spending ten hours going from Madrid to Granada. Of course, there are different classes of trains, but even the so-called "fast ones" really aren't.

EURAILPASS: Many in-the-know travelers to Europe have for years been taking advantage of one of its greatest travel bargains, the Eurailpass, which permits unlimited first-class travel in any country in Western Europe, except the British Isles. Passes are purchased for periods as short as 15 days or as long as three months.

Here's how it works. The pass is sold only in North America. Vacationers taking the 15-day low-cost air excursion may purchase a Eurailpass for $250; otherwise, a 21-day pass costs $320; a one-month pass, $390; two months, $530; three months, $650. Children under 4 may travel free, and children under 12 need pay only half fare.

Its advantages are tempting. No tickets, no supplements (simply show the pass to the ticket collector, then settle back to enjoy the European scenery). Seat reservations are required on some trains.

With your Eurailpass, you can also purchase bus and steamship tickets at a reduction. In Spain, for example, you are allowed 15% on certain tours. A pamphlet issued by Eurailpass gives all details.

Those under the age of 26 can purchase a **Eurail Youthpass,** entitling them to unlimited second-class transportation for two months for only $350, or one month for $270. These passes are nontransferable, and if there is any evidence of alteration, the pass is nullified.

Travel agents in all towns and railway agents in such major cities as New York, Montréal, Los Angeles, or Chicago sell the tickets. The Eurailpass is available at the offices of CIT Travel Service, the French National Railroads, the German Federal Railroads, and the Swiss Federal Railways.

If you plan to travel a great deal on the European railroads, you will do well to secure the latest copy of the Thomas Cook Continental Timetable of European Railroads. This comprehensive 500+ page timetable covers all of Europe's mainline rail services with great detail and accuracy. It is available exclusively in North America from Forsyth Travel Library, PO Box 2975, Shawnee Mission, KS 66201, at a cost of $15.95 including postage.

THE BUSES: The bus lines are numerous, low priced, and often most comfortable. Reader Jim Marrion, Holyoke, Massachusetts, writes: "If you are going less than 100 miles, the bus is the only way to travel. You get to see more because the trains always leave you outside the center of the city."

You'll rarely encounter a for-real bus terminal in Spain. Sometimes the hub of transportation is a café, a bar, the street in front of a hotel, or simply a spot at an intersection.

Typical prices include the following: from Madrid to Toledo, a distance of 44 miles (70 kilometers), 190 pesetas ($1.82) one way; from Madrid to Segovia, some 59 miles (95 kilometers), 250 pesetas ($2.40).

Compared to trains, bus service is often excellent. The choice between bus and train was obvious when one reader faced a four-hour run from Algeciras to Seville on the bus, or ten hours by train.

AIR TRAVEL WITHIN SPAIN: Two major airlines operate within the country: the big daddy **Iberia,** and a hard-working smaller sister, **Aviaco.**

Domestic air flights, for the most part, are inexpensive by European standards. For example, you can take a round-trip flight from Barcelona to Palma (the capital of Majorca), then go on to Ibiza (the other leading island in the Balearics), and return to Barcelona for $89.

CAR RENTALS: Whether you're planning an extensive tour of Spain—or have time to visit only the Imperial Cities in the environs of Madrid—I strongly recommend using a rented car. It can free you to explore that hilltop church, that hidden-away beach resort, that remote regional parador (government-run inn), which you'd never reach by train or bus. Naturally, the larger your party, the cheaper the car rental becomes.

Spain offers any number of car-rental firms, including the government-owned **ATESA.**

You can arrange rentals in the Madrid office of ATESA at 59 Gran Vía (tel. 247-73-00). Cars are offered with unlimited mileage—a cheap arrangment if you're planning to do a lot of driving. The typical rate in a Seat model (the Spanish version of Fiat) is 900 pesetas ($8.64) a day, plus 10 pesetas (10¢) per kilometer. Many weekend package deals are offered for 4000 pesetas ($38.40), which includes the first 300 kilometers free. The unlimited-mileage bargain costs 1800 pesetas ($17.28) per day, or else 12,000 pesetas ($115.20) per week. Gasoline, oil, and extra insurance are not included.

Avis is also well represented in Spain, with about 20 depots and kiosks at all the major airports including Barajas. In making a reservation in the United

States, you can call a toll-free number—800/331-2112. **Hertz** is just as efficient, and is also well represented in Spain. Before leaving America, you can make international reservations by calling this toll-free number—800/654-3134.

The curtain now rises on our next chapter, covering general comments on the scene in Spain.

Chapter II

THE SCENE IN SPAIN

From Bullfights to Hotels to Sangría

ENIGMATIC SPAIN is not Europe. Some have compared it to Africa, but it isn't Africa either. It is a unique country, a land that made an institution out of the bullfight, the flamenco dance, the fiesta, and the siesta. Spiritually, it's pitch black or blood red; it recognizes few other colors in its spectrum.

Spain is changing at a rapid rate. A few of its Mediterranean coastal cities are almost ceasing to be Spanish, and are turning instead into international melting pots. Yet in its inland cities, this land of lore is responding to the world interest in its past by restoring its castles and palaces that have rested in decay for hundreds of years. Tourism is like a shot of adrenalin to a country that once appeared to the Western world to have become disillusioned with itself.

Spain is hard to understand and almost impossible to generalize about. One reason for this is that Spain is made up of a group of nations: the Aragonese and the Castilians; the Catalans of the northeast and the Galicians of the northwest; the Basques, and the Andalusians.

THE SIGHTS OF SPAIN: The sights of Spain are staggering. It takes at least two months to see all the major cities—and even that calls for some fast moving. Most of us don't have such an allotment of time, however, and will want to get the most out of Spain in a shorter number of city visits.

It is with this in mind that a personal selection of the "Top Ten Cities" has been made below. This list, of course, should not be taken to imply that Spain does not have country scenery of interest.

But the romance and magic of Spain are to be found in its cities, of which it possesses more legendary ones than any country other than Italy. These have altered their makeup dozens of times through waves of invasions by alien conquerors (such as the Moors).

Here, in no particular order, are my nominations for glamor and greatness (El Escorial, of course, is not a city, but is included in the list, nevertheless): (1) Toledo; (2) Segovia; (3) Madrid; (4) El Escorial; (5) Salamanca; (6) Seville; (7) Granada; (8) Córdoba; (9) Barcelona; and (10) Santiago de Compostela.

PLANNING YOUR ITINERARY: From the standpoint of the visitor, Spain is roughly divided into these sections: **Madrid** and its environs; **Andalusia** (Seville, Córdoba, Granada, the Costa del Sol); **Barcelona,** a jumping-off point for Majorca and the Pyrenees; the **Atlantic Coast,** beginning in the east with San Sebastián and stretching west to La Coruña; and **Valencia** and the **Costa Blanca,** referred to as the **"Levante."**

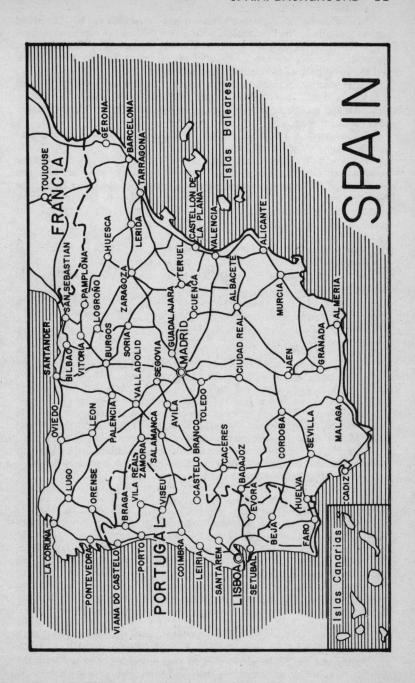

Madrid is the major gateway. But it is not—or should not be—the prime target for pilgrims. The Prado aside, what makes the Spanish capital so intriguing is that it makes such a good excursion base for several of Spain's major attractions: Toledo, Segovia, El Escorial, Ávila, Salamanca, Burgos, Cuenca, and the royal palaces at Aranjuez and La Granja.

After winding up an affair with the cities of the heartland, you might head next for the biggest lure of all, Andalusia, with stopovers at Córdoba, Seville, Granada; and an afternoon spent getting intoxicated (free) in the bodegas at Jerez de la Frontera.

If time remains, you might tie in a trip to Andalusia with an excursion to nearby Tangier on the northwestern coast of Africa.

But you won't know Spain until you've visited **Catalonia,** the **Basque Country,** and **Galicia.** The capital of Catalonia is Barcelona. From there, you can continue with excursions in all directions; north to the Costa Brava, the Pyrenees, and to the little principality of Andorra; then to the monastery of Montserrat; west to Zaragoza; south to the old Roman city of Tarragona; east to the vacation resorts of Majorca, Ibiza, and Minorca.

For readers with the time, a trip along the Atlantic Coast of Spain may also rank as an exceptional travel experience. Beginning at the summer capital and Basque center of San Sebastián, you can journey along this "green coast" to Galicia, with its capital at La Coruña and its major stopover at Santiago de Compostela.

On the way back to Madrid, you can combine the cathedral city of León; the Castilian plain of Zamora, the university city of Salamanca, and the walled city of Ávila.

Of the coastal resorts, the **Costa del Sol** is the winner (with Marbella, Torremolinos, and Málaga recommended, in that order, for places in the sun); the **Costa Brava** is runner-up (Tossá de Mar the brightest star on this sun strip); and the **Costa Blanca** comes in a poor third (with Benidorm and Alicante the chief centers). And one of the best spots, now that it's no longer a German colony, is Sitges, south of Barcelona, on the so-called **Gold Coast (Costa de Oro).** The beach cities of San Sebastián and Santander are quite lovely on the Atlantic Coast—but the Spanish virtually acquire squatters' rights to all the hotel rooms there in July and August.

Valencia, surrounded by orange groves and rice paddies, has many sight-seeing targets that can be shot down in a day—but it's not a place to linger in, as it's a big industrialized port city.

THE SEASONS: Summer: Hot, hot, and hot again, with the cities of Castile (Madrid) and the cities of Andalusia (Seville and Córdoba) stewing up the most scalding brew. Madrid has dry heat; the temperature can hover around 84 degrees Fahrenheit in July, 75 in September. Inland Seville has the dubious reputation of being about the hottest area in Spain in July and August, often baking under temperatures that average around 93 degrees.

Barcelona is humid. The temperature in Majorca in high summer often reaches 91 degrees. On the overcrowded Costa Brava, the essentially European clientele experiences around 81 degrees in July and August. The Costa del Sol has an average of 77-degree heat in summer. The coolest spot in Spain is the Atlantic Coast from San Sebastián to La Coruña, with temperatures in the 70s in July and August.

Spring and Fall: The ideal times to visit nearly all of Spain, with the possible exception of the Atlantic Coast, which experiences heavy rainfall in October and November.

Winter: The coast from Algeciras to Málaga is popular most of the winter, with temperatures reaching a warm 60 to 63 degrees. It gets cold in Madrid, as low as 34 degrees. Majorca is warmer, usually in the 50s, but often dipping into the 40s. Some of the mountain resorts have extreme cold.

Conclusion: May and October are the best months.

BULLFIGHTS—THE SPECTACLE OF DEATH:

A great number of Americans consider bullfighting a cruel and shocking sport. But Ernest Hemingway, in his encyclopedia of bullfighting, *Death in the Afternoon,* pointed out, "The bullfight is not a sport in the Anglo-Saxon sense of the word, that is, it is not an equal contest or an attempt at an equal contest between a bull and a man. Rather it is a tragedy; the death of the bull, which is played, more or less well, by the bull and the man involved and in which there is danger for the man but certain death for the bull." Hemingway, of course, became an aficionado. Perhaps you will, too.

The symbolic inner drama of the bullfight is acted out almost like a ballet—it's certainly an art form. There are those who are convinced that it is not cruelty, but a highly skilled activity calling forth some of man's most important qualities; survival, courage, and style.

Regardless of how you view it—cruel sport, tragedy, art form—this spectacle in the afternoon is an authentically Spanish experience, and, as such, has much to reveal about the character of the land and its people.

In fairness, it should be pointed out that many readers have expressed horror upon viewing a bullfight. I take no official position on it, as it is largely a matter of personal taste. Go at your own risk.

Season and Tickets

The season of the *corridas,* as the bullfights are called, takes place from early spring until the end of October. Fights are held in locations ranging from the oldest ring in remote Ronda to the big-time Plaza de Toros in Madrid. Sunday is corrida day in most major Spanish cities, although Madrid and Barcelona may have fights on Thursday. Other, smaller towns which can't afford many bulls have fights that coincide with their fairs or feast days.

How to purchase a ticket will be described in both the Madrid and Barcelona sections of this book, but these preliminary comments can be made. Tickets fall into three classifications: *Sol* (sun), *sombra* (shade), or *sol y sombra* (a mixture of two—half in the sun, half in the shade, when the sun starts to set). Naturally, the sombra seats are the most expensive; the sombra-y-sol ticket falls into the medium-priced range.

A bullring is called a *Plaza de Toros.* Don't refer to a bullfighter as a toreador. The one who kills the bull is a *matador.* All the use of the word toreador may prove—other than resulting in a laugh from a Spaniard—is that you've seen *Carmen.*

The Fight Itself

The corrida begins with a parade, in which all participants take part. For many viewers, this may be the high point in the afternoon's festivities, as all the bullfighters are clad in their costumes called "suits of light."

The fight begins when the lance-carrying *picadores* on horseback go after the bull and jab him. This is the point in the game at which the first-time viewer often raises objections. The horses are sometimes gored, even though protected by mattresses. If not this, the horse and its rider may be tossed into the air.

Next come the *banderilleros,* whose job is to puncture the bull with pairs of gaily colored darts. This is a major step in preparation for the kill. When the Matador places the darts, it is even more exciting, as chances are he'll be more stylized and skilled than the banderilleros.

After this fanfare, the action narrows down to the lone fighter and the bull. This is the highlight of the afternoon. Gone are the fancy capes. Instead, the matador uses what is known as a *muleta,* a small red cloth. He makes a challenge to the bull, perhaps one known as a *natural,* most often with the muleta held in his left hand. Hemingway called it "the fundamental pass of bullfighting, the simplest, capable of greatest purity of line and the most dangerous to make."

After a number of passes, the time comes for the kill, the "moment of truth." A truly skilled fighter may kill the bull in one thrust. However, a bullfighter's skill at killing is not judged by what happens to the bull after the sword thrust. Nevertheless, it's a common sight to see fighters who make repeated thrusts, arousing a spirit of revenge on the part of the audience. The angry spectators are likely to toss objects into the ring to vent their rage. After the bull drops dead, the highest official at the ring may award the matador an ear from the dead bull, or perhaps give him the tail. The bullfighter may be carried away as a hero, or, if he has displeased the crowd, be chased out of the ring by an angry mob.

Usually, six bulls are killed by three matadors in an afternoon.

FLAMENCO: From the lowliest taberna to the poshest nightclub, you are likely to hear heel clicking, foot stamping, castanet rattling, hand clapping, and the sound of sultry and tortured guitar music. This is flamenco. Its origins lie deep in the Orient, but the Spanish gypsy has given it an original and unique style.

It is a dance dramatizing inner tension. Performed by a great artist, flamenco can tear your heart out. But the growth and popularity of this art form have caused many a mediocre performer to enter the field, and these people are often more concerned with imitation and audience reaction than they are with any lost love. Occasionally you may have to sit through a parade of untalented performers, waiting for the true artist.

Chances are you are familiar with flamenco. But what most Americans consider flamenco is typical of Andalusia. Discovering variations on the theme may spark up many an evening for you.

The usual flamenco place in Spain is, in reality, a cabaret, where you pay a certain amount for the first drink—and this is tantamount to a cover charge.

Flamenco has no story line to follow. The leader, with insistent hand clapping, sets the pace, drawing each of the performers forward. He or she lurks behind and around the performers at all times, trying to infuse them with rhythm. If it is a good rhythm, it can be contagious. You may end up with the castanets yourself, stamping and crying out.

FIESTAS: Year in and year out, the Spaniard celebrates fiestas. Almost all of these events are religious in nature, but they offer entertainment to all, Catholic or not. Both religious and cultural motifs are combined to form this spectacle of Spanish life. Bullfights, parades of colorfully costumed locals, folk singing and dancing, concerts, games, and exhibits lift the fiesta out of merely regional interest.

During the fiesta, all semblance of a regularly scheduled life comes to a halt in the towns or cities. The gears shift rapidly, as the locals pour their energies and enthusiasms into these celebrations (the frenzied preparations leading up to them are almost as exciting as the actual events). When you see the hard life that many of the workers lead, you may better understand why the fiesta is such an important period in which to have an emotional overflow and release.

September, in particular, is one of the most crowded and varied months on the festival calendar, although August offers serious competition. **Semana Santa** (Holy Week), usually from April 11 to 18, is celebrated all over Spain. **Corpus Christi** is another colorful observance time throughout the country. But the calendar is loaded year round.

Many of these fiestas have major variations—and are known by other names. For example, a *romerías,* which you may see along the road, is a pilgrimage to a particular historic site (everybody packs food, as the romerías sometimes last two days). In contrast, a *verbena* is held in a city (Madrid has one) or a town. At a verbena, the nightlife is festive, with a special emphasis placed on folk dancing. Finally, a *fería* (literally, fair) is a special event dear to the Spanish soul. The best known one is the **Fería of Seville,** but there are countless others. Don't expect it to be devoted to cattle shows: singing and dancing are also the rule of the day.

How do you attend a fiesta? When and where are they held? Frankly, there are so many that it would take a thick volume to list and describe them. However, Tourist Bureaus throughout Spain distribute (free) a *Tourist Calendar,* which catalogues all of these folk traditions.

The most recent edition listed more than 3000 such events.

THE HOTEL OUTLOOK: The government regulates the price of hotel and pension rooms in Spain, and the client will not only find a sign listing these prices posted downstairs in the lobby, but an individual card posted in the bedroom, since some rooms, or course, are more expensive than others. The government allows a minimum and a maximum rate, and the prices quoted include taxes and services.

Theoretically, the maximum rate should apply for the better rooms and the peak season—but this is rarely the case. The maximum rate is generally in effect all year. However, at some resorts in the slow season, the rates may be lowered by the management to attract added business. In all instances in this book, I have quoted the higher rate. If you should arrive at a hotel that has decided to charge you the minimum, then you can consider this as an added bonus.

The rate for full board is arrived at simply by adding the price of the meals to the price of the room. There is no obligation, however, to accept full board, except at *pensions* (boarding houses). However, many hotels, hostels, and pensions are permitted to add a 20% surcharge to the price of a room if a guest does not take at least one main meal at the hotel. In such establishments, it's recommended that you take "demi-pension" (that is, breakfast plus either lunch or dinner). The Tourist Ministry also permits many hotels to charge you breakfast, even if you don't have it in the hotel. In other words, breakfast is usually obligatory.

If there are three or more in your party, you may want to ask for an additional bed in your room. In a single room, an additional bed can cost no more than 60% of the maximum price for the room (no more than 35% of the maximum price in a double room).

When you see the sign **Residencia,** it means you can't take any meal at the establishment other than breakfast.

If you have a serious complaint to make against any establishment, you can request the "Official Complaint Book"— *Libro do Reclamaciones.* The hotel management is obligated by law to turn your complaint over to the government authorities within 24 hours. The government does not put up with any nonsense; it wants visitors to be content—and will quickly bring an offender into line.

The Spanish government rates hotels by stars. The most outstanding hotels in Spain are rated five stars, or deluxe, with leading first-class establishments earning four stars. However, for our limited budget, we'll stay mainly with three-star hotels, dipping often into the one- or two-star field for cheaper lodgings.

In addition to hotels, the pensions are among the least expensive accommodations. A liberal sampling of the better pension establishments is included in this guide.

The cheapest places in Spain are designated by light-blue plaques outside the door, **CH** standing for *Casa Huespedes* and **F** for *Fonda.* These are invariably basic but respectable establishments, and some readers have found them "salubrious" as well. Readers John and Gail Pearce of Toronto say: "The magic word for finding cheap accommodation seems to be fonda rather than pension. A fonda proved a saving grace in Toledo."

Warning: As a general rule I always request a room in the rear if the hotel lies on a principal square or main artery. Spain, now that it's switched from the donkey to the automobile and motorcycle, has some of the noisiest city traffic I've encountered in Europe. Thundering buses rumbling through the major cities only add to the decibel count. Another alternative is to seek hotels on quieter side streets, and this guide has many of those.

Staying at Paradores and Albergues

The Spanish Department of Tourism has created some unique accommodations. Throughout the country, deserted castles, monasteries, and palaces have been taken over and turned into hotels. In some cases, first-class modern hotels have thus been created.

At great expense, modern baths, steam heat, and such have been added, yet the tradition that was and is Spain has been retained. These establishments have been furnished with antiques, excellent reproductions, and objects of art. Meals are also served in these government-run hotels. Whenever possible, typical dishes of the region are featured.

The more ambitious of the establishments are called *paradores,* and are in historic as well as scenic areas. The *albergues,* on the other hand, are modern and are built substantially in the Spanish fashion. They are comparable to motels, as they are along the roadside, existing in hotel-scarce sections for the convenience of passing motorists who want overnight stopovers. A client is not allowed to stay in an albergue for more than 48 hours, and the management does not like to accept reservations. But reservations during the peak months at paradores are essential.

In addition, the government also runs *refugios,* which are mostly in remote areas attracting hunters, fishermen, and mountain-climbers. One final establishment—a *hostería*—is a specialty restaurant, such as the one at Alcalá de Henares, near Madrid, which is decorated in the style of a particular province, and offers regional dishes at reasonable prices.

FOOD AND DRINK: For the North American, the Spanish cuisine presents a number of tempting surprises—enough to rate an *Olé*. It also offers a number of gastronomic nightmares, enough to make the palate cry uncle and the stomach rumble something unprintable. Matadors, horsemen, flamenco dancers, the Spaniards are. Great chefs they often are not.

Still, in spite of this drawback, the tastebuds of today's pilgrim are in for better flavors than ever before. Those who traveled in Spain in the '30s, '40s, and '50s could tell a story to make gastronomes swear off food for life. But today the Spanish chef or just plain cook in the tourist-trodden Spain is faced with a dilemma. Tastebuds tell the Spaniard one thing; the sharp-tongued foreigner often disagrees. Being essentially hospitable, the Spaniard tries to adapt. If a foreigner likes hamburgers, then hamburgers it will be. But the Spanish chef reacts with wide-eyed hurt when the diner sends the plate back with a question: "Why did you saturate that burger in all that olive oil?"

The foreigner may one day succeed in changing the Spanish cuisine. Already many hotels feature international cooking, which sometimes is another term to describe bland, uninspired fare.

By no means should you get the impression that all Spanish food is bad. Many dishes and regional specialties are excellent, as will be outlined later.

The food in Spain is often varied, the portions immense—and the price moderate by North American standards, but rising dangerously for the Spaniard. Don't travel looking for a Kansas City steak. However, the roast suckling pig is so sweet and tender it can often be cut with a fork. The Spanish have superb cuts of veal which are unknown in North America. The Spanish *lomo (de cerdo)*—a loin of pork—is unmatched anywhere.

Here are some general rules to help guide you:

Breakfast: One starts the day off lightly in Spain with a continental breakfast—either hot coffee, hot chocolate, or tea, with assorted rolls, butter and jam. The coffee is usually strong and black, served with hot milk. Some Americans consider it too strong and bitter for their tastes, and therefore ask for Nescafé, which seems to have a virtual monopoly in Spain. You'll get a pot of hot water and an envelope of powdered coffee. Breakfasts are served in your room or in the hotel restaurant, although the best buys are available at the so-called *cafeterías*. The cafeterías are found on all major streets in all Spanish cities. Breakfast is obtainable at almost any time you want it.

Lunch: This is an important meal in Spain, comparable to the farm-style noonday "dinner" in America. There is rarely anything dainty about Spanish lunches—no watercress sandwiches or scoops of chicken salad on toast. Luncheons usually include three or four courses, beginning with a choice of a big bowl of soup or several dishes of hors d'oeuvres called *entremeses*. Often a fish or egg dish is served following this, and then a meat entree with vegetables. Wine is always on the table. Dessert is usually a pastry, custard, or assorted fruit; this is followed by coffee. Lunch is late by American standards: 1:30 to 3:30. And now you know why the Spaniard has those little sandwiches at 11.

Tascas: After the early-evening promenade, many Spaniards head for their favorite tascas, or bars, where they drink wine and sample assorted *tapas,* such as bits of fish, eggs in mayonnaise, or olives.

Dinner: This is another extravaganza. A typical meal again starts with a big bowl of soup, followed by a second course, often a fish dish, and backed up by another entree, usually veal, beef, or pork, accompanied by vegetables. Again, desserts tend to run to fresh fruit, custard, or pastries. A large flask of wine always sits on the table, and you can generally drink as much as you want. Afterward, you might have demitasse and one of those fragrant Spanish brandies. The chic dining hour, even in one-donkey towns, is 10 or 10:30. Quite conceivably, you might get out by midnight. (In heavy tourist regions and hand-working Catalonia, you can usually get your dinner by 8:30 p.m.) In most middle-class establishments, most people dine no later than 9:30. It's really a matter of taste.

Warnings: Know that the Spaniard loves to eat from the first hour in the morning until midnight.

North Americans who plunge wholeheartedly (or whole hog) into this experience all at once may be headed for trouble. The Spaniard's stomach is made out of genuine, rust-free cast iron. Yours may not be. Those who start sampling all the specialties the first day and drinking far beyond their usual intake of wine invariably will be suffering "Toledo tummy" before the sun rises on the third day. Buy Tanagel, sold in all pharmacies, to stop this malady.

Furthermore, two heavy Spanish meals a day are definitely not recommended at any time. Throughout Spain are sprouting up modern cafeterias (not self-service), featuring what is essentially American-inspired food. It might be better to patronize one of these establishments, as the light lunch is virtually unknown elsewhere in Spain. Perhaps a toasted ham sandwich, some fresh fruit or melon, and a drink for lunch, instead of a four-courser ranging from chicken paella to squid cooked in its own ink. Then you may be in the mood for a big Spanish dinner.

As a final caution, if you do consume a heaping lunch, don't behave like mad dogs and Englishmen and rush out into the noon-day sun for a round of sightseeing, the Prado, the Royal Palace, Toledo at sunset. Do as the Spaniard does. Go home to sleep it off in a recuperative siesta.

Restaurants and Menus

The government controls menu prices, but no longer forces restaurants to provide a *menú turistico*. However, some restaurants elect to continue to offer this meal. Spain is currently undergoing a change in its eating habits, probably as a result of entertaining so many visitors. For many, the tourist menu was too large, too unwieldly, especially at lunch. Others, however, thought it the best bargain.

The *menú del día,* or *cubierto,* emerges as a more viable selection. Offering a complete meal at a set price, the menu of the day is the finest dining bargain in Spain, although it rarely features the best meals. Usually, it includes a first course, such as fish soup or hors d'oeuvres, followed by a main dish, plus dessert, bread, and the wine of the house. You won't have a large selection, but enough to dine well, nevertheless. For this set meal, the cook decides what are the best buys of the day at the market. Lunches, especially in Madrid, are becoming briefer. The siesta may one day be a thing of the past.

Of course, in all restaurants you can order à la carte. Certainly many visitors have found this preferable to ordering the more standardized set meals.

Finally, with very few exceptions, the cost of any dish on a Spanish menu includes the service charge, too, but it is customary to leave a 10% tip.

Most restaurants in Spain still adhere to the rigid Sunday closing. Have your hotel call ahead and check a particular establishment before heading there on a Sunday. On the other hand, hotel dining rooms are generally open seven days a week. There's always some food dispenser open, particularly in Madrid, Barcelona, and the Costa del Sol, but in smaller places staffs like a day of rest.

Cafeterías: Springing up everywhere. But don't expect self-service. Many of these cafeterías—rated one, two, or three cups—don't even serve hot meals. Others do. Many feature increasingly popular dishes known as combined plates

—say, fried eggs, french fries, veal, a lettuce-and-tomato salad. Some of these combined plates may be mismatched, others quite adequate.

The cafeterías are responsible for the biggest change presently occurring in the Spaniard's eating habits. Although many serve hot Spanish meals, their menus generally offer lighter items, such as hot dogs and hamburgers.

One of the best safeguards protecting tourists against flagrant abuses in restaurants is that welcome *Libro de Reclamaciones,* the complaint book. Asking for this book usually turns the waiter's face pale and brings the owner rushing over to see what is wrong. The reason is that very stiff fines are given to offenders, so that no one takes these books lightly. Nor, of course, should you resort to them except in extreme cases.

The Question of Olive Oil and Garlic

Garlic is an integral part of the Spanish diet, and after the cooking revolution that occurred in North America in the '60s and '70s, visitors are no longer as shy of its wonderful flavor as they once were. However, know that the Spaniard probably loves garlic more than you do, and it appears often in the oddest dishes. Since there are still some people around who can't abide it, in any form, it's important to learn the expression *No ajo* ("no ah-ho"). That tells the waiter (if he doesn't speak English) that you don't want garlic in your dish.

Olive oil is so expensive today that it's considered a luxury. But if you don't want it in a certain dish, and prefer, say, your fish grilled in butter, the word is *mantequilla.* In some instances, you'll be charged extra for the butter. Some dishes, such as paella, require the oil in their basic preparation—and therefore it can't be avoided.

One reader, John R. Miller, Jr., in the U.S. State Department in Rabat, Morocco, writes: "I found that olive oil added a distinct and hearty flavor to my eggs, and now prefer them cooked that way instead of with butter."

Perhaps, if you're not addicted already, Spain will convert you to olive oil and garlic.

Some Notes on the Cuisine

Whenever possible, you may want to partake of regional specialties, as during your visit to the Basque country or Galicia. But many dishes, including Andalusian gazpacho and Valencian paella, have transcended their region and have become dishes of the world. Some items you may want to avoid; others should be included as part of your Spanish experience, even though they may seem odd or sound unappetizing.

To begin with, soups are quite good, and are usually served in big bowls, although some hotels are catching on to the dainty cup. The creamed soups, such as asparagus and potato, can be top-notch, and bland enough to be soothing to delicate stomachs. In fact, they are often made of powdered envelope soups such as Knorr and Liebig. The already-mentioned *gazpacho,* on the other hand, is heavy but tasty. It is chilled soup, served year round, but particularly popular during the hot months. The combination is pleasant: olive oil, garlic, ground cucumbers, and raw tomatoes with a sprinkling of croutons. Spain also offers a variety of fish soups—*sopa de pescado*—in all of its provinces, and many of these are superb.

In the paradores and top restaurants, the hors d'oeuvres can be tempting. Sometimes as many as 15 tiny dishes are served. In lesser known places, these entremeses are something to be avoided, consisting as they often do of last year's sardines and bits and pieces of sausage left over from the Moorish

Conquest. In contrast, salads will probably be appreciated by most North Americans. They are usually fresh, with crisp lettuce and vine-ripened tomatoes.

Eggs—served in countless ways—loom large in the Spanish diet. An omelet is called a *tortilla*. But what is known as a Spanish omelet in America is not Spanish in Spain (they refer to it as Portuguese). A Spanish omelet—called a *tortilla española*—is one made with potatoes. A simple omelet is called a *tortilla francesa.*

In its fish dishes, Spain is a star. The residents prepare them in unique and tempting ways, varying from province to province. It is now possible to get safe fish even in inland cities, such as Zaragoza. Ice and speedy transportation have distributed the treats of the sea all over Spain. One of the most common types of fish offered is hake *(merluza);* it's sweet and white, quite good and very popular. *Langosta,* a variety of lobster, is seen everywhere—and it's a treat, although expensive.

The Portuguese, in particular, but some of the Spaniards too, go into rapture at the mention of barnacles. Gourmets eat them with gleaming eyes, and speak of the sea-water taste. Others find them a tasteless bore.

If you see *rape* suggested on a menu, don't be surprised. The Spanish Tourist Office defines it as a "sweet, wide-boned ocean fish, the texture of scallops."

Also recommended—at least once—are a few dozen half-inch baby eels. They rely heavily on olive oil and garlic for their flavor, but they're good to eat. Squid cooked in its own ink is suggested only to those who want to go native. A culinary delight, however, are charcoal-broiled sardines, a treat in the Basque provinces.

You can't go to Spain without trying *paella,* made in thousands of different ways (with whatever the chef happens to have in the kitchen). Flavored with saffron, paella is perhaps the most famous dish of Spain, obtainable almost anywhere. It is an aromatic and delightfully seasoned rice dish topped usually with shellfish, chicken, sausage, peppers, and other local spices. Served authentically, it comes in a metal pan called a *paellera* steaming hot from the kitchen. Incidentally, what is known in America as Spanish rice isn't Spanish at all. If you ask an English-speaking waiter for Spanish rice, he'll serve you paella.

As for chicken, it will sometimes qualify for the Olympics. Spit-roasted chicken, however, often can be quite flavorful. Beef, on the other hand, would not satisfy a Texas rancher, but it's possible to get a thinly cut steak that's not too tough. Pork is at its best when it is suckling pig, spit roasted, and served crisp on the outside, tender inside. Lamb chops and veal crop up on almost all menus, particularly veal.

Except in summer, vegetables are weak on the Spanish menu. Green fresh vegetables seem hard to come by, and the diner often gets canned string beans, peas, or artichokes. Potatoes are also a staple, although there is a tendency to saturate them in olive oil. Avoid mashed potatoes.

The Spanish resemble the Chinese in that they do not put great emphasis on desserts. *Flan* is a home-cooked egg custard, and it appears on all menus—sometimes with a burnt-caramel sauce. Otherwise, it's a good bet to ask for a basket of fresh fruit, which you will wash at your table. Homemade pastries are usually moist and not too sweet. Ice cream is featured on nearly all menus as well.

The Days of Wine, Sherry, and Solares

Unlike the European, the North American is a water drinker—and getting the stuff in Spain used to be a problem. It isn't any more. The water is safe to drink in all the major cities and tourist resorts. But if you're traveling in really remote areas, you might play it safe and order bottled water. On all other occasions, bottled water is a waste of money, yet it's thought of as a most fashionable drink.

One of the most popular noncarbonated bottled drinks in Spain is *Solares,* which comes from a town in northern Spain known for its pure waters. Nearly all restaurants and hotels have it. If you'd like your water with a little kick, then ask for *agua mineral.* You'll note that bottled water often costs more than the regional wine.

In the largest cities, you'll get bottled milk, but it loses a great deal of its flavor in the process of pasteurization and tastes cooked. In all cases, avoid untreated milk and milk products. Sometimes it's safe—and sometimes it isn't —but why take the chance? About the best brand of fresh milk is called **Lauki.**

Beer *(cerveza)* is not native to Spain, but is now drunk everywhere as commonly as in the U.S. Domestic brands include San Miguel, Mahou, Aguila, and Cruz Blanca.

Sherry *(Vino de Jerez),* made from grapes from the aristocratic vineyards at Jerez de la Frontera, south of Seville, has been called "the wine with a hundred souls." This is the drink to have before dinner (try the topaz-colored *finos,* a very pale sherry), or whenever you drop in to some old inn or bodega for refreshment. In many of them are rows of kegs with spigots. *Manzanilla,* incidentally, was extolled by no less an authority than Hemingway, who preferred it as an apéritif. Remembered from Edgar Allan Poe's *The Cask of Amontillado,* a golden-colored, medium-dry sherry of the same name is also extremely popular. The sweet cream sherries (Harvey's Bristol Cream, for example) are favorite after-dinner wines (called *oloroso).*

The French may be disdainful of Spanish wines, but they can be truly noble, especially two leading Spanish varieties, **Valdepeñas** and **La Rioja,** both from Castile. If you're fairly adventurous and not too demanding in your tastes, you can always ask for the *vino de la casa* (wine of the house) wherever you dine. The **Ampurdan** of Catalonia is heavy. From Andalusia comes the fruity **Montilla.** There are also some good local champagnes in Spain, such as **Freixenet.** One brand, **Benjamin,** also comes in individual-size bottles.

A word should also be said about Spanish cider *(sidra),* from the northern provinces. There are three basic types: (1) still cider which is poured in a special way, and is usually obtained in Asturian taverns specializing in this; (2) plain bottled cider, similar to that served in England or France; and (3) champagne cider, tasting a bit like champagne.

Sangría is the all-time favorite refreshing drink in Spain. It is a red wine punch that is festive looking, and mixed with oranges, lemons, seltzer, and sugar.

Imported whiskies are available at most Spanish bars, although they tend to be expensive. If you're a drinking person, it is better to switch to brandies and cognacs. The Spanish reign supreme with these two drinks. Try **Fundador,** made by the Pedro Domecq family in Jerez de la Frontera. If you're seeking a smooth cognac, ask for **"103"** white label.

You'll find many varieties of aromatic and potently sweet liqueurs—fine for after dinner if you have a sweet tooth.

Coca-Cola, and even Pepsi, have made inroads into Spain, but these drinks are more expensive than in America. In general, avoid the carbonated citrus drinks that are on sale almost anywhere. Most of them never saw an orange, much less a lemon. If you want a citrus drink, order old, reliable Schweppes. An excellent noncarbonated drink for the summer, now exported to France, is called **Tri-Naranjus** and comes in lemon and orange flavors. Your cheapest bet is getting a liter bottle of **gaseosa,** which comes in various flavors. In summer you should also try a drink I've had nowhere else outside Spain. It's called a *horchata,* a nutty, sweet milk-like beverage made of tubers called **chufas.**

Chapter III

MADRID

1. The ABCs of Madrid
2. Hotels in Madrid
3. The Restaurants of Madrid
4. The Top Sights
5. The Sporting Life
6. Shopping in Madrid
7. Madrid After Dark

AS SPANISH CITIES GO, Madrid is a young upstart. It was not significant until as late as 1561. It is the virtual nerve center of Spanish life; yet, at times, it seems so strangely removed from the country that the visitor would be left with only the dimmest impression of Spain if he or she saw only its capital city.

Once Barcelona was the major arrival and embarkment point for tourists to Spain, but that is no longer the case. The Castilians of Madrid have edged out the Cataláns of Barcelona, and Madrid has become the capital of the country—both in name and fact.

It is not my purpose to dispute the charm of either of these two venerated ladies. It's a question of preference and taste. However, if your time is pressed and you are forced to choose between them, then Madrid becomes the favored one, not only because of its own rich attractions, such as the Prado and the Royal Palace, but because of its satellites. Few European capitals are encircled with as many rich historical sites as Madrid.

Perhaps it was logical that Madrid became the capital: it is almost in the geographic center of the Iberian peninsula, which encompasses Portugal. As such, it is the loftiest capital city in Europe, sitting high on a plateau, some 2133 feet above sea level. It is modern, increasingly industrial, noisy, animated, and ringed by new "cities" or apartment houses. Parts of it, particularly Old Madrid, are architecturally appealing. Other sections are graced with wide boulevards and landscaped parks—and there are splashing fountains, water shortage or not.

It is big and crowded, with hordes of visitors intermixing with the Spaniards during the summer months. In a country where birth-control propaganda is received with little enthusiasm, Madrid's population figure has topped the three million mark.

During the peak promenade hours—6 to 7:30—on the **Gran Vía**, it would appear that every Spaniard in Castile goes out walking. For the most part, they are well dressed, animated, and apparently filled with so much to say that everybody seems to talk at once. The metallic sounds of conversation in the cafeterías, the tascas, or at the sidewalk tables are so overpowering that you may think a wholesale revolution is being organized. But nothing so dramatic. A wife's expenditures at the Galerías Preciados or the outrageously rising cost of langosta may send the Madrileño into a flight of fury. Such an outpouring of energy is often difficult for the more phlegmatic northern Europeans to understand. But how did it all begin?

A MINI-HISTORY: Madrid has never officially been recognized as a city. As astonishing as this may seem, it is indicative of the late development of the town, although mention of an outpost at the site goes back to the 10th century. Once in the 14th century and again in the 15th, parliament convened here, and Madrid also achieved some prominence as a royal hunting ground. However, as mentioned earlier, it wasn't until 1561 that Philip II made it the capital.

From then on, the life of the town underwent rapid and dramatic alterations. During the War of the Spanish Succession, Madrid changed hands many times, but its greatest sympathy lay with the Bourbons in opposition to the House of Hapsburg. Again, in opposition to Napoleon, a bloody uprising broke out in Madrid on May 2, 1808, that led to the Spanish War of Independence.

Following the war, Madrid, as the capital, entered upon a century of decline and defeat, presiding over the liquidation of an empire.

Madrid was the stronghold of the Republicans during the Spanish Civil War of 1936–1939, and it suffered the nightly raids of the German bombers. Large sections were destroyed, and others were bombarded when the Nationalists invaded in 1939. Franco made it his capital.

After the belt-tightening days of World War II, Madrid began to take on the appearance of a bustling metropolis, as the autonomy of the suburbs faded away. Nearly all traces of the destruction left by the Civil War vanished in the booming reconstruction days that followed.

INSTANT GEOGRAPHY: In modern Spain, all roads and rails—and all telephone lines—lead to Madrid, the center of a vast network of transportation and communication hookups. With such ever-increasing importance, the capital has overspilled whatever boundaries it may once have had—and is branching out in all directions. But the layout of this vast city need not perplex you, as there are many industrial and residential sections of Madrid that you probably will not concern yourself with as a visitor.

Every arrival must learn of the existence of the **Gran Vía,** which cuts a winding pathway across a large segment of the city beginning at the **Plaza de España,** containing one of the tallest skyscrapers in Europe, the **Edificio España.** Gran Vía was the original name of this street, although in recent years it was called Avenida de José Antonio. It has now reverted to the original designation. On this principal avenue in Madrid—Sinclair Lewis would have called it *Main Street*—you'll find the largest concentration of shops, hotels, restaurants, movie houses, whatever, of any other place in the city. The **Calle Serrano** with its many shops and restaurants is a runner-up.

South of the avenue lies a large square known as the **Puerta del Sol,** which used to have the significance of, say, Piccadilly Circus in London. All road distances from Spain are measured from this gate. James Michener called it "Beloved of Madrileños for centuries as the focus of their life in a way that the popular squares of old European capitals could not equal." However, the significance of the Puerta del Sol has declined as the mainstream of life shifted

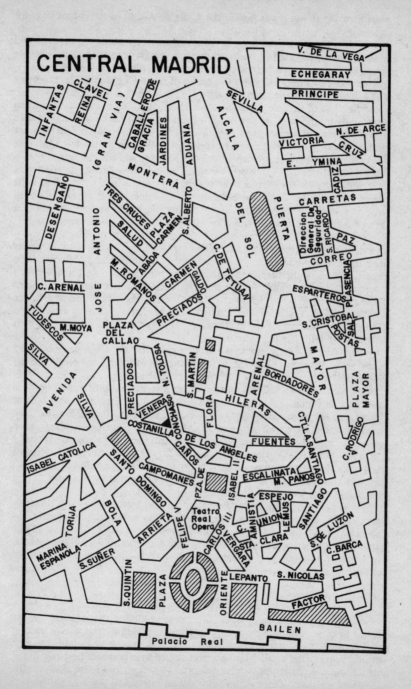

CENTRAL MADRID

elsewhere. At this gateway begins the **Calle de Alcalá,** a street that runs for 2½ miles.

Unlike the Puerta del Sol, the **Plaza Mayor** represents the heart of Old Madrid, enough so that I recommend that you treat it as an attraction. Whether it was an execution of a heretic or the scene of a bullfight, this huge square—ordered built by Philip III—was the center of life in Old Madrid. Its notoriety was achieved during the reign of Carlos II (1661–1700, called "The Bewitched One," the last of the line of the Spanish Hapsburgs). Under the reign of this supposedly insane king, an *auto-da-fé*—literally act of faith—was staged here in which nearly 20 persons lost their lives at the stake. Today the plaza is not addicted to violence and it doesn't necessarily look Spanish, but has a mixture of French and Georgian architecture. With its formality and tidiness, it makes for an interesting stroll—or a promenade. Through the arches pass pedestrians branching out onto the narrow streets of the old town, where one can find some of the capital's most intriguing restaurants and tascas. On the ground level of the plaza are colonnaded shops, many selling fun headgear such as that of a turn-of-the-century Spanish sailor or an officer in the kaiser's army.

Of all the sections of the capital, the area south of the Plaza Mayor—known as *barrios bajos*—merits the most exploration. The cobblestone streets are narrow and winding, the architecture often of the 16th and 17th centuries. Directly south of the plaza (reached by steps) is the **Arco de Cuchilleros,** a street of típico restaurants, such as the Casa Botín, flamenco clubs, and taverns—the poor people of Madrid, markets with fresh vegetables, *cuevas* (see the nightlife section), low dives with red lights and beaded curtains—it's the closest Madrid comes to evoking the rhythmic gypsy music and whirling dancers that *Carmen*-watching has led us to expect.

The Gran Vía ends its run when it merges with the Calle de Alcalá and becomes the **Plaza de la Cibeles,** with its fountain to Cybele, the mother of the Gods, and what has become known as the cathedral of post offices. From Cibeles, the wide **Paseo Calvo Sotelo** begins a short run until it marches into the **Plaza de Colón.** From this latter square rolls the serpentine **Paseo de la Castellana,** the boulevard that one day may take all the attention away from the Gran Vía, flanked as it is by sophisticated shops, apartment buildings, such luxury hotels as the Castellana, Villa Magna, and the Luz Palacio, and foreign embassies. Once it was peppered with town houses in which rich Madrileños lived in the 18th and 19th centuries—but many of these, regrettably, are being torn down to make way for New Madrid. The boulevard bypasses the public ministries on its journey to the frontiers of Madrid.

Back at Cibeles again: heading south is the **Paseo del Prado,** housing Spain's major sightseeing attraction, the Prado, as well as the Botanical Garden. This paseo leads into the **Atocha Railway Station.** To the west of the garden lies the **Parque del Retiro,** the finest in Madrid, with restaurants, nightclubs, a rose garden, statuary, and two lakes. Once it was reserved for royalty.

1. The ABCs of Madrid

Whatever your needs or travel problems, you'll find that Madrid has the answer to them. The single question is: How do you find what you're seeking quickly and conveniently? In an emergency, of course, your hotel is the best bet. But some of the smaller hotels aren't staffed with personnel entirely fluent in English; and sometimes—even if they are—the person at the desk can be amazingly apathetic about something of vital interest to you.

What follows, then, is an alphabetical listing of important miscellany—the data that can be crucial to a visitor. Typical queries, answered below, include: How much do I tip a porter? How do I make a telephone call? Find a doctor, etc.?

AIRPORTS: **Barajas** is the international airport of Madrid, and it's divided into two separate terminals—one for international flights, another for domestic. A shuttle bus runs between the two. For Barajas Airport information, telephone 205-40-90.

Air-conditioned yellow buses take you from right outside the arrival terminal at Barajas to the underground bus depot under the Plaza Colón. You can also get off at several points along the way, provided you don't have your suitcases stored in the hold. The cost of the service is 100 pesetas (96¢), and buses leave about every 20 minutes, either to or from the airport.

If you go by taxi into town, the approximate cost is 400 pesetas ($3.84), and the driver is entitled to assess a surcharge (either direction), not only for the trip but for baggage handling. If you should step into an unmetered limousine, it is important to negotiate the price in advance.

AMERICAN EXPRESS: For your mail or banking needs, the American Express office at the corner of the Marqués de Cubas and the Plaza de las Cortés (across the street from the Palace Hotel) draws the visiting Yankee. The office is open weekdays from 9 a.m. to 5:30 p.m. and on Saturday until noon.

BABYSITTERS: Nearly all major hotels in Madrid can arrange for babysitters. Usually, the concierge keeps a list of reliable nursemaids or young girls, and will get in touch with one of them for you, provided you give adequate notice. Rates vary considerably, but tend to be reasonable. More and more babysitters in Madrid speak English, but don't count on it. Chances are yours won't—although you can request it, of course.

BANKS: You get a better exchange rate here if you're exchanging dollars into pesetas than you do at any of the exchange bureaus around the city. Banks are open at 9:30 a.m. (but it's best to go after 10 a.m.) to 2 p.m. Monday to Friday. Banks are also open on Saturday from 9:30 a.m. to 1 p.m. The currency exchange at Chamartín railway station is open 24 hours and gives the best rates of exchange in the capital.

BOOKSTORES: There are many all over the city, selling both English- and Spanish-language editions, along with touring maps. Two good ones are **Aguilar,** 24 Serrano (tel. 226-05-38), and **Oxford,** 54 Avenida de la Havana (tel. 250-51-10). Others include the **Espasa Calpe,** 29 Gran Vía (tel. 221-19-32); **Librería Bucholz,** 20 Paseo General Martinez Compos (tel. 221-12-33); and **Editorial Hernando,** 11 Ferraz (tel. 247-62-27).

BUS TERMINALS: Madrid has two principal ones—**Auto Rest,** 6 Glorieta Conde de Casals (tel. 251-66-44), and the large **Estación Sur de Autobuses,** 17 Canarias (tel. 468-42-00). Buses to the environs of Madrid, such as Toledo and Segovia, leave from numerous other stations; it's best to telephone 401-99-00 for the latest information about departures.

A network of buses also traverses the city, fanning out to the suburbs. The route of each bus is clearly marked at each stop on a schematic diagram. Buses are fast and efficient, traveling along special lanes made for them all over the city. The fare is quite cheap: 20 pesetas (19¢). Micro-buses charge 30 pesetas (29¢). Incidentally, a new airport bus service is in effect.

CIGARETTES: A pack of American cigarettes costs around $1 to $1.50. Some Spanish filter cigarettes, on the other hand, begin at 25¢ a package. And you'd better be a tough hombre if you try one.

CLOTHING SIZES: For the most part, Spain uses the same sizes as the continent of Europe. The sizes of women's stockings and men's socks are international.

For Women

Junior Miss		Regular Dresses		Shoes	
U.S.	Spain	U.S.	Spain	U.S.	Spain
5	34	10	40	5	36
7	36	12	42	5½	36½
9	38	14	44	6½	37½
11	40	16	46	7½	38½
		18	48	8	39
		20	50	8½	39½
				9	40

For Men

Shirts		Slacks		Shoes	
U.S.	Spain	U.S.	Spain	U.S.	Spain
14	36	32	42	5	36
14½	37	34	44	6	37
15	38	36	46	7	38
15½	39	38	48	7½	39
15¾	40	40	50	8	40
16	41			9	41
16½	42			10	42
17	43			10½	43
				11	44
				12	45

Warning: This chart should be followed only as a very general outline, as in the same country there are big differences in sizes. If possible, try on all clothing or shoes before making a purchase. You'll be glad you did.

CONSULATES AND EMBASSIES: The **American Embassy** is at 75 Calle de Serrano (tel. 276-36-00), and the **Canadian Embassy** at 35 Nuñez de Balboa (tel. 225-91-19). The British Embassy is at 16 Fernando el Santo (tel. 419-02-00).

CRIME: It's on the upsurge, as any Madrileño will readily admit. Many will tell you that it's not safe to walk on the streets of Madrid after dark. I don't agree. Pickpockets are a nuisance, but Spain still lags far behind such European cities as Rome and Paris, especially in violent crime. It's relatively safe to be about, although discretion is always advised. Terrorism is a major political problem for the country, but, chances are, the average visitor can go into every province of Spain and never encounter a Basque terrorist or know that one exists.

CURRENCY: Spain's unit of currency is the **peseta,** worth about $.0096 in U.S. terms (as of this writing—*subject to change*). One U.S. dollar is worth about 103.55 pesetas. Spain also uses *centimos,* units of currency so low they're almost worthless. It takes 100 centimos to equal 1 peseta, which is worth about 1¢ in U.S. coinage.

Pesetas	U.S.$	Pesetas	U.S.$
1	$ .01	100	$ .96
2	.02	250	2.40
3	.03	300	2.88
4	.04	400	3.84
5	.05	500	4.80
10	.10	750	7.20
15	.14	1000	9.60
20	.19	1250	12.00
25	.24	1500	14.40
30	.29	1750	16.80
40	.38	2000	19.20
50	.48	2250	21.60
75	.72	2500	24.00

CUSTOMS: Spain permits you to bring in most personal effects and the following items duty free: two still cameras with ten rolls of film each, one movie camera, tobacco for personal use, one bottle each of wine and liquor per person, a portable radio, a tape recorder and a typewriter, a bicycle, golf clubs, tennis racquets, fishing gear, two hunting weapons with 100 cartridges each, skis and other sports equipment.

Upon leaving Spain, citizens of the United States who have been outside the country for 48 hours or more are allowed to bring in $300 worth of merchandise duty free—that is, if they have claimed no similar exemption within the past 30 days. Beyond this free allowance, the next $600 worth of merchandise is assessed at a flat rate of 10% duty. If you make purchases in Spain, it's important to keep your receipts.

DENTIST: For an English-speaking dentist, get in touch with the **American Embassy,** 75 Calle de Serrano (tel. 276-34-00), which has a list of recommended ones. If you have a dental emergency, you may have to call several before you can get an immediate appointment—hence, the need of a comprehensive list.

ELECTRIC CURRENT: Most establishments now have 200 volts, although older places may have 100 volts or 120 volts, 50 cycles. Carry your voltage adapter with you and always check at your hotel desk before plugging in any electrical equipment. It's best to travel with battery-operated equipment.

EMERGENCIES: If you need the police, call 091. In case of fire, dial 232-32-32, and if you need an ambulance, as in the case of an accident, telephone 256-02-00.

FILM: As one tourist official put it, film is "expensive as hell in Spain." Take in as much as Customs will allow. I suggest that you wait to process it until you return home. However, if you can't wait, and you'll be in Spain long enough to get your pictures back, you can take your undeveloped film to the leading department store, **Galerías Preciados,** 28 Preciados, right off the Gran Vía (tel. 222-96-78). There you'll find a department which will develop your film. Incidentally, you're not supposed to photograph policemen or military personnel in Spain.

GAS: Gas is easily obtainable and costs about $2.50 per gallon for regular, the normal fuel used in rented cars in Spain. The average Spanish vehicle—predominantly Seats or Fiats—get close to 45 miles a gallon.

HAIRDRESSERS: In Madrid women can patronize the **Peluquería Conti,** 11 Preciados (tel. 231-51-99), or the **Peluquería Emtine,** 74 Serrano (tel. 276-01-67).

HITCHHIKING: This is no longer smiled upon as much as it used to be. It may be technically illegal. However, people still do it, tourists tending to pick up tourists. Empty cars filled with Spaniards are not as frequent (they're often at capacity with friends or relatives). I don't recommend that you stick out your thumb in the presence of the Civil Guard.

HOLIDAYS: They include January 1 (New Year's Day); January 6 (The Epiphany); March 19 (Feast of St. Joseph); April 9 (Good Friday); April 12 (Easter Monday); May 1 (May Day); June 10 (Corpus Christi); June 29 (Feast of St. Peter and St. Paul); July 25 (Feast of St. James); August 15 (Feast of the Assumption); October 12 (Spain's National Day); November 1 (All Saint's Day); December 8 (Immaculate Conception), and December 25 (Christmas, of course). No matter how large or small, every city or town in Spain also celebrates its local saint's days. In Madrid it's on May 15 (Saint Isidro).

HOSPITAL: On the outskirts of Madrid, at University City, stands a thoroughly up-to-date and well-run establishment, the **Anglo-American Hospital,** 1 Paseo de Juan XXIII, Ciudad Universitaria (tel. 234-67-00). Emergency care can be rendered here, of course. Fees are payable in advance. They also take credit cards. In addition, the **U.S. Embassy,** 75 Calle de Serrano (tel. 276-36-00), will present you with a detailed list of doctors in Madrid, indicating their training and whether or not they speak English.

LANGUAGE: Spanish is the official language of the land, naturally, and French is also widely spoken in parts. In Madrid more and more people, especially the younger ones, are learning English. Nearly all major hotels and top restaurants are staffed with English-speaking persons. However, out in the country it is to be hoped you were a language major in school.

LAUNDRY: In most of the top hotels recommended in this guide, you need only fill out your laundry and dry-cleaning list and present it to your maid or valet. Same-day service usually costs from 25% to 50% more. If you don't have time, you can go directly to **Tintoría Embajadores,** 35 Ponferrada (tel. 201-20-44), in Madrid's old section.

LIQUOR: Almost anyone of any age can order a drink in Spain. I've seen gypsy shoeshine boys who looked no more than 8 years old go into a tasca and purchase a glass of wine with their newly acquired tip. Bars, taverns, cafeterías, whatever, generally open at 8 a.m., and many serve alcohol until around 1 or 2 a.m. Spain doesn't have many stores devoted entirely to selling liquor and wine. Rather, you can purchase alcoholic beverages in almost any market, along with cheese and other foodstuffs.

METRIC MEASURES: Here's your chance to learn metric measures before they're introduced to America.

Weights		Measures	
U.S.	*Spain*	*U.S.*	*Spain*
1 ounce = *28.3 grams*		*1 inch* = *2.54 centimeters*	
1 pound = *454 grams*		*1 foot* = *0.3 meters*	
2.20 pounds = *1 kilo (1000 grams)*		*1 yard* = *0.91 meters*	
1 pint = *0.47 liter*		*1.09 yards* = *1 meter*	
1 quart = *0.94 liter*		*1 mile* = *1.61 kilometers*	
1 gallon = *3.78 liters*		*0.62 mile* = *1 kilometer*	
		1 acre = *0.40 hectare*	
		2.47 acres = *1 hectare*	

NEWSPAPERS: Most newsstands along the Gran Vía or kiosks at the major hotels carry the latest edition of the *International Herald Tribune.* Spain also has an American weekly, a magazine known as the *Guidepost.* It is packed with information about late-breaking events in the Spanish capital; tips on movies shown in English, musical recitals, whatever. You may also want to become a regular reader of the *Iberian Daily Sun,* an English-language newspaper containing stories and listings of interest to both visitors from North America and Britain as well as expatriates. If you're traveling south, look out for *Lookout* magazine, a quality production in English with stories focused primarily on Spain's Sun Coast, although the staff also runs articles of general interest to the traveler to Spain.

PASSPORTS: A valid one is all an American, British, or Canadian citizen needs to enter Spain. You don't need an international driver's license if renting a car. Your local one from back home should suffice if it is up-to-date.

PETS: Better leave them at home. Otherwise, before departure you have to bring documents to the Spanish consulate nearest you, revealing licenses and shots. In normal circumstances pets aren't welcome at public places; certain hotels will accept them, however. But these arrangements should be made in advance.

PHARMACIES: Drugstores are scattered all over Madrid. If you're trying to locate one at an odd hour, note the list posted outside the door to any drugstore that's not open. On the list are the names and addresses of pharmacies which are in service. The Spanish government requires drugstores to operate on a rotating system of hours—thereby assuring you that some will be open at all times, even Sunday midnight.

POLITICS: In its post-Franco era, Spain now has a constitutional monarchy, and it won't disturb you unless you disturb it.

POST OFFICE: If you don't want to receive your mail at your hotel or American Express office, you can direct it to *Lista de Correos* at the central post office in Madrid. To pick up such mail, go to the window marked *Lista,* where you'll be asked to show your passport. The central office in Madrid is housed in what is known as "the cathedral of the post offices" at Plaza de la Cibeles (tel. 221-81-95). An airmail postcard to the United States costs 33 pesetas (32¢) if sent from Spain, and an airmail letter up to five grams goes for 43 pesetas (41¢).

RADIO AND TV: You're out of luck if you want to watch your favorite TV shows in English. Every television network broadcasts in Spanish. However, on the radio you can pick up the voice of the American Armed Forces, listening to music, hourly newscasts, and sports reporting. You'll also get a weather report if you're planning to go touring that day.

RAILWAY STATIONS: Madrid has two major railway stations—the Atocha and the Charmartín. At the **Atocha,** Glorieta de Carlos V, you can book passage for Lisbon, Toledo, Andalusia, the Levante (Valencia), and Aragón. The nearest Métro stop is Atocha. For trains to Barcelona and the French frontier, go to **Chamartín** in the northern suburbs at Agustín de Fox. For railway information, telephone 733-30-00.

Warning: In Madrid don't wait to buy your rail ticket or make a reservation at the train station. By this time there may be no tickets left—or at least no desirable tickets remaining. For most tickets, go to the principal **RENFE** office at 44 Alcalá (tel. 247-74-00). Although, in fairness, I must caution you that this place at times can be a veritable madhouse, packed with pushing, shoving people in no readily perceivable order. It's especially difficult for those who speak little Spanish. If you don't want to fight the crowds, you can purchase RENFE tickets from most travel agents in the capital.

RELIGIOUS SERVICES: Most churches and cathedrals in Madrid are Catholic, and they're found all over the city. The British chapel for the Church of England, known as the **Church of St. George,** is at 45 Hermosilla (tel. 274-51-55). A **Baptist church** stands at 4 Hernandez de Tejada (tel. 407-43-47). A **Jewish synagogue** lies on Calle de Balmes (tel. 445-98-43). It opened in the late 1960s, the first one to do so since the expulsion of Jews from Spain in 1492. Daily services are conducted.

REST ROOMS: Some are available, such as those in Retiro park in Madrid and on the Plaza del Oriente across from the Royal Palace. Otherwise, you can always go into a bar or tasca, but you really should order something—perhaps a small glass of beer or even a bag of peanuts.

SENIOR CITIZENS: Those traveling by rail get a 50% discount for trips exceeding 100 kilometers with the purchase of a *Tarjeta Dorado* (gold card), which is sold at RENFE ticket offices and train stations for 25 pesetas (24¢). Passport proof of age is necessary.

STORE HOURS: Major stores no longer take a siesta, and are open from 9:30 a.m. to 8 p.m. from Monday to Saturday. However, smaller stores, such as the "mama and papa" operations, still follow the old custom and do business from 9:30 a.m. to 1:30 p.m. and from 4:30 to 8 p.m.

SUBWAY (METRO): The system, first installed in 1919, is quite easy to learn, and you can travel in the underground if not comfortably, at least without any congestion or crushing, as in former years.

Line no. 7 is completely different from the rest, and as modern as some of Europe's newest underground systems. The future lines under construction will be the same type as no. 7. The central converging point of the subway is at the **Puerta del Sol**. The fares are 20 pesetas (19¢) for a single trip and only 30 pesetas (29¢) for a round-trip ticket. The Metro begins its runs at 6 a.m., shutting down at 1:30 a.m. It's best to try to avoid traveling on the subways during the rush hours, of course.

TAXES: Spain has no Value Added Tax, popularly known as VAT, as it is not a member of the Common Market. All prices in hotels, stores, and restaurants have the tax already "built into" the tariffs. However, there is a car-rental tax of 4½%, one of the lowest in Western Europe.

TAXIS: In Madrid the rates are still reasonable enough that the taxi becomes a recommended way of getting about. The legendary antiquated cabs of the capital have been replaced by speedier and more efficient models. The increase in taxi rates has been high in Madrid, but they were originally below rock bottom.

When you flag down a taxi, the meter should register 30 pesetas (29¢). Each extra kilometer is another 50 pesetas (48¢). But there are hidden extras that do not show up on the meter, which you are nevertheless obligated to pay. Trips to the railway stations and to the bullring carry an additional 30 pesetas (29¢) supplement, plus yet another supplement of 25 pesetas (24¢) on Sunday and holidays.

Warning: So many of the taxi drivers of Madrid seem like such honorable fellows that it's hard to throw stones without hitting some of the good guys. But petty bandits often can be more annoying than professional Mafia types. Make sure that the meter is turned down when you get into a taxi. Otherwise, some crooked drivers will "assess" the cost of the ride, and their assessment, you can be assured, is involved with higher mathematics. This is a flourishing racket. Keep your guard up and the meter down.

Also, there are many unmetered taxis in Madrid that hire out for the day or for the afternoon. These are perfectly legitimate vehicles, but some of the drivers of these hired cars—particularly if business is slow—will operate like gypsy cabs. Since they are unmetered, they can charge you a high rate for just a short distance. They are easy to avoid *if you stick to the black cabs with red bands around them.*

The exception to that general rule is the "mini" taxi system. These smaller cabs in blue, encircled by yellow bands, are much cheaper than the standard vehicles. Likewise, they are metered.

If you take a taxi outside the city limits, the driver is entitled to charge you twice the rate shown on the meter.

TELEGRAMS: Cables may be sent at the central post office building in Madrid at the Plaza de las Cibeles (tel. 221-81-95). However, the dialing number for international telegrams is 241-33-00. In Spain's it's cheaper to telephone within the country than it is to send a telegram.

TELEPHONES: If you don't speak Spanish, you'll find it easier to telephone from your hotel. Know, however, that this is often a very expensive way of doing it, as hotels impose a surcharge on every operator-assisted call. If you're more adventurous, you'll find street phone booths known as *cabinas,* with dialing instructions in English. Local calls can be made for 5 pesetas (5¢) if you don't talk more than three minutes. Some of these machines take 25-peseta (24¢) coins, giving you a chance to say a little more. However, it may be best for long-distance calls, especially transatlantic ones, to go to the main telephone exchange, **Central de Teléfonos,** 28 Gran Vía (tel. 004), where you'll find English-speaking operators.

TELEX: You can send Telex messages from the central post office building in Madrid, Plaza de la Cibeles (tel. 221-81-95) and from all major hotels.

TEMPERATURES: Average monthly temperatures in Madrid are as follows:

	High	Low		High	Low
January	46	34	July	91	65
February	48	34	August	90	66
March	52	39	September	76	65
April	65	45	October	65	52
May	75	52	November	55	48
June	78	58	December	50	41

TIME: Spain is six hours ahead of Eastern Standard Time in the U.S. In Madrid, dial 093 to learn the time.

TIPPING: It is not a problem if you follow certain guidelines, knowing that general rules are to be abandoned in the face of exceptional circumstances, such as someone performing a "life-saving feat." Tipping is simplified in Spain, since the government requires hotels and restaurants to include their service charges —usually 15% of the bill—in their tariffs or in the price of their food items. However, that doesn't mean you should skip out of a place without dispensing some extra pesetas. What follows are some guideline suggestions.

Hotels: A porter is tipped 25 pesetas (24¢) per piece of luggage he handles, but never less than 100 pesetas (96¢) even if you have only one small suitcase. If the maid has performed some extra task for you, you might give her 15 pesetas (14¢). In front-ranking hotels, the concierge will often submit a separate bill, reflecting your charges for newspapers, etc. If he's been helpful in performing extra services, such as wrapping packages or getting you tickets for the bullfight, you should tip him in addition to the bill he submits. Here I have no rule of thumb, as the tip will depend on the actual number of requests you have made of him.

Hairdressers: Both barbers and beauticians should be tipped at least 15% of the bill.

Taxis: Add about 12% to the fare as shown on the meter. However, if the driver personally unloads or loads your luggage, increase that to approximately 20%.

Porters: At airports such as Barajas and major terminals, the porter who handles your luggage will present you with a fixed-charge bill.

Restaurants: In both restaurants and nightclubs, 15% is added to the bill. To that, you should add another 3% to 5%, depending on the quality of the service. Waiters in deluxe restaurants and nightclubs are accustomed to the 5%—which means you'll end up tipping 20%. If that seems excessive, you must remember that the initial service charge reflected in the fixed price is distributed among all the help, including the dishwasher, so all of it does not go to your waiter.

Services: The little women who guard the washrooms get 5 pesetas (5¢) or 10 pesetas (10¢), and theater ushers—either at the bullfights or in movie houses or legitimate theaters—get from 5 pesetas (5¢) to 15 pesetas (14¢).

TOURIST OFFICE: The headquarters of the main tourist office in Madrid is 50 María de Molina (tel. 411-40-19). The staff there dispenses folders and travel information not only about Madrid and its environs, but for the entire country. English is spoken. There are also English-speaking officers at the Charmartín railway station during the day and early evening.

2. Hotels in Madrid

Virtually everyone from retired bullfighters to Civil War field commanders has rented a floor and opened up a hotel or pension in Madrid. On our $25-a-day budget, it's possible to stay at many of the city's three-star hotels, and have a private bath, too.

And if you're thinking I'm planning to hustle you off to the boondocks for this cheap living, you're wrong. For the most part, I'll stick to the pick of accommodations on the Gran Vía. Some of the hotels lie a block or two off the avenue—and this may be even better, as that location offers some protection against the noise of traffic. This section will be followed by hotels in and around the Prado Museum and the most central Atocha Railroad Station, as well as those that lie off the fashionable Paseo de la Castellana in the north of Madrid.

My lead-off listings represent the cream of Madrid's value-packed hotels. However, those on the strictest of budgets—even those desiring to live cheaper than our budget—should read from the bottom of the list, booking into a one- or two-star hotel, or perhaps a clean, livable, albeit plain, pension (boarding house).

THREE-STAR HOTELS: The principal feature of the following recommendations—in addition to the gracious and inexpensive living offered—is the sheer convenience of living on "Main Street," near the shops, movie houses, restaurants, bars, and cafeterías.

On or Near the Gran Vía

Lope de Vega, 59 Gran Vía (tel. 247-70-00), used to be a well-kept secret, attracting the Spanish gentry in town for the theater, fiestas, or shopping. Now it's gone international. But don't be misled by the entrance. Sandwiched between two shops, a tiny elevator will lift you to this well-run hotel. Once you enter the reception lounge and drawing room, you'll be in a world of graciousness and dignity. Attractive antiques are placed in the wood-paneled lounges and private rooms. A double with private bath rents for a maximum of 2300 pesetas ($22.08). Top price for a single with bath is 1800 pesetas ($17.28). Named after the great dramatist, the hotel has been owned since 1959 by an antique dealer, which explains the furnishings. The English-speaking manager, Enrique Luís Indeguy Olivar, has trained his staff well, making for the atmosphere of a private club rather than a hotel. There's an underground 700-car garage across the street. The hotel has an American Bar with television.

If you're a light sleeper, be duly warned that the front rooms opening onto the Gran Vía are noisy, of course.

Príncipe Pío (Holy Prince), 16 Onésimo Redondo (tel. 247-08-00). There are advantages as well as drawbacks to this selection. The whizzing traffic heard from the front rooms doesn't appeal to those seeking serenity. However, the location—within a short walk of the Royal Palace, the Plaza de España, and the Gran Vía—makes it bull's-eye center for many. In the words of one woman reader from Lowell, Massachusetts, "there's proper comfort and sanitation," a reference to the 167 modern bedrooms, all with private baths (many singles and doubles with showers, but no tub baths). The furnishings in both the public rooms and bedrooms are very much in the idiom of 1960s moderno. Doubles cost 3196 pesetas ($30.68); singles, 2128 pesetas ($20.43). Families may be interested in booking one of the triple rooms at 4121 pesetas ($39.56). A continental breakfast is an extra 200 pesetas ($1.92) per person, and a lunch or dinner goes for 765 pesetas ($7.34). Because of its excellent facilities and standards, the government gives the Príncipe a high rating.

Residencia Lar, 16 Valverde (tel. 221-65-92), is an 80-room hotel just off the Gran Vía. One gets personal attention here. Private baths go with every room, and the most you'll be asked to pay for a double is 2400 pesetas ($23.04). Singles, less preferred, rent for a maximum of 2000 pesetas ($19.20). The rooms are clean, although a little creaky in the corners. There is a small sunken lobby, but no dining room. A continental breakfast is brought to your room for an extra 160 pesetas ($1.54).

Hostal-Residencia Venecia, 6 Gran Vía (tel. 222-46-54), seems to have been created primarily for honeymooners, although nowadays nonnewlyweds and single persons are welcomed, too. The Venecia still has its matrimonial beds in some of the rooms. It is a hotel high up in one of the older buildings on the Gran Vía, and is reached by one of those old-fashioned elevators. A bevy of scrubbing and polishing maids keeps the hotel as clean as a nunnery. The staff and guests combine to create a congenial atmosphere. The accommodation rates are from 1500 pesetas ($14.40) to 2000 pesetas ($19.20) in a double with some form of private bath. A bathless double, however, costs only 1400 pesetas ($13.44). Depending on the plumbing, singles range from 900 pesetas ($8.64) to 1400 pesetas ($13.44). A continental breakfast is an additional 125 pesetas ($1.20) per person.

Hostal Metropol, 47 Montera (tel. 221-29-35), is an intriguing 19th-century building with a matching interior. For such a centrally located hotel (it adjoins the Gran Vía), the accommodations are a bargain: from 1800 pesetas ($17.28) to 2000 pesetas ($19.20) in a double, the higher price for a complete bath. Singles range from 1400 pesetas ($13.44) to 1800 pesetas ($17.28), the latter for complete bath. A vigorous management works hard to make guests comfortable. The decor in part is a mass of bold stripes and patterns, and everything is kept immaculately. A continental breakfast is 150 pesetas ($1.44) extra. It should be pointed out, however, that the accommodation for many will be only barely adequate, as it is rather noisy, lying on the corner of two busy streets.

At Chamartín Railway Station

Hotel Chamartín, at the Chamartín Railway Station (tel. 450-90-50), is a 378-room hotel rising nine stories, part of the major transportation and shopping complex in this modern train station. The owner of the hotel is RENFE, the government's railroad system, and it's operated by Entursa Hotels, which is an organization best known for deluxe "museum" hotels. The Chamartín is the first of the company's budget properties. The director, who oversees a large staff, is José C. Moya.

The hotel lies a 15-minute ride from the airport and a five-minute jaunt from the city's major business and sightseeing areas.

All guest rooms are air-conditioned, featuring TV, radio, a refrigerator/bar, a private safe, and specially insulated windows for maximum quiet and privacy. Eighteen one-bedroom suites, some with balconies, are also available. Rates in the regular rooms are 3100 pesetas ($29.76) in a single, from 4200 pesetas ($40.32) in a double.

Especially oriented to the business traveler, the Chamartín offers a currency exchange, travel agency, bank, car rental, and complete communication services. A screen in the lobby posting the arrival and departure of all trains affords special convenience to the traveler.

A coffee bar serves a continental breakfast daily, and room service is also available. A choice of drinks is featured at the bar off the main lobby. Guests can dine at a variety of restaurants and snackbars in the Chamartín complex.

Among the extensive facilities and services available to hotel guests are 13 shops, four movie theaters, a roller skating rink, a disco, and ample parking.

For more information and reservations, write Reservations Systems, Inc., 6 East 46th St., New York, NY 10017, or call 212/661-4540. The nationwide toll-free number is 800/223-1588.

Off the Paseo de la Castellana

Far removed from the narrow streets of Old Madrid, the "New City" is booming northward. Beginning at the Plaza de la Cibeles, the Paseo Calvo Sotelo runs into the Paseo de la Castellana, this wide boulevard wending northward. Once town houses stood in this principally residential sector of the city. Nowadays, luxury hotels such as the Villa Magna and the Luz Palacio line the avenue. Off this wide thoroughfare on quieter streets lies a modern hotel offering good value.

The **Sace,** 8 José/Abascal (tel. 447-40-00), doesn't make for a dramatic write-up. No famous people have stayed here, and it's too young to have much of a history or tradition. But for those seeking up-to-date amenities at moderate rates, the Sace is a leading contender. Owned by the Automobile Club, it contains 72 rather standardized and compact bedrooms, each with a private tiled bath. A double goes for 4000 pesetas ($38.40), a single for 2300 pesetas ($22.08). A continental breakfast is an extra 200 pesetas ($1.92) per person.

The Sace is a bit out of the center of Madrid, near the Paseo de la Castellana, in a primarily residential sector of the Spanish capital, but it's easy to get to important areas such as the Prado from here. It's almost like motel living, except you do get hotel service. There are a garage on the premises, a Victorian bar, and the Troika Restaurant.

Near the North Station

San Antonio de la Florida, 13 Paseo de la Florida (tel. 247-14-00). A lot depends on the room you get. Those preferred open onto the Manzanares River and the former royal hunting grounds (now a public park), the Casa de Campo. The front rooms face a wide, traffic-heavy avenue, across from the North Station, and are less desirable, of course. But whichever room you get, it will be fairly modern, as the hotel was built in 1964, complete with 100 freshly created bedrooms, all with private baths.

For those who don't mind being slightly out of the center, or for those who are motorists (there is a garage), the San Antonio might be the ideal headquarters. The rates are reasonable: 2600 pesetas ($24.96) in a double, 1510 pesetas ($14.50) in a single. Breakfast is extra. The bedroom furnishings are functional, not exceptional, the balconies adding an extra bit of glamor. The public rooms have a quiet style, in a warm, contemporary sense, and the dining room is inviting. There's a cocktail lounge for predinner drinks (where I recently met seven Americans, all in one evening), plus a grill room for light meals.

Near Glorieta Quevedo

Conde Duque, 5 Plaza Conde Valle Suchil (tel. 447-70-00), is a good-size (151 rooms) hotel which was modernized way back in the '50s. It opens onto a tree-filled little plaza where children play. Be warned that this hotel is a long way north (about 12 blocks) of the Plaza de España, off the Calle de San Bernardo, which starts its run at the Gran Vía—too long to walk but a subway stop, the San Bernardo, is nearby, taking you into the heart of the city in a few minutes.

You pay 2500 pesetas ($24) in a double room. All of these rooms contain well-maintained private baths. Only a few singles are available, costing 1500 pesetas ($14.40). A continental breakfast is an extra 170 pesetas ($1.63). The furnishings include modified reproductions of 19th-century English pieces and modern built-in headboards. There are bedside lights and telephones. The three-star hotel is near a branch of the Galerías Preciados department store, in a residential sector filled with apartment houses.

Near the Puerta del Sol

Hotel Residencia Cortezo, 3 Doctor Cortezo (tel. 239-38-00), is off the Calle de Atocha, which leads to the railroad station, and it is only a few minutes' walk from the Plaza Mayor and the Puerta del Sol. A double room with bath rents for 2750 pesetas ($26.40). Singles with bath are 1800 pesetas ($17.28). A continental breakfast is an extra 150 pesetas ($1.44) per person. The accommodation is not only comfortable but attractive. The beds are springy, the colors well chosen, the furniture pleasantly modern, and often there is a sitting area with a desk and armchair. The baths are slickly contemporary, and the public rooms match the bedrooms in freshness. The staff also furnishes guests with a lot of extras, such as an excellent map of the capital.

Gran Hotel Victoria, 7 Plaza del Angel (tel. 231-45-00), is another good-size refurbished hotel near the Puerta del Sol, and within easy reach of the little street of budget restaurants, the Ventura de la Vega. Even though the hotel is in a congested area, it opens onto its own little plaza, and has three tiers of bay windows, reminiscent of the architecture in northwestern Spain. The rate for a double room with private bath is 3130 pesetas ($30.05). A single with bath is 2200 pesetas ($21.12), with a continental breakfast costing 160 pesetas ($1.54) extra. The rooms are quite good, although not lavishly furnished, and a staid but polite atmosphere prevails. The Victoria rents out its banqueting room to middle-class Spanish families for wedding receptions.

Hostal Embajada, 5 Calle Santa Engracía (tel. 447-33-00), is a clean, pleasant three-star hotel about one block from the Plaza Alonso Martínez, a rather distinguished residential area. Still standing across the street is a great 19th-century palace. The Embajada has 84 rooms, and doubles with bath cost 3700 pesetas ($35.52). Singles go for 2800 pesetas ($26.88). Breakfast isn't included. You'll find the bedrooms tastefully decorated and the bathrooms modern. There's a modest lounge which has no bar.

Lisboa, 17 Ventura de la Vega (tel. 429-98-94), is perched right on Madrid's most famous restaurant street. My only warning is that during the evenings the milling crowd of tasca hoppers tends to be noisy. The three-star hotel is a neat and trim, modernized little town house, with compact rooms, each with private bath. Singles go for 1200 pesetas ($11.52), doubles with showers or private baths for 1600 pesetas ($15.36). The best equipped doubles are complete with sitting rooms, these renting for 2200 pesetas ($21.12).

In the cooler months, there is central heating. The staff speaks five languages, sometimes amusingly so: "Our guests must not werry for transportations." True, everything seems near: American Express, the airline offices, the Puerta del Sol. Over the years the hotel has grown shabby, but the friendly, helpful staff compensates. The Lisboa has no restaurant.

ONE-AND TWO-STAR HOTELS: For cheaper rates I'll have to desert the three-star hotels in favor of the one-star and two-star establishments, the latter roughly comparable to a second- or third-class hotel. These accommodations are usually older, their furnishings frayed, but all of these recommendations are clean and moderately comfortable.

Near the Atocha Station

Hotel Mercátor, 123 Atocha (tel. 429-05-00), does a good job of maintenance. Only about a three-minute stroll from the Prado, it draws a clientele seeking a good, modern hotel—orderly, well run, and clean, with enough comforts and conveniences to please the weary traveler. Some of the rooms are impersonal, but others are more inviting, especially those with desks and armchairs. Color is often utilized effectively. The best twin-bedded rooms with private bath rent for 2635 pesetas ($25.30). Singles peak at 1675 pesetas ($16.08). The lower floors, as one reader put it, "are cold in design as a Nordic winter—but I had a good bedfellow." The Mercátor has an adjacent parking lot, and is within walking distance of the Iberia air terminal and American Express.

Near the Plaza de Roma

Don Ramón de la Cruz, 94 Don Ramón de la Cruz (tel. 401-72-00), is a 102-room, 102-bath modern hotel, on a relatively quiet street, far from the noise of the madding crowd. It's just off the Plaza de Roma, which is reached from Retiro Park via the broad and attractive Calle de Alcalá. The subway, M. Becerra, stops near the hotel.

The rooms are large enough to spread out your paraphernalia (unless you're returning from an African safari). They're styled with English reproductions, mainly mahogany pieces, such as chests and armchairs. The rate in a double ranges from 1800 pesetas ($17.28) to 2200 pesetas ($21.12). Most singles with bath rent for 1600 pesetas ($15.36). Two elevators service the eight floors, and there's a small breakfast room, plus an air-conditioned public lounge (no restaurant). The staff is friendly and cooperative.

Near the Puerta del Sol

Hotel Residencia Santander, 1 Enchegaray (tel. 429-95-51), is a snug little hotel, just off the Puerta del Sol. You can get a fair to passable double room with private bath for 2200 pesetas ($21.12). A single rents for 1500 pesetas ($14.40), and you pay another 130 pesetas ($1.25) per person for a continental breakfast. The Santander is on a teeming street, but you may appreciate the atmosphere if you like people and local color. The Santander is a refurbished old house, with 38 rooms.

Hotel Internacional, 19 Arenal (tel. 248-18-00), is deceiving: on the outside it looks old-worldish, with its six stories of stone covered with ornate trim and balconies. At some time, however, modernization did take place. The lobby is marble and wood, with low, contemporary chairs set around coffee tables. The spacious dining room has mirror-striped pillars and scenic Spanish murals. Guests of various nationalities gather in the late afternoon in the wood-paneled lounge bar. The bedrooms are fairly pleasant and large. The furnishings, however, are leftovers or misfits, but somehow they all combine to make for what can be a comfortable stay. The price of a double room with private bath peaks at 2500 pesetas ($24). Single rooms with either private bath or shower rent for 1700 pesetas ($16.32). A continental breakfast is an additional 170 pesetas ($1.63).

Francisco I, 15 Arenal (tel. 248-02-04), offers 57 modern, clean rooms. Doubles with a shower-bath (sit-down tub) range from 2800 pesetas ($26.88). Singles—only four in this category—with similar baths go for 2300 pesetas ($22.08). There's a pleasant, if aseptic, lounge, a bar, Muzak, and on the sixth floor you'll find a comfortable, rustic-style restaurant where a set meal costs 740 pesetas ($7.10). Unfortunately, there's no view, but the spacious dining room is pleasantly decorated, nonetheless.

Near the Gran Vía

Mónaco, 5 Barbieri (tel. 222-46-30), is a hidden-away hotel on a teeming tasca-loaded street of Madrid, within an easy walk of the Gran Vía. It takes its name from a chic principality, although it is, in fact, an inexpensive hotel. Each of its bedrooms is different, but all have been refurbished and the plumbing updated. Much gilt, marquetry, and marble are used in the building, and there's a profusion of bronze and gilt chandeliers. Carpets and upholstery have been renewed. A single rents for 1750 pesetas ($16.80), a double for 2200 pesetas ($21.12), plus an additional 150 pesetas ($1.44) for a continental breakfast. There's a tiny stand-up bar and an enclosed breakfast room.

THE BEST PENSIONS: Now I turn to a decent bargain, the pensions, or boarding houses, of Madrid. In my opinion, they offer the cream of the crop in the Spanish capital. By and large, with notable exceptions, these accommodations are superior to the hotels rated one or two stars by the government.

Most of them occupy one large floor in an office or apartment building. All of them have fetching mid-city locations. Some serve breakfast only (and thus become an obvious lure for those who want to eat out); others dish up three meals a day.

Near American Express

Hostal Residencia Roso, 3 Plaza de la Cortés (tel. 429-83-29), is directly across the street from American Express, in an elevator building on the sixth floor. On my most recent visit, a student from Arizona who was living here volunteered the information that it was the best pension he'd found in Spain—and he had been in all the provinces. But the owner enlarged upon this a bit, maintaining that it was the cleanest and best-kept pension in Europe. Unquestionably, it is good, immaculate, and tidy. Friends who know Madrid recommend it as a "very special and inexpensive little place to stay." A bathless single room goes for only 675 pesetas ($6.48), a bathless double for 1150 pesetas ($11.04). Doubles with shower go for 1350 pesetas ($12.96), rising to 1500 pesetas ($14.40) with complete bath. No breakfast is served, and I extend my every good wish to the elevator.

Hostal Principado, 7 Zorilla (tel. 222-66-81), is rated two stars and it's a real find. In a well-kept town house, near the American Express, it is run by the gracious Sra. Maria Alonso Alohonso. She keeps everything immaculately clean, and has made many improvements since taking over the establishment. New tile, attractive bedspreads and curtains give everything a fresh look. A double with shower and water basin costs 1600 pesetas ($15.36), rising to 2200 pesetas ($21.12) in a double with complete bath. A bathless single rents for 1400 pesetas ($13.44). A continental breakfast costs an extra 125 pesetas ($1.20) per person here. One reader, Marty Delman, Los Angeles, California, said, "Turista-afflicted tourists can have hot tea and lots of sympathy." At the entrance downstairs, you'll see where the residents of old arrived in their carriages.

At Santa Bárbara

Santa Bárbara, 4 Plaza de Santa Bárbara (tel. 445-73-34), occupies the third floor of a building on a tree-lined street in a relatively remote section of Madrid. The owner, José Luís Rodríguez, is not allowed to put up a sign, so it is not quickly identified. He also pays for no advertisements, explaining he wants to keep prices as low as possible. The character of the large apartment-turned-small-hotel is old-fashioned, with the smallest, stuffiest reception in the Iberian peninsula. But the bedrooms are, for the most part, of generous size, many furnished with antique beds. You'll be charged 1400 pesetas ($13.44) in a bathless double, 950 pesetas ($9.12) in a single. A continental breakfast is included, and served in a room which is a study in golden oak furnishings. You can ride in the tiny iron-cage elevator.

Along the Gran Vía

The Gran Vía abounds in pensions, many of which are quite good. Others along the street are dubious as to service and facilities. The following represent what I consider the best buys in this classification. (Many of the boarding houses are not directly on the Gran Vía, but on streets jutting off from it.)

The Hotel Alcázar Regis, 61 Gran Vía (tel. 247-93-17), is part of the colorful past of Madrid. Conveniently perched on a corner—right in the midst of Madrid's best shops—it is an old-fashioned building, complete with a circular Greek-style temple as its crown. In a captivating atmosphere, you'll find long and beautiful rooms, wood paneling, leaded-glass windows, parquet floors, crystal chandeliers, and graciously proportioned bedrooms. There has been no chopping up of the rooms to install private baths. A double room with water basin rents for 900 pesetas ($8.64) per person, and one can have full board in the attractively decorated dining room at a rate of 1500 pesetas ($14.40) per person daily, based on double occupancy.

Hostal Gaos, 14 Mesonero Romanos (tel. 231-63-05), offers guests the chance to enjoy a comfortable standard of living at moderate rates. A double bedroom with private bath, memorable for its cleanliness and freshness, costs 1700 pesetas ($16.32), 1200 pesetas ($11.52) if bathless. This residencia is on the second, third, and fourth floors of a building just off the Gran Vía; it lies directly north of the Puerta del Sol. Across the street is the popular flamenco club Torre Bermejas. A continental breakfast is an extra 120 pesetas ($1.15) per person.

At the Puerta del Sol

Hostal Residencia Americano, 11 Puerta del Sol (tel. 222-28-22), is suitable for those who want to be in the bull's-eye center of Madrid, the Puerta del Sol, its so-called Times Square. Its owner-manager, A. V. Franceschi, has recently refurbished all the 42 bedrooms, which come with private baths. The hostal is surrounded by four streets, and 80% of the rooms are outside chambers with balconies facing the street. It's on the third floor of a five-story building, and Mr. Franceschi promises hot and cold running water 24 hours a day. The single rate is 1300 pesetas ($12.48), increasing to 1800 pesetas ($17.28) in a double. A continental breakfast is an extra 100 pesetas (96¢) per person.

Near the Cortés

Hostal Residencia Olga, 13 Calle Zorrilla (tel. 232-21-14). Jeffrey and Marsha Silverstein, living in Badajoz, Spain, highly recommended this place to me—and theirs is a good choice. The location is behind the Cortés (Spain's House of Deputies), and Jeffrey finds it as clean as "my grandmother's kitchen —and that's pretty clean." It's family run, a single room renting for 550 pesetas ($5.28), a double going for 1000 pesetas ($9.60). Most of the units come with showers. Because the location is behind the Congreso, it is a secure area, relatively free of crime as there is 24-hour-a-day guard service. The host is known to me only as "García," and he and his wife are friendly and helpful. They do much to ease your adjustment into the capital.

READERS' PENSION SELECTIONS: "The **Hotel La Perla Asturiana,** 3 Plaza de Santa Cruz (tel. 266-46-00), is centrally located adjacent to the Plaza Mayor in Old Madrid, yet only one block from the Puerta del Sol (American Express is only a ten-minute walk away). Singles cost 890 pesetas ($8.54); doubles, 1400 pesetas ($13.44) to 1600 pesetas ($15.36), the higher price for a room with complete bath" (Dominick Cincirpini, Pittsburgh, Pa.). . . . "The **Hostal Residencia Matute,** 11 Plaza Matute (tel. 228-69-04), is great. Here you get a full tile bath and shower, marble stairways—the works. Doubles with bath peak at 1800 pesetas ($17.28), and singles with shower go for 900 pesetas ($8.64). Mr. Gutierrez, who speaks English, runs a first-class and strictly clean operation. This is the best hotel at tourist rates we found" (John G. Sindorf, Palmer, Alaska). . . . "The **Hostal Don Juan,** 18 Calle Recoletos (tel. 275-00-64), is in central Madrid. Its location makes it especially suitable for families traveling with small children. The Don Juan is just a short block from El Retiro, the great park adjacent to the Prado. An underpass makes this park accessible from the hotel without the necessity of crossing a major street. In addition, the Don Juan is run by a couple who are most obliging in every respect (they procured a crib for our youngest daughter). The Don Juan charges a peak

1500 pesetas ($14.40) in a double with shower, 1200 pesetas ($11.52) in a single with shower, plus an extra 100 pesetas (96¢) per person for a continental breakfast" (Robert G. Schuur, New York, N.Y.). . . . "We stumbled upon the **Hostal Anton,** 4 Calle Muñoz Torrero (tel. 222-53-77), one block from the Gran Vía Metro, one block from the Calle de Barco and your good budget restaurants. The concierge, Carlos Navalón, speaks English and is more than willing to give information about Madrid and the surrounding area. We stayed in a double (very large) with bath for only 1750 pesetas ($16.80); doubles without bath are 1400 pesetas ($13.44). The rooms, although not luxurious, are well kept and clean. For those who want it, a continental breakfast is available at an extra 120 pesetas ($1.15) per person" (Randall Cooper, Wilmington, Del.) . . . "My hotel find was the **Hostal Baranjas,** 17 Augusto Figueroa (tel. 232-40-78), where a single with shower cost only 900 pesetas ($8.64); a double with shower (no toilet) was 1250 pesetas ($12), peaking at 2000 pesetas ($19.20) with private bath. A continental breakfast is an extra 120 pesetas ($1.15) per person" (T. K. Moy, Woodhaven, N.Y.). . . . "I highly recommend the **Hostal Varela,** 5 Valverde (tel. 221-20-00), which is centrally located. The street is behind the Sepu Department Store which is on the Gran Vía. The management speaks English. Most rooms have showers, heaters, and telephones. The charge begins at 900 pesetas ($8.64) per person daily. This includes a room and a continental breakfast" (Mrs. Jan Smalley, Scottsdale, Ariz.).

"The **Hostal La Macarena,** 8 Cava de San Miguel (tel. 265-92-21), is run by three generations of the family of Señor Antonio Juan. The entire family is fluent in Spanish and French. Their son is capable in handling English, and the family as a whole is learning a sufficient amount to attend to most needs. The attitude of the family is the best I have met in my travels. Here one feels like a guest rather than a cog in the tourist industry of Spain. The physical surroundings have not only been improved, but the family takes an interest in people to the point of lending an Australian 1000 pesetas ($9.60) when he arrived on a bank holiday and was unable to exchange any money. This was unsolicited. Another couple with a nine-month-old child was not only made welcome, but the grandmother of the family sat with the child to allow the couple a night on the town. In short, they provide the nicest possible introduction to Spain and the Spanish people. The rates, with a continental breakfast included, are: single, 1250 pesetas ($12); a double with bath, 1800 pesetas ($17.28); and a double without bath, only 1500 pesetas ($14.40)" (Lance Hansche, Bernardsville, N.J.). . . . "**Hostal Numancia,** 8 Magdalena (tel. 468-68-76), is one of the cleanest hostals in Madrid, and I saw plenty when I looked for a place. It is a one-star hostal, and the price is 1100 pesetas ($10.56) in a double, 650 pesetas ($6.24) for a single. Each unit is equipped with a lavatory. It is centrally located, five minutes' walking distance to Puerta del Sol and Plaza Mayor. Also there are a subway station and bus stops at the plaza almost in front of the place called Plaza de Tirso de Molina. The owner is a friendly woman who loves to advise on what to see and do in Madrid" (Glenda Day, Orlando, Fla.).

"**Hostal Arantza,** 7 Calle San Bartolomé (tel. 231-11-65), two blocks from the Gran Vía and around the corner from Restaurant El Criollo, is a well-run Basque hotel, centrally located and run by English-speaking Señora Arantza. Prices in a double with shower, including a continental breakfast, are 1500 pesetas ($14.40); without shower but with wash basin and breakfast, 1200 pesetas ($11.52). This is a good place for anyone attending the bullfights during San Isidro, as the Metro Chueca is a block and a half away, and it's only a five-stop, eight minute run to Ventas Plaza de Toros, the bullring" (William Carrie, St. Petersburg, Fla.). . . . "The **Hostal Rifer,** 5 Calle Mayor (tel. 232-31-97), is just a block from Puerta del Sol. It is on the fourth floor (not counting the ground floor) and may be reached by elevator. It has an impressive, all-marble entrance which is watched and kept clean by the doorman. The hostal has 12 rooms with two single beds or one matrimonial bed. The beds are firm and comfortable, and like the rooms, are kept scrupulously clean. Each room has its own radiator, a godsend in winter. There is a television for the guests. Here the atmosphere is pleasant and native, which lends to learning Spanish and Spanish customs. A room for two costs 1400 pesetas ($13.44) a day, but it's worth much more by comparison. There are no single rooms. The service is friendly and helpful. Doña Marisa, who manages the hostal, dispenses valuable information" (Joseph Vinci, Madrid, Spain).

"We were guests in a private apartment licensed to have tourists for 1250 pesetas ($12) a night for the room, **Señor Hugo Albornoz,** 12 Calle Hospital (tel. 230-32-82). Señor and Señora Albornoz have no children and are a young couple in their 30s. Señora Albornoz likes to be called by her first name, Marita, and made us feel like family. Those who stay here can eat with the family, paying the cost of their food, or they can have kitchen privileges to prepare their own meals. Marita showed us a store where wine is sold inexpensively by the liter from barrels and Marita and her husband, who works nights, are one of the frankest, most open and friendly couples we have met in our journeys through Europe. The apartment is on the fifth floor without an elevator. The couple speaks a little English, but for those who speak Spanish, here is an opportunity to meet a real philosopher. We stayed up till 4 a.m. talking (my wife and I speak Spanish) the first night we arrived. Don't expect a palace. It is a typical small apartment of a working family, but we really enjoyed this opportunity to get to know a Madrid family. They will accept reservations if you pay in advance" (Ed and Eva Brylawski, New York City, N.Y.). . . . "We stayed at the **Hostal-Residencia Fenix,** 6 Concepción Arenal (tel. 231-41-20), off the Gran Vía, near the department store Galerías Preciados. It is very pleasant and clean. A nice double room with shower (toilet a few steps down the hall) rented for 1750 pesetas ($16.80), a single for 1200 pesetas ($11.52)" (Lynne Sedgwick, Croton, N.Y.). . . . "In the heart of town, the **Hostal Marlasca,** 14 Cruz (tel. 221-48-33), offers at 1200 pesetas ($11.52) a single room, a continental breakfast, and the use of a shower. For a double with bath, expect to pay from 1700 pesetas ($16.32). In the family atmosphere of the Marlasca, flamenco dancing can often be observed as parents and children practice" (Joan Moffett, Albany, N.Y.). . . .

"The **Pension Aguadulce,** 3 Plaza de las Cortes, sixth floor (tel. 221-99-96), is a real find near the Prado. Very small (eight to ten rooms), it is owned by Dulce Navarro who runs it with her daughter, also named Dulce, who speaks very functional English. They charge 1750 pesetas ($16.80) per night for two, and that covers several hours of their company as they make you feel right at home in their sitting room, which is pleasant and comfortable with several art reproductions tastefully displayed. No meals other than a continental breakfast are served and our room had no bath, but the cost covers the price of showers. For us, fresh off the plane, it was a great initial experience with friendly Spanish people. They even invited us into their private quarters to watch a bullfight on TV. I'm certain that similar hospitality would be extended to anyone who takes the initiative in conversation" (James Wiley). . . . "We found an excellent little 15-room pension, the **Hostal Mondragón,** 32 Carrera San Jerónimo (tel. 429-68-16), midway between the Puerta del Sol and the Plaza de las Cortés. There is an elevator, as it is on the fourth floor. Our room had free hot showers and a small terrace. A bathless single rents for 500 pesetas ($4.80). Bathless doubles begin at 700 pesetas ($6.72), increasing to 800 pesetas ($7.68) with shower. Above all, our room was clean and quiet" (Dr. and Mrs. John Dabel, Dover, Del.).

"**Hostal Residencia María Molina** is in the heart of the city, 11 Carrera de San Jerónimo (tel. 259-60-88), just a couple of blocks from the Puerta del Sol. The rooms have been redecorated and are kept sparkling clean. No English is spoken, but the director and his wife are eager to help. Bathless singles with hot and cold water cost 550 pesetas ($5.28); doubles with shower, a better bargain, go for 725 pesetas ($6.96) to 825 pesetas ($7.92). A continental breakfast is an extra 75 pesetas (72¢) per person. This pension is also near a number of excellent low-budget restaurants on Calle Victoria, where the real heart of the Spanish people can be felt, and foreign visitors are most welcome" (Mary Lynn Chilbert, Camden, N.J.). . . . "We were delighted to discover the clean, comfortable, convenient **Hostal de Sonsoles** at 18 Fuencarral (tel. 232-16-35). It has a marble entry and wrought iron birdcage elevator. For 1800 pesetas ($17.28) a night, we had a twin-bedded double, tastefully furnished and well lighted, with a desk at which to write. Two chairs provide alternative seating from the beds, which are good and firm. In addition, there's a full tile bath with shower, hot water at all times, and large, thick towels. No meals are served, but just around the corner at Calle de las Infantas and Calle de la Horteleza is **Salaberry.** It's much nicer than hole-in-the-wall, stand-up bars. It has two long counters and a large bright, clean area with tables and chairs. A daily menu for 400 pesetas ($3.84) is presented" (Mr. and Mrs. James L. Isaacson, San Jose, Calif.).

"**Hostal Capricho,** 30 Calle de las Infantas, third floor (tel. 232-35-17), was the best find of my trip to Spain. This is a one-star hotel, kept immaculately clean by the owner, Señor de la Fuente, who speaks French and also understands 'sign language.' The hotel has ten doubles that go for 900 pesetas ($8.64) a night and three singles costing 600 pesetas ($5.76). Showers are an extra 125 pesetas ($1.20). The hotel is centrally located, only two short blocks from the Gran Vía, yet on a quiet side street" (Shelley Wachsmann, Carmel, Israel). . . . "Your readers may be interested in tourist apartments while on extended stays in Madrid. They offer more privacy than a pension and additional savings on meals by providing cooking facilities, even if used only for breakfast. At **Apartamentos Diamond Brick,** 30 Calle Ayala (tel. 225-40-30), for $12.50 (U.S.) a day, we had a charming single apartment which slept two and had a full private bath, kitchenette, and telephone. It is next to a large market, making grocery shopping easy. Daily maid service is provided. The location is only 2½ blocks from Calle Serrano and within walking distance of the terminus of the airport bus, Plaza Colón, for those not burdened with much luggage. A taxi costs about $1 from Plaza Colón to the building, including tip" (Bob Marlin, Los Angeles, Calif.).

A "CASA" OF BUDGET HOTELS: On the main drag Gran Vía, close to many of Madrid's shops and restaurants, is an old-fashioned, 19th-century building filled almost exclusively with small hotels and pensions. The address is **44 Gran Vía.** The building has more hotel beds than the old woman who lived in the shoe had children. And some of the chambers are so small you may be as cramped as that prolific woman's niños.

Still, for the pilgrim who hops off the train in tourist-packed Madrid— armed only with luggage and minus a reservation—the house of hotels is a good bet for doorbell ringing. In some cases, there are two hotels on the same floor. An elevator makes the search easier.

Hotel Continental, 44 Gran Vía (tel. 221-46-40), sprawls high, wide, and handsome over the entire third floor. The rooms are comfortable and tidy, the furnishings having undergone "a grand reform." Showers, baths, even paintings to enliven the decor, have been added. Two persons in a room with either shower or bath pay from 1850 pesetas ($17.76), including a continental breakfast. A single without bath costs 1000 pesetas ($9.60). The lobby is dignified, and the desk clerk speaks English. Plaudits to a management that has tried to create a pleasant house in which to lodge.

Hostal-Residencia Miami, 44 Gran Vía (tel. 221-14-64), enjoys the vista from the eighth floor. Only a continental breakfast at 100 pesetas (96¢) is served, which means you don't have to be slapped with the demi- or full-pension requirement. Bearing no resemblance to its namesake, the 1920-ish Miami is a good bet for peseta watchers, as it charges only 1200 pesetas ($11.52) for any one of its five doubles with water basins. Two of the special doubles, complete with private baths, rent for 1700 pesetas ($16.32). Bathless singles go for only 900 pesetas ($8.64). Although somewhat cluttered, the residencia is clean and has a helpful staff.

The **Hostal Residencia Tanger,** 44 Gran Vía (tel. 221-75-85), on the top-floor roost, emerges with the quietest and sunniest disposition. The lobby is small but tasteful, and there is pleasantly old-fashioned furniture in the bedrooms. The passion of Mercedes Bilbao Ducable for knickknacks softens the rough edges and imbues the Tanger with a homey touch. Doubles with a shower (but no toilet) tally up at 1400 pesetas ($13.44). Bathless doubles are 1200 pesetas ($11.52). Singles pay 650 pesetas ($6.24) in a bathless room, increasing to 750 pesetas ($7.20) in a room with a shower. Only a continental breakfast is served, at 90 pesetas (86¢).

STUDENT ACCOMMODATIONS: If you're a bona fide full-time student, your International Student Identity Card will be an open sesame for you in Madrid and the rest of Spain. The ISIC, which costs $6, entitles you to discounts and student reductions at some theaters and most museums; and it enables you to fly on intra-European student charter flights at one-third the regular commercial fare. It also gives you the opportunity to join low-cost student tours operated by student travel bureaus, and to stay at student hostels, as well as eat at student restaurants. For information about the ISIC and details about transportation and travel services, write to the **Council on International Educational Exchange,** 205 East 42nd St., New York, NY 10017 (tel. 212/661-1414). Another office is at 312 Sutter St., San Francisco, CA 94108. The identification card issued you will give you access to most of the student lodgings of Madrid, such as those maintained *in summer only* by the University of Madrid.

In the area of the Ciudad Universidad, my only recommendation is the **Colegio Mayor José Antonio,** Avenida Séneca (tel. 243-26-00), an impressive brick structure, surrounded by park-like grounds. A total of 204 beds is offered to both men and women. The full-board rate ranges from 1500 pesetas ($14.40) in a single to 1200 pesetas ($11.52) per person, based on double occupancy. You're required to book for at least three days. To reach the dormitory, take bus 12 or the Metro (although it's a good ten-minute hike from the Moncloa subway stop).

3. The Restaurants of Madrid

The capital of Spain wraps a fringed shawl around a maze of restaurants. Most of my recommendations are in the heart of town, although restaurants have sprouted up almost overnight in every suburb. Time was when a traveler to Spain had to eat Spanish food almost exclusively. That is no longer true. Madrid has gone international, offering a wide spectrum of restaurants that range around the globe in cooking styles. They even do American food.

TOP-OF-THE-BUDGET DINING: My very favorite—and most expensive— recommendations will come first.

Casa Botín, 17 Calle de Cuchilleros (tel. 266-42-17), was founded in 1725, and is probably the most famous restaurant in Spain. Ernest Hemingway fanned the fires of its reputation when, in the final pages of *The Sun Also Rises,* Jake invited Brett to Botín to dine on roast suckling pig from Segovia and to drink rioja alta wine. "It is one of the best restaurants in the world," the author wrote. If that wasn't enough publicity, again, in *Death in the Afternoon,* he invited his mythical Old Lady there, preferring once again the suckling pig, rather than thinking "of casualties my friends have suffered."

Actually, the restaurant has everything on its side, especially its location near an edge of the Plaza Mayor, as well as its structure—an old building with beautifully preserved rooms that are furnished with imagination. Don't miss the early 18th-century oven; all visitors eventually inspect it. Out of that oven comes the justly praised roast suckling pig, that dish of Old Castile. Or if you prefer, the second-ranking dish is cordero asado (roast baby lamb). Don Antonio, one of the owners, assists with the language problem; he's greeted thousands of North Americans—so don't hesitate to call on him.

The service is tops, and a menú of the house goes for 1150 pesetas ($11.04). This menú is offered only in autumn and winter, and includes garlic soup with egg, roast suckling pig, melon, or a small pitcher of wine or a glass of beer (mineral water if you prefer). Once in Madrid, it's worth going if not whole hog, at least a little bit the pig. If so, you'll pay 850 pesetas ($8.16) for the cochinillo asado on the à la carte menu. Less expensive but very good dishes on the à la carte menu include half stewed partridge, 530 pesetas ($5.09), and chicken in a casserole with vegetables, 350 pesetas ($3.36). The fish dishes are most recommendable, including a mixed fish in a casserole, Spanish-fisherman style, 475 pesetas ($4.32).

Classified as the two-fork restaurant, Botín has superb chefs, and you won't get any unpleasant surprises here. Lunch is served from 1 to 4 p.m., dinner from 8 p.m. to midnight. There is a small Andalusian bodega downstairs, where you can also order a complete meal (however, you can't drop in and tie up a table by ordering just a glass of wine). Nice atmosphere, as Papa would say.

La Toja, 3 Siete de Julio, near the Plaza Mayor (tel. 266-46-64), is a leading seafood restaurant in Madrid. Although buried deep in the heart of Spain, Madrid has some of the freshest seafood in the country. The reason: it's flown in fresh within an hour or so from both Mediterranean and Atlantic ports. In Spain gourmets consider the paella the secret barometer of a chef's skill, and here he redeems his reputation, a large platter—served to two persons —costing 1500 pesetas ($14.40). The paella is studded with tasty bits of succulent morsels of seafood, and the other "fruits of the sea" dishes are distinguished as well.

If you're not seeking seafood, you'll find a variety of beef, pork, and veal specialties, prepared more or less well. La Toja is definitely a splurge, a complete meal costing around 1600 pesetas ($15.36) per person.

If you dine in this part of Old Madrid, it can be a memorable experience. Perhaps some mandolin-playing troubadours will come around to entertain you, as you sit out on the Plaza Mayor. I suggest you go here for an apéritif before dinner. Madrileños look upon the square with feelings of pride and affection, and you'll easily understand why. Since La Toja is a favorite spot with foreigners and Spaniards alike, it's wise to have your hotel telephone for reservations before striking out for old town.

El Callejón, 6 Tenera (tel. 231-91-95), was Hemingway's "other favorite." It lies on a tiny street right in the heart of Madrid, off the Gran Vía. Before leaving Madrid, a close friend was advised by Papa to go to the Prado to see his favorite paintings, then take a "last supper" at Callejón. The restaurant, still going strong today, serves some of the tastiest Spanish dishes in town. For example, it features regional dishes on set days of the week. On Tuesday and Saturday, you can order stewed veal, but you have to go here on Thursday for that Spanish soul-food dish, red beans with rice. Openers might include the classic garlic soup, or shrimp Bilbao style. Main courses include the special steak or calf sweetbreads. Eggs Callejón and half a roast chicken are much cheaper. The least expensive way to dine here is to stick to the three-course menu of the day. For dessert, try either the cherries with fresh cream or the fried bananas. If you dine à la carte, expect the tab to range from 1200 pesetas ($11.52) to 1800 pesetas ($17.28).

La Hostería Piamontesa, 18 Costanilla de Los Angeles (tel. 248-34-14), is in a town house which has been converted into an Italian restaurant. Its trio of dining rooms are on the second floor, above a bar on the street level. Little remains of the former drawing room, except the parquet floors and crystal chandeliers. Hit-and-miss paintings and bric-a-brac decorate the walls, making it cheery and homey.

Best of all, however, is the cooking, augmented by the sizable portions and the low prices. While there is a traditional menú turístico at 875 pesetas ($8.40), many diners prefer to order à la carte, paying about 1100 pesetas ($10.56) for a complete meal. The waitresses on request bring in a large bowl of Roman-style stracciatella to get things started. That and one of the pastas make a full meal. Try the lasagne verde al horno—homemade, rich, and oozing with cheese. For those desiring meat or fowl, the saltimboccas (literally, jump-in-your-mouth) à la Romana are good. If you order the latter, you'll receive bowls with at least five different vegetables. The zuppa inglese, a dessert, makes a good finish. The staff takes a holiday in August and shuts down on Monday.

Chez Lou, 6 Pedro Muguruza (tel. 250-34-16), near the Eurobuilding Hotel in the northern sector of Madrid, stands near the huge mural by Joan Miró, which alone would be worth the trek up here. Quite different from most restaurants in Madrid, this cozy little place is run by a French woman. In fact, it evokes a small French inn—say, in Burgundy and Morvan. The restaurant appeals to an in-the-know international set, and it's a good idea to make reservations early in the day, especially because Chez Lou is not large.

In this intimate setting, you get well-prepared and reasonably priced French food. The restaurant serves pâté as an appetizer, then a large range of crêpes with many different fillings. Folded envelope style, the crêpes are not tea-room size, but perfectly adequate as a main course.

I've sampled several variations on the crêpe theme, finding the ingredients nicely blended, yet distinct enough to retain their identity. A favorite is the large crêpe stuffed with minced onions, cream, and smoked salmon. The ham and cheese is also tasty. Crêpes cost from 425 pesetas ($3.85), and the price of your dessert and drink is extra.

Come here if you're seeking a light supper when it's too hot for one of those table-groaning Spanish meals. Chez Lou opens at 6:30 p.m. for dinner, which is wildly early for Madrid, and it also serves lunch except on Saturday. It closes completely on Monday.

Valencia, 44 Gran Vía (tel. 232-01-50), offers some of the best typically Spanish cookery on this main drag. One flight up, it has tables overlooking floor-to-ceiling windows that give you a bird's-eye view of shoppers on the street below. As you may know, Valencia is a city known for its paella. The restaurant not only aptly bears the name, but lives up to the reputation of the dish. The paella here is one of the highlights of a culinary adventure in Spain. It is endlessly generous, and has all sorts of fish and meats cut up in it. The most economical way to dine here is to order the menú de la casa at 500 pesetas ($4.80), which includes two dishes, bread, sangría, and a dessert. It is always astonishing to see Spaniards treat this enormous dish as one of several courses. The Valencia closes down on Monday.

Mesón las Meigas, 6 Barbieri (tel. 221-07-57), provides a lively Galician tavern atmosphere. It's on a short street of tascas, flamenco clubs, and low-priced restaurants (none of which lives up to the standards of this mesón). In the early evening, Barbieri becomes a virtual mall of pedestrians (mostly men), wandering from tasca to tasca, imbibing their favorite sherry along with bits of squid or some such tapas.

The front room of the mesón is like a country inn, with a heavy emphasis on local color: strings of garlic, sausages, and many smoked hams. In the rear, the dining room continues the same rural ambience, with its hay forks, oxen yokes, and open fireplace with an iron crane for pots of Galician soup—in all, a comfortable, friendly atmosphere, with spirited waiters. These young men will chop off hunks of whole-grained crusty bread, putting them down beside a jug of wine at your table.

There is a menú del día for only 850 pesetas ($8.16), a different one offered for each day of the week. On the à la carte menu, I recommend the caldo gallego, a hearty soup of greens and potatoes. Another regional specialty is the lacón con grelos, a boiled ham hock with greens. An appropriate beverage is the sangría de vino ribeiro. On the à la carte menu, expect to pay from 650 pesetas ($6.24) to 1500 pesetas ($14.40) per person.

La Bola, 5 Bola, just north of the Teatro Real. If you'd like to savor the Madrid of the 19th century, then this taberna is an inspired choice. It's one of the few (if not the only) restaurants left in Madrid that's painted with a blood-red facade. Once nearly all fashionable restaurants were so coated. La Bola hangs on to tradition like a tenacious bull. Time has galloped forward, but not inside this restaurant, where the soft, traditional atmosphere, the gentle and polite old-world retainer-type waiters, and the Venetian crystal, the Carmen-red draperies, the aging velvet preserve a yesteryear.

Ava Gardner, with her entourage of bullfighters, used to patronize this establishment, but it was her discovery and remained relatively unknown to tourists. That's surprising, in that the food is good, and not at all expensive. A specialty is the sopa Wamba, which is soothing to those who have had too much rich fare, made as it is with ham and rice in a broth, over which chopped hard-boiled eggs are sprinkled. The roast chicken (pollo asado) is always reliable as is the sole *(lenguado)* meunière. Depending on your selections, the cost of a complete meal ranges in price from 700 pesetas ($6.72) to 1000 pesetas ($9.60).

As visiting Berliners and Viennese can tell you, there is a worthwhile fatherland restaurant in Madrid: the **Edelweiss**, 7 Jovellanos (tel. 221-03-26), a Spanish conception of a Munich beer hall. Established in Madrid after the war, it specializes in Germanic dishes, a welcome respite from the Spanish cuisine. There's a good reason why this place is always jammed—portions here are big, waiters friendly on the whole, and service efficient. In addition there's a large menu to choose from. Lunch is served from 1 until 4 p.m. and dinner from 7 p.m. (early eaters take note) to midnight. A meal—wine and service included—will cost from 1500 pesetas ($14.40) to 2500 pesetas ($24) per person. Soups are hearty and homemade, and among the main-course selections roast veal and goulash are traditionally featured. The best known dish of the restaurant is eisbein (pork leg specially prepared in the German style). It's served with sauerkraut and mashed potatoes. For dessert, I'd suggest the apple tart with whipped cream. Actually, the Edelweiss may not break your budget after all. If you consume all this at 3 o'clock in the afternoon, chances are you'll skip dinner unless you're Orson Welles. The restaurant is in a corner building near American Express. Closed in August and on Sunday night.

Continuing the international theme, you might also like to patronize **Jada**, 3 Corredera Baja de Pablo, off the Gran Vía (tel. 222-96-67). This place has a devoted following because of its fine, low-priced food, with complete meals, with wine or beer, coming to around 750 pesetas ($7.20) per head. Most diners seem to begin their meals with eggrolls, and the chef does them well, filling the crackly shells with shrimp, pork, and crisp vegetables. The management relies on crisp, fresh ingredients, making Jada far superior to the host of bad Chinese restaurants that have opened in recent years in Madrid. Service is attentive and not overbearing. If you don't like to wait around until 9:30 p.m. to dine with the Spaniards, you can slip in here with fellow tourists at 7 p.m. and order dinner. Just arrive on the doorstep. I've shown up at various hours and always found a table available.

La Trucha (The Trout), 3 Manuel Fernández González, is the recreation of an old tavern from the owner's hometown, the port city of Cádiz. The atmosphere is typically Andalusian, with a street-floor arched dining room decorated with pigtails of garlic, red peppers, and onions. You'll find iron signs of the bullfight. On the lower level is a *cueva* (cave) with a bar and another dining room in the same style.

The bar is made with thick slabs of wood; on display are the kinds of fish brought in from Málaga and Cádiz. The prices are so reasonable that many Madrileño middle-class families eat here regularly. The menu of the day goes for 750 pesetas ($7.20), and includes a choice of two plates, plus bread and wine.

However, I gravitate to the platos del día, a different one offered for each day of the week, and peaking at 600 pesetas ($5.76). A savory stew (called "glorious" in the province of Asturias) is fabada, made with beans, Galician ham, black sausage, and smoked bacon.

Back in the old part of town, there are two candidates for those who like good beef and good meat. **Casa Paco,** 11 Puerta Cerrada (tel. 266-31-66), has been known to Madrileños and foreigners for decades. Despite the tourist invasion, its owners have kept up the quality of food and efficiency of service. The restaurant is actually an old tavern, with dining rooms downstairs and upstairs. The tourist menu is 700 pesetas ($6.72), but the reason most people come here is to order one of the deliciously thick steaks, priced according to weight and served sizzling hot on a wooden board. Figure about 1500 pesetas ($14.40) for this delicacy. If you can't spend that much, order the roast lamb for 1000 pesetas ($9.60), or a simple roast chicken for 450 pesetas ($4.32). Since Casa Paco is so well known, expect at least a half-hour wait, even on a weekday evening. However, at lunchtime, you can usually get a table right away.

Casa Paco's rival, two blocks down, is **El Schotis,** 11 Cava Baja. Equally famous for its meat, the restaurant specializes in a churrasco Schotis for 700 pesetas ($6.72) or a large veal chop for 550 pesetas ($5.28). There's also a menú del día for 750 pesetas ($7.20), but you're better off ordering à la carte, paying from 1000 pesetas ($9.60). Closed in August.

STATESIDE SPECIALTIES: A popular hangout for locals and visiting Yanks is **Hollywood,** 1 Calle Magallanes (tel. 448-91-65). It's a California-style hamburger extravaganza, a fashionable place to eat and be seen, serving, according to many travelers, "the best American food in Europe." It is owned and operated by an American couple from Detroit. Outside you can sit in director's chairs on the terrace, with the name of a movie star on the back. You will find this one of the most comfortable and best people-watching sites in Madrid, while you enjoy sangría or your back-home favorite. Inside, it's nostalgia time, with bentwood chairs and many framed photographs and posters. Some Spaniards have encountered problems in eating the hamburgers, as indeed would anyone not familiar with devouring food five inches high. Hamburgers weigh in at one-half pound, and range in price from 250 pesetas ($2.40) to 355 pesetas ($3.41), the latter with cheese, bacon strips, and Russian dressing. These orders are served with french fries and salad. Other Stateside treats are chili con carne at 180 pesetas ($1.73), homemade apple pie at 160 pesetas ($1.54), cheesecake at 195 pesetas ($1.87), and, as recently reported in the *New York Times,* "probably the best onion rings in the world."

The same food is also available at Hollywood's other locations at 3 Apolonia Morales (tel. 457-79-11), in the Castellana area near the Eurobuilding and Melía Castilla Hotels, and at 1 Tamayo y Baus (tel. 231-51-15), close to Plaza de Cibeles and the Prado.

Burger King, 4 Orense (tel. 455-83-18), is Yankee all the way—the same Whoppers, Whalers, french fries, and jaunty colors, with hats on the pretty waitresses. It seems a little strange to see the nearly all-Spanish clientele standing in line, filling their trays with American-style "quickie food." The prices are modest for such a Madrid import: Whoppers are 175 pesetas ($1.68); regular hamburgers, 100 pesetas (96¢); Whalers, 160 pesetas ($1.54); french fries, 75 pesetas (72¢); and all soda drinks, 75 pesetas also. Burger King dispenses its wares at other locations: 3 Princesa, 4 Arenal, 96 Conde de Peñalver, 48 Lagasca, and 123 San Bernardo.

LOW-BUDGET DINING: As of this writing, the **Calle del Barco** is about the best all-around street for the reader who wants to keep his budget within the strictest limits of the $25-a-day allotment. This narrow street is one of the most colorful in the center of the city, with its wrought-iron balconies gracing old town houses, an occasional elaborately carved oak door opening onto a musty courtyard that speaks of better days. You'll see sheets flapping from the windows of upper-floor apartments, pushcarts rolling across cobblestones. Wrinkled old women, draped in black, hobble past on canes, trailed by their screaming grandchildren. Delivery boys hurry by with boxes of iced red mullet perched on their shoulders.

The landmark for locating this street is the SEPU Department Store on the Gran Vía. From there, walk up a one-block street known as the Calle Jimenez de Quesada, which becomes the Calle del Barco. My preferred choice on "bistro alley" is:

Pagasarri, 7 Barco. The management's head is still swimming from the onslaught of foreign invaders. In fact, there's likely to be a line waiting outside for the 1 p.m. opening. Once known only to the Spanish, Pagasarri now attracts modern diners who have been known to ask for (gasp!) a Coke with dinner. The waiters ask: "Do you comprehend Spanish?" The dining room is like a corridor, getting larger at the rear. It's a family-style atmosphere, and you are often asked to share tables where you can eavesdrop to your heart's content. Nice to know—it's air-conditioned.

At lunch from 1 to 4 p.m., or at supper from 8:30 to 11:30 p.m., you can usually fare well here for about 450 pesetas ($4.32) to 700 pesetas ($6.72). You can also experiment with the à la carte choices. Paella is served as an appetizer on Thursday and Sunday for 225 pesetas ($2.16). The chef prepares a pretty good omelet (about a dozen different varieties) going for 140 pesetas ($1.34).

Should the Pagasarri be closed or too crowded, continue down the street to **Capri,** 27 Barco. This is the Spanish equivalent of a French bistro. The food is típico, and foreigners are welcomed, but not catered to in the way the more commercially oriented establishments tend to treat their new customers. The restaurant's housed in a glass-fronted, modernized ground-floor section of an old town house. (Incidentally, the El Barco Bar next door is a good place to stop for a predinner sherry.)

On my latest summer trek, I arrived just as the melons did—and fresh, vine-ripened ones they were at that, including that rarity in Spain, watermelon. The chef's sopa de mariscos (seafood soup) at 95 pesetas (86¢) is about the cheapest tab on that delicacy I've found anywhere in Madrid. The roast half chicken was a golden brown, the freshly sliced tomatoes ordered as a salad a good buy, too. Best bet—select your main dish from Capri's plates of the day. For an average meal, expect to pay from 400 pesetas ($3.84) to 700 pesetas ($6.72) per person.

Near the Plaza de España

Behind the Plaza de España, with its landmark Edificio España (the skyscraper Hotel Plaza sits here), is an old standby for hungry, budget-minded Americans, the **Vera Cruz,** 5 Calle San Leonardo (tel. 247-54-41). This is a simple "económico," but the food is outstanding and the service friendly. The menú del día costs only 300 pesetas ($2.88), and usually includes a soup or hors d'oeuvres, followed by a meat or fish dish, then cheese or fruit, plus bread and wine. The Vera Cruz also has daily specials—for example, paella for 200 pesetas ($1.92), or a typical Madrid dish made of chick peas, sausage, cabbage, and potatoes, called cocido, for 250 pesetas ($2.40).

Near American Express

Lázaro, 9 Zorrilla (tel. 222-14-08), is a little restaurant offering meals so low in price that I don't understand how the proprietor pays his mortgage. The location, near American Express, is about a five-minute walk from the Prado. The decor? There isn't any. It's plain, but the cleanliness and the white-coated waiters serving simply prepared, nutritious food make it worthwhile for typically Spanish meals. The menu of the day goes for only 570 pesetas ($5.47), and includes three courses, plus the wine of the house. It's more like a small village inn than a big-city restaurant. Because of its simplicity and price, clients eat here regularly. (Spanish-speaking friends once told me, "We even got invited home to taste the paella prepared by the wife of one of the waiters—much better, by the way, than that offered at the restaurant.") Closed in August.

In Old Madrid

La Casa Ciriaco, 84 Calle Mayor (tel. 248-06-20), is a special restaurant near the Plaza Mayor and the old Town Hall, in one of the most romantic parts of old Madrid. It enjoys associations with the Spanish painter, Ignacio Zuloaga. La Casa's definitely not out for the tourist traffic—in fact, foreigners are still regarded with a certain curiosity around here. Female travelers take note: the atmosphere is rather chauvinistic. Autographed bullfighter pictures attest to its popularity with aficionados. Unshaven workmen mix democratically with gray-suited businessmen, plus an occasional priest.

The chef features dishes from Navarre and Andalusia, although Castilian specialties predominate. On the à la carte menu, you can order such main courses as trout in the style of Navarre or tender slices of veal. A good gazpacho makes a fine opener. An average repast here will bring the tab to anywhere from 700 pesetas ($6.72) to 1000 pesetas ($9.60).

On and Around the Ventura de la Vega

The Ventura de la Vega, in the heart of Madrid, is one of the cheapest restaurant streets in Europe. Right after the war, you could dine there for only 10 pesetas, a complete meal including wine and service. But those days have faded into history (also it was alleged that in those lean years horsemeat was served instead of beef). Today, the Ventura de la Vega is the most popular budget restaurant street in Madrid, its establishments as plentiful as shrimp in a family-size paella. One final warning: Watch for those August closings.

Luarques, 16 Ventura de la Vega (tel. 429-61-74), dishes up some of the most savory viands on this street. It's a winner in the Mr. Clean sweepstakes, too. But it's not the cheapest, offering a set meal of four platos, plus bread and wine, for 600 pesetas ($5.76). Considering what you get, it's a fair buy. The restaurant offers all the standard dishes that are the hallmark of the Spanish cuisine: gazpacho, paella, flan, sopa de pescado, and roast chicken.

The **Restaurant Hylogui,** 3 Ventura de la Vega (tel. 429-73-57), offers a 570-peseta ($5.47) dinner. It is one of the largest dining rooms along the street, but has many arches and nooks for those who want to escape their public. In frankness, it must be admitted that the cuisine here has scored with some budgeteers, really struck out with others. One intrepid, globe-trotting American schoolteacher wrote enthusiastically that he took all his meals here while in Madrid, finding the soup pleasant and rich, the flan soothing, the regional wine dry.

El Gran Triunfo, 13 Echegaray (tel. 429-64-80), is by far the cheapest Chinese restaurant in Madrid. There is no decor to speak of (20 tables under fluorescent lighting), but it offers a 400-peseta ($3.84) menu that consists of egg drop soup or hot-and-sour soup, eggrolls, sweet-and-sour pork or fish, and fried rice, plus bread, wine, and ice cream.

El LaCon Restaurante, 8 Manuel Fernández González (tel. 232-49-40), is a large, colorful country inn restaurant on three levels. You get excellent food, a rustic atmosphere, and moderate prices, considering that it has been so expensively and recently created. There are rough white beams, hanging hams, lanterns, crude tables, and an antique gun collection. Before dining on the mezzanine, you can order tapas in an old-world-style bar in the cellar. One of the chef's specialties is bacalao vizcaina, codfish prepared Basque style. The clams in a marinara sauce are also tasty, as are the shrimp with garlic. Another typical dish is ham hock with greens. Expect to pay about 900 pesetas ($8.64) for a most filling repast.

Running parallel to the Ventura de la Vega is a street housing the **Casa Sevillano,** 33 Príncipe (tel. 232-01-85), a short stroll from the Spanish Theater, which lures its budget-conscious patrons in with the promise of a real bargain: a 450-peseta ($4.32) cubierto populár. Unlike most of the set meals offered throughout Spain, the choice here is large. For a starter you can choose those tasty white beans, a cream of mushroom soup, the sopa de la casa, Andalusian gazpacho, a consommé or hors d'oeuvres. Main courses are equally varied, and a salad of freshly chopped fruit is occasionally featured for dessert. The cubierto, incidentally, includes bread and wine. Bypass the unattractive front room and head for the rear.

In the Goya Shopping Area

Casa Cirilo, 36 Calle General Pardiñas, is handy for those in the Goya shopping area. You enter Cirilo through a small bar, which leads into two tiny downstairs dining rooms, and another one upstairs. The decor is simple: tiled walls, bentwood chairs, and fluorescent lights; but the restaurant is well patronized by knowledgeable Spaniards. The specialty here is pollo riojano, a half chicken prepared with heaps of red peppers, mushrooms, sausage, and served with french fries. An à la carte meal costs from 750 pesetas ($7.20) to 1000 pesetas ($9.60). The tourist menu goes for 750 pesetas ($7.20), which will get you, for example, hors d'oeuvres or lentils, followed by fish or roast chicken, then custard for dessert, plus bread and wine.

Riofrío, Centro Colón, 1 Plaza Colón (tel. 419-29-77), where you can pause to refresh, is an ideal, central place for on-the-run snacks and drinks. Its terrace, overlooking the Columbus Circle of Madrid, is favored on sunny days. Otherwise, there is a more formal interior restaurant where you can get more substantial meals, as well as a self-service section. Club sandwiches go for 400 pesetas ($3.84) and an appetizing combination plate for 550 pesetas ($5.28). Spanish coffee is 75 pesetas (72¢), and a presnack drink such as a scotch is 350 pesetas ($3.36). Prices are raised slightly if you sit outside on the terrace.

Time out for tea? If you're in the area, I'd suggest the **Embassy,** at the corner of Ayala and the Paseo de la Castellana, one block north of the Plaza Colón. You can't miss it, as it's a virtual landmark with Madrileños living in this part of town. It's been called the Schrafft's of Spain. From 4 o'clock in the afternoon on, its a rendezvous point for those hoping to relax and talk over a wide assortment of well-stuffed sandwiches, canapés, and rich pastries. Those little "tea sandwiches" cost from 85 pesetas (82¢) each.

In the Rastro Area

In the area of Madrid's popular flea market, the Rastro, your best bet is **La Esquinita,** 16 Plaza Cascorro, where you can eat a whole roast chicken for 500 pesetas ($4.80). Otherwise, try the roast quail or a squid sandwich—that's right! La Esquinita is more of a bar than a restaurant, although there are some tables.

"The Cheapest Restaurant in the World"

El Criollo, 21 Barbieri, is an anachronism, a simple working person's place without frills that actually serves a dinner for 150 pesetas ($1.44). The genial proprietor, Don Alejandro Yubero, doesn't seem to be out to add anything to his bank account or take away much from yours. For this price, you get, say, pea soup, a meat entree with potatoes, followed by a plate of custard for dessert. Although it's a puzzle to know how he does it without a grant, I extend my best wishes to Don Alejandro. I hope he never has to face the realities of the inflationary 20th century. The restaurant is open from 1 to 4 p.m. and from 8:30 p.m. till midnight.

The Cafeterías

The cafetería is the fastest growing eating institution in Madrid, patronized not only by foreigners, but by a legion of modern señoritas and their beaus who want to get into the culinary swing of the Western world. These generally modern, American-style, slick establishments are misleadingly known as cafeterias (only one of them in Madrid is self-service). The biggest and most popular is:

The **Cafetería California,** 49 Gran Vía (tel. 231-51-51), a base for visitors, as well as for the smart young Madrileño seeking "exotic" tastes. The California, a chain of cafeterías, caters to the ever-growing need to satisfy a taste for derivative dishes from the United States—milkshakes, cheeseburgers, club sandwiches. A hamburger costs 300 pesetas ($2.88) at the counter; a club sandwich, 300 pesetas also; a hot dog, 150 pesetas ($1.44); and pancakes with caramel syrup and whipped cream, 200 pesetas ($1.92).

Two other California cafeterías are at 21 (tel. 435-12-27) and 47 Goya (tel. 435-69-79), and yet another is at 39 Gran Vía. The cafeterías are generally open from 8 a.m. until 1:30 a.m. Other cafetería chains include **Morrison** and **Manila.**

THE OLIVER AREA: A whole slew of as yet untouristy restaurants are within a few blocks' radius of the famous bar **Oliver.** In addition to the nearby Cafe Gijón, there are:

Casa Gades, 4 Conde de Xiqueña (tel. 232-30-51), run by flamenco dancer Antonio Gades, a favorite hangout for show-biz people, journalists, and artists. The small restaurant is built on several levels. Around the walls are placed posters, paintings, and autographed photographs. The ambience is warm, the prices of dishes relatively inexpensive. A set menu costs 575 pesetas ($5.52), although many guests prefer to come here for the pizzas, ranging in price from 220 pesetas ($2.11) to 350 pesetas ($3.36). A typical menu, including a salad, veal scaloppine, and flan (caramel custard), will cost 750 pesetas ($7.20), not including your choice of wine.

El Communista, 35 Augusto Figueroa. Although officially this restaurant is known as Tienda de Vinos (Wine Shop), in-the-know Madrileños have dubbed it "The Communist," Lord knows why. This rather rickety old wine shop, with a few tables in the back, has become quite fashionable with actors, journalists, and people in the arts looking for simple Spanish fare without frills. There is a menu, but no one ever thinks of asking for it. You simply ask one of the two waiters "What do you have today?" and he tells you. Nor do you get a bill; you're just told how much. There's no sign outside the restaurant to tell you "this is it," just a rather yellow, decrepit wooden facade, an awning, and old bottles in the window. Inside, you sit at wooden tables and on wooden chairs and benches placed around the walls. The walls are decorated with old posters, calendars, pennants, and clocks. You can start by ordering a garlic or vegetable soup or lentils for 90 pesetas (86¢), followed by lamb chops, 350 pesetas ($3.36). An average meal here will cost from 400 pesetas ($3.84) to 750 pesetas ($7.20).

La Argentina, 8 Válgame Dios, corner of Calle Gravina (tel. 221-37-63), is about two blocks away from Oliver. Its owner, Sr. Rodríguez, is always there to watch over clients. Although he lived many years in Argentina, he hails originally from Asturias. La Argentina only has 16 tables, but the food is tops, decor is simple and clean, and you're usually served by one of the two waitresses who have been there for a number of years. Best bets here are: cannelloni Rossini, noodle soup, and creamed spinach. Meat dishes are tops, including entrecôte or roast veal. Chicken villaroy is another special. The regular tourist menu goes for 600 pesetas ($5.76). All dishes are served with mashed *and* french-fried potatoes. For dessert, have a baked apple or rice pudding. À la carte meals range in price from 475 pesetas ($4.56) to 750 pesetas ($7.20).

The last of the restaurants near Oliver is a top-notch económico called **Bogotá,** 20 Calle de Belén (tel. 419-50-12). Here, on Bethlehem Street, in a no-frills restaurant with tiled walls and a television set, you can have a tourist menu for 425 pesetas ($4.08). Soups are rich and hearty, and the chef does a good villaroy chicken (breaded breast of chicken). I'm also fond of his large steak known here as churresco de cebon. There are also several platos combinados as well. An à la carte meal costs from 400 pesetas ($3.84) all the way to 1000 pesetas ($9.60) if you want to order the expensive steak.

MISCELLANEOUS: Kentucky Fried Chicken, the American-owned restaurant chain, has a good place in Madrid at 13 Juan Hurtado de Mendoza (tel. 259-10-94). It's in the "Dr. Fleming" area, where many foreigners live and dine. The Kentucky has a counter, and an adjoining restaurant with tables. At the tables, a two-piece chicken lunch costs 300 pesetas ($2.88); a three-piece one, 400 pesetas ($3.84); and a jumbo (five pieces), 700 pesetas ($6.72), which includes chicken, mashed potatoes, cole slaw, bread, wine, and fruit.

Kuopin Restaurante Chino, 6 Valverde, is an interesting Chinese restaurant, only 100 long strides from the busy Gran Vía, reached by metro. It's approached through a long hallway in an old Madrid building. Inside you'll find the usual Chinese decor with large lanterns. Many of your fellow diners will be Chinese, a fairly good gauge of authenticity and value. The chef offers a special budget dinner for 325 pesetas ($3.12), offering, for example, egg-drop soup, sweet-and-sour pork, and ice cream with walnuts. Bread and a beverage are included. À la carte temptations are sweet corn, egg, and chicken soup for 125 pesetas ($1.20); Cantonese shrimp, 300 pesetas ($2.88); and roast pork, Cantonese style, 255 pesetas ($2.45). Kuopin is open from noon to 4 p.m. and from 8 p.m. to midnight, and all the waiters speak English.

Restaurante Trafalgar, 7 Trafalgar, is one of the best all-round budget restaurants in Madrid. On a quiet, wide street, off the Calle Luchana (a couple of blocks from the Drugstore and the Café Commercial), it has a neat, trim, clean dining room. In summer, a row of tables is placed outdoors for al fresco dining. Food and service are tops, and the portions are generous. Although there is a tourist menu, you're best ordering such à la carte specialties as paella, roast veal, and villaroy chicken. Your tab should be in the neighborhood of 400 pesetas ($3.84) to 700 pesetas ($6.72).

If you're addicted, as I am, to pizza at least once a week, you're in luck in Madrid if you go to the **Pizza Hut,** 11 Orense, in the northern sector of the city. This has to be one of the most attractive Pizza Huts you are likely to find. It's styled in a contemporary Iberian rustic theme, using bentwood chairs and wicker baskets, with shadings of salmon pink and green. The pies here are cooked to order and haven't been waiting around all night. Count on spending about 750 pesetas ($7.20) per person, and you'll be quite filled for dinner. Service is daily from noon to midnight.

READERS' RESTAURANT SUGGESTIONS: "Costa del Sol, 6 Tres Cruces, gives a full three-course meal, wine and bread included, for 450 pesetas ($4.32), and believe me, the food is delicious! I went there several times and I found it great. The only disadvantage is that it is usually full, as it's small. You usually have to wait a while before you can get a table, but it's worth it" (Olga Duarte, Salamanca, Spain). . . . **"Restaurant Chino-Prado,** 5 Jesus y María (tel. 227-00-66), is a good find for those readers who like Oriental food at low prices in pleasant surroundings. The proprietor, Mr. Ho-Choong-Han, is an affable fellow who learned some English in Hong Kong. He and his family have moved to Madrid and are making a go of it. A three-course meal (soup, beef chop suey, bread, wine, and dessert) costs 450 pesetas ($4.32). À la carte selections are also reasonably priced, and the food is tasty and well prepared. This little restaurant is on a quiet street, less than a ten-minute walk from the Plaza Mayor" (J. Hobson, New Orleans, La.). . . . "A Japanese friend took us to what he described (and we agree) is the best Japanese restaurant in town. **Restaurante Japones-Donzoko,** 9 Echegaray (tel. 429-62-24), near Puerta del Sol. You can have steak Japanese style with a wonderful salad and vegetables for 500 pesetas ($4.80). Their beef is the greatest. Tempura is 480 pesetas ($4.61), which was just right for me but may be a skimpy portion for the American male. Donzoko is beautifully clean, uncluttered, and quiet. It's open from 1:30 to 4 p.m. and from 8 to 11:30 p.m. You may see the chef later at the Princess disco" (Dayna Smalley, Scottsdale, Ariz.).

"Right off Plaza Mayor is a neat little place with very clean restrooms, and it is *climatizado* (air-conditioned). It's **Los Galayos,** 5 Calle de Botoneeras (tel. 266-30-28). They take American Express cards. A meal with wine is 1100 pesetas ($10.56). Gazpacho is very good. Outside you are served plenty of sangría. It is worth going there just to sit outside and enjoy the sangría, as you can watch all that is going on in Plaza Mayor while being secluded from it" (Mrs. Jan Smalley, Scottsdale, Ariz.). . . . "Near Puerta del Sol is **El Club,** Restaurante, Cervecería & Jamonería, 4 Calle Victoria. The beer is very cold, and at an outside table where you are charged an extra service charge, it costs 100 pesetas (96¢). Paella is 400 pesetas ($3.84). El Club is right across the street from where you can buy bullfight tickets" (Dayna Smalley, Scottsdale, Ariz.).

"Mesón las Descalzas, 3 Postego San Martín (tel. 222-72-12), is a smallish restaurant with a tavern atmosphere, where our meal was served by an attentive, jolly waiter who entered into the fun as we translated the Spanish menu and ordered our meal in Spanish. The gazpacho was the best we had in Spain and the helping was generous. This was followed by zarzuela, a fish stew to which I give full praise. A full three-course meal with entremeses and wine and coffee for two costs 2000 pesetas ($19.20). I highly recommend this restaurant. . . . One enters **Mesón D'a Morrina,** 33 Leganitos (tel. 247-10-62), past a window in which fresh, pink suckling pigs are hanging by their back feet. Inside, the counter is lined with exotic food. Flames leap from the kitchen stoves as meats are grilled. The atmosphere is jolly and full of good humor. The food is excellent, and the suckling pig is a specialty. It melts in your mouth and is well worth the 780 pesetas ($7.49). While you eat and absorb the atmosphere, a band of Mandregos comes in to play on guitars and mandolins and sing. My advice is: don't miss it" (Dr. and Mrs. C. H. Chaffey, Dapto, N.S.W., Australia).

"Across the street from the ticket office for bullfights, at 9 Victoria, is the **Pasaje Mateu,** a one-block-long pedestrian mall loaded with inexpensive tapas bars and restaurants. I bought a round of five beers and two glasses of wine for less than $1 (U.S.). It attracts a rather bohemian crowd but is quite safe" (Bob Marlin, Los Angeles, Calif.).

... "For Basque cooking, try the busy and crowded **Taberna Batela** on the square off Calle de la Luna, not too far from the Gran Vía. Their mussels for 175 pesetas ($1.68) are especially good" (Joseph W. Zdenek, Rock Hill, S.C.).... "For a real splurge, seafood lovers should try **El Pozo de Monterrey** on Alcalá near the Puerta del Sol. The dining room is upstairs. You can dine here for less than 1200 pesetas ($11.52) if you order carefully. The shellfish is excellent, and I heartily recommend the merluza al horno. They also have fine manchego cheese and good sangría. Don't order more than one dish unless you have a gargantuan appetite.... The buffet at **El Corte Inglés** (a large department store on Calle Preciados) is just the thing for those large appetites. The food is good, you can eat all you want for 750 pesetas ($7.20), the selection is enormous, and they start serving early and continue to serve later than most restaurants" (Ileane Kine, Huntington Beach, Calif.).... "Two restaurants that deserve mention are the **OK Cafetería** and the **Ballosteros.** The first of these, the OK Cafetería, is one flight up on the corner of the Gran Vía and Callao. It is self-service and clean, spacious, inexpensive, and has excellent freshly cooked food. It is particularly helpful for people who have just come to Spain and are not too sure about the names of the various dishes. The Ballosteros, a small restaurant at 4 Ventura de Vega, off San Gironimo, was a real find. The food is superb and the prices reasonable. I was recommended to this restaurant by a Spanish student with whom I became friendly, and after the first dinner, I returned every night that I could. The sangría is excellent, and the garlic and mushroom in oil a rare treat. The place has not been 'discovered' yet, and the waiters speak no English. As I speak passable Spanish, I had no problems" (Ranes C. Chakravorty, Salem, Va.).

TASCA HOPPING: If you think you'll be tightening your belt or devouring your nails before the fashionable 9:30 dining hour in Madrid, you've been misinformed. The Madrileños aren't walking around with a lean and hungry gleam in their eyes: they're out eating, as usual. Throughout Madrid you'll find the ever-popular *tascas,* bar-like establishments that usually serve wine and platters of tempting hors d'oeuvres, both hot and cold. These tidbits are known as *tapas,* meaning covers. A small glass of wine is called a *chato* (if you ask for a martini in some of these establishments, you'll be served a vermouth that goes by that name).

For around 35 pesetas (34¢) to 60 pesetas (58¢) you can have both a snack and a glass of wine. The food offered is varied: mushrooms, baby eels, shrimp, salads, lobster, mussels, sausage, ham—and, in one establishment at least, the testicles of a bull. But stick to the more familiar items for your first visit. The average Spaniard consumes an unbelievable amount of food in these places and then sits down to a course-heavy meal. Incidentally, you can often save pesetas by ordering at the bar.

You may call these nightly rounds "tasca crawling"—the equivalent of the English pub crawling—or "tasca hopping." Whether you crawl or hop depends entirely on how much wine you've had to drink.

The tasca goes way back into Spanish history, but now the custom is beginning to catch on with foreign visitors. Conversations are volatile in these places, and it's a fine way to spend the time before dinner.

In many of the "ethnic" tascas, refrigeration seems questionable, particularly in regard to the fish dishes, so stick to my recommendations.

By the way, the Spanish have a wonderful toast: *Salud, amor, y pesetas, y tiempo para gustarlos* ("Health, love, and wealth, and the time to enjoy all of them").

Los Motivos (Impulse), 10 Ventura de la Vega (tel. 429-67-29), offers about two dozen different platters of tasty tapas every evening. It's one of the most frequented bars in Madrid; its smart and relatively sophisticated crowd of Madrileños start filing in nightly around 8. It's decorated like an old tavern: hand-hewn beams, strings of garlic, wine bottles hanging from the ceiling, and crude wood stools and tables. The food at the bar is under glass—so it's most sanitary. Tapas range in price from 100 pesetas (96¢) to 200 pesetas ($1.92). A glass of wine? Only 25 pesetas (24¢). Incidentally, should you wish to stay on for dinner, the cubierto of the day goes for 500 pesetas ($4.80). Los Motivos is rated as a three-fork restaurant.

Taberna Toscana, 22 Ventura de la Vega (tel. 222-70-22), sits on the previously explored budget restaurant street of Madrid. Many Madrileños begin their nightly tasca crawl at this point. The aura is that of a village inn, far removed from 20th-century Madrid. You sit on crude country stools, under time-darkened beams from which hang sausages, pimientos, and sheaves of golden wheat. The tiled tasca bar is long and loaded with tasty tidbits, including the house specialties: lacón y cecina (boiled ham); habas (broad beans) with Spanish ham; and chorizo (a red pepper and pork sausage). These are almost meals in themselves. Especially delectable are the almejas à la marinera (clams) at 250 pesetas ($2.40). Beer in a stein is offered, although a chato of red wine at 20 pesetas (19¢) is more popular. If you're with a party, you can order a jarra de vino.

La Casona, 3 Calle Echegaray, is a personal favorite, a well-designed setting for regional wine and tapas. It's usually less crowded than the above recommendation and clean—if you ignore the traditional Spanish custom of dropping shrimp shells on the floor. The specialty of the house is "patatas Casona," crunchy fried potatoes with a hot red sauce. Specialties cost from 75 pesetas (72¢) to 300 pesetas ($2.88), the latter for charcoal-grilled shrimp. To wash it down, you can order a chato of wine for 25 pesetas (24¢).

Cervecería Alemana, 6 Plaza Santa Ana (tel. 231-50-66), was intended as a German beer hall, but it became Spanish somewhere along the way. Young Madrileños are fond of stopping in for a mug of draft beer at 25 pesetas (24¢). Opening directly onto one of the liveliest little plazas of Madrid, it clings to its turn-of-the-century traditions. Here you can sit at one of the tables, leisurely sipping your beer or wine, as the waiters make no attempt to have you drink up and press on. The beer hall draws a wide assortment of people, but the dress is decidedly casual. To accompany your beverage, try the fried sardines at 90 pesetas (86¢) or a Spanish omelet at 70 pesetas (67¢).

La Torre del Oro, 26 Plaza Mayor (tel. 266-30-16). The location is unbeatable: on the most historic square in Madrid, where Carlos II ("The Bewitched One") organized his auto-da-fé spectacles. The place drips with character: Andalusian tiles, old heavy beams darkened by the years, that old standby, hanging garlic. The waiters are all dolled up in red and green sashes. Stop in here for that North African specialty, pinchos morunos, a small shish kebab on a skewer, costing 125 pesetas ($1.20), and deep-fried sea minnows at 250 pesetas ($2.40).

Cervecería Santa Bárbara, 8 Plaza de Santa Bárbara, is unique in Madrid. It's an outlet for a beer factory—and beer isn't exactly a beverage traditionally associated with Spain. In recent years, the management has pumped much loot into making it modern and inviting, and a frieze of brightly lit lanterns welcomes you. You go here for beer, of course: la cerveza negra (black beer) costing 30 pesetas (29¢), cerveza dorada (golden beer), 30 pesetas also. The local brew is best accompanied by delicious homemade potato chips, a plate of them for 100 pesetas (96¢). Fresh shrimp, lobster, crabmeat, and barnacles are also served. The interior is quite large, dominated by a long counter and filled with huge tables. You can go directly to one of the wooden tables for waiter service, or stand at the counter. The nearest Metro stop is Alonso Martínez, and the hours are 11 a.m. till 11 p.m.

CIDER DRINKING: Casa Mingo, 2 Paseo de la Florida (tel. 247-79-18), is a rarity in Madrid, left over from another era. It's a tavern-style cider bar, where you can order refreshing Asturian cider, hard or sweet, accompanied by crusty bread and goat cheese. The drink is served authentically. The waiter holds the glass as low as he can in his left hand, and the bottle of cider as high as he can in his right. He then pours. Don't bother about the drops that may fall on the floor. You're participating in an age-old ritual. The "bubbly champagne" type cider costs 110 pesetas ($1.06). However, a bottle of the ordinary cider goes for 80 pesetas (77¢). The accompanying *cabrales* (goat cheese) and bread is another 80 pesetas. The decor is rustic, with wooden casks lining one wall. In fair weather, you can enjoy your drink at one of the sidewalk tables. The old tavern is across the street from the Goya Pantheon.

4. The Top Sights

In sightseeing, Madrid is as lean as a Spanish dog when compared to Paris, London, or Rome. Nevertheless, getting to know this Iberian mistress takes a long time, a lot of shoe leather, and an almost fanatical probing on the part of the stranger who wants to see what is hidden behind the fan.

Except for the Prado, you might visit Madrid and never set foot inside a museum. Not that Madrid proper is that lovely. She isn't. Her face is marred by dowdy, 19th-century relics, such as those lining the Gran Vía—monuments more to bulk than style.

Of course, Madrid has wide paseos, parks, and fountains, but this is her public face. You won't learn much about Madrid walking around the Retiro. But you may learn a great deal if you stroll the teeming nighttime streets of her old town.

Madrid lives concealed in the shadows of her narrow streets, but emerges prudishly respectable when she promenades along her paseos.

Pretentious, stubborn, she is a city to be experienced for the sensations of the moment, even though sensuality isn't her forte. Walk her streets, smell her smells, listen to her sounds. Hear the indiscreet breaking of confidences over glasses of wine in the tascas; have your nostrils assailed by the smell of baby eels cooking in olive oil; feel the hot, baking streets in the midafternoon when it seems that you're strolling aimlessly around a pale ghost city under the Castilian sun; or experience the cold biting winds that sweep across the plains in the winter, punishing the faces of denizen and stranger alike.

Gradually, like a patchwork quilt, the pieces come together into a meaningful whole. After a while Madrid takes on a certain coherence. The dirt and squalor of her old town counterbalance the antiseptic apartment houses springing up on her skirttails; the bubbling fountains offset the harshness of the dry dust in summer; the shrill voices at night crack the deadly stillness that settles in the afternoon; the sheer dreariness of some of her buildings forms a better showcase to reveal the rich decorations of her architectural surprises.

Madrid does not invite unqualified admiration, as she is a fiercely arrogant city, her personality shaped by her proud, passionate Castilians.

THE PRADO: There is a legend in Spain that all great art is shipped to Madrid. This is an exaggeration, and there are some notable exceptions to disprove it (El Escorial, Toledo), but the claim does point up the outstanding reputation of this museum. The Prado (tel. 239-80-23) is one of the most important repositories of art in the world, with its more than 3000 paintings.

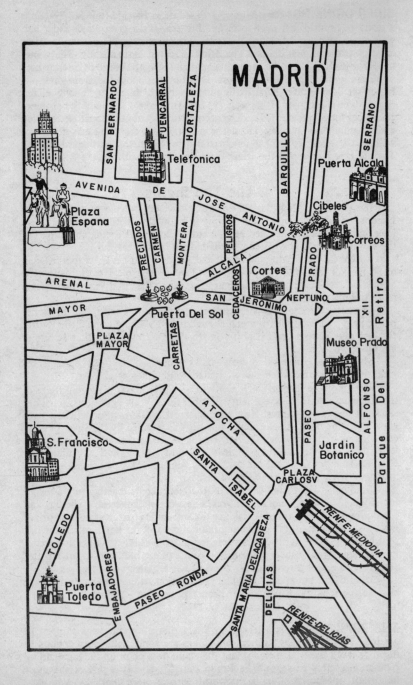

Even the Prado's severest critics admit that it's in third or fourth position among the world's museums.

This treasury of art began as a private collection of the Spanish kings, and was enhanced by the Hapsburgs, especially Carlos V, and later the Bourbons. The paintings were carefully purchased by the royal collectors one by one, never stolen or expropriated. The kings and queens who loved art never bought entire collections but rather individual works of art. In paintings of the Spanish school, the Prado has no equal.

The Prado is housed in a colossus of an 18-century building littered with arcades and colonnades. The museum is not a storehouse of national art; it is a world museum, with works by many famed European painters. Still, on your first visit, you'll want to concentrate most heavily on the Spanish masters (Velázquez, Goya, El Greco, and, to a lesser degree, Murillo). The average traveler can "do" the Prado in two visits of perhaps two or three hours' duration. Better yet, two weeks.

The Prado is open daily except Monday from 10 a.m. to 5 p.m. (in summer until 6 p.m.); until 2 p.m. on Sunday. On weekdays it charges 200 pesetas ($1.92) per person. The museum is closed on Good Friday, as well as on January 1 and December 25. From June 1 to September 15 the Prado is open right through from 10 a.m. to 6 p.m. The Prado now has new galleries dedicated to the Spanish masters of the 19th century and the impressionists, among others. They are in the Casón del Buen Retiro, two blocks behind the Prado, on Calle Alfonso XII, opposite the Retiro Park.

Currently, the painting stirring up the most excitement is Picasso's *Guernica.* Long banned in Spain, the painting rested for years in the Museum of Modern Art in New York before it was returned to Spain. Picasso's work reflected his sadness at Generalissimo Franco's bombing of Guernica, a little Basque town. Picasso requested that *Guernica* not be returned to Spain until the death of Franco and the "reestablishment of public liberties." Behind a glass barrier, the painting covers almost a whole wall—some 12 feet high and about 25 feet long. Visitors are kept at a distance of some 25 feet from the world masterpiece.

The casón is open on Tuesday, Thursday, Friday, and Saturday from 10 a.m. to 6 p.m., April to September. Its off-season hours are from 10 a.m. to 5 p.m. On Wednesday it is open from 3 to 9 p.m., and on Sunday from 10 a.m. to 2 p.m. It is closed on Monday and charges 200 pesetas ($1.92) for admission.

For visitors who must see the Prado quickly (by far the majority), I have compiled a list below of a representative collection of outstanding paintings from the various schools.

With many notable exceptions (Goya's sketches), most of the major works of the Prado are exhibited on the first floor. You may want to head there first before your viewing power begins to fade.

Rooms II through V are devoted to Italian masters—such artists as Raphael, Botticelli, Mantegna, and Andrea del Sarto, along with Correggio. None of the works at the Prado represents the best of the output of these great artists, although in Room IV an *Annunciation* is typical of the style of Fra Angelico (1400–1455).

Rooms VII through X continue the Italian cavalcade of art, with the Venetian artists featured this time. Perhaps the most celebrated work here is Titian's voluptuous Venus being watched by a musician who can't keep his eyes on his work (two different versions: one in Room VIII and another in Room X).

Room IXB takes us to Spain and the work of El Greco (1524–1614), the Crete-born artist who lived much of his life in Toledo. Philip II, a great patron of the arts, didn't take to El Greco's strangely distorted and elongated figures through which the artist expressed his spirituality. Although he was born in Greece and studied in Italy, many art historians have expressed the opinion that he was the most Spanish of all artists (Goya aficionados may differ). In Rooms IXB and XB we see a parade of "The Greek's" saints, Madonnas, Holy Families—even a ghostly *John the Baptist*. But El Greco's masterpiece hangs in a little church in Toledo (next chapter).

Rooms XIII and XVIII treat us to the five-star showcase of the Prado, the incomparable Velázquez (1599–1660), a "warts-and-all" type painter who got away with many an unflattering portrait of his patron, Philip IV—the king even learned to like his likeness. The world, of course, considers Velázquez one of the all-time great painters. Spaniards, however, consider him *the* greatest. The Prado has the most splendid array of his works—notably the already-mentioned portraits of Philip IV, the highly praised *Drunkards*, and his series of four dwarfs. One of his best portraits is the little girl in the hoop dress, Margarita of Austria, daughter of his patron.

In Room XVII is the most famous painting in all of the Prado—and it's Velázquez's masterpiece. Entitled *Las Meninas*, it is considered by art critics to be a triumph in the use of light effects. Like so many of Velázquez's works, the painting contains a fascinating dwarf woman. The faces of the queen and king (presumably we are looking at the scene through their eyes) are reflected in the mirror in the painting itself. The artist in the background? Velázquez, of course. On center stage is Princess Margarita.

In Room XXVIII is displayed Rubens's peacock-blue *Garden of Love*, and his rendition of the *Three Graces*.

Room XIB takes us back to Spain . . . this time to Ribera (1591–1652), a Valencia-born artist who during his long sojourn in Italy refined and polished his tortured world on canvas. His best work is the *Martyrdom of St. Philip* in which we feel the somber tragedy of Spain.

In Rooms XXV and XXVI we see Murillo's work including *Bartholomé* (1617–1682). This Seville-born artist—often referred to as the "painter of Madonnas"—is not my favorite. A number of critics consider him extremely dated, at least for modern tastes. The sentimental cardmakers of yesteryear relied heavily on his works at Christmas. The most notable of his three Immaculate Conceptions displayed here is *La Immaculada de Soult*, returned to Spain by the French government during World War II.

The Prado contains one of the world's outstanding collections of Hieronymus Bosch, the Flemish genius who was born sometime in the mid-15th century and died in 1516. Through his paintings parade all the citizens of Hell—imps, hobgoblins, ghouls, ogres and ogresses, pigwidgeons, wraiths, and all sorts of creeping, crawling fiends—some only with a ghoulish head and a pair of mischievous legs trotting off to do no good. In the middle of Room XLIII is Bosch's table of the *Seven Deadly Sins* (stuff your eyes on gluttony). Also in this salon is one of the Bosch's most famous works, his triptych, *The Hay Wagon*. Each selfish, greedy soul—even the pope—is trying to grab his share and more from the "hay wagon" of life as it rolls to Hell. Don't miss Pieter Brueghel's *Triumph of Death*. Brueghel, another Flemish painter, continues Bosch's ghoulish work.

In Room XLIV is one of "El Bosco's" finest triptychs (surely his best known work), *The Garden of Earthly Delights*, which reveals his three stages of interpretation: (1) creation, (2) the struggle, and (3) hell.

The ground floor of the Prado is also rich in paintings and sculpture. But the first-timer, already exhausted, may want to confine his search to some sketches and paintings by Goya.

Rooms LIV and LVII are the Goya exhibition. Francisco de Goya (1746–1828) was considered a strange and eccentric genius, ranking along with Velázquez and El Greco in the trio of great Spanish artists. Hanging here also are the cruel portraits that Goya did of his patron, Charles IV, and his family. The queen looks like a chicken, the king a shadowy version of an overstuffed George Washington. Even a stallion and a chic riding costume couldn't disguise the fact that Maria Louisa Teresa looked like a scrubwoman. Goya painted at both the literal and figurative expense of royalty. Incidentally, the Goya paintings *Maja Vestida,* lying seductively clad in a white gown, and *Maja Desnuda* (the *Naked Maja,* believed to have been posed by the Duchess of Alba—and, later, on the screen by Ava Gardner), are on the ground floor in Room LVIIA.

In Room LIII we see the beginning of a series of sketches by Goya. Some of them, depicting the cancer of 18th-century Spain, caused the dragon fire of the Inquisition to breathe down Goya's neck. Room LVA contains one of the artist's most reproduced works, *The Third of May (1808),* recognizable by the outstretched arms of the man facing the firing squad. The scene is from the Napoleonic invasion of Spain. In addition, we see another important work, the battle scene from the *Second of May* revealing a bloody event in 1808, as the Madrileños tried desperately to fight off the invaders. Room LVIA houses one of the strangest, gloomiest exhibits in the Prado—Goya in a black mood. And when Goya was in a black mood, he could make a painter such as Ribera look like a stand-up comic. The so-called "black paintings"—all expressionistic—were made at his country casa when Goya was deaf, perhaps even mad. To borrow the title from *Whistler's Mother,* the Goya paintings were arrangements in grays and blacks. After viewing these, you will have seen the best of his work, as well as the best of the Prado.

Buses going to the museum are numbered 10, 14, 27, 34, 37, and 45. Metro stations are Banco, Atocha, and Prado.

THE ROYAL PALACE: Owing a heavy debt to French architects, this 2800-room royal palace (tel. 248-74-04) was begun in 1737, on the site of the Madrid Alcázar, which burned to the ground in the Christmas of 1734. Of its approximately 2800 rooms—which that "Enlightened Despot" Charles III called home—some are open to the public, while others are still used for state business.

You are conducted through the royal showcase on a guided tour. Just say "Inglés" to the doorman who takes your ticket, so you'll hook up to an English-speaking tour. The inclusive tour encompasses the Tapestry Gallery, the Reception Room, the State Apartments, the Armory, the Royal Pharmacy, and the Library.

The reception rooms and state apartments should get priority here if you're rushed. They embrace a rococo room with a diamond clock, a porcelain salon, a Royal Chapel that is used whenever a new cardinal is sent to Spain, a Banquet Room where receptions for heads of state are held, and a Throne Room with a chair on which Franco never sat.

The rooms are literally stuffed with objects of art and antiques—forming salon after salon of monumental grandeur, with no apologies for the opulence of a bygone era (damask, mosaics, stucco, Tiepoloesque ceilings, gilt and bronze, chandeliers, paintings, tapestries, and the inevitable chinoiserie).

The miles and miles of tapestries, both Flemish and Spanish, in the Tapestry Gallery comprise an impressive collection numbering in the hundreds. Many date back to the 15th century.

After viewing the tapestries, you move on for a peek at the private rooms of Alfonso XIII, which were damaged during the Civil War, later restored by the Franco government. The palace was last used as a royal residence in 1931, before the unsteady king and his wife Victoria Eugénie fled Spain.

(King Juan Carlos and Queen Sofia are more modest in their requirements. They have turned the Royal Palace over to history, choosing not to live there but in a much smaller palace, the Zarzuela, named after the Spanish operetta or musical comedy. Their palace is suburban.)

After this, a short walk across the courtyard will bring you to the armory, where you'll see the finest collection in Spain, perhaps the world. Many of the items—powder flasks, shields, lances, helmets, saddles—are from the collection of Charles V (Charles I of Spain).

From here, the comprehensive tour takes you into the Royal Library, with volume after leather-bound volume, and the less interesting pharmacy containing bottles in which—conceivably—concoctions might have been mixed to help cranky Maria Josefa's migraines.

To visit all these sights, you pay 300 pesetas ($2.88), and the hours are 10 a.m. to 1:30 p.m. and 4 to 6 p.m. Monday to Saturday; Sunday 10 a.m. to 1:30 p.m. If you want to visit only the Armory, the charge is 50 pesetas (48¢). A ticket for just the private apartments and the palace goes for 150 pesetas ($1.44) per person.

Also known as the Palacio de Oriente, the Royal Palace is on the same-name Plaza de Oriente, a short ride from the center of town. The nearest Metro stop is called Opera, a healthy walk away.

Incidentally, you may also want to visit the Carriage Museum (Carrozas), also at the Royal Palace, to see some of the grand old relics that Spanish aristocrats have been riding around in for the past two centuries. It keeps the same hours as the palace, 50 pesetas (48¢) entrance. Metro stop: Ópera.

THE ROYAL FACTORY OF TAPESTRIES: At this factory, the age-old process of making exquisite (and very expensive) tapestries is still carried out with consummate skill. Goya is the superstar around here: nearly every tapestry seems to be based on one of his cartoons.

The artist, of course, was the most famous person who ever worked for the factory—employed between 1775 and 1792. During those years, he designed more than four dozen "cartoons" which were used as models for tapestries. Many of these same patterns—such as El Cacharrero (The Pottery Salesman)—are still in production today. (To see Goya's original cartoons, you must go to the Prado.) Many of the other designs were based on cartoons by Francisco Bayeu, Goya's brother-in-law.

In 1835, the factory—known as Santa Bárbara when it was founded by Philip IV—was shut down. Now the industry's happily revived. Many of the workers hardly look at the pattern, they know it so well. Other more cautious artisans prefer to use a mirror.

As a superstitious lot, the artists may not want to show too much pride in their work. They remember Arachne, the Lydian maiden of Greek mythology who boasted of her weaving skill with such arrogance (even challenging Athene to a contest) that she was turned into a spider.

Admission is 25 pesetas (24¢). The factory, at 2 Fuenterrabia, is open from 9:30 a.m. to 12:30 p.m. Closed on Saturday and Sunday, the house also shuts down August 1 through September 1. Metro stop: Atocha or Pelayo.

GOYA MUSEUM AND PANTHEON: Here, at the tomb of Goya, you can see one of his masterpieces, an elaborately beautiful fresco depicting the miracles of St. Anthony on the dome and cupola of the little hermitage of San Antonio de la Florida, which is on the Paseo de San Antonio de la Florida.

The tomb and fresco are in one of the twin chapels (visit the one on the right), which were built in the latter part of the 18th century. Discreetly placed mirrors will help you see the ceiling better. One of the figures in the paintings—a woman draped in fabric—is the best known segment of the fresco, used to symbolize Spain in travel posters throughout America and Europe. The hermitage is in a remote part of town (below the North Station), but it's on several bus lines. From July through September, the museum is open from 10 a.m. to 1 p.m. and 4 p.m. to 7 p.m. Hours from October through June are 11 a.m. to 1:30 p.m. and 3 to 6 p.m. (closed Tuesday). Admission is 50 pesetas (48¢).

BULLFIGHTING MUSEUM (MUSEO TAURINO): At the Plaza de Toros de las Ventas, this museum—the best of its kind in Spain—may serve as a fitting introduction to bullfighting before you actually see an event in the ring. Here you'll find such items as the death costume of Manolete, the traje de luce (suit of light) that he wore when he was gored to death at the age of 30 in Madrid's Plaza de Toros. The year: 1947. As one aficionado said at the time: "Manolete's fortunes were in the millions. He didn't know when to quit."

Other memorabilia evoke the heyday of Juan Belmonte, the Andalusian who in 1914 revolutionized bullfighting by performing so close to the horns that he became world-renowned for his bravery. His friend and rival, Joselito (José Gómez), is also represented, that matador who was gored 54 times. A bull finally ended the career of Joselito in 1920, although Belmonte retired and became (you guessed it) a bull breeder. Other exhibits include a Goya painting of a bullfighter (a guide will elaborately show you where to stand so that you may better appreciate the painting). Photographs and relics of the ring trace the history of bullfighting in Spain from its ancient origin to the present day. For admission, go to the rear of the Plaza de Toros any time between 10 a.m. and 1 p.m. and 3:30 and 7 p.m. Admission is 50 pesetas (48¢).

MUSEUM OF LÁZARO GALDIANO: Imagine 37 rooms in a well-preserved 19th-century mansion of the aristocracy bulging with artworks—including many by the most famous old masters of Europe.

Most visitors take the elevator to the top floor, then begin their descent, lingering long over many of the mementos. At the beginning of the collection, the hand-woven vestments (some dating from the 15th century), the display of swords (surely more than El Cid's army had), the daggers, the seals of kings (even one from Napoleon), hardly suggest what is in store. Case after case of Spanish fans are only mildly interesting (one belonged to Isabella II, who, the court considered, was in dire need of something to hide behind).

However, in Salon 20 are two works by the incomparable Bosch evoking his own peculiar brand of horror, his canvases peopled with creepy fiends devouring human flesh. Unexpectedly, Rembrandt's *Self-Portrait* adorns a wall in Salon 21. The Spanish masters, naturally, are the best represented—a whole galaxy of them: Velázquez, El Greco, Zurbarán, Ribera, Murillo, and Valdés Leal.

Rare in Spanish museums is the section here devoted to works by English portrait and landscape artists: Sir Joshua Reynolds, Gainsborough, Gilbert Stuart (the American painter, noted for his three likenesses of George Washington), and Constable (one of his many interpretations of *Dedham Vale* in East Anglia). Italian artists exhibited include Tiepolo and Guardi, the latter with one of his never-ending, but always fascinating, scenes of Venice. Salon 30—for many, the most interesting—is devoted to Goya, and includes some of the paintings of his "black period" and a portrait of the cuckold, the weak Charles IV, and his unattractive but amorous Queen Maria Louisa.

Other exhibitions include enamel works (unsurpassed in Spain), 16th-century crystal from Limoges, French and Italian carvings from the 14th and 15th centuries (one of the most remarkable collections in the country); Byzantine jewelry; a Maltese cross from the 15th century; Italian bronzes from the Roman days to the Renaissance; and medieval suits of armor. In Salon 6 hangs a small portrait of a woman encased in a green velvet frame. Although the museum attributes this painting to Leonardo da Vinci, many art historians dispute this claim. The painting is more generally attributed to Ambrogio de Predis of Milan, with whom da Vinci lived his first years in that Lombard city. Calling it a da Vinci was denounced by one critic as "unwarranted and disturbing sensationalism."

At 122 Serrano, the museum (tel. 261-60-84) may be visited from 9:15 a.m. to 1:45 p.m. daily. The regular admission is 200 pesetas ($1.92), dropping to 100 pesetas (96¢) on Sunday. Metro stop: Maranon.

CONVENT OF LAS DESCALZAS REALES: Following in the footsteps of Charles V's daughter, Juana of Austria, "gentle ladies" of the aristocracy—disappointed in love or "wanting to be the bride of Christ"—stole away to this mid-16th-century convent to take the veil. Of course, all of them brought a dowry, making the so-called "Royal Barefoots" one of the richest convents in the land.

However, by the mid-20th century, the ladies of nobility were no longer in ascendancy, and recent arrivals had no problem at all taking the vow of poverty. True, the convent still contained a collection of art treasures valuable enough to have financed a revolution. But portraits by El Greco or Velázquez don't buy rice for the paella unless sold—and the sisters were forbidden to auction off anything. In sad fact, they were starving—the exposure of which brought on a nationwide scandal.

The state intervened, and the pope granted special dispensation to open the monastery as a museum. The good sisters, about 30 in all, are eating once again, happy to report; and much of the public is enthralled to get a look behind the walls of what was once a mysterious edifice on one of the most beautiful squares in Old Madrid.

An English-speaking guide will show you through. In the Reliquary are housed the dowries brought by the nobel ladies, such as the last wife of Philip II. One of the relics is said to contain bits of wood from the cross on which Christ was crucified; another is alleged to hold some of the bones of St. Sebastian. The most valuable painting is Titian's *Caesar's Money*, valued in the millions (of pesetas). The Flemish Hall shelters the finest works, including one of a processional by Hans Van Baker. Other paintings are by Brueghel the Elder and Bernardino Luini, the Lombard artist. Sardonically, portraits of the sisters of Emperor Charles V reveal them to have the same faces as their ugly brother.

Many of the tapestries were based on Rubens's cartoons, displaying his chubby matrons. Gold and silver threads were woven into some of the vestments, dating mainly from the 16th and 17th centuries. In the cloisters, a guide will conduct you to the Chapel of Our Lady of Guadalupe, known for its Virgin sculpted in lead.

The monastery (tel. 222-06-87), open daily from 10:30 a.m. until 1:30 p.m. and 4 to 6 p.m., charges 100 pesetas (96¢) admission. It stands on the Plaza de las Descalzas Reales, reached by heading down the Postigo de San Martín (so narrow the walls close in) from the Gran Vía. Metro stop: Plaza del Sol.

SOME MORE ATTRACTIONS: Those with more time for Madrid might want to check out the following sights:

Church of San Francisco El Grande

Ironically, Madrid, capital of cathedral-rich Spain, does not in itself possess a proper cathedral. But it does have an important church, with a dome larger than that of St. Paul's in London. At the Plaza de San Francisco El Grande (1 San Buenaventura), this 18th-century church is filled with a number of ecclesiastical works of art, notably a Goya painting of St. Bernardino of Siena. A guide will show you through the building, taking you through the museum and pointing out the most interesting features in the chapels. The church is open from 11 a.m. to 1 p.m. and 4 to 7 p.m. except Sunday and Monday.

Admission is 10 pesetas (10¢). In summer, the afternoon hours are 5 to 8. On late fall or winter afternoons, you sometimes have to insist that the lights be turned on, or you'll see little. Metro: La Latina.

The Rastro

If you're in the market for a gigantic wire figure of Don Quixote, or a two-seater German motorcycle from World War II, then by all means visit the Rastro, the flea market of Madrid, which runs up and down several hilly streets south of the Plaza de Cascorro. You don't have to be in the market for anything. The Rastro is something to experience. The life of Madrid spills out here. There are legendary stories told about the discovery of fortunes in art treasures, but don't expect to uncover any such finds; instead, you'll often come up with interesting little things that can make ideal gifts, such as antique keys to castles. You can start a new vogue in America by placing them on your coffee tables; of course, you'll have to make up a spectacular story concerning their origins. But if you're interested in buying, there are many items that might tempt you, although frankly, most of the little thrown-together stalls are filled with plain unadulterated junk. For example, the Spanish government requires that a soldier return his boots after his tour of duty. They come here, trade their good pair in for an old scruffy pair—and pocket the difference. One Spaniard claimed that someone stripped his motorcycle of parts on a Saturday night. On Sunday, he went to the flea market and, after an exhaustive search, found the stolen parts on sale. By 2 in the afternoon, most of the stallkeepers start shutting down. Often this is the best time to make quick purchases, as their desire to sell reaches a fever pitch then. **Bargain.**

READER'S SHOPPING TIP: "The **Rastro** has now added the popular Indian clothes to its wares. These garments are quite expensive in the stores, both in the United States and in Spain, but they can be purchased at the Rastro for half the price or less, depending on your bargaining skills. There are many stalls so the selection is wide. Also, I suggest you go on a weekday morning around 11 o'clock, when there are only a few shoppers, and the vendors are more likely to give you a better buy because they are more anxious to make a sale. Around 1 to 2 p.m., most vendors pack up their goods and head for the bars to spend the rest of the day eating, drinking, and talking—a very important part of Spanish life" (Bertie Green, Columbia, S.C.).

The Retiro

Here in the heart of Madrid is a vast, shaded, once-royal park, which may be necessary to visit when the summer heat in Madrid becomes unbearable. A reminder of some of the large forests that once stood proudly in Castile, the park is filled with numerous fountains (one dedicated to an artichoke), statues (one honors Lucifer, strangely heretical in Catholic Spain), and a large lake where soldiers meet their girls during the hotter months.

In summer, the rose gardens are worth the visit. There are two restaurants in the park, the Florida and Pavilion, but they're much too expensive for our budget; you'll find a number of other places where you can have inexpensive snacks and drinks.

From 8 a.m. to 8 p.m., you can rent a rowboat in the Retiro, costing 25 pesetas (24¢). If you're not so inclined, then a ride on one of the motorboats may make you completely forget that mean August sun. What to do afterward? Take a promenade.

The House of Lope de Vega

What Shakespeare is to the English-speaking world, Lope de Vega is to the Spanish. One of the most prolific writers who ever lived, this Madrid-born author dramatized Hapsburg Spain as no one ever had before, earning a lasting position in Spanish letters. A reconstruction of his medieval house stands on a narrow street, ironically named Cervantes (knock on the ancient door at no. 11). It is within walking distance of the Prado. The dank, dark house is furnished with relics of the period, although one can't be sure that any of the furnishings or possessions actually belonged to this 16th-century genius. After a guide shows you through the house, you can visit the gardens out back. It is open from 11 a.m. to 2 p.m. except Monday, and the price of admission is 50 pesetas (48¢). From mid-July to mid-September, the house (tel. 222-88-25) is closed to the public.

Fine Arts Museum

In the **San Fernando Fine Arts Academy,** 22 el Paseo de Recoletos (a short walk from the Puerta del Sol), is exhibited a universe of Spanish masters, from the brightest light on the Milky Way (Goya) to a twinkle (Zubarán) and a fading glow (José Perovani). The first room you enter contains a splendid array, devoted to Goya.

Here you'll find Goya's self-portrait, soft, subdued, kindly realistic to himself. No. 670 is Goya's interpretation of Manuel de Godoy, lover of Queen Maria Louisa, wife of Charles IV. Two of Goya's best known paintings—*The Crazy House* and a *Scene from the Inquisition*—are in this salon. Painting in diffused colors, the artist turned his vivid mind and advanced technique to the all-consuming terror of Spain. The result is horrifyingly brilliant.

Room 2 (to the left) is graced with a number of Zurbarán portraits of robed monks. In these paintings, we see how he skillfully combined spirituality with realism.

The gallery also contains minor works by Murillo and Ribera, as well as a Rubens painting of Susanna and the lecherous elders. The academy is open from 10 a.m. to 2 p.m.; it charges 50 pesetas (48¢) admission.

Convent of La Encarnación

Finished in 1616, in the reign of Philip III and his Queen Margaret (sister of the emperor, Ferdinand II), this convent and its adjoining church stand on one of the most charming squares in Old Madrid, right down from La Bola restaurant, a short walk from the Plaza de España.

The original architect was Juan Gómez de Mora, although work in another century was carried out by Ventura Rodríguez. A Spanish-speaking guide will show you around, pointing out the most important ecclesiastical paintings and a *John the Baptist* by Ribera. Other works include a gory Christ with serpentine hair by Georgio Fernández. In the Reliquary rest a relic of St. Margaret and a skull said to be that of St. Alexander.

The cloisters are filled with richly decorated chapels, one in the Pompeiian style. The convent is open daily from 10:30 a.m. to 1:30 p.m. and 4 to 6 p.m., and charges 100 pesetas (96¢) admission. On Sunday, it is open from 10:30 a.m. till 1:30 p.m.

MUSEUM MISCELLANY: For those of you who have extra sightseeing time in Madrid, there are a number of museums that might be visited:

Cerralbo Museum

Picture a town house dripping with the gilt and red-velvet romanticism of the 19th century—a place once inhabited by staunch nobility who posed stiff backed and straitlaced for their family portraits. The family of the Marquis of Cerralbo lived in this splendid Madrileño mansion until the 1920s, filling its every nook and cranny with decorative bric-a-brac or art treasures. No one stinted on the crystal chandeliers or the then-fashionable, opulently colored glass imported from the factories of Venice where it was made to order.

The Cerralbo clan were art collectors as well, purchasing well-known works from celebrated artists: Zurbarán (an *Immaculate Conception*) or Ribera *(Jacob with the Lamb)* or El Greco *(St. Francis).* Every noble household had to be richly endowed with tapestries, antique furniture, ecclesiastical sculpture from the Middle Ages, armor, marble busts, gilt mirrors, terracotta clocks, baby-fat cherubs, cabinets made of porcelain (really exquisite), and chinoiserie, and this family was no exception. The Cerralbos apparently also had an interest in armaments, as exemplified by their pistols, helmets, and rifles. The diet is almost too rich for one visit. Especially intriguing is the library and study of the late marquis, remaining as he left it.

The town house—turned over to the state and now run as a rare, little-visited museum—is at 17 Ventura Rodríguez, within walking distance of the Plaza de España. Charging 100 pesetas (96¢) for admission, it is open daily, except Tuesday, from 9 a.m. to 2 p.m. Regrettably, it closes during the entire month of August. Metro stop: Plaza de España.

National Archeological Museum

For some reason, Iberian archeological museums tend to be dull—surprisingly, since so many civilizations (prehistoric, Roman, Visigothic, Moslem) have conquered the peninsula. An exception, however, to that generalization is this stately mansion in Madrid, a storehouse of artifacts from prehistoric times to the heyday of the baroque. One of the prime exhibits here is the Iberian statue *La Dama de Elche,* a piece of primitive carving—probably from the fourth century B.C.—that was discovered on the southeastern coast of Spain, as well as the splendidly polychromed *Dama de Baza* recently discovered in Granada Province, also from the same date.

A cache of treasures from the discovery of some of the finest Punic relics in Europe on the Balearic island of Ibiza is displayed, many of them found in a Carthaginian and Roman necropolis.

Excavations from Paestum, Italy, enhance Room 4: some of the statuary of Imperial Rome, including a statue of Tiberius enthroned as well as one of the controversial Livia, wife of Augustus.

The collection of Spanish Renaissance lusterware, as well as Talavera pottery and Retiro porcelain, is shown to good advantage, along with some rare 16th- and 17th-century Andalusian glassware.

Although the "classic" artifacts are impressive, the contributions from medieval days up through the 16th century are highly laudable. Many of the exhibits were ecclesiastical treasures removed from churches and monasteries. A much-photographed choir stall from Palencia—hand-painted and crude, but remarkable, nevertheless—dates from the 14th century and is displayed in Room 7.

At 13 Calle de Serrano, on the major shopping artery, the museum may be visited every day from 9:30 a.m. to 1:30 p.m. for 110 pesetas ($1.06). Worthy of a look are the reproductions of the Altamira cave paintings discovered near Santander in northern Spain in 1868. Joseph Déchelette called them "the Sistine Chapel of Quaternary art." The man-made *cuevas* in Madrid simulate the lateral chamber at Altamira—but with far more neck-craning room. The paintings—in blacks, reds, and violets—are chiefly of bison, horses, and wild boars. The caves may be visited between 9:30 a.m. and 1:30 p.m.

Museum of Sorolla

Sorolla is an acquired taste. He was born Joaquín in Valencia in 1863, and died in Madrid in 1923. In his day he was celebrated, as autographed portraits from King Afonso XIII and U.S. President Taft reveal. From 1912, he and his family occupied this elegant Madrileño town house off the Paseo de la Castellana. Two years after his death, his widow turned it over to the government—and it is now maintained as a memorial to the painter, inaugurated in 1932.

Except for the faded furniture and portraits, much of the house remains as Sorolla left it, right down to his stained paint brushes and pipes. In the museum wing, however, is displayed a representative collection of the artist's paintings. All of the works owned by the museum can't be exhibited, however, because of the lack of space.

Although Sorolla painted portraits of Spanish aristocrats, he was essentially interested in "the people," often in their native costumes, such as those once worn in Ávila and Salamanca. He was expecially fond of painting beach scenes on what is now the Costa Blanca. His favorite subjects are depicted either "before" or "after" their bath, and he was interested in the subtle variations of the Spanish sunlight. One critic wrote that Sorolla "may fail to please certain individuals, contaminated by an unhealthy leaning towards things decadent, pessimistic and tragic."

Seek out not only the artist's self-portrait, but the paintings of Madame Sorolla and their handsome son.

Entered through an Andalusian-style patio, the museum is at 37 General Martinez Campos. It is open daily except Monday from 10 a.m. to 2 p.m. and charges 150 pesetas ($1.44).

The Romantic Museum

Of special interest and limited appeal, this museum attracts those seeking the romanticism of the 19th century. Decorative arts festoon the mansion in which the museum is housed: crystal chandeliers, faded portraits, oils from Goya to Sorolla, opulent furnishings, porcelain, jewelry, ceramics, even *la grande toilette*. Many of the exhibitions date from the days of Isabella II, the high-living, fun-loving queen who was forced into exile and eventual abdication of her throne (she lived in Paris until her death in 1904).

At 13 San Mateo, the **Museo Romantico** is open daily from 10 a.m. to 6 p.m., to 2 p.m. on Sunday. It charges 75 pesetas (72¢) for admission. It is closed on Monday and from August 1 to September 15.

The Museum of Bottles

In Madrid, Señor Chicote became a legend. His bar at 12 Gran Vía (tel. 232-15-12) is a mecca for foreigners and Spaniards alike, and was especially popular with Hemingway. In the cellar of the bar, the good señor collected beer, liquor, and wine bottles from all over the world. Many of the bottles were presented by celebrities, including Doña Fabiola de Mora y Aragón, who married the Belgian king, Baudouin; Cantinflas of Mexico; Onassis; Selassie; as well as Tyrone Power and Ava Gardner, stars of *The Sun Also Rises*.

In all, there are more than 23,000 bottles, including one in the shape of a lightbulb, the gift of Phillips. Bottles come in odd shapes and sizes: one like a Rolls-Royce tank, another in the form of Charlie Chaplin. Many contain vintage whiskies, such as an 1820 Johnnie Walker. One bottle alone is worth more than $2400.

Although Señor Chicote has willed his fabulous collection to the state, it is, at present, private. If you wish to see it, your best bet is to inquire at the bar, preferably after you've ordered a drink or two. You'll be allowed to descend with a boy who'll guide you around (tip expected, of course).

The Wax Museum

The **Museo Colón**, Plaza Colón, is the newest on my list of museums. Housed in the Centro Colón, it charges a steep 250 pesetas ($2.40) for adults, 150 pesetas ($1.44) for children. The museum is a bit like London's Madame Tussaud's or Paris's Musée Grevin; there are scenes depicting events in Spanish history, such as Columbus calling on Ferdinand and Isabella. Contemporary international figures aren't neglected either. Thus, we see Jacqueline Onassis having champagne at a supper club and Garbo all alone. The heroes and villains of World War II—everybody from Eisenhower to Hitler—are enlivened by the presence of the "Blue Angel," Marlene Dietrich, singing "Lili Marlene." Out-of-work filmmakers created the 400 figures in 38 tableaux, succeeding best with backdrops, falling shortest in the depiction of contemporary celebrities. Hours are from 10:30 a.m. to 1:30 p.m. and 4 to 8:30 p.m.

Templo de Debod

This Egyptian temple once stood in the Valley of the Nile, 19 miles from Aswan. When the new dam built there was going to overrun its site with water, the Egyptian government agreed to have it dismantled and presented to the Spanish people. It was taken down stone by stone in 1969 and 1970, then shipped to Valencia. From that Mediterranean port, it was sent by rail to Madrid where it was reconstructed and opened to the public in 1971. Photos upstairs in the temple depict its long history. It stands right off the Plaza de

España, and can be visited daily from 10 a.m. to 1 p.m. and 5 to 8 p.m. (on Sunday, to 3 p.m.) for an admission of 20 pesetas (19¢).

Museum of America

This museum, in University City, of Hispanic America reflects the influence of Spain on the Americas and the Philippines, tracing the important cultural influence the colonial power had in the New World. Inaugurated by Franco in 1965, the museum numbers among its finest exhibits a reproduction of the tent used by Queen Isabella I during the conquest of Granada.

However, most of the displays come from the New World: Inca art, and a Maya codex from Mexico; Chimu, Mochica, and Nazca ceramics from Peru; pre-Hispanic gold objects, such as the treasury of "Los Quimbayas" of Columbia; pre-Columbian art from Costa Rica and Nicaragua; and shrunken heads from the Jivaros of Ecuador.

Artifacts are displayed from the Caribbean and the Philippines, along with feather tapestries, pictures with mother-of-pearl inlay depicting the conquest of Mexico by Cortés, red-colored ceramics from Guadalájara. A map shows the string of Franciscan missions founded in California. You can also press buttons to light up a map that pinpoints Columbus's four voyages to America.

In one wing is a popular art exhibition from the Americas and the Philippines. The museum is open daily from 10 a.m. to 2 p.m., and charges 80 pesetas (77¢) entrance. Students and teachers are admitted free.

The Casa de Campo

Most people aren't in Madrid too long before they hear about that once-royal park, the Retiro. But many tourists never make it to the former royal hunting grounds, the **Casa de Campo,** miles and miles of parkland lying south of the Royal Palace, across the Manzanares. You can see the gate through which the kings rode out of the palace grounds—either on horses or in carriages —and headed for the park. You, of course, will have to take less elegant transportation: the Metro to El Lago or El Batán.

The park has a variety of trees and a lake, which is usually filled with rowers. You can have drinks and light refreshments around the lake, or you can go swimming in an excellent, municipally operated pool for 150 pesetas ($1.44).

The Madrileños like to keep the place to themselves; on a hot night or a Sunday morning, the park throngs with people trying to escape the heat. If you have an automobile you can go for a drive, as the grounds are extensive. The park is open until around 11 p.m. It's cool, pleasant, refreshing—a cheap way to spend an evening. In addition, the park has an ultra modern zoo.

At the edge of the park is the Parque de Atracciones, previewed separately in the nightlife section. Take Autobus 33 from Plaza de Isabel, the Teleférico bus, or, on Saturday and holidays, buses from Ventas, Estrecho, and Puente de Vallecas.

Some readers have found the zoo at the park the rival of the National Zoological Park in Washington. However, it's expensive, charging an entrance fee of 250 pesetas ($2.40). To be admitted to the children's zoo costs another 150 pesetas ($1.44), and you're charged yet another 40 pesetas (38¢) to take the zoo train. The zoo is well laid out and, as a special feature, has grottos without bars allowing you to be virtually eyeball-to-eyeball with the animals. If you don't like crowds, visit between 2 to 5 p.m. when no sane Spaniard would venture there.

ORGANIZED TOURS: For general tours of Madrid, **Wagon-Lits Viajes,** 23 Alcalá (tel. 433-56-00), is a good bet. All of its tours depart from its bus terminal at 8 Plaza de Oriente, near the Royal Palace. Although not terribly imaginative, the trips hit the high spots, not only in Madrid, but in the major cities that form a wheel around the capital.

A morning sightseeing tour leaves the terminal at 9:30 a.m., costs 1300 pesetas ($12.48) and takes in the Prado and the Royal Palace—quite a mouthful for one spree. For 925 pesetas ($8.88), a far less interesting afternoon trip takes in such secondary sights as the bullring, Retiro Park, and the Spanish University. The tour usually departs at 3 p.m.; but, out of deference to the heat, in summer the coach leaves at 3:30 p.m.-

Of all the excursions outside Madrid, the full-day trek to Toledo is the most popular. Costing 2100 pesetas ($20.16), the tour leaves all year at 9:30 a.m., taking in the cathedral as well as a factory that makes the celebrated swords of the Imperial City, and includes lunch. The second most popular excursion is to El Escorial, the monastery built by Philip II that is the pantheon of Spanish kings, and to the Valley of the Fallen, a memorial commemorating those men who lost their lives in the Civil War. This full-day tour costs 2800 pesetas ($26.88), operates year round, and leaves at 8:30 a.m. Lunch is provided at a typical restaurant in Escorial.

READER'S SIGHTSEEING TIP: "I visited the military and naval museums in Madrid and tried to include the railroad museum as well. The **Military Museum** at 1 Mendez Nuñez is far and away the best, and I would recommend that any persons interested in visiting it allow two or three hours there. The **Naval Museum** at 2 Montalban, nearby, is much smaller, and it is composed primarily of pre-1700 and post-1945 material. An hour is sufficient for it" (John V. Fels, Phoenix, Ariz.).

5. The Sporting Life

The Madrileños have a tremendous interest in action-packed events, an interest that reaches its peak in the bullring. But jai alai is another popular diversion. Read on:

THE BULLFIGHT: Chances are you'll see your first bullfight in Madrid, and you couldn't be more fortunate, because the capital draws the finest matadors in Spain. If a matador hasn't proved his worth in the major ring in Madrid, he just hasn't been recognized as a top-flight artist. The big season begins during the Feast of San Isidore, the patron saint of Madrid, on the 15th of May. This is the occasion for a series of fights, during which time the audience is filled with talent scouts. The men who distinguish themselves in the ring are signed up for Majorca, Málaga, or wherever.

If possible, try to buy your tickets where you see the official sign; otherwise, you pay 20% more. Sometimes, however, the official center is out of tickets, and then you'll have to throw yourself upon the mercy of the scalpers if you're eager to see a particular fight.

For tickets to the biggest bullring in Madrid, the 26,000-seat **Plaza de Toros** at 237 Calle de Alcalá, go to the office at 9 Victoria; to reach it, head east from the Puerta del Sol, then walk two blocks down the Carrera de San Jerónimo, then turn south onto Victoria. You can save approximately one-fourth of the price of the ticket if you ask for *sombre y sol,* which means that during part of the fight you'll be in the sun.

Front-row seats, known as *barreras,* can cost anywhere from 1500 pesetas ($14.40) to 3300 pesetas ($31.68). *Delanteras*—third-row seats—are available in both the *alta* (high) and *baja* (low) sections, and range from 500 pesetas ($4.80) to 2600 pesetas ($24.96). However, you can often get quite a passable *filas* for anywhere from 200 pesetas ($1.92) to 1750 pesetas ($16.80), the latter a most desirable perch. Bullfights are held on Sunday at 7 p.m. (also on holidays), from Easter to October. Fights by neophyte matadors are sometimes staged at 11 on Saturday evening as well. These fights are less expensive.

On the day of the fight, take the Metro to Ventas, although you may be killed in the stampede if you arrive late in the afternoon shortly before the fight begins. Of course, you can take a taxi, although you'll never get one back unless you have the driver wait. A suggestion is that you take the Metro out early; that way you'll avoid the last-minute rush. After the fight, you can wait until the first two or three trains have gone before venturing underground.

If you find that you're becoming an aficionado, then you may want to purchase a ticket to a fight at the **Vista-Alegre,** the second-choice ring in Madrid, for which tickets are sold at 3 Victoria near the main ticket office. This is a small bullring, but a number of Spaniards maintain that they often see better fights here.

READER'S SUGGESTION FOR PURCHASING TICKETS: "To avoid paying the 20% broker's fee tacked on when you buy a ticket at the downtown office, I suggest the tourist go down to the bullring, a few hours before the fight, and purchase a ticket at the window, *not* at the brown huts in front of the bullring, which also add a 20% surcharge. The seats are the same no matter where you obtain your tickets. Arriving within an hour of the bullfight will force one to stand in a terribly long line, and the better seats may no longer be available. For this reason, it is important to arrive at least two hours before the fight. To while away any time you have before the event, you can spend a delightful couple of hours at El Retiro park which is full of people Sunday afternoon. If you don't feel up to the half hour or so walk, the subway will take you there in a minute" (Kevin Corrigan, Miami University, European Center, Luxembourg).

MINOR SPORTS: A popular Spanish diversion that originated in the Basque country is jai alai or *pelota,* a ball game with the fastest action around. The **Frontón Madrid,** 10 Dr. Cortezo (tel. 239-10-37), is a major center for this exciting sport, and seats are low-priced: from 100 pesetas (96¢) to 200 pesetas ($1.92). Naturally, that charge is just to keep anybody from simply straying in, because the house really makes its money on betting. But until you learn the game, you'd better skip the gambling and concentrate on the action. Once you've seen a game, you might try your luck with a 50-peseta (48¢) bet. Games are played at 4:30 p.m., and on Saturday there are games at 11 a.m. and 1 p.m. as well.

6. Shopping in Madrid

Rivaled but not surpassed by Barcelona, Madrid offers the best buys for the bargain hunter of any city in Spain. Thousands of tourists pass through the Spanish capital yearly; and, frankly, many shops are designed chiefly for what the proprietors think the well-heeled foreigner will like.

On the other hand, Madrid is chiefly an industrial and commercial capital, in which the majority of the stores and shops exist primarily for the patronage of Spaniards. As the average income of a Spanish family is far below that of an American, Canadian, English, or Scandinavian, managers or shopkeepers must keep prices in line with what they think the local traffic will bear. Consequently, the city offers some of the lowest priced high-quality merchandise of any European capital.

HANDICRAFT EXHIBITIONS: Artespaña (Empresa Nacional de Artesanía), 32 Gran Vía, 14 Hermosilla, 3 Plaza de las Cortés, and 33 D. Ramón de la Cruz, are the government-sponsored exhibition and sales centers for Spanish handicrafts, some of the best establishments at which to purchase handmade furniture and decorative items from all the regions of Spain. The buyers know their country well, bringing to their showrooms excellently made items. You'll find furniture reproductions, Toledo damascene work, wrought-iron work, ceramics, glassware, carved wood, jewelry, and hundreds of other accessories.

Much of the jewelry is made of sterling silver. Córdoban filigree boxes are a good buy. Other displays include tin lanterns (with inserts of ruby-red, amber, or midnight-blue glass), pewter ashtrays, handmade regional dolls, ecclesiastical woodcarvings, fringed pillow covers and bedspreads, handmade Catalán chairs, and Córdoban leather goods.

The showrooms are supervised by English-speaking attendants, who can arrange for packing and shipping. The hours are from 9:30 a.m. to 1:30 p.m., and 4:30 to 8 p.m. For information, telephone 411-13-62 or 261-64-00.

Kreisler, 19 Serrano (tel. 276-53-38), is owned and operated by a seemingly tireless American midwesterner from Akron, Ohio, Edward Kreisler, a skillful entrepreneur of Spanish decorative handicrafts. Through his grapevine, he keeps in touch with artisans in obscure villages and towns, presenting their wares in his jam-packed galleries in the Serrano shopping district. Within are most of the Spanish items that the North American visitor wants, including olive-wood articles, "El Greco chairs," handmade mantillas, Toledo damascene work, woodcarvings, wrought iron, Spanish fans, purses in grained leather, and tapestry needlework.

Kreisler is also an official agency for Majorcan pearls and Lladró porcelain. The section of Lladró porcelain has been enlarged and is perhaps the most complete in Madrid. Prices are very competitive because Kreisler doesn't add on any percentage for commissions to guides. Purchases can be packed and shipped anywhere in the world.

At the **Galería Kreisler,** in a separate section, some of the fine painters and sculptors in the country have found an important showcase for their talents. Here you'll find both the old master and the avant-garde artist represented. The gallery features Spain's most reputable artists whose works are often in the permanent collection of the National Museum of Contemporary Art. Kreisler has another art gallery, **Galería Kreisler Dos,** showing only avant-garde artists, including works by Miró, Picasso, and Juan Gris. The address is 8 Hermosilla (tel. 226-42-64). It's about 75 years around the corner from 19 Serrano.

WOMEN'S CLOTHING: One of the most popular retail outlets for women's clothing is **Herrero,** 33 Gran Vía (tel. 222-03-10), on the main street of Madrid. Seven other retail branches are found in the capital as well, each carrying the same merchandise. The stores feature an especially good line of suede, leather dresses, and coats—custom-made, if you desire.

MADRID'S LEADING DEPARTMENT STORES: Galerías Preciados, 28 Preciados (tel. 222-96-78), right off the Gran Vía, has greatly expanded and improved in recent years. It's really two stores now, connected by an underground passageway. It's more Macy's than Lord & Taylor, with quite presentable readymade clothing for men, women, and children. There's a top-floor snackbar and restaurant, with a *guardería infantil* where you can park your infant while you shop at your leisure. Some good buys I noted recently include guitars, men's suede jackets, Spanish capes for men, women's full-length suede coats (the colors are exciting, including royal blue, kelly green, olive, and violet).

Men's suits: In the second-floor tailoring department, you can order a suit in five working days. You're fitted with one of the basic "try-on" suits. The goodly selection of fabrics—plaids, solids, herringbones—are made into whatever style you prefer.

On the lower level is a department jam-packed with regional handicrafts, including ship models made in Catalonia, historical sword reproductions, regional dolls, tooled leather from Córdoba, damascene work from Toledo, Lladró porcelain figurines from Valencia, blown glass from Majorca, white ceramic pieces from Manises, handicrafts from Galacia, and ceramics from Gerona and Valencia.

The other big department store chain is **El Corte Inglés** (tel. 232-81-00), with outlets all around the country, including Málaga. At present, branches in Madrid are on Calle Precíados, near the Puerta del Sol in the center of the city; on the Calle Goya, where it crosses the Calle de Alcalá; on the Calle Raimundo Fernández Villaverde, right off the Avenida del Castellana, plus a newer one in Princesa Street. Rather than running about from boutique to tourist shop to boutique, many visitors will find it easier and often cheaper to make all their purchases in a department store. For example, at El Corte Inglés, you can buy a handsome Toledo sword or typical gypsy doll, or one of the well-known Spanish mantillas.

SOME BOUTIQUES: Don Carlos, 92 Serrano (tel. 275-75-07), is on the best street for elegant shopping in Madrid. This boutique features an excellent selection of clothing for both men and women. . . . Also good is **Blanco,** 26 Velázquez (tel. 226-61-27), a most up-to-date boutique that is more popular with the younger set. . . . Finally, **Berhanyer,** 25 Juan de Mena (tel. 231-41-77), is Spain's top designer, offering a wide selection of his ready-to-wear apparel in this handsome boutique. It's highly recommended for quality merchandise, but only if you can afford it.

ORIGINAL OILS BY SPANISH ARTISTS: Spanish Painters Society, 68 Alcalá (tel. 231-65-96), is the largest art gallery in Europe. It was the brain child of Javier Martinez, who was captivated by the idea of presenting the works of unknown, traditional Spanish artists at low rates. You can pick up a small oil painting for as little as $60 (U.S.), although most canvases are in the $300 bracket; some go as high as $4000.

Two hundred artists—many from the School of Fine Arts—are exhibited at the Painters Association. Note: Some of the artists are only moderately talented; a few are frankly mediocre; but others show skill and imagination. It's easy and inexpensive to ship purchases to North America: a canvas is rolled safely in a strong metal tube. The gallery is open all day, from 9:30 a.m. to 8:30 p.m. (also on Sunday morning).

HANDMADE WOMEN'S GLOVES: Vargas, 21 Calle de Cerretas, down from the Puerta del Sol, is a good, all-around place at which to purchase a wide assortment of gloves, ranging from fashionable selections to industrial ones for Spanish working people. The prices at this shop are very reasonable. No one is paying for a fancy address or stylish decor. The Vargas specialty is color: robin's-egg blue to burgundy to beige to Carmen red to shocking pink to saffron to olive. Materials include suede, leather, and fabrics such as lace.

CUSTOM TAILORING: Valdivia, 86 Gran Vía (tel. 247-96-40), is in the Edificio España (the Plaza Hotel building) at the Plaza de España. Mariano Valdivia inherited his skill and business from his father, and has won the respect and patronage of many a Spanish businessman or diplomat by turning out skillfully tailored suits for men. His staff can produce a suit in four or five working days, if you're available for fittings. Their shop offers an excellent choice of fabrics in all weather weights. Everything is made by hand, even the button holes. They can give you a conservative banker's look or outfit you in more provocatively styled clothing. A good selection of custom shirts is also available.

FOR MAJORCAN PEARLS: The agency for **Perlas Majorica,** the registered trademark for what are considered the finest artificial pearls in the world, is at 5 Plaza del Callao (tel. 222-52-47). This outlet offers the pearls in a wide variety of necklaces, bracelets, earrings, rings, and pins in different colors and combinations. Fine pieces of jewelry are also on sale.

FUNKY HEADGEAR: Casa Yustas, 30 Plaza Mayor (tel. 266-50-84), is an extraordinary hat emporium, especially popular in this day of strange headgear. If your sessions with the analyst have revealed a hang-up for unusual hats, you can satisfy your inclinations here. Picture yourself a Congo explorer, a Spanish sailor, an officer in the Kaiser's army, a Rough Rider, a priest, even Napoleon. A straw sombrero is a conversation piece, and a black beret will return you to the Montmartre of the 1920s.

ANTELOPE AND LEATHER GOODS: Boutique Shalóm, 45 Gran Vía (tel. 247-17-39), specializes in antelope and leather as well as suede. This third-floor shop will make any design you want: bring in a sketch or photograph, and the workers will turn it out within 24 to 36 hours. The shop also does work in napalán (sheepskin), wool, silk, and cotton. There is a variety of antelope jackets for men and women, as well as beautiful suede jackets. In addition, the shop displays any number of accessories, including boots, handbags, and gloves.

HANDICRAFTS AND GIFTS: Sefarad Shopping Center, 54 Gran Vía (tel. 247-61-42), is the largest official distributor of Lladró porcelain in Madrid. More than 40,000 articles of all sorts have been assembled in relatively small quarters, on the first and third floors. Some of the items included in this array are 18K gold, silver, costume jewelry, ceramics, Majorca pearls, typical Spanish souvenirs, handicrafts from every region of Spain, judaica, oil paintings, and mantillas. It also has a big selection of all sorts of leather travel goods in the finest skins.

Aleixandre, 23 Gran Vía (tel. 221-29-20). At three different locations in Madrid, Aleixandre offers one of the most tasteful selections of gifts in the Spanish capital. Shopping is made even more enjoyable by the elegant, salon-like setting, combined with flattering, personalized service. The merchandise includes a wide selection of 18th- and 19th-century fans, jewelry, costume jewelry, leather goods, perfume, mantillas, Toledo ware, and Perlas (pearls) Majorica. The other Madrid shops are at 5 Plaza Canalejas and 39 Velázquez.

READER'S SHOPPING TIP: "For people who would like Nao or Lladró porcelain at a reduced price, on the lower level of the **Galerías Preciados** in the regional handicrafts section, find the corner that has damaged pieces. These have been repaired very skillfully. Take the one you like to the salesperson, who will take it to her supervisor, who will give you a discount price. You don't have to buy it if you don't agree with the price. I got a 2200-peseta ($21.12) item for 1240 pesetas ($11.90)" (Lauretta B. Freeman, Montclair, N.J.).

7. Madrid After Dark

Madrid abounds with dance halls, tascas, cafés, theaters, movie houses, music halls, and nightclubs—but you have to proceed carefully through this maze, as many of these nightly offerings are strictly for the residents, or for Spanish-speaking people.

For the bizarre, you have to go to Hamburg or Paris, but if a good time is what you're looking for, Madrid won't let you down. The average visitor will want to find the flamenco places, as this is the highlight of Spanish nightlife, but there are other offerings that intrigue, too.

The rules of the game: Spanish nightlife may not always offend the Bible belt, but one marvelously compensating factor is that it's cheap. In most clubs a one-drink minimum is the rule, and you can nurse your drink through the entire evening's entertainment. It's a perfectly acceptable custom.

Because dinner is served late in Spain, nightlife doesn't really get under way until after 11, and it generally lasts till around 3 a.m. If you arrive at 9:30 at a club, you'll probably find that you have the place all to yourself.

Because Madrileños are said to be fond of prowling around at night, they are known throughout Spain as *gatos* (cats).

FLAMENCO SHOWS: The strum of a guitar, the sound of hands clapping rhythmically . . . and you know that flamenco is about to start. Soon colorfully dressed women, occasionally men, flounce onto the stage to swirl in time with the music. The staccato beat of castanets and the tapping of heels make the rafters ring. Flamenco . . . the incomparable Spanish art form.

Most of the major clubs in Madrid are patronized almost exclusively by foreigners. Hence, some of the very top ones are beyond the means of most budgeteers. However, two other leading and less expensive flamenco nightspots are Torres Bermejas and Arco de Cuchilleros. Neither one of them is cheap—but then you need only purchase one drink, as there is no minimum or cover charge.

Café de Chinitas, 7 Torija (tel. 248-51-35), is swanky and expensive, a four-fork restaurant and flamenco club in Old Madrid, between the Ópera and Gran Vía. The setting is tasteful, with paneling in olive and geranium red. No amateurs play here. Rather, La Chunga is the featured dancer, as well as Serranito, the guitarist. These and 37 other performers make up what is called a cuadro. The first show is at 11 p.m., although the festivities usually last until 3:30 a.m. The minimum is 1400 pesetas ($13.44), and this entitles you to a drink at a table. It's also possible to attend dinner at 9:30 p.m., then stay to watch the show. À la carte main dishes average around 1000 pesetas ($9.60) to 1400 pesetas ($13.44).

Las Brujas ("The Witches"), 15 Norte, off Calle San Bernardo (tel. 222-53-25), is an authentic flamenco spot in Madrid. The entry is a reasonable facsimile of a country courtyard, with an open grill fireplace and cobblestones. The three-course tourist menu, not including drinks, is 2000 pesetas ($19.20). But if you want to watch the show and have drinks only, you need pay only 900 pesetas ($8.64) for the first drink, 600 pesetas ($5.76) for the second. The tables are small, and it's likely to be crowded. Don't let the waiter seat you behind the pillars which block part of the show.

Torres Bermejas, 11 Mesonero Romanos (tel. 232-33-22), right off the Gran Vía, is an underground cellar decorated in the style of a harem from old Granada. Some of the best flamenco dancers in Spain appear here, usually a trio of gypsy stars. For 2500 pesetas ($24), you can order a set meal, including wine, and you must pay a supplement for the show. After 11:30 p.m., until 3 a.m., you can attend by ordering just a drink at 1200 pesetas ($11.52).

If you're still on the flamenco trail, then you might try **Arco de Cuchilleros,** 7 Cuchilleros (tel. 266-58-67), near the Botín Restaurant. Lots of single men and women come here. A flamenco show with a girlie twist is often presented. All in all, it's fun to be here if you don't take the proceedings too seriously. The one-drink minimum will cost you 1000 pesetas ($9.60).

To go Spanish, you might enjoy attending a *zarzuela,* a Spanish musical variety show. Often these vaudevillian presentations sandwich flamenco numbers and musical revues between their regular acts. Even if you don't see any flamenco dancing, you'll find attending a *zarzuela* is . . . well, an experience. The best showplace in town for a *zarzuela* is the interesting old-style theater, **Teatro Calderón,** 18 Calle de Atocha, opposite a little plaza, Jacinto Benavente (with underground parking). There are numerous good seats which range in price from 400 pesetas ($3.84) to 1000 pesetas ($9.60).

Head for the **Teatro de la Zarzuela,** 4 Calle de Jovellanos (tel. 221-98-95), for more traditional *zarzuela* fare. It is at the Zarzuela Theater that Madrid's opera and ballet festivals are held each spring.

Note: For chamber and symphonic music, go to the **Teatro Real** (tel. 241-97-39), on the Plaza Isabel II.

DISCOS: The Spanish disco takes its inspiration from other Western capitals —in fact, many have English names. In Madrid, most of these clubs open around 6 p.m. for what is called a matinee. They usually go till 9 p.m., when they shut down to allow their young patrons to go out for dinner. Then around 11 p.m. they reopen, although they don't generally start to rock till around midnight.

Bocaccio, 16 Marqués de la Ensenada, off the Plaza Colón (tel. 419-10-08), is an offshoot of the celebrated same-name disco in Barcelona. It is the poshest disco in the Spanish capital, done in glittering art nouveau, with tufted red velvet banquettes. In this elegant setting, you'll pay 450 pesetas ($4.32) for a first drink, although the charge is reduced to 300 pesetas ($2.88) for each drink thereafter. It's open daily from 7 p.m. to 3:30 a.m.

Cerebro, 3 Calle Princesa (tel. 448-20-13), a block away from the Plaza de España, is the best disco in Madrid. It's in a hugh modern complex, that includes several cafeterías. There are, in fact, four Cerebros in Madrid: one at 1 Calle Magallanes—the original disco—and three near the Plaza de España— one of which is a disco, and another a theater where offbeat musicals are staged, but which presently operates as a disco as well. The third is a small, cozy place for the young with the latest musical hits from all over the world. The entrance of the so-called Cerebro Two is down a flight of glass stairs, extended over pools of bubbling water. Although doors open at 7 p.m., I suggest that you postpone your visit until midnight. The club stays open until 10 p.m., then reopens at

11 p.m. and closes at 4 a.m. The latest rock is played, but the disc jockey varies the musical diet. On one recent occasion, and for no particular reason at all, he played three Viennese waltzes. The charge is 500 pesetas ($4.80) for the first drink. Subsequent drinks cost 300 pesetas ($2.88). For this set fee, you are entitled to dance all night. Usually waiters come around in the wee hours with free sandwiches or canapés for those hungry after all that dancing.

J.J. (Hota-Hota), 4 Plaza del Callao (tel. 232-04-29), off the Gran Vía, honors a famed Spanish duo. In some respects, it is Madrid's most frenetic psychedelic statement, right in the heartbeat center of the capital, entered alongside a movie theater. Built like a theater in the round, the disco has tables arranged by tier around the floor and stage, where live groups often (but not always) appear. The young woman in the cage is a disc jockey (looking as if she's launching herself into outer space) directing the intricate electronic lighting, the flashing and blinking strobes, causing on one occasion one older client to exclaim, "Loco, loco." Singles pay 750 pesetas ($7.20); couples, 1200 pesetas ($11.52).

New Royal, 43 Gran Vía, is on the lower level of the Rex Hotel, right in mainstream Madrid. When the music reaches its peak, it's loud. But sometimes, incongruously, a Spanish couple will move in slow rhythm to the fast-paced sounds. The early sessions—the matinees—cost only 250 pesetas ($2.40) per drink; it's 500 pesetas ($4.80) after dinner. The disco is open from 7 p.m. to 3 a.m.

SPECTACLES: In the post-Franco era, nightclub entrepreneurs have discovered nudity, and are presenting an array of glossy cabarets and what one reviewer called "super sexy hi-fi shows."

The most beauties on nightly display are found at the **Lido,** 20 Alcalá (tel. 232-21-01), which is a direct spin-off from its famous namesake in Paris. It never attains the quality of the Lido in Paris, but what you get in Madrid isn't bad. At least it's the best such show staged in Spain today. Men even take their wives to the 10:45 show, and perhaps even to the 1:15 a.m. spectacle, but on my last visit, I saw not one woman in the audience for the "super-sexy" show which went on at the ungodly hour of 3:15 a.m. A drink costs 1750 pesetas ($16.80), which serves as your entrance fee to the show. The costumes are extravagant, with lots of feathers which eventually are removed—that is, if you're willing to wait around.

More international sex shows are offered at the **Music Hall Pirandello,** 7 Ventura Rodríguez (tel. 247-63-12), where eroticism attains high levels for Madrid, and the price of entrance is your first drink which goes for 1200 pesetas ($11.52). The loud, racy show goes on at 1:15 a.m., although the club opens at 11:30 p.m., closing at 4 a.m. Here you'll encounter some of the least inhibited women in the Spanish capital.

Xairo, 11 Paz (tel. 231-24-40), is even more daring, offering, on occasion, what the management bills as a "sadamasoquisimo sexual" spectacle. Show times are at 11:45 p.m. and 1:30 a.m., and the cost of your first drink is 1000 pesetas ($9.60).

JAZZ: **Whisky Jazz,** 7 Diego de León (tel. 261-11-65), has the beat—in fact, it's Madrid's leading jazz center. It lies off the Calle de Serrano near the American Embassy. There is no number on the oak door (you may feel like you're attending a speakeasy of old, so tight is the security at the door). Inside the two-level brick structure is a main floor, with a bar at the rear, plus an open staircase leading to a mezzanine of tables.

The memorabilia on the walls and in the glass case reveals a reverence for jazz. Encased are letters and faded photographs of the "greats" from New Orleans, Kansas City, Chicago. Jazz groups appear with frequency; otherwise, the management plays recordings of their works. In the early part of the evening, you pay 300 pesetas ($2.88), that tab increasing to 500 pesetas ($4.80) in the early morning when the live groups usually appear. On weekends and holidays, the charge is 700 pesetas ($6.72).

CAVE CRAWLING: To capture a peculiar Madrid joie de vivre of the 18th century, you can tune in the circuit of *mesones* and *cuevas,* many found in the Old Town, known as *barrios bajos.* From the Plaza Major, walk down the Arco de Cuchilleros until you find a gypsy-like cave that fits your fancy. Young people especially love to meet in the taverns and caves of Old Madrid for communal drinking and songfests. The sangría flows freely, the atmosphere is charged, the room usually packed, the guitars strummed into the night air. Sometimes strolling bands of singing students (known as *tuna*) go from bar to bar, colorfully attired, with ribbons fluttering from their outfits.

A favorite of readers is the **Mesón de la Guitarra,** 11 Cavade de San Miguel, recommended by Jerold Freier of Cambridge, Mass.: "The crowd is made up of workmen, couples, and tourists, attracted by the sound of three songs all going at once. Yankee Stadium sounds quiet by comparison. Like an English pub, many of the people here are regulars, coming on a particular night each week to meet their friends and sing. As a result, it is loud, exciting entertainment, almost any night of the week. Like most things in Madrid, it doesn't really get rolling until after 10:30 p.m. The mesón consists of three levels. The higher up and the farther you go, the louder it gets. Don't be afraid to begin singing an American song, if it has a fast rhythm. You'll find that 60 people have joined in, even if they don't known the words. There is no admission charge, and a small jug of wine (about four glasses) is 1250 pesetas ($12)."

Mesón de Austrias, Cava San Miguel II, near the Mesón de la Guitarra, is the delight of many of our readers, especially Joan Ellen Pick of Syracuse, N.Y., who writes: "I spent countless evenings mesón-hopping, having wine for very few pesetas, and tapas, cheese, mushrooms, or olives. The accordion player here is the Louis Armstrong of Spain (in looks and voice). The food is delicious, the people friendly." John N. Davis of Nottingham, England, says that if you are looking for a decent place, cleanliness, good quality, and waiters with notions of English, this is the mesón for you. A whole tortilla suitable for four people goes for 250 pesetas ($2.40) and a pitcher of sangría for 300 pesetas ($2.88) at a table. It is a cozy place, with coved brick ceilings, four rooms in all, and in wintertime, the favored spot is in front of the open fire in the front room.

Some other mesones on the block are the **Mesón del Boquerón, Mesón de la Tortilla, Mesón del Champiñón, La Mazorra,** and **Mesón de las Infantas,** all with similar prices.

Sesamo (Sesame), 7 Calle del Príncipe (tel. 232-91-91), is in a class all by itself. It is the personal statement of art-loving Tomás Cruz Diaz, who started this cueva back in the early 1950s, drawing a clientele of young painters and writers to its ambience, described by the proprietor as "cosmopolita y bohemia." Hemingway was one of those early visitors (a plaque commemorates him).

When you first see it, you think you're walking into a tiny snackbar—and you are. But proceed down the flight of steps to the cellar. The walls are covered with contemporary paintings, and there are quotations from such writers as Byron or from such scholars as Unamuno. At squatty stools and tables, an international assortment of young people listens to piano music, perhaps folk singing, guitar playing—nothing formal. Conversation is also important. It's customary to order a pitcher of sangría for four at 350 pesetas ($3.36) or a beer at 65 pesetas (62¢).

READER'S TASCA SUGGESTION: "In the tasca classification, we recommend the new **Mesón Asturias,** 5 Alvarez Gato. This was our first tasca, and we ate almost everything in sight on the night we arrived, after a visit to the Valley of the Fallen. We had lamb shanks, a mushroom dish, a sausage plate, and baby eels, sharing dishes as in a Chinese restaurant. The total tab for four was about 4000 pesetas ($38.40). Even more outstanding than the food was the friendliness of the owner. He told us he was open until 1 a.m., so the next night we dropped in at about 11 o'clock. The place was just closing, but he insisted that we come in and have a glass of wine. It turned into a party with him and his wife and a discussion of the operation of a tasca. We saw no greater friendliness anywhere in Spain" (John V. Fels, Phoenix, Ariz.).

SOUTH AMERICAN FOLKLORE: **Malambo,** 3 Jardines (tel. 232-64-90), features various types of live shows, but most of them South American folklore. Every night at 11:15, the club offers four different groups, each doing two numbers. The show's over around 4 a.m. You go down a flight of stairs and come to a fairly large room with a stage, and tables and chairs for about 150 people. The minimum (for a drink) is 360 pesetas ($3.46). Very few Europeans or Yanks attend. The audience is almost entirely South American and Spanish. Entertainment is only vocal and instrumental. Closed Monday.

Irlanda Pub, 46 Alberto Alcocer, is not really an Irish pub, but an intimate bar where you can enjoy soft, South American music in a friendly atmosphere, consisting mostly of couples and groups. Drinks run around 450 pesetas ($4.32) to 700 pesetas ($6.72) when there is entertainment. At the piano bar you are likely to hear songs of all styles. It's a good place to spend the better part of an evening.

"DISNEYLANDIA": That's what the press of Madrid screamed when the **Parque de Atracciones,** Madrid's festive fun park, opened in 1969. There is a típico restaurant, a disco, an outdoor dance hall, a Greek theater presenting free concerts and flamenco, boats on canals, and many pleasure rides. Open all year, the park invites revelry.

To reach the park (on the edge of the **Casa de Campo,** the former royal hunting grounds, now a public park) you can take a cable car from the intersection of the Paseo del Pintor Rosales and the Calle Marques de Urgillo. Along the grassy parkway, there is a large overhead sign in yellow and orange (Teleférico) which you pass under, down along a path to the cable station which is at the rear of the new cafetería built on the hillside ledge. The ride takes about 11 minutes. A round-trip ticket costs 130 pesetas ($1.25); a one-way, 90 pesetas (86¢). The cable car operates from 11 a.m. to 2 p.m. and 4 to 9 p.m. in good weather only. For a group of three or four, a taxi would be more convenient and less expensive. The park is open from 6:30 p.m. to 1 a.m. on weekdays, from 6 p.m. to 2 a.m. on Saturday (rides shut down between 3 and 4 p.m.), and from noon to 1 a.m. on Sunday (again rides stop between 3 and 4 p.m.). The general admission is 50 pesetas (48¢) for adults, 25 pesetas (24¢) for children ages 3 to 10. The park is closed on Monday. Rides are paid by buying tickets, with most adventures costing two or three tickets.

Some of the better rides, such as the Russian Mountain (in reality, a modified roller coaster), cost four tickets. Speedboats operate on the narrow canals, cutting through the grounds, past straw-thatched houses, twisted trees, and under bridges. There's an auto racetrack, with miniature cars and banks of rubber tires to ease the bumps. It's all here: "shoot the chute," a pond with boats for juvenile yachting types; a merry-go-round with stylized animals; a flight through "space," antique cars, a carousel, and maze of glass. You can ride throughout the grounds on an elongated puppy dog (a group of cars), or go writhing on an octopus (El Pulpo). At the center of everything is an illuminated tower, offering a bird's-eye view of the city, a miniature elevator taking you to the summit.

A final attraction is the Greek-style **Teatro,** which is free. This open-air theater has cast cement seats facing the bowl. Colored water displays shoot from the fountains, picked up by a reflection pool. From flamenco to ballet, from classic to comic, the bill of fare is wide. Weather permitting, one-hour shows are performed at 7:30 and 10:30 p.m. from May till the end of September.

A restaurant lies within the grounds. Although not super-expensive, its prices are high enough to make it a splurge.

READER'S RESTAURANT SUGGESTION: "If you are not in the mood to make a splurge of your supper when visiting the Parque de Atracciones, I'd suggest you go to the **Autoservicío del Teatro,** a few steps away from the theater, and enjoy your meal in the open air, with beautiful views of the illuminated park. We had tortilla Paula, ternera en salsa con puré de patatas, ensalada de lechuga y tomate, quesillo, bread, and dessert. All that costs only 400 pesetas ($3.84), and it's very tasty" (R. Depreitere, Kortrijk, Belgium).

A short walk from the Amusement Park is the **Madrid Zoo,** charmingly laid out, which is open from 10 a.m. to sunset and charges 225 pesetas ($2.16) for adults and 115 pesetas ($1.10) for children from 3 to 8 years old. (Children under 3 go free.) The zoo is stocked with all the classical animals, as well as several rare varieties such as the okapi. Most animals are in the open, separated from visitors by moats or freely strolling along the paths. There's a children's zoo within and a Papagayo Club in which these colorful birds show off their astonishing prowess. A train will take you around the principal route and the kiddies can ride on ponies or camels, visit the children's theater, and see the seals being fed and other attractions.

The zoo now has a pair of panda bears, a gift to the king and queen. Not many zoos have pandas, so these are of special interest. During the hottest part of the day, the bears are in seclusion.

THE PICK OF THE BARS: In *Papa Hemingway,* A. E. Hotchner called the **Palace Hotel Bar** (tel. 429-75-51) " . . . the nerve center of Madrid's social intrigue, where every woman looks like a successful spy." Even today, it holds to its established position, attracting Spanish nobility and fashionable foreigners alike. Everything is low key, in the old-world tradition: grainy marble panels mellowed with age, chairs you can lose yourself in, waiters who never interfere except to pounce when a guest needs a light—everything reflecting the lofty position of this pre-World War I "Grand Hotel."

For many, Hemingway was responsible for much of the fame of the **Palace Bar** at 7 Plaza de las Cortés. In the closing pages of his 1926 novel, *The Sun Also Rises,* he had Jake invite Brett to the bar for a final drink. The heroine delivered her famous line while enjoying a martini: "Barmen and jockeys are the only people who are polite any more." The martinis still taste just fine, and you can sample one for yourself between 1 and 3 p.m. and 8 to 10 p.m. Reader Clayton McDaniel, Key West, Florida, says, "Good martinis seem to be a matter of pride with hotel bartenders. In Madrid, Seville, Granada, and Valencia, they are outstanding—better than their counterparts in the U.S." A martini costs 250 pesetas ($2.40), although a brand-name scotch goes for 475 pesetas ($4.56).

Oliver's, 3 Calle del Conde Xiqueña, off the Paseo de la Castellana (tel. 221-73-79). Would you like a private club for your headquarters in Madrid? Oliver's is a hangout for show-biz people, with a good sprinkling of foreign personalities dropping by as well. It's all run by Jorge Fiestas, who writes a gossip column in one of Spain's movie magazines. The co-owner is director-actor Adolfo Marsillach. Oliver's is like a drawing room or the library-study of someone's town house. There are two club rooms, each with its own personality. The street floor seems like a tasteful, although faded, stage setting, with sofas and comfortable armchairs arranged for homelike conversational gatherings—the tone set by the scenic mural on the ceiling, which is left over from the old grocery shop that used to occupy this site. On either side of the fireplace stand recessed shelves, with an eclectic collection of hi-fi records (you can pick the ones you want played), books on the theater, movies, and painting. Drinks (and tapas) are brought unobtrusively to your table, and average 200 pesetas ($1.92) apiece. Scotch is 300 pesetas ($2.88). Reached by a graceful curving stairway, the downstairs room is softer, more secluded, with a pianist playing persuasive background music. Meet you at Oliver's. The bar is open from 8 p.m. till 3 a.m.

Chicote, 12 Gran Vía (tel. 232-15-12), attracts with its aura of a gentleman's club. It belonged to the now-legendary Señor Chicote (see my description of his "Museum of Bottles" earlier in the chapter). For thousands of English-speaking readers, Hemingway made this bar famous; here he sat entertaining his friends with such remarks as "Spain is a country for living and not for dying." Most alcoholic drinks are in the 90-peseta (86¢) to 200-peseta ($1.92) range.

Pickwick Club, 48 Paseo Pintor Rosales (tel. 248-51-85), draws homesick English expatriates. No other establishment in Madrid recaptures the "pubby" atmosphere better. On the walls hang framed prints of characters from Dickens, brass hunting horns, pewter and ceramic beer mugs, even horse brasses. Loners can drink at the bar, or at one of the small tables, sinking into the soft sofas and armchairs. The doorman is clad in "New Forest" green, and the Spanish waiters join the act with their tartan jackets. Most alcoholic drinks cost 125 pesetas ($1.20), including your tapas, usually salted nuts and Andalusian olives. The pub is about a ten-minute walk from the Plaza de España, and is open from 6 p.m. until 1:30 a.m.

New Pepe's Coctel-Bar, 72 Castellana (tel. 261-11-32), is a favorite hang-out for American expatriates who roost at the bar, sip vodka and tonics at 250 pesetas ($2.40) at the tables, and chat in the subdued lighting. The atmosphere is on the elegant side. A whisky costs from 250 pesetas ($2.40). Pepe's is open till 3 a.m.

The Red Lion, 9 Juan Hurtado de Mendoza, is a magnet to visitors with twangy accents from England, Scotland, Wales, and Australia. It's the expatriate heartbeat area in the Dr. Fleming area in the northern residential section of Madrid. It also has a *Sun Also Rises* atmosphere. The exterior has been given a Tudoresque facade by owner John Gray. Inside it's a miniature museum of memorabilia from Great Britain. There's a dart board and a few inside tables, but the guests prefer the sidewalk tables in good weather. The women who wait on you are English, with delightfully friendly manners. At the tables a brandy costs 80 pesetas (77¢). The favorite of habitués is anis at 80 pesetas also. The Red Lion is one block from the Castellana, and has a modest little Red Lion sign outside for identification.

Drug Store, 101 Feuncarral (tel.231-26-00), is as close as Madrid comes to possessing an American drugstore hangout. Launched in 1972, it's actually the counterpart of its more famous siblings in Paris. The Drug Store is open 24 hours a day and sells everything from records, books, and newspapers to groceries and clothing. There are several snackbars, a psychedelic restaurant with oddly shaped booths, even an associated movie house. The food and service are not especially good, so plan on just a hamburger at 225 pesetas ($2.16) and coffee or some of the pastries rather than a full meal. Most flavors of ice cream go for 85 pesetas (82¢) to 120 pesetas ($1.15).

Cuevas del Duque, 9 Duque de Liria, is an unusual and interesting bar, standing in front of the Duke of Alba's palace, a short walk from the heartbeat Plaza de España (walk along the Calle Princesa). This is really an underground bar and a small, ten-table mesón, serving such simple Spanish dishes as fababa (with ham and beans), gazpacho, and roast meat. Meals average around 1100 pesetas ($10.56). But most patrons come here to order drinks. In fair weather a few tables are set outside, beside a tiny triangular-shaped garden. Other tables line the Calle Princesa side, and make an enjoyable roost for an afternoon drink, ranging in price from 300 pesetas ($2.88) to 500 pesetas ($4.80).

READER'S BAR SELECTION: "At the corner of Calle Bailen and Calle Mayor is the **Anciano Rey de los Vinos,** near the Royal Palace. For about 15¢ a glass, you can savor the same excellent wine that drove the sister of Isabella II to don commoner's robes and sneak out of the palace to this historic bar" (Bob Marlin, Los Angeles, Calif.).

A FAMOUS OLD COFFEEHOUSE: Gran Café de Gijón, 21 Paseo de Calvo Sotelo (tel. 231-91-21). All old European capitals have a coffeehouse that traditionally has attracted the literati. In Madrid, the counterpart of Les Deux Magots in Paris or the Antico Caffè in Rome is Gijón, which opened in 1890 in the heyday of Madrid's *bella época*. Artists and writers (some look like Spanish versions of Tennessee Williams) patronize this venerated old café on one of Madrid's major boulevards. Many of them spend hours over one cup of coffee. The coffeehouse has open street windows looking out onto the wide paseo as well as a large terrace for sun-worshippers and birdwatchers. Along one side of the café is a stand-up bar, and on the lower level is a restaurant. A Cuba libre goes for 100 pesetas (96¢) although certain whisky drinks will cost 200 pesetas ($1.92).

READER'S NIGHTCLUB SELECTION: "**El Biombo Chino,** 6 Isabel la Católica, off the Gran Vía (tel. 248-12-82), is a sparkling new nightclub with a first-rate show for those who understand Spanish fairly well. Admission is 1200 pesetas ($11.52). You can sit here until about 3:30 or 4 a.m." (Ileane Kine, Huntington Beach, Calif.).

Chapter IV

RING AROUND MADRID

1. Toledo
2. Aranjuez
3. El Escorial and the Valley of the Fallen
4. Segovia and La Granja
5. Alcalá de Henares and El Pardo
6. Ávila
7. Guadalupe
8. Mérida
9. Zafra
10. Badajoz

MADRID IS ENCIRCLED by some of the major sightseeing treasures of Spain. As pointed out in the introduction to the capital, the most important reason for basing in Madrid is not only to view its own offerings, but the surrounding ones as well. In this chapter, we'll take a tour of the environs of Madrid, on every major artery, shooting out in all directions from the capital. The distances are short enough—9 miles for the quickest one, 68 for the longest—so that you can leave Madrid in the morning, journey to a town and see its major sights, yet be back in your hotel by nightfall.

However, if you should want to stay over in any town along the way, I've included the best of the budget hotels in every place. The restaurants and the sights, however, will be the primary concerns of the average visitor.

The first four tours encompass the National Monument cities of **Toledo, Aranjuez,** and **Segovia,** and a monastery that is a wonder of the world, **El Escorial.**

The next two tours are included for those who have a couple of extra days to spend outside Madrid. Those who are so blessed can visit the beautiful little town where Franco used to rule Spain, **El Pardo,** and they can go to the ancient university city that produced Cervantes, **Alcalá de Henares.** In addition, the walled city of Ávila looms heavily on many agendas. Finally, those with even more time can visit the **Monastery of Guadalupe** in the Extremadura and the Roman ruins at **Mérida** on the road to Portugal, perhaps stopping off in **Badajoz.**

All of these sites can be reached either by train or bus on a do-it-yourself basis.

1. Toledo

If El Greco were to return to Toledo today, I suspect he would not be shocked or even surprised at the appearance of the city that was the inspiration for so many of his paintings in the 16th century. Toledo—officially declared a National Monument city—has remained that unchanged. The residents dress differently, and El Greco might be puzzled at the strange hordes of camera-carrying tourists who pack into the city, but he could stroll through the familiar streets that are, in many instances, only alleyways, hardly big enough for a man and his donkey—much less an automobile.

Toledo still occupies its royal position, sitting like a queen on a high-hilled throne, overlooking the sparsely vegetated plains of New Castile. Surrounded on three sides by a loop of the River Tagus, it was an obvious choice as the capital of Spain, as it is a natural fortress near the geographic heart of Iberia. Even though Toledo is no longer the political center of the country, it remains the religious center, being the seat of the Primate of Spain.

Back in the 1500s, Toledo resembled an old and faithful wife who had been deserted by an errant husband (Philip II) in favor of a simple young thing (Madrid). Toledo lost its status as the capital of Spain—and was never to regain it, although an attempt was made. But time has paid its alimony checks to this venerated city, which might safely be called a country town today, following its massive loss of population. If Toledo had remained the capital, the chances are that much of it would have been torn down and altered to keep pace with the expanding needs of modern Spain.

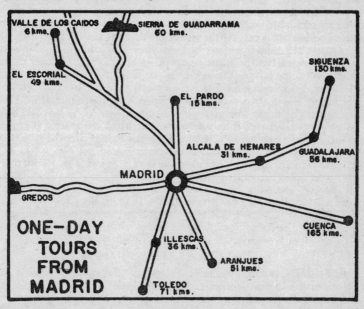

If you land in Madrid and your absurdly tight schedule allows you only one day for an excursion outside the capital, then that trip should be to Toledo. You still will not know Spain, but you will have seen a blending of the elements —Arab, Jewish, Christian, even Roman and Visigothic—that made Toledo great centuries before Columbus sailed to America.

GETTING THERE: The ideal way to go, of course, is in your own car—but many readers won't be able to afford that. The worst possible way to go is by train. Of all the means of transportation, the least expensive is:

By Bus: This means of transportation is shorter and more direct than the train, which goes through Aranjuez and leaves you too far from the heart of the city. The **Continental Auto** line (tel. 227-29-61) leaves from Estación Sur de Autobuses, 17 Calle Canarias (take Metro to Palos de Moguer) in Madrid at 9 or 9:30 a.m. in both summer and winter (take the "directo" bus), and the trip takes about an hour and 15 minutes. Cost: 250 pesetas ($2.40) one way or 450 pesetas ($4.32) round trip. The same bus leaves from the Explanada de San Miguel in Toledo at 6, 7, and 7:30 p.m. in summer, at 5:30, 6 and 7 p.m. in winter. Check this in advance. You purchase tickets upstairs, and the bus leaves from Madrid at the lower level. To be sure of a seat, it is necessary to purchase your ticket in Madrid the evening before your desired trip. You can take the Metro to the Palos de Moguer stop and enter the bus station directly from the platform.

By Car: As your own driver, you will go through the Toledo Gate in Madrid on the road south. A little more than halfway, you'll come to the unspoiled medieval village of **Illescas,** where a stopover is recommended at the **Hospital and Sanctuary of Our Lady of Caridad.** The nuns who live here will show you their proud possessions, five paintings by El Greco. Admission is 25 pesetas (24¢). The view is worth far more.

Then it's on to Toledo. If you take your car inside the city gates, you must accustom yourself to blowing your horn gently—or driving slowly around the corners. Incidentally, remember to have some peseta pieces handy if you take your car around to some of the major sites, as there are many little old men there opening car doors. At the end of the day, the cost will be small.

About 3½ miles from the city, the skyline of Toledo will come into view. It is spectacular. But the greatest surprise—and a moment of richer enchantment—will come later in the day when you cross over the 14th-century San Martín bridge spanning the Tagus for a view of the city from the other side. The setting is evocative of the moody, melancholy, storm-threatened *View of Toledo* hanging in the Metropolitan Museum in New York. It is said that El Greco painted that view from a hillside site on which the Spanish government has opened a new parador, the **Conde de Orgaz,** named after the subject of El Greco's masterpiece (which, incidentally, is in Toledo, not New York). If you arrive at the right time, you can sit on the terrace, enjoying an apéritif in what have been called the violet sunsets of Toledo.

Perhaps more important than all the sights outlined below is a road, known as the **Carretera de Circunvalación,** running along the Tagus in part and all around the city. Clinging to the hillsides are the rustic dwellings, the *cigarrales* of the Imperial City, immortalized by the 17th-century dramatist Tirso de Molina, who named his trilogy *Los Cigarrales de Toledo.*

THE SIGHTS: If you're like most visitors, you'll want to get the most out of Toledo in the shortest possible time. With these thoughts in mind, I have narrowed the sights down to those that can be covered in one day:

The Cathedral

This ancient structure of many styles is the most treasured in Spain. As a Gothic cathedral, it ranks among the greatest in all of Europe, having been constructed in part, ironically, by the Moors. The cathedral was begun in 1226 on the site of a Visigothic church, but was not completed until one year after Columbus sailed to America, which partially explains its many styles.

Spanish history has passed through its portals—moments to remember and those to forget, the latter including the proclamation of "Juana la Loca" (Joan the Mad) and her husband, "Felipe el Hermoso"(Philip the Handsome), heirs to the throne of Spain.

Of its many treasures, its **transparente** stands out (often called "outlandish" and once "outrageous pomp"). Light pours in from a hole in the ceiling, gracing the high-riding angels, a "Last Supper" in polychrome, and a Virgin in ascension. Originally, no one could see this wall of marble and florid baroque alabaster sculpture—the cathedral was too dark. Then a hole was cut through the ceiling, which aroused a storm of protest amoung Toledans, who charged that the renovation would cause the cathedral to collapse. They were wrong, and the hole was décorated like a Rubens painting. The sculptor was Narcisco Tome, and it was a family affair, as he put his talented sons to work on it as well.

Also contained within the cathedral are the *Twelve Apostles* by El Greco, which Herbert R. Lottman found "in the modern vein of a Giacometti or a Francis Bacon." In the Sacristy hangs El Greco's *Spoliation of Christ,* depicting Jesus in flaming scarlet, a bit of "sacrilege" that offended the narrow minds of the artist's day (he was even hauled into court). James A. Michener wrote that one could "discover something about the soul of Spain" from this painting. Look also for Goya's arrest of Christ on the Mount of Olives.

A curiosity of the cathedral is the **Capilla Mozárabe,** built in the 16th century and containing works by Juan de Borgona. A mass is still held there today which employs mozarabic liturgy. Among the outstanding features of the **Treasure Room** is a 500-pound gilded monstrance created in the 15th century, and still carried through the streets of Toledo on the feast day of Corpus Christi. The monstrance is alleged to have been made with gold brought back from the New World by Columbus. If possible, look at the beautiful rose windows at sunset, and see the Renaissance-style **Choir Room,** with its elaborate woodcarvings.

The cathedral is open from 10:30 a.m. to 1 p.m. and 3:30 till 7 p.m. in summer, charging 85 pesetas (82¢) for admission. In winter, its hours are from 10:30 a.m. to 1 p.m. and 3:30 to 6 p.m. It costs 40 pesetas (38¢) extra to climb the tower.

The Alcázar

One of the most dominant sites of the Toledo skyline is the Alcázar, which became world famous at the beginning of the Spanish Civil War, during a 70-day siege in 1936. What person familiar with those events will ever forget the telephone call placed to the Nationalist general inside the Alcázar? The rebels had the son of the general and were going to kill him if the Nationalists didn't surrender the fortress. The general refused to surrender. The siege lasted from July 21 to September 28.

The Alcázar was practically destroyed, but this fortress had been devastated many times before that. Today it has been rebuilt, and has been turned into an Army Museum, housing such exhibits as a plastic model of what the fortress looked like following the Civil War, electronic equipment used during the siege, and photographs taken during the height of the battle.

In front of the museum is a monument honoring the heroes of the Alcázar. Admission is 75 pesetas (72¢), and the summer visiting hours are from 9:30 a.m. to 7:30 p.m. (till 6 p.m. in winter). The location is on the Plaza de

Zocodover. A walking tour is laid out, giving a dramatic and realistic picture of the siege. Allow about an hour for a visit.

Museum of Santa Cruz

Formerly a 16th-century hospital, this magnificent Greco-Roman palace practically competes with the art it protects. It is a storehouse of the art treasures of Toledo. Built in the form of a Greek cross, the plateresque hospice was founded by Cardinal Mendoza, that dramatic nobleman—sometimes called "the third king of Spain"—who helped Ferdinand and Isabella gain the throne.

His handsomely constructed hospital, complete with paneled ceilings, is now a museum of fine arts and archeology. However, for all the cultures— Moorish, Visigothic—that have swept over Toledo, the city is weak in the latter. A rather unprepossessing display of Visigothic artifacts remains.

Look for El Greco's justly praised *The Assumption of the Virgin.* Goya and Ribera are also represented, along with a display of gold, opulent antique furnishings, and somewhat unimpressive Flemish tapestries.

A short walk from the Plaza de Zocodover, the museum, on Calle de Cervantes, is open daily from 10 a.m. till 6:30 p.m. Admission is 150 pesetas ($1.44), which also entitles you to visit the nearby **Museo de los Concilios y de la Cultura Visigoda.**

The House of El Greco

In the old Jewish quarter of Toledo (known as the *"antiguo barrio judio"*) stands **Casa del Greco** on tiny Calle Samuel Leví. This building honors the artist (real name: Domenico Theotokopulos), who settled into Toledo in 1577 and lived there for most of his life until 1614. He lived with what could either have been his wife or mistress, Doña Jerónima, a noted beauty. Her face is said to have inspired El Greco's madonnas.

In 1585 he is known to have moved into one of the rundown palace apartments belonging to the Marquis of Villena. Pedro the Cruel's chancellor of the exchequer, Samuel ha-Leví, is said to have built a home on the same site in the 14th century. It was riddled with subterranean passages to hide his riches. In time the house was occupied by Don Enrique de Villena, who became notorious as a sorcerer. In the underground cellars he was said to have practiced black magic and alchemy.

The main part of the palace was rented to El Greco. From the windows he could look out onto his favorite views of the Tagus. He was to live at other Toledan addresses, although he returned to the Villena palace in 1604, remaining there until his death.

In the early part of the 20th century, the so-called Villena apartments were badly deteriorated and were torn down. However, the Marqués de la Vega-Inclán saved the only remaining part of El Greco's dwelling place. This was a small Moorish house, once believed to have been occupied by ha-Leví. In time it, along with a neighboring house, became the El Greco museum. Today it's furnished with authentic period pieces.

Without a guide, you can visit the studio of El Greco, complete with a painting by the artist. The garden and especially the kitchen merit your attention, as does a sitting room in the Moorish style. Jorge Manuel, the son of El Greco, also fancied himself an artist, as you'll see. The museum contains one of El Greco's *The Apostles,* as well as paintings of St. Francis, St. Bernardino, a view of Toledo, and three portraits, plus many pictures of various Spanish artists of the 17th century. For 75 pesetas (72¢) admission fee, the house may be viewed from 10 a.m. to 2 p.m. and 3:30 till 7 p.m. Off-season hours are 10 a.m. to 2 p.m. and 3:30 to 6 p.m. The house is closed Monday.

The Transito Synagogue

Down the street from El Greco's museum on the Plaza del Greco is this once important worshipping place for the large Jewish population that used to inhabit the city, living peacefully with both Christians and Arabs. This 14th-century building is noted for its superb stucco and Hebrew inscriptions. There are some psalms along the top of the walls and on the east wall a poetic description of this temple. The building of the synagogue was ordered by the chancellor of the exchequer to Pedro the Cruel, Don Samuel ha-Leví. The name of the king appears clearly in a frame in the Hebrew inscription.

The synagogue is the most important part of the **Sephardí Museum** (Museo Sefardí), which was inaugurated in 1981 and contains in other rooms the tombstones with Hebrew epigraphy of the Jews of Spain before 1492, as well as other art pieces. The museum and synagogue can be visited from 10 a.m. to 2 p.m. and 3:30 till 7 p.m. in summer, until 6 p.m. in winter. Admission is 75 pesetas (72¢).

San Juan de los Reyes

This church on the Calle de los Reyes Católicos was founded by King Ferdinand and Queen Isabella to commemorate their triumph over the Portuguese at Toro in 1476. Its construction was started in 1477, according to the plans of architect Juan Guas. It was finished, together with the splendid cloisters in 1504, dedicated to St. John the Evangelist, and used, from the very beginning, by the Franciscan friars. It is a perfect example of the Gothic-Spanish-Flemish style.

San Juan de los Reyes has recently been restored after being damaged in the invasion of Napoleon and abandoned in 1835. Actually, the national monument has been entrusted again to the Franciscans since 1954. The price of admission is 25 pesetas (24¢). You can visit the church from 10 a.m. to 1 p.m. and 3 to 7 p.m. in summer (it closes an hour earlier in winter).

The Church of Santo Tomé—Exposición Anexa

In a city that has as many historical sites as Toledo, this modest little 14th-century chapel on Calle de Santo Tomé would have been overlooked if it did not possess El Greco's masterpiece, *The Burial of the Count of Orgaz*. In this painting, the spirituality of El Greco is revealed as never before; his elongated figures are at their most beautiful. The soul of the dead count is seen as an innocent baby ascending to heaven. The body of the count is surrounded by his friends (perhaps including El Greco), the men clad in black with starched white collars, totally unaware of the robed angels and *putti* appearing over their heads. El Greco did the work in 1586, although the count himself reportedly died in 1323. You buy your ticket at the church for 35 pesetas (34¢), then sit in one of the hard-backed chairs placed in front of the painting. The longer you look at it, the more you realize its wealth of subtle details. The church, with its mudéjar tower, is open from 10 a.m. to 2 p.m. and 3:30 to 6:30 p.m. in summer (closes an hour earlier in winter).

The Synagogue of Santa María la Blanca

In the closing part of the 12th century, the Jews of Toledo erected an important synagogue, in an art style known as almohade, which employs graceful horseshoe arches and ornamental horizontal moldings. However, by the early 15th century, it had been converted into a Christian church. Much of its original look remains, nevertheless, and consists of five naves and elaborate mudéjar decorations—almost mosque-like in effect. Cloistered nuns have replaced its former Jewish occupants, and they're quite poor, judging by the signs outside advertising their embroidery. The synagogue is open in summer from 10 a.m. to 2 p.m. and 3:30 to 7 p.m.; from 10 a.m. to 1 p.m. and 3:30 to 6 p.m. in winter. Admission is 20 pesetas (19¢).

Hospital de Tavera

At the outskirts of the city, this private museum is near the Puerta Bisagra, off the Paseo de Madrid. A 16th-century Greco-Roman palace, it is the privately owned museum of the Duchess of Lerma. Cardinal Tavera, who had the "ear of the royal family," originally built the place, ordering a facade called plateresque in Spain. Almost as if to perpetuate the aristocratic living style of the 16th century, the duchess owns a spectacular art collection.

In the **Banqueting Hall** hangs a portrait of Charles V by Titian, and the collection of books in the **Library** has been called priceless. She owns five paintings by El Greco, including his *Holy Family,* the *Baptism of Christ,* and portraits of St. Francis, St. Peter, and Cardinal Tavera, the founding father of the hospital.

Ribera's freakish painting, *The Bearded Woman,* attracts many doctors who study it in detail. The hirsute female is nursing a baby, and the agonized look on the face of her husband reveals a lot.

The museum is open from 10 a.m. to 1:30 p.m. and 4 to 6:30 p.m. summer and winter. The entrance fee is 50 pesetas (48¢). In the nearby church is the mausoleum of Cardinal Tavera, designed by Alonso de Berruguete.

WHERE TO EAT: Somewhere in the middle of your tour, you'll want to take time out for lunch. This wonderful old city has several recommended restaurants, but the prices seem high—particularly for a lunch.

The Best Bargains

Maravilla ("Wonder"), 5–7 Barrio Rey (tel. 22-33-00), is a restaurant in a seasoned hotel that sits on a small satellite square of the historic Plaza de Zocodover, whose sidewalk cafés are featured heavily in Spanish novels and plays. The so-called Barrio Rey, the "quarter of the king," is friendlier and more intimate. It's like a living room somehow, filled with cheap restaurants and cafés that seemingly change their names so often it's virtually impossible to keep track of them.

Entered from the tiny cobblestoned plaza, the hotel hides behind its bays and grillwork. The food in its dining room is quite good—in fact, considering the price asked and the quality of the cuisine, it's about the best all-around dining bargain. You can get a four-course dinner (extremely generous portions), including a carafe of the local wine, bread, and service for less than 900 pesetas ($8.64).

Casa Aurelio, 6 Sinagoga, between the cathedral and the Plaza de Zocodover (tel. 22-20-97), is an intimate yet bustling little restaurant, which has long been popular with visitors, students, and locals. There are three or four small rooms, tile floors, walls covered with hides, burlap cloth, and bric-a-brac such as bulls' heads. The lighting is soft, and air conditioning is provided in summer. The menú del día at 675 pesetas ($6.48) includes a Castilian soup or hors d'oeuvres, then a steak with french fries or hake, followed by fruit or ice cream, bread, and wine. You enter the dining area through a small bar which is usually crowded with people.

El Emperador Restaurant, 1 Carretera del Valle (tel. 22-46-91), is a modern restaurant on the outskirts of Toledo, reached via an arched bridge and by car. Its terraces overlook that memorable vista, the river below and the towers of Toledo. Inside, it is modified tavern style, with a spacious, attractive dining room with leather and wooden chairs, heavy beams, and wrought-iron chandeliers, and attentive service. Best news is that there is a 575-peseta ($5.52) set meal, which might include a choice of three kinds of soup (beef, vegetable, or noodle) followed by a small steak with french-fried potatoes, then fresh fruit and wine. El Emperador is favored by the chauffeur guides from Madrid who almost always order from the à la carte menu the mountainous plate of roast lamb. It comes with potatoes, and one hardly needs any other food. If you order à la carte, expect to pay from 550 pesetas ($5.28) to 800 pesetas ($7.68).

The Super-Splurges

The **Parador Conde de Orgaz,** Cerro del Emperador (tel. 22-18-50), combines some of the best Castilian regional cuisine with what surely must rank as one of the most spectacular views from any restaurant in Europe. Sheltered in one of the Spanish government's finest paradors, the restaurant is on the crest of a hill—said to be the spot that El Greco selected for his *View of Toledo.* From the heart of the city, you can either drive your car or take a taxi (the scenery along the way is well worth the extra pesetas).

On the upper level is a bar for an apéritif. Later, sitting in a chair upholstered with red velvet, you can select either a luncheon or dinner, both 1200 pesetas ($11.52). Of course, you can order à la carte, but the fixed-price meal is cheaper, and can include, for example, some tasty Spanish hors d'oeuvres, followed by hake (a sweet white fish), then perhaps either veal or beef grilled on an open fire, plus dessert (some moist and light cakes here). If you're dining light (highly recommended on a hot August day), try a local specialty, tortilla española con magra.

The **Venta de Aires,** 25 Circo Romano (tel. 22-05-45), is outside the city gates. Since 1891, when it was only a little roadside inn (*venta* means roadside inn), hungry Spaniards have made their way here to sample the pièce de résistance of Toledo, perdiz (partridge). "The French," confides a waiter, "know what a great dish this is. The Americans think it's spoiled or bad tasting. They're happy with roast chicken. But there are those exceptions. It always makes me happy when a Norteamericano likes our perdiz." As a curiosity, see former President Nixon's entry in the guest book after he ate here in 1963.

This sought-after game dish, on the à la carte menu, is best with the red wine of Méntrida. However, if you want to keep your tab low, you'd better stick to the 750 peseta ($7.20) set meal. For dessert you must try the marzipan, virtually an institution in Toledo and said to have been created by the Arabs who lived here. To dine here à la carte would cost from 1200 pesetas ($11.52) to 1800 pesetas ($17.28).

READERS' RESTAURANT SUGGESTIONS: "Two restaurants we liked are **El Casino,** along Barrio Rey past the Maravilla, 2 Plaza de la Magdalena, and **El Aljibe** at Plaza Padre Juan de Mariana, near the Visigoth Museum. At El Casino, you can order a 500-peseta ($4.80) menú del día with choices such as paella or green beans in tomato sauce, meat balls or fish or pork chop, plus half a bottle of wine per person, bread, and dessert. At El Aljibe, the 515-peseta ($4.94) menú del día order will include fish soup or gazpacho, paella or fish or beefsteak, plus bread, wine, and ice cream with caramel sauce. Go through the bar and down the stairs into a series of caves" (Norriss Hetherington, Berkeley, Calif.). . . . "Just down the street from the Plácido is the **Bolivia** at 15 Calle Santo Tomé, upstairs over a bar. The menú del día is 325 pesetas ($3.12) and includes a thick soup, omelet, bread, wine, and orange. The staff is very pleasant, and the place is jammed with foreign students and older local women" (Diana Hanson, Bethesda, Md.).

STAYING OVERNIGHT: If you are among the fortunate few who can spend the night in Toledo, you will have a choice of widely varying accommodations. You can either stay in the city or across the river.

The **Hotel Carlos V**, 2 Plaza Horno de Magdalena (tel. 22-21-00), is an old favorite with visitors to Toledo. If you're driving, it's best to park at the garage on the Plaza de Zocodover, then walk to the hotel. Overlooking the cathedral, the hotel has a personality just as somber. But its rooms are well appointed and the service fine. When you see the handsome exterior of the Carlos V, you may be scared off, thinking it higher priced than it is. The half-board tariff ranges in price from 3000 pesetas ($28.80) in a single to 4500 pesetas ($43.20) for two in a double. A lunch or dinner, ordered separately, costs 1500 pesetas ($14.40).

Residencia Imperio (Empire), 7 Cadenas, off the Calle de la Planta, just two minutes from the heartbeat Plaza de Zocodover (tel. 22-76-50), is the best bet for those who must keep costs rock-bottom. Run by Don José Gómez Priento, it opened in 1967, and immediately attracted the attention of pesetawise visitors.

Most of the bedrooms overlook a little church with a wall overgrown with wisteria. You pay 1785 pesetas ($17.14) for a double with private bath, 1630 pesetas ($15.65) for one with a shower. Singles with shower go for 1035 pesetas ($9.94). A continental breakfast costs an extra 150 pesetas ($1.44) per person. The rooms are not too large, but are fresh and comfortable.

Hotel Maravilla, 7 Barrio Rey (tel. 22-33-00), is a tiny bit of Spain that modern tourism is passing by. If your taste runs to small, very Spanish hotels with local color, then this will probably please you. First of all, it's 30 feet off the main square of Toledo, with its coffeehouses and sidewalk tables. The little old hotel, which was semi-modernized in 1971, opens directly onto a miniature cobblestone plaza where three excellent "local" restaurants set out tables during fair weather. Would that you could get a front room overlooking this. The building has many bay windows, the bedrooms are modest but adequate, and the furnishings are so-so. The cost for a double with bath is 3000 pesetas ($28.80); singles with the same plumbing cost 1500 pesetas ($14.40). A continental breakfast is an extra 220 pesetas ($2.11) per person, and you can order lunch for 725 pesetas ($6.96), dinner for 850 pesetas ($8.16). You can hang out your laundry on the roof, and, on occasion, use an iron in the laundry room downstairs.

Across the Tagus

For readers who have a car or who don't mind one or two taxi rides a day, there are excellent accommodations in this area.

La Almazara, 47 Carretera de Piedrabuena (road number C781; tel. 22-38-66), takes its name from an old olive-oil mill that used to stand at this location. Providing one of the most offbeat accommodations in and around Toledo, it is hidden away up in the hills, discreetly approached via a private road. If you follow the road to the Parador or Ciudad Real, C781 turns off with road signs to Cuerva, about two kilometers out of the city. You arrive at an old-fashioned country villa, with its own courtyards and vineyards—a rare opportunity to soak up the atmosphere of old Spain, far removed from the pace of city life (exceptional view of Toledo).

La Almazara offers 22 rooms—20 doubles and 2 singles. A double with private bath costs 2200 pesetas ($21.12); a single with private bath, 1800 pesetas ($17.28). Only a continental breakfast, at 160 pesetas ($1.54), is served. You may be assigned either a spacious chamber in the main house, or a bedroom in the annex. The hotel is open from April to October.

The Big Splurge

Parador Conde de Orgaz, Paseo de los Cigarrales (tel. 77-00-51), is proof that when the Spanish government decides to recapture the spirit of the past—but with all the modern comforts of this century—it has no peer. Named after the subject of El Greco's masterpiece, this parador was recommended earlier for its restaurant. However, it also offers the most luxuriously appointed bedrooms in all of Toledo. On the ridge of a rugged hill, it was built on the spot where, as mentioned, El Greco is said to have painted his *View of Toledo* (although the artist arbitrarily turned a few buildings around to suit his sense of composition).

The Parador sits like a glorious large country inn, its spacious entry hall containing a long refectory table. A stairway and balcony lead to dark oak-paneled doors opening onto the bedrooms. The accommodations are spacious and beautifully furnished, each with reproductions of regional antique pieces. You pay 4000 pesetas ($38.40) for a double room with private bath, 2500 pesetas ($24) for a single with bath. A continental breakfast is an extra 250 pesetas ($2.40) per person. Reserve well in advance.

The main living room-lounge has fine furniture, a wall of glass, old chests, brown leather chairs, thick-topped tables—all opening onto a sun terrace overlooking the Imperial City. On chilly nights, guests seek out the cozy recessed fireplace area.

READERS' HOTEL SELECTIONS: "We stayed at the **Hostal del Cardenal,** 24 Paseo de Recaredo (tel. 22-49-00), built right up against the Moorish walls. It is run by the Botín brothers, who own the well-known restaurant in Madrid. A lovely double room with a continental breakfast costs 3440 pesetas ($33.02). A single goes for 2145 pesetas ($20.59). The restaurant is quite elegant, and the food and service fine. Dinner for two was a splurge, costing almost as much as the night's lodging. There is a charming garden where meals are served, weather permitting" (Rose Schuyler, Rego Park, N.Y.). . . . **"Fonda Segovia,** 4 Calle de Recoletos, is one minute's walk from the Plaza de Zocodover. Take the second right off Calle de la Silería, which starts on the northeast side of the Zocodover, and go to the bottom of the square which opens up on your right. It's clean, friendly, and inexpensive. A double with water basin costs 850 pesetas ($8.16)" (Mr. and Mrs. John Pearce, Toronto, Ontario, Canada).

WHEN NIGHT FALLS: Most people staying over have only one night to spend in Toledo, and they shouldn't lament the fact that the city's nightlife isn't terribly flamboyant. Toledo has something far more thrilling than flamenco: the walk through the old city on a trail that Cervantes might have taken. A strange air, bordering on the mystical, blankets the city at night, when it takes on an almost Oriental look. When the hordes of visitors have gone, when the sidewalk hawkers have closed down for the day, a mood descends that is both soothing yet curiously disturbing. The old city seems haunted, as if it had witnessed too much violence or had hidden too many secrets behind its walls. When the glare of the sun fades, the buildings become like silent ghosts leering down at you. The narrow streets at first appear foreboding, but they're safe—even though you might occasionally pass a figure in a long cape and a Napoleonic hat (a policeman). To spend the night in Toledo and to walk its deserted and ancient streets is to journey back into the Middle Ages.

2. Aranjuez

This Castilian town, about 29 miles south of Madrid, was the spring and fall home of the Bourbon kings, who found it too hot for the summer months (they headed then for La Granja near Segovia). With its manicured shrubbery, its stately elms, fountains and statues, Aranjuez still remains a regal garden oasis in what is otherwise an unimpressive agricultural flatland producing a great abundance of the strawberries and asparagus for Castilians.

An arm of the Tagus River cuts through the town on its way to Toledo. The Royal Palace goes back to the days of Philip II (1561), and is often compared with Versailles.

GETTING THERE: Aranjuez is easy to reach from Madrid. The road is good, and the trip takes less than an hour. If you do not have a car, and you're on the do-it-yourself tour, then you can take a bus run by **Automnibus Interurbaños, S.A.**, 18 Paseo de las Delicias (tel. 230-46-07). Buses depart from the Estación Sur de Autobuses de Madrid, 17 Calle Canarias, at 8 and 9 a.m. and 1, 4, 5:30, 7 and 8:45 p.m. The cost of a one-way ticket is 175 pesetas ($1.68).

Tip: On the way to Aranjuez, look for what is known as **Cerro de los Angeles** (Angels' Hill), the geographic center of the Iberian peninsula. A huge white statue of Christ dominates the mountain.

THE SIGHTS: On your arrival in Aranjuez, it's best to purchase a ticket for 125 pesetas ($1.20) allowing you to visit the sleepy town's trio of attractions, including the **Royal Palace,** the **Garden of the Island** adjoining it, and the **Casita del Labrador** in the **Jardín del Príncipe.**

The Royal Palace

"Deception . . . its dominant note," wrote an expatriate American. "In almost each of its widely varying rooms there is at least one thing that isn't what it first appears," William Lyon accurately put it. To prove his case, he cites mosaics that are made to fool the eye into thinking they are oils, or a flat ceiling in trompe l'oeil that achieves a startling three-dimensional effect.

As you enter the cobblestoned courtyard, you can tell—just by the massive bulk of the palace—that you're going to see something spectacular. Ferdinand and Isabella came this way, as did Philip II (the former traveling about so much it was hardly possible for them to have a favorite oasis, the latter preferring the life he had created for himself at El Escorial). The Bourbons were the main force behind the flowering of Aranjuez. Philip V and Charles III were also fond of life as it was easily lived here.

The structure you see today dates principally from 1778 (the previous buildings were swept by fire). Throughout its salons parade the opulence of a bygone era, room after room a royal extravaganza. If it strikes you as a bit garish, remember that royalty in those days didn't have to apologize for ostentation.

Many styles, furnishings, and decorations are blended here: Spanish, Italian, Moorish, French. Of course, no royal palace would be complete without an Oriental salon, reflecting the popularity of chinoiserie that once swept over Europe. Of special interest also is the Porcelain Salon. The painting collection, relatively unimportant, does contain works by José Ribera and Lucas Jordan.

A guide conducts you through the huge complex and will expect a tip. The hours are 10 a.m. to 1 p.m. and 3:30 to 7 p.m. in summer (till 6 p.m. in winter).

Afterward, you're turned out on your own for an enchanting promenade through:

The Garden of the Island

It appears somehow forgotten, its mood melancholic. In back of the Royal Garden, it lies quietly, its special magic hard to convey. There once lived a Spanish impressionist, Santiago Rusiñol, who captured on canvas its evasive quality. One Spanish writer said it was "as if softly lulled by a sweet 18th-century sonata, beautifully portrayed by the composer Joaquín Rodrigo in his world-famous *Concierto de Aranjuez.*" "Non Plus Ultra" fountain is dazzling, although one observer found the black jasper fountain of Bacchus "orgiastic." Under linden trees, the fountain of Apollo is romantic, and others honor the king of the sea as well as Cybele, goddess of agriculture.

On your approach to the island, you may want to stroll through the **Parterre,** in front of the palace—much better kept than the Garden of the Island, but somehow not as romantic.

The Casita del Labrador

"The little house of the worker" is a classic example of understatement. Actually, it was modeled after the Petit Trianon at Versailles. If you visit the Royal Palace in the morning, you can spend the afternoon here. Those with a car can motor to it through the tranquil **Jardín del Príncipe,** with its black poplars, for a fee of 50 pesetas (48¢). However, if you're on foot, go to the Hotel Delicias, 2 Carretera de Madrid, where you can board a boat for 30 pesetas (29¢) which will take you for a pleasant ride up the Tagus.

The little palace was built in 1803 by Charles IV, who later abdicated in Aranjuez. The queen came here with her youthful lover, Godoy (whom she had elevated to the position of prime minister), and the feeble-minded Charles didn't seem to mind a bit. Surrounded by beautiful gardens, the "bedless" palace is lavishly furnished in the grand style of the 18th and 19th centuries. The marble floors represent some of the finest workmanship of that day. The brocaded walls emphasize the luxurious living—and the royal john is a sight to behold (in those days, royalty preferred an audience). The clock here is one of the treasures of the house.

WHERE TO EAT: Between palace-hopping, you'll want to take time out for lunch. Be forewarned that most of Aranjuez's tourist-financed restaurants—especially those along the river—jack up their prices as high as the government will allow.

But in the heart of town is a good low-cost dining recommendation, the **Casa Pablo,** 20 Almibar (tel. 891-14-51). Tables are set outside under a shade canopy, and as you dine here in garden chairs, you can enjoy the street of trees and plants, the beds of roses, the red and pink geraniums. Usually, lottery sellers squat nearby, peddling their tickets. In cooler weather, you walk through the tasca to a cozy and clean dining room in the rear, or the one upstairs.

The two-fork tavern offers a complete meal for 650 pesetas ($6.24), including a carafe of wine, bread, and service. It it's a hot day and you don't want a heavy dinner, try a shrimp omelet, or half a roast chicken. Once, in asparagus season, I simply ordered a plate of those fresh morsels accompanied by white wine. If you want a superb dish, try a fish called mero (a Mediterranean pollack of delicate flavor), grilled over an open fire. If you dine à la carte, expect to pay from 800 pesetas ($7.68) to 1400 pesetas ($13.44).

For the more affluent, the traditional choice remains **La Rana Verde** (The Green Frog), 12 Príncipe. The setting is next to a small bridge spanning the Tagus. The restaurant looks like somebody's summer house—the beamed ceiling stretching high and soft ferns drooping from hanging baskets. The preferred spots for dining are in the nooks overlooking the river (which eventually makes its lazy way to Portugal.)

The least expensive way to eat here is to order a three-course set meal at 700 pesetas ($6.72). Strawberries are served with sugar or with orange juice or ice cream. Asparagus, as in all the restaurants of Aranjuez, is a special feature. Especially recommended in season are the game dishes, particularly partridge, quail, and pigeon. Under the fish dishes, the fried hake is good as is the fried sole. Ordering à la carte will bring the tab up to 800 pesetas ($7.68) to 1200 pesetas ($11.52).

Across the river is the cheaper **Alegría de la Huerta,** with a simple no-decor dining room and a pleasant garden for summer dining. The tourist menu is 700 pesetas ($6.70) and features hors d'oeuvres or beans, chicken with salad, fruit, bread, and wine.

READER'S HOTEL SELECTION: "If you're in search of a clean hotel with modern furniture and plumbing, you might stop at the **Hostal Infantas,** 4 Avenida Infantas (tel. 891-13-41). We paid as little as 1600 pesetas ($15.36) for a nice double room with private shower and toilet, and 1800 pesetas ($17.28) for a triple. The hotel is in a quiet area and yet only a five-minute walk from the Royal Palacio. You can park your car in front of the house. Next door is a cafetería, where you may have your breakfast" (R. Depreitere, Kortrijk, Belgium).

3. El Escorial and the Valley of the Fallen

Ranking next to Toledo as the most important excursion from Madrid is the austere monastery of El Escorial. Philip II ordered the construction of this granite-and-slate rectangular monster, and the building was begun in 1563, two years after the king moved the capital to Madrid. This combination palace-royal mausoleum is 30 miles from Madrid, on the slopes of the Guadarrama Mountains. A trip there is usually combined with an excursion to the Valley of the Fallen (nine miles away).

For years the haunt of aristocratic Spaniards, El Escorial has long been a summer resort. When the atmosphere of Madrid becomes unbearable, the air of El Escorial is like a tonic. Hotels and restaurants flourish in summer, as hundreds flock here to escape the heat of the capital.

GETTING THERE: If you're on the do-it-yourself tour, you can take either a train or bus. The **Empresa Herranz,** 7 Paseo de Moret (near the Air Ministry in the vicinity of the University; tel. 243-81-67), has a bus leaving Madrid from 10 Calle Isaac Ferral at 9:30 a.m. and 2:30, 7 and 9 p.m. A one-way ticket costs 152 pesetas ($1.46). From El Escorial, the same line goes to the Valley of the

Fallen, a round-trip fare costing 165 pesetas ($1.58). On holidays, the hours are likely to be different, so check in advance.

Trains leave Madrid from Atocha Station, and during the summer extra coaches are added to handle the overflow. Starting at 8:30 a.m., trains leave nearly every hour. For exact schedules and travel costs, consult the **RENFE** offices or the Spanish Tourism Office opposite the Palace Hotel.

A VISIT TO THE MONASTERY: The **Royal Monastery of San Lorenzo del Escorial** is a huge granite fortress that houses a wealth of paintings and tapestries, and serves as a final resting place for Spanish kings. It is made foreboding, both inside and out, by its sheer size and institutional look, an aspect broken only by its steeples and towers. Made from rock from the nearby mountains, El Escorial took 21 years to complete, a remarkably fast time considering the bulk of the building and construction methods in those days.

El Escorial can proudly boast the following: 1200 doors, 2593 windows (if a guide tells you 2673 windows, don't debate the point; his Spanish pride may force you into counting them), 86 staircases, 89 fountains, 16 courtyards or patios, and 300 cells. In addition, it contains more than 1600 paintings and murals, including works by El Greco, Velázquez, Bosch, Titian, Tintoretto, to name only a few, as well as tapestries by Goya.

The minimum time that one should allow—even for the most cursory visit—is two hours, although three would be more suitable, and even at that you'd be pushing it. The visiting hours are 10 a.m. to 1 p.m. and 3:30 to 4:30 p.m. The comprehensive admission ticket is 175 pesetas ($1.68), but there are four different admissions and sights from which to choose.

Because the palace-monastery is so vast, you simply can't see it all—don't even try. But here are some of the highlights:

The **New Museo** is the picture gallery, containing the monastery's art collection. Philip II, who collected many of the paintings exhibited here, definitely did not like the mysticism of El Greco, and turned instead to his pet, Titian, for inspiration. Nevertheless, you'll find El Greco's *The Martyrdom of St. Maurice* rescued from the mothballs where Philip stored it. In addition, you'll see El Greco's *St. Peter,* Titian's *Last Supper,* Velázquez's *The Tunic of Joseph,* and *The Hay Wagon* by Bosch.

The **Royal Library** contains a priceless collection of books, estimated at 60,000 volumes—one of the most significant library storehouses in the world. Here you'll see displays ranging from the handwriting of St. Teresa to medieval instructions on how to play chess. Discover, in particular, the Moslem codices and a Gothic "Cantigas" from the reign of Alfonso X ("The Wise") in the 13th century.

You can also visit the **Philip II Apartments,** the so-called "cell for my humble self" that he ordered built in this "palace for God." By that time, Philip had become a religious fanatic, and requested his bedroom erected overlooking the altar. The apartments are strictly monastic, and you'll find Bosch's copy of his own work, *The Seven Capital Sins.* Its dome based on Michelangelo's drawings for St. Peter's, the **Basilica** has four organs, and measures approximately 300 feet from floor to ceiling. The choir contains a crucifix by Benvenuto Cellini.

The **Throne Room** is, by comparison, simple. On the walls are many ancient maps.

The **Apartments of the Bourbon Kings** break from Philip's bleakness, and are more lavishly decorated in keeping with the latter-day tenants' taste for luxury. The tapestries displayed look like paintings until they are examined closely. Under the altar of the church you'll find the octagonal **Royal Pantheon,** where most of the kings of Spain from Charles I to Alfonso XII, including Philip II, lie buried. Here, too, are the tombs of the queens, the mothers of kings. This is one of the most regal mausoleums in the world (nearby, on a lower floor, is the "Wedding Cake" tomb for children).

Just watch what you say in the **Whispering Hall,** and you may enjoy your visit to El Escorial.

Just as Philip II ordered it, El Escorial is dedicated to St. Lawrence, martyred by burning, and it commemorates the triumph of the soldiers of the Hapsburg monarch at San Quintín in 1557. Juan Bautista de Toledo, the original architect, was replaced after his death by Juan de Herrera, the greatest architect of Renaissance Spain, who completed it in the shape of a gridiron. The total legacy of these men was summed up by a critic of European architecture as" . . . overwhelming, moving no doubt, but frightening."

If time (and interest) remains, you might visit the **Casita del Príncipe** (Prince's Cottage), a small but elaborately decorated 18th-century palace that was a hunting lodge. The so-called cottage was built for Charles III by Juan de Villanueva. Near the gateway is a cafetería. *Warning:* It's almost impossible to visit the monastery and prince's cottage in the morning—at least before the casita closes for its staff to have lunch at 12:30 p.m. Most visitors stay in El Escorial for lunch, visiting the cottage when it reopens in the afternoon.

WHERE TO EAT: If you're not on an organized tour, you'll have to fend for yourself at lunch. And in El Escorial that can be a real problem. Some of the local eateries, spoiled by the busloads of tourists who arrive as frequently as the rains in Galicia, try to extract your gold fillings when they tally up the luncheon tab.

The diner seeking an economical noonday repast should bypass the highly advertised restaurants with their fat-cat menus and head instead for Plaza Generalísimo, right in the center of town. The restaurants here specialize in Castilian cooking, using the local produce and wines.

Castilla, 2 Plaza Generalísimo (tel. 896-10-46), stands right in the center of town; in summer tables are placed outdoors—in the shade, of course. The dishes featured here are typically Spanish, including a reliable paella for 500 pesetas ($4.80). Another good-tasting dish is the veal scaloppine at 550 pesetas ($5.28). Everything tastes better when you order a large pitcher of sangría, costing 350 pesetas ($3.36). Expect to spend from 950 pesetas ($9.12) to 1700 pesetas ($16.32) if you order à la carte. The latter price is for the more expensive beef dishes.

Cafetería del Arte, 14 Floridablanca (tel. 896-07-23), is right next to the tourist office. This air-conditioned place has the usual platos combinados, ranging from 260 pesetas ($2.50) for fried eggs, rice, and frankfurters, to 400 pesetas ($3.84) for grilled tomato, chorizo sausages, veal sandwich, potatoes, and string beans. Muzak is featured, paintings are placed along the walls, and sunshades protect the al fresco tables.

The Big Splurge

Mesón La Cueva (The Cave), 4 San Antón, (tel. 890-15-16), recaptures the world of old Castile. Built around an enclosed courtyard, it is a típico mesón. Everywhere you look it's nostalgia time—stained-glass windows, antique chests, scenic murals, a 19th-century bullfighting collage, time-soiled engravings, paneled doors, iron balconies.

The cooking is on target, the portions are generous. Some of the best-known regional specialties in Spain are served, including Valencian paella and fabada asturiana (the pork-sausage-and-bean dish). But a simple fresh trout broiled in butter may be the best of all. The most expensive items on the menu are roast suckling pig and roast lamb (tender inside, crisp on the outside, in the manner of Segovia). The tab here will range from 950 pesetas ($9.12) to 1600 pesetas ($15.36).

Opening off the courtyard, and entered through a separate doorway, is La Cueva's tasca, brimming over with Castilians in pursuit of their favorite predinner drinks (many ending up not having dinner at all).

READER'S RESTAURANT SUGGESTION: "While visiting El Escorial, we stopped for dinner at a small (six tables) restaurant, **El Caserio,** 2 Reina Victoria (tel. 896-14-58), on the upper floor of a café. Its owner, Señor Dionisio Ruíz Calvo, is most helpful, tending to everyone's needs. The quality of the food is excellent" (George Linper).

STAYING OVERNIGHT: If you'd like to break up your stay in Madrid, you might spend a night or two at El Escorial—or more if you have the time. The temperature in the summer is quite cool, primarily because of the bracing mountain air. What to do during the day need not be a problem. El Escorial makes an ideal base for visiting the cities and towns of Segovia and Ávila, the royal palace at La Granja, the Valley of the Fallen—or even the more distant university city of Salamanca. The hotels here are pleasant enough, and the rates are moderate.

Miranda & Suizo, 20 Floridablanca (tel. 896-00-00), is one of the leading two-star hotels, offering a double room with private bath for 2000 pesetas ($19.20) to 2200 pesetas ($21.12), singles—12 in this category—for 1500 pesetas ($14.40), also including bath. A continental breakfast is an extra 170 pesetas ($1.63) per person. On a tree-lined street in the heart of town, this hotel is within easy walking distance of the monastery. An excellent middle-class establishment, the Miranda & Suizo is a simple, 50-room, Victorian-style building with balconies. Some of the quite good bedrooms open onto terraces. The rooms are amply furnished with comfortable pieces; the beds are often made of brass and sometimes you'll find fresh flowers on the table. In summer, tables and chairs are placed outside for dining.

Hostal Príncipe, 6 Floridablanca (tel. 896-16-11), is an old-fashioned hotel with oodles of charm. Downstairs is the bar, where a large, wood-paneled and carved fireplace adds to the homey atmosphere. The Príncipe has ten double rooms with bath renting for 1500 pesetas ($14.40). Add on the usual 20% if no meals are eaten here. A continental breakfast costs 120 pesetas ($1.15). The quite good lunches or dinners go for 625 pesetas ($6) each.

READERS' HOTEL SELECTION: "**Hostal Malagón,** 2 Calle San Francisco (tel. 890-15-76), is plain but comfortable, a third-floor hostal only three minutes' walk from El Escorial. A double with water basin costs 850 pesetas ($8.16). A continental breakfast goes for 90 pesetas (86¢)" (Mr. and Mrs. John Pearce, Toronto, Ontario, Canada).

Whether you're planning to stay over—or are visiting El Escorial for the day—at some point most visitors head for:

THE VALLEY OF THE FALLEN: This architectural marvel—two decades in the making—might be called Franco's Escorial. It is dedicated to those who died in the Spanish Civil War. Its severest critics might suggest that this monument represents all the worst of neo-Fascist design; its kindest sympathizers say they have found renewed inspiration by coming here. Others not involved in the Spanish civil struggle might see it as a gigantic reminder of the folly of war.

A gargantuan cross, nearly 500 feet high, dominates the **Rock of Nava,** a peak of the Guadarrama Mountains. The funicular to the foot of the cross costs 50 pesetas (48¢) and is well worth it. Directly under the cross is a basilica in mosaic, completed in 1959. Here is where the body of José Antonio, the founder of the Falangist Party, is buried. When this Nationalist hero was buried at El Escorial, a storm of protest arose—particularly from influential monarchists—who pointed up the fact that José Antonio was not royalty. Obviously infuriated, Franco decided to erect another monument. Originally, it was slated to honor the dead on the Nationalist side only, but the intervention of several parties led to a decision to include all the caídos, so that in time the mausoleum claimed Franco as well.

On your way to the basilica, you'll walk through six chapels. It's like going through a huge tunnel to the center of a mountain. By all means, wear your walking shoes.

If you go by car, you'll have to pay 150 pesetas ($1.44) to drive up the mountain to the monument. However, there is no charge for entering it. It's open from 10 a.m. to 7 p.m.

Valle de los Caídos, a three-fork restaurant (tel. 896-02-01), has been installed in this dramatic location, halfway up the mountainside. After passing through the entrance gates, it's on your left and reachable only by car. It's a mammoth, ultra modern structure, with wide suspended terraces and ceiling-to-floor picture windows. The menú del día is 650 pesetas ($6.24), which could include cannelloni Rossini as an opener, then pork chops with potatoes, a dessert, and, of course, wine.

On the other side of the mountain is a monastery that has sometimes been dubbed "the Hilton of monasteries," because of its seeming luxury. It is inhabited by Benedictine monks.

4. Segovia and La Granja

Nowhere does the faded glory of Old Castile shine more brightly than in Segovia. Wherever you look, you'll see remains of a greater day, whether it be the most spectacular Alcázar on the Iberian peninsula or the well-preserved, still-functioning Roman aqueduct. The parade of armies of occupation—Romans, Visigoths, Moors—has disappeared, and Segovia is peaceful. It has little of the commercialism of Toledo, and the modern visitor can probe into the past at leisure.

Segovia lies on the slope of the Guadarrama Mountains. Two rivers, the Eresma and the Clamores, converge in the city.

Warning: If you're visiting in the early spring, wear warm clothes. It's cold at those altitudes.

GETTING THERE: If you go by automobile, the ride between Madrid and Segovia to the northwest will be approximately 54 miles by one road, 63 by another. At Villalba, the road forks and you have a choice of routes. Consider taking the southern one to reach it, returning via the northern route, but budgeting enough time for a stopover at La Granja.

If you're without an automobile, then you can catch a morning train at the Atocha Station in Madrid. You will be delivered to the train station in Segovia, where you can board a bus to the Plaza Mayor, the heart of the city.

It is also possible to go by bus. The Empresa La Sepulvedana, 11 Paseo Florida, runs a daily bus except Sunday and holidays at 7:45 and 11:45 a.m.; a return bus leaves Segovia at 4:45 and 7:45 p.m. (Sunday 8:15 a.m. from Madrid and return at 4:45 and 7:45 p.m.). The price of a one-way ticket is 295 pesetas ($2.83).

THE SIGHTS: This ancient city, whose history goes back to the dim Iberian past, lies in the center of the most castle-rich part of Castile. A major moment in its history came when Isabella was proclaimed Queen of Castile here in 1474. Walls still encircle the old part of town, but they are not as impressive as the ones that you'll see at Ávila.

The narrow, winding streets of this hill city must be covered on foot if you're to have the experience that is uniquely Segovian. Basically, Segovia is a city rich in historical buildings—Romanesque churches, old mansions, 15th-century palaces.

Of the multitude of attractions in Segovia, I have selected six that I feel best represent the city.

Alcázar

If you've ever dreamed of castles in the air, then all the fairytale romance of childhood will return when you view this structure. Many have waxed poetic about it, comparing it to a giant boat sailing through the clouds. See it first from down below, at the junction of the Clamores and Eresma Rivers. It is on the west side of Segovia, and you may not spot it when you first enter the city. But that's part of the surprise.

The castle dates back many hundreds of years—perhaps to the 12th century. But a large segment of it—notably its Moorish ceilings—was destroyed by fire in 1862. Over the years, under an ambitious plan, the Alcázar has been restored.

Inside, you'll discover a facsimile of Isabella's dank bedroom. It was at the Alcázar that she first met Ferdinand, preferring him to the more "fatherly" king of Portugal. But she wasn't foolish enough to surrender her "equal rights" after marriage. In the Throne Room, with its replica chairs, you'll note that both seats are equally proportioned. Royal romance continued to flower at the Alcázar. Philip II married his fourth wife, Anne of Austria, here.

After you inspect the polish on some medieval armor inside, you may want to walk the battlements of this once-impregnable castle, whose former occupants poured boiling oil over the ramparts onto their uninvited guests below. Or you can climb the tower, originally built by Isabella's father as a prison, for a view supreme of Segovia. In particular, note the so-called pregnant-woman mountain.

The fortress is open from 10:30 a.m. to 7:30 p.m. (closes at 6 p.m. in winter). Admission is 30 pesetas (29¢).

The Roman Aqueduct

This aqueduct, an architectural marvel, is still used to carry water, even though it was constructed by the Romans almost 2000 years ago. It is not only the most colossal reminder of Roman glory in Spain, but one of the best-preserved Roman architectural achievements in the world. It consists of 118 arches, and in one two-tiered section—its highest point—it soars to some 95 feet. Another fact: You'll find no mortar in these granite blocks, brought from the Guadarrama Mountains. The Spanish call it **El Puente,** and it spans the

Plaza del Azoguejo, the old market square, stretching out to a distance of nearly 800 yards. When the Moors took Segovia in 1072, they destroyed 36 arches. However, Ferdinand and Isabella ordered that they be rebuilt in 1484.

There are no visiting hours, of course; you can see it at any time night or day. It's an integral landmark of Segovia.

"The Lady of the Cathedrals"

This 16th-century structure lays claim to being the last Gothic cathedral built in Spain. Fronting the historic Plaza Mayor, it stands on the spot where Isabella I was proclaimed Queen of Castile. It's affectionately called *"la dama de las cathedrales."* Inside, it contains numerous treasures, such as the Blessed Sacrament Chapel (created by the flamboyant Churriguera), stained-glass windows, elaborately carved choir stalls, 16th- and 17th-century paintings, including a reredos portraying the deposition of Christ from the cross by Juan de Juni. Older than the cathedral are the cloisters, belonging to a former church destroyed in the "War of the Communeros." The museum of the cathedral contains jewelry, paintings, and a rare collection of antique manuscripts, along with the inevitable vestments. If you want to visit the cloisters, the museum, and the chapel room, the charge is 30 pesetas (29¢). In summer, the cathedral is open from 9 a.m. to 7 p.m. (from 9 to 1 and 3 to 6 in winter).

Church of Vera Cruz

Of all the Romanesque churches of Segovia, the one called Vera Cruz is the most fascinating. Built in either the 11th or 12th century by the Knights Templar, it has an isolated view of Segovia, overlooking the Alcázar. Its major feature is its 12 sides. (The unusual design of this polygonal church is believed to have been taken from the Church of the Holy Sepulchre in Jerusalem.) Although the city was walled and protective, the knights boldly built this edifice outside. This is a gem of a Romanesque building. Inside there's a fascinating inner temple, rising two floors. It was here that the Knights Templar conducted a night-long vigil as part of their initiation rites.

The Monastery of El Parral

The "monastery of the grape" enjoys a lonely position across the Eresma River—sitting as if abandoned (in fact, it has been recently restored). You arrive at the gateway like a pilgrim calling for his dole. Behind its plateresque facade, it is a church of many styles, including Gothic and Renaissance. It was established for the Hironymites by Henry IV, a Castilian king (1425-1474) known as "The Impotent." The chief art treasure of the monastery is a large retable, the work of Juan Rodríguez in 1528. The same artist also did the sarcophagi of the Segovian aristocratic family, the Villena clan. A robed monk shows you through. To reach the monastery, head out the Calle del Marqués de Villena any time from 9 a.m. to 1 p.m. and 3:30 to 6:30 p.m. (from 9 a.m. to noon and 3 to 6 p.m. on Sunday and holidays). By all means, make a contribution to the cause.

The Church of San Martín

On the trail from the cathedral to the Roman Aqueduct is the Church of San Martín, which was, at one time, among the most outstanding in Old Castile. A Romanesque structure from the 12th century, it is characterized by its outside porticoes. Except for the rare altar, the interior is less interesting.

The square on which the church stands, the Plaza de la Sirenas, was modeled after the Piazza di Spagna in Rome. A fountain commemorates the legend of Juan Bravo, the hero of the War of the Communeros against Charles V. Nearby is the 15th-century **Mansion of Arias Davila,** one of the old houses of the Segovian aristocracy.

A MEAL IN OLD CASTILE: The natives of Segovia take a special pride in preparing roast suckling pig (cochinillo asado). Although this dish is popular throughout both Castiles, Segovia has acquired a particular reputation for it. Perhaps you'd like to try it here; at any rate, you'll probably want to sample some of the Old Castilian cooking.

For years, the **Mesón de Cándido,** 5 Plaza del Azoguejo (tel. 42-81-02), has maintained a monopoly on the tourist trade. An old Spanish inn, it is quite beautiful, and its popularity can be judged by the flocks of hungry diners who fill every one of the half-dozen dining rooms. In the shadow of the aqueduct, it offers an à la carte menu that includes cordero asado (roast baby lamb) or cochinillo asado. For a complete repast, including the local specialties cited, expect to spend from 1400 pesetas ($13.44) to 1900 pesetas ($18.24). The proprietor of "The House of Cándido" is known as *mesonero mayor de Castilla* (the major innkeeper of Castile). He's been decorated with more medals and has won more honors than paella has grains of rice, and has entertained everyone from King Hussein to Hemingway. His restaurant is open from 12:30 p.m. to midnight.

Less expensive is **Casa Duque,** 12 Calle Cervantes (tel. 41-17-07), founded in 1895. Below in the tavern decorated in the típico style, you may order a sherry or other predinner drink before sitting down to your huge noonday repast. Duque, the *maestro asador,* as he calls himself, supervises the roasting of the pigs.

The waitresses, wearing the traditional costume of the mayoress of Zamarramala, will serve you a menú del día for 1000 pesetas ($9.60). If you want to enjoy Segovian gastronomic specialties, ask for sopa castellana, made with ham, sausage, bread, egg, garlic, and much more. For the main dish, roast suckling pig is the house specialty, although you may prefer roast lamb. To finish off, try a cake known as ponche alcazar. An à la carte choice will cost you anywhere from 1000 pesetas ($9.60) to 1800 pesetas ($17.28).

Another good budget choice is **El Bernardino,** 2 Calle Cervantes (tel. 41-31-75), where Ireno Alvarez offers a menú del día for 700 pesetas ($6.72) that includes a huge paella (or hors d'oeuvres if you prefer), roast veal with potatoes, flan or ice cream, plus bread and wine. Expect to spend 1200 pesetas ($11.52) if you order à la carte. El Bernardino is built like an old tavern, with lanterns hanging from the beamed ceilings, and a delightful view over the red tiled rooftops of the city. The place is impeccable, the service excellent.

STAYING OVERNIGHT: Segovia is much cooler than Madrid, and for that reason it is ringed by a number of summer resorts, popular mostly with the Spanish. However, the hotels within the city are relatively modest, both in decor and price.

Gran Hotel Las Sirenas (The Sirens), 30 Juan Bravo (tel. 41-18-97), stands on the most charming old plaza of Segovia, opposite the Church of San Martín. Although modest, it's one of the leading hotels of Segovia, attracting those with traditional taste. Each well-kept accommodation—around 50 in all—has its own bath, telephone, and such contemporary fittings as bedside reading lamps. Its matrimonial doubles go for 2200 pesetas ($21.12) to 2600 pesetas ($24.96); singles, 1500 pesetas ($14.40) to 1800 pesetas ($17.24). A continental breakfast at 150 pesetas ($1.44) per person will be brought to your room, although a more preferred spot is the drawing room's balcony, with its pots of red geraniums and a view of orange trees. A modest dining room offers full dinners (French-Spanish cuisine), and in the Brasserie you can enjoy a before-dinner drink.

Hotel Acueducto, 4 Padre Claret (tel. 42-48-00), was built in the shadow of the Roman aqueduct in 1963. Behind its bandbox-modern facade are 77 bedrooms, most with streamlined furnishings and bed headboards with reading lamps and telephones. For the most expensive double rooms, you pay 3000 pesetas ($28.80); singles average 2000 pesetas ($19.20), although a few with complete bath go for 2500 pesetas ($24). A continental breakfast is an extra 175 pesetas ($1.68) per person. The dining room serves three complete meals a day, including a five-course luncheon or dinner costing 800 pesetas ($7.68).

READER'S HOTEL SELECTION: "I would recommend the **Hostal Florida,** 4 Calle Santa (tel. 42-48-23). It costs 1100 pesetas ($10.56) for a bathless room for two. A continental breakfast at 100 pesetas (96¢) and hot showers are extra. The owners of the hostal are extremely friendly. When I was cold, they informed me that there was no heat in May, and instead I was offered a glass of wine to warm me up. When they found out we were from California, we were asked to bring some candies to their California friends" (Carol Simon, Oakland, Calif.).

LA GRANJA: Homesick for France, the Bourbon kings created a miniature slice of Versailles in Castile, with the snow-capped Guadarrama Mountains in the background. The founder of the Bourbon dynasty in Spain, Philip V, grandson of Louis XIV, was born at Versailles on December 19, 1683. For his own gardens and summer palace in Spain, he chose a modest name, La Granja, meaning grange or farmhouse (a small farm originally stood on the site). In time, La Granja became Philip's mausoleum (he is buried here, along with the body of his second queen, Isabel de Franesio, in the Collegiate Church).

La Granja is richly stocked with paintings and antique furnishings, mostly Empire. It is mainly noted for its tapestries, many of which were based on Flemish designs (others on cartoons by Goya), made at the Royal Factory of Tapestries in Madrid.

However, the gardens—studded with elms and chestnuts—remain the abiding attraction of La Granja, luring tourists from the hot streets of Madrid every year. If you come either on a Thursday, Saturday, or Sunday afternoon (May through October), you'll see the fountains spewing forth. Gods, goddesses, and nymphs—captured in stone—cavort beneath the waters.

The palace is open from 10 a.m. to 1 p.m. and 2 to 6 p.m. (until 7 p.m. in summer), charging an admission of 75 pesetas (72¢). The entrance to the gardens is free, except when the fountains are turned on; then you pay 30 pesetas (29¢) for the privilege of strolling through, at 5:30 p.m. only.

Buses run throughout the day between Segovia and La Granja, a distance of seven miles. La Sepulvedana, 21 Ezequiel González, operates regular service (check at the Tourist Office in Segovia for schedules). From Madrid, La Sepulvedana (3 Emilio Carrere) runs a bus, in summer, to La Granja by way of the Puerto de Navacerrada. It leaves Madrid at 8:30 a.m. and returns at 7:30 p.m.

LEAVING THE AREA: After visiting La Granja, you can head back to Madrid via **Puerto de Navacerrada** (15 miles away), perched at an altitude of more than 6000 feet. This mountain pass, somewhat reminiscent of Austria, has, for years, been the most popular skiing resort for Madrileños, and is jammed on winter weekends.

5. Alcalá de Henares and El Pardo

It is a strange combination, but in less than a day, you can visit El Pardo, the site of Franco's former palace, and Alcalá de Henares, a sadly neglected town that gave the world Cervantes and Catherine of Aragon, the unfortunate first wife of Henry VIII. Perhaps you'll want to visit Alcalá de Henares first—maybe have lunch there—then go to El Pardo later in the afternoon.

ALCALÁ DE HENARES: Time has been unkind to this ancient town, which once flourished with colleges and monasteries, even palaces. A university was founded here in the 15th century, and Alcalá became a cultural and intellectual center. But in the 1800s everything was shut down, and a blanket of gloom and provincialism settled over the town. Decay destroyed most of the old buildings, and the bloody Civil War didn't help either.

However, the last handful of years, Alcalá has begun to attract visitors who come out from Madrid for the day, mainly to see the birthplace of the creater of *Don Quixote*, Cervantes, who was born here in 1547. Who knows? The town may soon experience a much-overdue renaissance.

The main stopover, then, is the rebuilt **Casa de Cervantes,** on Calle Mayor, an interesting Castilian house constructed around a courtyard with pillars and an old well. The house, maintained by the Ministry of Culture, is open from 10 a.m. to 2 p.m. and 4 to 8 p.m., and charges 50 pesetas (48¢) for admission. It is closed on Monday. On Sunday, hours are from 10 a.m. to 2 p.m.

After visiting this shrine, you should see the university, which adjoins one of the most interesting regional restaurants in Spain. Lope de Vega, and many other famous Spaniards, studied at the university; you can see some of their names engraved in plaques in the examination room. The university has a facade of plateresque, a style of ornamentation popular in the 16th century.

Reader Maria Telesco writes, "Alcalá de Henares has acquired another claim to fame besides the Cervantes house. It is fondly known as 'Little America' by the thousand or more American air force families living there, who seem to get along quite well with the permanent residents. The Spaniards take this 'invasion' in stride, and are universally friendly, courteous, and helpful.

"When you step outside the Alcalá station, you are on the Calle Marqués de Ibarra. Walk a block, cross Calle Ferraz, and on your left is a most striking building—a neo-Mudejar Moorish castle of red brick, about 100 years old. This building alone is worth a trip to Alcalá. It was used as a hotel in the 1930s.

"Keep walking past this building in the same direction (away from the train station), and at the next corner make a left. Walk two or three blocks to a tiny alley called Calle Goya, where in solitary splendor, behind a mesón, is the **Restaurante Reinosa,** 6 Goya (tel. 889-09-98). This little two-forker has delusions of being a four-forker in quality and service, but not in price. The menú del día is 550 pesetas ($5.28), but the à la carte items are worth a splurge. The paella is without peer, the spaghetti fantastic (although oily), the Stroganoff well prepared and seasoned. The waiters are the best. They make a ceremony of serving everything, as if you were guest of honor at a royal banquet."

You may want to visit the **Hostería del Estudiante,** 3 Calle de los Colegios (tel. 888-03-30), a remarkable example of a 15th-century Castilian inn, an attraction in its own right (in fact, many visitors drive up from Madrid just to eat here). If you arrive early, you can lounge in front of a 15-foot open fireplace during the cooler months. At other times, you may welcome this inn as a cool respite from the burning sun of Castile. Oil lamps hang from the ceiling; pigskins are filled with the locally made wine, and rope-covered chairs and high-backed carved settees capture the spirit of the past.

The restaurant is run by the Tourist Bureau, and offers a huge three-course lunch or dinner for 950 pesetas ($9.12), including every thing. The restaurant features regional specialties such as the cocido Madrileño, the hearty stew of Madrid, or trout in the style of Navarre. To finish, try the cheese of La Mancha. The food, although quite good, reflects a heavy Castilian hand. If you venture into the à la carte selections, expect to spend from 1500 pesetas ($14.40) for a complete meal. The restaurant is closed Christmas through January.

After lunch, you might want to walk through the cloisters (floodlit at night for after-dinner strolls).

READER'S SIGHTSEEING TIPS: "A few stops east on the train from Alcalá de Henares is **Guadalajara,** which is worth a short trip. There are a fine arts museum and a number of old churches that are a delight to sketch or photograph.

"Finally, **Chinchon.** If you have a car and want to go from Alcalá to Toledo, you bypass Madrid and take the N-111, which is a delightful country road. About halfway, signs advertise the Cuevas (caves) of Chinchon. This is a medieval walled town, a zillion years old and breathtaking. The Plaza Mayor sits in a little valley and takes you back a thousand years in time. Up the hill are the caves, which house a restaurant. We ate at one of the two-forkers in the Plaza, and it was a real treat. The Anis de Chinchon is manufactured here and is sold in the Plaza very inexpensively" (Maria Telesco, Inglewood, Calif.).

EL PARDO: After your visit to Alcalá de Henares, you should have time left for an afternoon jaunt to El Pardo (not to be confused with the Prado Museum), which lies about eight miles north of Madrid on another road. The short run to the little town of El Pardo is lined with trees, and is reminiscent of the opening scenes in the film *To Die in Madrid.* Indeed, dying was what a lot of Spaniards did in and around here during the Civil War. Much of the town was destroyed during the famous advance toward University City. But there's no trace of destruction today—the country is sleepy and peaceful. During Franco's reign, El Pardo—and not the capital—was the seat of government.

Palacio de El Pardo

The palace, the residence of Franco until his death, was opened to the viewing public in August 1976. Almost overnight it become one of the most popular sights around Madrid, with more than 2000 people daily going through 30 of its 100 rooms from 10 a.m. to 12:30 and 4 to 6:30 (holidays, 10 a.m. to 1 p.m.). An entrance fee of 30 pesetas (29¢) is charged.

The palace's exterior is like a large French-style château, which does little to reveal the surprising grandeur inside. It has been a royal residence since medieval times. Over the years it has been furnished lavishly, mostly with Empire pieces, and it boasts an outstanding collection of Flemish and Spanish tapestries.

Franco took over in 1940. Perhaps as an imperial conceit, he had many small salons to screen visitors before they were admitted to the reception hall. The former dictator's ornate gilt throne reveals royal pretensions.

Of particular interest are mementos left by the Franco family, including an extensive wardrobe; see especially ten wax dummies modeling Franco's most important state uniforms. The tour takes about 45 minutes.

Highlights include a Tapestry Room, its 18th-century collection lit by a glittering bronze and crystal chandelier. Visiting ministers were received here.

In the Salon de Consejos, with its 19th-century coved ceiling, ministers would gather for conferences or else Franco would preside at large family dinners. Tapestries were based on cartoons by Goya, Bayeu, Aguirre, and González Ruíz.

The next room is the office where Franco received ambassadors. While seated at his elaborately decorated and bronze-trimmed desk, he received more than 70,000 people. His most prized possession here was a 15th-century sideboard which once belonged to Queen Isabella.

A passageway takes you to a once-private room with English furnishings, used as a library. Next is the Goya Tapestry Salon, once a general reception area, mainly for friends of the general's wife.

In the family dining room to follow, only lunch was served. The walls are covered with silk embroidery, the fabric matched on the chairs. The room is decorated with 17th-century Flemish paintings.

Other salons include a room used for after-dinner coffee, with many personal family photographs; an oddly shaped music room with classic English furniture; a private, simple Gothic chapel, which was the former bedroom of Alfonso XII who died there in 1884. Generalísimo and Mrs. Franco prayed there daily.

What follows is a four-room suite once used by Franco's daughter. Her bedroom is painted entirely in raspberry pink.

Franco's former bedroom, with its green silk walls, has twin beds. But during the dictator's long illness, a hospital bed was substituted. Next comes the official salon for Mrs. Franco, with its Louis XIII–style furnishings and Oriental chandelier.

Franco's private theater is in white, red, and gold—classic and well designed, a family gathering point for Sunday night motion pictures.

Finally, the rooms Franco reserved for his most important overnight guests are perhaps the most tastefully decorated in the palace, done in the Marie Antoinette style.

Outside the palace chapel is the place where Franco's body lay in state.

In back of Franco's former palace is the **Casita del Príncipe** (Prince's Cottage), a small hunting-lodge kind of palace that was built during the reign of Charles III in the 18th century. It was actually ordered by his son, the prince, or probably more accurately by his strong-willed wife, who was noted for needing a hideaway or two (the one at Aranjuez was simply too far away for quick "sneak-aways" in the night).

Designed by architect López Corona, the cottage is lavishly furnished, including such adornments as embroidered silk walls. Eight paintings by Lucas Jordan are displayed, embracing six mythological scenes, an *Adoration of the Kings*, and *The Triumph of the Virgin*. Many of the furnishings are in the styles of Louis XV and Louis XVI, as well as Empire.

The small palace is open from 10 a.m. to 1:30 p.m. and 3:30 to 6 p.m. Admission is 30 pesetas (29¢). In the summer, the afternoon hours are 4 to 8 p.m. By the way, if you haven't been to the Goya Pantheon in Madrid yet, ask for a free pass for it when you pay your entrance fee here, thereby saving yourself 30 pesetas (29¢) at the Pantheon.

El Pardo means a very dark green, and the surrounding countryside lives up to its title. If possible, go to the top of the hill and soak up the views in all directions. There are many places in the town where you can sit outside and have a cool drink.

WHERE TO DINE: La Marquesita, Avenida de La Guardia (tel. 736-03-77), is one of a group of competing restaurants on the main boulevard, with an interior dining room and tables set across the street under a canopy for al fresco meals. It's a summer delight to dine under shady trees, a winter pleasure to have a meal in front of the inside fireplace. The front room is turned over to a tasca, where diners traditionally order a Tío Pepe before their meal. All the elements are there to suggest a Castilian inn, the crude regional chairs at the tables, the hams hanging from the beamed ceilings, even a see-through kitchen.

If you want a large dinner, consider the set meal for 500 pesetas ($4.80), including wine, bread, and service. On the à la carte menu, the fish dishes are fresh, especially the trout in the style of Navarre, or the grilled sole with potatoes. The most expensive items in the chef's repertoire are the roast suckling pig and tournedos. The paella de mariscos (shellfish) for two is a savory treat, as is the fish soup, a light meal. An average dinner, selected from the à la carte menu, will cost from 750 pesetas ($7.20) to 1400 pesetas ($13.44). El Pardo is easily reached by frequent bus service from Madrid.

6. Ávila

The ancient walled city of Ávila, 68 miles west of Madrid, is completely encircled by its preserved 11th-century walls, which are among the most important medieval relics in all of Europe. The city has been declared a National Monument, and there is little wonder why. The walls aren't the only attraction, however: Ávila was the birthplace of St. Teresa of Jesus, and has a number of age-worn Romanesque churches, Gothic-style palaces, and a fortified cathedral.

Perhaps you've seen the walls already—for that was no Hollywood-created city in the Sinatra film *The Pride and the Passion.* When the citizens of Ávila ceased to be afraid, they started to move outside the city and erected houses backed up against the wall—but that was long ago, and all of those shanties have been ripped down. It is possible to drive the entire length of the walls, roughly about 1½ miles.

In all, the walls have about 88 semicircular towers and more than 2300 battlements. The walls, which took nine years to build, were completed right before the dawn of the 12th century.

Warning: I sounded a warning to visitors going to Segovia in the early spring, and I'll sound the same warning here. Wear warm clothes as it's cold at these altitudes.

GETTING THERE: Ávila is about a two-hour train ride from Madrid. The 8:30 a.m. train from Atocha Station, arriving in Ávila at 10:22 a.m., is recommended. There are later morning trains and afternoon departures as well.

La Empresa Larrea, S.A., 4 Calle de Martín de los Héroes in Madrid (take the Metro to the Plaza de España; tel. 248-47-84), runs a bus to Ávila daily, except Sunday and holidays, leaving at 9:30 a.m. The bus returns from Ávila at 4:45 p.m. On Sunday it leaves Madrid at 9:30 a.m., returning from Ávila at 7 p.m. The cost of a one-way ticket is 363 pesetas ($3.49).

THE SIGHTS: Ávila lays claim to being the highest city in Spain (3708 feet above sea level). It has changed hands many times—Romans, Visigoths, Moors —but in all the history of this walled city, no one has become more linked to its spirit and legend than St. Teresa, who was born here in 1515. This Carmelite nun, instrumental in the defeat of the Reformation, was a mystic, given to trances in which she conjured up the vision of the devil and of angels sticking burning hot lances into her heart. She also wrote about them. She was severely attacked and criticized in her lifetime (once she was imprisoned in Toledo), and she founded a number of convents, as she opposed the so-called looseness of the Carmelite order. Many legends sprang up after her death, including the belief that a hand severed from her body could perform miracles. Souvenir collectors later made keepsakes of her remains. In 1622 she was canonized. It is said that she developed an intense antagonism toward Ávila because of the harsh treatment she received there. However, one of the city's most interesting sights is the . . .

Convent of St. Teresa

This 17th-century convent and baroque church grew up on the site of the birthplace of this most important saint. It contains a number of relics associated with her life, including a finger that belonged to her right hand. One of the most bizarre displays in the church is the glass-enclosed body of a monk. You figure out if it is a real body or a clever reproduction. Look for some fine altars and sculpture by Gregorio Hernández. The convent is open from 9:30 a.m. to 1:15 p.m. and 3 to 8:15 p.m.; there is no charge.

The Cathedral

This is both a cathedral and a fortress. Built into the old ramparts of Ávila, it is cold and austere, bridging the gap between the Romanesque and the Gothic—and, as such, enjoys a certain distinction in Spanish architecture. One local writer likened it to a granite mountain. However, the interior is among the most unusual in Spain, built of a mottled red-and-white stone.

As in most European cathedrals, Ávila's has lost the purity of its original design, giving way to new chapels and wings (one completely in the Renaissance mode). The apse was built right into the walls, forming a large tower with machicolations. A Dutch artist, Cornelius, designed the seats of the choir stalls in the Renaissance style, and the principal chapel holds a reredos showing the life of Christ by Pedro Berruguete, Juan de Borgoña, and Santa Cruz. In back of the chapel is the tomb of Bishop Alonso de Madrigal (called "El Tostado" or "the parched one," owing to its brownish complexion)—the work a masterpiece of Vasco de Zarza.

The **Museum of the Cathedral** contains a ceiling laminated with gold, a 15th-century triptych, a copy of an El Greco painting, as well as "grande" vestments and 15th-century song books. The *Great Custodia* is by Juan de Arfe (1573). Admission to the museum is 30 pesetas (29¢).

The cathedral is open from 10 a.m. to 1:30 p.m. and 3 to 7 p.m. in summer, including holidays (till 5:30 p.m. in winter).

The Basilica of St. Vincent

Outside the city walls, this Romanesque-Gothic church, in faded sandstone, is the most interesting in Ávila. It consists of a nave and a trio of apses of monumental size. Like its mother church, the cathedral, it bridges the gap between Romanesque and Gothic, encompassing styles from the 12th to the 14th centuries. On the southern portal, a cornice depicts the enternal struggle between good and evil. The western portal dates from the 13th century, and contains excellent Romanesque carvings.

The interior houses the tomb of St. Vincent, martyred on this site in the fourth century. The medieval carvings on the tomb, depicting his torture and subsequent martyrdom, are fascinating. Charging 10 pesetas (10¢) for admission, the church is open from 11 a.m. to 1 p.m. and 4 to 6 p.m. On Sunday it's open from 12:30 to 1 p.m. and 4 to 6 p.m.

Church and Monastery of St. Tomás

Also outside the city walls, this Gothic-style monastery was built in the 15th century. Once it was the headquarters of the feared Inquisition in Ávila. For three centuries it had the dubious distinction of housing the tomb of Torquemada, the first Grand Inquisitor, whose zeal in prosecuting (or persecuting) the "unfaithful" made him a notorious figure in Spanish history.

In 1836, a mob of Torquemada haters ransacked the tomb and burnt the remains somewhere outside the city walls. The ashes were then cast upon the fields. According to an official of the convent, no one at present "knows exactly where the tomb was."

Prince John, the only son of Ferdinand and Isabella, is also buried here, in a tomb in the transept of the church. The little cupids—part of the sculptured tomb— were decapitated during the French invasion. What sorry fun that must have been for the soldiers! Don't miss a visit to the **Royal Cloisters,** in many respects the most interesting architectural feature of the place. St. Tomás may be visited from 10 a.m. to 1 p.m. and 4:30 to 7:30 p.m. The cost for both the monastery and the cloisters is 15 pesetas (14¢). For 50 pesetas (48¢) more, you may visit the **Museum of the Far East** in the upper part of the third cloister. It exhibits curios and relics from Vietnam, China, Japan, and other Oriental nations.

At this point in our journey, that bell you hear ringing is for dinner.

WHERE TO EAT: El Rastro, 1 Plaza del Rastro (tel. 21-12-19), is an old Castilian inn built right into the 11th-century town wall. From time unknown it has been an inn, putting up travelers for the night and feeding them well on the local produce.

At the "Slaughterhouse," the dishes are typically Castilian, with more attention paid to the proper preparation of local produce than to tricky culinary maneuvers. You can enjoy a good meal for around 1000 pesetas ($9.60). However, you'll pay more if you order the casa's specialties, such as cordero asado at 850 pesetas ($8.16). The one supreme dish in Ávila is tender white veal, also 850 pesetas. The dessert specialties originally came from recipes developed by nuns in the convent. Try, for example, the yemas de Santa Teresa (St. Teresa's candied egg yolk), 150 pesetas ($1.44).

Pepillo, 10 Plaza Santa Teresa (tel. 21-31-06), may be outside the city walls, but it's definitely "in" when it comes to bargain dining in Ávila. Quality isn't sacrificed either, as good produce is used. Pepillo's popular cubierto is offered for 550 pesetas ($5.28), and includes on its typical menu, fish soup, roast veal, flan, bread, and wine. The air conditioning is a plus in summer.

STAYING OVERNIGHT: Ávila is a summer resort. From its lofty plateau as Spain's highest city, it is cool in the hot months, and in Castile this is an attraction.

The hotels are few in number, comfortable without being spectacular— that is, all except the new paradors, which is reason enough to make the trip to Ávila, even if, like Jericho, its walls came tumbling down. There is, as well, the four-star Palacio Valderrabanos. *Warning:* The Spanish book nearly all the hotel space in July and August, and it is hard to get an accommodation then without a reservation.

The **Parador Nacionale Raimundo de Borgoña,** 16 Marqués de Canales de Chozas (tel. 21-13-40), is another triumph among the Spanish paradors. Within the ancient walls, skilled craftsmen have constructed an old-style inn, using salvaged stones, tiles, pillars, and timbers. The hotel is graced with a dignified entranceway for automobiles, and most of its public lounges open onto a central courtyard with an inner row of old columns. The furnishings are tastefully appropriate: tall stone fireplaces, highly polished tile floors, old chests, leather armchairs, paintings, and discreet sculpture. The price of the luxurious double bedrooms with private baths is 3800 pesetas ($36.48) a night. Singles pay 2800 pesetas ($26.88). The dining room, with its leaded-glass windows opening onto a terraced garden, serves good-tasting Castilian dishes. A large three-course dinner is wheeled out for 950 pesetas ($9.12). A continental breakfast is an extra 250 pesetas ($2.40) per person.

If the Parador is booked, try your luck at the **Hotel Reina Isabel,** 17 Avenida de José Antonio (tel. 22-02-00), once the most preferred choice in town—until the opening of the government Parador. Near the railway station, outside the city walls, it charges 1800 pesetas ($17.28) to 2000 pesetas ($19.20) for a double with private bath. The most expensive singles with private baths cost 1300 pesetas ($12.48). A continental breakfast is an additional 150 pesetas ($1.44) per person. The Reina Isabel, in spite of its regal name, is a good, substantial middle-class hotel—suitable for a night's stay.

Hotel Jardín, 38 San Segundo (tel. 21-10-74), has, as its name indicates, a small garden (in front). In this town of narrow streets and stone buildings, it is refreshing to see a little greenery. The Jardin is in a small park-like area near one of the old city gates. For 1500 pesetas ($14.40) to 1800 pesetas ($17.28), a couple can stay here in a clean double room with private bath. The other doubles, with less plumbing, are even more inexpensive at 1250 pesetas ($12) to 1400 pesetas ($13.44). Singles peak at 1100 pesetas without bath. The accomodations are utilitarian, not the least bit fancy. A continental breakfast is an extra 150 pesetas ($1.44) per person. Meals are served in a skylit dining room: 570 pesetas ($5.47) for either lunch or dinner.

El Rastro, 1 Plaza del Rastro (tel. 21-12-19), is the best choice for the bargain hunter. The Rastro is my dining recommendation, too, but few tourists know that they can spend the night at this old Castilian inn built right into the city wall. A double room with a private bath comes to only 1500 pesetas ($14.40) a night. But if you're satisfied with a most basic, but clean, double room with a water basin—and the use of the bathroom in the corridor—then the rate for two is only 1200 pesetas ($11.52) a night. For as little as 950 pesetas ($9.12), you can have a single room with water basin only. A continental breakfast costs another 125 pesetas ($1.20) per person.

READER'S HOTEL SELECTION: "**Albergue Nacional de Carretera,** Carretera Nacional IV, km. 83 (tel. 10-70-00), Villacastin, stands halfway between Segovia and Ávila, and not far from El Escorial. A lovely room for two costs 2400 pesetas ($23.04) to 3000 pesetas ($28.80); a complete meal, 950 pesetas ($9.12). A continental breakfast is another 250 pesetas ($2.40) per person. And if the señora would like to venture over to the village square to the hairdresser for a wash and set, she'll come back with a story to tell her husband" (Dick and Doris Menkes, West Orange, N.J.). . . . "Not 30 yeards from the Albergue, on the same side of the highway, is to be found the **Hosteria El Pilar** (tel. 10-70-50). The rooms here are almost as good as the Albergue for about one-third of the price, and the cuisine is, in our opinion, superior. Prices are 1600 pesetas ($15.36) for a double room with bath, 1100 pesetas ($10.56) for a double without bath, and 750 pesetas ($7.20) for a single. A continental breakfast is another 150 pesetas ($1.44) per person. The really excellent cochinillo (roast suckling pig), a specialty of the district, costs 750 pesetas ($7.20), and a first-class mixed salad is 240 pesetas ($2.30)" (P. B. Baker and G. C. Jones, London, England).

Our final goals are far afield from Madrid and require overnight stopovers:

7. Guadalupe

The most inaccessible destination listed in this guide, Guadalupe—in the province of Cáceres, 1500 feet above sea level—is 117 miles west of Toledo. The road you take to reach it (C401) is poor, but the wild scenery of the Extremadura Mountains is spectacular.

Reader Cork Millner writes,"The rough cobblestone streets that twist, a few yards wide, up and down the hills are stacked with tattered cottages that could have welcomed a serf centuries ago. The people are cheerful and contented, living on terms of friendship with the hens, pigs, and cows that inhabit the cottages with them. The only incongruity is the ubiquitous television antennas that crop up atop the cottages."

THE SIGHTS: The **Monastery of Guadalupe** (tel. 1) is a treasure. In 1325 a shepherd searching for a stray lamb reportedly spotted a statue of the Virgin in the soil. In time, it was to become venerated throughout many parts of the world, honored in Spain by such personages as Isabella, Columbus, and Cervantes. Known as the Dark Virgin of Guadalupe, it is said to have been carved by St. Luke. You can see the Virgin enthroned above the altar.

A shrine was built to commemorate the statue. Riches of tribute poured in from all over the world, making Guadalupe one of the wealthiest foundations in Christendom. (The monastery of Hieronymites, founded by Alfonso XI in 1340, is now run by Franciscan friars.)

An expert on the subject, Walter P. Corrigan, North Miami Beach, Fla., writes: "The statue itself of Our Lady of Guadalupe with its magnificent treasure is very possibly one of the most remarkably beautiful pieces of religious art work in all of Christendom."

High above the altar in a small alcove, the Virgin is turned around to face her "subjects." The more devout among the audience can touch or kiss the jeweled garment.

In the magnificently decorated sacristy are eight 17th-century masterpieces by Zurbarán. Despite the uninspired subject matter forced on the artist —bald-haired friars connected with the monastery—he achieved richly imaginative canvases.

The Gothic cloister, dating from the 14th century, is in flamboyant style, with two galleries, a patio, and coffered ceilings. But the pièce de résistance, the mudéjar cloister, is the most stunning of all. In its center is a Gothic mudéjar shrine in brick and tiles from 1405. The Moorish fountain is from the 14th century.

In the form of a Latin cross, the church is noted for the wrought-iron railings in its naves. Be sure to see the museums devoted to ecclesiastical vestments and the choir books produced by 16th-century miniaturists. For 85 pesetas (82¢), you can visit the museum and the sacristy of the monastery.

WHERE TO STAY: In Guadalupe, the major hotel is the **Parador Nacional Zurburán**, 10 Marqués de la Romana (tel. 36-70-75), which has 20 rooms. A double with bath costs 2400 pesetas ($23.04) to 3000 pesetas ($28.80); a single with bath 2200 pesetas ($21.12). A continental breakfast costs 250 pesetas ($2.40), and lunch or dinner, 950 pesetas ($9.12). There's a pleasant garden, a swimming pool, and a bar. The hotel is in the center of town in a scenic spot.

The alternative to the parador is **Hospederia Real Monasterio** (tel. 36-70-00), once a way station for weary pilgrims visiting the shrine. Back then, lodging was granted in return for a small donation. Times have changed, but the prices remain low at this two-star hotel which, I think, deserves a higher rating. Some of the rooms contain high-vaulted ceilings. Doubles with bath range in price from 1970 pesetas ($18.91). Singles with private bath go for 1260 pesetas ($12.10). A continental breakfast is an additional 160 pesetas ($1.54). There is a bar as well, and visitors are generally pleased with the meals, a complete luncheon or dinner going for 900 pesetas ($8.64). Closed from January 10 to February 10.

8. Mérida

Once called Rome in miniature, Mérida was known as Augusta Emerita when it was founded in 25 B.C. Thirty miles east of the border town of Badajoz and 273 miles from Madrid, Mérida was the capital of Lusitania—and considered one of the most splendid cities of Iberia. It once ranked as the ninth town in importance in the Roman Empire.

THE SIGHTS: As a Roman city, Mérida was three times its present size. In western Spain in the province of Badajoz, its monuments, temples, and public works (such as aqueducts) have earned it a reputation for the finest Roman ruins on the Iberian peninsula. Michener wrote that a visit here "is like a trip to ancient Rome." An exaggeration, but Mérida is worthy, nevertheless.

The **Roman bridge** over the Guadiana was the longest in Roman Spain, consisting of 81 arches. It was constructed of granite under either Trajan or Augustus, then restored by the Visigoths in 686. Philip II ordered further restoration in 1610, and work was also done in the 19th century. It's about half a mile long.

At the head of the bridge, and guarding the entrace to town, is the **Alcázar,** commonly known as the Conventual or the Alcazaba. Built by the Moors, it is a square structure that was granted to the Order of Santiago in the 12th century.

The **Roman theater** is the greatest treasure of antiquity, and has been called "one of the best preserved Roman ruins in the world today." It was built by Agrippa in 18 B.C. to house an audience of 5000 persons. Decorated even today with Corinthian columns and statues, it was one of the most celebrated buildings in Roman Spain. Today it's also the setting for classic dramatic presentations. Next to the theater is the **amphitheater,** dating from A.D. 8, and once seating about 15,000 spectators who thrilled at the sight of slaves being fed to the lions.

Both the theater and the amphitheater may be visited for 75 pesetas (72¢).

Other sights of interest include the old hippodrome or **Circus Maximus** which could seat about 30,000 people who were drawn to watch chariot races or boats engaged in naval battles (its basin could be flooded); the 50-foot-high **Trajan's Arch** (often called Arco de Santiago); the **aqueducts;** and some remnants of the **Roman wall** that once encircled the city.

An **Archeological Museum,** open both mornings and afternoons, has been installed in one of the ancient convents—this one dedicated to Santa Clara. In the center of the city, it is noted for its collection of Roman statues, although other exhibits include sarcophagi, columns, glass, and pottery, as well as Visigothic artifacts.

The latest monument to be excavated is the **Temple of Diana** (actually it was dedicated to Caesar Augustus). Squeezed between houses on a narrow residential street, it was converted in the 17th century into the private residence of a nobleman. He used four of the original Corinthian columns in his architectural plans.

READER'S SIGHTSEEING TIP: "After the theater, by far the most impressive other Roman remain is at the **Mithraeum,** a glorious second-century mosaic kept under cover in a locked shed. There are various other mosaics open to view (and to the elements), but make sure the curator unlocks the door to show you this exceptional one" (Mr. and Mrs. John Pearce, Toronto, Ontario, Canada).

WHERE TO STAY: The **Parador Vía de la Plata,** 3 Plaza Queipo de Llano (tel. 30-15-40), is in the heart of town, installed in the former Convento de los Frailes de Jesus. Opened in 1966, it offers air-conditioned rooms on different levels. Old stone stairs lead to the bedrooms, and in the cloister a salon has been installed. A double with bath costs 3900 pesetas ($37.44), and a single with bath rents for 3120 pesetas ($29.95). In addition you must pay 250 pesetas ($2.40) for a continental breakfast. Should you want meals, the charge is 1200 pesetas ($11.52) per person. In the center is a garden studded with shrubbery and flowers. The parador also contains a garage and bar.

The **Hotel Emperatriz,** 19 Plaza de España (tel. 30-26-40), is older, but a good value for a three-star hotel. Its doubles rent for 2425 pesetas ($23.28), its singles for 1325 pesetas ($12.72). All accommodations contain private baths. You can have a complete meal for 800 pesetas ($7.68). On the premises is a nightclub as well as a bar. Try to get a room facing the plaza where the intense activity of the locals can be watched until after midnight. On the rooftops around the square are many stork nests, and these birds seem to take a similar interest in all the activity.

READER'S HOTEL SELECTION: "Walk straight up the hill in front of the railway station to the **Hostal Guadalupe,** 17 Calle José Antonio (about two blocks). The charge is 550 pesetas ($5.28) for a single. A continental breakfast is an extra 75 pesetas (72¢). Hot showers are another 100 pesetas (96¢)" (Charles McGimsey, Jr., Mamaroneck, N.Y.).

9. Zafra

One of the most interesting sightseeing targets in Extremadura, Zafra is filled with old streets and squares in the Moorish style. It lies 38 miles from Mérida. Its fair of San Miguel, on October 4, is famous throughout Spain. The Castle of the dukes of Fería is the most important in the province. It is characterized by its sumptuous 16th-century Herrerian patio and its Sala Dorada with a richly paneled ceiling. The Ministry of Information and Tourism has opened a government-run parador in the restored castle.

It's the **Parador Hernán Cortés,** Place Corazón de María (tel. 55-02-00), named after a former guest of the castle, one of the conquerors of Mexico. Cortés stayed with the dukes of Fería for a time before his departure to the recently discovered New World. The castle was originally built in 1437, on a square plan with four round towers. The interior of the parador is decorated in a beautiful, but restrained, style. It contains the chapel of the Alcázar, with an octagonal Gothic dome.

In addition to being decorated in splendid taste, the parador offers much comfort in its 21 double rooms which rent for 2750 pesetas ($26.40) to 3300 pesetas ($31.68) and its five singles which go for 2300 pesetas ($22.08). All accommodations contain private baths. A continental breakfast is an extra 250 pesetas ($2.40) per person. The magnificently decorated dining room offers regional meals for 950 pesetas ($9.12). In additional, there is a bar, a large lounge, a patio, a garden, and a swimming pool—first-class comforts in a setting of antiquity.

Finally, let me conclude with a suggestion from readers.

10. Badajoz

"Badajoz is an interesting place to stay. The old city is full of color and ancient walls. A plaque in the main plaza commemorates the Revolution. Badajoz is on the Guadiana River on the Spanish side of the Portuguese border. An old Roman bridge crosses the river.

"Near the new bridge on the Madrid–Lisbon highway is a good hotel, the **Residencia Río,** Avenida de Elvas (tel. 23-76-00). It has recently been redecorated and much improved, and doubles rent for 2000 pesetas ($19.20) to 2500 pesetas ($24). A continental breakfast costs 175 pesetas ($1.68) extra. The hotel does not serve meals, but there is a restaurant in the corner of the building, evidently under different management, and you are given a voucher honored there for your breakfast. We also enjoyed an excellent meal of swordfish there. There is a grove of eucalyptus trees between the hotel and the river where gypsies camp. Don't sit outside at the restaurant, because gypsy children spend their time begging from everyone in sight.

"For side trips in the **Extremadura,** land of the Conquistadores, there is a trio of towns to visit.

"**Jerez de los Caballeros** is an interesting journey from either Badajoz (75 kilometers south on N432) or Mérida (99 kilometers southwest on N360). It is a small town of white houses extending from a cathedral on a hilltop down into a valley below. Vasco Núñez de Balboa was born there, the first European to look westward on the Pacific Ocean. A statue in a small square at the bottom of the town commemorates him. Legend has it that he was born nearby in a small whitewashed house at 10 Calle Capitán Cortéz.

"**Medellín,** 40 kilometers east of Mérida, is a little town where Hernán Cortés, conqueror of Mexico, was born. The road approaches through irrigated farmland from which you get a first glimpse of the old whitewashed town on the opposite side of the Guadiana River. An old ruined castle on the adjacent hill dominates the town. The river is crossed on a Roman stone bridge. The cobbled town plaza is surrounded by old stone buildings. In the center is a monument to Cortés, with the impressive ruined castle in the background. There is truly the atmosphere of ancient Spain here.

"**Trujillo** is an interesting city with many Roman and medieval ruins, 90 kilometers east of Mérida. This is the birthplace of Francisco Pizarro, conqueror of Peru. The old stone family house still stands in the corner of the plaza, complete with coat-of-arms. Opposite, in front of the cathedral, a bronze

Pizarro sits astride a horse in the act of riding out to conquer" (Dr. and Mrs. C. H. Chaffey, Dapto, N.S.W., Australia).

Now for a little culture, let's head for the university city of Salamanca.

Chapter V

CITIES OF THE HEARTLAND

1. Salamanca
2. Zamora
3. León
4. Valladolid
5. Burgos
6. Cuenca

FROM THE ARID plains of Old Castile and the kingdom of León (and from Aragón) emerged the austere people who were to unify, and ultimately dominate, all of Spain. Modern Spain was conceived when Isabella of Castile married Ferdinand of Aragón on October 19, 1469. Five years later she was proclaimed Queen of Castile and of León. The chasing of the Moors from Granada, the conquest of all of Spain, the sailing of Columbus to America—all this would in time transpire because of these Catholic monarchs.

This proud and highly moral queen and her unscrupulous husband inherited a land largely treeless, with golden-brown plains. From this they fashioned an empire whose influence was to extend not only over all Spain, but throughout Europe and to the New World. The power once held by Old Castile shifted long ago to Madrid, but there have remained many reminders of a fabulous past.

The ancient kingdom of León once embraced the first three cities we are slated to visit: **Salamanca, Zamora,** and the provincial capital of **León.** Eventually, this kingdom was annexed to the growing might of Castile. The district has been called the most castle-rich part of Spain. Walls of defense also grew up around the cities, particularly those near the Portuguese border, Salamanca and Zamora, although the walls at Ávila are the only well-preserved ones.

In Old Castile, we'll visit the inland provincial capital of **Valladolid.** It was here that a broken-hearted Columbus died on May 19, 1506. On a happier day, Isabella married Ferdinand in this city. From there, we journey to **Burgos,** once the capital of Old Castile. In a small town near here, Vivar, arose El Cid, Spain's greatest national hero. The Campeador was later to conquer the Moorish kingdom of Valencia.

Finally, we'll go to **Cuenca** in New Castile. Cuenca, of course, will not be visited because of any historical significance, but because it is an isolated, geographic freak (as you will soon discover).

1. Salamanca

This ancient university city is one of the most beautiful of Europe. It has passed its period of glory, but wears its fall from grace and prestige handsomely. Its fame began in the early 1200s when Alfonso IX founded a university here.

Today it is a well-preserved city, with many colleges that once attracted scholars from all over Europe; turreted palaces, faded convents, and Romanesque churches. Great men have crossed the ancient Roman bridge that spans the Tormes, one of the routes leading into the city. Columbus came this way seeking—but not finding—support for his dreams. In this century, the Basque, Unamuno, Spain's greatest scholar, spoke out against the actions of both the Nationalists and Republicans in 1936, but his voice was drowned by the clash of the Civil War. Broken and defeated, he died that year in Salamanca.

Now, in a more enlightened Spain, a large statue of Unamuno stands in one of the squares in the old part of town.

THE SIGHTS: After much visiting and eliminating, I have compiled the following list of "The Top Seven." All of them could be visited on one very busy day. I'll begin with . . .

The University

This, the oldest university in Spain, was the chief source of Salamanca's former glory. At one time, it was considered the greatest university in Europe. In front of the plateresque facade of the building, a statue honors Fray Luís de León, who is connected with the university's best known legend. Once arrested on suspicion of being a heretic, Fray Luís was away for five years before he was finally cleared. When he returned, he began his first lecture (so the story goes): "As I was saying yesterday. . . ."

Inside this old building you can visit, first, the 16th-century classroom, cluttered with crude wooden benches. Light is practically nowhere to be seen. The remains of Fray Luís are kept in the chapel, which is worth a visit. The library is upstairs, but it cannot be visited. The university can be visited from 9:30 a.m. to 1:30 p.m. and 4 to 7 p.m. In winter, the afternoon hours are 4 to 6 p.m.; on Sunday 10 a.m. to 1 p.m. Admission is 50 pesetas (48¢).

The New Cathedral

One would hesitate to call this a new cathedral at all—its origins, in fact, go back to 1513. It took so long to build a cathedral in those days (this one was completed in 1733) that the edifice represents many styles, but, roughly, it could be classified as late Gothic, although baroque and plateresque features are most evident. Churriguera with his rococo style also dabbled in this melting pot of architecture. The building has a grandly beautiful facade: gold on beige sandstone. It has elegant chapels, the best decorated dome in Spain, and bas-relief columns that look like a palm-tree cluster. Unfortunately, its stained glass is severely damaged. It doesn't cost anything to visit the cathedral, and you may do so from 10 a.m. till 1 p.m. and 3:30 till 6:30 p.m. (in winter, however, it closes at 5).

The Old Cathedral

Adjoining the new cathedral is this older version, which was begun in the 12th century, predating the university. Its simplicity is in dramatic contrast to the ornamentation of its younger, but bigger sister. It is a Spanish version of

Romanesque. Be sure to see the huge stone that once fell on a workman's head, but didn't kill him, causing the townspeople to claim it as a miracle. After inspecting the interior of the cathedral, venture forth into the enclosed cloisters with their Gothic-style tombs of long-forgotten bishops. The chapels here are of special architectural interest. The old cathedral, which keeps the same hours as the new one, charges 30 pesetas (29¢) for admission.

Casa de las Conchas

The 15th-century House of Shells was built by a doctor. The focal point of interest is its facade of simulated sea shells, which creates a dramatic effect. The house is owned by Count Santa Coloma of Madrid and Seville. He rents his casa to the city of Salamanca for the symbolic sum of 1 peseta a year. Casa de las Conchas is presently being restored, and the job may take a few years to complete.

Fine Arts Museum

The **Casa de los Doctores de la Reina,** 2 Patio de Escuelas, was built in the late 15th century by one of Queen Isabella's doctors. Along with the Casa de las Conchas, it is one of the most representative examples of the Spanish plateresque style. The Fine Arts Museum is housed here, with a selection of paintings and sculptures ranging from the 15th to the 20th centuries. Hours are 10 a.m. to 1:30 p.m. and 4 to 6 p.m. On Sunday it's only open in the morning. The museum is closed on Monday. Admission is 75 pesetas (72¢).

Convent of San Esteban

Few will have the time to visit all the old churches of Salamanca, but if you tour this one, you will have had the best. This edifice competes with the cathedral in magnificence—notably in its golden-brown plateresque facade. The late Gothic church was built in the 16th century. Inside, José de Churriguera created a six-columned and garlanded high altar that is one of the greatest art treasures of Salamanca. By all means, visit the Gothic cloisters, which are open from 9:30 a.m. to 1 p.m. and 4 to 7:30 p.m., charging 30 pesetas (29¢) for admission.

The Plaza Mayor

This square is widely acclaimed as the most beautiful public plaza in all of Spain. It has enjoyed this reputation for a very long time, and I have no desire to dispute or detract from it. The plaza represents the 18th-century Spanish baroque style. No trip to the university city is complete unless at some point in your adventure you come here to walk through the arcaded shops and feast your eyes on the honey-colored buildings. After this inspection, you can understand why the Plaza Mayor (Town Square) is such an integral part of Spanish life.

STAYING OVERNIGHT: The **Hotel Alfonso X,** 64 Toro (tel. 21-44-00), is attached in Siamese fashion to its more expensive sister, the Monterrey. Both are under the management of Don Pablo Ferrando, an inn-keeper who extends a hearty welcome. Centrally positioned, about a four-minute walk from the Plaza Mayor, the Alfonso X offers a total of 66 rooms, each with private bath. For a double, the price is 2600 pesetas ($24.96) to 3000 pesetas ($28.80) nightly; it's 2300 pesetas ($22.08) in a single. An added bonus—you can enjoy the facilities of the better equipped Monterrey, especially its outside terrace and open-air swimming pool, ideal for summer splashes. There's no restaurant, and the obligatory breakfast costs 200 pesetas ($1.92).

Hotel Clavero, 15 Consuelo (tel. 21-81-08), is a good little modernized hotel near the 15th-century Torre del Clavero, a landmark tower of Salamanca. The hotel's location is top-notch, within walking distance of most of the city's major monuments. It's usually quiet and peaceful around here, and the hotel lies just off a small tree-decked plaza. A recent modernization job was carried out with reasonable skill, and the bedrooms are tidy, with suitable furnishings, plus a sprinkling of antique reproductions. For a double with private bath, you pay 1800 pesetas ($17.28). Singles without bath cost 1000 pesetas ($9.60). Half board is an extra 1500 pesetas ($14.40) per person.

Hotel Universal, 13–15 Rua Mayor (tel. 21-20-06), offers an Andalusian-style accommodation. Its position is near the House of Shells and only a short walk from the Plaza Mayor. Built in the style of the 1880s, the hotel is blessed with a covered courtyard. The spacious bedrooms open onto rambling corridors and galleries—a slice of old Spain. The commodious doubles, many with brass beds, retain some of their original antique furnishings. For a double with bath, the rate ranges from 1600 pesetas ($15.36) to 2000 pesetas ($19.20). The most expensive singles cost 1400 pesetas ($13.44). For 1400 pesetas ($13.44), you can take all three meals here. No English is spoken, but the Universal is a find if you're not too demanding.

Las Torres is a small (37 rooms) hotel one flight up at 47 Plaza Mayor (tel. 21-21-00), which combines good comfort, low prices, and an unbeatable position. If you're lucky enough to get one of the rooms overlooking the Plaza Mayor, you're in for a treat indeed. A double with bath goes for 1500 pesetas ($14.40); a single with shower, 1000 pesetas ($9.60). The obligatory continental breakfast is 110 pesetas ($1.06). Downstairs is a large cafetería bustling with activity in the evenings. A lunch or dinner costs 450 pesetas ($4.32).

READER'S HOTEL SELECTION: "Hostal Laguna, 13 Consuelo (tel. 21-53-82), opposite the Clavero tower, offers a double with shower and breakfast for 1200 pesetas ($11.52). Parking is possible on the street in front of the hostal, which has an excellent location, directly in the center of medieval Salamanca, within walking distance of everything you might want to see" (Mrs. H. Chadim, Curtin, Australia).

WHERE TO EAT: The **Restaurant Felix,** 8 Pozo Amarillo (tel. 21-72-81). is the best all-around economy dining spot in Salamanca—known for its good meals and generous portions. It is right off the Plaza del Mercado, a satellite square of the Plaza Mayor; and once you find it, you'll need rose-colored glasses when appraising the decor, as the restaurant ignores fanfare, concentrating instead on its 600-peseta ($5.76) set meal. Typical fare might include a bowl of fish soup, roast pork, a Spanish melon for dessert, plus bread, wine, and service. The friendly waiter customarily addresses all male customers as "caballero" without being the least bit obsequious. Especially good here is the ensaladilla à la vinagreta, a huge portion of onions, tuna fish, peas, peppers, string beans, and potatoes in vinegar, almost a meal in itself. If you order à la carte, expect to pay from 600 pesetas ($5.76) to 1000 pesetas ($9.60) per person. Before selecting a table, have a predinner drink at the bar up front. You'll surely get your money's worth here.

For more expensive dining, try **El Nuevo Candil,** 1 Plaza de la Reina (tel. 21-90-27). The emphasis is on quality Castilian cuisine—and the portions aren't skimpy either. Its commendable and recommendable 600-peseta ($5.76) dinner is served complete with "pan and vino," plus service. The fresh-tasting fish dishes always come as a surprise in inland Salamanca. El Candil is like a bodega, in the típico tavern sense, complete with stuffed bull's head. The roast suckling pig with parsley in its mouth spreads the word that the food is good. Most à la carte bills range between 1200 pesetas ($11.52) and 2000 pesetas ($19.20).

In addition, let's sample the wares at **El Mesón,** 10 Plaza Poeta Iglesias (tel. 21-72-22), opposite the Gran Hotel near the Plaza Mayor. One of the finest restaurants in the city, El Mesón serves good Spanish cooking in an inviting atmosphere. The 750-peseta ($7.20) set meal might include a choice of clam soup or gazpacho, followed by chicken cooked in its own juice or a breaded veal cutlet, and finally, fruit or flan, plus bread, wine, and service. I've observed the expertise of the cooks in the back for hours at a time; they act like they're cooking chow for the French Foreign Legion, but by the time the waiter gets the plates to the dining room, the food manages to taste more like viands worthy of . . . a sheik at least. The average à la carte bill is 800 pesetas ($7.68) to 1500 pesetas ($14.40). Happy news: The Mesón is air-conditioned. Other rock-bottom budget restaurants include:

El Dorado, 1 Calle del Clavel (near Casa Felix and the Plaza Mayor), offering a tourist menu for only 450 pesetas ($4.32). A typical meal might include paella, hors d'oeuvres, or soup as an appetizer, then veal or pork, and finally dessert, with bread and wine thrown in, too. The dining room is tiny, with only six tables, and the adjoining bar is bound to be jammed with munching students and locals.

A whole slew of inexpensive restaurants can be found in the old part of town. Thus, opposite the Casa de las Conchas is **Las Conchas,** with a tourist menu for 475 pesetas ($4.56).

Next to the Casa de las Muertas (opposite the Unamuno statue) is **Casa Nandi,** 8 Calle Bordadores, offering a set meal for about 700 pesetas ($6.72).

A SIDE TRIP TO CIUDAD RODRIGO: On the way to Portugal, Ciudad Rodrigo makes an ideal stopover, and it's a good day trip from Salamanca if you're based there. The ancient walled town is 54 miles from Salamanca.

Flanking its narrow streets are town houses from the 16th and 17th centuries, built by followers of the "Conquistadors." The cathedral dates from the 12th century, with some fine woodwork in the chancel by Rodrigo Aleman. The Plaza Mayor is a showpiece of 17th century architecture.

Installed in a 15th century fortress is one of the handsomest paradors in Spain, the **Parador Nacional Enrique II,** Plaza del Castillo (tel. 46-01-50). It offers 28 beautifully furnished rooms, doubles with private baths costing between 2400 pesetas ($23.04) and 3000 pesetas ($28.80). Singles are rented for the nightly rate of 2200 pesetas ($21.12) to 2400 pesetas ($23.04). A continental breakfast is an extra 250 pesetas ($2.40) per person. The food is well prepared, and the service is friendly and polite. A complete lunch or dinner costs from 950 pesetas ($9.12).

READER'S TOURING TIP: "**Candelario** is a mountain village 2½ miles out of Bejar, in the province of Salamanca. This charming village is a mecca for Spanish tourists, especially in the month of August, when the heat is insufferable at lower altitudes. It is virtually undiscovered by foreign visitors, which means that prices are still low. Reservations must be made well in advance for the month of August. There is nothing to do in Candelario except explore the village and the surrounding grandeur of the Sierra, but for the traveler who wants peace and quiet off the beaten track (to put it tritely), the village is unsurpassed" (Johnnie Ruth Aldrich, Salamanca, Spain). [*Author's Note:* I'd suggest seeking an accommodation at the **Hotel Cristi,** 1 Plaza Bejar (tel. 40-29-76). The price for a double room with water basin ranges from 1000 pesetas ($9.60) to 1750 pesetas

($16.80). A continental breakfast is an additional 120 pesetas ($1.15). A complete meal costs an additional 950 pesetas ($9.12).]

From Salamanca, we now head to Zamora, about 40 miles to the north. There is daily bus service from Salmanca's bus station at 27 Avenida Héroes de Brunete. Inquire at the Tourist Bureau for the exact time of departure. Some Zamora-bound trains also leave from Salamanca.

2. Zamora

Little known by tourists, Zamora (prounounced "tha-mora") is a most representative city of Old Castile. A blend of the old and the new, it has traces of its ancient city wall, yet is quite modern and commercial in parts. Capital of Zamora province, the frontier medieval city rises up starkly on the Castile flatlands, a reminder of life swept by, of conquering monarchs and forgotten kingdoms.

This is another city in which you're advised to walk and explore on your own. Stroll along the arcaded main square, walk across the arched Roman bridge built in the 1300s, pass by the decaying Romanesque churches. The river Duero flows peacefully by, and toward sunset it reflects the glow from the honey-colored stone buildings.

The one building that should be viewed from the interior is the 12th-century **cathedral.** Here, in this edifice topped by a gold and white Oriental-looking dome, you'll find rich hangings, interesting chapels, and intricately carved choir stalls. Later architectural styles have been added to the original Romanesque features, but this indiscriminate mixing and blending of periods is typical of Spanish cathedrals—as you've probably noticed by now.

WHERE TO STAY AND EAT: Since Zamora is not on the main tourist route, its hotel and restaurant situation is sadly behind the times. But that situation has begun to change, especially since the opening of the following recommendation:

The **Parador Nacional Condes de Alba y Aliste,** 1 Plaza de Canovas, **Paral** (tel. 51-44-97), is a government-owned and run four-star parador. The tourist traffic didn't merit a large place in remote Zamora, so the planners wisely kept the rooms down to 19—each, of course, with private bath.

This magnificent parador, one of the most impressive in Spain, is right in the heart of the old part of Zamora, two blocks away from the Plaza Mayor. It is housed in a sumptuous old palace formerly belonging to the counts of Alba y Aliste, who built it in the late Middle Ages on the site of the Alcazaba. The palace was ordered by Enrique de Mendoza, first count and the uncle of King Ferdinand II of Aragon and Castile. The mansion was rebuilt in the 16th century. The parador reminds one of the New York Cloisters, with its splendid armor, antique furniture, tapestries, and old clocks. There is a large inner patio with a well in it, which is closed off by glass partitions in the winter. The lounges and public rooms have all been splendidly furnished with period pieces, carpets, comfortable chairs, plants, wood paneling, fireplaces, old mirrors, and chests, and no cluttering. The dining room is also furnished in what might be termed sumptuous rusticity, and provides a view of the swimming pool and surrounding countryside. There's also a cozy wood-paneled bar (open 12:30 to 11 p.m.). Doubles cost 3400 pesetas ($32.64) to 3900 pesetas ($37.44); singles go for 2800 pesetas (26.88) to 3200 pesetas ($30.72). A continental breakfast is 250 pesetas ($2.40) extra. You can order a dinner for 950 pesetas ($9.12).

The **Cuatro Naciones** (Four Nations), 7 Avenida de José Antonio (tel. 51-22-75), is one of the leading hotels in town, granted two stars by the government. Relatively small (40 rooms), it offers a double with complete private bath for 2250 pesetas ($21.60). The best single rooms with private showers go for 1350 pesetas ($12.96). The furnishings aren't inviting enough for more than an overnight stay, but they are adequate and comfortable, and many of the rooms are spacious. The food is also quite presentable, a complete luncheon or dinner costing 900 pesetas ($8.64).

If you don't want to eat at either the main hotel or the parador, you'll find a number of regional restaurants, patronized mostly by the locals, serving fair and reasonably priced food.

Neptuno, 4 San Pablo, offers a four-course meal for 650 pesetas ($6.24), which includes wine and service.

Those on a starvation budget should head to **El Alcázar,** 1 Sacramento (corner Calle Reina), where a complete meal costs only 475 pesetas ($4.56). This might include noodle soup, loin of pork, dessert, bread, and wine; or consommé, veal steak, dessert, bread, and wine. The most expensive dishes on the menu are the two braised pigeons and the milk-fed baby lamb.

Cheapest of all is the **Chillon,** 5 Sacramento, which is completely without frills—a kitchen-like decor. However, food is prepared well, and everything is served up in generous portions. Try, for example, the fish soup as an appetizer, followed perhaps by paella or veal in tomato sauce. At certain times of the year the cook also does rabbit, and lamb, perhaps from Segovia province, is another feature. Expect to spend from 450 pesetas ($4.32) to 600 pesetas ($5.76) for a complete meal.

READER'S RESTAURANT SUGGESTION: "In a lovely city which has too few restaurants, I found the **Café Serafim,** which is near the Plaza Sagasta. The Serafim is a three-forker, so perhaps out of line with the expectations of some readers, but although the waiters are pretty snooty, which seems to be the rule in such fancy places, the food, surroundings, and prices are absolutely unbeatable, i.e., in terms of the quality of the food and the excellence of the ambience" (James L. Busey, Manitou Springs, Colo.).

3. León

Once this was the leading city of Christian Spain. The old cathedral town was also the capital of the kingdom of the same name, a centuries-old empire that began to decline when it was united with Castile. León today is a sort of dividing point between the last remnants of Old Castile and the northwestern routes of Galicia. The principal interest in León focuses on the stained-glass windows of the cathedral, one of the most spectacular sights in Spain.

THE SIGHTS: Like most Spanish cities, León is divided into an old and a new quarter. The modern, commercialized León holds little interest (Papa H hated it), but the old quarter is well worth the visit.

The Cathedral

This 13th-century, early Gothic cathedral is called the **Santa María de Regla.** Its cloisters, towers, flying buttresses—the usual architectural elements that one looks for in a cathedral—are virtually ignored, as one stands in awe of the yards of preserved stained-glass windows. To see a sunset through a rose window here is like watching the cathedral go up in incredibly beautiful flames. In summer the cathedral is open from 8:30 a.m. to 8:30 p.m., and in winter from 8:30 a.m. to 1:30 p.m. and 4 to 8:30 p.m., and it doesn't cost anything to visit,

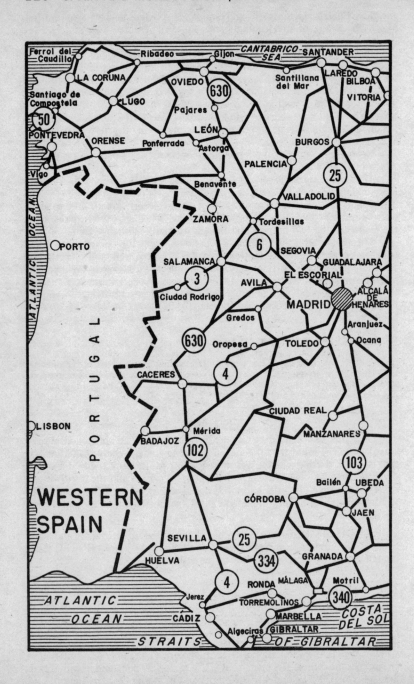

although the museum charge is 100 pesetas (96¢). After you visit here, you may want to see the second major sight in town . . .

The Royal Pantheon of St. Isidor

Here the flower of Spanish Romanesque blooms fully. The church was dedicated to San Isidoro de Sevilla in 1063, and contains as many as 23 tombs of Leonese kings. The pantheon marked the beginning of Romanesque art in León and Castile. It was mainly built in the 11th century, later embellished by the craftsmen and artists employed by Ferdinand I. The columns are magnificent, the capitals splendidly decorated. Covering the vaults are murals from the 12th century. See especially the ornate architecture of the southern portal and the central nave, as well as two portals at either end of the lateral naves.

Ferdinand I ordered that a new Romanesque church be erected on the foundations of a church built by Alphonsus V. Its consecration was to tie in with the arrival of the body of its patron saint from Seville. Unique in Spain, the **Treasury** holds such rare finds as a 10th-century Scandinavian ivory, an 11th-century chalice decorated with chalcedony, as well as an important collection of Oriental cloths from the 10th to the 12th centuries.

The **Library** alone contains many ancient manuscripts and rare books, including a Book of Job from 951 and a Visigothic Bible from the same period, as well as an 1162 Bible, plus dozens of miniatures.

The attractions may be visited in summer from 9 a.m. to 2 p.m. and 3:30 to 7:30 p.m. (in winter from 10 a.m. to 1:30 p.m. and 4 to 6:30 p.m.), for 100 pesetas (96¢) admission fee. On Sunday, hours are from 10 a.m. to noon, and no admission is charged.

STAYING OVERNIGHT: The **Hotel de San Marcos,** Plaza de San Marcos (tel. 23-73-00), is a former 16th-century monastery, once a top tourist attraction of León. But the Spanish government, at great expense, remodeled it, installing such luxury trappings as private baths, extravagant and authentic antiques, and quality reproductions. Operated for a while as one of the showcase paradors of the country, it was eventually turned into a super-splurge hotel run by private management.

The old "hostal" used to put up pilgrims bound for Santiago de Compostela. It still does today—but not for the same amount of money the 17th-century pilgrims paid. A sumptuous double room with private bath goes for 6300 pesetas ($60.48), with each additional person in the room paying 2200 pesetas ($21.12). Singles cost 3900 pesetas ($37.44). The price of a complete dinner here runs to 1500 pesetas ($14.40).

WHERE TO EAT: About the best all-round budget restaurant in León, long popular with the locals, is **Los Pazos,** 3 Arco de Animas. You enter through a bar, and in the back is a medium-size dining room. Service is fast and friendly, and the food is good. Specialties include scrambled mushrooms, besugo (sea bream), blood sausage with potatoes, and roast lamb. For dessert, have the copa special or Irish coffee. An average à la carte meal will cost from 500 pesetas ($4.80) to 1000 pesetas ($9.60), depending on your selection.

If you want something cheaper, go next door to **Los Pelayos,** 5 Arco de Animas, featuring a tourist menu for only 450 pesetas ($4.32) that includes paella, chicken, fruit, and wine. However, there are only four tables.

Excellent meals can also be had at **Los Candiles,** 11 Independencia, where there's a complete repast for 600 pesetas ($5.76). À la carte dishes include a heaping noodle soup (served from a tureen), creamed spinach, hake, roast veal with peas, and kidneys in sherry. The dining room is small, pleasant, scrupulously clean, and homey. On my last visit, I had a large noodle soup, roast veal with potatoes and peas, a mixed salad, a half bottle of wine, flan, and bread. Such à la carte meals range in price from 550 pesetas ($5.28) to 950 pesetas ($9.12) per person.

READER'S RESTAURANT SUGGESTION: "An excellent but low-priced restaurant is **Tornos**, 8 Calle Cid in León. We had an extremely good and substantial dinner there. The paella was gigantic. Two other examples: You get a delicate, tender steak which covers your whole plate or else two large trout. French fries are served with both the steak and trout. In this recommendable two-fork restaurant you get an average meal for a cost ranging from 550 pesetas ($5.28) to 900 pesetas ($8.64). Service is fast, and the waiters are helpful and friendly. The atmosphere is elegant, the decor clean and attractive" (Michael Breidenbach, Cologne, W. Germany).

READER'S TRAVEL TIP: "A train trip in Spain for the adventurous that is not listed in 'Cook's Continental Timetable' or in Spanish RENFE schedules is from León to **Bilboa** via a narrow-gauge railroad.

"The 210-mile or 335-kilometer journey starts in León at 8:50 a.m. and arrives in Bilboa at 6:52 p.m., or starts in Bilboa at 8:45 a.m. arriving in León at 7:10 p.m. The 54-plus stops give one an insight into rural northern Spain, where you see beautiful scenery in the Picos de Europa and the Elbalse de Ebro (headquarters of the mighty Ebro). Although a lunch stop is indicated at Mataporquera, travelers are advised to take full food and drinks for the entire trip. The cost is less than $15 (U.S.) per person in first class. There is also third class available" (Brook Hill Snow, Orlando, Fla.)

While the world is still rosy from the reflection of the stained glass in León, our tour of Old Castile moves to another provincial capital, that of . . .

4. Valladolid

From the 13th century until its eventual decay in the early 17th century, Valladolid was the on-again, off-again center of royalty (it saw the wedding of Isabella and Ferdinand, as was mentioned, and the birth of Philip II). Men who would one day be called saints came from Valladolid. Dreamers and philosophers searched to find reality, or escape it, here.

And, finally, came explorers, notably one named Columbus, who died here on May 19, 1506, broken in spirit and body. He was dead two years after the demise of his former patron, Isabella, and one year following the refusal of Ferdinand to reinstate him as a governor of the Indies. The death of Columbus somehow seems symbolic of Valladolid . . . of something lost, the golden opportunity in the New World that went astray, as Spain pursued short-sighted goals instead of long-term policies.

Valladolid lies in the heart of Old Castile, some 125 miles from Madrid. It is harshly cold in winter, harshly hot in summer.

Valladolid, a city that has seen greater days, is now living—perhaps grudgingly—with the realities of the present. Cervantes, Columbus, Philip II, the Catholic kings, are gone forever. After centuries of decline, the city is finding, not renewed glory, but greater economic health in such products as flour, ironware, and a huge Renault factory.

Many of Valladolid's treasures are buried in pollution, noise, and unimaginative structures of an industrialized city that seems to be swallowing up its historical past. Old parts of the city have given way to mindless, utilitarian structures, but there are also a number of quite obviously ancient structures scattered about here and there.

STAYING OVERNIGHT: The **Inglaterra**, 2 María de Molina (tel. 22-22-19), is a two-star hotel. Don't be put off by its prison-gray exterior; it warms considerably inside, although you shouldn't expect a bonfire. The bedrooms are neat and tidy, with a minimum of furnishings. If the hotel isn't superb, its prices are. The best doubles—those with complete private bath—rent for 2200 pesetas ($21.12) nightly. Singles with bath are 1800 pesetas ($17.28), but only 1400 pesetas ($13.44) with shower. In all, it's a good stopover possibility to wash off the Valladolid dust and get a good night's sleep. There's an old-fashioned dining room with chandeliers, large mirrors, and curious-looking radiators with doors on them for keeping the food warm when you have one of the 800 peseta ($7.68) meals. A continental breakfast goes for 175 pesetas ($1.68) per person. There's also a pleasant coffeeshop, plus a bar downstairs.

WHERE TO EAT: **Hostería de la Cueva**, 4 Correo, reigns supreme in the Valladolid underground as the undisputed bargain restaurant. This cueva (cave) is preening-proud of its four-course dinner. To warm up your appetite, begin with a bowl of soup, or try paella. Then you have a choice of fish or egg dishes. For the main plate, roast pork or veal make for good fare. Finally, a Spanish melon or pineapple for dessert. The three-course dinner is 450 pesetas ($4.32); the four-courser, 700 pesetas ($6.72).

The cuisine of the hostería is típico—that is, such specialties as sardines grilled on the stove, sopa de pescado (fish soup), Valencian paella, anguilas (baby eels), langostino (large shrimp), even the hors d'oeuvres. The cave is early Neanderthal, graced with stone walls, beamed ceilings, and wrought-iron chandeliers. So many dark nooks encourage amorous dalliance . . . or whatever else you had in mind. Less adventurous diners may be attracted to:

The **Cafetería Maga**, 29 Calle de Santiago, a thoroughly modern, air-conditioned cafetería. In reality, a four-fork restaurant, the Maga on its downstairs level dispenses combined plates costing anywhere from 300 pesetas ($2.88) to 475 pesetas ($4.56) including, for example, rice, green peas, ham, a fried egg, sausage, and a salad, as well as bread, wine, and service. The cookery is sound, although nothing is fancy, and the cafetería stays open until midnight.

Even cheaper are several inexpensive restaurants on the Calle Correo. The **Mesón Combarros** has a menú for 495 pesetas ($4.75) that includes paella, roast veal, dessert, bread, and wine. The **Rif** has a menú for only 450 pesetas ($4.32) which will get you a soup or fish dish, followed by a choice of meat, and winding up with a Spanish dessert such as flan or ice cream. Bread and wine, of course, are included. Farther down the Calle Correo is the **Troya**, featuring a menu for 400 pesetas ($3.84).

READER'S RESTAURANT SUGGESTIONS: "I found several good eating places, all of which I recommend in their separate categories. **El Fogon** (two forks) is near the post office in the Plaza de los Leones de Castilla, and has a varied Spanish menu. . . . The **Bar Ceyjo**, 3 José Antonio Primo de Rivera, offers all kinds of tapas, tartaletas (pressed, toasted sandwiches), and a specialty, ceyjos (frankfurters wrapped in bacon). . . . After tapas, you might try the **Salon de Té Cubero**, 7 Passion, near the main square, for desserts to be eaten at the bar or at the tables, tea, chocolate, or regular bar drinks. . . . Another good restaurant on Calle Correos is the **Zamora**, with a menu for 500 pesetas ($4.80)" (Joseph W. Zdenek, Rock Hill, S.C.).

THE SIGHTS: The College of San Gregorio, near the Plaza de San Pablo, houses the **National Museum of Sculpture**. Gracing its galleries is illustrious, gilded, polychrome sculpture, an art form that reached its pinnacle in Valladolid. First, the figures were carved from wood, then painted with consummate skill and grace, achieving lifelike dimensions.

Examples of this original and imaginative work that blended together the artistry of the painter and the sculptor are on display in the first three rooms of the museum. The most significant works here are those by Alonso Berruguete (1480–1561), son of Pedro, one of the great painters of Spain.

From 1527 to 1532, the younger Berruguete labored over a retable for the altar of the convent of San Benito. This work, housed at the museum, is considered a masterpiece. In particular, see his *Crucifix with the Virgin and St. John* in Room II and his *Sacrfice of Isaac* in Room III. Works by other artists such as Juan de Juni and Gregorio Frenández are also displayed.

After visiting the galleries, you may want to explore the two-story cloisters. The ground floor represents controlled simplicity, but the upper level is in the florid style, with jutting gargoyles and fleurs-de-lis. Then you may want to see the chapel where the confessor to Isabella I (Fray Alonso de Burgos) was buried. While here, you can't miss the gruesome sculpture of that favorite subject of Spain, *Death*.

The museum may be visited from 10 a.m. to 1:30 p.m. and 4 to 6:30 p.m. for 150 pesetas ($1.44). On Sunday it is open only from 10 a.m. to 1:30 p.m.

Adjoining the college is the **Church of San Pablo** (St. Paul), which was once a 17th-century Dominican monastery. Its facade—built in so-called "Isabelline-Gothic"—is similar to that of the college above, but is more remarkable. Flanked by two towers, the main door supports level after level of lacy stone sculpture. The church may be visited from 7:30 a.m. to 1 p.m. and 5 to 9:30 p.m. (free).

There are a number of other churches and sights of interest in addition to San Gregorio and San Pablo. You can, as for example, visit the cathedral and the **Museo Diocesano** (Diocesan Museum), in the heart of the old quarter. The Calle Cascajares leads to it. Regrettably, this great cathedral seems to be in disrepair and is gradually falling to pieces. The reredos over the main altar is the work of Juan de Juni, and the Diocesan Museum contains numerous relics of artistic value (in particular the remains of collegiate churches built during the Romanesque and Gothic periods). For 50 pesetas (48¢), you can visit from 9:30 a.m. to noon and 3 to 7 p.m.

Las Huelgas Reales or the monastery of Las Huelgas Reales is one of the most famous in Spain, both because of its past history and its privileges. It was once the palace of the queen, María de Molina, and she is, in fact, buried here in a 14th-century tomb. The reredos over the high altar is one vast sculptural masterpiece, the creation of Gregorio Fernández. On the outside is a mudéjar arch of exceptional value. Hours are from 10:30 a.m. to 12:30 p.m.; admission, 50 pesetas (48¢). The Calle de Cristóbal Colón leads to this church.

You can also make a quick tour through the house once occupied by Miguel de Cervantes, the immortal author of *Don Quixote,* who did much of his writing in Valladolid. The **Casa de Cervantes,** 14 Calle del Rastro, was occupied by Cervantes and his family (first-floor rooms) in 1605. It is now a museum, open from 10 a.m. to 7 p.m. in summer (to 5:30 p.m. off-season), charging 50 pesetas (48¢) for admission.

5. Burgos

This Gothic city grandly lives up to its well-earned reputation as the "cradle of Castile," having sallied forth into life in the ninth century. Just as the Tuscans are credited with speaking the most perfect Italian, so the denizens of Burgos with their distinctive lisp ("El Theed" for El Cid) are supposed to speak the most eloquent Castilian.

When the Andalusians first heard that lisp, they thought the men of Burgos were rather an affected lot . . . until the heroism and valor of these lisping Castilians quickly dispelled that notion. And when I speak of heroism. El Cid Campeador marches into focus. The chivalrous knight is forever linked in legend and blurred reality to the city of Burgos. Spain's greatest national hero was born near here, and his remains are in the city's principal sightseeing attraction, its grand cathedral. El Cid was immortalized as the hero of the epic *El Cantar de Mío Cid.*

Like all the great cities of Old Castile that experienced early glory, Burgos declined seriously in the 16th century, to be revived later. In 1936, during the Civil War, right-wing Burgos was the headquarters of Franco's Nationalist army.

The city lies in the Arlanzón River valley, about 150 miles north of the once- rebellious Madrid, and at almost equal distance from the French border. From Madrid, Burgos is easily reached by rail on the fast **TER** train.

Burgos is apt to be a cauldron in July and August. Following usually brilliant autumn days (the best time to visit), Burgos is likely to experience a long hard winter, with freezing cold winds rushing across the flat Castilian plains. Spring tends to be as clear as crystal, with the oak and beech forests in the provinces renewing their life under a luminous sky.

STAYING OVERNIGHT: Hotel **España,** 32 Paseo del Espoleón (tel. 20-63-40), is the best budget choice in Burgos. It lies at the end of the city's major paseo, lined with sidewalk tables and full of promenading Castilians early in the evening. The bedrooms are adequate, lacking style and imagination, but completely comfortable. The prices are reasonable. The best double rooms with private bath cost 2590 pesetas ($24.86). The choicest singles, with complete bath, go for 1590 pesetas ($15.26). I extend a bravo to the cooperative and friendly management (when the España is filled to the rafters, desk personnel have been known to ring up other hostelries to find rooms for stranded tourists). A continental breakfast is an extra 136 pesetas ($1.31) per person, and a lunch or dinner is 765 pesetas ($7.34).

The **Hotel Norte y Londres,** 10 Plaza Alonso Martínez (tel. 20-05-45). On a pleasant square deep in the heart of Burgos, the hotel possesses traces of its faded grandeur in its stained glass, leaded windows, and crystal chandeliers. Guests are assigned to good-size bedrooms, with basic furnishings. The super-size bathrooms come equipped with yesteryear's finest plumbing. Two persons in a room with private bath pay 2000 pesetas (19.20); singles in rooms with shower bath are charged 1100 pesetas ($10.56). The cheapest singles cost 950 pesetas ($9.12). A continental breakfast is obligatory at 150 pesetas ($1.44). English is spoken by the director.

WHERE TO EAT: The restaurants in the heart of Burgos—that is, surrounding the cathedral—usually feature prices that soar as high as a Gothic spire. Exceptions to that statement include . . .

Restaurant Villaluenga, 20 Laín Clavo. Although it will not walk off with any prizes for decor or imagination in cuisine, the Villaluenga will deliver a menú del día for 600 pesetas ($5.76). That will include, perhaps, a salad, a pork chop, ice cream or fruit, plus bread, wine, and service. A short walk from the cathedral, the two-fork restaurant is a dependable choice for big eaters. But, be warned of its utter simplicity. The dining room enclosure is in the back, by the way.

Rincon de España, 18 General Mola, a stone's throw from the cathedral, is a family-type restaurant which also draws many discerning visitors. You can eat indoors in a rustic-type dining room, or outdoors under a large awning closed off by glass when the weather threatens. A special menu here costs 675 pesetas ($6.48) and includes an omelet, roast veal, flan, wine, and bread. The Spanish Corner also offers platos combinados. A more extensive special menu costs 995 pesetas ($9.55) and might include a spinach omelet, roast veal, ice cream, bread, and wine. The food here is fair, the portions large, the vegetables fresh, and the service friendly.

The Big Splurge

Casa Ojeda, 5 Vitoria (tel. 20-64-40), is a top-notch restaurant which combines excellent Burgalese fare, cozy inn-like decor, friendly service, and medium prices. Downstairs there's a large, odd-shaped bar made of polished wood. Moorish-type tiles and low ceilings set a pleasant ambience for meals or munching. There are intimate nooks, old lanterns and fixtures, trellis work, and carpeting wherever you tread. Upstairs is the restaurant, which is divided into two sections; one overlooking the street and the other the Casa del Cordón where the Catholic monarchs received Columbus after his second trip to America, on April 23, 1497.

A menú del día costs 900 pesetas ($8.64), and might feature a Castilian soup, pork filets, dessert (ice cream, flan, fruit), bread, and wine. À la carte dishes are roast lamb (a specialty here), Basque-style hake, sole Harlequin, and chicken in garlic. However, if you order from this menu, the charge is likely to be 1100 pesetas ($10.56) to 1800 pesetas ($17.28).

THE SIGHTS: From limestone quarries in 1221 came the first stones for the **Cathedral of Santa María** in Burgos, an ecclesiastical structure destined to become one of the most celebrated cathedrals in all of Europe. Built in the flamboyant Gothic style, the cathedral was in the works for three centuries.

The exterior competes with the interior in sheer artistry and design. The three main doorways are flanked by two 15th-century ornamented, 275-foot-high bell towers by John of Cologne. Inside, the cathedral is cross-shaped, with enough chapels and appurtenances to create an architectural maze. The overall bastardized appearance stuns. Somehow, the effect of all the diversification of styles tends to heighten the drama and the impact on the first-timer.

Of all the chapels, the most outstanding is the 16th-century **Chapel of Condestable,** behind the main altar. This is one of the best examples of the so-called Isabelline-Gothic style of architecture, relying heavily on such rich decorations as heraldic emblems with elaborate coats-of-arms, a sculptured filigree doorway, figures of apostles and saints, balconies, and an eight-sided "star" stained-glass window. The chapel contains the tomb of its founding Condestable and his wife.

Equally elegant are the two-story, 14th-century cloisters (note the splendid entrance) filled with some excellent examples of Spanish Gothic sculpture. The tapestries displayed, including one well-known Gobelin, are rich in art and detail. In one of the chapels is an old chest linked to the legend of El Cid. According to the story, it was filled with gravel, but used as security by the warrior to trick moneylenders into thinking that it contained great wealth.

In the **Chapel of El Santísimo Cristo** is a figure of Christ that, according to legend, was the work of Nicodemus. The model? Christ himself! (Spanish cathedrals are big on claims.) But this one is particularly interesting in a macabre way, in that it seems to be made of cowhide with what appears to be human hair.

Under the octagonal dome—often compared to a lantern—are buried the remains of El Cid and his wife, Doña Ximena. Finally, you may want to see the double **Escalera Dorada** (Stairway of Gold) in the north transept. This elaborate stairway was built in the 16th century, the work of Diego de Siloé.

From March to November, the cathedral is open from 9 a.m. to 1 p.m. and 3 to 7 p.m. (winter hours are 10 a.m. to 1 p.m. and 3 to 5 p.m.). For 30 pesetas (29¢) you can buy a ticket that entitles you to visit the chapels, the cloisters, and the treasury. This purchase is recommended, as many of the most important art treasures are behind bars. Stroll by at night, incidentally, as the cathedral is illuminated then.

At least one more sight in Burgos deserves a visit. It is the **Royal Monastery of Las Huelgas.** For a monastery whose name means restful retreat, this convent outside Burgos has seen a lot of action. Built in the 12th century in a grand and richly ornamented style, it was once "a summer place" for Castilian royalty, as well as a retreat for nuns of royal blood. But today its old grandeur is just a shadow of itself, and it houses a small band of nuns of any blood type—that is, if they're Cistercian.

Inside, the Gothic church is built in the shape of a Latin cross. Despite some unfortunate mixing of Gothic and baroque, it contains much of interest—notably some 14th- and 16th-century French tapestries and a pulpit that revolves on a swivel. The tomb of the founder, Alfonso VIII, and his queen, the daughter of Henry II of England, lies in the Choir Room. A novelty is a photograph of the skeleton of the king's son, 13-year-old Henry I, revealing that he suffered an operation performed on his head.

Through the 13th-century doors we pass into the first cloisters, an appendage of the monastery. The cloisters were built in the 13th century in a blend of the Gothic and mudéjar styles. The ceiling is severely damaged, but remains of Persian peacock designs are visible. In 1937 Franco and the Falangists met in the simple but beautiful **Chapter Room,** with its unusual 12th-century standard of the Moors (war booty). The second cloisters were built in the 12th century and were originally part of the palace.

Finally, the **Museo de Ricas Telas** is devoted to costumes—mostly 13th-century—that were removed from the tombs. These remarkably preserved textiles give us a rare look at medieval dress.

The nunnery is reached by going out the Valladolid road for more than a mile (the turnoff is clearly marked). From the Plaza de José Antonio in Burgos, a bus bound for Las Huelgas leaves every 20 minutes. The convent is open from 11 a.m. to 2 p.m. and 4 to 6 p.m. Admission is 35 pesetas (34¢).

READER'S TOURING SUGGESTION: " About 42 miles from Burgos on the main road to Lagrono lies the remarkable city of **Santo Domingo de la Calzada.** Here the place to stay is the **Parador Nacional** (tel. 34-03-00), installed in a medieval building which originally housed pilgrims on their long journey to Santiago de Compostela. The parador is at 3 Plaza del Santo immediately opposite the cathedral and is well up to the extremely high standard set by all these government-owned inns. It is most luxuriously furnished, and has excellent bedrooms all with private bathrooms. There are 25 double rooms which cost from 2650 pesetas ($25.44) to 3300 pesetas ($31.68), and two singles at 2000 pesetas ($19.20) to 2400 pesetas ($23.04). A meal costs 950 pesetas ($9.12), and a continental breakfast is an additional 250 pesetas ($2.40) per person. The tomb of Saint Dominic, for whom the city is named, is in the cathedral, which is worth visiting. In honor of a fantastic centries-old legend, which is vividly recounted by James Michener in his book *Iberia*, a live rooster and hen are kept in a large cage high up on a wall within the cathedral. During mass the rooster often crows loudly, and indeed we were startled to hear him crow several times when we visited the cathedral" (Dr. and Mrs. E. McC. Callan, Canberra, Australia).

For our next and final stopover, we leave Old Castile and head for what is known as "New Castile."

6. Cuenca

At last, the word is out—Cuenca is one of the most interesting towns in Spain. The citizens of this long-forgotten town—some 100 miles east of Madrid —could have spread the word years ago, but somehow they didn't, even though they could use a few tourist dollars around here. People sigh "Isn't it quaint?" after seeing Cuenca.

This medieval town—once dominated by the Arabs—has what the Spanish call *casas colgadas*, or what we would call cliff-hanging houses. With their multiple terraces, they are a sight to behold. The rivers Júcar and Huécar meet at the bottom of the deep ravine, and if you ever go inside one of these cliff dwellings, you'll really expect to take a sudden plunge to your death in one of the gorges that split Cuenca.

Cuenca-bound trains leave from Atocha Station in Madrid. Trains originating in Valencia also stop off at Cuenca to pick up passengers en route to the Spanish capital.

THE SIGHTS: The chief sight of Cuenca is Cuenca itself. It is cut off and isolated from the rest of Spain. One of the reasons for the belated interest is that it requires a northern detour from the heavily traveled Valencia-Madrid road. The gorges give it a quality of unreality, and about eight old bridges span the two rivers, connecting the ancient parts with the growing new. One of the bridges is suspended over a 200-foot drop.

What you do in Cuenca is walk and explore. The streets are narrow and steep, often cobbled, and even the most athletic tire quickly. But you shouldn't miss it, even if you have to stop and rest periodically. At night you're in for a special treat when the casas colgadas are illuminated.

When you enter the town, you know what is in store for you. The outskirts have an industrialized tinge, but press on. The best is yet to come. Stop off at the **Oficina de Información** at 34 Colón (tel. 22-22-31) and pick up a map of the town. You'll need one.

You should try to drive practically to the top of the castle-dominated hill, although the road gets rough as you near the end. The view is worth it, however. You'll notice that the gorges make the town appear freakish, somewhat reminiscent of little Ronda in Andalusia.

In summer, the mountain breezes are cool here; in winter you freeze. Fall and spring, too, can be nippy.

The one architectural site that merits a special visit is the Gothic cathedral begun in the 12th century. It bears a resemblance to England's Norman style. Part of it collapsed in this century, but it has been restored. The cathedral, a National Monument filled with religious art treasures, can be visited from 9 to 11 a.m. and 4:45 to 7 p.m. On Sunday it is open from 10 a.m. to 1:30 p.m. and 4:45 to 7 p.m.

Spain's Most Modern Art Gallery

In this relatively obscure and remote town rests the **Museum of Spanish Abstract Art,** on Calle los Canónigos. The finest of its kind in Spain, it has been called "a rare gem" by critics. The setting is totally incongruous, with heavily laden burros moving by slowly outside, led by weather-beaten old women draped in black. Yet behind the iron knocker on the oak door is a world whose art is as modern as tomorrow.

The museum is housed in one of the cliff-hanging dwellings; the salons are well arranged, particularly to allow the natural Spanish light in to illuminate the paintings whenever possible. Many visitors (and they're coming from all over the world now) erroneously attribute this museum to the government. Actually, it's financially independent, an idea born in the mind of painter Fernando Zóbel.

The most outstanding abstract Spanish painters are represented, including Rafael Canogar (especially his *Toledo*), Luís Feito, Zóbel himself, Tapies, Eduardo Chillida, Gustavo Torner, Gerardo Rueda, Millares, Sempere, Cuixart, Antonio Saura (see his grotesque *Geraldine Chaplin* and his study of Brigitte Bardot, a vision of horror, making the French actress look like an escapist from Picasso's *Guernica*). In one room, by contrast, there's a 15th-century mural discovered during the restoration of the building representing *The Banquet.*

Closed Monday, the museum is open weekdays and Sunday from 11 a.m. to 2 p.m. and 4 to 6 p.m. It is open Saturday from 4 to 10 p.m. only. Admission is 60 pesetas (58¢).

Toledo was originally considered as the site of the museum; admittedly, the "Imperial City" would have brought far more visitors. But Cuenca was chosen—lucky for Cuenca, and even more so for you if you can make the pilgrimage.

READER'S SIGHTSEEING TIP: "Just by luck, I stumbled on Cuenca's answer to Pamplona. One Saturday in September, they boarded up the shop fronts and turned a couple of bulls loose to let the young bucks display their bravado. Almost everybody there seemed to be local, and it was a pleasant afternoon. Everybody was carrying around their wineskins getting gloriously drunk" (D.E. Waggener, APO, New York, N.Y.).

A Side Trip to an Enchanted City

If you're staying over in Cuenca—or otherwise have the time—you can visit what the citizens of Cuenca call their **Ciudad Encantada,** about 25 miles northeast of the capital. Here, a windy, rainy, violent Mother Nature fancied herself a sculptor. Backed up by her "artist's helpers" (underground waters), she created a city out of these large rocks and boulders, shaping them into bizarre designs. You don't have to accept the names that others have given to these images, comparing them to the likeness of such things as a seal, an elephant, a Roman bridge. Let your own imagination go to work.

WHERE TO STAY AND EAT: Xúcar, 17 Cervantes (tel. 22-45-11), is the best economy bet for Cuenca—a modern little (28 rooms) hotel, built in the late '60s. Everything is immaculate, and the staff keeps the atmosphere informal. All the rooms contain private tiled baths, and rent for 1600 pesetas ($15.36) to 2000 pesetas ($19.20) in a double, 1400 pesetas ($13.44) in a single. A continental breakfast is an additional 165 pesetas ($1.58) per person.

On the second floor is a lounge with TV, and the hotel boasts an elevator as well as a country-style dining room, with a tasca in front. Wood beams, fresh linen on the tables, and best of all, the friendly personal service make it inviting.

The **Mesón Casas Colgadas,** 3 Calle los Canónigos (tel. 21-18-22), offers one of the most spectacular dining rooms in Spain. The restaurant stands (rather, clings) to one of the most precarious projected points in Cuenca. It's built five stories high, with sturdy supporting walls and beams. Its pine balconies and windows overlook the ravine below and the hills beyond. In fact, it's the most photographed "suspended house" in town. Worth every centimo, the least expensive set meal begins at 1000 pesetas ($9.60), although you could easily spend 1800 pesetas ($17.28). The menu includes the most typical regional dishes and a wide variety of international cuisine. Before-dinner drinks are served in the tavern room on the street-floor level, which stays open till midnight. Even if you're not dining here, you may want to drop in for a drink, and take in that view. (The abstract art museum is next door, incidentally, so why not combine the two?)

Las Torcas, 6 Avenida República Argentina (tel. 21-29-26), is one of the least expensive restaurants in Cuenca. It offers homemade cooking in a simpático atmosphere. A mezzanine dining room overlooks the tasca bar— as clean as soap. The paintings on the walls, the wood paneling, the open staircase make it attractive. A good bargain is the 600-peseta ($5.76) menú de la casa. On the à la carte list, some offerings worth considering are the sopa de mariscos (shellfish soup), the trout with ham, and the loin of pork prepared over hot coals. The meal will probably run you about 900 pesetas ($8.64), including bread, wine, and dessert. Closed in November.

READERS' HOTEL SELECTION: "There is a two-star hostal residencia, **Avenida,** at 39 Avenida José Antonio (tel. 21-43-43). You have to look sharp to see the sign. It is comfortable, clean, and the service is good and friendly—all Spanish, of course, Tourism has barely touched the place. A room with bath is 1400 pesetas ($13.44) to 2000 pesetas ($19.20) for two. A continental breakfast is 150 pesetas ($1.40) per person" (I. E. Orton, Ottawa, Canada. . . . **"Hostal-Residencia Castilla,** 4 Diego Jiménez (tel. 21-23-92), offers a double with bath (no breakfast) for 1200 pesetas ($11.52). This is a nice hostal in a modern apartment house. Parking is not too difficult on the street in front" (Mrs. H. Chadim, Curtin, Australia).

READER'S HOTEL SELECTION (LA ALMARCHA): "There is a **Hostal San Cristóbal,** Km. 155 (tel. 24), in the village of La Almarcha on the Madrid to Valencia highway, which is only about 30 miles from Cuenca and lets you stay where you can make a quick departure in the morning. My single, with dinner and morning coffee and cupcakes, was 1200 pesetas ($11.52). Be sure to ask for a room in the back however, because they have a sign out front that would light up Times Square" (D. E. Waggener, APO, New York, N.Y.).

———————

Those of you who didn't fall in the gorge at Cuenca can now journey with us to a region that is Spain's greatest tourist attraction.

Chapter VI

ANDALUSIA

1. Jaén, Baeza, and Úbeda
2. Córdoba
3. Seville
4. Jerez and Cádiz
5. The Huelva District
6. Ronda
7. Granada

ANDALUSIA is a pagan land. This vast, wild, rugged tract of southern Spain—quite interestingly—lives up to all the clichés you've ever heard about. It's as if—for once—those travel posters didn't lie. Silvery olive trees vibrate in the wind; the scent of orange blossoms hangs in the air; mantilla-wearing señoritas, with carnations in their hair, run through the narrow streets on fiesta days; gypsies rattle their castenets in caves thousands of years old; and young men serenade their girls under balconies on hot Spanish nights.

This once-great stronghold of Moslem Spain is also rich in history and tradition. Of all the sections of Spain, it has the most celebrated sightseeing treasures: the world-famous Mesquita (mosque) at **Córdoba**, the Alhambra Palace at **Granada**, the great Gothic cathedral at **Seville**. It also has towns of which you may never have heard—places like **Úbeda**, castle-dominated **Jaén**, gorge-split **Ronda, Jerez de la Frontera** (the home of sherry), and the gleaming white port city of **Cádiz**. Give Andalusia at least a week, and know then you will have skimmed only the surface of its many offerings.

This dry, mountainous region also embraces the **Costa del Sol** (Málaga and Torremolinos), but this popular strip of Spain is dealt with separately in the following chapter. Go to the Costa del Sol for beach resorts, nightlife, and relaxation; visit Andalusia for its architectural wonders, its beauty, and a life that has come to symbolize—quite erroneously—Spain itself.

Crime alert: Anyone driving south into Andalusia and the Costa del Sol should be warned about thieves. Once one of the safest and most crime-free districts of Europe, southern Spain is now beset with break-ins. A major problem is breaking into cars. Many motorists park their cars with all their luggage in it only to return from a sightseeing attraction to find they've been robbed.

Daylight robberies are very commonplace, especially in such cities as Seville, Córdoba, and Granada. Also, it is usual for a car to be broken into while tourists are enjoying lunch in a restaurant. Some establishments have solved the problem by having guards (a service for which you should tip, of course).

Under no circumstances should you ever leave passports and travelers checks unguarded in a car.

1. Jaén, Baeza, and Úbeda

The province of Jaén, with its three principal centers—the capital city of Jaén, Baeza, and Úbeda—lies in one of the most recently discovered tourist sections of Spain. But this country, at long last, is beginning to be accorded its proper interest. For too many years, visitors whizzed through Jaén on their way south to Granada, or bypassed it altogether on the southwest route to Córdoba and Seville. But the government is beefing up the sad lot of the hotels in the province with its excellent paradors, which now provide some of the best living accommodations in Spain. If you have an extra day, it is recommended that you spend it touring the capital city of Jaén and its two stepdaughters, Baeza and Úbeda.

To reach Jaén, take a train from the Atocha Station in Madrid, which will deliver you to the Linares and Baeza station. From this point, you can then make frequent bus or electric train connections to either Úbeda or Jaén.

For our first stopover in the province, we'll pay our respects to the capital.

JAÉN: This city lies in the center of the major olive-growing district in Spain. It is sandwiched between Córdoba and Granada (each lying about 60 miles away in opposite directions). Some 210 miles south of Madrid, the history-rich town of Jaén has been traditionally considered a gateway to Castile or a gateway to Andalusia, depending on which way one was headed. It has a bustling modern section of little interest to visitors, but its Moorish-influenced older part is reason enough for going there. A castle high on the hill dominates the capital, and it has been turned into a first-class parador. On a clear day, you can see the snow-covered peaks of the Sierra Nevada.

A historical note: The Christian forces gathered in their stronghold here before marching on Granada to oust the Moors in 1492.

The Sights

Jaén's most important National Monument is its honey-brown **cathedral**, a blend of both baroque and Gothic architectural features, with a Romanesque facade—in all, an unfortunate wedding of styles that occurs too frequently in Spanish cathedrals. The interior is dominated by a huge dome. The formality and grandeur of the cathedral attest to Jaén's importance in days gone by. The building is open from 7:30 to 11 a.m. and 5:30 to 9 p.m.; no admission charge.

In addition to its cathedral, Jaén has a number of historic churches, but **La Magdalena** is the most interesting. A Gothic church, it was once an Arab mosque, and can be visited from 8 a.m. to 2 p.m. and 5 to 8 p.m. (free). The city also has numerous mansions left over from the heyday of Spanish aristocracy that contrast dramatically with the Arabesque white and purple-washed tile-roofed dwellings. Its narrow, cobblestone streets hug the mountainside.

Where to Stay

The **Parador Castillo de Santa Catalina** (tel. 23-22-87), a castle on the hill overlooking Jaén, is one of the government's showplace paradors. Just to stay here is a good enough reason for coming to Jaén. In the tenth century the castle was a Moslem fortress, surrounded by high protective walls and approached by a steep, winding road. When Christians did approach, the Moors were fond of throwing them overboard. The castle is still reached by the same road, but the hospitality has improved remarkably.

Visitors enter through a three-story-high baronial hallway. The polite staff shows guests to their balconied bedrooms (doubles only), all of which have been tastefully furnished, and with an eye to both comfort and style. The spick and span tiled private baths (and the heating in winter) make living in this castle bearable after all. And the price for all this is about 3500 pesetas ($33.60) for two persons, plus another 250 pesetas ($2.40) per person for a continental breakfast.

Dining at the castle is dramatic, both in atmosphere and cuisine. The high-vaulted dining chamber looks like a small cathedral, with its wrought-iron chandeliers, stone arches, a raised hearth, and a collection of copper kettles and ceramics. On either side of this lofty room are arched windows, opening onto a terrace on one side and a view of Jaén on the other.

A big luncheon or dinner here, costing 1000 pesetas ($9.60), includes the regional wine of Jaén province. The food is adequately prepared, especially the paella. The hors d'oeuvres consist of 20 tiny plates, including, of course, the olives for which Jaén is famous. The fried hake is a good fish choice. For your third course, you're given a selection of meat dishes, such as liver sauteed with onions or perhaps a breaded veal cutlet. The basket of fruit is tempting, as are the homemade pastries, especially the typical dish of the region, cheese with honey or quince.

Hotel Rey Fernando, 7 Plaza Coca de la Piñera (tel. 21-18-40), is a fairly modernized establishment, a two-star hotel in Jaén. It's close to the monuments and transportation center, and makes for a comfortable overnight stay. Plain but livable doubles, with bathrooms, go for 2000 pesetas ($19.20) to 2200 pesetas ($21.12); singles are in the 1000-peseta ($9.60) to 1300-peseta ($12.48) range. While not a glamorous hotel, it is clean, and offers a good dining room where you can have either lunch or dinner for 850 pesetas ($8.16).

For those on a tight budget, there's the very plain, but nonetheless charming, **Hostal San Lorenzo,** 1 Madre de Dios (tel. 23-38-73), near the cathedral. The simply furnished rooms are entered directly from an Andulasian patio with a fountain, tiled floors, potted plants, and the ubiquitous small statue of the Holy Virgin. In all, there are 15 rooms. Doubles (sans shower bath) cost only 600 pesetas ($5.76), and singles go for 450 pesetas ($4.32). A continental breakfast is an extra 75 pesetas (72¢) per person.

Where to Eat

For plain eating without frills, try **Las Vegas,** 4 Generalísimo (tel. 23-41-85), where you can get a meal for 600 pesetas ($5.76) that might include ham-and-egg soup, Andalusian-style hake, a quarter bottle of wine, bread, and fruit. The restaurant serves until midnight.

After lunch or an overnight stopover in Jaén, our tour continues to Baeza, 28 miles north.

BAEZA: This historic old town of Gothic and plateresque buildings and cobblestone streets is one of the least spoiled in Spain, a fit rival for its bigger sister, Úbeda. In many respects, Baeza is like a fantasy of a small Andalusian town come true. At twilight lanterns hang on walls of plastered stone, flickering against the darkening sky and lighting the narrow streets.

The main square, a two-story open colonnade, is a good point to begin your exploration. But you may soon gravitate to the section bordering the

cathedral, the most interesting area. Built in the 16th-century, the cathedral is a blend of Gothic and Renaissance architectural styles.

Even more enticing a sight is the **Palace of San Felipe,** with its intricately sculptured Gothic facade. Now a seminary, it contains a modern chapel opening off its 16th-century courtyard. A baroque stairway leads to another mosaic chapel. But in Baeza one doesn't want to spend too much time inspecting the interior of buildings, regardless of how fascinating. The town as a whole provides the architectural interest and drama.

After a walking tour, it's only six miles by bus northeast to . . .

ÚBEDA: This former stronghold of the Arabs is a Spanish National Monument, a town filled with golden-brown Renaissance palaces, tile-roofed dwellings bathed in whitewash, and narrow cobblestone streets. Like its neighbor, Baeza, it offers the visitor a chance to see a relatively untouched, aristocratic Andalusian town. You can cut off the Madrid-Córdoba road and head east for Linares, then on to Úbeda, a detour of 26 miles. The government has installed a parador here in a ducal palace—so you might make it a luncheon stopover if you're pressed for time.

The palaces and churches of the city are almost endless. For centuries, a web of decay and dust has fallen over them, but now many are being restored. At present you can view the churches, but you'll have to settle for staring at the outside of the mansions. The charm of this town is to be discovered by wandering through its streets, and this charm isn't necessarily reflected in one particular sight. You'll probably get lost—but that's all right, too.

The Sights

To give you a more intimate experience in the town, I've narrowed the sights down to three specific ones: a palace (the government parador coming up in the next section), a hospital, and a church.

The **Hospital of Santiago,** on the edge of town, was completed in 1575, and it's still in use. Over the years, it has earned a reputation as the "Escorial of Andalusia," and although the title is misleading, it does point up the grandeur that this building once possessed. Happily, you can simply walk into its courtyard: no one charges admission.

Santa María de los Reales Alcázares is the most intriguing of Úbeda's many churches. The cloisters, with their fan vaulting, are Gothic, and the interior with its tiled and painted ceiling is a blend of Gothic and mudéjar. It stands on the ground that once held an Arab mosque. Inside the church you'll find a gruesome statue of a mutilated Christ—a real horror movie.

Living and Dining in a Ducal Palace

The **Parador Nacional del Condestable Dávalos,** Plaza de V. de Molina (tel. 75-03-45), provides guests with a chance to live in a 16th-century palace, in a style superior to that of the duke who originally inhabited it back in the golden days of this ancient town. The palace shares an old paved plaza, deep in the heart of Úbeda, with La Iglesia del Salvador, a church with a dazzling **facade.**

A formal entrance to this Renaissance structure leads into an enclosed patio, encircled by two levels of Moorish arches. Pots of palms and plants rest upon the tiled floors. An inner staircase leads to the balcony, off which lie the upper-level rooms. The bedrooms are nearly two stories high, and have beamed ceilings and tall windows. Antiques have been combined with reproductions:

the beds are comfortable; and the private baths are roomy. The charge for all of this is 2700 pesetas ($25.92) to 3300 pesetas ($31.68) in a double room with private bath, 2400 pesetas ($23.04) in a single with a private bath.

Before lunch or dinner, you might go into the low-beamed wine cellar, old and tavern-like, with stone arches, crude stools and tables, three giant kegs of wine, and a wall covered with a collection of ceramic vases and dishes. Dinner is served on the ground floor in a room representing restrained taste. Costumed waitresses bring good Spanish dishes to your table, and the bill for a luncheon or dinner is 950 pesetas ($9.12). This includes the wine and service, and it's well worth the splurge. Why not have your after-dinner coffee in either of the living rooms, perhaps near the fireplace?

An Alternate Hotel Choice

Frankly, if you can stay at the parador, there doesn't seem to be any earthly reason for living elsewhere—unless you arrive without a reservation only to find the hotel fully booked. In that case, head for the **Hotel Consuelo,** 12 Avenida Ramón y Cajal (tel. 75-08-40). Not luxurious, but absolutely comfortable and utilitarian, this is a fairly modern, three-story building, with a simple dining room where good meals cost 600 pesetas ($5.76). The Consuelo's greatest asset, however, is its low rate structure: only 1400 pesetas ($13.44) to 1800 pesetas ($17.28) for a double room with complete bath. The most expensive singles, those with private bath, rent for 1200 pesetas ($11.52). A continental breakfast is an extra 125 pesetas ($1.20) per person. The Consuelo is on the other side of Úbeda from the parador, across from the Institute of Enseñanza Media.

Now we move on. If you spend the night in the province of Jaén, you'll need to go 65 to 75 miles (depending on where you stayed) the next day to reach one of my most highly recommended "Top Ten Cities."

2. Córdoba

Ten centuries ago, Córdoba was one of the greatest cities in the world: it then had a population close to 900,000. The capital of Moslem Spain, it was not only Europe's largest city, but a cultural and intellectual center as well. Córdoba, the seat of the Western Caliphate, flourished with public baths, mosques, a great library, and palaces. But a lot of greedy, sacking hordes have since passed through Córdoba, tearing down its ancient buildings, carting off its art treasures, and pillaging its riches. Perhaps the proof of Córdoba's greatness lies in the fact that—despite these assaults—it still has enough traces of its former glory to make it a rival of Seville and Granada, and a contender for the title of the most fascinating city in Andalusia.

Today, this provincial capital is known chiefly for its mosque, but it abounds with other artistic and architectural riches, especially its domestic dwellings. The old Arab and Jewish quarters are filled with streets narrower than most sidewalks. Like Seville, Córdoba is famed for its flower-filled patios, and it's perfectly acceptable to walk along the streets, gazing into the courtyards. This is rarely considered an invasion of privacy; rather, the citizens of Córdoba take pride in showing off their patios, part of the tradition of the city. For the most part, these homes are whitewashed, and plants hang from balconies.

If you are bypassing the province of Jaén and heading directly from Madrid to Córdoba, the distance is about 260 miles, a good day's drive from the capital. Córdoba lies on that much-traveled route between Madrid and

Seville. Consequently, reaching it by rail from many centers in Spain is easy. It is serviced by both a **TER** and a slow train. The train trip from Madrid to Córdoba is through some of Spain's most beautiful countryside. The **TALGO** is a fast, comfortable, and inexpensive ride—about 3500 pesetas ($33.60) for a first-class, reserved seat.

Before I highlight the treasures of Córdoba, let's find a hotel.

WHERE TO STAY: The hotel situation here is varied. There are several that are modern and relatively impersonal; others more atmospheric and charming, and a few in both categories that are inexpensive.

Hotel Residencia Marisa, 6 Cardenal Herrero (tel. 22-63-17), is a real find. Right opposite the mosque, it is a simple, friendly, and clean 28-room hotel where you can get double with bath or shower for 1800 pesetas ($17.28), a single for 1300 pesetas ($12.48). No meals are served except a continental breakfast, at 175 pesetas ($1.68). The rooms are comfortable and well furnished, and there's a pleasant lounge in the Castilian fashion. The service is polite and efficient.

Hotel Cuatro Naciones, 4 García Morato (tel. 22-39-25), is the place for you if you like to sleep in a giant brass bed, or walk in a courtyard filled with potted plants and lots of geraniums. The hotel, known primarily to discriminating Spaniards, is a reminder of the traditions of Andalusia. Fortunately, the owner hasn't succumbed to modernization, and the hotel proudly maintains its vintage charm. But never fear, private bathrooms have been installed in some of the rooms, and these doubles rent for 1800 pesetas ($17.28). The best singles (with shower baths) go for 1200 pesetas ($11.52). Breakfast, the only meal served, is an extra 135 pesetas ($1.30). The dining room opens off the courtyard, and has elaborately tiled walls, crystal chandeliers, and straight-back provincial chairs. The hotel is centrally located, but difficult to reach. It is on a narrow street in the heart of the city, engulfed by Córdoba's shopping and business district. You'll have to park your car down the street, go to the hotel, summon the porters, and have them make the long trek with your luggage. This third-class hotel is only a two-minute walk from the Plaza de José Antonio.

Hotel El Brillante, 91 Carretera del Brillante (tel. 27-58-00), is a third-class hotel, five minutes from the heart of the city, at the foot of a hill that leads to the government's first-class parador. A typically Andalusian building, with white plaster and green trim. El Brillante has the characteristics of an old inn, with a patio (canopied in summer) filled with vines and potted plants.

You'll be led up a staircase to a balcony, which winds around to the simple bedrooms. A double with bath rents for 1800 pesetas ($17.28). Singles range in price from 1000 pesetas ($9.60) to 1400 pesetas ($13.44). But be warned: sleep only with bedmates you're romatically interested in—in some of the double beds you'll sink into the middle. A continental breakfast is an extra 110 pesetas ($1.06) per person. And the hotel, like so many of Córdoba's hostelries, is hot enough to make eye shadow run in summer. It's best to take your own soap and towels. The hotel is reached by bypassing the railway station and heading north up the Avenida de América. Cross the railway bridge and continue for half a mile. El Brillante is at the clearly marked turnoff to the parador.

Hotel Granada, 21 Avenida de América (tel. 22-18-64), is not the most elaborate or chicest hotel in Córdoba, but it shouldn't be written off. It's only a one-star hotel, across the street from a railway station—but what a railway station. Set back from the avenue, the station is charming and colorful, with trees and a little flower garden. The Granada is also well built, fairly modern, and huddles beside this tree-lined avenue, luring guests with its combination bar-lounge at the entrance.

The bedrooms are simply but adequately furnished. For a good-size double with private bath, the charge is 1750 pesetas ($16.80). The best singles (with shower, no toilet) tally up to 950 pesetas ($9.12). For 120 pesetas ($1.15), a continental breakfast is served. Lunch or dinner costs 600 pesetas ($5.76) extra, including, for example, cream of mushroom soup, fried fish, filet of veal with vegetables, plus a choice of desserts.

Andalucía, 3 José Zorrilla (tel. 22-18-55), has made many friends since opening its doors in the late '60s. Off the Gran Capitán, it lies near the cathedral, making a presentable first impression with its admittedly modest trappings. "It always seems to be full," was one typical comment. "The word must be out." The word is that you can get a clean and comfortable double room for just 1550 pesetas ($14.88), a single with shower bath for 950 pesetas ($9.12). The Andalucía serves breakfast only, costing 135 pesetas ($1.30) extra.

The Big Splurge

Parador Nacional La Arruzafa, Avenida de la Arruzafa (tel. 27-59-00), is serenely placed on the rise of the Sierra de Córdoba, at the outskirts of the city. For its reasonable rates, it offers the conveniences and facilities of a luxurious resort hotel. It's one of the finest paradors in all of Spain, commanding not only the best view in Córdoba but featuring a swimming pool as well.

The bedrooms—82 in all—are spacious and furnished in finely styled dark wood pieces. Some of the rooms have balconies for taking breakfast or relaxing over a drink. Doubles—all with complete private baths—cost from 3400 pesetas ($32.64) to 5300 pesetas ($50.88). A double rented to a single person goes for 2800 pesetas ($26.88).

Los Gallos, 7 Avenida de Medina Azahara (tel. 23-55-00), is a recently built hotel set in the midst of this ancient city. But it comes off winningly, perhaps because of its taste level and streamlined design. Half a block from a wide, tree-shaded boulevard, it stands eight floors high, crowned by an informal roof garden.

The lifesavers in summer are the outdoor swimming pool and the air-conditioned bedrooms. For a double room with private bath, the charge is 2800 pesetas ($26.88) to 3400 pesetas ($32.64). The rooms have many built-in comforts and contain balconies. Finally, the hotel offers many additional facilities, such as a restaurant, a drinking lounge, and a spacious public lobby.

Residencia Maimonides, 4 Torrijos (tel. 22-38-53), is a three-star contender just opposite the mosque. The 61 somewhat antiseptic rooms are spotless and comfortable. Amenities include telephones in each room, air conditioning, a bar, and a garage. The Maimonides is named after a Jewish philosopher, doctor, and theologian who lived in Córdoba. It charges 3100 pesetas ($29.76) for a double with bath. A continental breakfast is another 230 pesetas ($2.21) per person.

READERS' PENSION SELECTIONS: "A great economic find is the **Hostal Perales,** 19 Avenida Mozárabes (tel. 23-21-12). I got a very nice single room for only 450 pesetas ($4.32). Doubles go for 750 pesetas ($7.20). Rooms are bathless, but the use of the corridor shower is free. A continental breakfast is an extra 90 pesetas (86¢) per person. Go right from the main entrance to the railroad station, turn left at the second street (Mozárabes), which is immediately after you cross a park. It's right there on the corner" (David Zarri). . . . "There is a good three-star hotel, **El Califa,** 14 Lope de Hoces (tel. 22-84-00), on the east side of the park, more conveniently located than the parador. It's within five minutes' walk of the mosque. The charge is 3000 pesetas ($28.80) for a double,

1800 pesetas ($17.28) for a single, both with bath. The hotel has air conditioning and a garage. One block up the street, a fine restaurant, Ciro's, offers excellent food in large portions and fine service" (Joseph W. Zdenek, Rock Hill, S.C.).

WHERE TO EAT: By all means, shake free of your hotel for at least one meal a day while you're in Córdoba. The restaurants are more like an evening adventure than they are places to pick up a quick bite. Often they combine food with flamenco—so make an evening of it.

Los Califas (The Caliphs), 9 Deanes, lures its customers to the old Jewish Quarter, and here a covered patio and fountain recreate the feel of Andalusia. The two-fork restaurant offers meals at 650 pesetas ($6.24) and 950 pesetas ($9.12). For this, you're likely to get a salad or gazpacho, paella, roast chicken, plus ice cream and sangría. Incidentally, Los Califas is one place in Spain where you can order the tail of a bull (rabo de toro) as a main course, 480 pesetas ($4.61). Don't waste your time wondering how fish can taste so fresh in inland Córdoba—it just does—especially the sole cooked over coals, or swordfish in the Córdoba style. If you order from the à la carte menu, expect to spend from 900 pesetas ($8.64) for a complete meal. Closed Wednesday.

El Caballo Rojo, entrances at 28 Cardenal Herrero, Plaza de la Hoguera, and 4 Judería (tel. 22-38-04), is another atmospheric establishment within walking distance of the Mezquita in the old part of town. One of its entrances is through a bar, where rows of hors d'oeuvres have been lined up to accompany predinner drinks. The other entrance, 6 Romero, is through a colorful courtyard, with a winding staircase. The dining room is a delight, its three large arched windows opening onto the patio. In summer, guests either dine in the patio under a grape arbor, or enjoy the air conditioning inside. On cool evenings, the smell of burning logs is in the air.

At "The Red Horse," a complete meal begins at 1000 pesetas ($9.60), and a typical one might include gazpacho, paella, a main dish of chicken, then ice cream and sangría. It's also easy to spend 2000 pesetas ($19.20) for a dinner here.

Readers Lolli and Brian Sherry, Northfield, Illinois, had this added note: "Our mixed salad covered a dinner-size plate, and we had a delicious smoked pork chop about three-quarter inches thick, unlike the quarter-inch slivers we usually received. Dinner was accompanied by sangría and followed by ice cream. This was without a doubt the outstanding dinner of our trip."

Off the main Plaza de José Antonio is the **Calle Victoriano Rivera,** where several budget restaurants, all with outside tables, are to be found. The **Plata,** for example, offers a three-course meal for only 500 pesetas ($4.80). And for that you get soup, hors d'oeuvres, or a salad; then a potato omelet or paella; veal with sherry, fried fish, or a breaded veal cutlet; plus dessert, wine, and bread.

READERS' RESTAURANT SUGGESTIONS: "Taberna del Potro, 2 Coronel Cascajo (tel. 22-34-95), is a crazy place—fair cooking, very Spanish, and untouristy. The least expensive cubierto goes for 400 pesetas ($3.84). Only lunch is served" (Mrs. Diane Keeling, Ottawa, Canada). . . . "When arriving hungry and thirsty at Córdoba at noon with your car, coming from Seville, Málaga, or Granada, don't face the traffic jams of unknown inner Córdoba. Why not stay on the other side of the Guadalquivir River, before the Seville road enters the ancient city, and stop at the **Restaurante del Puente Nuevo,** 60 Avenida de Cádiz, as we did? Buy yourself a good lunch in the modern, air-conditioned restaurant. I'd suggest you begin with the tasty entremeses. Continue with a merluza, ternera con tomate, or dos chuletas de cordero. A big bottle of mineral water (one litro) will kill your thirst, unless you prefer to drink wine, but remember, you'll have to drive your car to the hotel. For a dessert, you might choose ice cream, watermelon, or flan. A complete meal here ranges in price between 550 pesetas ($5.28) and 900 pesetas ($8.64). By the time you finish your lunch, it will be siesta hour in Córdoba, traffic will slow down under the warm sun, and you'll have no trouble at all finding a hotel" (R. Depreitere, Kortrijk, Belgium).

"For a break from a big supper, you might try **Cafetería Albolafia,** 5 Deanes, near the mosque, a very clean, handsomely decororated bar, featuring a nice variety of tapas and raciones" (Joseph W. Zdenek, Rock Hill, S.C.). . . . "A friend found a really good restaurant, half hidden in a little street off the Calle Judíos in Córdoba, the **Mesón de la Luna.** We had a mixed grill of lamb, port, and chorizos, a large plate of mixed vegetables, bread, and good red wine. I don't remember the exact tab, but it was under 1200 pesetas ($11.52) for the two of us. This was good food in a city where restaurant food is often mediocre. . . . **Los Patios,** 16 Cardenal Herrera, is a self-service restaurant across from the mosque. This is not gourmet fare, but the price is right for people on a budget: all you care to heap on your plate for 500 pesetas ($4.80). Drinks are extra. I had an excellent vino dulce for 35 pesetas (34¢). I saw a young man come out with a full tray which he split with his wife— two meals for 500 pesetas ($4.80). The patios are pleasant places to sit" (Ileane Kine, Huntington Beach, Calif.).

Wine-Tasting at a Bodega

Bodega Campos, 32 Coronel Cascajo, is the most festive-looking old tavern and wine cellar in Córdoba. It is accustomed to foreigners, who constantly seek it out near the Plaza del Potro (the entrance is by the little church of San Francisco). You can ramble through the long-beamed room, explore the rows of high-stacked barrels of aging wine, then perhaps have a glass of sherry in the courtyard, with its balcony and trailing flowers and vines. Don't miss the old iron gateway, or the well with its rope and bucket. The bodega receives visitors after 5 p.m. Count yourself lucky if you hear some spontaneous flamenco while you're there. Incidentally, if you have visited the Bullfight Museum, you will be given a signed ticket, allowing you two samples (free) of sherry. If you like a sweet one, try Chunga.

THE SIGHTS: The principal reason for visiting Córdoba is its Mezquita, now a cathedral. But the old Alcázar, an ancient synagogue, museums, and galleries will round out your day. There's a lot to absorb, and visitors with more time may want to spend at least two days here. We'll begin with the star attraction.

The Mezquita

The origins of this mosque go back to the eighth century. It was the crowning architectural achievement of the Moslems in the West, rivaled only by the mosque at Mecca. It is a fantastic labyrinth of red-and-white, peppermint-striped pillars. Wandering inside is like taking a journey through an enchanted forest of jasper and marble.

To the shock and astonishment of most visitors, a cathedral sits awkwardly in the middle of this mosque, mauling the purity of the lines. The cathedral, mostly 16th century plus a lot of other styles, is impressive enough, what with its intricately carved ceiling and baroque choir stalls. But who can forgive it—or its builders—for desecrating one of the most magnificent architectural treasures in Europe? Additional ill-conceived annexes later turned the Mezquita into one of the freak architectural sights of the world. The one most interesting feature of the mosque is the *mihrab,* a domed chapel-shrine of Byzantine mosaics that once housed the Koran.

The weird combination cathedral-mosque has some pretty weird hours to go with it. It is open all year in the mornings from 10:30 a.m. to 1:30 p.m. But its afternoon hours are staggered. From October to March, it's open from 3:30

to 6 p.m. The rest of the year it may be visited from 3:30 to 7 p.m. Admission is 100 pesetas (96¢).

After your exploration of the interior, you may want to stroll through the Courtyard of the Orange Trees, which has a beautiful fountain. My heartiest readers will climb a 16th-century tower that was built here on the base of a Moorish minaret. The tower is high, and offers a panoramic view of Córdoba and its environs.

The Alcázar of the Christian Kings

Started in 1328 by Alfonso XI ("The Just"), the Alcázar de los Reyes Cristianos is one of the best examples of military architecture of its day. This fortress on the river was once lived in by Ferdinand and Isabella, who governed Castile from here, and made preparations for the reconquest of Granada, the last Moorish stronghold in Spain. Columbus journeyed this way round about then to fill Isabella's ears with his plans for discovery.

The building is a quadrangle, characterized by powerful walls and a trio of towers—the Tower of the Lions, the Tower of Allegiance, and the Tower of the River. The walls of the Tower of the Lions (Leones) contain ogival ceilings that are intricately decorated, and considered the most notable example of Gothic architecture in Andalusia.

The Alcázar is visited in particular for its beautiful gardens, which are illuminated at night, and for its Moorish baths. Of the many patios of the Alcázar, the Patio Morisco is perhaps the loveliest, its pavement decorated with the arms of León and Castile. Also while here, be sure to seek out a distinguished Roman sarcophagus, representative of the funereal art of the second and third centuries A.D. The collection of Roman mosaics is also outstanding —especially in a unique piece dedicated to Polifemo and Galatea.

The Alcázar is open year round from 9:30 a.m. to 1:30 p.m. In the afternoon from May 1 to September 30, it is open from 5 to 8. From October 1 to April 30, its afternoon hours are from 4 to 7. The admission is 50 pesetas (48¢). The gardens, incidentally, are illuminated from May 1 to September 30 from 10 p.m. till 1 a.m. and it'll cost you a well-spent 50 pesetas (48¢) to stroll through.

The Synagogue

Córdoba possesses the most famous synagogue in Spain, one of three still remaining in the country (the other two are in Toledo). The mudéjar edifice was built in 1350 in the Barrio Judío (Jewish Quarter). The synagogue is noted particularly for its stucco work. The east wall contains a large orifice where the Tabernacle once was placed (inside were kept the scrolls of the Pentateuch). At the time Columbus was discovering America, the Jews were being expelled from Spain. The synagogue was then turned into a hospital, a role it played until 1588 when it became a Catholic chapel. The building may be visited during the day. No admission is charged, but the attendant will expect a tip.

The Fine Arts Museum

Housed in an old hospital founded by the Catholic monarchs, this picture gallery is at the Plaza del Potro ("Pony Square"). It contains the works of a number of the artists, including Zurbarán and Valdés Leal, Goya, Ribera, and Murillo. One salon is devoted to the works (or else reproductions of them) of locally born sculptor Mateo Inurria.

You enter through an Andalusian courtyard, and the visit makes for a cool and refreshing late-morning or afternoon interlude. It is open in the morning (all year) from 10 a.m. to 1:30 p.m. In July and August, as well as Sunday, it is open to 2 p.m. In November, December, and January, the afternoon hours are from 3:30 to 5 p.m.; in February, 3:30 to 7:30 p.m.; in March and October, 3:30 to 6 p.m.; and in April, May, June, and September, 4 to 7 p.m. The admission is 30 pesetas (29¢).

Museum of Julio Romero de Torres

Reached across the patio from the Fine Arts gallery, this museum honors a Córdoba-born artist who died in 1930. It has a certain novelty interest, for the artist particularly liked to paint nude women, such as the one seen in the celebrated *Naranjas y Limones* (orange and lemons). When you glimpse this nude, figure out which are the lemons. Other notable works include *The Little Girl Who Sells Fuel, El Pecado* (Sin), and *A Dedication to the Art of the Bullfight.* A corner of the studio that the artist once occupied in Madrid has been reproduced in one of the rooms, displaying paintings left unfinished at his death.

Incidentally, **La Plaza del Potro,** on which the museum stands, is one of the most characteristic of Córdoba. It is noted for its fountain, built in 1557, standing at one end of the square. The young stallion of the fountain has his forelegs raised, holding the shield of Córdoba. The gallery keeps the same hours as its sister museum (see above). There is no admission charge.

The Bullfight Museum (Museum Municipal de Arte Cordobés)

Near the Zoco, in an Andalusian-style, 16th-century building, this museum contains an impressive collection of bullfight paraphernalia, with memorabilia of the great Córdoban bullfighters, including stuffed bulls' heads, "suits of light," and pictures, trophies, and posters. That's Manolete over there in repose. You'll also see the blood-smeared uniform of El Cordobés. Both of the famed bullfighters came from Córdoba. The museum, at the Plazuela de Maimonides, may be visited from 9:30 a.m. to 1:30 p.m. The afternoon hours are 5 to 8 p.m. from May 1 through September 30; 4 to 7 p.m. from October 1 through April 30. Admission is 50 pesetas (48¢).

Other Sights

Córdoba also contains a **Roman bridge,** believed to date from the time of Emperor Augustus. It's hardly Roman anymore, as none of the 16 arches that support the bridge is original. In addition, the sculptor Bernabé Gómez del Río erected a statue to Saint Raphael in the middle of the bridge in 1651. On the other side of the Roman bridge is the **Tower of the Calahorra.** Henry II of Trastámara ordered this tower built in 1369 to protect him from his brother, Peter I. The tower betrays mudéjar architectural influences, as reflected in the arched ceilings of the chambers. In all, there are 14 good-size rooms, and the city of Córdoba uses them to house a museum of the town's history. For example, in one chamber are the three charters granted Córdoba by Ferdinand III. Another chamber honors Gonzalo Fernández de Córdoba, the Gran Capitán. Finally, one large room is called the Hall of the Americas. The tower keeps the same hours as the Alcázar, but admission here is 50 pesetas (48¢).

The Provincial Archeological Museum is one of the three most important archeological museums in Spain (it's rated just behind those of Madrid and Barcelona). It's housed in a palace dating from 1505 that once belonged to Páez de Castillejo. Arranged chronologically, the collection depicts the goods left behind by the various people and conquerors who have swept through the province of Córdoba—everything from Iberian hand weapons to Roman sarcophagi. Especially interesting are some Visigothic artifacts. The most outstanding collection, however, is devoted to Arabian art and records the entire Moslem occupation. In between exhibits, take a few minutes to relax in one of the patios, with its fountains and ponds. Admission is 25 pesetas (24¢).

One of the newest museums to open in Córdoba is the **Palacio de Viana** on the Plaza de Don Gome, which is open to the public from 9 a.m. to noon, charging 100 pesetas (96¢) for admission. Córdoba was once known for its palatial palaces, but few of them are open to the public. Visitors are shown into a carriage house, where the elegant vehicles of another era are displayed. In a city famed for its leather, these carriages have much leather decoration. In the elegant rooms, look for the leather wall hangings, some of which date from the period of the reconquest by the Christians. There's also a collection of leather paintings.

SHOPPING: In Moorish times Córdoboa was known for a peculiar kind of leather. This leather took its name from the city, whence is derived the word "cordwainer." This Córdoboan leather, so highly valued in 15th-century Europe, was studded with gold and silver ornaments, then painted with embossed designs *(guadamacil)*. These large panels from Córdoboa were used in many palaces in lieu of tapestries. Today the industry has fallen into great decline, the market filled with cheap imitations.

However, one shop in Córdoboa continues the old traditions **Meryan,** at 2 Calleja de las Flores, one of the most colorful streets in the city, is run by Angel Lopez-Obrero, aided by his two skilled sons, Alejandro and Carlos. They operate near the mosque in a building some 2 ½ centuries old. Their workshops are at the same address, and you can see artisans plying the age-old craft.

Usually items are custom ordered, but as a commercial retail outlet a selection of ready-to-go items are also sold, including cigarette boxes, jewel cases, attaché cases, book and folio covers, and ottoman covers, along with a large selection of other leather goods.

READER'S HOTEL SELECTION (CARMONA): "Between Seville and Córdoba is the small town of **Carmona.** At the southeastern edge of the ancient alcazaba wall sits the magnificent **Parador Alcázar del Rey Don Pedro** (tel. 14-10-10). The rooms are spacious, air-conditioned, and furnished with leather chairs, carved wooden pieces, animal hide rugs, and woven wall hangings. The common lounges have luxurious authentic furnishings. A large swimming pool surrounded by flowers (and overrun with bees) lies beneath the walls on the hillside. The parador's restaurant offers dishes native to the region, and the service is impeccable. A double room costs 3500 pesetas ($33.60); lunch or dinner, 950 pesetas ($9.12); and a continental breakfast, 250 pesetas ($2.40). On the other side of town is a Roman necropolis (cemetery) which contains the remains of 800 families who lived in the area about 2000 years ago. A 12-year-old guide gives a 30- or 60-minute tour in basic Spanish at a cost of approximately 50 pesetas (48¢) per person, plus tip. There's an archeological museum on the site. A large Roman amphitheater is being excavated" (Ronnee Lipman, Glen Rock, N. J.).

3. Seville

Once in a great while, a city emerges with a personality so unique it becomes famed throughout the world for its beauty and romance. Seville, the capital of Andalusia, is such a place. It is the most charming of Spanish cities, because its mysteries cannot be unveiled in a night, or even in a month of nights.

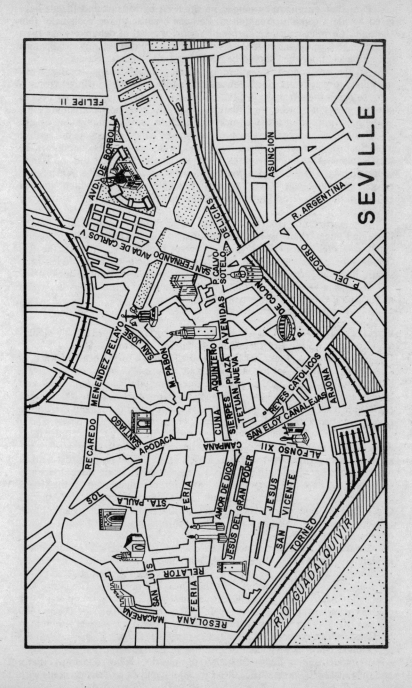

Don Juan and Carmen—aided no small bit by Mozart and Bizet—have given Seville a romantic reputation. Perhaps because of the acclaim of *Don Giovanni, Carmen,* and *The Barber of Seville,* a cabal of debunkers has risen to challenge this reputation of the city. But if a visitor can see only two Spanish cities in a lifetime, they should be Seville first and Toledo second.

All the words used to conjure up an image of Andalusia—orange trees, mantillas, lovesick toreadors, flower-filled patios, castanet-rattling gypsies—seem to reach their fruition in Seville. But it is no mere fluff of a city decked out for tourists; it is rather a substantial, progressive river port, containing some of the most important artistic works and architectural monuments in Spain.

Seville has undergone radical change at the hands of history, but, unlike most Spanish cities, it has fared rather well under most of its conquerors, be they Romans, Arabs, or Christians. Pedro the Cruel and Ferdinand and Isabella are only some of the many monarchs who have held court here. When Spain entered its Golden Age in the 16th century, Seville was the city which funneled gold from the New World into Spain. Columbus docked here after his journey to America.

Seville, romantic city that it is, was planned in my opinion more for the horse and buggy than the modern motorist of today. Driving within its precincts is a nightmare. Nearly all the streets run one way toward the Río Guadalquivir. Locating a hard-to-find restaurant or hotel on a hidden little square might require more than patience, and even a little bit of luck.

It takes at least two days to see most of the major sights of Seville, which means you'll need a roof over your head—

WHERE TO STAY: Seville's hotels, unlike its restaurants, are usually moderate in price—and most of them have Andalusian charm and style.

Hotel América, Plaza del Duque (tel. 22-09-51), in the heart of town, is a 100-bedroom hotel that has many superior features. All units contain private baths, as well as phones and radios. The hotel is mercifully air-conditioned, and in high season it charges 3400 pesetas ($32.64) in a double, from 1800 pesetas ($17.28) in a single. Rooms are small, usually with tiled floors, and everything is spic and span. Other superior features include wall-to-wall carpeting, and if you're there in winter, an individual heat control that works. One reader liked the "real beds that are long enough—not the usual hammock you get in Spain." Relaxing from sightseeing trips, you can rest in the TV lounge or order a drink in the Duque bar. Beside the hotel is a large car park, rising three floors and sheltering 600 cars (it's dangerous to leave your car unguarded on the streets of Seville at night). Although it doesn't have a major restaurant, the América does offer a tea room, cafetería, and snackbar, and if you're planning a shopping expedition, one of Spain's major chain department stores, El Corte Inglés, opens onto the same square.

Residencia Sevilla, 5 Daoiz (tel. 38-41-61), is a quietly secluded and moderately priced hotel. On a little plaza in the center of the city, it's typically Andalusian, with all the features that implies—a central glass-covered courtyard, a shaded patio, balconies, hanging vines, lots of plants. The entire first floor has old-fashioned, home-like furnishings. The comfortable and attractive double rooms with private bath peak at 2100 pesetas ($20.16); singles pay 1400 pesetas ($13.44) for rooms with showers. No meals are served other than breakfast, which costs an additional 125 pesetas ($1.20).

Hostal Ducal Residencia, 14 Plaza de la Encarnación (tel. 21-51-07), is a fairly modern hotel. Each of its airy, spacious double bedrooms has a bath, and the rate is 2300 pesetas ($22.08). Likewise, the five single rooms come with bath, and are 1500 pesetas ($14.40). The furnishings are a combination of provincial and utilitarian, efficient but with no particular style. Each room has its own telephone, as well as central heating (it does get cold in Seville). A continental breakfast can be brought to your room for an extra 130 pesetas ($1.25), but no other meals are served. English is spoken. The location is handy to many of those specialty shops along narrow streets. Several buses stop nearby.

Fleming, 3 Calles Sierra Nevada y Concepción (tel. 36-19-00), lies at the end of a cul-de-sac in the Puerta de Carmona sector. Although snugly tucked away, it is, nevertheless, within walking distance of Old Seville. You get airy, well-furnished, and comfortable bedrooms, and doubles with private bath rent for 3000 pesetas ($28.80), singles with shower baths for 2400 pesetas ($23.04). For another 200 pesetas ($1.92) per person, a continental breakfast is served. If you like natural woods combined with chalk-white walls; long, low built-in headboards with bedside lights; room telephones; and air conditioning—then the Fleming is for you.

The lounges, including the bar, are also modern, with leather chairs and wood paneling. Guests gather on the rooftop solarium, enjoying views of the old narrow streets. On the premises is a snackbar and restaurant, serving three meals a day.

Hotel Simón, 19 García de Vinuesa (tel. 22-66-60), is a one-star hotel at the rear end of the Giralda, suitable for some who can stand the noise. The side street seems to be what one reader called "the local drag strip for Vespa motor scooters." If you can stand that, you'll find the hotel an old-fashioned charmer. Before its present reincarnation, the hotel was a fine Sevillian private mansion, typical of those built in the city in the 18th and 19th centuries. Transformed to meet the standards of a hotel with up-to-date requirements, it is on a side street. The best singles rent for 650 pesetas ($6.24), the price going up to 1100 pesetas ($10.56) in a double, plus another 110 pesetas ($1.06) per person for a continental breakfast. The best arrangement is to stay here on the full-board plan, costing 1250 pesetas ($12) per person daily, based on double occupancy. The food is good, and the service is excellent. The chandelier-lit dining room is in the old Moorish style.

Residencia Murillo, 7 Lope de Rueda (tel. 21-60-95), is tucked away deep in the heart of Santa Cruz, the old quarter. In fact, it's almost next to the gardens of the Alcazar on a street so narrow you can practically peer into the bedroom in the house across the way—the houses in the "barrio" are that close together.

The Murillo is named after the artist who used to live in this district. Inside, the lounges harbor some fine architectural characteristics and antique reproductions. Behind a grilled screen is a retreat for drinks.

A double room with private bath rents for 2200 pesetas ($21.12); singles pay 1600 pesetas ($15.36) for rooms with bath, 1300 pesetas ($12.48) with shower only. A continental breakfast is an extra 150 pesetas ($1.44) per person. Many of the rooms I recently inspected were cheerless and gloomy, so ask to have a look before checking in. Like all the hotels of Seville, the Murillo is in a noisy area.

You can reach this residencia from the Menéndez Pelayo, a wide avenue that lies west of María Luisa Park, where there's a sign that will take you through the Murillo Gardens on the left. Motorists should try to park in the Plaza de Santa Cruz. You can then walk two blocks to the hotel, which will send a bellhop back to the car to pick up your suitcases.

READERS' HOTEL SELECTIONS: "**Hostal Residencia Jentoft,** 2 Benidorm (tel. 22-09-81), charges 600 pesetas ($5.76) in a single, 950 pesetas ($9.12) in a double. A continental breakfast is an extra 100 pesetas (96¢) per person. It may be difficult to find—it is about two blocks from the Plaza de Armas railroad station. Take the street that angles off from the right side of the station, turn right into the narrow street just past the large Michelin sign. The hotel is indicated by Residencia Z. H. Walk upstairs to the first door on the right" (L. L. Farkas, Tucson, Ariz.). . . . "Our outstanding find has been the **Hostal Linense,** 66 Calle Gravina (tel. 22-92-85). The hostal is maintained in spotless condition, and the meals are excellent. For our midday meal, we had paella, grilled fish, eggs, ham, and fruit salad. The inclusive tariff for a double room with wash basin, hot and cold water, and three meals is 1550 pesetas ($14.88) per day per person, based on double occupancy. The bathroom and toilet are kept in spotless order" (F. Wherritt, London, England). . . . "The **Casa Moreno Hostal,** 15 Avenida de Cádiz (tel. 23-47-95), is within sight of the Cádiz Station. The owners speak no English, but are good at sign language and understanding broken Spanish—very friendly and helpful. They charge 750 pesetas ($7.20) for a double, 1100 pesetas ($10.56) for a triple. A continental breakfast is another 100 pesetas (96¢) per person" (R. E. Shelgren, Paris, France). . . . "I highly recommend the **Hostal Residencia Alcázar,** 10 Menéndez Pelayo (tel. 23-19-91). A nice double room with bath and breakfast costs 3000 pesetas ($28.80). The concierge speaks good English. Excellently located, it is on the main road through Seville for traveling north or south. Behind the hotel is a street that leads directly to the nearby train station, and on this street halfway down the block on the left is an enclosed garage with all-night guards to watch your car. Across the street from the hotel is a nice park, and this is where one can hire one of the horse-drawn open carriages for a fun tour of the city" (John R. Miller, Jr., Washington, D.C.).

WHERE TO EAT: Nearly all of the major restaurants known and frequented by tourists in Seville have increased their prices considerably in the past few years. In response to the trend, budget-seeking Europeans have turned to other restaurants, seeking out less-frequented establishments where the Sevillians have been blissfully eating for years. Let's get off the main trail and follow their lead. I'll begin, as usual, with the budget choices, then follow with a big splurge.

Casa Cavillo, 64 Sierpes, is one of the best all-around budget restaurants in Seville, noted for such Andalusian treats as gazpacho and fried fish. Even the paella, borrowed from the Valencian kitchen, is good. This casa sits smack dab in the middle of Seville, in the heart of its most popular shopping district. The streets in this section are so narrow that only pedestrians are allowed on them. For only 600 pesetas ($5.76), a three-course cubierto is featured that on my last trip included paella, chicken, and croquettes—but it must be eaten standing up at the bar. For 800 pesetas ($7.68), big eaters can get a more varied repast, plus one extra course, and a chair. The Casa Calvillo has more dining nooks than Seville has beautiful señoritas. It is a virtual maze of dining rooms, and its al fresco tables monopolize the sidewalks.

La Isla, 23 Arfe (tel. 21-26-31), extremely noisy, is unquestionably popular, although it's gone a bit high hat on us, adding such refinements as air conditioning. Once little more than a workingperson's dining spot, the Isla now appeals to tourists also. A set meal costs 650 pesetas ($6.24), and for that price, you get reasonably good cooking—including such typical dishes as sole covered with a tasty sauce, grilled liver, chicken croquettes. At an appealing bar at the front, guests can order a before-dinner sherry. The restaurant huddles close to a food market, giving you a view into the daily lives of Sevillians.

El Puerto Restaurant, 59 Betis (tel. 27-03-60), with its multilevel dining terrace, has the best ventilation in town. It is across the river in Triana, its many tables sloping right down to the waterfront. Connoisseurs of Andalusian dishes have been navigating their way here for years. The food is served in a surrounding of shrubbery, palms, and vines. Recorded music plays softly, and in summer it's cool and relaxed here, except on Sunday and holidays when a carnival-like atmosphere prevails. The restaurant's more than creditable cuisine is for those who take their food seriously. Usually reliable dishes include the special paella, sole and red mullet, a cazuela de mariscos (casserole of shellfish), baked lamb, and a varied fish fry. The special menú del día costs 650 pesetas ($6.24), including wine. Closed Monday.

Casa Senra, 41 Bécquer, about three blocks from the Marcarena gate, is an old standby for knowledgeable Sevillians. Although unprepossessing from the outside, once you are through the tapas-loaded bar, you find a pleasant, beamed-ceiling dining room with checkered tablecloths, white arches, air conditioning, and hams hanging from the rafters. For 650 pesetas ($6.24), you get a bowl of seafood soup (sopa de picadillo); followed by a rodaballo (fish) so big you can hardly finish it; beer, bread, and dessert. À la carte specialties go a bit higher and might include gazpacho, a seafood omelet, trout in sherry, Basque-style hake, and paella for two. For dessert, try the baked apple or fruit salad. If you order à la carte, expect to pay from 650 pesetas ($6.24) to 1000 pesetas ($9.60) per person. The clientele is mostly well-to-do locals.

El Bodegón Torre del Oro, 29 Santander, merits a resounding olé. The specialties of this three-fork house include Andalusian gazpacho (only in spring and summer), paella de arroz Bodegón (made with chicken, vegetables, and varied shellfish), and the most popular dish of all, pollo al ajillo (chicken cooked with garlic).

You'll undoubtedly like the rustic atmosphere here—Spain itself, reflected in the hanging hams, the old oil paintings, crude tables and simple chairs. The evening begins in the bar section, where all sorts of wines are available, along with the traditional tapas of prawns, lobsters, etc. The Torre del Oro also offers a 550-peseta ($5.28) menu that includes gazpacho; then veal or paella; and flan at the end. You can also eat at the bar, which is cheaper. There, half a roast chicken is 270 pesetas ($2.59); entrecôte, 650 pesetas ($6.24); and squid, 450 pesetas ($4.32).

READERS' RESTAURANT SUGGESTIONS: "We found a tiny restaurant (only about 12 tables), **Los Duendes,** 45 Contero, on a little side street near the cathedral. The food is very good, especially the veal cooked in its own juice. We had an excellent dinner here for about 650 pesetas ($6.24) per person. It looks like a long gypsy cave, and the staff is very friendly and attentive. We got the impression that the bar across the street was connected to this restaurant in some way; and the waiters would hurry across the street and come back with beer or ice cream on a tray, having picked up same in the bar. It made the service interesting to watch" (Mrs. William P. Duggan, Burlington, Ontario, Canada). . . . "For a good dinner in interesting surroundings, we recommend the **Hostería del Laurel,** 5 Plaza de los Venerables (tel. 22-02-95), which is in the Old City (Barrio de Santa Cruz). There is a bar and dining area on the first floor. We chose the second floor, which is strictly the dining room. The food is excellent, and the prices are reasonable. A set meal costs 750 pesetas ($7.20)" (Mr. and Mrs. John E. Freeland, Winter Haven, Fla.). . . . "While in Seville we ate one night at a restaurant recommended by James Michener in *Iberia.* **El Mesón** (The Inn), 26 Calle del Dos de Mayo (tel. 21-83-65), within easy walking distance of the Residencia Murillo where we stayed. For dessert we had membrillo and manchego cheese which were suggested by Michener and now called 'The Michener Combination' on the menu. The restaurant is decorated with pictures of John Fulton (the American bullfighter), Kenneth Vanderford (the poor man's Hemingway), Michener, and other celebrities. There are also several excellent drawings of bulls and Spanish cowboys by John Fulton. With meals costing 550 pesetas ($5.28) to 750 pesetas ($7.20), the restaurant certainly deserves to be in your book" (Mrs. John H. MacKenzie, American Embassy ATO).

"Try the **Casa Diego** at 7 Place Curtidores. There is a tourist dinner for 475 pesetas ($4.56). It's a small place and they only speak Spanish, but the food is good and you can't equal the price" (R. E. Shelgren, Paris, France). . . . "Add the air-conditioned restaurant **Los Robles** (tel. 21-31-50), 58 Calle Alvarez Quintero (the same street, incidentally, as the restaurant Los Duendes, since Alvarez Quintero and Contero have a common stem), in the shadow of the cathedral. Four adults had a splendid meal here, including a preliminary drink, soups, an excellent Sevillana assortment of fried fish, some escalloped veal, a delightful grilled sole, desserts which included a specially aged manchego cheese, coffee, a first-rate (at the price) house wine, and bread—all at an average price of about 1000 pesetas ($9.60) per person. The excellent menú del día is only 500 pesetas ($4.80), and the service is impeccable" (J. F. R. Taylor, Winnipeg, Manitoba, Canada). . . . "The **Mesón Don Raimundo,** 26 Argote de Molina (tel.22-33-55), offers an excellent menu of the day for only 950 pesetas ($9.12) each. For the first of the three courses we both had a good gazpacho. We followed this with a tasty veal casserole and hake. For dessert I had a fresh, fresh fruit salad, and my companion had homemade ice cream. The usual carafe of house wine and crisp bread rolls were in the overall charge. We were particularly pleased with the ambience. Based in a tastefully converted old house, the dining room was spacious and scrupulously clean, with a charming decor. Many fascinating antique objects—old copper, pottery, and wrought-iron work—backed up the warm glow from the open fire in the center. The service was faultless, and the toilets were the most attractive I saw in Spain" (Emma Wood, London, England). . . . "For those who crave ice cream, I suggest **Horchata Fillol,** Calle de Sierpes. There you can order a nice sundae for 85 pesetas (82¢), strawberries with whipped cream for 115 pesetas ($1.10), and ice cream cones, as well as horchata. . . . For tapas, I recommend the **Bar Modesto,** at the northern end of Murillo Park, for excellent seafood hors d'oeuvres and a great variety of others, averaging 75 pesetas (72¢) to 125 pesetas ($1.20) a serving, and **Bodegón Pez de Espada,** between Calle Colón and Calle Cabo Noval, near the cathedral for generous portions of seafood at 75 pesetas (72¢) to 100 pesetas (96¢)" (Joseph W. Zdenek, Rock Hill, S.C.).

"**Mesón El Tenorio,** 11 Mateos Gago (tel. 21-40-30), is a small restaurant just behind the cathedral which keeps very busy. It is full of atmosphere, and if you can get a table you can dine on excellent food, each course plentiful and cheap. The food is prepared and cooked at the back of the restaurant and the smells are most attractive and mouthwatering. Specialties are roast lamb and fresh fish. We had a three-course meal with coffee and wine for 700 pesetas ($6.72) each" (Dr. and Mrs. C. H. Chaffey, Dapto, N.S.W., Australia). . . . "What a blessing to find the **Cafetería Restaurante Nuevo Coliséo,** 3 Plaza Calvo Sotelo and 17 Almirante Lobo (tel. 22-96-42). Everything is spotlessly clean, the menu is in English, the employees are efficient and helpful, and the dishes are all appetizing and not floating in oil. There are outside tables, and inside, there is a stand-up bar. But the trick is to go upstairs where there is a cafetería counter. The chicken salad is delicious. The menú del día goes for 575 pesetas ($5.52). The restaurant is right on the corner of a street that goes by the river, near the Puente San Telmo (middle bridge). Follow Avenida de José Antonio from the cathedral to the river. It's a short walk" (Mrs. Elson E. Flowers, Orlando, Fla.). . . . "We were pleased with the large number of choices on the menú del día and with the quality of the food at **Los Alcazares,** 10 Miguel de Manara (tel. 21-31-03), between the Alcázar and the Archives of the Indies. Salad Andaluz, with tomato, green pepper, and onion in about equal proportions, olive oil, and vinegar, was especially good at 225 pesetas ($2.16). Most main dishes are priced from 400 pesetas ($3.84) to 500 pesetas ($4.80). A complete meal here will cost from 900 pesetas ($8.64) to 1500 pesetas ($14.40)" (Norriss Hetherington, Berkeley, Calif.).

THE TOP SIGHTS: Seville has an astonishing number of palaces, churches, cathedrals, towers, and historic hospitals. Since it would take a great deal of time to visit all of them, I have narrowed the sights down to a handful of representative ones, which include all of the most famous and frequented places.

The Cathedral

This huge Gothic building, at the Plaza V. de los Reyes, ranks with St. Paul's in London and St. Peter's in Rome in size. Work began on it in the late 1400s, and it took centuries to complete. Built on the site of an ancient mosque, the cathedral claims that it contains the remains of Columbus, his tomb mounted on four sculptured men. (A digression: Many historians believe the remains of Columbus were taken to what is now the Dominican Republic sometime in the mid-16th century. However, in correspondence with me, the Secretary of the Metropolitan Chapter maintains that the remains were moved to the Cathedral of Havana, Cuba, and finally, at the beginning of this century, in 1902, were shipped to the Seville cathedral. The Metropolitan Chapter keeps documents to this effect.)

The cathedral abounds in artistic works, many of them architectural, such as the stained-glass windows (some dating from the 15th century); the rejas (the iron screens closing off the chapels); the 15th-century choir stalls—gilt and velvet and elaborately carved; and, finally, the Gothic reredos above the main altar, a beautiful carving begun in the 15th century. During Corpus Christi and the Immaculate Conception observances, the altar boys do their dance of the castanets in front of the High Altar.

In the treasury you'll find minor works by Goya, Murillo, and Zurbarán; and here, in glass cases, a touch of the macabre shows up in the display of skulls.

After your tour of the dark interior, you can emerge into the sunlight again by entering the Patio of Orange Trees, with its fresh citrus scents and chirping birds. The cathedral soars into the sky, creating a sense of infinity. At night it is illuminated, and the effect of the Gothic fantasy is complete.

The cathedral may be visited from 10:30 a.m. to 12:30 p.m. and 4 to 6:30 p.m. In winter, the afternoon hours are 4 to 6. Admission is 75 pesetas (72¢).

La Giralda Tower

This Moorish tower is the city's most famous monument. Erected as a minaret in the 12th century, it has seen later additions, such as 16th-century bells. Just as the Big Ben tower symbolizes London, La Giralda conjures up Seville. It is that important a landmark. To climb it is to take one of the walks of a lifetime. There are no steps—you ascend a ramp that seems endless. Should you make it to the top, the view of Seville is dazzling. The city is literally spread out at your feet. The old rule forbidding persons to go up alone has been done away with; authorities now assume you won't jump. Admission is 25 pesetas (24¢).

The Alcázar

This is a magnificent mudéjar palace, built in the 14th century by Pedro the Cruel. From the Dolls' Court to the Maidens' Court through the domed Ambassadors' Room, it contains some of the finest work of Sevillian craftsmen. Isabella and Ferdinand, who used to live here, also influenced its architectural evolution, as did Carlos V. On the top floor, the Oratory of the Catholic monarchs has a fine altar in polychrome tiles made by Pisano in 1504.

The mudéjar style as exemplified by the facade was developed by Moslems working in Christian Spain following the final ousting of the Moors from Granada. Thus inspiration of the style is both Gothic and Moslem. This lavish palace in Seville is considered by some to be worthy of comparison with the Alhambra at Granada.

The well-kept gardens, filled with beautiful flowers, shrubbery, and fruit trees, are alone worth the visit. Hours are 9 a.m. to 12:45 p.m. year round; 4 to 6:30 on summer afternoons; 3 to 5:30 in winter. On Sunday it is open only in the morning. Admission is 105 pesetas ($1.01) to the palace. If you wish to view only the gardens, the charge is 35 pesetas (34¢).

Hospital de la Santa Carídad

This 17th-century hospital is intricately linked to the legend of Miguel Manara. Such French writers as Dumas and Prosper Mérimée have portrayed him as a scandalous Don Juan. It has been suggested that he built this institution to atone for his sins. However, this has proved false. Manara had a "brave and chivalrous youth," but the death of his young and beautiful wife in 1661 caused such grief, he retired from society and entered the "Charity Brotherhood." There he spent the rest of his life, burying corpses of the sick and diseased as well as condemned and executed criminals. Today the members of this brotherhood of Saint Charity, as did their founder, tend the poor, old, and invalids who have no one else to help them. Nuns show you through the courtyard, which is festive in colors of orange and sienna, and of different architectural styles. The baroque chapel contains works by Murillo and Valdés Leal, a 17th-century Spanish painter. As you're leaving the chapel, look over the exit door. Here you'll find one of the most macabre pictures I've ever seen—that of an archbishop being devoured by maggots. Somehow Leal's worms compensate for Murillo's pink cherubs. The hospital is open from 10 a.m. to 1 p.m. and from 3:15 to 7 p.m. all year. Admission is 50 pesetas (48¢).

OTHER SIGHTS: The 12-sided **Tower of Gold** overlooks the Guadalquivir River. Its lower base was built in the 13th century. Originally, it was covered with gold tiles—hence, its name—but someone long ago made off with them. Recently restored, the tower has been turned into a maritime museum. It is open from 10 a.m. to 2 p.m. daily, except Monday (on Sunday the tower closes at 1 p.m.). The price of admission is 20 pesetas (19¢).

To go to Seville and miss seeing an Andalusian palace would be a sad state of affairs. The Duchess of Alba no longer allows tourists to traipse through her inner sanctum, but it's quite easy to visit the **Casa de Pilatos,** the 16th-century palace of the dukes of Medinaceli, 1 Plaza de Pilatos (tel. 22-52-98).

Recapturing the splendor of the past, it combines the styles of Gothic, mudéjar, and plateresque in its courtyards, fountains, and salons. According to tradition, this house was supposed to be a reproduction of Pilate's House in Jerusalem. Don't miss the two wonderful old carriages, or the rooms filled with Greek and Roman statues. The painting collection includes works by Carreño, Pantoja de la Cruz, Sebastiano del Piombo, Lucas Jordan, Batalloli, Pacheco, and Goya. At the Plaza de Pilatos, the mansion may be visited from 9 a.m. to 1 p.m. and 4 to 8 p.m. in summer, from 10 a.m. to 1 p.m. and 3 to 6 p.m. in winter. The fee is 100 pesetas (96¢).

Continuing our exploration, in the lovely old convent off the Calle de Alfonso XII you'll find one of the most important art collections in Spain, housed in the **Museo de Bellas Artes** (Fine Arts Museum). A whole gallery here is devoted to one painting by El Greco of his son, but Seville-born Murillo and his devoutly religious paintings are the highlights. Works by Zurbarán are also exhibited. The 17th-century artist Valdés Leal with his dramatic, macabre paintings is represented as well, with an entire wing devoted to his works. He did not believe in subtlety: in his painting of John the Baptist's head on a platter, he included his knife—in case you didn't get the point. I find the top floor less interesting, with its so-called modern paintings.

The art gallery is open from 10 a.m. to 2 p.m. all year. It's closed on Monday. Admission is 150 pesetas ($1.44).

No sightseeing trip to Seville would be complete without a . . .

Stroll through Santa Cruz

What was once a ghetto of Spanish Jewry is now the aristocratic quarter of Old Seville. The streets of Santa Cruz are no bigger than alleyways, and have such names as "Vida" or "Muerte" (Life, Death). Flower-filled balconies with draping bougainvillea jut out over this labyrinth, shading you from the noonday sun or lunar rays. Here you can look through numerous wrought-iron gates into the patios filled with fountains and plants. In the evening, it is a common sight to see Sevillians sitting outside drinking icy sangria under the glow of lanterns. This old district, where Murillo used to live, can be entered through several streets, but the main one is northeast of the Alcázar. Its whitewashed houses are within easy walking distance of most of my hotel recommendations.

Now we head up the Avenida de Isabel la Católica for the . . .

Park of María Luisa

This vast tract of parkland in the eastern part of the city was once the private grounds of a palace. In 1929, Seville was to host the Spanish-American Exhibition, and many pavilions from the countries in the western hemisphere were erected here. The worldwide Depression brought havoc to the exhibition, but the pavilions still stand.

The principal one, at the Plaza de España, is a crescent-shaped building, accompanied by an arch-shaped lagoon with five arched and tiled bridges leading to it. It's a fantastic palace, and I commend the Sevillians for preserving it. Strollers come here on hot summer nights, enjoying the fountains and the many lovers' lanes.

The **Archeological Museum** is in the park at the Plaza de América, and it contains many artifacts from prehistoric times (Carambolo Treasure) and the days of the Romans, Visigoths, and Moors. It may be visited from 10 a.m. to 2 p.m., except Monday, for an admission fee of 150 pesetas ($1.44).

That Famous Tobacco Factory

At this point in your visit, you may wonder what happened to Carmen's tobacco factory (known more formally as the **Real Fábrica de Tabacos).** If you continue up the Calle San Fernando, you'll discover that the factory has gone to college . . . and so can we.

When Carmen waltzed out of the tobacco factory in the first act of Bizet's opera, this 18th-century building became world famous. But if you go there today, you'll find that serious students have replaced the "free-loving, cigarette-smoking Andalusian beauties."

By all means, explore the building at your leisure (although you may find it closed during part of the summer). It is near the landmark luxury hotel, the Alfonso XII. So far, no one charges admission.

The April Fair and Holy Week

Many tourists consider attending the April Fair in Seville reason enough for coming to Europe. Seville's April Fair is the most famous one in the country, although it was inaugurated as "recently" as 1847, unlike some of the age-old fairs in Spain. The Andalusians—perhaps more so than most people—seem to know how to prepare a proper greeting for spring.

Holy Week comes first, from Palm Sunday until Easter. Through the streets of Seville are paraded the wooden figures called *pasos.* But by far the most interesting processions are those of the hooded and robed penitents, who look like—but certainly are not—members of the KKK.

The fería usually begins in mid-April, lasting less than a week. The Andalusian women wear their traditional costumes; floats and carriages are festooned with flowers; horseback-riding men and their señoritas gallop through the traffic-free streets.

The April Fair is a showcase of Spanish folklore and customs, from bullfights (the best) to flamenco. Festively decorated tent-like pavilions—called *casetas*—are set up by the Sevillians, and they go camping until the fair is over. Lucky is the visitor who gets invited by one of the locals to his temporary home. Wine and food are constantly being served. At night, the fair is illuminated by miles of colored lights . . . a magnificent carnival atmosphere.

Despite all this gaiety and glamour, don't go to Seville at that time unless you have reservations (make them months in advance). Virtually every tourist on two continents, it would seem, including the Spaniards, floods into the city, occupying every accomodation from the most luxurious suite to the dankest room in the lowliest pension. To arrive for the fair without a reservation would be foolish indeed, unless you plan to book accomodations in a neighboring city and commute.

At any time of the year, however, you can enjoy:

FLAMENCO: When the moon is high in Seville—and the scent of orange blossoms is in the air—it's time to walk through the alleyways of Santa Cruz in search of the sound of castanets.

Los Gallos (The Roosters), 11 Plaza de Santa Cruz (tel. 21-69-81), is in a converted town house, transformed to provide a showcase for flamenco artists. In air-conditioned comfort, you can hear flamenco from 10 p.m. till dawn. Many clients sit transfixed throughout the night. You pay a total of 1000 pesetas ($9.60), including the cover charge and your first drink. Marie J. Low of Anaheim, California, wrote: "There is absolutely no pressure to buy another drink. I consider it money very well spent." All of the seats have a clear view, even those on the tiny mezzanine. Reservations should be made before 6 p.m.

El Patio Sevillano, 11 Paseo de Cristóbal Colón (tel. 21-41-20), is a showcase of Spanish folk. The presentation may take the form of flamenco or Andalusian songs, or perhaps classical Spanish music and dance, with works by Falla, Albéniz, Granados, and Chueca. Two shows are presented nightly, one at 9:30 and another at 11:30. Sometimes an early show is performed at 7:30 p.m.

The entrance fee and cover charge is 1000 pesetas ($9.60), although you'll pay 250 pesetas ($2.40) for your second drink. Near the Guadalquivir River in the center of the city, the club faces the Triana quarter and the Torre del Oro (Tower of Gold).

READER'S FLAMENCO RECOMMENDATION: "**La Trocha,** 23–25 Ronda de Capuchinos (tel. 355-028), has a mixed revue, including flamenco, popular Spanish songs, and Sevillian songs and dances. The crowd includes a good sprinkling of tourists but is far more solidly Sevillian than the crowd at Los Gallos where I doubt there is even one Spaniard in the audience. Los Gallos bills itself as *puro flamenco,* and this may be true. For performer-audience rapport, however, La Trocha is much more fun. We were advised to take taxis because of an unpredictable neighborhood" (John R. Miles, Malibu, Calif.).

READER'S SIGHTSEEING TIPS: "The ruins of the Roman city of **Italica** are well worth a visit. They lie on a hill about six miles northwest of Seville, near the village of Santiponce on the main road to Lisbon, and are easily reached by car or bus. Italica was founded in 206 B.C. and was the first important Roman settlement in the Iberian peninsula. The renowned emperors Trajan and Hadrian were both born of noble families in Italica. After about the fourth century Italica was abandoned, and in the Middle Ages the city was mercilessly plundered. Serious excavations started in about the mid-19th century. The great amphitheater is one of the finest in existence, and the recently excavated theater and streets, lined with patrician houses of magnificent colored mosaics, are memorable" (Dr. and Mrs. E. McC. Callan, Canberra, Australia). . . . "To reach Italica, take a bus at the Paseo de Cristóbal Colón, in front of Casa Luís. Your bus is the Coche de Santiponce, costing 30 pesetas (29¢). It runs every half hour, the trip taking a half hour to the ruins, where a return bus leaves every half hour. Admission is 60 pesetas (58¢), and it's well worth it. There's an amphitheater, as well as a small museum. Don't miss the mosaics of the birds, gods, and days of the week. There are also original Roman lead pipes, and waterways from the amphitheater connecting directly with the Guadalquivir River. If you're very lucky, a small, enthusiastic Spaniard will pick you up and give you a complete, detailed guided tour—all in his accented Sevillian Spanish. Bring a dictionary. He will refuse any recompense. This could be one of the highpoints of your visit to Spain" (Dr. D. Duberman, Southampton, N.Y.). . . . "If you are interested in Spanish customs, take the local bus which stops on one of the corners of the Plaza Encarnación marked 'Cemetery' on a Sunday morning. I have never witnessed anything as spectacular as the droves of people bringing fresh flowers to the graves, as well as the scrubbing, painting, and maintenance by each family of its own marble grave sites. The landscaping is beautiful, with huge cedars and lovely shrubs—all immaculately cared for" (Shirley Dichtl, Warrenville, Ohio).

READER'S RESTAURANT SUGGESTION (OUTSIDE SEVILLE): "Directly across the road from the entrance to Italica is a delightful restaurant named **Bentorrillo Canario.** We were attracted by the delicious smells of the mojo picón—cuts of meat which are grilled as one chooses them. You pay by the weight of the meat. It may be a slight splurge, but four of us had eight-ounce steaks, a large communal salad with regional olives, french fries in addition to the small baked potato which accompanies the meat, fresh bread, wine, and Pepsis for about 850 pesetas ($8.16) each. The decor is rustic—fireplace, rough stone walls, and wagon-wheel windows. It is very clean and frequented by many Spaniards, as it is definitely not a "tourist trap" (Debi Grout, Madrid, Spain).

4. Jerez and Cádiz

After leaving Seville, those who have an extra day can take a change-of-pace adventure and visit the bodegas at Jerez (Sherry) de la Frontera as well as the Atlantic port city of Cádiz. We'll begin with Jerez, about 60 miles south of Seville.

JEREZ DE LA FRONTERA: This is that charming little Andalusian town that has made a bridge to England with the thousands and thousands of casks of golden sherry it has shipped there over the centuries. Steeped in the past, with origins going back nearly 3000 years, Jerez today is primarily a modern, progressive town with wide boulevards, although it does have an interesting old quarter. Yet the reason that busloads of visitors pour in every year is to get those free drinks at one of the bodegas where wine is aged and bottled.

The town is pronounced either "Herez" or "Her-eth," depending on whether you're Andalusian or Castilian. The French, the Moors, etc., have called it various names—Hérès, Scheris—and somehow, as they are wont, the English corrupted this to Sherry (the "valour" of sherry was extolled by no less an authority than Shakespeare).

Jerez is easily reached by bus or rail from Seville. We'll begin our exploration with . . .

Touring the Bodegas

Jerez is surrounded by the aristocratic vineyards of Spain, and the ideal time to visit is during the grape harvest in September. However, visitors are assured of the finest in hospitality all year, because Jerez is widely known for its warm welcome.

There must be more than a hundred bodegas in and around Jerez, where you can not only see how sherries are made, bottled, and aged, but where you can get free samples as well. Among the most famous brands are Pedro Domecq and Gonzalez Byass, the maker of Tío Pepe.

On a typical visit to a bodega, you are shown through several high-ceilinged buildings which house all of the makings of the sherries and brandies. One building will have facilities for the pressing and sorting of grapes; another will be a bottling plant; a third will be filled with thousands of large oak casks (probably imported from America).

Sometimes you are taken to a bodega or wine tavern and shown some bottles of the oldest wine in Jerez. Sometimes such personages as Juan Carlos I, King of Spain, have come through here and autographed their favorite barrels.

After a typical tour, guests may go to an attractive bar where variously colored and different-tasting sherries—amber, dark gold, cream, something red, sweet, and velvety—can be sampled. *Warning:* These sherries are more potent that one might at first suspect. If offered, try the very dry La Ina or the brandy, Fundador, one of the most popular in the world.

If you're here at harvest time in the fall, by all means pay a visit to the vineyards, one of the most fascinating sights in Spain.

When you arrive in town, go to the **Tourist Office** (Turismo) on Alamede Cristina (tel. 34-20-37), to learn what bodegas are open and which ones are welcoming visitors. Most often you'll have to take a taxi from the Tourist Office to the bodega, where you'll be assigned a guide.

Regrettably, many of the bodegas are closed in August (some shut down in July). However, many reopen by the third week of August, although several others are closed until the first of September when the wine festival gets going.

Since many people come to Jerez just to visit a bodega, they can be seriously disappointed. To avoid being thwarted, you can make a side trip to the village of **Lebrija,** lying about halfway between Jerez and Seville, 8½ miles west of the main highway.

Lebrija is a local winemaking center where some very fine sherries are made. At one small bodega, that of Juan García, you are courteously escorted around by the owner. However, there are several other bodegas in Lebrija, and the local citizens will gladly point them out to you if asked.

At Lebrija you can get a glimpse of rural Spain.

Where to Stay

The town has no nightlife to speak of, and a minimum of hotels—but this works out reasonably well, since most bodega-hopping visitors come just for the day, then press on to Cádiz by nightfall, or head back to Seville. However, for readers staying over, here are my recommendations.

Nuevo Hostal, 23 Angel Mayo (as there is no street sign, look for a plaque which says "Manzana 219" off the Plaza de los Reyes Católicos; tel. 33-16-30), is a little peseta saver, frequented mostly by Spaniards. Rates are 1500 pesetas ($14.40) for the best double rooms with shower, 1150 pesetas ($11.04) for a double with less plumbing. Singles rent for 800 pesetas ($7.68). A 20% supplement is charged if you don't take your meals here. At the three-meals-a-day rate of 1150 pesetas ($11.04), few can afford to say no (meals are large and good). The entrance has superb 12-foot-high doors, with grillwork like a town house. Inside, the small lobby is three floors high and covered with glass in the

Andalusian style. The bedrooms are large for the most part, pleasingly old-fashioned.

One of the best streets for those shopping around for budget hotels is the Calle Higueras, off Calle Fermin Aranda, and Calle Juan C. Duran.

Here you'll find such "hostals" as **Las Palomas,** 17 Higueras (tel. 34-37-73), where a bathless single room ranges in price from 700 pesetas ($6.72) to 900 pesetas ($8.64); and doubles, also bathless, are priced anywhere from 1100 pesetas ($10.56) to 1400 pesetas ($13.44). A continental breakfast is an extra 125 pesetas ($1.20) per person.

Another good possibility, **Joma,** 22 Juan C. Duran (tel. 34-98-69), offers bathless singles at 700 pesetas ($6.72) and doubles with private baths for 1400 pesetas ($13.44) to 2200 pesetas ($21.12). A continental breakfast is an extra 125 pesetas ($1.20) per person.

The **Alhambra,** 20 Higueras (tel. 34-98-95), is another bargain in that it offers bathless doubles for 1000 pesetas ($9.60), bathless singles for 600 pesetas ($5.76). For 90 pesetas (86¢) per person, a continental breakfast will be served.

Best, but plastic new, is the **Mica,** 7 Juan Carlos Duran (tel. 34-07-00). Eight of its 38 rooms are singles. All have air conditioning, bath, and telephone. There's a pleasant bar downstairs for those espresso coffees, and a very modern breakfast lounge. Mica rates only two stars, and it certainly deserves three. Rooms cost 1500 pesetas ($14.40) to 2000 pesetas ($19.20) for a double, 1200 pesetas ($11.52) for a single. A continental breakfast is 125 pesetas ($1.20) extra.

READERS' HOTEL SELECTIONS: The Ávila Hostal, 3 Ávila (tel. 33-48-08), was our first experience in a hostal in over a year of traveling, and we found we were just as comfortable as in many three-star hotels. The entrance to the building couldn't have been more off-putting, but our room was adequately furnished and heated, and spotlessly clean. We also had a good private bathroom with the hottest hot water we encountered anywhere. Price of a double room with bath is 1700 pesetas ($16.32). With shower, it is 1500 pesetas ($14.40), but only 1350 pesetas ($12.96) in a bathless double. A continental breakfast is an extra 125 pesetas ($1.20) per person" (Margaret Fels, Turramurra, N.S.W., Australia). . . . **"Hotel Residencia Capele,** 58 General Franco (tel. 36-64-00), is a modern hotel with well-furnished rooms. The hotel is clean and convenient, being only one block from the center of the city. There is no parking, but the car was safe all night in the next block. Parking is restricted nearer the hotel. A double with bath rents for 2800 pesetas ($26.88) to 3300 pesetas ($31.68), and a continental breakfast, the only meal provided, is an extra 250 pesetas ($2.40) each. A single rents for 2300 pesetas ($22.08) to 2800 pesetas ($26.88)" (Dr. and Mrs. C. H. Chaffey, Dapto, N.S.W., Australia). . . . "We arrived at Jerez without a reservation. The two three-star hotels, the Jerez and the Capele, as well as the Mica, were full, and so we ended up at the **Motel Aloha,** Carretera de Circunvalación (tel. 33-25-04). The rooms cost 2500 pesetas ($24) in a double. This is a quite adequate hotel with high marks for its personal service and its dining room. One note of warning: There is a tourist map of Jerez distributed by one of the wineries. It shows the Motel Aloha about a kilometer southeast of where it actually is, which makes for a great deal of confusion when you are looking for it at night" (John V. Fels, Phoenix, Ariz.).

For Fast Food

For sandwiches, snacks, and combined plates, try **La Vega,** on the Plaza Esteve, a short walk from the Hotel Los Cisnes. This cafetería spreads its simpler wares on the downstairs level, while its more expensive sister upstairs dispenses more savory viands. La Vega is air-conditioned (but there's a lot of hot air in the machine). In cooler weather, you may prefer to dine outside at the sidewalk tables. The cafetería is popular with modern señoritas and their guys, drawn here by the sandwiches such as ham on toast, 150 pesetas ($1.44) at a table, 140 pesetas ($1.34) at the counter. During the day, this place is crowded with old men smoking cigars and talking loudly.

READER'S RESTAURANT SUGGESTION: "Restaurante San Francisco, 2 Plaza Esteve (tel. 34-49-14), is an excellent place to dine. The waiter on our visit there was congenial, helpful, and efficient. The food came in the largest helpings we had in Spain. A very plentiful three-course meal costs from 800 pesetas ($7.68) to 1500 pesetas ($14.40). We had sherry first and a bottle of special wine. We can highly recommend this as a place to dine leisurely on good food" (Dr. and Mrs. C. H. Chaffey, Dapto, N.S.W., Australia).

Arcos de la Frontera

Only about 20 miles east of Jerez de la Frontera, this old Arab town was built in the form of an amphitheater. Sitting on a rock and surrounded by the Guadalete on three sides, it contains many houses which have been hollowed out of this formation. From the old city, it opens onto a high-in-the-clouds view which some visitors have found without rival on the Iberian Peninsula.

The city is filled with whitewashed walls and narrow winding streets which disappear into steps. It holds a lot of historical interest, and has a beautiful lake complete with paddle boats and a Mississippi riverboat. One can take the bus from Seville, Cádiz, or Jerez de la Frontera, as there is no train service to this little bit of paradise.

The best place to stay is the **Parador Casa del Corregidor,** Plaza de España (tel. 70-05-00), the government-run parador. From the balconies of the parador, one has views of the Valley of Guadalete, filled with farms, plains, and the river below. In good weather you can take your meals on one of these balconies (try the pork with garlic). Either lunch or dinner costs 950 pesetas ($9.12).

Reader William C. Sano, Swampscott, Massachusetts, writes: "I spent one whole day reading my paperback novel on the balcony of our room, drinking in the view and watching the sun create unusual images in shadows as it moved across the sky. Then I went out exploring the Old Town at night." The parador offers 21 accomodations, some doubles with ballroom-size baths. Doubles rent for 3700 pesetas ($35.52) to 4300 pesetas ($41.28), including a better-than-continental breakfast served right on the main square.

After our stopover in sherry country, we head south to the port city of—

CÁDIZ: This modern, bustling Atlantic port is a kind of Spanish Marseilles. It's a melting pot of Americans, Africans, and Europeans who dock or pass through here. The old quarter teems with native life, little dives, and seaport alleyways through which sailors from many lands wander in their search for adventure. But despite the thriving life, it is devoid of major interest, and has far more successful competitor cities in Andalusia.

At the end of a peninsula, Cádiz separates the Bay of Cádiz from the Atlantic. From numerous sea walls around the town, you have views of the ocean, to which the denizens of Cádiz have always looked. In fact, Columbus set out from here on his second voyage to the New World, on September 25, 1493. "Convert the infidels, settle the land," Isabella ordered him. She probably commanded that he speed up the gold shipments as well. Seventeen vessels were manned by anywhere from 1000 to 1500 men, including priests, doctors, even Chris's brother.

This ancient port city of Cádiz enjoyed varying states of prosperity, particularly after the discovery of the New World. Its origins go back into antiquity: Did Hercules really found the city? Or was it the trading Phoenicians?

Arabs, Visigoths, Romans, and Carthaginians have passed through Cádiz, all leaving their imprints.

The most convenient point for a walking tour is Plaza de San Juan de Dios, which could easily provide the background for a movie about a North African port city. Anchor later at one of the sidewalk cafés, and watch the people pass by. Or perhaps stroll up San Antonio Abad for a glimpse of the seamy side of life. One reader from Bethesda, Maryland, found "the whorehouses all quite tidy and freshly painted, with pots of geraniums at the end of the San Antonio Abad." A right turn brought her to the homosexual street. But before we do too much exploring, let's settle into Cádiz.

Where to Stay

Cádiz has a number of budget accommodations, some of which are quite poor. However, on our budget, we can afford some of the finest lodgings in the city.

Hotel Francia y Paris, 2 Plaza de San Francisco (tel. 21-23-18), is about a five-minute walk from the waterfront, on one of Cádiz's attractive tree-filled plazas, in the heart of the old town. It's a modern structure of fair design; most of the bedroom windows are fitted with striped awnings to keep out the strong sun (Cádiz is called the "City of Light"). Fairly comfortable and medium-size double rooms with private baths rent for 2700 pesetas ($25.92). Singles pay 1800 pesetas ($17.28) in rooms with private bath. A continental breakfast is another 175 pesetas ($1.68). The hotel is run in a somewhat *comme ci, comme ça* manner. Many of the staff members speak English; and there is a cozy, wood-paneled bar and lounge.

Imares, 9 San Francisco (tel. 21-22-57), is most Andalusian, an older hotel with a large entrance patio, a marble staircase, balcony, and all. The rooms in general are large and well kept; there are 37 in all, with a wide variation of plumbing. The most expensive doubles, with complete bath, are 2000 pesetas ($19.20), 1700 pesetas ($16.32) in a double with a shower bath. Singles go for 1000 pesetas ($9.60). A continental breakfast is another 150 pesetas ($1.44) per person. The hotel is run by a "simpatico" staff who give good service. The only drawback is that since all the rooms face a cavernous inside patio, any noise reverberates through the whole building. Light sleepers, take note. The street sign for the hotel now only reads "Residencia" in white on red vertical letters.

Across the Bay

Hotel Puertobahía, Playa de Valdelagrana, Puerto de Santa María (tel. 86-27-21), is an important three-star hotel built directly on the beach, opposite the port of Cádiz. Near the Rota Naval Station, it offers 330 spacious rooms, each having its own bath and sun terrace. It's a self-contained resort, with two swimming pools, a sauna, tennis courts, sandy beach, plus two restaurants and a disco. A twin-bedded room with bath is 3250 pesetas ($31.20), dropping to 2100 pesetas ($20.16) in a single with bath. A set luncheon or dinner is an extra 1000 pesetas ($9.60).

Where to Eat

Head to the heart of the city, the **Plaza de San Juan de Dios,** for good economy dinners. But here you must pick and choose carefully, as a number of eating establishments in Cádiz are more used to serving a rough-and-ready fleet than Mr. and Mrs. Smith of Lawrence, Kansas.

Casa Manuel, 14 Plaza de San Juan de Dios (tel. 23-30-29), opens onto this central square. You can dine outside at the café tables and watch the parade go by (and Cádiz puts on a good one). The restaurant features a menú del día for 550 pesetas ($4.28) that usually begins with Valencian paella, a beefsteak for a main course, and ends with fresh fruit. Manuel's Place is a kind of social center, especially on hot summer nights. It was recently modernized, so that it is all white tablecloths, bustling waiters, and lots of light.

La Caleta, 1 Plaza de San Juan de Dios. This restaurant offers a good 500-peseta ($4.80) menú de la casa. A typical meal might consist of fish soup, then liver or fried steak with french fries, followed by mixed fruit. Sailors feel at home here, as the interior is decorated like the inside of a ship. If you prefer visual dining, go to one of the outside tables, where you can generally watch heavily made-up women plying that age-old trade. Harbor-rat troubadours pretend to entertain you—an excuse to pass around the collection plate.

Restaurante El 9 is for real starvation budgeteers. It's on the Calle San Fernando, off the Plaza San Juan de Dios, and here you can get a meal for 250 pesetas ($2.40). I recently had a dish of rice with seafood, an egg (or a thin steak), a roll, a glass of wine, and some fruit for that sum. À la carte dishes are as follows: noodle soup, 55 pesetas (53¢); a plate of lentils, 60 pesetas (58¢); macaroni, 55 pesetas (53¢); a meat and potato stew, 120 pesetas ($1.15).

Next door is another budget restaurant, the **Económica,** where a plate of lentils, paella, macaroni, or fish goes for 75 pesetas (72¢). Two eggs and potatoes go for only 90 pesetas (86¢). Both the El 9 and the Económica have white tile walls and neon lights, but in some strange way exude a kind of budget charm all their own. ˙

The Sights

The principal artistic treasures are found in the **Fine Arts** and **Archeological Museums,** both in the same building at 5 Plaza Generalísimo. The Fine Arts Museum houses one of Spain's most important Zurbarán collections, including a series he did of a monk, as well as paintings by Rubens and Murillo (his picture of Christ is one of his most important works). The Museum of Archeology is known for its Roman, Phoenician, and Carthaginian collections. Both museums are open from 9:30 a.m. to 2 p.m. every day except Monday, and charge 75 pesetas (72¢).

The **cathedral** is a magnificent baroque-style building in the Plaza Pio XII, built in the 18th century by the architect Vicente Acero. The interior, composed of the finest materials, is in the neoclassic style forming an impressive group dominated by its outstanding apse-aisle. In its splendid crypt with a level vault lies the tomb of the Cádiz-born composer Manuel de Falla. The treasure museum contains a priceless collection of Spanish silver, embroidery, and fine paintings belonging to the Spanish, Flemish, and Italian schools.

Unless it is closed for repairs, the cathedral can be visited, together with the treasure museum, from 10 a.m. to 1 p.m. and 4 to 6 p.m. in winter. In summer, the afternoon visiting hours are 5 to 7 p.m. (no Sunday visiting hours). Admission fee is 30 pesetas (29¢) to the museum, 15 pesetas (14¢) to the crypt.

Branching out from the cathedral, incidentally, are cobblestone streets which will lead you to some of the most interesting alleyways in the old barrio.

READERS' SIGHTSEEING TIP: "Do mention the delightful park along the waterfront in the old quarter. It's straight out of *Alice in Wonderland,* with tropical plantings and fir trees sculptured into incredible corkscrew shapes. There's a little stand with tables where you can get beer, sherry, and simple tapas" (Lolli and Brian Sherry, Northfield, Ill.).

5. The Huelva District

West of Cádiz, moving toward Huelva and the Portuguese frontier, lies the rapidly developing **Costa de la Luz** (Coast of Light), which is hoping to pick up some of the overflow from the Costa del Sol. The "Luz" coast stretches from the mouth of the Guadiana River, forming the boundary with Portugal, to Tarifa Point on the Straits of Gibraltar. Characterizing the coast are long stretches of sand, pine trees, fishermen's cottages, and lazy whitewashed villages.

The area, as of this writing, is a predominantly German resort area. The food, atmosphere, signs, and language are often German. Sometimes even the shows at the hotels are presented in German. Therefore, if you're seeking typically Spanish flavor, stay clear.

At **Huelva** is a large statue on the west bank of the river commemorating the departure of Christopher Columbus on his voyage of discovery of the New World.

About seven kilometers up the Río Tinto, on the east bank on the waterfront of the little, sleepy town of **Palos de la Frontera,** is the actual spot from which Columbus departed. Here a monument marks the place.

His ships were anchored off this bank where the final victualing was carried out. About six kilometers south is the **Convento de la Rabida.** In the little white chapel in the convent grounds, Columbus prayed all night for the success of his voyage on the eve of his departure. The chapel may be visited. From both places, the large white statue of Columbus at Huelva can be seen across the water downstream.

One of the best accommodations in the area is the **Parador Nacional Cristóbal Colón,** Carretera Mazagón-Moguer (tel. 37-60-00), at Mazagón (Palos de la Frontera), 12 miles from Huelva, a cheerful Andalusian town, with several churches dating from the 16th century. Open all year, this parador charges 3100 pesetas ($29.76) to 3900 pesetas ($37.44) in a double room, 2700 pesetas ($25.92) in a single, all with private bath. One reader, Dr. A. C. Tarjan, Lake Alfred, Florida, writes: "The best place we've ever stayed at in Spain. Accommodations are quite good, with air conditioning, and there's a good view of the Mediterranean. Although a swimming pool is available, there is access to 40 miles of desolate beach. In the rooms are small refrigerators stocked with drinks (you pay as you go). The food prices are high—950 pesetas ($9.12) for a set menu—although what is offered is simple."

A Side Trip to Medina Sidonia

This survivor of the Middle Ages is one of the most unspoiled of the hillside villages of Spain. It's about 29 miles east of Cádiz, 22 miles southeast of Jerez de la Frontera.

Medina Sidonia is one of those villages that time forgot. It has cobblestone streets, white tile-roofed buildings that cascade down the hillside, a Gothic church, a Moorish gate, and steep alleyways on which little old women in black and men on donkeys descend. The Arab influence is everywhere.

The surrounding countryside is wild and seldom visited. Pockets of fog sometimes settle over the land, and sunrise is often reminiscent of greeting the morning on the Yorkshire moors.

From Medina Sidonia, it's a 2½-hour drive to the port city of Algeciras, or you can take the Jerez road back to Seville.

6. Ronda

This little town, which sits proudly as a principality high (2300 feet above sea level) in the Serrania de Ronda Mountains, is one of the oldest and most aristocratic towns in Spain. But that's not the chief reason it's visited. Ronda is split by a deep (500-foot) gorge, which in turn is spanned by a Roman stone bridge. On both sides of this "hole in the earth" are cliff-hanging houses, which look as if—with the slightest push—they'd plunge into the chasm.

Ronda is an incredible sight. The road to Ronda, once difficult to drive, is now a wide highway with guard rails. The town and the surrounding mountains were the legendary hideouts of bandits and smugglers, but today the Guardia Civil has put an end to that occupation. Smugglers today, it seems, either retire or become horse trainers.

You'll discover a town divided by the gorge into an older part, the Moorish and aristocratic quarter, and the newer part, on the southern side of the gorge, the section built principally after the Reconquest. The older quarter is by far the more fascinating; it contains narrow, rough streets, and buildings that show a marked Moorish influence (watch for the minaret). After the lazy sunny resort living of the Costa del Sol, a side excursion for the day to Ronda, with its unique beauty and refreshing mountain air, is like a tonic.

Ronda is great for the explorer. A native boy or two may attach himself to you as a guide: actually, if you give one a few pesetas, it might be worth it, since weaving your way in and out of the narrow streets may be a problem. There are the remains of the **Moorish baths;** the **bullring,** built in the 1700s, the oldest in Spain; the interesting **Palacio de Marqués de Salvatierra;** and the **Palacio de Mondragón,** overlooking the cliff, where the Moorish king lived before Isabella and Ferdinand moved in. However, at the latter, only the gardens can be visited, and they are not well maintained.

Ronda is a three-hour ride from Algeciras.

STAYING OVERNIGHT: The **Hotel Reina Victoria,** 25 Jerez (tel. 87-12-40), with its spacious lounges and airy bedrooms, is similar to an English country home. It's at the edge of town, with terraces that hang right over the precipice. Each bedroom has all the modern amenities, the rooms are big and comfortable; some with complete living room, including sofas, chairs, and tables. Outside many of the bedrooms is a private terrace with garden furniture. The beds are sumptuous, and the bathrooms have all the latest improvements. The simpler double rooms with bath rent for 3200 pesetas ($30.72), the "semi-suites" for 3600 pesetas ($34.56). The best singles, with private tub baths, cost 2000 pesetas ($19.20). A continental breakfast is another 200 pesetas ($1.92) per person. Dining here is recommendable, as the food is well cooked, a set meal going for 950 pesetas ($9.12).

Hostal Residencia Royal, 52 Virgen de la Paz (tel. 87-11-41), is the best choice for those who want to spend the night in an ancient section of Ronda. It is near the old bull arena, on a tiny cliff-edge plaza. From here you can easily reach most points of interest in the town. Every room of this comfortably conservative, Sevillian-style hotel has its own balcony, and you can enjoy the sunsets. Double rooms with bath cost 2100 pesetas ($20.16). A single with bath (only two in this category) is 1400 pesetas ($13.44). A continental breakfast is another 150 pesetas ($1.44) per person. Rooms are reasonably well furnished.

Hotel Residencia Polo, 8 Mariano Soubirón (tel. 87-24-47), lies right in the heart of Ronda, close to a big shopping arcade for pedestrians. The Polo is run with professionalism, and its accomodations are pleasantly—not elegantly—decorated and are well kept. Bedrooms are spacious; even the closets and private bathrooms are large enough for your needs. You get good value here: 2000 pesetas ($19.20) nightly in a double. You can order typically Andalusian fare at the adjoining restaurant, the two-fork Restaurante Polo (tel. 87-26-69), where meals begin at 500 pesetas ($4.80).

READER'S HOTEL SELECTION: "We were fortunate to find a room in a small pension named **La Española Huespedes**, just off the Plaza de España on the new town side of the upper bridge, only a two-minute walk from the gorge. It isn't on a street, but on a walkway just to the left of the Tourist Office on the plaza. The cost is only 650 pesetas ($6.24) for a double without bath, and, while simple, the accommodations are very clean. The showers are free. Just ask for the *llave* to the *ducha*. Meals are available, inexpensive, but not required. A set meal costs 450 pesetas ($4.32), a continental breakfast going for 90 pesetas (86¢)" (James Wiley). [*Author's Note:* This accommodation is recommended only in an emergency.]

WHERE TO DINE: **Don Miguel Restaurant,** 4 Villanuova, stands at the end of the bridge, with vistas of the upper gorge. A three-fork restaurant, it has tables set outside on two levels, enough to seat some 300 persons. The various set menus range in price from 750 pesetas ($7.20) to 1200 pesetas ($11.52). The food is fairly good, the rest rooms clean, and the chairs in the typical Andalusian style. The waiters are polite and speak enough English to get by. There is also a pleasant bar if you want to drop in just for a drink. Even if the food at Don Miguel weren't good (which it is), I'd still go here just to enjoy drinks and tapas (hors d'oeuvres) "inside the bridge," the old renovated prison. During the summer it's a bustling place. The restaurant closes from January 15 until February 20.

Don Miguel also owns the **Mesón del Puente,** Plaza del Ayuntamiento, which is a bar built into the ancient bridge spanning the gorge. It makes an interesting stopover for refreshments. The Saturday night flamenco sessions attract mainly the locals.

La Gloria, 3 Calle Corrales y 3 Ríos Rosas (tel. 87-10-03), can also be safely recommended. A two-fork restaurant, it is very clean, and the location isn't far from the famous bullring. For a first course, you are usually offered a choice of hors d'oeuvres, hot soup, or a salad. Next you can make your selection from, say, a ham omelet, hake, kidneys cooked in sherry, roast lamb (or, alternatively, roast chicken), finishing off with the typical fruit or ice cream. All this should cost no more than 500 pesetas ($4.80).

READERS' RESTAURANT SUGGESTIONS: "May I suggest your readers try the restaurant **Pedro Romero** on Virgen de la Paz (tel. 87-10-27), just down from the Hostal Residencia Royal? I had positively the best filet of sole in my life there on the recommendation of a Dutch film crew who had been there for several weeks. The menú del día costs 620 pesetas ($5.95). It's across from the bullring" (Nick Chickering, Nevada City, Calif.). . . . "During our stay in Ronda, the best budget restaurant we found was **Las Canas,** 2 Duque de la Victoria (tel. 87-10-08). This is a small, simple place on the corner of the Plaza del Socorro, only a short walk from the old bullring. There is a TV in the corner, and the place is plain in the extreme, but the food is good and the waiter most friendly and helpful. The menú del día costs 410 pesetas ($3.94), and includes soup or salad, fish, omelet or other main dish, fruit, bread, and wine" (Dr. and Mrs. E. McC. Callan, Canberra, Australia).

Exploring in the Environs

The Cueva de la Pileta, lying eight miles west of Ronda near Benoaján, in the province of Málaga, has been compared to the Caves of Altamira, near Santander in the north of Spain. In an area of wild beauty, known as the Serranía de Ronda, the caves were discovered in 1905 by José Bullón Lobato,

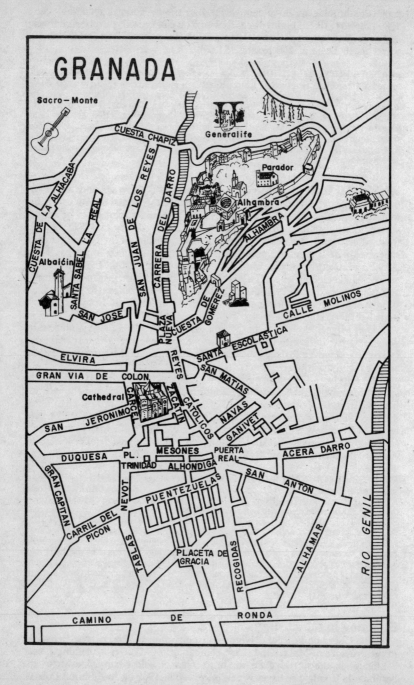

grandfather of the present owners. More than a mile in length and filled with oddly and beautifully shaped stalagmites and stalactites, the caves contained five fossilized human and two animal skeletons.

In the mysterious darkness, cave paintings have been discovered, dating back to prehistoric times and depicting animals in yellow, red, black, and ochre. Many of the drawings contain symbols whose meaning is obscure. One of the highlights of the tour is a trip to the "chamber of the fish," a wall painting of a great black seal-like fish about three feet in length. The fish chamber is the innermost heart of the cave, ending in a precipice which drops vertically nearly 250 feet.

The easiest way to reach the cave is to drive there from Ronda. However, those without private transport can take the train to Benoaján. But, be warned, the cave lies at least an hour's walk from where the train deposits you. In the valley, just below the cave, lives a guide who will conduct you around the chambers, carrying artificial light to illuminate the paintings. You'll spend at least an hour here, and the cost is a well-spent 125 pesetas ($1.20).

Our next adventure is Granada, one of the top four tourist cities of Spain.

7. Granada

This former stronghold of Moorish Spain, at the foothills of the snow-capped Sierra Nevada mountain range, is part of the folklore of the world. Washington Irving *(Tales of the Alhambra)* used the image of this city of the pomegranate *(granada)* to conjure up a spirit of romance.

Perhaps because of all this excessive sentimentality, Granada, like Seville, has its debunkers. Admittedly, if Granada were to be judged by its 19th-century Lower City, it would be a dull, grayish Spanish town. Dozens of ill-conceived buildings were erected after the senseless destruction of the large Moorish part of the city. But the spirit of Granada is reflected more in its purple-red Alhambra, the 13th-century Moorish palace that is one of the most celebrated edifices in the world. Sitting high on a hill overlooking Granada, it is the city's crowning achievement.

Granada has played host to many "visitors," such as the Romans and the Visigoths; but it was the Moslem invaders who left the biggest imprint on the city. In 1492, after Isabella and Ferdinand took over this last remaining stronghold of the Arabs, the city entered a sad decline. But in the last century, the Granadines began to prosper again, and they are not living exclusively off their glorious past. Granada today is one of the most important commercial cities of Spain.

Enjoying a mild climate, it is some 2200 feet above sea level. It sprawls over two main hills, the Alhambra and the Albaicin, and it is crossed by two rivers, the Genil and Darro.

There are any number of ways to reach Granada. One of the most frequented routes is between Madrid and Granada, or Granada and Seville, or from the Costa del Sol. If you are visiting Granada from Madrid, it is suggested that you stop off at Jaén. But if this is impossible, then you can board a train at the Atocha Station in Madrid that will take you directly to Granada. In addition, regular scheduled Iberia Airlines flights go from Madrid to Granada's airport. In summer, in particular, many visit Granada from Málaga or Torremolinos. There is both train and bus service from Málaga. See the local RENFE or tourist offices about those constantly changing times of departure and return.

A warning note: A popular scam in Granada, usually practiced by gypsies, is to approach you, thrust a flower in your jacket, then pour out a rapid incantation (purportedly fortune-telling). You'll pay dearly for the experience, but only if you allow it.

WHERE TO STAY: The hotel and pension outlook is bright in Granada, and the choice of different styles of living is wide.

Splurging in a Former Convent

The **Parador Nacional San Francisco,** near the Alhambra (tel. 22-14-93), is one of the finest places at which to stay in Spain. The reasons are many, each crowding the others to be mentioned first. It is definitely romantic-style living, and the best double rooms rent for 5500 pesetas ($52.80). It is imperative that you reserve in advance, as this is one of the most sought-after places in the country.

The parador is part of the greater compound of the Alhambra, and that is recommendation enough. Its history goes back to the 15th century, when it was built as a convent following the reconquest of Granada by the Catholic kings. Queen Isabella was temporarily buried here, until her tomb in the Royal Chapel could be completed.

The larger, Moorish-inspired patio at the parador is the older one, planted with time-aged vines and trees. The long gallery, opening onto the patio, must have been a chapel or a meeting hall; it is now a comfortable living room furnished with a mixture of antiques and upholstered pieces. The angular dining hall has remained the same, except that local women have replaced the nuns as waitresses.

The accommodations differ widely, the choice rooms being grabbed up first, of course. Many are large antique-filled bedrooms, although there are smaller and more simply furnished ones in the newer wing. From every window, you get a picture-postcard view.

As for the food, most of the excellent dishes served are native to the province. You have assurance about the cleanliness of the food preparation, and you can come here to dine even if you aren't staying at the parador. A complete luncheon or dinner costs 950 pesetas ($9.12).

Before your meal, join the guests by having a drink in the lounge.

The Top Budget Hotels

Gran Hotel Brasilia, 7 Recogidas (tel. 25-84-50), is smack in the center of Granada, providing many comforts such as full air conditioning. The rooms are well-furnished; the hotel is efficient; the staff polite (English is spoken). In short, it's one of the best hotels in the city. All of the rooms, both single and double, have private tub-shower baths. Couples pay 3100 pesetas ($29.76) to 4000 pesetas ($38.40); singles, 1900 pesetas ($18.24). A continental breakfast is an extra 160 pesetas ($1.54) per person. You'll find other important facilities, such as an American bar, a roof terrace, and a grill for light snacks. The location is fine for shopping, too—only three blocks from the Puerta Real.

Macia, 4 Plaza Nueva (tel. 22-75-33), is an attractive modern hotel, right at the bottom of the hill going up to the Alhambra. Its 40 rooms rate two stars, so you're getting a real bargain in what I think should be a three-star hotel. All rooms have heating, private bath, phone, and are clean and functional, with fluorescent lighting and stone floors. Doubles cost 2200 pesetas ($21.12), and singles run 1400 pesetas ($13.44). If there are three in your party, the manager will rent you a triple at 2950 pesetas ($28.32). There's no restaurant.

Sudán, 60 Avenida José Antonio (tel. 25-84-00), is a two-star hotel, only a five-minute walk from the Puerta Real in modern Granada. A clean, comfortable, substantial hotel, it is one of the best places in the city: doubles cost from 2500 pesetas ($24) daily. Singles with private baths rent for 1500 pesetas ($14.40). Be sure to ask for one of the front rooms with bay windows, as they are the superior accommodations. The entire staff is most cooperative, and the food is quite good, with a lunch or dinner averaging 900 pesetas ($8.64).

Residencia Anacapri, 7 Joaquin Costa (tel. 22-55-62), is a quietly situated hotel, right off the Reyes Católicos in the heart of the modern city. The rooms are comfortable, nicely furnished; the hotel is well run, and has a look of old-world elegance to it. Doubles with private bath cost from 2200 pesetas ($21.12) to 3100 pesetas ($29.76). Singles with private bath start at 1900 pesetas ($18.24), but are few in number.

A continental breakfast, costing 160 pesetas ($1.54) extra, will be delivered to your room, but no other meals are served. However, this need not be a problem, as the Anacapri is near many of Granada's budget restaurants. Because it is on a secluded street, the hotel offers rooms protected from the traffic noises of bustling Granada, the plague of most of the city's major hotels. You'll also be right in the center of the shopping section.

Hotel Inglaterra, 6 Cetti Meriem (tel. 22-15-59), is right near the cathedral, the peal of bells awakening you to another day in Granada. A corner hotel, it is built in an Andalusian style, with a glass-covered lobby. Recent modernization has brightened it up considerably, although it still languishes in a sort of turn-of-the-century ambience. It offers the fine service of bygone days. Not so old are the bathrooms, assigned to each bedroom. A double with bath goes for 2200 pesetas ($21.12). Only three singles are offered, those with private baths costing 1800 pesetas ($17.28). Triple rooms with bath rent for 2600 pesetas ($24.96), plus another 160 pesetas ($1.54) per person for a continental breakfast.

Hostal Carlos V, 4 Plaza de los Campos Elíseos (tel. 22-15-87), is an unpretentious, comfortable hotel on the upper floor of a building. Several of its rooms have balconies boasting some spectacular views of the city, and a double room with bath goes for 1980 pesetas ($19.01), 1430 pesetas ($13.73) without bath but with a terrace. Singles are 1100 pesetas ($10.56). Normally you're expected to have some meals in the hotel. These cost 770 pesetas ($7.39) for either lunch or dinner, plus an additional 155 pesetas ($1.49) for a continental breakfast. The owner says he has special accomodations for four people, and all rooms have telephones.

Hotel Manuel de Falla, 16 Antequeruela Baja (tel. 22-75-45), is a secret gem, known to discerning travelers. Within walking distance of the Alhambra, it is perched on a hill overlooking the city, and is built like a California home, on several levels with gardens. The view is perfect, and living here is like being a part of the life of a tiny village, far removed from the modern part of Granada.

But don't expect a pad like Hugh Hefner's. Its bedrooms are basic, with decent furnishings and fairly reliable plumbing. For a double with private bath the rate is 2100 pesetas ($20.16). Singles with shower baths are 1400 pesetas ($13.44). You can take all three meals here for an additional charge of 1400 pesetas.

Hostal América, 53 Real de la Alhambra (tel. 22-74-71), within the ancient Alhambra walls, is one of the leading pensions of Granada. You walk through a covered entryway right into the shady patio of what once was probably the villa of a wealthy family. It is both lively and intimate, with large trees, many potted plants and ferns. The plants run up the white plastered walls, leap over the doorways and windows, and twine themselves around the ornate grillwork. Garden chairs and tables are set out for the excellent, home-cooked Spanish meals. This little oasis is a personal, homey retreat.

The living room is graced with a collection of decorative objects from the region. The bedrooms occasionally have Andalusian reproductions, personal and pleasing, but without distinction. The cost of the best double room with private bath is 2025 pesetas ($19.44); bathless singles go for 1260 pesetas ($12.10). A complete lunch or dinner is an extra 720 pesetas ($6.91). It is open March 1 to October 31.

Pension California, 37 Cuesta Gomérez (tel. 22-40-56), is too often passed up as one whizzes up the hill toward the Alhambra. But don't miss it (on your left) if you're in need of an inexpensive and typically Spanish accommodation. It is run in an informal, family-like manner, totally unlike a hotel. The bedrooms are simply furnished, but well kept. A number of double accomodations with showers rent for only 1150 pesetas ($11.04). Single rooms, with water basins only, cost just 800 pesetas ($7.68). A set lunch or dinner goes for 575 pesetas ($5.52), and a continental breakfast is yet another 90 pesetas (86¢).

READERS' HOTEL SELECTIONS: "**Hotel Guadalupe,** Avenida de los Alijares (tel. 22-34-23), opened in 1969. Listed as a three-star hotel, it offers air-conditioned rooms that are just excellent. The price is 2645 pesetas ($25.39) in a double room with bath; 1800 pesetas ($17.28) in a single with a shower bath. It is right across the street from the Generalife. The meals—if one chooses to eat here—are the best we found in any hotel. A complete lunch or dinner costs 795 pesetas ($7.63). I recommend it highly for those who might like to go a bit higher now and then. The owner and his wife are absolutely charming—and so anxious to help us in every way" (Mrs. William P. Duggan, Burlington, Ontario, Canada). . . . "The **Hostal Residencia Britz,** Plaza Nueva and 1 Gomérez (tel. 22-36-52), rents its twin-bedded rooms for 1100 pesetas ($10.56) a night. Showers and bath are down the hall. A continental breakfast costs another 100 pesetas (96¢) per person. The hostal is at the very foot of the hill leading to the Alhambra. Take bus 11 from the railway station" (Edward H. Pietraszek, Chicago, Ill.). . . . "We found **Hostal Los Carmenes,** 2 Isaac Albeniz (tel. 23-19-05), very near the railway station and several cheap restaurants. The charge is 1000 pesetas ($9.60) in a bathless double. A continental breakfast is another 100 pesetas (96¢) per person. The management will book you for a visit to a gypsy cave and a nightly show for a very low charge" (Ms. Ofelia Adair, Miami, Fla.). . . . "**Hotel Kenia,** 65 Molinos (tel. 22-75-06), was once a spacious old Spanish home and has been carefully modernized to retain the same atmosphere. The buildings are surrounded by gardens. The rooms are large and have a good-size bath and are very clean. The owner is helpful and speaks English. This hotel is a family enterprise, and the members work to keep the guests happy. The Kenia is quiet, something to be praised in Spain, and relatively convenient to the old city and the Alhambra, just ten minutes' walk up the hill. One can visit Manuel de Falla's carmen (old rustic cottage) and the new Manuel de Falla concert hall on the way up to the Alhambra, a minute's deviation down Antequeruela Alta. While we were there, a band of Mandregos stopped on the road outside the hotel at 2 o'clock one morning and played and sang ancient music. Windows were raised all around, and after the concert the listeners raised hearty applause and rained down pesetas on the happy musicians below. This was a pleasant experience for us in Spain. The hotel charges 2400 pesetas ($23.04) for a double with bath, only 1300 pesetas ($12.48) in a single. A lunch or dinner, ordered separately, goes for 800 pesetas ($7.68), or else you may take half-board terms at a charge of 2200 pesetas ($21.12) per person daily, based on double occupancy" (Dr. and Mrs. C. H. Chaffey, Dapto, N.S.W., Australia).

"A beautiful accommodation I found was the **Hostal Loren,** 2 Alvaro de Bazan (tel. 27-65-00), near the cathedral, one block off the Gran Vía de Colón. Here I spoke Spanish and English with the owner's son. The rooms are perhaps the cleanest and nicest in Spain, and each has a speaker with an on-off switch, playing American music. The single rate is 900 pesetas ($8.64)" (Daniel Klein, New York, N.Y.). . . . "**Hostal Suecia,** Calle Molinos (tel. 22-50-44), is next to the Hotel Kenia. A double with breakfast is 1500 pesetas ($14.40), with unlimited use of the adjacent bathroom. The hostal is a converted villa. You can sit under shade trees on the entrance terrace and park in front off the main street. The señora who owns it is nice and helpful with suggestions on what to see in

Granada besides the Alhambra. It's an excellent find and highly recommended" (Mrs. H. Chadim, Curtin, Australia).

WHERE TO EAT: From the heights of the Alhambra to the narrow, dark streets in the heart of the city, feasting on the rich and plentiful Andalusian cuisine is an important part of the day's activity in Granada. The lead-off restaurant recommendation is the government-run parador, **San Francisco,** Alhambra (tel. 22-14-93), with its splurge dinners for 1200 pesetas ($11.52). In summer, meals are served on a terrace overlooking the illuminated Generalife. But for inexpensive dining in Granada, here are some cheaper recommendations:

La Florida, 21 Elvira (tel. 22-64-93), near the cathedral, is in an old building around the corner from the Hotel Inglaterra. High standards prevail at this simple Spanish restaurant. Nothing is posh here, but you can decorate your palate with mouthwatering scenery such as pasta, meat, and fish dishes. It's a grade above average in dinner fare, but its all-inclusive menú del día is only 575 pesetas ($5.52), which might include a paella, an omelet, a fish dish, bread, wine, and a dessert. The noise coming from the kitchen may sound like the far side of Dante's *Inferno,* but you can chalk this up to atmosphere to compensate for the lackluster decor.

Jandilla, 1 Puente del Carbón, is on a horse-and-buggy street in the heart of modern Granada. It offers a típico Andalusian dinner for 615 pesetas ($5.90), sometimes featuring gazpacho. Try rape as an entree—one translator defined it as "eel-pout." But you may want to stick to more familiar items, notably the seafood soup, followed by grilled lamb cutlets with potatoes. You can dine outside in summer at the sidewalk tables. Since the Jandilla leads a double life as a bar, why not start off your meal with a glass of dry, light sherry, Manzanilla?

Polinario, Real de la Alhambra, is a simple two-fork restaurant within the ancient walls of the Alhambra, across the way from the Palace of Charles V. The Spanish cooking is reasonably good, and a complete meal will set you back 700 pesetas ($6.72), including service and wine. This altitudinous restaurant earns its chief credits for its Andalusian dishes, such as chilled gazpacho, always a favorite with the summer crowd who flit in and out of here with copies of Washington Irving's book. Its rooms have been decorated with nondescript restraint, but this provides a soothing background for such dishes as lamb chops, ragoût, or hake fried Roman style. The inevitable but always welcome flan is served for dessert. In summer, like the caliphs of old, diners eat in the garden. The restaurant closes at 5 p.m.

La Nueva Bodega, 9 Cetti Meriem (tel. 22-59-34), is one of the most economical restaurants of Granada. The New Bodega attracts peseta-watchers who beat a hasty path to its attractive door. The restaurant is near the cathedral and around the corner from the Inglaterra Hotel.

The 525-peseta ($5.04) menú de la casa includes fish soup, a ham omelet, veal cutlet milanesa, flan, bread, and wine. A much cheaper and less elaborate meal at the bar goes for 375 pesetas ($3.60). This latter might be an ideal luncheon choice, as it offers a choice of paella or a French omelet with tomato sauce, bread, and flan.

Restaurant Sevilla, 14 Oficios (tel. 22-46-64), opposite the Royal Chapel, is the Lorelei of Granada, luring a mixed crowd that spans the generation gap. The Sevilla, in the center of the city, is definitely típico with an upbeat elegance —like an owner's conception of what the foreign tourist wants an Andalusian decor to be.

The menú del día goes for 950 pesetas ($9.12), and is available at either luncheon or dinner. My most recent repast included gazpacho, Andalusian veal, and a selection of desserts, such as caramel custard or fresh fruit, bread and the wine of Valdepeñas. If you order à la carte, expect to spend from 1400 pesetas ($13.44). You can dine inside, where it is pleasantly decorated, or have a meal on the terrace. Sevilla also has a bar.

Los Manueles, 4 Zaragoza, is an old Granada standby on a narrow side street. It is unpretentious, with colorfully tiled walls and floors, and fans alternate with lanterns hanging from the ceiling. Above the counter hang dozens of tempting Seranno hams. There are two small dining rooms, or you can sit on the no-traffic street outside in the summer. The tourist menu is 625 pesetas ($6), although the portions are somewhat parsimonious. À la carte specialties include the pescada Manueles, which is hake with all kinds of peas, shrimp, and a sauce. Finish with strawberries and cream or quince jelly. Ordering à la carte will cost from 750 pesetas ($7.20) to 1400 pesetas ($13.44), the latter price for the more expensive beef dishes.

Colombia, 1 Antequeruela Baja (tel. 22-74-33), is a típico restaurant in the Alhambra. The public rooms are air-conditioned in summer, and serenading guitarists come around at meal times in the Andalusian-style large dining room. The least expensive way to dine at this three-fork restaurant is to order one of the set menus, the cheapest of which goes for 750 pesetas ($7.20). On my latest rounds, I was served cream of asparagus soup, followed by hake in the Roman style, then York ham in port wine with a garnish of cream of spinach in a béchamel sauce, plus a selection of various fruits, even a carafe of red Valdepeñas wine and Spanish coffee. The restaurant is air-conditioned, and from its terrace you can enjoy a good view over Granada and the Sierra Nevada.

Finally, I have found that one of the best lunches in Spain is served in any city that has a **Galerías Preciados** department store. Granada is no exception. For the shopper in a rush, it offers a regular table menú for 400 pesetas ($3.84), which I consider one of the best bargains in the city. The meal begins with soup, and follows with, say, breast of chicken and french fries. For that low price, you also get bread and wine (or else beer or mineral water). If you want the "special menu," the cost goes up to 500 pesetas ($4.80). For that higher price, you get a fish course to open with (mine was fried hake), followed by beef with vegetables, bread, and wine. There's also a children's menu at 250 pesetas ($2.40). The least expensive way to eat here is to ask the waiter for the express menu at 350 pesetas ($3.36). To wash it down, I'd order a bottle of Rioja red wine. Perhaps you will, too.

READERS' RESTAURANT SUGGESTIONS: "After nearly two months' travel in Spain, I found the best economy restaurant in one of the most touristy (i.e., expensive) cities of all, Granada. The **Nuevo Restaurante,** 33 Calle de Navas, right off the Plaza del Carmen, has a vast assortment of excellent, three-course menus with wine and bread for only 450 pesetas ($4.32) to 600 pesetas ($5.76), served at the bar. In the restaurant are offered several different three- and four-course menús del día, ranging in price from 550 pesetas ($5.28) to 750 pesetas ($7.20). All the menus include bread and wine, and the choice offered is almost overwhelming. My favorite dish was the San Jacobo steak, a beef filet stuffed with ham and cheese. Be warned that if you arrive during the prime lunch hour, there may be a wait. The Granadines know a good thing when they have it" (David Colden, Encino, Calif.). . . . "The area behind the Plaza Nueva and behind the Hotel Inglaterra is a maze of little streets, which are dotted with good, inexpensive restaurants that cater to local clientele. Most of these are bars with a few tables. Don't expect to find anyone who speaks English. Eat at the bar whenever possible, and you should be able to get a good meal for under 500 pesetas ($4.80). Unfortunately, I don't remember the names of most of these places, but I didn't have a bad meal anywhere in Granada, no matter how little I paid. The **Mesón Andaluz** on Cetti Meriem serves set plates at the bar for about 200 pesetas ($1.92) to 250 pesetas ($2.40). The food is good and the atmosphere pleasant" (Ileane Kine, Huntington Beach, Calif.).

THE SIGHTS: The sights of Granada don't end with the Alhambra, they begin with it.

The Alhambra

When you first see the Alhambra, don't be surprised by its somewhat somber exterior. Remember that the Arabs applied the same principle to architecture that they did to their women: they kept the outside parts veiled. You have to walk across the threshold to discover the true treasures.

The Moorish palace is entered through the incongruous 14th-century **Gateway to Justice.** Tickets are sold in the office next to the uncompleted palace of the Hapsburg king, Charles V. A comprehensive ticket, including both the Alhambra and the Generalife, costs 250 pesetas ($2.40). The Alhambra may be visited in summer from 9 a.m. until 7 p.m. In winter, it opens at 10 a.m. and closes at 6 p.m. The average visitor does not need the services of an expensive guide, but should be content to stroll along in a quietly contemplative mood through the richly ornamented open-air rooms, with their lace-like walls and courtyards with fountains. Most of the Arabic inscriptions seem to translate: "Only Allah is conqueror."

The most photographed part of the palace is the **Court of Lions,** containing a highly stylized fountain of lions. This was the heart of the palace, the most private section, where the sultan wanted to be alone to enjoy his harem. Opening onto the court are such rooms as the **Hall of the Two Sisters,** where the favorite of the moment was kept, or the **Gossip Room,** that factory of intrigue. In the dancing room in the **Hall of Kings,** an early version of the striptease was performed nightly to amuse the sultan's party. In all, it's like a theater, around which the eunuchs of old guarded the gems of the harem. Apparently, these eunuchs weren't too diligent one night. One sultan, according to legend, beheaded 36 Moorish princes because one of them was suspected of having been intimate with his favorite.

You can see the room where Washington Irving lived (in the chambers of Charles V) when he was compiling his *Tales of the Alhambra*—the best known of which is the legend of the three beautiful princesses, Zayda, Zorayada, and Zorahayda, who fell in love with three captured Spanish soldiers outside their "La Torre de las Infantas." Irving did more than any other writer to publicize the Alhambra to the English-speaking world.

Although Irving credits the French with saving the Alhambra for posterity, these invaders blew up seven of the towers in 1812, but a Spanish soldier cut the fuse before more damage could be done. When the Duke of Wellington arrived a few years later, he chased out the chickens, the gypsies, and the transient beggars who were using the Alhambra as a king of tenement dwelling, and set up housekeeping here himself.

Incidentally, don't miss the Roman-inspired **Royal Baths,** and the 13th-century **Alcazaba,** which is in ruins.

Charles V may have been horrified when he saw the cathedral placed in the middle of the great mosque at Córdoba, but he had his hand involved in some architectural incongruity as well. He built a Renaissance palace at the Alhambra. Although quite beautiful, it seems to have as much reason here as Anne Hathaway's cottage would at Times Square. Today it houses a **Museum of Fine Arts,** which you can visit for 75 pesetas (72¢), open from 10 a.m. to 2 p.m. daily except Sunday. It also shelters a National Museum devoted to

Hispanic-Muslim art, which keeps the same hours, charging an additional 75 pesetas (72¢) admission. You can visit the Alhambra on Saturday evening when it is illuminated at an admission of 180 pesetas ($1.73).

From the Alhambra, you can proceed up the hill (road clearly marked) to . . .

The Generalife

The sultans spent their summers here at this palace, safely and serenely locked away with their dancing girls. Built in the 13th century to overlook the Alhambra, the Generalife depends on its gardens and courtyards for its glory. Don't expect an Alhambra in miniature: the Generalife was always meant to be a retreat, even from the splendors of the Alhambra. This palace was the setting of the story of the prince locked away from love in Irving's *Tales of the Alhambra*. It is open from 9 a.m. until 7 p.m. It opens at 10 a.m. in winter, closing at 6 p.m. The comprehensive ticket of 250 pesetas ($2.40), which most visitors purchase at the Alhambra, entitles you to admission to the Generalife.

The Cathedral and Royal Chapel

This richly ornate Spanish Renaissance cathedral, with its spectacular altar, is one of the great cathedrals of Spain. It is acclaimed primarily for its beautiful facade and interior gold and white decor. Work on it began in the 16th century, roughly some 30 years after Isabella and Ferdinand reclaimed the city. It is in the lower city, off the principal avenue, Gran Vía de Colón.

In back of the cathedral (entered separately) is the flamboyantly Gothic **Royal Chapel,** where Isabella and Ferdinand are buried. It was their wish to be buried in recaptured Granada, and not Castile or Aragón. The coffins are remarkably tiny by today's standards, which is a reminder of how short folks used to be. The tombs are properly accented by a wrought-iron grill, a masterpiece. Occupying much larger tombs are the remains of their daughter, Joan the Mad, and her husband, Philip the Handsome. Both the chapel and cathedral can be visited from 11 a.m. to 1 p.m. and 4 to 6 p.m.; the charge is 40 pesetas (38¢) for each monument.

The Albaicín

This old Arab quarter doesn't belong to the Granada of the 19th-century buildings and wide boulevards. It, and the surrounding gypsy caves of Sacro-Monte, are holdovers from the past. The Albaicín once flourished as the residential section of the Moors, even after the reconquest of the city, but it declined when the Christians finally declared the Moslems intolerable and drove them from the city. A narrow labyrinth of crooked streets, the Albaicín was spared the fate that many parts of Granada suffered when they were torn down in the name of progress. Happily, it has been preserved, as have its old cisterns, fountains, plazas, whitewashed houses, an occasional villa, and the decaying remnants of the old city gate. One catches a glimpse of a private patio filled with fountains and plants, a traditional way of life handsomely continuing. Be sure to follow the sign to the old Arab baths (free).

Shopping in a Moorish Market

The **Alcaicería,** which huddles close to the cathedral in the lower city, is a rebuilt Moorish-style village of shops in the heart of Granada. Its narrow streets are filled with shops selling the típico arts and crafts of Granada province. For the souvenir hunter, the Alcaicería offers one of the most splendid assortments in Spain—everything from tiles to castanets to wire figures of Don Quixote chasing windmills. Lots of Spanish jewelry is to be found here, comparing favorably to the finest of Toledo work. For the window shopper in particular, it makes for a pleasant stroll. In former days, the Alcaicería was the silk market of the Moors.

The Gypsy Caves of Sacro-Monte

These inhabited gypsy caves have been the subject of much controversy. Admittedly, they are a tourist trap, one of the most obviously commercial and shadowy rackets in all of Spain. Still, the caves are a potent enough attraction, if you follow some rules.

Once thousands of gypsies lived in the caves of the "Holy Mountain," so named because of several Christians martyred here. However, many of the caves were heavily damaged in the flood-like rains of 1962, forcing hundreds of the occupants to seek shelter elsewhere. Nearly all of the gypsies remaining are in one way or another involved with tourism. As one newspaper writer put it, "Some gypsies do not even remain in the caves overnight. When the last bus has departed, they leave, too, for a modern apartment elsewhere in the city."

When evening settles over Granada, visitors in heavy loads descend on these caves near the Albaicín, the old Arab section. In every cave, you'll hear the rattle of castanets and the sound of guitars. Everybody in the gypsy family is doing an act.

Popularly known as the *zambra*, this can be intriguing entertainment *only* if you have an appreciation of the grotesque. Whenever a gypsy boy or girl comes along with a genuine talent, he or she is often grabbed up and hustled off to the more expensive clubs. Those left at home often amuse with their pathetic attempts to assume the image of glamor.

One of the main reasons for going, of course, is to see the caves. If you're expecting primitive living, you may be in for a surprise. Many are quite comfortable, with such conveniences as telephones and electricity, and often they are decorated with copper and ceramic items—and the gypsies need no encouragement to sell them to you.

If you want to see the caves, you can walk up the hill by yourself. By smoke signals or whatever, your approach will already be advertised before you get there. Attempts will be made to lure you inside one of the caves—and to get whatever money from you these cave-dwellers can.

You can also book one of the organized tours, arranged by the travel agencies in Granada. Even at the end of one of these organized tours—all expenses are theoretically paid in advance—there is likely to be another attempt (on the part of the gypsies, not the travel agencies) to extract more money from you. As soon as the *zambra* ends, hustle yourself out of the cave as quickly as possible. Even so, some señorita may chase you down the hill, jabbing her finger in your ribs and screaming, "Money, amigo, money." Readers have been critical of these tours. A typical comment, from a Syracuse University student: "The entire evening was unprofessional and un-typically Spanish and over-priced for the entertainment we received."

During the *zambra*, refuse to accept a pair of castanets, even if offered under the friendly guise of having you join in the fun. If you accept them, the chances are that you'll later be asked to pay for them. Buying anything in these caves is not recommended. Leave all your jewelry at your hotel (in itself risky), but don't take more money to the caves than you're prepared to let light-fingered Luís have.

A different point of view is reflected in the following letter:

"Several of the gypsies had superb figures, and they danced with fire in their feet. They were friendly to the tourists, offering them free drinks and castanets. The audience, which consisted mostly of Americans, sat rigidly and frigidly in their seats, contemptuously rejecting all attempts by the gypsies to establish friendly communications. Understandably, the gypsies were offended and hurt by the tourists' uncalled-for attitude of fear, hostility, and scorn. Though they felt rejected, the gypsies performed brilliantly—and all the while the audience looked guarded as if they were sitting in a robber's lair. It was painful to see. My wife and I feel very strongly that many of the gypsy performers, both in the Sacro-Monte caves and the nightclubs, are talented artists, the heirs of a colorful tradition, and worthy of our respect. As for the tourists, they will be well advised to show better manners. Otherwise, the gypsies have every right to regard them as barbarians" (Dr. Alfred Dorn, Long Island City, N.Y.).

READER'S SIGHTSEEING TIP: "La Cartuja is a 16th-century monastery right off the Albaicín, where Napoleon's armies killed Saint Bruno. It is said to be the only monument of its kind in the world. The price of admission is 20 pesetas (19¢) per person. For that, one will see a museum of paintings, a church, a garden, and a few real surprises. As a matter of fact, a Carthusian monk gave me a guided tour absolutely free" (Charles B. Le Mieux, Oak Park, Ill.). [*Author's Note:* La Cartuja is sometimes called "the Christian answer to the Alhambra," owing to its ornate stucco and marble. Its most notable paintings are by Bocanegra, its outstanding sculpture by Mora. It is open daily from 10 to 1 p.m. and from 4 p.m. until sunset.]

READER'S TIP ON MOUNTAIN AND OCEAN SCENERY: "The traveler in his or her own car is able to drive up the highest mountain road in Europe, south of Granada, to a thousand feet below the highest peak in Spain, in the Sierra Nevada mountains, 11,500 feet high. Another magnificent road runs from Granada south to Lotril. The mountains rival those of Austria and Switzerland in their majesty, great cliffs, and deep gorges. The road from Lotril, which is on the sea, is another fine adventure, as it winds along the coast with many hairpin turns. Each curve presents a new view of the hills and the sea" (Calvin Keene, Lewisburg, Pa.).

THE TOP NIGHTSPOT: The best all-around flamenco show in Granada is staged at **Jardines Neptuno,** Calle Arabial (tel. 25-11-12). Maybe it's not the same show dancing girls performed for sultans centuries ago, but these acts are still "torrid," even though toned down considerably for today's audiences. In addition to flamenco, performers attired in their regional garb do folk dances and give guitar concerts. The show is in a garden setting and breezily expensive, as much as 1000 pesetas ($9.60) for your first drink. But you can nurse it all evening, and that means three solid hours of entertainment. Don't arrive before 11 p.m.

Chapter VII

THE COSTA DEL SOL

1. Algeciras
2. Tarifa
3. Estepona
4. Puerto Banús
5. San Pedro de Alcantara
6. Marbella
7. Fuengirola and Los Boliches
8. Mijas
9. Torremolinos
10. Málaga
11. Nerja
12. Almería

NOWHERE IS THE Spanish tourist boom more booming than on the sun strip named the Costa del Sol. This razzle-dazzle stretch of Mediterranean shoreline begins at the western frontier harbor city of **Algeciras** (gateway to Tangier), and stretches all the way east to the up-an-coming port city of **Almería.**

Sandwiched between these two points is a generally steep and rugged coastline, with poor-to-fair beaches, set against the Sierra Nevada. Along this stretch of land, you'll find sandy coves, whitewashed hamlets, olive trees, old farms, new apartment houses, fishing boats, golf courses, and a widely varied flora—both human and vegetable. In all, the Sun Coast's mild climate in winter and its virtually guaranteed sunshine in summer have made it a year-round attraction.

What were once sleepy fishing villages, with naked niños and little stoop-shouldered women in mourning black, have been knocked out of their slumber by the sound of the jukebox and the honking of a million horns. Blond frauleins, Viking daughters, frisky mademoiselles, and pink-cheeked English girls are today's "children," and they're still running around practically naked, in bikinis.

Hotels, once scarce, are plentiful. Even the remotest, the most provincial of the villages, are erecting hotels. Once the men fished for squid. Now their nets are turning up two-legged land creatures. With many exceptions, style and grace (two elements well known to the Andalusians) have gone the way of García Lorca (he was executed) in this part of the world.

Many of the sun spots along the coast are stricly for low-income Europeans. For the average fun-loving gringo, I suggest **Marbella** and **Torremolinos,** although many sun-seekers find historic **Málaga** more suitable.

From June until deep in the heart of October, the coast is mobbed. If you should arrive during the peak months, make sure you've nailed down a reservation. If you go at other times, chances are the innkeeper will roll out the red carpet, kiss your hand, polish your shoes, and carry you to your pick of a chamber.

The Costa del Sol is traversed by two bus lines, the best means of transportation for those planning to go resort hopping. The major run is from Málaga to Algeciras via Torremolinos and Marbella. If you're flying to the Costa del Sol from Madrid (Iberia has daily connections), you'll land at the Málaga airport. We'll begin our trip up this coast at:

1. Algeciras

This port town is the jumping-off point for Africa (it takes about three hours to reach either Tangier or Spanish Morocco). Algeciras reflects a heavy North African influence. It is a modern, efficient, and clean-looking port city. If you're planning a trip to Tangier from Algeciras, there is a baggage storage depot at the ferry terminal which is very inexpensive—only 15¢ (U.S.) down and 10¢ a day to hold each piece of your luggage.

Algeciras used to be a base for day trips to Gibraltar, and it may be again by the time of your visit. Britain and Spain announced (1982) that the 14-year Spanish blockade of Gibraltar will be lifted. However, remember that agreements are subject to change, and you really should check at the Turismo office on Muelle (tel. 67-17-61) if you're contemplating a trip to "The Rock." There you'll be advised of the latest border-crossing situation.

Even if you don't have time to make the trip to Gibraltar, the habit of Gibraltar watching has always been popular in Algeciras. There it sits, in plain view, six miles out in the Bay of Algeciras. Gathering at the Algeciras docks, tourists aim either their binoculars or cameras at the formidable rock.

WHERE TO STAY: Algeciras is okay for the night, but is not recommended for long stopovers. If you must stay, try the following . . .

Hotel Término, 6 Avenida Villanueva (tel. 67-14-90), a short walk from the docking area. Some of its only fair bedrooms have views of the docks. For a double room with private bath, the charge ranges from 1400 pesetas ($13.44) to 1800 pesetas ($17.28); the best single rooms (with bath) cost 1200 pesetas ($11.52). The dining room is on the ground floor, and there's a terrace for drinks on the second landing. A continental breakfast costs 125 pesetas ($1.20) per person; a luncheon or dinner goes for 625 pesetas ($6). Término is a clean, comfortable, and cheap hotel.

Those wanting to get away from the port area should consider the three-star **Hotel Alarde,** 4 Alfonso XI (tel. 660-408). A hotel which opened in 1971 in a quiet commercial area, it has double rooms with bath and balcony for 3250 pesetas ($31.20). There's a snackbar, but no restaurant. In the center of Algeciras, the residencia is near the Park of María Cristina. Its furnishings are in the pure Toledan style, with antique railings. The main floor is completely air-conditioned, unusual for Algeciras. On my most recent stay, I was left with a very favorable impression of the staff and the homey atmosphere created by management.

READERS' HOTEL SUGGESTIONS: "In four weeks of touring Spain, the cheapest double I found was at the **Hostal Residencia Rua,** 6 Calle Cristo (tel. 67-30-81), which rents a double for 750 pesetas ($7.20) with a shower and wash basin. A continental breakfast is another 100 pesetas (96¢). It's very close to the railroad station, bus terminal, and harbor, and is in the center of town, although it's suprisingly very quiet" (Edward H. Pietraszek, Chicago, Ill.). . . . "The **San Roque Motel,** Km. 124, San Roque (tel. 78-01-00), is about 20 kilometers out of Algeciras between Algeciras and Marbella. It's directly on the highway in a wooded area on a hillside. It has a nice pool, so-so restaurant, and double cabins with small kitchens, lushly flowered individual patios, and shower at 1700 pesetas ($16.32). A continental breakfast is an extra 125 pesetas ($1.20) per person, and a luncheon or dinner costs another 650 pesetas ($6.24) if you want to depend on the motel restaurant" (Mrs. F. M. Nelson, FPO, N.Y.).

WHERE TO EAT: The **Casa Sanchez,** Calle Moret (tel. 67-12-24), is a simple bar and restaurant, near the docks and along the canal, where you can get a meal for 500 pesetas ($4.80) that will include soup or an egg dish, plus paella or macaroni, fruit, bread, and wine. There's a TV blaring away in the evenings, but if you don't mind it, you're all right.

Across the canal is the **Casa Alfonso,** 4 Juan de la Cierva (tel. 67-12-39). For 400 pesetas ($3.84), you can get paella or bean soup, fried fish, a beefsteak with potatoes, bread, wine, and fruit. It's simple and unpretentious, an excellent bargain.

READERS' RESTAURANT SUGGESTIONS: "At the **Restaurante Montes,** 36 Castella (tel. 65-69-05), we found the best value in six cities. There are two Restaurantes Montes under the same ownership, a block apart, about three blocks in from the market. There are guide signs from the market. Both restaurants serve similar four-course meals with wine and bread. One has linen tablecloths and air conditioning, and charges 600 pesetas ($5.76). The other, which has fewer tourists but English-speaking waiters, charges 550 pesetas ($5.28) for the four-course meal. Both restaurants are spotless, and the food and service are excellent" (Mrs. J. Kemp, London, Ontario, Canada). . . . "I have found **Pollo Caporal,** 39 Avenida Virgen del Carmen, on the Paseo Marítimo, about 300 yards in a northeasterly direction from the Portillo bus station, to be a consistently good restaurant. It is similar to a Kentucky Fried Chicken franchise and is quite inexpensive. It is an ideal haunt for those in transit through Algeciras, since you can take away boxed quantities of the succulent chicken if your boat or bus departure is imminent. Set dinners start at 300 pesetas ($2.88), and there are both draft beer and Coca-Cola available. The decor is brash and modern, and this is not a restaurant for gastromones perhaps, but it has tasty food at good prices" (J. M. P. Nichols, Marbella, Spain).

READER'S SIGHTSEEING TIPS: "**Getares** is a small village three kilometers south of Algeciras on the coast, with a lovely uncrowded beach with great views of the Rock. We seemed to be about the only foreigners on the beach.

"**Casares,** 8½ miles off the coast highway just south of Estepona, is a beautiful detour for those working their way north or south along the Costa del Sol. It is a small, unspoiled village in a spectacular setting against the Sierra Bermeja. Casares could be considered a prototype of the Andalusian village, glistening white, all hills, and topped by the ruins of an old fortress. The ride in from the coast offers outstanding views of the town" (James Wiley).

2. Tarifa

If you're in Algeciras, instead of rushing east along the Costa del Sol, I'd suggest a visit west to Tarifa, an old Moorish town that is the southernmost point in Europe. After leaving Algeciras, the roads climb steeply. In the distance you can view Gibraltar, the straits, and the "green hills" of Africa. In fact, you can actually see houses in Ceuta and Tangier on the Moroccan coastline. This road, between Tarifa and Algeciras, is one of the most splendid coastal routes in Spain, maybe in all of Europe.

Tarifa has retained much of its Moorish character, more so than any other town in Andalusia. Narrow, cobblestone streets lead to charming patios filled with flowers. The town was named for Tarik, one of the leaders of the Moorish forces.

At Tarifa is a five-mile-long beach. At one point this beautiful white sandy beach is a quarter of a mile wide. Tarifa is still a Spanish military zone, and that has hindered development, but a major resort is in the making.

Mesón de Sancho, 340 Carretera General Cádiz-Málaga, Km. 94 (tel. 68-49-00), is a rambling, informal, hacienda-style inn, where you'll find a restful atmosphere, plus a swimming pool set out in the midst of olive trees and terraces. It's about ten miles southwest of Algeciras on the Cádiz road. A double with bath rents for 2200 pesetas ($21.12). There are no singles as such; however, one person occupying a double room pays only 1760 pesetas ($16.90). An intercommunicating two-room apartment with bath carries the highest price tag: 3500 pesetas ($33.60) for four persons. Whenever I stay here, I request a bungalow, reached along a shady path, going for 2000 pesetas ($19.20) nightly for two persons, plus another 165 pesetas ($1.58) for a continental breakfast.

The room furnishings are modest-contemporary, with headboards, telephones, tiled baths, and steam heating in the cooler months. Here you can relax in the afternoon, enjoying the potted geraniums, the flowering oleander, the graceful eucalyptus trees. In the country-style dining room, its walls of windows overlooking the garden, a complete luncheon or dinner is served for 850 pesetas ($8.16).

3. Estepona

A town of Roman origin, Estepona is a budding beach resort, 53 miles from Málaga. It is more unpretentious and less developed than Marbella or Torremolinos, and many prefer it for that reason, especially Europeans. Estepona contains an interesting 15th-century parish church and the ruins of an old aqueduct are nearby at Salduba.

Its new recreational port is an attraction, as is its nude beach, Costa Natura, the first legal nude beach along the Costa del Sol. Its other beaches are La Rada, two miles long, and El Cristo, which stretches only 600 yards. One major reason for recommending Estepona is that it contains some of the major bargain stopovers along the Costa del Sol.

ACCOMMODATIONS: In the town, your best bet, if you want to spend the money, is **Caracas,** 50 San Lorenzo (tel. 80-08-00), which lies just off the coastal highway. It is a gleaming white, five-story modern building with balconies. Lying about 150 feet from the beach, in the heart of Estepona, it offers 40 double bedrooms in the modern idiom. The rooms have no style, but are of generous size. A single rents for 1700 pesetas ($16.32); a double, 2600 pesetas ($24.96). The atmosphere is clean and jazzy bright. A complete luncheon or dinner goes for 750 pesetas ($7.20).

Buenavista, 118 Paseo Marítimo (tel. 80-01-37), is a friendly, comfortable little residencia right on the coastal road. It's recommended for an overnight stopover or a modest holiday. Rooms are clean, but likely to be noisy in summer from the heavy traffic. Singles rent for 850 pesetas ($8.16); doubles, from 1200 pesetas ($11.52) to 1800 pesetas ($17.28). A continental breakfast is an extra 125 pesetas ($1.20) per person, and either lunch or dinner goes for 600 pesetas ($5.76).

El Pilar, 22 Plaza José Antonio (tel. 80-00-18), is a modest, two-story, tile-roofed hostal, opening onto the prettiest square in the village. There are tables set out for refreshments in the midst of orange trees and bougainvillea. The dining room is very provincial, and you can eat somewhat family style. A complete lunch or dinner costs 600 pesetas ($5.76). A single is 850 pesetas ($8.16) without bath; a double, 1400 pesetas ($13.44) if bathless to 1800 pesetas ($17.28) with shower bath. A continental breakfast is an extra 125 pesetas ($1.20) per person. The rooms are quite basic, but clean, opening onto a covered central area. The bedrooms have water basins only, although there are toilets in the corridor.

La Malagueña, 1 Calle Castillo (tel. 80-00-11), is a very modest low-budget hostal. Many of its rooms open onto a three-story-high, glassed-in courtyard or else onto the street, overlooking the Plaza las Flores, with its border of orange-bearing trees. The courtyard of La Malagueña is rather simple with a fountain in the Andalusian style. The rooms are stripped-down basic, with water basins only and old beds. Linoleum covers the floors. The rates are low enough to attract low-paid Spanish working people—1200 pesetas ($11.52) in a double, 750 pesetas ($7.20) in a single. A meal, taken separately, costs 480 pesetas ($4.61), though you can stay here on full-board terms for 1800 pesetas ($17.28) per person, based on double occupancy.

After all the pesetas you've saved at these simple inns, you may be ready for some—

SPLURGE DINING: At **Le Castel,** Urbanización Bahía Dorada, Carretera de Cádiz (tel. 80-05-46), on the western fringes of Estepona, you'll enjoy an excellent French and Belgian cuisine. The chef-owner, Michael Witmeur, is from Belgium, and his wife is Spanish. Their waterfront restaurant is a tile-roofed villa on the highway. You enter a living-room bar, with an open copper-hooded fireplace, with clusters of hanging pierced tin lanterns. The dining rooms are on a lower level, with sloping ceilings and windows overlooking the tiled roofs of the encircling development and the sea. Clusters of lanterns illuminate the two dining rooms.

The chef provides an individualized international cuisine, and many nouvelle cuisine specialties. If you order his fresh fish soup, you're given toast and a small bowl of curried garlic mayonnaise to eat with it. Other good appetizers are the mussels bourguignonnes or the hors d'oeuvres Castel. Hot rolls are brought out to accompany your main dish—sole meunière, rabbit, and (in season) quail with cherries. You can even get fried chicken and curry sauce with the accompanying condiments. Try his monk fish with pink peppercorns, his peppersteak, roast suckling pig, and meat and chicken from the charcoal grill. A classic ending is the peach Melba. Expect to spend from 1200 pesetas ($11.52) to 2000 pesetas ($19.20) if you dine here. On Wednesday night in season (from June to September), a program of flamenco is presented. The restaurant is closed in February and on Tuesday from November to January.

El Molino, Urbanización El Saladillo (tel. 80-09-49), is set back from the coastal highway. It is named after a towering white windmill, surrounded by thick shrubbery and pine trees. Its two dining rooms are tavern style, with rustic furnishings and ceiling beams. In fair weather you can dine on the vine-covered terrace at the rear. Meals are offered every evening between 8 and 11:30 p.m. However, the restaurant is closed from January 10 to April 8, and on Tuesday. The cuisine is mainly French. I'd suggest, to get you started, shrimp cocktail at 380 pesetas ($3.65); pâté of the casa, also 380 pesetas; the snails at 350 pesetas ($3.36); or perhaps turtle soup, 325 pesetas ($3.12). For a main dish, you might prefer rack of lamb at 680 pesetas ($6.53); veal chop at 750 pesetas ($7.20); or the fish filets at 700 pesetas ($6.72); which are always good. At the end of your meal, you may be tempted by the lemon sorbet at 250 pesetas ($2.40), or the fresh raspberries or wild strawberries in cream at 450 pesetas ($4.32). Expect to spend from 1350 pesetas ($12.96) to 2300 pesetas ($22.08) for a complete meal.

4. Puerto Banús

This marine village, near Marbella, is a favorite resort of celebrities from all over the world. Almost overnight a village was created in the traditional Mediterranean style. There is no sameness here. Each building appears different in design, yet everything blends into a harmonious whole. Yachts can be moored at your doorstep. Along the harbor front is an array of sophisticated bars and restaurants, all of which are expensive.

Try, if you can, to wander through the quiet back streets as well, past elegant archways, grilled patios, and flower-filled plazas. The rich and the elegant rent apartments in this village for the season.

However, there are no inns that I know of, just restaurants. Surprisingly, a few of the dining rooms—not those on the waterfront—offer bargain meals. Go here for lunch or dinner and for sightseeing. It's a dream-like village, a Disneyworld creation of what a Costa del Sol fishing village looks like.

RESTAURANTS, BARS, AND DISCOS: **El Dolar,** reached by walking up a stairway from the port, is a bargain oasis in this high-priced, tab-happy port. A simple tavern, it specializes in Basque cookery, and does so very well. There are only a few tables, so it's likely to be crowded in high season. Expect to spend around 1200 pesetas ($11.52) for a big meal, including the house wine. Each day a plato del día is featured, and it's invariably fresh. Paella is the chef's specialty, but he also does a selection of various tapas which you might want to nibble on before eating your main course. He also does a well-prepared codfish in the Basque style, as well as some interesting shellfish dishes. Try his sole gratin or his mixed fish fry of Mediterranean sea creatures. It's open only in season.

El Mesón Grill, Puerto de José Banús, is an attractive restaurant, with a mezzanine courtyard patio and a rambling group of dining rooms under a coved stucco ceiling. At its entrance is a raised charcoal-burning fireplace. The color scheme is yellow and white, with raffia-seated provincial chairs. You can get half a grilled chicken here for 400 pesetas ($3.84), and the Costa del Sol version of the American hamburger at 400 pesetas also. Deep-fried hake is a fine choice, and cigalas (crayfish) are priced according to weight. The chef's specialty, also priced according to weight, is dorada (dory) which is cooked in salt. A carafe of the house wine starts at 280 pesetas ($2.69) to 400 pesetas ($3.84), and an average meal here will cost from 700 pesetas ($6.72) to 1200 pesetas ($11.52). The mesón is open only during the summer season.

Pizza y Pasta, Casa o Local, 11 Calle de Ribera, is a fast-paced little establishment whose name tells it all. If you're a person who considers a pizza a full meal, then this little trattoria will accomodate. Pizzas range in price from 300 pesetas ($2.88) to 450 pesetas ($4.32), including the popular calzone. The crust is thick, and the cheese and marinara center juicy with flavor. The pasta is good, especially the pasta al pesto. The lasagne is first rate, as is the tortellini. Most of the pasta plates cost between 350 pesetas ($2.88) and 400 pesetas

($3.84). Closed Monday. Again, this place only operates during the summer
season.

Sinatra Bar, Muelle Ribera, is gravity center for people-watching. Here
residents of the nearby apartments meet for early-morning coffee or drinks late
in the evening. The preferred spot, if the weather is right, is on one of the white
bamboo chairs set out on the sidewalk. Only a few feet away, rows of luxury
yachts await your inspection. Tables are usually shared, and piped music tells
you, among other things, "what it's like down in Louisiana." Drinks range
from 60 pesetas (58¢) for coffee up to 250 pesetas ($2.40) for a local whisky.
Go here in the summer months only.

From 11 p.m. nightly, you can visit **Andrea,** Puerto de José Banús, which,
as of this writing, is the major disco in the port, offering drinks for 600 pesetas
($5.76). In between dancing and music, you can enjoy such Italian dishes as
pizza, spaghetti, pasta fagioli (beans), cakes, and ice creams. Light meals begin
at 750 pesetas ($7.20). Andrea is strictly a summer-only establishment.

GAMBLING: At the **Casino Nueva Andalucía Marbella,** Nueva Andalucía,
on the outskirts of Puerto Banús (tel. 81-13-44), the Costa del Sol approaches
the glamor and nightlife excitement of the French Riviera. At this deluxe club,
a host of facilities are available in addition to gambling. Swimming pools, a
private beach, a nightclub, a drinking lounge, a first-class restaurant are but
some of the luxurious facilities awaiting the big spender who can afford to
partake. For at least one evening during your stay, it's fun to dress up for a
night on the town. At the casino, guests play American roulette (also the
French variety) as well as black jack and chemin-de-fer. You'll need your
passport to get in, as well as 400 pesetas ($3.84) shelled out for the entrance
fee. In summer the casino is open from 8 p.m. till 5 a.m., and in winter from
6 p.m. to 3 a.m.

5. San Pedro de Alcantara

Between Marbella and Estepona, this attractive village, 43 miles west of
Málaga, contains interesting Roman remains officially classified as a National
Monument. In recent years it has been extensively developed as a resort suburb
of Marbella, containing some colorful hotels, previewed below.

Pueblo Andaluz, Carretera de Cádiz, Km. 179 (tel. 81-16-42), is built in
the style of an Andalusian village, with patios and gardens planted with flowering shrubbery and trees. This self-contained resort world lies about a five-mile
drive west from Marbella in the direction of Algeciras. However, the beach is
only a five-minute walk from your bedroom door. It makes a good bet for
families, as there's a special playground reserved for children, as well as a
paddling pool. Bedrooms are decorated in the Spanish traditional style, costing
1200 pesetas ($11.52) to 1800 pesetas ($17.28) in a double, that tariff dropping
to only 950 pesetas ($9.12) in a bathless single. In the regional-style dining
room, built like a hacienda, only breakfast at 150 pesetas ($1.44) is offered. The
hotel is open from April 1 to October 31.

Cortijo Blanco, San Pedro de Alcantara (tel. 81-14-40), a few kilometers
west of Marbella toward Gibraltar, offers 107 bedrooms overlooking miniature
patios overgrown with bougainvillea, canna, and roses. Built in the Andalusian
hacienda style, it offers modern accommodations, each with private bath.
Tariffs vary according to the season, the highest rates in effect from March 1
to October 31. Singles range from 1600 pesetas ($15.36) to 2100 pesetas
($20.16); doubles, 2400 pesetas ($23.04) to 2800 pesetas ($26.88), plus 1500

pesetas ($14.40) per person extra for half board. Luncheon is served under a long covered garden pergola, dinner in the more formal dining hall, where the walls are lined with oils and tables surrounded by high-backed gilt and red Valencian chairs. During the day, the social center revolves around a large open-air swimming pool.

6. Marbella

Although it enjoys a broad base of tourism, Marbella is still, in part, the most exclusive resort along the Costa del Sol, ranking number two to Torremolinos in popularity. Once English expatriates and French countesses inhabited its shaded villas, and many still do. However, in recent years much Arab money has been pumped into Marbella.

Marbella, a beach town in transition, is the first major resort the motorist approaches after heading east on the road from Algeciras (it's about 50 miles from Gibraltar). If it's approached from the east, it is about 37 miles from Málaga, 28 miles from Torremolinos. The big attraction is the beaches in and around Marbella— **El Fuerte** and **La Fontanilla** the two chief ones. But there are others, perhaps more secluded, if you have transportation and care to branch out. Yet keep in mind that the myth of a little hidden spot on the Sun Coast is becoming just that: **a myth.**

Despite its overbundance of tourists, Marbella is a pleasant Andalusian town at the foot of the Sierra Blanca. It's bustling and modern, but there are traces of the old, such as its palace-like town hall, its medieval ruins, and old Moorish walls. Like most Spanish towns, its greatest charm is to be found in its old quarter, with its narrow cobblestone streets and Arabesque houses. However, many of the old houses have been hastily converted into shops that sell merchandise at inflated prices. Still, it makes for a good late-afternoon or before-dinner stroll.

WHERE TO STAY: Marbella, which is noted for charging about 15% higher prices than other places along the strip, quite surprisingly features a number of excellent budget hotels.

Hotel Guadalpín, Carretera 340 Cádiz-Málaga, Km. 186 (tel. 77-11-00), is right on the rugged coast, only 300 yards from the beach (a mile from the center of Marbella). You can live here at this three-star hotel for 2200 pesetas ($21.12) to 3000 pesetas ($28.80) in a double room with private bath. For a single with a full bath, the rate is 1800 pesetas ($17.28) to 2000 pesetas ($19.20), but only ten rooms are available in this category. A continental breakfast is an extra 185 pesetas ($1.78) per person, and a complete lunch or dinner costs another 800 pesetas ($7.68).

Guests spend many hours relaxing around two swimming pools; or they walk along a private pathway lined with fir trees to the Mediterranean. The dining room has large windows overlooking the patio and pool, and the main lounge has been designed in ranch style with round marble tables and occasional leather armchairs arranged for conversational groups.

The bar area of the spacious lounge is brick and natural wood, making it warm and attractive. Each room has not only two terraces, but a living room and bedroom combined; most of the rooms are furnished in "new ranch" style. They have all of the conveniences, such as telephones and central heating during the cooler months.

El Rodeo, 2 Victor de la Serna (tel. 77-51-00), is a modern hotel, just off the main coastal road of Marbella, yet it is quiet and cut off from traffic noises.

It's a seven-story structure, with a swimming pool and sunbathing area at its crown. Two elevators whisk you to the second-floor lounges which are spacious, sunny, and furnished as in a country house. Stark white bamboo is used effectively in some areas, and the breakfast room is cheerful, with ladderback chairs and decorative fabric at the windows. There's also a bar with tropical bamboo chairs and tables. The bedrooms are well styled, with several shuttered closets and lounge chairs, white desks, and bentwood chairs. Each has a private bath. The highest tariffs are charged from April 1 to October 31, although the hotel is open all year. A single room with bath and terrace costs 1850 pesetas ($17.76), rising to 2400 pesetas ($23.04) in a double, also with bath and terrace. A continental breakfast at 150 pesetas ($1.44) is the only meal served. El Rodeo stands about a five-minute walk from the beach, another five-minute stroll to the old section with its chic boutiques and restaurants.

Residencia Alfil, 19 Avenida Ricardo Soriano (tel. 77-23-50), in the middle of Marbella is one of the brightest additions to the resort's skyline. The style here is slick and modern, but the eight-floor Alfil handles it well. Both the public rooms and the well-furnished, spacious bedrooms are thoughtfully designed, often utilizing Spanish reproductions (richly paneled door, chairs with leather and nailheads).

The charge for a double room with private bath is 2000 pesetas ($19.20), 1500 pesetas ($14.40) in a single with private bath. All but ten rooms have private balconies, many with views of the Mediterranean. A continental breakfast costs 150 pesetas ($1.44). There's garage space.

Sportclub, Paseo Marítimo (tel. 77-29-00), stands right on the water, with its own beach, sharing space with a waterfront restaurant. The club-hotel has a dignified entrance with a stained-glass panel and plants, and on its sea side is a wide terrace for sunbathing which is also ideal for sunset drinks. Rooms are attractively furnished and well kept, costing 2400 pesetas ($23.04) in a double with bath, 2000 pesetas ($19.20) in a single with the same plumbing. Meals are 850 pesetas ($8.16) each. In the Sportclub Restaurant, you can order excellently prepared fish dishes from an à la carte menu—Málaga fish fry, chanquetes, squid with lemon, and grilled swordfish. Most main dishes range in price from 400 pesetas ($3.84) to 850 pesetas ($8.16).

Residencia Lima, 2 Avenida Antonio Belón (tel. 77-05-00), a short skip to the sea, is a little bit more secluded, tucked away in a residential section of Marbella. Quite a modern structure, it stacks up its bedrooms for a least eight stories, then encircles them with private balconies. The Lima's furnishings, both in the good bedrooms and the lounges, lean heavily on Spanish provincial.

Open year round, the Lima charges a peak of 2300 pesetas ($22.08) for a double with bath; 2150 pesetas ($20.64) for a double with shower bath (there are four in this category). Singles with shower baths rent for 1600 pesetas ($15.36). A continental breakfast is an extra 150 pesetas ($1.44) per person.

Residencia Finlandia, Finlandia (tel. 77-07-00), is oddly placed in the "Huerta Grande," a residential section suitable for peace and quiet. Yet it's only a five-minute walk to the center of town, and a two-minute jaunt to the Mediterranean. This small, well-kept hotel is a decent place in which to hole up for a while. It's very clean, modern, and if run by a friendly management. The rates are friendly, too—1650 pesetas ($15.84) for a double with bath, and 1250 pesetas ($12) for a single. The rooms are airy, spacious, and equipped with modern furnishings. You'll find your bed turned down at night, and you can have your continental breakfast on the terrace in the morning. The breakfast is obligatory at 125 pesetas ($1.20) per person. No other meals are served, however.

Residencia San Cristóbal, 18 Ramón y Cajal (tel. 77-12-50), in the heart of Marbella, is a fine hotel—modern to the teeth, but not antiseptically so. Its five floors have long, wide terrace balconies, with window boxes filled with vines and flowers. Each bedroom contains many refinements, such as walnut headboards with telephones and overhead individual reading lamps. Room dividers separate the comfortable beds from the small living room area. An added plus is the private terrace beyond—just right for a continental breakfast in the Marbella sunshine. Double accomodations with clean baths rent for 2100 pesetas ($20.16). Only a continental breakfast at 200 pesetas ($1.92) is served.

El Castillo, 2 Plaza San Barnabé (tel. 77-17-39), is perhaps the smallest hotel in town, perched in the old narrow-streeted town, at the foot of the castle, opening onto a minuscule triangular square used by an adjoining convent and school as a playground in the afternoon. There's a small covered courtyard, and the second-floor bedrooms have only inner windows. The spartan rooms are scrubbed clean, and contain white tiled baths. Rates are 1400 pesetas ($13.44) in a double, 1000 pesetas ($9.60) in a single. No morning meal is served, and not one word of English is spoken. It's for the adventurous only.

Hostal Residencia Gogar, 5 Joaquím Chillida (tel. 77-00-11), is a tiny place right in the heart of Marbella. It's a gem if you can get in, and you stand a good chance, as it hasn't been discovered yet. It's ultra clean and utterly simple, but you're right in the heart of the action, near Orange Tree Square. Only Spanish is spoken, but you can easily manage here. The señora who runs it is friendly and polite, proudly showing off her immaculate rooms, for which she charges just 1100 pesetas ($10.56) in a bathless double, 800 pesetas ($7.68) in a single. A continental breakfast is another 100 pesetas (96¢) per person. Pots of geraniums are placed out on the balconies, and a jungle of bougainvillea climbs up the whitewashed walls.

Nagüeles, Carretera de Cádiz, Km. 184, 3½ kilometers from Marbella, heading west (tel. 77-16-50), stands near the luxurious Marbella Club on the fringes of Marbella, right on the main coastal road. Its entrance and restaurant are on the busy highway, but the two-story, white-washed brick hotel has bedrooms set back from the traffic and protected by orange and willow trees. Red bougainvillea vines crawl through the railings of the balconies. There are 17 nicely, but simply, furnished bedrooms, which are clean and contain private baths. The rate is 1400 pesetas ($13.44) in a single, 1800 pesetas ($17.28) in a double. A continental breakfast is an extra 150 pesetas ($1.44) per person. The hotel is open only from April to October.

Residencia Munich, 5 Virgen del Pilar (tel. 77-24-61), is an unassuming rather basic little three-story hotel, just a short walk from the water. It's owned by a German woman, Anna Luise Gasteiger, who offers some rooms with private baths, some with balconies. A continental breakfast at 125 pesetas ($1.20) is the only meal she serves. The residencia is set back from the street, shielded by banana and palm trees. The little lounge and breakfast room are cluttered with knickknacks, a mixture of old and new furniture. There is definitely a homelike atmosphere. Doubles with showers or private baths peak at 1200 pesetas ($11.52) and singles, also with private plumbing, go for 900 pesetas ($8.64).

The **Hostal Mena,** 10 Plaza del Generalísimo Franco (tel. 77-40-60), is the best boarding house for those seeking real economy. The Mena is on an attractive plaza of citrus trees and flowers in the old town. It's modest, with a little covered courtyard, but the forever-scrubbing maids keep it immaculate. None of the basic rooms has a private bath, but they are equipped with water basins. Rarely is a complaint heard when it comes to pay the bill: 850

pesetas ($8.16) for a double room, only 650 pesetas ($6.24) for a single. A continental breakfast is an extra 100 pesetas (96¢) per person.

WHERE TO EAT: Restaurant prices are soaring in Marbella. In many instances, your hotel remains a good bet, but since so many of Marbella's hosteries are residencias, you'll need to seek out independent budget dining spots. I'll lead off with . . .

La Cancela, 6 Misericordia (tel. 77-00-73), is owned by Mrs. Linda Horton. The cozy restaurant features a large ivy-covered patio for al fresco dining and a pleasant bar where you can enjoy your favorite drink. Its open fireplace and beamed ceilings contribute to its typical old Andalusian atmosphere. The menu varies according to the season, with reputed specialties such as roast lamb and mint sauce for 525 pesetas ($5.04), stuffed pork for 500 pesetas ($4.80), and a variety of inexpensive local fish dishes from 350 pesetas ($3.36) to 650 pesetas ($6.24). Desserts include profiteroles for 125 pesetas ($1.20). Reservations are advised. Closed Tuesday.

Posada Puerta del Mar, 4 San Juan de Dios, is an unpretentious little Spanish restaurant, the kind that is hard to come by in cosmopolitan Marbella. Actually, the place was an old buggy inn, which has now been adorned with flowers and potted plants. You can eat indoors or on the pleasant patio. Soup here is fresh, prepared daily, and the chef informs me that the most popular fish dish is hake; the best loved meat dish, steak and potatoes. Flan, predictably, is the preferred dessert. An average meal here costs around 600 pesetas ($5.76).

Metropol, 21 Avenida Ricardo Soriano (tel. 77-11-39), stands right on the main street. Its Dutch patron, René Lith, will welcome you. He has taught his Spanish chef the skills he learned when he ran another restaurant in his native Netherlands. I've been dropping in here regularly for nearly 15 years, and have found the cookery consistently good—in fact, much improved in recent years. The atmosphere is friendly and cozy, the ambience enhanced by soft-playing music in the background. Mr. Lith's cooking repertoire is international. Try, for example, his large shrimps l'Orly, served with tartar sauce, and his superb chicken. I'd also suggest the filet of halibut, cooked au gratin in a well-flavored sauce. The paella is also good. Expect to pay about 1000 pesetas ($9.60) to 2000 pesetas ($19.20) for a meal at both lunch and dinner.

Bodegón Asturiano, Avenida de la Fontanilla, stands on the western fringe of Marbella, on the ground floor of a modern apartment building. The province of Asturias, in northwest Spain, is noted for its hearty, provincial cookery. No dish is more typical of this province than fabada, a variety of beans cooked with pork, having some resemblance to the French cassoulet. Other main courses include veal from Ávila, which is tender, white veal, the best in Spain. Also good is hake cooked Basque style. To begin your meal, you have a choice of such savory appetizers as sopa de ajo, a soup made with garlic, or snails with garlic. Flan finishes the repast nicely. Everything tastes better when washed down with the classic Asturian cider. The cost of a complete meal ranges in price from 750 pesetas ($7.20) to 900 pesetas ($8.64).

Crepería Marbella, 11 Plaza de los Naranjos (tel. 77-51-49), is the first of its kind in Marbella, set in the old town, overlooking Orange Tree Square. Against the backdrop of an old-world atmosphere, it offers a variety of well-stuffed crêpes—both for your main course and dessert—prepared in the French manner. You might begin with French onion soup, or a mixed green salad. Main-course crêpes are likely to include everything from spinach soufflé to seafood (invariably featured). If you don't want a crêpe, or would rather save the experience for dessert, then you can ask for chicken Maryland. The dessert crêpes are spectacular (I've sampled apple, banana, and chocolate mint). Prices for the main dishes range from 300 pesetas ($2.88) to 520 pesetas ($4.99). Crêpes cost from 245 pesetas ($2.35) to 345 pesetas ($3.31). The crepería is reached by climbing a flight of stairs. It's entered through an arcaded patio with balconies. What you find is a small provincial room with a beamed ceiling, an overscale open fireplace, and Valencian chairs. Closed Sunday.

Casa Eladio, 6 Virgen Dolores, a two-minute walk from Orange Tree Square, has a simple setting, with plastic-covered tables. But it serves a modest dinner for just 400 pesetas ($3.84), one of the best bargains in Marbella. The ambience, what there is of it, is dimly lit and snug, a popular gathering place for families, particularly on a Sunday afternoon. Rich aromas filter back from the kitchen, where such local dishes are being prepared as Andalusian tripe, eggs flamenco style, swordfish with salad, and kidneys with sherry. A specialty is grilled sea bream. The menu is in English. For dessert, nearly everybody orders pudding. If you dine à la carte, expect a tab ranging in price from 500 pesetas ($4.80) to 700 pesetas ($6.72). Closed Wednesday.

The **Pizzería Sanremo,** Edificio Mediterraneo (tel. 77-43-33), on the Paseo Marítimo, right on the beach, draws devotees of the Italian kitchen who like to sample the viands of the owner, Stefano Vella. The menu is presented in English, and most diners prefer one of the pizzas, costing around 250 pesetas ($2.40), or perhaps one of the various spaghetti concoctions, averaging about 325 pesetas ($3.12) per plate. The raw carrot salad is an unusual item on menus in Spain, and the veal dishes are well prepared. For a complete meal, expect to pay about 800 pesetas ($7.68). If you're in the resort on a Thursday, you can come here to order couscous, the North African specialty, costing 750 pesetas ($7.20).

The Big Splurge

La Triciclette, 16 Buitrago (tel. 82-35-77), is one of the most popular dining spots in Marbella. It is a converted home, courtyard and all, on a narrow street in the old part of town. It's easy to find if you ask, as it has become a local landmark. The customers come from all over Europe and North America. Sofas provide a living-room ambience in the bar, and twisting stairs lead up to an intimate dining room and an open terrace dining patio which is delightful except in the chilly months. The food is exceptionally good with a continental menu selection. A good beginning would be spinach crêpes or a house specialty, cheese (Gruyere) croquettes. Fresh sole, grilled or meunière, or a moussaka is offered. Chocolate mousse is the favorite dessert. An average meal here costs between 1200 pesetas ($11.52) and 2000 pesetas ($19.20). The wine list is extensive and reasonable. Reservations can be made between 8 p.m. to 1 a.m.; closed Sunday.

Gran Marisquería Santiago, 5 Paseo Marítimo Duque de Ahumada (tel. 77-00-78), stands right on the waterfront, up from the beach. It has the best prepared and the freshest shellfish and fish dishes in Marbella, but you have to pay a high price for some of the most delectable creatures of the Mediterranean. The least expensive way to dine here is to order the set menu for 800 pesetas ($7.68), which includes either hors d'oeuvres or seafood soup (savory, spicy), followed by a small entrecôte or else the fresh fish of the day, climaxed by dessert. If you're ordering à la carte, you'll find such specialties as raw mussels which make an excellent appetizer, although the true Spaniard selects the baby eels—cooked with garlic and bubbling hot olive oil. Chanquetes, those tiny fish found along the Mediterranean coast—a kind of local whitebait—is another specialty, as is the unique fried fish of Málaga. At the end of your meal, you may prefer the Manchego cheese. À la carte meals usually mean a bill in the neighborhood of 1800 pesetas ($17.28).

El Puchero Vasco, 1 Panadería (tel. 77-33-37), offers Basque cookery in a typical mesón setting. A sophisticated tavern atmosphere prevails. The walls contain a collection of paintings, and some tables are set on an open patio surrounded by plants. In cooler months logs burn in an open fireplace. The food is quite good, and the service exceptional. Your meal can be expensive, depending on what you order. You might begin with leek-and-potato soup, then follow with roast baby chicken or perhaps squid cooked in its own ink. The lemon curd tart is a good dessert. Complete meals begin at 850 pesetas ($8.16). Closed Sunday.

FLAMENCO: Marbella flamenco spots come and go with frequency, and those that survive are often "in" one year, "out" the next. However, at the moment **La Caneta Pagoda Gitana,** Carretera de Cádiz, enjoys favor. This Oriental-style place is just a mile from the heart of the city (call 82-40-42 for reservations). You should arrive after 10:30 p.m., as that's when the "gypsy blood" gets going. Skilled artists frequently appear; usually, there's a team of half a dozen singers, as well as a *gran cantadora* and Spanish guitarists. For your entrance fee and first drink, you usually are charged 1000 pesetas ($9.60). The clients are likely to be as intriguing as the show, everybody from Portuguese gigolos with American widows to Brunhildes and their Spanish Don Juans.

The challenger to the above recommendation is **Fiesta,** 8 Calle Valentunana (tel. 77-37-43). Usually featured as star performer here is Manolita Cano, called "the first vedette of Spanish song and rumba." Backing up the star are cantores and some fine Spanish guitarists. Shows are nightly from 10:45 to 12:45 and from 1:15 and 2:45, at a cost of 800 pesetas ($7.68) for the first drink, 500 pesetas ($4.80) thereafter.

POPULAR BARS: El Club, 8 Calle Príncipe (tel. 77-15-23), is in Old Marbella, near Horcher's La Fonda. It has rapidly become "a home away from home" for expatriates, both British and American. Owner Ray Holland, from Nottingham, runs the bar much like a house party. With its old walls, the house is charming, with Moorish stone archways and intimate candlelit patios. You enter, past a bottomless well, to a maze of tiny rooms which are furnished comfortably. Aside from the bar, the most sought-after place is in front of the open fireplace. The decor is eclectic, suggesting an informal hominess. Mr. Holland is well informed about the latest restaurants and nightlife. El Club is open from 8 p.m. daily, except Sunday. The upstairs L-shaped room has been converted into a small and intimate restaurant, seating only two dozen guests.

Bacchus Bar, 18 Avenida del Fuerte (tel. 77-22-00), is a small, friendly Irish bar which will give you a warm welcome. Underneath the Torre de Marbella building, it offers you, besides your favorite cocktail, local drinks such as sangría. Light snacks, apéritifs, liqueurs, coffee, and, of course, Irish coffee are also offered at reasonable prices. The owner, Mrs. Linda Hutton, would be more than pleased to give you any information you require to help make your stay in the area more enjoyable. Closed Tuesday.

IN THE SIERRA BLANCA: If the summer heat has got you, you may want to retreat north into the Sierra Blanca to the **Refugio de Juanar,** 12½ miles north of Marbella on C337, outside Ojen (tel. 88-10-00). Reached by a winding road, the parador is sponsored by the Spanish government, offering very comfortable accommodations and excellent regional cookery. Most motorists come up only for the day, enjoying the mountain scenery and a complete luncheon or dinner for 950 pesetas ($9.12). Meals are served in a rustic-style dining room, and there is an open terrace for drinks offering views of the Sierras. The Refugio is not unlike a fine Spanish villa, with a tiled roof and iron grillwork at its windows. The lounge features an open fireplace and comfortable armchairs, along with a few antiques and Oriental scatter rugs. There are nine bedrooms, most of which contain private baths. Each is handsomely styled and immaculately kept. Doubles with bath rent for 3000 pesetas ($28.80), but only 2400 pesetas ($23.04) if bathless. Singles cost ($23.04). A continental breakfast is an extra 250 pesetas ($2.40) per person.

7. Fuengirola and Los Boliches

The twin fishing towns of Fuengirola and Los Boliches lie halfway between the more famous resorts of Marbella and Torremolinos, about 20 miles from Málaga. The promenade along the water stretches some 2½ miles. With their chalk-white houses and friendly residents, Fuengirola and Los Boliches don't have the facilities and drama of Torremolinos, nor the chicness of Marbella. But Fuengirola is cheaper, and that has attracted a horde of economy-minded European tourists.

On a promontory overlooking the sea, the ruins of San Isidro Castle can be seen. Los Boliches is just half a mile from Fuengirola and is less developed. The Santa Amalja, Carvajal, and Las Gaviotas beaches are broad and clean, and have fine sands.

WHERE TO STAY AND EAT: Florida, Paseo Marítimo (tel. 47-61-00), is a garden spot opening right onto the sea. In front of the hotel is a detached semitropical garden, providing areas for sunbathing and refreshments served under a wide, vine-covered pergola. The hotel offers 111 double or twin-bedded rooms, with bath and shower. Most of them have a balcony overlooking the sea or mountains. The floors are tiled, and the furnishings, particularly in the lounge, make much use of plastic. The cost of staying here for two persons, including a continental breakfast, is 2700 pesetas ($25.92). Singles with breakfast are 1800 pesetas ($17.28). The half-board rate for two persons is 4100 pesetas ($39.36).

Hostal Sedeno, Benavente (tel. 46-17-78), occupies a tucked-away position three minutes from the beach, in the heart of town. Running between two streets, its entrance lobby is modest, although it leads to a larger adjoining lounge furnished with antiques and reproductions. You pass a small open courtyard, with stairs leading to the second- and third-floor bedrooms with balconies. These accommodations overlook a small garden with fig and palm trees, plus a glassed-in dining room with terrace. It's not unlike an early modern Florida motel. Doubles with full bath go for 1800 pesetas ($17.28), but only 1400 pesetas ($13.44) with shower. Singles range in price from 1000 pesetas ($9.60) to 1200 pesetas ($11.52). Full board is an additional 1400 pesetas ($13.44) per person. The continental breakfast at 150 pesetas ($1.44) per person is obligatory. The hostal is closed from December 10 to January 10.

READERS' HOTEL SELECTIONS: "A small hostal in Los Boliches is the **Hostal Residencia Nevada,** 3 Santa Rosa (tel. 47-56-98), a block from the Don Bigote Restaurant. A double with complete bath costs $18 (U.S.) A handful of bathless singles rent for only $12. The rooms are well furnished and very clean, with central heating. There are parking facilities, a coffeeshop, and a bar. The manager, José Centeno, is fond of Americans and speaks excellent English. In addition, good and tasty homemade Spanish food is available at reasonable prices" (Dr. and Mrs. H. W. Goebert, Kailua, Hi.).

Meals at Fuengirola

Restaurante Romy, Calle Moncayo, is a bustling place with tables outside which quickly fill up in the evenings with happy, chattering diners. Owner Pepe Moreno sees to it that the food is good, and if you're interested in any special dish, ask and he might have it prepared for you, if possible. His menú del día costs only 280 pesetas ($1.73). On my latest rounds, I enjoyed sopa de ajo (garlic), the hors d'oeuvres, consisting of potato salad, chopped green pepper, tomatoes, and onions with dressing, as well as cauliflower and broiled sardines in a sauce. If featured, the shellfish soup is also recommendable. For a main course, I'd suggest merluza (hake) in a sauce, prepared "Romy" style.

La Chuleta Flamenca, Calle Miguel de Cervantes, Perla 2 (tel. 47-38-70), is a typical mesón with tables out front under a canopy in an arcade a half a block from the waterfront. At this two-fork restaurant, service tends to be friendly and courteous, but perhaps a little too forgetful during the rush of the tourist season in summer. The least expensive way to dine here is to order the menú del día for 400 pesetas ($3.84). For that, you get one fish- or meat-based dish, plus dessert and wine.

The chef does a good job with steak, preparing it both Basque style and Provençale. For an appetizer, his pâté is a favorite, or you can select among an assortment of shrimp or snails. The chicken curry is also recommendable. For dessert, the homemade ice cream Grand Marnier is tempting, as is the Dame Blanche (ice cream with a hot chocolate sauce). If you wish to sample the à la carte specialties, you can expect to spend from 700 pesetas ($6.72) to 1000 pesetas ($9.60).

Casa Zafra, 6 Perla, Paseo Marítimo, (tel. 47-05-94) a typical mesón with outside tables, standing right on the port. It's a central gathering point, particularly at night, attracting an international crowd who come here mainly for the fish dishes. The wafting aromas of fish frying in olive oil drifts down to the beach. Pleasant, lively, and colorful, the "casa" offers shellfish soup, although many guests in summer prefer gazpacho instead. Clams marinara is also good, as is the fried squid. The chef's specialty is his fish fry which always manages to taste more original and distinctive along the Costa del Sol than anywhere else in Spain. For dessert? You guessed it. Flan. Expect a bill in the neighborhood of 650 pesetas ($6.24) to 900 pesetas ($8.64).

Sin Igual, Carretera de Cádiz, Km. 217 (tel. 46-50-69), at Fuengirola, is run by Juan Fernández, a photographer whose pictures of Morocco are mounted on the walls. Try to get a seat on the sun porch, with its picture windows. Mr. Fernández and his wife, Jacqueline, were born in Morocco (they ran a restaurant in the environs of Fez for many years). At their Fuengirola restaurant, they enjoy faithful patronage by their habitués, plus a large collection of tourists who have heard of their good food which is often exotic in flavor. Try, for example, their mutton and prunes, a popular dish they used to serve in Morocco. Herb-flavored shish kebab à la Greque is their specialty, although they also do a crêpe au gratin (stuffed with fresh spinach), the latter a good choice for lunch on a hot day. Desserts are rich and calorie loaded. Sin Igual is open daily except Tuesday, a complete meal costing around 950 pesetas ($9.12) to 1400 pesetas ($13.44).

READER'S RESTAURANT SUGGESTION: "**Los Amigos,** Calle Miguel de Cervantes. From the town fish market docks, walk to the second street from the shore, turn left, and walk south to Calle Miguel de Cervantes and look for the sign. This restaurant is frequented mostly by the local people, who enjoy reasonable prices. Four adults in our party had dinner for 500 pesetas ($4.80) each. Two of us had fried shrimp, two had fried mero, two tossed salads (one salad was almost too much for two people), fried potatoes for four, bread and butter, and something to drink. The service is good, as is the food, not too greasy like most fried food in Spain" (Margaret W. Rogers).

If you're motoring along the coast, an ideal spot for a luncheon or dinner is the following recommendation in Los Boliches:

Splurge Dining in Los Boliches

Don Bigote (Mister Mustache), Los Boliches (tel. 47-50-94), is a "labor of love" created by its owners Roy and Vera Wykes, and their son Martin. The family sold their advertising agency in London in the early '60s to head south to the easy life on the Costa del Sol. Accustomed to creativity, they soon put their ingenuity to work on Don Bigote, a fine restaurant about two blocks from the beach on a difficult-to-find, one-way street (but well worth the search). They took over a deserted sardine factory and turned it into a lofty-raftered restaurant and bar.

As Mr. Wykes describes it, "We searched Spain for choice ceramics and ornaments. From one of the few remaining artisan factories, we had carpets and materials hand-loomed to authentic Andalusian designs. From demolished buildings, we acquired beautiful wrought-iron grills, railings, columns, and lamps. Old country masons were employed to convert and recreate graceful arches, great thick walls, and pebble-paved floors. Nurseries were raided for plants and trees—the sweet-perfumed 'lady of the night,' subtropical bougainvillea and hibiscus, climbing morning glory, and exotic palms. Most of the tiles and plaques were handpainted in Seville, perfect examples of a fast-dying craft."

During the winter months a blazing log fire and intimate candlelight make for a perfect setting for dining. In summer, the doors open toward a splashing fountain in the garden patio. Over the front door is a portrait of Mr. Wykes, who happens to sport a grandiose mustache—hence, the moniker.

You can enjoy a dry martini, 100 pesetas (96¢), or a frosted jug of sangría at 225 pesetas ($2.16).

A three-course table d'hôte, including wine, goes for just 660 pesetas ($6.37). On the à la carte list, outstanding selections include vichyssoise at 175 pesetas ($1.68); English steak-and-kidney pie, chicken-and-mushroom pie, or fish-and-egg pie, at 430 pesetas ($4.13); fried jumbo prawns, 500 pesetas ($4.80); even a banana or pineapple split, 250 pesetas ($2.40). The restaurant is open for lunch from noon to 4 p.m., and for dinner from 8 p.m. to midnight (the bar is open until 1 a.m.).

8. Mijas

Just five miles up from the Costa del Sol perches a village known as White Mijas because of its marble-white Andalusian-style houses. Mijas is at the foot of a sierra near the turnoff at the emerging resort of Fuengirola. From its lofty precincts at 1476 feet above sea level, a panoramic view of the Mediterranean unfolds.

Celts, Phoenicians, and Moors, as well as today's intrepid tourist, have traversed its cobblestone streets. The easiest way to get around town is to rent a burro taxi. All of Mijas is an attraction, and it's overrun with souvenir shops, but if you're seeking out a single destination head for a park at the top of Cuesta de la Villa. There you'll see the ruins of a Moorish fortress dating from 833.

If you're in Mijas for a fiesta, you'll be attending the only square bullring in the country.

WHERE TO STAY: Hotel Mijas, Carretera Benalmádena (tel. 48-58-00), is one of the most charming hotels on the Costa del Sol. Built hacienda style, it sits on the slope of a mountain, with a flower patio that's partially enclosed. On white wicker furniture, you can rest on the terrace and enjoy the view. The drinking tavern is in the Andalusian style, with large kegs of wine. The more athletically inclined enjoy the swimming pool and tennis court. Later in the evening, the guests retreat to the handsome lounge, furnished with inlaid chests and antiques, including an especially interesting collection of fans. The bedrooms maintain this stylish living, complete with private baths. Singles go for 4465 pesetas ($42.86); doubles, 3400 pesetas ($32.64) per person. For such a small hotel, there is a wide range of facilities, including a sauna, gymnasium, boutique, hairdresser, barber, and a barbecue. Entertainment is provided (in season) in the evenings, and during the day guests can play at the 18-hole Mijas golf course.

Those on the most limited of budgets, however, will prefer to seek lodgings at **Del Mirlo Blanco**, 13 Plaza Queipo de Llano (tel. 48-50-94), a little five-room establishment, right off the main square. The hostal's kitchen is known for serving a particularly good Basque cuisine—and the Basques are some of the finest cooks in Spain. Therefore, you might want to take the full-board rate of 1650 pesetas ($15.84) per person. Visitors can drop in for a set meal at a cost of 575 pesetas ($5.52). Those seeking rooms will find a single with bath, costing 950 pesetas ($9.12); a double with bath, 1250 pesetas ($12). A continental breakfast is an extra 125 pesetas ($1.20) per person.

The inn has a whitewashed exterior with black wrought-iron balconies and red shutters. Inside it is provincial style, with high-backed dining chairs. At the entrance stands a rack of home-baked desserts. A cozy living room has crescent-shaped couches and a fireplace. A rear dining room is bodega style, with an open fireplace. The aroma of good food permeates the atmosphere. During mealtimes the dueña of the house sits behind the tiny cash register, serenely smiling, wearing her hair up high on her head. English is spoken.

WHERE TO DINE: El Escudo de Mijas, Pescadores (tel. 48-50-25). Owner Rico Ritasso will welcome you in almost any language, as he speaks at least 12 fluently. His food is good and the atmosphere warm. Small tables with cloth napkins add a touch of taste. The service is first class as well. The menu of the day goes for 550 pesetas ($5.28), although you may prefer to try some of the specialties on the à la carte menu. These include assorted hors d'oeuvres, fried squid, and a house tart made by Mrs. Ritasso, a German woman. With a bottle of the local wine, plus coffee, you'll probably spend 1500 pesetas ($14.40) for a substantial meal.

The **Casa Jaime** (tel. 48-51-92), in the center of Mijas, serves one of the least expensive meals in the village. For just 450 pesetas ($4.32), you can order from the menú del día. On my latest rounds, this set meal began with a bowl of soup, followed by a baked white fish and salad, plus plenty of bread, a quarter of a liter of wine, and a basket of fresh fruit for dessert. The few outside tables go quickly in summer. Inside, the local men gather to watch bullfights on TV. The street is filled with souvenir shops, so you can combine a meal at Casa Jaime with a shopping excursion. If you're flush, try the pepper steak at 650 pesetas ($6.24). The restaurant is run by Antonio Jaime Blanco, who is a very pleasant character.

Continuing east, we come to the biggest resort on the Costa del Sol.

9. Torremolinos

This jet-age Mediterranean beach resort has become world famous in the past few years—so famous and so discovered, in fact, that the arbiters of that which is chic have abandoned it and turned elsewhere for more fashionable oases. In summer, it is a gathering spa for international visitors and their fringe friends. That stringy-haired girl boarding the Yugoslavian freighter for Tangier will make it to Torremolinos before the summer is out. Similarly, the Hamburg hitchhiker with a backpack is probably heading here, too.

It is a melting pot of Europeans and Americans who come from places ranging from North Dakota to the Boul' Mich, from Soho to Berlin. Many Americans have found Torremolinos the perfect place to relax after a whirlwind tour of Europe. The living's easy, the people fun, and you don't have to worry about visiting a lot of historical monuments.

Thus, the sleepy fishing village that formerly was Torremolinos has been engulfed in a cluster of resort hotels. One visitor called the general style of the place "Andalusian Miamic." Prices have been on the upsurge in boom-town Torremolinos. Nevertheless, the town remains one of the vacation bargains of Europe, if you hunt and pick carefully through the ever-increasing maze of hotels. Comparable accommodations in Cannes would cost four times as much —maybe more.

Overlooking a bay, Torremolinos lies at the foot of the Sierra Mijas. It is nine miles west of Málaga, and it has a five-mile beach, its chief selling point. Once a summer resort, it has now arrived as an all-year-round vacation spot. For example, airplanes are flown in loaded down with low-income Danes, waving their meal tickets and stubs from en masse hotel bookings. At the prices they pay in winter off-season, they save by *leaving* Copenhagen.

The sun does disappear occasionally, however, in Torremolinos, and the wind can blow hard and cold in winter. It is not unusual to see a woman decked out in a fur coat standing shivering on the windy central plaza, while others are lying in some secluded spot on the beach in the scantiest bikinis.

In summer, the resort flourishes with latter-day Ryan O'Neal look-alikes, bikini-clad blondes, artists, writers, German war widows, and English secretaries. It's also a potent attraction to the oily-haired, hollow-cheeked Spanish youths from surrounding Andalusia and Castile who fancy themselves conquistadores. They leave their farms and villages behind, and flock to this most sophisticated of Spanish towns, hoping to meet that legendary, love-starved Swedish blonde.

Love somehow manages to bloom every so often amid all this tinsel. The only ones to get left out of the high life are, as usual, the pure and pristine among the Spanish maidens. These unlucky señoritas often are deserted by their fickle beaus, who waltz off in pursuit of those unchaperoned imports from Germany, Scandinavia, England, and America.

The old inhabitants who remember Torremolinos in the "hard" days cast a disdainful eye on these vacationing hordes. The attitude of the natives was best summed up by a black-shrouded Spanish dueña, who crossed herself at the sight of three German girls in briefer-than-brief bikinis strolling down the street on a shopping expedition.

WHERE TO STAY: The competition is tough in Torremolinos. Consequently, a hotel generally has to be new—or look it—to compete successfully. The three-star hotels, for the most part, are superb, some of the finest resort accommodations in Spain today. The only catch is that when tourists are jumping as high as marlin, many of these establishments may insist on full pension or at least half board (breakfast, plus one other meal).

La Caracola, Playa Bajondillo Paseo Marítimo (tel. 38-44-66), is a three-in-one hotel complex edging right up to the sandy beach with one of the most unusual petal-shaped pools on the coast. *El Pescador* (The Fisherman), facing the mountain, is the older of the buildings, although completely modernized, and it has simple but tasteful rooms. The *Casa al Mar* (House at the Sea) is a compound of bungalows on several levels, providing open terraces with seaview vistas. The central and last member of the trio, *La Caracola* (The Snail), is the newest, and it overlooks the swimming pool and the palm-fringed lawn. Here most of the rooms have sleeping alcoves with divider draperies off a full-size living room done in the Castilian idiom—natural heavy wood, leather upholstery. Private sun balconies are also available.

For what you get, the cost of staying here is low: 2100 pesetas ($20.16) to 2400 pesetas ($23.04) in a double room with private bath, 1400 pesetas ($13.44) to 1800 pesetas ($17.28) in a single room with shower bath. A continental breakfast is an extra 200 pesetas ($1.92) per person.

The major objection here is the section of town, which many readers have found "hot" and "dirty."

Alta Vista, Plaza del Mercado (tel. 38-76-00), on the old marketplace, is right in the heart of Torremolinos, surrounded by little lanes of boutiques and flower-filled patios with coffeeshops. It's a few minutes' walk from the beach, but the rooms have small balconies projected into the Costa del Sol sun. The entire roof is a tiled solarium with festive umbrella tables, lounge chairs, and a bar.

For a double with private bath, the charge is 1750 pesetas ($7.20), 1100 pesetas ($10.56) in a single with bath. There are 100 twin-bedded rooms, offering ornate wrought-iron beds draped in decorative fabrics, reed-seated chairs, telephone, and bedside reading lamps.

In the well-styled lounge (Andalusian wood and leather furnishings), guests gather for reading, conversation, or letter writing. The bar is inviting with its beamed ceiling and tiles. Lunches or dinners are served in a stylish dining room.

Hotel Amaragua, Los Nidos (tel. 38-46-33), is right on the beach in the middle of the residential area of Torremolinos-Montemar, with a total of 198 rooms (12 of which are suites), all with complete bath, terrace, and sea view. The hotel has lounges, television, a bar, three large swimming pools (one heated), gardens, water sports, a children's playground, a sauna, parking facilities, and a tennis court. In a double with private bath, the rate is 2800 pesetas ($26.88), 1900 pesetas ($18.24) in a single with shower bath.

Los Nidos (tel. 38-04-00) is in the residential area of Torremolinos-Montemar, next to the beach. It's in the style of a small Andalusian village, with 70 rooms and bungalows, all with bath, central heating, private entrances, and terraces. Forty have lounges and safes. Double rooms with private baths rent for 2200 pesetas ($21.12) nightly, singles for 1500 pesetas ($14.40).

The **Hotel Edén,** 36 Bajondillo, below the new town (tel. 38-46-00), is built on many levels on a cliff (the entrance is on the eighth floor). Two elevators take you down to the bedrooms—a "descent into the catacombs," as one reader put it. All of the 94 bedrooms have private terraces, which overlook the rooftops, a cultivated field, a stable renting riding horses, all climaxed by a vista of the Mediterranean. In a double with a complete private bath facing the beach, you pay 3100 pesetas ($29.76), with taxes and service included. In a single, the rate is 2500 pesetas ($24). A continental breakfast is an extra 250 pesetas ($2.40) per person.

The rooms are often decorated in resorty colors, but they're utilitarian and comfortable, although plumbing and maintenance may be shaky at times. On the lower level is a swimming pool and an adjoining terrace. An open veranda restaurant overlooks the sea.

One final temptation: Occasionally there is flamenco in the bar. Perhaps a gypsy guitarist will walk around the room singing, before a stamping, gaily costumed dancer goes into her act.

Sidi Lago Rojo, 5 Miami (tel. 38-76-66), stands in the heart of the still preserved fishing village of La Carihuela, only 150 feet from the beach with its waterside fish restaurants and bars. The hotel, newly built and the finest place to stay in the fishing village, has its own surrounding gardens and swimming pool, along with terraces for sunbathing and a refreshment bar. The modern hotel offers studio-style rooms, tastefully appointed. The furnishings are contemporary Spanish, with excellent tiled baths and terraces with views. Other facilities include radios, phones, air conditioning, and refrigerators. For a single with shower or bath, the charge is 1200 pesetas ($11.52) to 1500 pesetas ($14.40), rising to 2000 pesetas ($19.20) to 2400 pesetas ($23.04) in a double. Full board costs an extra 2400 pesetas ($23.04) per person. A continental breakfast is an extra 175 pesetas ($1.68) per person, and set meals are offered for 675 pesetas ($6.48), at either lunch or dinner. The bar is a popular gathering point, with a sophisticated decor. In the late evening, there is disco dancing.

Hotel Plata, 1 Pasaje Pizarro (tel. 38-00-70), is central, right on the coastal road to Málaga. It is surrounded on three sides by private terraces with folding chairs and tables set out for breakfast or drinks. The oddly shaped rooms are large; there's enough space to add extra beds if required.

The attractively furnished, modern doubles with bath rent for 1500 pesetas ($14.40) and 1800 pesetas ($17.28). Two singles, with shower only, go for 1000 pesetas ($9.60). Each bed has its own table and reading lamp. The air-conditioned dining room, which serves reasonably good meals, captures the Andalusian spirit with its beamed ceiling, crude yet comfortable chairs, and lots of bric-a-brac. In July and August, full board is required at an extra cost of 1400 pesetas ($13.44) daily.

Hotel Los Arcos, 70 Carlotta Alessandri (tel. 38-08-22), was once a grand old villa at the edge of what used to be a fishing village. It is somehow reminiscent of the Old Spanish houses built for movie stars in Beverly Hills in the '20s.

Oddsy-endsy type furnishings are placed throughout. However, the reasonably pleasant bedrooms attract a homing-pigeon clientele flying here in no small part because of the price: 1400 pesetas ($13.44) for a double room with private bath; single rooms with private baths are 850 pesetas ($8.16). A complete luncheon or dinner is an extra 500 pesetas ($4.80), and a continental breakfast is yet another 150 pesetas ($1.44) per person. All rooms have garden views, telephones, and balconies.

Hotel Bristol, 112 Avenida Montemar (tel. 38-28-00), is built in the modern motel style, each room with a private balcony overlooking the freeform swimming pool. Perched on the far western frontier of Torremolinos, it may escape the bedlam of the center of town, but it doesn't avoid the trucks and cement mixers roaring past its door. It is set off the main coast road, on an embankment covered with bushes and flowers.

It is frequented by Nordic tour groups who want to return to Scandinavia sunburned and well fed. The Bristol's lobby is rather uninspired, although neat and streamlined. The spacious bedrooms are reasonable priced—1600 pesetas ($15.36) for doubles with private baths, 1400 pesetas ($13.44) for doubles with private shower baths. A continental breakfast is another 150 pesetas ($1.44) per person.

Hotel Don Juan, 8 Cauce (tel. 38-35-55), purports to be an exact copy of the 14th-century Moslem Zacatín at Granada. That may be true, but the interior is expressly designed for modern tastes. The 130 bedrooms contain private baths, central heating, and telephones, and rent for 1400 pesetas ($13.44) in a double room, 1000 pesetas ($9.60) in a single. A continental breakfast is an extra 150 pesetas ($1.44) per person. You can have a complete meal for 575 pesetas ($5.52) per person in the Panoramic Restaurant on the top floor. Not only is it air-conditioned, but it offers a view of Málaga Bay and Torremolinos. In addition, two bars and lounges are air-conditioned. One entrance to the Don Juan is from the coast road, the other from one of the arcade streets crowded with boutiques and restaurants. You have to go up to the roof to get the direct sun in the solarium. Those who remain downstairs will generally find the lobby as busy as Times Square on New Year's Eve.

Hostal Los Riscos, 40 Loma de los Riscos (tel. 38-14-20), is a redone private villa on the side of a hill, in a residential area of Torremolinos—not too far from the beach or the center of town. Canadian owned, it has been well adapted to its present function of providing home-like accommodations at a low rate. True, it's a modern place—set back from the street by a low stone wall and an iron gate. It has a front portico, and the rooms open onto a small garden at the side. Guests like to gather here for a restful chat under the banana trees and bright umbrellas. The staff enjoys providing simple but nourishing home-cooked meals. You pay 1000 pesetas ($9.60) for a double with private bath. A continental breakfast is available at 125 pesetas ($1.20) per person. The hostal also has a restaurant, serving à la carte meals from 250 pesetas ($2.40) up.

Hostal Los Jazmines, Avenida del Lido (tel. 38-50-33), right on one of the best beaches in Torremolinos, at the foot of the shady Avenida del Lido, is a paradise for sunseekers who try not to get burned by sun or expense. It charges 1800 pesetas ($17.28) to 2200 pesetas ($21.12) in a double room with private bath. A complete meal costs 700 pesetas ($6.72).

The hostal faces a plaza, and consists of a compound of modern buildings erected around terraces, lawns, and an odd-shaped swimming pool. Meals are served on the open-air terrace, or inside the appealing dining room, furnished with Spanish reproductions. The bedrooms themselves are more impersonal, but they have their own little balconies, coordinated colors, and compact baths. It's a good hike up the hill to the center of town from here.

Samba, Urbanización La Colina (tel. 38-58-66), is a modern hillside hotel in a development just below the coast road to Málaga, about five minutes from the airport. Buses stop right outside the project; and the Torremolinos mini-rail has a stop in La Colina. Most of its no-frills bedrooms have projecting balconies and picture windows fronting the coastline. All rooms have full private baths. Singles rent for 950 pesetas ($9.12), and doubles are modestly priced at 1600 pesetas ($15.36). A continental breakfast is an extra 150 pesetas ($1.44) per person. The lounge and dining room open off a lower floor onto a swimming pool play area. Within La Colina estate is a shopping complex with a supermarket, shops, boutiques, a drugstore, two cafeterías, and three restaurants, plus a disco for evening entertainment. Horseback riding and tennis courts are also available inside the estate, about a half-minute walk from Samba.

Miami, 10 Calle Aladino (tel. 38-23-45), is near the Carihuela section. It's the domain of Señora Vignale Gomez, who has furnished each accommodation differently, with dignity, style, comfort, and traditional trappings. Every room contains its own balcony and private bath. For all this, the high-season rate in a single is 1075 pesetas ($10.32), rising to 1700 pesetas ($16.32) in a double. A continental breakfast at 110 pesetas ($1.06) is the only meal served. The house, reminiscent of those built in Hollywood, California, is isolated by high walls and a private garden. There's even a small swimming pool. In the rear patio bougainvillea climbs over arches, and the tile terrace is used for sunbathing and refreshments. The living room is country rustic, with a walk-in fireplace, plus lots of brass and copper.

Your Own Apartment

La Nogalera, La Nogalera (tel. 38-17-50), in the bull's-eye center, is a complex covering at least three small blocks of fashionably styled buildings, with lush gardens, a pair of swimming pools, teahouses, a playground for children, a mini-golf course, several nice restaurants, garages, bodegas, even a small supermarket. The five-building community is linked by pedestrian bridges. You can rent an apartment, readily settling into your fully equipped kitchen or sun terrace. Apartments come in five price brackets, the cost depending on the season and number of occupants. For example, the peak August rate ranges from 3000 pesetas ($28.80) for two persons to 6000 pesetas ($57.60) for six. Tariffs are lower the rest of the year. Apartments are pleasantly furnished, with wood-paneled bookcases, marble coffee tables, armoires, conservative but stylish upholstered furniture, often a raised stone fireplace, plus a bar area complete with glassware. Original etchings and oil paintings give a homey touch.

READERS' APARTMENT SELECTION: "Our apartment hotel, **Los Olimpos,** at Carvajal, was roughly ten miles from Torremolinos, right on the Mediterranean. It has three large buildings—each floor of each division has only two apartments, complete with two bedrooms, two baths, a large living room, and kitchen. Everything's furnished, including maid service, glassware of every description, lovely dishes, ironing board, plus balcony facing the sea with four chairs and a table. Swimming pool, paddle boats, Tahiti-style umbrellas, breakwater, plus a restaurant which is rather expensive for not-so-good food. The apartments rent for 4200 pesetas ($40.32) a day and could hold at least five persons. A minimum stay of one week is required. Several restaurants and small groceries are nearby. It's on a four-lane highway edging the coast, and frequent buses to Málaga, Marbella, Torremolinos, and Fuengirola pass by" (Mrs. Elizabeth B. Melvin, St. Augustine, Fla.). . . . "Have you ever considered a nice, quiet apartment on the beach, with two large swimming pools plus one kiddies' pool? We found a fantastic place, clean and perfectly equipped, yet only a short bus ride from Tivoli amusement park and more adult fun in Torremolinos. We stayed for the entire month of June, hating to leave. Prices jump in July, but the weather in May and June was perfect, and we paid only 1850 pesetas ($17.76) a day for a single bedroom, living-dining room, nice-size kitchen, modern bathroom, and balcony overlooking the sea. In July and August, the rate is 2500 pesetas ($24) a day. The two-bedroom apartments are 3000 pesetas ($28.80) in May and June, 4200 pesetas ($40.32) in July and August. A minimum one-week stay is required. Many supermarkets, two open 24 hours, and many family-type restaurants are close by. The place is **Belamadina-Costa,** and our building was named Tamarindos" (Sylvia and Sam Shanker, Willowdale, Ontario, Canada).

WHERE TO EAT: The cuisine in Torremolinos, although somewhat slapdash, is varied, with lots of borrowing from America as well as continental Europe. The hotels often serve elaborate four-course meals, but at some point you may want to break free to sample the local offerings. At least the surroundings will be colorful, and the restaurants are clustered near each other, so you can do some window shopping in advance, waiting for that far-off fashionable dining hour of 9:30. Many establishments are quite expensive, but if you follow my clues, you'll find some good food bargains.

Restaurant Florida, 15 Calle Casablanca, La Nogalera (tel. 38-50-95), is a Danish and international restaurant on the lower level of a modern shopping complex, owned and run by a Dane, Jorn Lauvrits Hansen. The decor is South Seas, and the spread laid out inside is gargantuan, one of the best food values in Torremolinos. From 1 to 4 p.m. you can enjoy smörgåsbord, a vast array of dishes for just 700 pesetas ($6.72). Between 7 and 11 p.m., another deluxe buffet is offered at the same price, and you get to listen to piano music until around midnight. Many diners go early and linger late, getting up for occasional forays to that groaning table. You get fine herrings, tasty salads, cold meats, and hot dishes, plus a lot of plates of food. A spread of cheeses and fruits is offered along with desserts. It's quite a bounty.

Mesón El Gato Viudo, 8 Calle Nogalera, is a two-fork restaurant with sidewalk tables, right in the teeming heart of the action. The restaurant is decorated in the tavern style, with Kelly-green Spanish chairs and tartan cloths. The chef specializes in Spanish cookery, offering a set menu for just 425 pesetas ($4.08). The à la carte menu, in English, is small but interesting, including the familiar repertoire of national dishes—shellfish soup, paella, and roast chicken. Fresh fruit is your best bet to finish your meal. On the à la carte arrangement, the average meal ranges in price from 550 pesetas ($5.28) to 700 pesetas ($6.72). The atmosphere is informal, and the international clientele shows up in all range of attire.

The **Grill Room,** on the ground floor of the Hotel Plata, 1 Paseje Pizarro, right off the Plaza de Costa del Sol, offers most civilized dining—a complete meal for 600 pesetas ($5.76). This is good value, as you'll usually be served cream of vegetable soup, a veal dish, and Spanish melon for dessert, plus bread, wine, and service. The air-conditioned Grill Room is decorated in "Hollywood Andalusian."

Hong Kong, Calle del Cauce (tel. 38-41-29), is the only restaurant along the Costa del Sol serving an Indonesian rijsttafel, literally a rice table. You're served a large bowl of rice with a selection of highly spiced side dishes. Among the Chinese dishes offered are hot spiced pork with vegetables and chop suey. The menú del día goes for 400 pesetas ($3.84). The Oriental restaurant is on a busy street of milling visitors. The street is a virtual open-air dining room.

Restaurante Canton, 23 Plaza de la Gamba Alegre, began as a hole-in-the-wall in the Edificio Begoña, but its popularity forced a move. For 500 pesetas ($4.80), you can order a complete dinner, including, for example, an eggroll, beef with onions, steamed white rice, and fresh fruit. Two specialties are the sweet-and-sour pork and the diced chicken with almonds. The wonton soup costs 175 pesetas ($1.68); the chicken fried rice goes for 250 pesetas ($2.40); and the sweet-and-sour fish is 250 pesetas also. Richard K. Chang of Hamden, Connecticut, wrote: "Being Chinese, we are always quite critical of Chinese restaurants recommended by non-Chinese. However, the cuisine we enjoyed in the restaurant certainly came as a surprise (pleasantly so)." "The Canton is open from 1 till 4 p.m. and from 7:30 p.m. till midnight, except Tuesday.

Salud Vegetarian Restaurant, Pueblo Blanco, Calle Casablanca. Maud welcomes you to this little hole-in-the-wall, tucked away in a beautiful, but obscure, corner of Torremolinos where the milling throngs rarely go. Maud is from Sweden and she runs this inviting little charmer. For your drink, you're offered a choice of fresh juices such as orange, apple, and carrot for 75 pesetas (72¢) small, 140 pesetas ($1.34) large. Each day a hot soup is featured at 85 pesetas (82¢) or 140 pesetas ($1.34), as well as a salad at 130 pesetas ($1.25). One hot dish of the day is also on the menu—on my most recent visit, a cauliflower-and-mushroom casserole, 200 pesetas ($1.92). You sit on natural-wood shield-back chairs (very tiny). Maud doesn't like to call her place a health-food restaurant. She says, "It's not health food—it's the way people used to eat." The restaurant is closed on Sunday.

The major gathering place in Torremolinos for the patrons of restaurants, boutiques, cafés, whatever, is called **La Nogalera.** Lying between the coast road and the beach (reached by walking down Calle del Cauce), this is a compound of modern, whitewashed buildings, with Andalusian flavor.

Open to pedestrian traffic only, it features a maze of colorful passageways, courtyards, patios for dining, fountains, trees, flowers—and lots and lots of people. If you're seeking anything from sandwiches to Belgian waffles to scrambled eggs to pizzas, you're likely to find it here.

At **Lanjarón,** Calle Queipo de Llano, up the hill from the Plaza del Mercado, a tourist menu is offered for 425 pesetas ($4.08), which includes soup, an omelet or fish dish, steak and potatoes, fruit, bread, and wine.

Seafood at La Carihuela

If you want to get away from the brash high-rises and Coney Island–type honky-tonk, head to nearby Carihuela Village, where some of the best bargain restaurants are found. Tops with locals and visitors alike is **Casa Prudencio,** 41 Carmen (tel. 38-14-52), on the beach. Àla carte dishes include gazpacho, lentils or soup, shrimp omelet, swordfish, and shish kebab. Try the special paella and strawberries with whipped cream (in the spring). The atmosphere is cordial, and you may make friends at the long tables where everyone sits together. There are also tables for four for the more fastidious. The boardwalk tables are almost always taken. If you want to splurge, order a lubina à la sal—a huge, boneless fish packed under a layer of salt, which is then prepared at your table and makes a singular gastronomical treat. Complete meals begin at 1100 pesetas ($10.56).

El Cangrejo, 25 Calle Bulto (tel. 39-04-79), is a country-style tavern, with a beamed ceiling, open fireplace, and ships' models. Right in the colorful heart of La Carihuela, it has a picture-window view of the sea. One entrance is on the street (Calle Bulto) that runs parallel to the beach. Ignore the piles of shrimp heads and anchovy tails which often find their way to the floor. This is the perfect place for a big seafood dinner, and often Spanish families fill up all the tables, gorging themselves on such seafood as grilled shrimps, sea bass on a skewer, shellfish zarzuela, or chanquetes (a kind of local whitebait). For an appetizer, I'd suggest the shellfish soup. A half bottle of sangría is a good touch. The immense variety of seafood dishes is staggering, and you will probably be, too, when you leave "The Crab." A full repast will cost from 650 pesetas ($6.24) to 1100 pesetas ($10.56).

For the best bargain dining at La Carihuela, leave the more expensively priced restaurants along the waterfront (where the sea view is practically added onto your tab) and head for one of the popular family taverns on one of the back streets. The best one I know is **Hermanos,** 11 Calle Carmen, where for just 400 pesetas ($3.84) you can order a menu of the day. It's simple, but adequate if you're really watching your pesetas. Waiters make their way through the hungry throngs, carrying clams in garlic sauce, chanquetes, or tiny shrimp cooked in their shells. On the à la carte menu, I'd endorse the red mullet, which seems to have a very distinctive flavor in La Carihuela, or the grilled swordfish. For that set meal I mentioned, I most recently faced a choice of fabada Asturiana (a bean-and-ham dish) or shellfish soup, followed by either veal or fried fish, wine, and bread. Most fish plates range in price from 200 pesetas ($1.92) to 350 pesetas ($3.36). The food is good, there's plenty of it, and no one complains when the bill comes.

READERS' RESTAURANT SUGGESTIONS: "Add to your list of delightful inexpensive recommendations the **Viking,** practically at the end of Calle San Miguel on Calle Casablanca (tel. 38-10-11). This restaurant is hosted by Tove Jensen who successfully competes with many local establishments by offering a menú del día for 650 pesetas ($6.24). The first night we tried the plate of the day and had frikadeller (meatballs) with potato salad and pickled cucumbers, a plate of Spanish rolls, and one-quarter of a liter of wine per person, as well as a dish of peaches for dessert. The pleasant surroundings are charmingly decorated with a Viking decor, and red and white tablecloths make the atmosphere intimate and cozy. We were so pleased we returned a second night, and would highly recommend this for those who especially enjoy Danish cuisine" (Les Snyder, Orange, Calif.). . . . "I recommend **El Bodegón,** 4 Calle del Cauce (tel. 38-20-12), very highly. You have your choice of sitting inside or out, and there's a full variety of Spanish and French cooking. A meal will cost about 700 pesetas ($6.72). The sangría and paella are excellent and the service very good. It is closed from January 5 to March 1" (C. J. Gordon, Thornhill, Ontario, Canada). . . . "Our recommendation is **Moncho** in La Carihuela, on Calle Bulto. Unfortunately we were unable to find a street number on the building, but the street is short and it runs right along the waterfront. One has a choice of eating either inside or out. For 500 pesetas ($4.80), we had a choice from three soups and three entrees, salad, bread, wine, and dessert. The service is excellent, and the food is superb. Unlike many Spanish restaurants, this one starts serving dinner at 6 p.m." (Mrs. Marianne Muse, Pullman, Wash.).

"The 12-table restaurant **Colorado,** on the Via Colorado north of the Playamar intersection, is run by a husband and wife who really make a meal memorable. Get a table at the rear, and you can watch the wife prepare Cordon Bleu dishes over seven fires, each dish a masterpiece and lovingly prepared. Among the offerings are crêpes, and a good-tasting onion soup. An average meal will cost from 500 pesetas ($4.80) to 750 pesetas ($7.20). The restaurant opens at 7 p.m. Be there on time, as it takes about two hours to enjoy a meal and the company" (Rev. David O'Leary, Zenda, Kans.). . . . "Our best find in restaurants in price, quantity, and quality of food was **Robinson's.** It is just off Pasaje Pizarro (no. 7) which runs parallel to and north of the large street, San Miguel. Coming off the Plaza del Sol onto Pizarro, take the second small street on the left. Run by a family, in a small, clean building, Robinson's provides excellent home-cooked meals in large portions. The first course offers a dozen soups and salads. The main course lists some score of the usual meals of meat and fish but also unusual ones such as meatballs in gravy and Hungarian goulash. Dessert consists of flan, ice cream, or fruit. The total cost, including tip, is only 480 pesetas ($4.61)" (Calvin Keene, Lewisburg, Pa.). . . . "We found **Ciao-Ciao,** 55 Calle Bulto, which offers a menú del día for 250 pesetas ($2.40). Also enjoyable there is the small pizza, 125 pesetas ($1.20); oven-baked onion soup with cheese, 125 pesetas also; and spaghetti with tomato sauce, 125 pesetas. The restaurant is extremely pleasant, with many outside dining tables adjoining the boardwalk" (Mrs. Daniel Hunter, Buffalo, N.Y.).

TORREMOLINOS AFTER DARK: The nightlife of Torremolinos can be a romp. The scene of the action changes so rapidly in this town that it's hard to keep up with it. The fickle clique that decides what's hot seems to come up with a new cabaret two or three times a season.

The Bars

Although the hub of guitar-playing activity used to be at the Plaza Costa del Sol, the only place still hanging on there is the **VIP Club.** The rest have been crowded out by hamburger joints and neon-lit snackbars. Activity has now largely shifted over to the nearby Plaza Andalucía, where the **Bar Central** has opened up in new premises and is again the place to have a coffee, chat, and meet people. There's a counter, and many wooden tables and chairs where you can while away the hours.

The **Bar El Toro,** 32 San Miguel, is for aficionados (the bullfight theme is everywhere). Kegs of beer, stools, and outside tables make it perfect for drinking a before-dinner sherry, or an after-dinner beer. At "The Bull," you can order such typical tapas as the tortilla and pinchito for about 75 pesetas (72¢). As a special attraction, the staff prepares a bullfight poster, with your name between those of two famous matadors, for 250 pesetas ($2.40).

La Boveda, 8 Cuesta del Tajo (tel. 38-11-85) (walk down a steep hill from the end of Calle San Miguel), is a fun spot with the accent on folk singing, flamenco, and South American songs. A 90-minute program is presented nightly. You can sit in cave-like decor, at wooden tables, surrounded by old chests, beamed ceilings, cobbled floors, in big vaulted rooms. A flamenco show is presented at 10:30 p.m., and you can attend for 750 pesetas ($7.20) which includes the price of your first drink. (The place was a 16th-century watermill, and the word "Torremolinos" comes from it.) There is dancing indoors and outdoors nightly. Outside you can sip a cognac and dance in a pleasant garden. You can also order food here, the chef specializing in meat and grilled fish such as sea bass. A complete meal is likely to run about 800 pesetas ($7.68), maybe more.

Before dinner, I'd suggest a visit to **Quitapenas,** 34 San Miguel. There you can order 12 grilled shrimp at 250 pesetas ($2.40)—and they are tasty, made all the better when washed down with a glass of wine at only 35 pesetas (34¢). Wine is dispensed from large ceramic crocks. The bar is likely to be crowded, and it always seems easy to meet people.

Flamenco

El Jaleo at the Plaza de la Gamba Alegre offers one of the best "tablao flamenco" showcases on the Costa del Sol, featuring singers, guitarists, and dancers. The price of a first drink (and this includes your cover) is 900 pesetas ($8.64), dropping to 600 pesetas ($5.76) the second time around. It is open from 10:30 p.m. till 2 a.m.

The Nightclubs

Los Violines (The Violins), near the Residencial Las Estrellas (tel. 38-31-40), is considered the only restaurant nightclub along the Costa del Sol. However, you can go just for drinks. The charge is 1000 pesetas ($9.60). Otherwise, the charge for dinner and show will run as high as 2500 pesetas ($24) per person. Featured nightly is an international show, often spotlighting Spanish dancing and ballet.

Cleopatra, Avenida Montemar (tel. 38-30-15), is the challenger as the leading nightclub along the Costa del Sol. It dramatizes Egypt in the days of Tutankhamen. Mummies and plaster sphinxes are used throughout. Dancing is to orchestra music, but two international floor shows are staged nightly at 11:30 p.m. and 1:15 a.m. The sexy show is reserved for those who wait up till 3 a.m. In between these slices of action, anything is possible, even the showing of a silent film. The door charge and the price of your first drink are included in the entrance fee of 1000 pesetas ($9.60).

El Madrigal, at Benalmádena-Costa, Carretera Cádiz, Km. 228 (tel. 44-11-17), presents the best shows along the Costa del Sol. You'll see an international show biz cast performing a Spanish ballet, an international floor show, and a sexy show. Your first drink costs 1000 pesetas ($9.60). Three spectacles are staged nightly, at 11:15 p.m. and at 1 and 2:15 a.m. The lighting and sound equipment are up to date.

Discos

Piper's Club, Plaza Costa del Sol, is a fun palace resembling a subterranean world, with ramps and tunnels connecting the various grottos. Music, mostly for young tastes, is piped in on four dance floors under strobe lighting reflecting fountains and pools. The place is usually intimate and packed. In all, it's evocative of the disco heyday of the late '60s. Open nightly, the club charges 650 pesetas ($6.24) for your first drink and 400 pesetas ($3.84) thereafter.

Tabu, 231 Carretera de Cádiz (tel. 38-10-20), close to the Carihuela Palace, provides inside dancing to records, but also has a summer terrace to cool off under the stars. There is no live orchestra, but lots of animation from the guests. It is a lively, entertaining candidate for an evening's fun at a cost of 600 pesetas ($5.76) for your first drink, 400 pesetas ($3.84) for the second. The excitement gets under way around 10:30 p.m., folding around 4:30 a.m.

Boga-Boga, 2 Barrio de los Naranjos (tel. 38-10-76), is a dance palace. Guests sit at multilevel tables before selecting one of three dance floors, the smallest one spotlit from underneath for those who like to let it all hang out. The decor is warm-toned conservative, but psychedelic lighting and "blast off" music enliven the scene. Doors open at 10 p.m., and the entrance fee of 1000 pesetas ($9.60) includes your first drink. Additional drinks are 450 pesetas ($4.32) each.

Gatsby, 68 Avenida Montemar (tel. 38-53-72), stands on a major, traffic-choked boulevard, and, wisely, has its own private parking. Taking its theme from Fitzgerald's 1920s, Gatsby has a loud, distortion-free sound system. The illumination employs strobes and spots, as you dance to up-to-the-instant disc selections. For your first drink, you pay 600 pesetas ($5.76). The attractive clientele seeks out the romantic tables.

A Wax Museum

One slightly offbeat way to spend some time before dinner in Torremolinos is to go to the London Wax Museum, called the **Museo de Cera de Londres,** 17 Carretera de Cádiz, opposite the railway station on the main road (tel. 38-25-02), which is open daily from 10 a.m. to 10 p.m. In summer the museum is open from 10 a.m. to 2 p.m. and 4 p.m. to midnight. In 28 settings, it features almost a hundred lifelike wax figures—including bullfighters, famous painters, movie stars, plus the inevitable chamber of horrors. Adults are charged 200 pesetas ($1.92) for admission; children, 100 pesetas (96¢).

Carihuela After Dark

For those who want to avoid the frenzied scene uptown, the little fishing village and beach district of La Carihuela is a nighttime target, much of the district evoking scenes in James Michener's *The Drifters.*

The center of action is **La Bodega Jerezana,** 9 Calle Carmen, in a modern building, with a whitewashed cobblestone entrance. Just follow the sound of laughter. It will lead you to the doorstep. The bodega owner, Agustín, is also the star attraction, amusing his guests with his earthy humor. He even puts down the audience, most of whom seem to enjoy it. For most of the jokes, you'll need to know Spanish, although Agustín also does mime routines from his large repertoire. Occasional "tuna" bands show up here, and drinks are cheap.

Most tourists who drift down here go over to **El Trocadero,** 30 Calle Bulto, which is entered through an arcade. There, drinks cost 250 pesetas ($2.40). The club is near a large restaurant with the same name (don't confuse the two). Flamenco ballet and guitarists are presented nightly. The dancers are sizzling, their sensuous rhythms and piercing voices filling the room.

Nearby I'd suggest **La Casita,** 44 Calle Bulto, where drinks cost only 200 pesetas ($1.92). This is really a flamenco bar occupying what used to be a little fisherman's cottage. Shouts of *"Viva Andalucía!"* echo through the night. You're so close to the flamenco dancers at this bar that you'll feel part of the show yourself.

———————

With Torremolinos behind us, we now head east to Málaga. It's a distance of only 9 physical miles, but at least 100 miles in spirit.

10. Málaga

This Mediterranean port city is first a bustling commercial and residential center, then a resort. Unlike Torremolinos, it could go on existing even if the sun-seekers disappeared suddenly, although tourism has undeniably beefed up the local economy considerably. Torremolinos is the unofficial queen of the Costa del Sol. Málaga, on the other hand, is official royalty.

The chief drawing card in Málaga is its mild off-season climate (summer can be a bit sticky); otherwise, it is devoid of a great deal of interest (its beaches are poor—the best one, **Baos del Carmen**).

Ranking next to Seville as the largest Andalusian city, Málaga has experienced a steady growth in population.

The city abounds with orange trees, flower markets, fishing boats, shops on narrow streets in the medieval section, hotels, parks, restaurants, and sidewalk cafés—and all this makes for a pleasant interlude.

The most festive time to visit Málaga is around the first week in August when the capital of the province celebrates the conquest of the city by the Catholic monarchs in 1487. This is an occasion for parades, bullfights, and a big *feria* (fair). A major, tree-shaded boulevard of the city, the **Paseo del Parque,** then becomes the scene of much building activity, as the avenida is transformed into a fairground featuring restaurants and amusements aimed at all purses.

Málaga's most famous son is Pablo Picasso, who was born here in 1881 at Plaza de la Merced, the center of the city. This co-founder of cubism, who would one day paint his mural *Guernica* to express his horror of war, left little of his spirit in the city of his birth, and even less of his work. The **Fine Arts Museum** in Málaga owns two of his most fledgling, teenage dabblings (the indomitable Picasso is better represented in Barcelona).

WHERE TO STAY: Málaga has a limited number of old villas in its fashionable eastern residential district that have been converted into quite good hotels, charging prices compatible with our budget.

Parador Nacional de Gibralfaro, Monte Gibralfaro (tel. 22-19-02), has everything one could possible desire in a Spanish accommodation: luxury, economy, seclusion, history, romance, and beauty. It sits high on a plateau, near the site of an old fortified castle, overlooking the city and the Mediterranean, with views of the bullring, mountains, and beaches. Originally a famous restaurant, the parador has been converted into one of the finest hotels in Spain.

Built mostly of old stone, it is elegant—but the cost of a double accommodation with private bath is 3300 pesetas ($31.68) a day. Singles pay 2475 pesetas ($23.76).

The bedroom suites have their own entranceway, a private bath, a combination bed-living room, tall and wide glass doors opening onto private sun terraces, complete with garden furniture. The decor of cowhide, handsome draperies, and the like, is tasteful; the furnishings are modern yet accented by reproductions of Spanish antiques; and all the necessities and several added amenities, such as armchairs, sofas, coffee tables, and a desk, enhance the comfort of guests. There are two dining rooms.

The parador is reached via a winding road through streets of old and new villas. If you have a car, drive north along the coastal road, Paseo de Reding. This becomes Avenida Casa de Pries, which in turn becomes the Paseo de Sancha. Turn left on Camino Nuevo, toward the hill.

La Maestranza, Cánovas del Castillo (tel. 21-36-10), is an efficiency apartment building which provides ideal accommodations for families on a budget. The units are self-contained, with private baths, heaters, refrigerator, kitchenette, and private terraces that open onto views of the sea, the mountains, the bullring at Málaga, and the Alcazaba. In most of the apartments the sofas make into beds. The cost is 2100 pesetas ($20.16) if one person occupies an apartment, going up to 2625 pesetas ($25.20) for two guests, and 2825 pesetas ($27.12) for a trio. Downstairs is a cafetería, a bar, and a TV lounge.

Astoria, 3 Avenida Comandante Benitez (tel. 22-45-00), can be useful as a styleless hotel when you need an inexpensive place to sleep, and no glamor. It's a ten-minute walk from the center of town, opening onto the river, overlooking a wide street and gasoline station. There is no lounge, just a check-in counter. At this substantial, eight-floor hotel, rooms are simply furnished and clean, a single with shower (no toilet) ranging from 1200 pesetas ($11.52). Doubles, either with private showers or complete baths, range in price from 1800 pesetas ($17.28) to 2100 pesetas ($20.16). A continental breakfast goes for an additional 150 pesetas ($1.44). If you have a car, you'll generally find street parking.

Casala, 3 Alameda de Colón (tel. 21-15-84), is suggested as an emergency shelter when a good bed and a clean room are all that you require. The hostal is near the river, within walking distance of the city center. The entrance is from a palm-tree-lined avenue. You enter a dark little lounge with an elevator which takes you to the simple, modest bedrooms. The prices are among the lowest in Málaga—singles with bath (hall toilet) cost 1200 pesetas ($11.52). Doubles, also with bath (but no private toilets), go for 1600 pesetas ($15.36) to 2000 pesetas ($19.20). A continental breakfast at 125 pesetas ($1.20) is the only meal served.

El Cenachero, 1 Barroso (tel. 22-40-88), on the third floor, is a modest little (only 14 bedrooms) modern hotel. Each room is different and nicely carpeted—and all contain showers. A double room with bath or shower costs 1500 pesetas ($14.40). Doubles with less plumbing go for 1300 pesetas ($12.48). Singles with bath cost 900 pesetas ($8.64). Everything is kept clean. No meals are served. The little hostal, opened in 1969, is five blocks from Alameda.

Hostal Residencia Derby, 1 San Juan de Dios (tel. 221-301), is a recommendable boarding house on the fourth floor (take the elevator up). Right in the heart of Málaga on a main square, it overlooks fountains and the harbor. Some of the units have excellent views of the Mediterranean and the port of Málaga. On one recent visit guests crowded around to watch a Russian cruise ship come into port. The hostal is quite clean, and all rooms have hot and cold running water. The charge is 850 pesetas ($8.16) per person, with a continental breakfast included. The Derby is a real find in these inflationary times, and it's handy to transportation. It was discovered for me by Steven Malycke, of Mount Union College, Alliance, Ohio.

READERS' HOTEL SELECTIONS: "**Hostal Carlos V,** 6 Cister Street (tel. 21-11-98), has hot water all day, heat which you can turn on any time of the day with a flick of a switch, and clean, comfortable rooms. It is also a new hotel, and the cost of a double room with bath is 1750 pesetas ($16.80)" (Mr. and Mrs. M. Landau, Stayner, Ontario, Canada). . . . "Arriving in Málaga late one balmy evening without reservations, we were getting desperate until we stumbled across the **Hotel Lis,** 7 Calle Córdoba (tel. 22-73-00). The helpful manager, Sr. Juan Doña Díaz, quickly installed us in a spacious corner room, with a balcony overlooking the harbor. The bathroom was almost as large as the room and just as spotless. The double room, with a continental breakfast, costs 1600 pesetas ($15.36). Sr. Díaz can arrange a variety of one-day bus tours. I can recommend the one to Ronda, especially. The bus will pick you up at the door of the Lis" (L. L. Brown, Davis, Calif.). . . . "I was pleased with **Hostal Residencia Carambolo,** 7 Marin García (tel. 22-84-00), right next to Woolworth's. Everything is new and spotlessly clean, and a room for two with bath costs 1600 pesetas ($15.36), a continental breakfast going for an extra 125 pesetas ($1.20)" (Robert R. Miller, Brooklyn, N.Y.).

WHERE TO EAT: The best dining is generally offered at my recommended hotels, but Málaga has a number of restaurants in its city center which are within our price range.

Restaurant Tormes, 2 Calle de San José, is a two-fork restaurant in front of the Fine Arts Museum that features a 550-peseta ($5.28) cubierto, including the works. For an appetizer, gazpacho is the most popular dish, although you may prefer the mixed hors d'oeuvres, or spaghetti. The *segundo plato* usually consists of fish, such as mero (the delicately flavored Mediterranean pollack), followed by a poultry course, such as roast chicken, then dessert. The service is friendly, and so is the proprietor, Antonio Ramírez Macias.

El Cenachero, 5 Strachan (tel. 22-30-13), is the Málaga home of paella, served here with tender chunks of chicken, shellfish, peppers, olives, all delicately saffron flavored. This is an old-world restaurant, with tables on the mezzanine. At the ornately marbled counter, you can order various cubiertos at prices ranging from 250 pesetas ($2.40) to 600 pesetas ($5.76). The atmosphere is one of local color, with decorative azulejos (tiles). Many tapas are available to be nibbled along with your wine. *Muy español aquí.*

The **Café Central,** Plaza José Antonio, is tops for snacks and small meals. Tables are placed outside on the sidewalk for watching the Málaga bustle go by. At the counter, you can have a paella for 250 pesetas ($2.40), 300 pesetas ($2.88) at a sidewalk table; a cocido at the counter, 175 pesetas ($1.68); even half a chicken for 350 pesetas ($3.36). A ham-and-cheese sandwich rings up at 150 pesetas ($1.44).

Mesón Danes (Faarup), 1 Calle Barroso, provides Danish and Spanish snacks at medium prices. There's a menu for 475 pesetas ($4.56) that might include Danish or Spanish soup, fish, meat, and bread. The Danish House stays open until midnight except on Sunday. It closes for vacation all of August.

A Big-Splurge Restaurant

The **Parador Gibralfaro,** Monte Gibralfaro (tel. 22-19-02), has long been the most exciting restaurant in Málaga. It enjoys a top-notch reputation for its fish dishes. From its hilltop retreat overlooking the city and the Mediterranean, it offers its guests a choice of two dining rooms. One is inside with walls of windows opening into the wide, covered terrace; the other is in the open air, with pleasant garden chairs and tables. The complete tourist menu, including wine and service, costs 950 pesetas ($9.12), a splurge well advised. At night, as the lights of Málaga go on, you can sip your Andalusian wine and look out over the world—you may be willing to pay the extra money for this kind of enchantment alone.

Drinks and Tapas

El **Boquerón de Plata,** 6 Alarco Lujan, has long been one of the most famous bars of Málaga. You go there for good Spanish wine and tapas. If you're a local, the latest gossip will be the order of the day. Most guests have a beer and a helping of the prawns. The fish depends on the catch of the day—it's invariably fresh. A plate of the day ranges from 300 pesetas ($2.88) to 450 pesetas ($4.32). *Warning:* There are two other places in the region touting the same name.

READERS' RESTAURANT SUGGESTIONS: "The restaurant **Pension Maite,** 3 Espartero, is in the middle of the city, up from the bus station (southbound) about four blocks on a small alley off the shopping area. It is a pension-restaurant, quite clean and pleasant. As a sample of the menu, we had soup, veal, french fries, salad, paella, and wine for 550 pesetas ($5.28) per person, and were both more than satisfied with the service and the portions" (Robert and Ann Leclair, West Springfield, Mass.). . . . "An excellent budget restaurant is **Kapi 13,** on Málaga Ciudad de Invierno, one block from Calle Larios. Here you can have a good three-course menu (we had entremeses, merluza, and a dessert) for 425 pesetas ($4.08), and we ate there several nights, sampling various dishes for the same price" (Nick Chickering, Nevada City, Calif.). . . . "Value for money, as the English say, is received at **Restaurante Maite,** 2 Angel Genivet. There is no menú del Día, but á la carte prices are low. Expect to pay from 150 pesetas ($1.44) to 200 pesetas ($1.92) for such typical dishes as sopa de marisco (shellfish soup), paella, merluza (hake), as well as most meat and fish plates. We'd compare this restaurant with that budget wonder of Madrid, El Criollo. Prices are a bit higher, but the servings are larger. Angel Genivet runs into Calle Esparteros, which runs into Mesón de Velez which runs along the back of the Gómez Raggio Hermanos department store fronting on Calle Larios" (Norriss Hetherington, Berkeley, Calif.).

"**Cafetería Maestranza,** Maestranza, opposite the east end of the park, has a varied menu, good food, and friendly service. The dining area is behind large windows and very clean. It is air-conditioned in summer. The menú del día is 525 pesetas ($5.04)" (Charles H. Wahl, Rochester, N.Y.). . . . "We ate several times at the **Hostal Restaurante** on Calle San Andres, not far from the railway tracks and the Mediterranean. On the menú del día for 450 pesetas ($4.32), I had enough wine and paella for two people, not one. The chicken soup with mint should be in *Bon Appétit.* The main course was hamburger, potato, and lettuce. Dessert was ice cream or fruit. The restaurant opens at 1 p.m. It is clean and cheap" (Joanne Groshardt, Knoxville, Tenn.). . . . "I had a memorable dining experience at **Tío Pepe,** 18 Juan de Padilla. This is a family-run establishment where, even though no English is spoken, the people outdo themselves to make their guests feel comfortable by creating a warm atmosphere. Moreover, the dinner was superb. A full four-course meal, including bread, house wine, a typical dessert (flan), and entrees such as chicken in Italian-style gravy, vegetables, and salad comes to 400 pesetas ($3.84). The portions are very generous, and the service is great" (Mary Lynn Chilbert, Camden, N.J.).

THREE HISTORICAL SIGHTS: Unlike the rest of the Costa del Sol, Málaga has several historical sites of interest:

The Alcazaba

The remains of this ancient palace of the Moorish rulers of Málaga are within easy walking distance of the heart of the city (with plenty of signs to point the way up the hill). The government has improved the local landscape around it, and orange trees and purple bougainvillea make it look even more beautiful. The view overlooking the city and the bay from the palace is among the best on the Costa del Sol. This fortress was probably erected in the ninth or tenth century, although there have been later additions and reconstructions. Isabella and Ferdinand stayed here when they reconquered the city. Inside it is installed an **Archeological Museum.** The Alcazaba may be visited from 11 a.m. to 1 p.m. all year and from 5 to 8 p.m. in summer, 4 to 7 p.m. in winter. Admission is 50 pesetas (48¢).

The Cathedral

In the center of Málaga, this 16th-century Renaissance cathedral suffered damage during the Civil War, but it remains impressive—big and vast, reflecting changing styles of interior architecture. Its most notable attribute is its richly ornamented choir stalls. The cathedral has been declared a National Monument. One statue of a lounging cardinal is definitely religioso camp. The cathedral, built on the site of a great mosque, may be visited from 10:30 a.m. to 1 p.m. and 3:30 to 7 p.m. all year. To see the choir by Ortiz, Mena, and Michael costs 25 pesetas (24¢).

Gibralfaro Castle

On a hill overlooking Málaga and the blue Mediterranean bay are the ruins of this ancient Moorish castle-fortress, the origins of which are unknown. It is near the government-run parador (a visit to the castle might be tied in with a luncheon stopover. You can enter the old Arabic gate that leads to the inside of this fortress any time of the day free). *Warning:* Do not walk to Gibralfaro Castle from the town. Several readers have reported muggings along the way, and the area surrounding the castle is now considered dangerous.

THE TIVOLI-WORLD OF THE COSTA DEL SOL: Built on the site of what was once an Andalusian olive grove, it is unique. Much has been done to avoid the Coney Island–type atmosphere: In essence, it is a public pleasure garden, with rides, a roller coaster, a disco, attractions such as regional folk dances staged in an Andalusian square, a Chinese pagoda, and a miniature Wild West frontier town, complete with can-can shows. Among the 16 water fountains, there is one with coordinated light- and water-dancing cascades.

You can eat anything from a light snack to a gourmet dinner in one of the many restaurants and snackbars, or have a drink in a variety of settings. The biggest attraction, however, is the 4000-seat theater where national and international stars perform daily. Practically all shows and rides are included in the entrance price, which is abour $4.50 (U.S.) for adults and $3.50 for children.

The park is open from April to October from 6 p.m. daily. Check at your hotel before heading there, however. The Tivoli is 2½ miles from the heart of Torremolinos, about a ten-minute run by bus or taxi. Buses and trains from all over the Costa del Sol connect with Tivoli-World.

READER'S SIGHTSEEING TIP: "I took a local bus from Málaga to Coín. It leaves south of the statue *Boy with the Baskets,* on a street that borders the fenced-off area where terminal buildings for the harbor stand. This town still retains some typical Spanish scenes—donkeys, old cobblestone streets, and women in black. The shoes in Coín's shoe stores are reasonably priced. At a nice little park, we made our own sandwiches with purchases from the local stores" (Shirley Dichtl, Warrenville, Ill.).

11. Nerja

Nerja dramatically perches on its handsome nest known as "The Balcony of Europe." Nearby is one of Spain's greatest attractions, the Cave of Nerja, a paleolithic panorama (see below). Nerja is some 32 miles east of Málaga.

The resort is known to hordes of European and North American vacationers who like its good beaches and small coves, its seclusion (off the main coastal route), and its atmosphere of narrow streets, courtyards, whitewashed, flat roofed houses.

WHERE TO STAY: Nerja may still be fairly small, but like David, it is a formidable contender for such Goliaths as Torremolinos. Its accommodations are excellent—top hotels, a luxurious government-run parador, and a scattering of moderately priced hostelries.

Hotel Portofino, 1 Puerta del Mar (tel. 52-01-50), is love at first sight. Everything conspires to work for it. First, it is on a sleepy, tree-filled plaza at the edge of a cliff, a sandy and rocky cove of the Mediterranean below. Its main lounge and terrace dining room offer an unblemished view of the coast. The nicely furnished bedrooms are staggered down the cliff. In addition, they have private baths and seaview balconies. Doubles with shower go for 1800 pesetas ($17.28), increasing to 2000 pesetas ($19.20) with bath. No singles are available. From May to October, full board is obligatory, at 1800 pesetas ($17.28) per person extra. Otherwise, a set meal costs 750 pesetas ($7.20); a continental breakfast goes for 175 pesetas ($1.68) per person.

The inn is family run, and it looks it. An Italian, Georges Torriglia, and his French wife Therese have put their personal stamp on everything, making the hotel almost an extension of their private home. Throughout the public rooms are placed many contemporary paintings, some the gifts of guests who tried to capture the beauty of the view. There's a raised hearth for the fireplace, and a goodly selection of provincial furnishings. The catch is, it's so fully booked in high season that you run a poor chance of getting a room

Hostal Fontainebleau, Calle Alejandro Bueno (tel. 52-09-39), is a personal favorite. The ownership is English (directed by Peter and Marlene Bainbridge), and the atmosphere is family-like. Each of the 26 pleasantly furnished rooms contains a private bath with shower, the singles renting for 925 pesetas ($8.88) and the doubles for 1550 pesetas ($14.88). Some family rooms suitable for three persons are offered for 2145 pesetas ($20.59). A continental breakfast is included in the room rates. A cooked breakfast is available on request as an optional extra, and a 100-peseta (96¢) allowance on its price is made, offsetting the continental breakfast. All of the accommodations open onto an attractive central patio. Weather permitting, breakfast is served al fresco. In a large, comfortable, air-conditioned bar, you can order home-cooked bar food, plus an array of drinks which, of course, are served till late at night. For your entertainment, there is a color TV salon, and in the high season, live shows. The hostal is about a 15-minute walk from the main beach and an eight-minute walk to the center of town, and is open all year except for the month of January.

Cala-Bela, 10 Puerta del Mar (tel. 52-07-00), is a miniature hotel, just a one-minute walk from the Balcony of Europe. Like its more expensive next-door neighbor, it, too, has bedrooms opening onto the sea. The lounge and reception area are as small as a compact car. For a double with bath, the charge is 1600 pesetas ($15.36), dropping to 1200 pesetas ($11.52) in a single. The rooms may be small, but they're clean—and what a view! Seated in a bone-white Valencian chair, you are served three meals in a seafront dining room at a cost of 1400 pesetas ($13.44).

Villa Flamenca, in the Urbanización Nueva Nerja (tel. 52-18-69), offering a total of 88 rooms, was opened in 1969. The villa is a completely modern building near the beach, convenient for those quick dips. Guests are received all year, and the charge for doubles with bath is 1400 pesetas ($13.44). No singles are available. The cost of three meals a day is an additional 800 pesetas ($7.68) per person daily.

The **Mena,** 15 Alemania (tel. 52-05-41), is a modest little residencia (breakfast only), with only ten bedrooms. The best doubles—those with bath—cost 1900 pesetas ($18.24), dropping to 1200 pesetas ($11.52) if bathless. Singles with water basins only are 850 pesetas ($8.16). A continental breakfast is an extra 125 pesetas ($1.20) per person. The rooms are basically furnished—no twin beds, strictly "matrimonial" around here. The Mena represents most abbreviated living, suitable only if your requirements are simple.

Montesol, 230 General Franco (tel. 52-00-14). Four of the bedrooms of this humble guest house contain private baths, the other three are fitted only with water basins. Owned by Manuel Guerrero Castillo, the house is quite modern and well kept (there is a vigorous ritual of scrubbing and polishing every day). Doubles without bath rent for 1100 pesetas ($10.56), singles for 750 pesetas ($7.20). You can take all three meals here for just 1250 pesetas ($12) per person extra.

A Super Splurge

The **Parador Nacional de Nerja,** outside of town (tel. 52-00-50), is worth saving up for. It's like an elegant California motel, blending modern concepts with traditional Spanish elements. Built low on the edge of a cliff, the parador is surrounded by lawns, spacious and sprawling, plus an outdoor swimming pool (or, if you prefer, an elevator will take you to the sandy beach below).

The air-conditioned interior utilizes suitable furnishings, placed against a backdrop of beamed ceilings, tiled floors, and homespun draperies. In high season (March through October), the rate is 4500 pesetas ($43.20) in a double room with private bath. Singles pay 3600 pesetas ($34.56). The double bed-chambers are (1) worthy of a honeymoon, (2) worthy of a second honeymoon, or (3) reason enough to get married in the first place.

If you can't stay here, maybe you'll want to have a splurge dinner—three big courses—after viewing the nearby caves. The price is 1000 pesetas ($9.60), and a typical repast might include a shrimp cocktail, veal cooked in its own juice, accompanied by vegetables, and topped off by a piece of homemade cake. Before or after a meal, you can go for a swim, nonresidents paying 350 pesetas ($3.36) for the privilege.

Pepe Rico Apartamentos Restaurante, 28 Almirante Ferrandiz (tel. 52-02-47), gets an enthusiastic recommendation, both as a restaurant and as a secluded place to stay in a friendly atmosphere. It's the joint creation of handsome Robert W. Holder and his wife, Kathy. German-born Holder worked in hotels and restaurants in Scotland, England, Greece, Switzerland, and France before finding his place in the sun in Nerja. He's also a remarkable amateur photographer, and, with technical advice from his photographer father, produced a popular book, *Nerja—Balcón de Europa.*

Their attractive, comfortable, recently remodeled apartments are priced on a daily basis, but no reservations are accepted for less than a week. Each has a bedroom with twin beds and a living room, with daily maid service. The lowest rates are charged from January through March. Rates peak in July, August, and September. Apartments cost 885 pesetas ($8.50) per day in winter, rising to 1365 pesetas ($13.10) per day in summer. The apartments are for two persons. It is closed in November.

Pepe Rico is a gleaming white, Spanish-style building right on the street, with grill windows and little balconies. The rooms open onto a long rear balcony, overlooking a flower-filled courtyard. Dining is in a tavern-style room, half wood paneled, with handmade wooden chairs, rough plaster walls, and ivy vines. These vines creep in from the patio, where you can also order meals al fresco. Only dinner is served; and it's offered daily from 7 until 11 p.m. However, the restaurant shuts down on Thursday in May, October, and December.

Holder himself does the cooking with the help of one chef. The menu is international, and offers a separate specialty of the day which might be a Spanish, German, Swiss, or French dish. These range from the Holders' own cold almond and garlic soup to Andalusian gazpacho, available only in the summertime. The list of hor d'oeuvres is impressive—Pepe Rico salad, smoked swordfish, an elegant selection, or else the pâté maison. Filet of pork, served Nerja style, and Hungarian kebab are popular main dishes. Also favored is the trout with almonds. Considering the quality of the food, these prices are extremely reasonable—that is, from 1200 pesetas ($11.52) for a meal, although you could spend more, of course, if you order more expensively priced main dishes such as peppersteak.

THE CAVE OF NERJA: The most popular outing from Málaga, or Nerja itself, is to the **Cueva de Nerja,** which scientists believe was inhabited perhaps from 100,000 to 40,000 B.C. This prehistoric freakishly shaped stalactite and stalagmite cave lay hidden from the world until as late as 1959, when it was exposed by a handful of men on a routine exploring mission from the nearby hamlet of Maro.

When fully opened, it revealed a wealth of treasures left from the days of the cave-dwellers, including some paleolithic paintings believed to be as old as 15,000 years. The paintings depict animals such as horses and deer, and the archeological museum in the cave contains a number of prehistoric artifacts. By all means, walk through its stupendous galleries, considered to resemble a drippy Gothic cathedral. In the **Hall of the Cataclysm,** the ceiling soars to a height of about 200 feet. From May 1 to September 1, hours are 9 a.m. to 9 p.m. Otherwise, the caves are open from 10 a.m. to 2 p.m. and 4 to 7 p.m. Admission is 100 pesetas (96¢).

Nerja-bound buses leave from the Plaza Queipo de Llano in Málaga at 10 a.m. and again at noon, returning at 3 and 4:45 p.m. *Be warned:* The bus trip takes two hours each way as the bus stops again and again between Málaga and Nerja.

12. Almería

This town is known as the Spanish Hollywood. Its light is so pure and bright that it has attracted a large colony of film people who make epics in and around the town. When the celluloid folk aren't around, Almería can be dull. At first it appears to belong to a stretch of North African landscape. Actually it lies at the far eastern stretch of the Costa del Sol, a frontier outpost for many motorists traveling to and from Granada and Torremolinos.

This hot, provincial capital is dominated by the **Alcazaba,** its Moorish castle, and the **Castle of San Cristóbal.** Undoubtedly the most Oriental-looking city in southern Spain, it still reflects its Andalusian heritage as well in its narrow streets and white houses ending in terraces. To the Arabs it was known as the "Mirror of the Sea." Flowers grow abundantly, and orange groves and palm trees give the city a certain grace.

The province of Almería is traversed by a series of high mountains, separated by narrow valleys, giving it a rugged relief. The coast is high and rocky.

WHERE TO STAY: A suitable hotel is the **Costasol,** 58 Paseo del Generalísimo Franco (tel. 23-40-11), which is modern and functional, offering reasonable comfort. It doesn't have a restaurant, serving breakfast only. The first-class hotel is in the center of town, and makes a decent overnight stop. It charges 1500 pesetas ($14.40) to 1750 pesetas ($16.80) in a single, 2130 pesetas ($20.45) to 2590 pesetas ($24.86) in a double. Most units contain private baths or showers.

READER'S HOTEL SELECTION: "The best bargain we could find in all of Almería was the **Nixar,** 14 Antonio Vico (tel. 23-72-55). At first the name was a turnoff, but we ventured inside anyway to receive a warm welcome and an adequate, clean room for just 1300 pesetas ($12.48) for two persons with bath. Some bathless doubles are offered at 850 pesetas ($8.16). Had we wanted a single, we could have found one for 675 pesetas ($6.48). It's not the kind of place you'd want to linger in, but next morning after breakfast—the only meal served—we pressed on to Granada" (Ralph Vallone, Los Angeles, Calif.).

WHERE TO DINE: Rincón de Juan Pedro, 2 Frederico de Castro (tel. 23-58-19), is the best place to dine in Almería, and it can be expensive, too, depending on what you order. Pure, simple regional cookery is featured, and the atmosphere is immaculate, inviting, and pleasant enough. Located in a coastal province, the restaurant relies heavily on a varied fist repertoire, its typical dishes served with olive oil and plenty of spices. The cuisine is not only rich, but the ingredients are well prepared. In season, you might be able to order partridge, prepared in many different ways. Set meals begin at 750 pesetas ($7.20), although if you order à la carte your tab could easily reach 1200 pesetas ($11.52) to 1500 pesetas ($14.40).

READER'S RESTAURANT SELECTION: "We ate at the **Imperial Restaurant,** 5 Puerta de Purchena (tel. 23-17-10), on the main square of town. It goes through a triangle at the intersection to have entrances on two streets. It was full of local people ordering fresh fish at lunchtime. The menú del casa at 675 pesetas ($6.48) offered a choice of fish soup or fried fish for the first course. The fish was a large plateful, a meal in itself, of calamares, flounder, and another fried fish. The second course was a choice of pork roast with orange sauce or veal, both with potatoes. The meal also included bread, wine, and flan. Both food and atmosphere made it a winner in addition to the low price. However, if you order á la carte, you can spend as much as 700 pesetas ($6.72) to 1000 pesetas ($9.60)" (Katherine Philipp, Columbia, Md.).

Chapter VIII

VALENCIA AND THE COSTA BLANCA

1. Valencia
2. Benidorm
3. Alicante
4. Elche
5. Murcia

VALENCIA AND PARTICULARLY the Costa Blanca are Johnny-come-latelies in Spain's beach resort sweepstakes. As such, they are picking up a lot of the overflow from the more popular and extremely overcrowded Costa del Sol and Costa Brava, their chief competitors for tourists.

The Costa Blanca begins rather unappealingly at Valencia, but improves considerably as it winds its way south toward Alicante. It is dotted with little fishing villages and towns known chiefly to vacationing Europeans or Spaniards who shun the carnival-like atmosphere of Torremolinos or the Costa Brava.

Every visitor to Spain seems to make it to **Valencia:** it's on the road to so many other points. But **Benidorm,** on the other hand, is more fitting for a longer stay. The success of Benidorm is fairly recent. It's the old story of Torremolinos again—a fishing village turned into an international resort.

Alicante is the official capital of the Costa Blanca. This provincial city enjoys a reputation as a winter resort because of its mild Mediterranean climate. **Murcia** is inland, but on the main road to the Costa del Sol; consequently, hordes of motorists pass through it. It makes for a pleasant stopover, as it's one of the most interesting cities in the Levante, a loose term, meaning east, often used to describe this part of Spain.

1. Valencia

The charms of Valencia—or lack of them—have been much debated. There are those who claim the city, where El Cid chased out the Moors, is one of the most beautiful on the Mediterranean. Others write it off as drab, provincial, and industrial. The truth lies somewhere in between.

Set in the midst of orange trees and rice paddies, Valencia sidles up to Barcelona and Madrid for the title of Spain's third city. Admittedly, its reputation as a romantic city seems to be justified more by its past than its present looks. At one time, for instance, it was a walled city, and was believed to have been founded by the Romans.

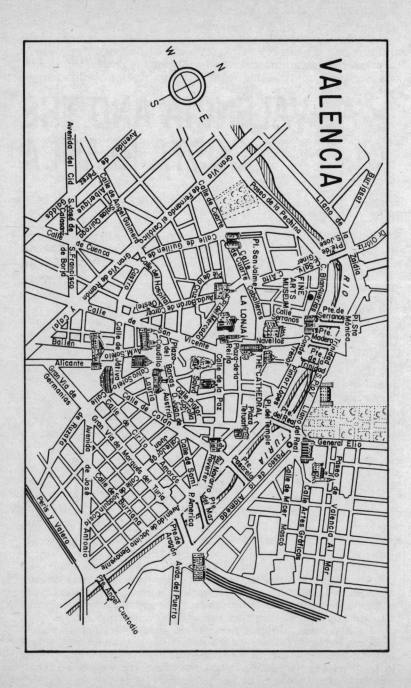

Hidden between the modern office buildings and monotonous apartment house architecture are considerable remains of its illustrious past. However, nature, in the way of floods, and man, in the way of war, have been cruel to Valencia. The Valencianos have torn down a lot of buildings that today would be considered architectural treasures. But they are a determined and industrious people; you may recall that Valencia, the capital of the Loyalists, was the last to succumb to Franco's troops.

In the evening, the city assumes a festive air, as throngs fill the streets for their nightly promenade. The scene is the liveliest at the central **Plaza del Caudillo,** where you can walk through a heavily scented flower market.

With its life and vitality, Valencia makes for a suitable stopover, either on the way north from the Costa del Sol or south from Barcelona. However, its beach area, two miles away, is somewhat shabby—definitely third rate.

WHERE TO STAY: You have your choice of living inside the city or by the sea. I'll begin with my top recommendations.

Llar, 46 Colón (tel. 322-72-96), fills a gap in the accommodation picture in Valencia. Built in 1967, the Llar was awarded three stars by the government, yet it charges reasonable rates. You pay 2900 pesetas ($27.84) in a double room with private bath, 2200 pesetas ($21.12) in a single, also with private bath. A continental breakfast is an extra 150 pesetas ($1.44).

The Spanish modern lounge is decorated with tasteful and comfortable armchairs, a wrought-iron divider separates it from the bar. *Note:* Rooms in the back tend to be very stuffy (there's no air conditioning), and those facing the street noisy. So you'll have to choose which bothers you least.

The **Hotel Inglés,** 6 Marqués de Dos Aguas (tel. 321-45-55), is for traditionalists. Placed in the heart of old Valencia, it stands right opposite a churrigueresque palace. The turn-of-the-century hotel has aged well by dint of care and respect. Most of its bedrooms have clear views of the tree-lined street below, and offer many old-fashioned comforts. The charge is 3000 pesetas ($28.80) in a double room with private bath. No singles are available. The obligatory continental breakfast costs 150 pesetas ($1.44). The lounge and dining room have been nicely kept; the old furnishings have been retained— chandeliers, gilt mirrors, provincial armchairs, and murals. Spaniards who want the best of restrained service have been stopping here for years.

Sorolla, 5 Convento Santa Clara (tel. 322-31-45), is named after the famous Spanish painter. Built in 1968, it is a seven-floor modern hotel in the center of the city, near the Plaza del Caudillo and the Plaza de Toros. Most of its 50 bedrooms have narrow balconies and compactly placed and utilitarian furnishings. Comfort, not style, is the keynote, and everything is kept scrupulously clean. A double with private bath rents for 3000 pesetas ($28.80); singles, also with baths, cost a peak 2000 pesetas ($19.20). No breakfast is served. However, there's a restaurant and snackbar on the ground floor.

Hotel Metropol, 23 Játiva (tel. 321-44-85), a three-star choice, is in front of the railway station, directly opposite the bullring, and only two blocks from the Plaza del Caudillo. At first glance, one would never suspect the hotel is so modern and well organized inside; its exterior suggests the architecture of a century ago, when builders incorporated balconies with tall French doors opening onto them. Most of the bedrooms are unusually large, even for Spain, and they are well furnished. Wall-to-wall draperies separate the sleeping area from the living room and its upholstered pieces.

All the double rooms contain private baths and cost 2900 pesetas ($27.84) nightly. Singles with bath pay a top 1900 pesetas ($18.24). All along the front of the Metropol are tables and chairs set out for drinks and meals. A continental breakfast is 150 pesetas ($1.44).

Hotel Bristol, 3 Abadía San Martín (tel. 322-48-95), is clean, comfortable, and on a quietly secluded narrow street in the older part of the city, near the Church of San Martín. It is only a three-minute walk to the central shopping district. All of the doubles have either private tub baths or showers, and rent for anywhere from 2500 pesetas ($24) to 2900 pesetas ($27.84). Eight singles with bath or shower are available at 1900 pesetas ($18.24). A continental breakfast at 150 pesetas ($1.44) per person is obligatory.

Sleeping by the Sea

The **Playa de Levante,** the Valencian beach, is about two miles from the city, although it might be equally at home on the New Jersey coast. On the **Avenida de Neptuno** is a string of hotels, restaurants, and bathhouses, their backs facing the sands and the sea. The restaurants along here are expensive, the hotels inexpensive (many rooms cost what you'd pay for locker space at some resorts on either the French or Italian Riviera).

The **Hostal Chicote,** 34 Playa Levante (tel. 371-61-51), is a fine place to stay when the temperature in the city starts keeping your plate of Valencian paella hot all evening. Decidedly unchic, as are all the "boarding houses" here, the Chicote offers rooms that are bare but clean, fairly comfortable, and a bargain. Most of the doubles contain private shower baths and cost 2000 pesetas ($19.20) nightly. Singles with shower baths rent for 1400 pesetas ($13.44). A continental breakfast is another 150 pesetas ($1.44).

Residencia La Pepica, 2 Avenida de Neptuno (tel. 371-41-11), is another good choice on the Playa de Levante, featuring bedrooms with views of the sea. It is early Miami in decor—no great compliment; still, it's a lifesaver for those who want to follow the sun, but not suffocate from it. La Pepica's comfortable and breezy doubles are only 1750 pesetas ($16.80), 1200 pesetas ($11.52) for singles. All of these rooms are decked out with private tub baths, and many open onto balconies. A continental breakfast is an extra 125 pesetas ($1.20) per person.

A Big Splurge for Drivers

The **Parador Nacional "Luís Vives,"** Carretera de Alicante, Km. 6 (tel. 323-68-50), at El Saler, about 12 miles south of Valencia, is a government-owned and operated parador, created by some of Spain's best architects and decorators. Many of the Spanish paradors try to evoke the romance and pageantry of medieval Spain; but this one prefers to be modern, in a restrained and classic way. A double with private bath and terrace rents for 4500 pesetas ($43.20). A continental breakfast is an extra 250 pesetas ($2.40) per person.

The air-conditioned parador is right on the coast, in the midst of sand dunes and a golf course. The oceanside terrace, wide and handsome, has a pathway leading through the dunes to the ever-pounding surf . . . one's own private beach. In all, it's just like a country club.

Inside, the lounges are intimate and comfortable. The dining room on the ground floor has a good view; the kitchen manages to turn out distinguished food, with a big dinner costing 1050 pesetas ($10.08).

The bedrooms are mammoth (ask for the ones at the back), with soft beds and large baths and "his and her" toilets. The furnishings throughout incorporate natural wood, leather, and homespun fabrics.

READERS' HOTEL SELECTIONS: "Hostal Lyon, 10 Calle Játiva (tel. 321-72-47), is a lovely, clean place, decorated with bright-colored wallpaper. The owners are nice and offer their full hospitality. Breakfast is not included, but there is an inexpensive restaurant downstairs called El Naranjo, serving a tourist menu for 500 pesetas ($4.80). The charge is 1400 pesetas ($13.44) in a double room with a shower" (Ms. Ofelia Adair, Miami, Fla.). ... "We found the Hostal Kroko, on the fifth floor (with elevator) of 28 Bailén (tel. 321-47-69)—the street that runs along the side of the train station. The owners speak French but no English, and are very friendly and helpful. A double with basin is 1200 pesetas ($11.52); a single with basin, only 750 pesetas ($7.20). No breakfast is available. There are many other hostals on this street too" (R. E. Shelgren, Paris, France). ... "We tried the Pension Moratín, 15 Moratín (tel. 322-12-20). The pension is run by three brothers, Javier, Antonio, and Benito, who are very nice people. For 1800 pesetas ($17.28) per person you get full board. This is our selection for a very nice place to hang your hat for a few days" (K. Nixon, Richmond, B.C., Canada). ... "Hostal Residencia Bisbal, 9 Pie de la Cruz (tel. 331-70-84), is owner-run by a husband and wife, both of whom speak excellent English and are ready to help. The hotel is sparkling clean and conveniently located in the old city near the market and other points of interest. Although no breakfast or other meals are served, this is not an inconvenience as the Bisbal is near numerous bars and restaurants. A double room with bath costs $19 (U.S.) per day. Rooms without bath are about $13. This is one of the best accommodations we found anyplace" (D. H. Rood, Atlanta, Ga.).

WHERE TO EAT: Valencia has a lot of big sprawling restaurants, most emphasizing those combination plates that are popular in Europe. Often the hotels offer good enough dining; but the sidewalk café restaurants usually have greater life and poorer food, generally speaking. The one dish to have in Valencia is paella—it's at home here. Follow the wafting aromas to:

Casa Cesáreo, 15 Guillén de Castro (tel. 321-42-14), is a discovery, an old-world tavern where you can eat very well. This long-established restaurant, within walking distance of the bullring and railway station, is on two floors. On the street level are counters and tables; and if you choose a table, the special paella Cesáreo is 400 pesetas ($3.84). If you order at the counter, prices are considerably cheaper—you're given a choice on the menu of *mostrador* (counter) or *mesa* (table). The menú del día—three plates, including bread and wine—costs 550 pesetas ($5.28) at the counter. Chef's specialties (ordered at the table) include grilled red mullet, mariscada Cesáreo, and half a chicken cooked with garlic. For a complete meal on the à la carte menu, the charge is likely to range from 600 pesetas ($5.76) to 1200 pesetas ($11.52). The Casa Cesáreo features a cuisine as typically Spanish as flamenco. Its walls are tiled, its furnishings provincial, its guests colorful—in all, a memorable experience.

Ateneo Bar, 18 Plaza del Pais Valenciano (tel. 321-01-54), is another bar-restaurant, this one opening onto the central square. It is a sort of international gathering spa for the flocks of European and American tourists who pass through Valencia every year. Its food is not exactly lavish, but in summer it can be so noisy and animated here that that detail is easily forgotten or forgiven. The fairly good 575-peseta ($5.52) "no extras" tourist dinner is honest at least. In the restaurant's terminology: "without tips, without any surprises." For that price you'll get three dishes, plus bread, wine, and dessert. If you're snacking light, I dare you to try the "Blimpy," a veal hamburger with onions for 150 pesetas ($1.44). And it wouldn't be a Valencian restaurant if it didn't serve the ubiquitous paella. Wandering among the à la carte specialties will mean a tab ranging in price from 950 pesetas ($9.12) to 1500 pesetas ($14.40). The restaurant is air-conditioned.

Cheaper and less snobbish than the Ateneo is the Casa Balanza, on the Plaza del Pais Valenciano at the corner of Calle José Calvo Sotelo, offering a menú del día for 425 pesetas ($4.08). For that you might have hake, a Spanish omelet, tomato and lettuce, bread, fruit, and coffee or a quarter liter of wine. It's a brasserie-type place, with tables indoors and out.

Across from the Ateneo is Valencia's answer to the super-deli, the **Barrachina,** Plaza del Pais Valenciano (tel. 321-12-70). Only this is also a restaurant. The Barrachina must have one of the best selections of goodies in all of Spain; it's certainly got room for them, as it spreads maze-like over a whole block. Outside are café chairs and tables; inside are such specialties as sweets and candies, croissants, delicious apple tarts, milkshakes *batidos* in all flavors for 30 pesetas (29¢), about 25 combination plates for around 300 pesetas ($2.88) to 500 pesetas ($4.80) each. The place has a bit of a Coney Island atmosphere to it, right down to the odor of frying sweets. Of course, there's sangría and horchata (which Valencia is famous for), hot dogs and sandwiches, cakes, and glazed fruit. Napoleons (called *mil-hojas* in Spain) are good as are the eclairs with whipped-cream filling (called *palonata*). There are several counters to sit at, and upstairs in a belle époque terrace are more chairs and tables.

There's also a separate restaurant which is open till 2 a.m. Here for 950 pesetas ($9.12) you get a salad, gazpacho, or other soup; macaroni gratin; hake or a quarter chicken; bread; wine or beer; and one of the excellent desserts. The least expensive paella is served with chicken, and you'll pay more for the version with shellfish. Ordering à la carte is likely to cost you from 1400 pesetas ($13.44) to 2200 pesetas ($21.12), the latter price for the expensive shellfish selections. At the Barrachina counter, there's a daily combination plate special which includes an omelet, veal steak with tomatoes and lettuce, plus bread, dessert, and wine.

Restaurante Alcañiz, 10 Calle Bailén (tel. 322-86-33), next to the Hotel Internacional and on the side of the railroad station, has a set meal for 500 pesetas ($4.80), which includes soup or salad, paella or a meat dish, dessert, bread, and wine. The Alcañiz is as plain as can be, with plastic table tops.

Tres Estrellas, 6 Convento Jerusalem, is a rock-bottom Chinese restaurant offering a tourist menu for 350 pesetas ($3.36), which includes chicken chop suey, sweet-and-sour pork, and white rice. On the à la carte menu, the dishes are typical of those found in any average Chinese restaurant—egg drop soup, eggrolls, pork with bamboo shoots, and fried rice. The cost of most of these dishes ranges from 130 pesetas ($1.25) to 350 pesetas ($3.36). The place is open from 1 to 4 p.m. and 8 p.m. to midnight. The decor consists of low ceilings and three rows of tables. It's simple but pleasant, not far from the railroad station, off Calle Jativa.

Horchaterías

When in Valencia, you should stop at least once in one of the city's famous horchaterías, a kind of oldtime café where Valencianos drink that milky, nut-flavored beverage called horchata. The two best known horchaterías are the turn-of-the-century **El Siglo,** 11 Calle Santa Catalina (tel. 331-84-66), serving regular horchata for 40 pesetas (38¢) to 70 pesetas (67¢), or the **Horchatería Santa Catalina,** 6 Calle Santa Catalina (tel. 332-22-28), which, a large plaque on a table assures us, was visited by royalty in 1903. Both places are open till about 9:30 p.m.

READER'S RESTAURANT SUGGESTION: "At 5 Plaza Mariano Benlliure, the self-service cafetería **Topics** serves a wide variety of excellent Spanish cuisine from 12:30 to 4 p.m. and 8:30 to 11:30 p.m. For 425 pesetas ($4.08), you can get a good, full meal. There is a bar that serves a delicious cafe con leche to wash down your meal" (Edward H. Pietraszek, Chicago, Ill.).

THE SIGHTS: From churrigueresque palaces to colorful city markets, to exquisitely styled Gothic buildings, Valencia offers a number of important historical attractions, all of which can be covered in a day. I'll begin with:

The Cathedral

In the heart of the city, at the Plaza de la Reina, this 13th-century cathedral, La Seo, represents a number of diversified styles. But the Gothic wins out. Its huge arches have been restored, and in back is a handsome domed basilica. Fortunate are those who visit it during one of the incense-burning ceremonies, a ritual little changed since the Middle Ages.

Of all the claims made by Spanish or Italian cathedrals, few exceed this one in Valencia. The cathedral for the past 500 years has had in its possession what it claims is the Holy Grail, that chalice used by Christ at the Last Supper. The subject of countless legends, the Holy Grail traditionally was used by Joseph of Arimathea to collect drops of Christ's blood as they fell from his body on the cross. It looms large in Sir Thomas Malory's *Mort d'Arthur,* Tennyson's *Idylls of the King,* and Wagner's *Parsifal.* In relatively recent times, it got the Hollywood treatment in *The Silver Chalice.*

After seeing the cathedral, for 30 pesetas (29¢) you can scale an uncompleted Gothic tower—known as **Miguelete**—for a panoramic view of the city and the fertile Huerta beyond. This octagonal tower is approximately 155 feet high. You may visit the **museum** of the cathedral (two works by Goya) from 10 a.m. to 1 p.m. throughout the year. However, the afternoon hours are from 4 to 7 p.m., June through September. Otherwise, the tower closes at 6 p.m., and it's also closed on Sunday, holidays, and for the months of January, February, and December. The cathedral is free, but it costs 30 pesetas (29¢) for the museum.

Generalidad

Built in the 15th and 16th centuries, this palace with its two square towers is one of the most fascinating in Spain. It has been handsomely furnished and restored, and is known for its carved wooden gallery. A Mediterranean Gothic building, this place is the headquarters of the Provincial Court, and may be visited for an admission of 15 pesetas (14¢) from 10 a.m. to 1 p.m. and 4 to 7 p.m. It is on the Calle de Caballeros in the old aristocratic quarter of Valencia.

La Lonja

At the Plaza del Mercado is the most splendid example of secular Gothic in Spain, completed in the 15th century. A beautiful, tasteful building, La Lonja has twisted spiral columns inside and stained-glass windows. Once it was a silk market. It may be visited (free) from 9 a.m. to 1 p.m. and 4 to 6 p.m.

The City Market

Across the street from La Lonja is one of the most fascinating city markets you're likely to encounter anywhere. When you see its more than 1200 stalls (a rough estimate), you may never want to shop in a supermarket again. It has everything: dried herbs, homemade soap, black blood sausage, ungracefully nude poulets. To see the women of Valencia shop is sight enough. The market is in a giant railway station-like building, of stained glass, no less.

Ceramics Museum

At the Palace del Marqués de Dos Aguas, you can see what looks like a surrealist decorator's masterpiece: a palace of rococo and churrigueresque. A bizarre building, its rooms compete with their exhibits. Next door to the Hotel Inglés, the palace has a vast collection of ceramics: lizards on plates, frogs on the backs of lambs. In addition, it has a Gallery of Humorists, with caricatures of everybody from Einstein on down. In keeping with its theme of unrelated items, it has a carriage museum and armor room downstairs. It may be visited from 10 a.m. to 2 p.m. and 4 to 6 p.m. daily except on Monday when it's closed, and on holidays when hours are from 10 a.m. to 2 p.m. The price of admission is 150 pesetas ($1.44).

Fine Arts Museum

A treasure house of paintings and sculpture stands on the north bank of the Turia River, reached on the Calle de San Pío V. The collection is rich in Flemish artists, as well as the home-grown variety from Valencia—the latter school reflected especially in the 14th- and 15th-century Valencia "primitives." On the ground floor the archeological collection is displayed, including early Iberian, Roman, and early Christian finds. The most celebrated painting is a self-portrait by Velázquez, and you'll also see a whole room filled with works by Goya. Other paintings are by Morales, El Greco, Ribera, Murillo, Pinturicchio, Sorolla, and "El Bosco" (Bosch). Furthermore, the museum was given some important sculpture by Mariano Benlliure. Of special interest is a salon devoted to the works of contemporary Valencian painters. The visiting hours are daily including Sunday from 10 a.m. to 2 p.m.; the admission, 150 pesetas ($1.44).

OUT-OF-TOWN-EXCURSIONS: A great deal of the charm of Valencia is to be found in its environs, particularly in the fertile **Huerta** and the **Albufera** (a freshwater lake south of the city). The Huerta is Valencia's giant orchard of orange trees, alongside its rice paddies. The rice is grown here for Valencian paella. A trip makes for a pleasant afternoon or morning outing. It can be tied in with a visit to Albufera's **El Saler** beach (far superior to the Levante).

In the village of El Saler, you might want to have Valencian paella for lunch or dinner. The **Restaurant Jaime,** 6 Calle Pinares (tel. 323-69-40), offers a complete dinner for 600 pesetas ($5.76), although wine is extra. From an English menu, you can order a Valencian salad or steamed mussels for an appetizer; then the shellfish paella (tastes as if it were delivered fresh from the sea and the rice paddies), followed by a dessert such as a tart or Manchego cheese. If ordered separately, the shellfish paella costs 350 pesetas ($3.36) and is a meal in itself.

Behind the main street is a tiny docking area, where it's possible to board boats for a cruise of the lake. Negotiate with the owner about price.

VALENCIA NIGHTLIFE: Valencia suffers from provincialism, and that is reflected, of course, in its nightlife. However, there are some diversions. For the best flamenco shows in the city, head for **El Colmao,** 6 Doctor Manuel Candela (tel. 323-63-05), where a thoroughly Spanish setting—murals, drawings of bulls, wrought-iron grillwork—provides the proper atmosphere for the dancing and singing of these Andalusian-inspired shows. For your first drink, you pay 850 pesetas ($8.16). The flamenco show begins at 11 p.m.

About the most popular place for the student crowd to go is **La Casa Vella,** 25 Roteros (just off the Plaza del Carmen). This bar-cum-cocktail lounge is equipped with loud hi-fi music, small tables, green carpeting, reproductions of old paintings on the walls, and several dimly lit rooms suitable for amor. There's no name sign outside the place; just follow the young Valencianos who sidle in every day of the week from 6 p.m. till 3 a.m. A beer here will set you back 100 pesetas (96¢), 150 pesetas ($1.44) if imported. Local whisky is 175 pesetas ($1.68); scotch, 250 pesetas ($2.40).

2. Benidorm

A gemütlich atmosphere prevails here as the yearly invasion from Germany keeps coming. Until West German marks started beefing up the economy, Benidorm was the tiniest of fishing villages. But in the summer, for every dozen natives, 12 dozen foreigners pour in. The French and English have also heard of its charm, its moderately priced hotels, and nightlife. It now awaits the Americans, who, so far, have just stuck a toe in the door.

The hotel builders of Benidorm must rock around the clock; you retire in the evening, and by the time you wake up, a new hotel has opened. Well, almost. Benidorm, because of its European influence, cracks through Spanish provincialism (or ignores it), and is the most sophisticated town this side of Torremolinos. It's recommended for stopovers or for longer stays—but reserve in advance for any stay between mid-June and September.

The town is reached by train from Alicante, also by bus from either Valencia or Alicante.

WHERE TO STAY: Benidorm, as mentioned, is increasingly being endowed with more and more hastily erected hotels—although no amount of building, it seems, can keep up with the popularity in the peak of the season. Pilgrims without reservations are practically laughed at when they innocently inquire for a room.

Since most of the hotel managers operate in a seller's market from June through September, they can slap the full-board requirement on their guests, despite protests by said guests that they simply don't want two stretch-your-girdle Spanish four-coursers a day. The way to beat the board requirement is to book into one of my residencia recommendations. But residencias are rare in Benidorm. Every hotel proprietor either hires a chef, or fancies himself one . . . or is forced into giving the job to his mother-in-law.

I've avoided the hotels springing up along the coastal road, after having spend sleepless nights in them, watching and listening to the rumbling trucks going back and forth between Barcelona and the road south.

Hotel La Peña, Avenida Gerona (tel. 85-06-94), is a modern hotel that (for the price) offers accommodations almost unequaled in Benidorm. First, it serves three good meals a day. Second, its bedrooms are streamlined, utilizing contemporary furnishings that, in part, were inspired by Spanish antiques—a tasteful, artful change of pace from the rashly impersonal decor of most of Benidorm's hostelries.

Next, all of the rooms have air conditioning, plus telephone, large built-in wardrobes, and slickly functional and attractive bathrooms. The price is 1500 pesetas ($14.40) to 2100 pesetas ($20.16) for a double room, 1400 pesetas ($13.44) in a single. The lounge is restrained (in a nice sense), spacious and cool; the terrace opens onto a long private swimming pool, in case you prefer fresh water. In all, the six floors of seaview rooms with balconies at La Peña accommodate 182 sun-seekers year round, who pay an additional 1700 pesetas ($16.32) per person daily for full board.

Hotel Les Dunes, Avenida de Madrid (tel. 85-24-00), is like a big beach club. Built in 1958 on the Playa de Levante, this 110-room (all with private tubs or showers), completely modern hotel is suitable for those who like plenty of activity, such as swimming . . . or whatever. In overall quality, the fairly spacious but simple bedrooms are above reproach. Many have Juliet balconies opening onto Benidorm's greatest Romeo, the almost guaranteed sunshine.

A guest pays 2400 pesetas ($23.04) for a double room. Full board is an extra 1800 pesetas ($17.28) per person. Les Dunes is graced with a front terrace swimming pool, near which is the dining area. Two bars take care of liquid sustenance. The hotel remains open all year (off-season reductions granted from November through February), and is heavily booked in summer by vacationers from Bristol, Bath, and Birmingham.

Hotel Brisa, Playa de Levante (tel. 85-54-00). From its beachfront perch, it is spotless, soulless, and simple, heavily outfitted with plumbing (private bath or shower in every room). This is a reasonable accommodation for both young and old moderns. The double rooms go for 1800 pesetas ($17.28) to 2200 pesetas ($21.12) a night, singles for 1400 pesetas ($13.44). A continental breakfast is an additional 150 pesetas ($1.44) per person. The rooms are bright, airy, and contain the necessary gadgets. There is elevator service, and a dining room where you can order one main meal a day for 750 pesetas ($7.20) per person extra. Its proudest feature is its swimming pool. The "Breeze" is open year round.

Residencia Madrid, Avenida de Madrid (tel. 85-08-03), resides on the Playa de Levante. All of its completely modern but impersonally furnished doubles contain private baths. Two persons can stay here at a cost ranging from 1800 pesetas ($17.28) to 2000 pesetas ($19.20). Singles are rented for 1500 pesetas ($14.40), and a continental breakfast is an additional 150 pesetas ($1.44).

Note: You may confuse the residencia with the **Hotel Madriles,** 3 Avenida de Madrid (tel. 85-32-00), which is under the same management and is close by. The Madriles is open only from April 1 to October 31. The Madrid, however, is open all year. At the Madriles, the cost of a double with shower is 1500 pesetas ($14.40) nightly, with a continental breakfast going for an extra 150 pesetas ($1.44).

Residencia Don José, 2 Carretera del Alt (tel. 85-50-50), is rare as the dodo, in that it was built as a residencia to serve only breakfast—a definite plus as this pleasant little hotel is in the hub of a district containing Benidorm's best budget restaurants (and some intriguing, but touristy, shops). Lying a short walk from the sea, the Don José is a white brick multibalconied building. Its neat and clean bedrooms, up-to-date and attractively furnished, rent for 1400 pesetas ($13.44) daily for doubles with private bath, 950 pesetas ($9.12) for singles. A continental breakfast is an extra 125 pesetas ($1.20). The hotel closes down from October 21 till Holy Week.

Hotel Canfali, 1 Plaza de San Jaime (tel. 85-08-18), is a seaside villa, one of the best of the smaller hotels. Its position is a scene-stealer—at the end of the esplanade, perched on a low cliff, with a staircase winding down to the beach. The Canfali's functional, inviting doubles with private bath (either shower or tub) go for 1250 pesetas ($12) to 1750 pesetas ($16.80), the more expensive offering balconies with sea view. Just three singles with bath are available renting for 1000 pesetas ($9.60). A continental breakfast is an extra 125 pesetas ($1.20). The hotel, open from April through October, is spacious and comfortable, but undistinguished in decor (its garden furniture of bamboo and plastic a case in point). Terraces overlook the sea, a perfect spot for morning coffee.

Hotel Levante, 4 Avenida de Martínez Alejos (tel. 85-36-62), a one-star hotel, won't romance you with glamor or special comforts—but its prices might. One of the older hotels of Benidorm—built back in the days (1958) when the resort was a target for German neocolonial activities—the Levante prices its doubles at only 1250 pesetas ($12) to 1700 pesetas ($16.32). Some of the rooms have showers (no toilets); others have water basins only. A few singles contain private baths, renting for 900 pesetas ($8.64). A continental breakfast is an extra 125 pesetas ($1.20).

The hotel's utter simplicity is not helped by a formidable use of chrome and plastic, although the rooms open interestingly onto a courtyard. The hotel is open April 1 to October 31.

The Pick of the Pensions

Residencia Bristol, 1 Avenida de Martínez Alejos (tel. 85-40-28), is a winning little (32 rooms) one-star pension in the heart of Benidorm. Open from April to October, it is sheltered in a modernized elevator building that contains fairly comfortable bedrooms renting for 1500 pesetas ($14.40) a night to couples (with private bath). However, most of the other adequately furnished bedrooms contain showers (but no toilet), and these are offered at a reduced rate. Singles, for example, are only 900 pesetas ($8.64), with a continental breakfast costing another 125 pesetas ($1.20). The best rooms, parceled out on a first-come, first-served basis, are the front locations with the view.

Hostal del Mar, 4 Pintor Lozano (tel. 85-08-21), is only half a block away from the Playa de Levante. This homey, friendly hotel and restaurant has 23 rooms providing the bare essentials for overnighting. A double with bath rents for only 1100 pesetas ($10.56), a single for 750 pesetas ($7.20). A continental breakfast is an extra 125 pesetas ($1.20) per person. The hostal has a pleasant, old-world dining room decorated with arches, wallpaper, an antique clock, crossed oars on the walls, and gilded mirrors. The tourist menu, costing 450 pesetas ($4.32), includes a special salad or consommé with egg, paella, pork chop, or chicken meunière.

On the Outskirts at Calpe

Paradero de Ifach, 81 Paradero de Ifach (tel. Calpe 83-03-00), is thrust out on the coast, 13 miles north of Benidorm, set back about two miles from the principal Valencia–Alicante highway. It huddles close to the giant Rock of Ifach (Alicante's Gibraltar). Built in the white flat-roofed North African style, the "paradero" offers sun-terrace living at moderate rates. Its living room is like a country home—traditional furnishings and groups of chairs arranged near the large sea-view window.

Most of the 29 bedrooms are handsomely designed, making living here a pleasure. You pay 2200 pesetas ($21.12) for a double room with bath; 1800 pesetas ($17.28) in a room with a shower bath. Singles with bath rent for a maximum of 1250 pesetas ($12), slightly less with shower. The bedrooms can be quite special—some contain antiques. Hopefully, you'll get a bed with a painted cut-out headboard and swan's neck footposts.

For dining, you can choose between a room with a beamed ceiling, an open fireplace, red and white tablecloths, or the sun-room greenhouse, with its red tiled floors, rows of arched windows overlooking the sea, a jungle of potted plants, hanging vines and ferns, and cages of singing birds. For all three meals, you pay 1500 pesetas ($14.40) per person, in addition to the room rate.

WHERE TO DINE: Planesia, 6 Plaza San Jaime (tel. 85-59-50), in the hotel of the same name, serves a good luncheon for 675 pesetas ($6.48). It includes hors d'oeuvres (plate of Russian salad, cheese, bologna, lettuce, tomato, ham, egg) or fruit juice, spaghetti or poached eggs, breaded veal cutlet or braised pork, and dessert of fruit or ice cream. There are about 15 tables, all impeccably laid out with white tablecloths and napkins. But the highlight of this eatery is its stunning view of the ocean and the whole stretch of the Playa de Levante far below. The two-star hotel perched atop the promontory rents doubles with bath for 1800 pesetas ($17.28), singles for 1400 pesetas ($13.44). A continental breakfast is 150 pesetas ($1.44).

Gambo, on the beach, dispenses the more traditional and routine "cafetería fare"—better suited for luncheons than dinners. The cafetería, with its sidewalk tables, is actually an annex of one of the most expensive four-fork restaurants in Benidorm. But for only 425 pesetas ($4.08), it serves a combined plate of hake fried Roman style, green beans, Russian salad; lettuce and tomato; plus fresh fruit, bread, and wine at the counter.

Gigi, 12 Calle de la Palma (tel. 85-05-85), has a set menu for 500 pesetas ($4.80) which includes soup, a meat dish, ice cream, wine, and bread. The owner is a Dutchman, Jack Take, who speaks good English and does the cooking himself. À la carte ordering here, however, can become expensive. The cuisine is international, with an accent on French cooking.

For Italian food, head for the **Pizzería Venetia,** Calle del Alt, a pleasant, rustic-decorative place where pizzas go for 250 pesetas ($2.40) to 350 pesetas ($3.36).

If you're looking for a plain, budget-priced Spanish restaurant in this town filled with four-language-menu clip joints, try the **Olimpico,** where the locals go, on 7 Calle de la Palma. A meal here costs 420 pesetas ($4.03) and includes a salad or consommé, macaroni and cheese or peas with ham, either franks and french fries or a mushroom omelet, then fruit or custard, bread, wine, or beer. The place has a TV in the corner, simple plastic-topped tables, and no decor to speak of. But the food is good and cheap.

Strictly for Splurging

Mesón Felipe V, Plaza del Ayuntamiento, 1 Avenida Gambo (tel. 85-75-57), perches on a low cliff of rocks over the Mediterranean. Entered from the street, the mesón is on two levels—the bottom an Andalusian-style bodega, with old weathered beams, terracotta floors, and regional stools and wooden tables set in front of oceanview windows. The 17th-century-style upper dining room, again with windowside tables to soak up the lapping waves, features a raised open hearth for charcoal-broiling meats, and a small terrace with tables and a view of the ocean and the town. Try the special hors d'oeuvres (entremeses) Felipe V, followed, perhaps, by a paella or a fish known as mero. Wind up with some crêpes suzettes with ice cream inside. On my last visit, I had the entremeses, mero, crêpes, coffee, wine, and mineral water, all for 1000 pesetas ($9.60).

The restaurant's 575-peseta ($5.52) set meal offers a main dish, such as beef or chicken, even the fish for the day, accompanied by a salad or vegetable, then followed by fruit or ice cream. At night you dine by candlelight.

BENIDORM NIGHTLIFE: As in Torremolinos, the nightlife in Benidorm has all the permanency of a sand castle. But here's the lay of the land as of this writing:

The **Granada,** Avenida Dr. Orts Llorca (tel. 85-20-38), on the edge of town, a five-minute ride from the center, conjures up the romance of the city of the pomegranate with its flamenco shows. It opens at 10 p.m. all year (best to go later). In summer the flamenco shows and dancing take place in the garden. For 800 pesetas ($7.68), which is the price of your first drink, you can stay and see a complete floor show, then dance to two bands nightly.

The two most popular discos are the **007** and the **Madeira Club,** both of them on the Plaza Triangular. The former is entered through a huge, simulated safe door, the latter through a steel bulkhead from a ship. Both charge about 500 pesetas ($4.80) per drink, which can be nursed through the evening.

The **Club Sirena,** huddled underneath **La Peña Hotel,** on Avenida Gerona (tel. 85-06-94), is a disco enhanced by the bobbing blond heads from Nordic lands who converge here in the early evening. For 350 pesetas ($3.36)—the price of a drink—young people rock to records. After 10 p.m., many of the more vine-ripened guests from the hotel come down, nosing out all the young and beautiful people. On Sunday, a so-called matinee lasts from 7 to 10 p.m.

La Canción del Mar, 50 Carretera Santa Fe, is high up in the prettiest part of the old town. It is, in fact, a restored manor house which now features a potpourri of entertainment ranging from flamenco to guitar strumming. Open every night from 9 p.m. to 1 a.m., it charges 800 pesetas ($7.68) for the show. The price entitles you to drink as much wine or sangría as you want. The decor is típico, with beamed ceiling, tiles, knickknacks, flowers, lanterns, nooks, paintings, and red-cushioned wicker chairs, and ornate lamps on each table. The club is closed from November to March.

READERS' TRAVEL TIP (ALTEA): "We longed for a small city or town where the visitors we encountered would be few in number, and we found one which came close to our hopes. About ten miles north of Benidorm, en route to Valencia, Altea is a sizable city but has a relatively undeveloped beachfront, and because of this, it seems to be less attractive to tourists. However, Benidorm is so close that for those who enjoy the more popular spots, a stay in Altea will provide the best of both worlds.

"While there, we stayed at the **Hotel Altaya,** 113 Generalísimo (tel. 84-08-00), just off the beach with terraces providing a view of the sea. This two-star hotel was one of the least expensive and nicest for the money that we ran into. We had a large, spacious room for two, costing 1500 pesetas ($14.40), with bath. Singles rent for 850 pesetas ($8.16). Although we did not have our meals at the hotel, the prices are: breakfast, 125 pesetas ($1.20); lunch and/or dinner, 650 pesetas ($6.24).

"We found a good and inexpensive restaurant just a short distance south of the hotel, **Mesón de Jaime,** where for 400 pesetas ($3.84) one can have the meal of the day, including salad, fish, bread, wine, and dessert. The restaurant is behind the Heladería al Puerto, a wonderful ice cream parlor on the Paseo Marítimo" (Maureen and Bruce Barnett, Elkhart, Ind.).

3. Alicante

Often compared to Nice in France, Alicante for some visitors is the best all-around city in Spain. It is popular not only in summer but in winter, as it is one of the warmest spots on the Mediterranean Coast. Its position is 50 miles from Murcia to the north, and about 25 miles from Benidorm. There is direct rail service from Murcia, Valencia, and Granada, as well as extensive bus connections. If you're traveling up and down the Costa Blanca, it's better to stick to the buses, as they run more frequently.

With its wide, palm-lined avenues, it is a city that takes the promenade seriously in the early evening. The magnificent **Explanada de España** extends around part of the yacht harbor and also includes the great promenade under the palms with mosaic sidewalks. I suggest that you get out and walk it (or else jog), even if you're used to driving down to the corner in your hometown.

San Juan is the largest beach in Alicante, lying a short distance from the capital. A good promenade runs parallel to the sea, and it's lined with villas, hotels, and restaurants. The bay of Alicante has two capes, and on the bay is Postiguet Beach. The bay stretches all the way to the Cape of Santa Pola, a town with two good beaches, a 14th-century castle, and several seafood restaurants.

Like an amphitheater, Alicante rises from the seashore up a hill until it reaches the Castle of Santa Bárbara, which towers over the bay and the provincial capital. The Greeks called it "Akra Leuka" (White Peak), and its original defenses were believed to have been erected by the Carthaginians in 400 B.C. In time it was also used by the Romans and Arabs.

The size and grandeur of this fortress is evident in its moats, drawbridges, bastions with their embrasures and merlons, tunneled entrances, guardrooms, bakery, cisterns, underground storerooms, hospitals, batteries, powder stores, barracks, ruins of the former governor's quarters, the Matanza Tower and the Keep, high breastworks, deep dungeons, and barrel-vaulted entrance leading to the underground passage connecting the castle to the beach.

From here, there is a very impressive view over land and sea from the top of the castle. Access is either by asphalt road or by an elevator which one boards on the Explanada de España. In winter the castle is open from 9 a.m. to 7 p.m., in summer from 9 a.m. to 2 p.m. and 5 to 10:30 p.m.

Just north of the entrance to Santa Bárbara is the station of a 93-kilometer narrow-gauge train which takes people up along the sometimes wild, always beautiful rocky, sandy beach-lined coast to Denia.

The train passes through such places as Villajoyosa, Benidorm, Altea, and 26 other stations, almost all of which would be worth a visit. Just north along the coast, the first stations are at what appear to be endless sand beaches. Then you come to rocky inlets and ports which alternate with beaches. Various vacation houses and villages dot the landscape.

Now a tourist center, Denia is lively and bustling, stretching from the slopes of a hill to the seashore. It was inhabited by the Greeks, and its name, Denia, comes from an ancient temple that was dedicated to the goddess Diana. In the town hall, a building which dates from the beginning of the 16th century, there are remains of the temple. You'll also find the remnants of an old Iberian settlement and a great Moorish castle. Denia has fine beaches, and its fishing port is one of the best in the region.

Back in Alicante, you can explore on your own. I'd recommend checking out the Barrio de Santa Cruz, on the slopes of the Castle of Santa Bárbara. The section lies behind the cathedral and forms part of the Villa Vieja (as the old quarter of Alicante is called). It is a colorful sector with wrought-iron grilles on the windows, particularly the "bulging variety." Streets wind about, and one can view the entire harbor while dodging sheets hanging from the windows, or admire blocks of flowers.

In Alicante you'll also find several big and small plazas, some of which are paved with marble. The Castillo de San Fernándo has a panoramic view and can be visited during the day. It's not as awesome as Santa Bárbara, but impressive enough.

The city is characterized by its already-mentioned wide boulevards, all of which are clean and lined with shops and bookstores of every description. Alicante boasts seemingly unlimited shopping facilities, including its leading department store, Galerías Preciados, where you may find what you're seeking without being trampled to death by the mobs as in Madrid.

The traffic is easy-going—uncrowded and unhurried, so that one can wander about the city with a good chance of not getting killed. Along the way you'll encounter beautifully planted parks and apparently endless lines of palms and gardens. There are many pedestrian malls, some of them paved with marble or tile.

When it's time to eat you'll find shellfish and fish taking up a large part of the menu. Many restaurants which are close to the sea offer a wide variety of fish, as well as lobster and Dublin Bay prawns. The characteristic dish of Alicante is rice, which is served in many different ways. The most usual sauce is *allioli*, a kind of mayonnaise made from oil and garlic. Alicante rice is served with chicken, lean pork, and greens; there is an enormous variety of rice dishes with "fruits of the sea." But the greatest variety in the food line on the Costa Blanca is in desserts; Spanish nougat is the most popular of all.

WHERE TO STAY: Cristal, 11 López Torregrosa (tel. 20-96-00), is a seven-floor hotel with an all-glass facade, one of the best designed hotels to be erected in Alicante. Your bedroom (all have private bath) may have chalk-white walls, moss-green draperies, and matching counterpanes, beds set against the built-in headboards, telephones, reading lamps, service bells, and stereo music. Doubles rent for 2200 pesetas ($21.12) to 2600 pesetas ($24.96), singles for 1800 pesetas ($17.28). A continental breakfast is an extra 175 pesetas ($1.68) per person.

In cooler months, there is central heating. The reception lounge is spacious, the comfortable furnishings arranged on islands of hand-loomed circular rugs. For drinks, there is a red and gold bar with low Chinese-style chairs and stools. The Cristal doesn't have a restaurant, but there's a snackbar on the premises. Built in the heart of Alicante, the hotel is, nevertheless, only a five-minute walk to the inner harbor and the esplanade.

Residencia Navas, 30 Calle de las Navas (tel. 20-40-11), is a winner in the bargain sweepstakes in Alicante. Built in 1965, this 40-room hotel gets only a one-star rating from the government, but that is primarily because it serves only breakfast (a blessing really) and has only water basins in its fair-size single rooms—which rent, incidentally, for 700 pesetas ($6.72).

Its clean, comfortable, and fairly handsome doubles carry a 1850-peseta ($17.76) price tag. If you're determined to get blood out of every centavo, ask for one of the 24 doubles with water basin only—1400 pesetas ($13.44) for two. A continental breakfast is an extra 150 pesetas ($1.44). Most rooms have their own balconies.

Portugal, 26 Portugal (tel. 22-32-44), opened in 1969, is modest and has 18 rooms spreading across its second floor. The accommodations are furnished in tasteful modern, and are kept immaculate. The most expensive doubles—those with private bath—go for 1200 pesetas ($11.52). The few singles (with water basins only) rent for 550 pesetas ($5.28), whereas a double room with wash basin costs only 950 pesetas ($9.12). Only breakfast is provided, at a cost of 150 pesetas ($1.44). The Portugal is a corner hotel, one block from the bus station, about four blocks from the railway station, and a three-minute walk from the harbor.

Hotel Residencia San Remo, 30 Navas (tel. 20-95-00), is another low-budget selection. Most of its bedrooms offer private baths. A white-plastered, seven-floor corner building, the residencia (breakfast only) offers clean, unpretentious, reasonably comfortable doubles for a peak 1600 pesetas ($15.36). The singles with shower baths go for 950 pesetas ($9.12). A continental breakfast costs an extra 125 pesetas ($1.20) per person. Some of the rooms have their own balconies.

WHERE TO DINE: Simple, rustic, but my top choice for budget dining is the **Mesón del Pollo**, 11 Sanjurjo, which features a 525-peseta ($5.04) meal that might include noodle soup with chick peas, a pork chop with potatoes, plus bread, wine, and dessert. The chicken, after which the restaurant is named, costs 275 pesetas ($2.64) for half a bird. You enter the mesón through a bar with the typical beamed ceiling and lined with five huge wine barrels (filled with Montilla, Comillas, and other wines). The dining room in back has ten tables, and the walls are decorated with photographs.

Those not wanting to spend their pesetas in the plush cafeterías on the Paseo Marítimo should head for the neighborhood around the bus depot. There you'll find the **Popeye**, 13 Calle Pintor Lorenzo Casanova, a typical económico whose prices may make your eyes pop. For 350 pesetas ($3.36), you'll get a soup or guisado, followed by that ubiquitos hake or pork, plus a dessert. Bread and wine, of course, are included. A second choice for the same tab might feature a plate of macaroni or beans; eggs or a tortilla with potatoes; bread, wine, and dessert. The Popeye is a clean, neon-lit place with no frills.

Around the corner is the equally inexpensive **Bar Río**, 24 Calle Portugal. It has a similar 375-peseta ($3.60) menu, but is a bit more brash than the Popeye.

Good cafeteria-type meals can be eaten at **Bar Montana**, 21 General Castaños, where you'll get a combination plate for 300 pesetas ($2.88) that'll include mero (a white fish), roast pork, asparagus, mushrooms, bread, wine, or sangría, as well as fruit.

with red cloths and lamps. We enjoyed watching the exciting à la carte specialties being cooked in the open air by an impressive headwaiter who was something of a showman, aided by an assistant. An à la carte dinner is likely to range in price from 900 pesetas ($8.64) to 1500 pesetas ($14.40). . . . We found a tiny, unpretentious restaurant, **Casa Tomasa**, 11 Virgen de Belén, a little side street in Alicante, which is not too easy to find but provided good comidas económicas for 300 pesetas ($2.88). There are only half a dozen tables with bright checked tablecloths. You are served by a young, smiling señorita, the daughter of the house. The cubierto is a bowl of soup or salad, a main dish, and fruit, wine and bread included. We ate there several times and found the fish dishes, such as salmonete (red mullet), especially good" (Dr. and Mrs. E. McC. Callan, Canberra, Australia). . . . "There's a good 350-peseta ($3.36) menu available at the **Restaurant Cafetería Piano Pub**, right on the Explanada de España, at no. 14" (Joseph W. Zdenek, Rock Hill, S.C.).

4. Elche

Between Alicante (13 miles away) and Murcia is the little town of Elche, famous for both its age-old Mystery Play and the groves of date palms that grow in profusion. The play is reputedly the oldest dramatic liturgy performed in Europe. But unless you're visiting from August 13 to 15 when it's presented, the date palms will be the major attraction.

The palm forest is unrivaled anywhere in Europe. Many Spanish towns couldn't celebrate Palm Sunday properly if it weren't for this forest. But the local people don't sit around worshipping palms all day; shoe and sandalmaking are the other occupations around here. La Dama de Elche, the primitive sculptured bust in the Madrid Archeological Museum, was dug up in this area.

When you see the whitewashed houses, in the setting of an immense date forest, you may feel you've been transplanted to an African, even an Oriental oasis. Take time out to visit the gardens, which have been declared a national treasure.

The best place to stay is at the parador, **Huerto del Cura**, 14 Federico García Sanchez (tel. 45-80-40), which stands in the so-called priest's orchard. From your bedroom window, you'll have lovely views of the palm trees. The parador consists of a number of cabins in the date palm grove. Each cabin has four double rooms with private baths. The rate is 2900 pesetas ($27.84) in a single, 4200 pesetas ($40.32) in a double. Although these tabs are high, it's a lovely, unique experience. Everything is beautifully furnished and immaculately kept, and the level of service is high. Built under the palms, a swimming pool separates the cabins from the main structure of the hotel. In the main building there is an attractive bar and an upstairs dining room where the food is well prepared. You look out over the pool and date grove while dining. Dinner costs 950 pesetas ($9.12) per person, and a continental breakfast goes for an additional 250 pesetas ($2.40).

Peseta-watchers would be better advised to stay at the simple little **Residencia Cartagena**, 12 Gabriel Moro (tel. 46-15-50), which lies across the river in the more commercial part of town. The hotel is pleasant and comfortable enough, and is open all year except in July. Singles are rented for 1400 pesetas ($13.44), doubles rising to 2400 pesetas ($23.04). A continental breakfast is an extra 250 ($2.40) per person.

For dining, the locals prefer the **Parque Municipal**, Paseo de la Estación (tel. 45-34-15), which is a large open-air restaurant and café, right in the middle of a public park. It's a good place to go for meals or drinks, and you'll get to study the people and the palms. Service is relaxed, the food of standard quality. Expect to spend from 1000 pesetas ($9.60) to 1600 pesetas ($15.36) for a complete meal here.

After a visit to the forest, we continue on to:

5. Murcia

This ancient Moorish city of sienna-colored buildings is an inland provincial capital on the main road between Valencia and Granada. Most motorists making this trip pass through it, and it's well worth a stopover. It lies about 52 miles from Alicante on the Costa Blanca.

The city abounds in grand houses built in the 1700s, but has many modern aspects as well, which have sprouted up at the expense of the old. Its principal artistic treasure is its 14th-century cathedral, a bastardized mixture of Gothic, baroque, and Renaissance. The Holy Week celebration here is known all over Spain, and this would be the ideal time to visit Murcia.

WHERE TO STAY: Residencia Rincón de Pepe, 34 Plaza de Apóstoles (tel. 21-22-39), is a surprise: a modern hotel hidden on a narrow street in the heart of the old quarter. Its entranceway is accented with marble, glass, and plants; there is a good-size lounge with many conversational areas, as well as a bar. The bedrooms are as up-to-date as the lobby, and they have many built-in conveniences. A double costs from 3200 pesetas ($30.72) nightly, a single going for 2500 pesetas ($24). Units are most comfortable, with air conditioning and complete baths. A continental breakfast at 250 ($2.40) is the only meal served. Yet the residencia owns my first dining recommendation:

WHERE TO EAT: Restaurant Rincón de Pepe, 34 Plaza de Apóstoles (tel. 21-22-39), is a tavern patronized by in-the-know diners of Murcia. Its long, low rooms are primitive, with large overhead oak beams, one wall of old wine kegs, and an open kitchen where you can see huge copper pots bubbling away. Diners usually start their meals at a long counter lined with plates of hors d'oeuvres.

For 1000 pesetas ($9.60), a menú del día is offered, including a wide choice—perhaps beginning with a Russian salad, stuffed peppers as a main course, followed by dessert. You can also order à la carte. A special paella, a meal itself, is served on Monday, Wednesday, and Saturday. Complete à la carte meals are likely to be expensive, from 2000 pesetas ($19.20) to 3000 pesetas ($28.80) per person.

For the least expensive dining in Murcia, cross the bridge to the **Taberna del Conde**, 18 Princesa, a modest hostal offering good food at good prices. Diners should be warned of the utter lack of decor, but the compensatingly traditional Spanish kitchen is decked out better. For 575 pesetas ($5.52), a cubierto is featured that offers a choice of soup of the day or gazpacho, followed by meat or fish, usually veal escalope or hake, then flan or fruit. The helpings are generous.

READERS' RESTAURANT SUGGESTION: "We found **Casa Emilio**, 22 Plaza Calvo Sotelo (tel. 21-13-25), a two-forker with white linen cloths, napkins, and jacketed waiters. We had paella for two at 600 pesetas ($5.76), and it was outstanding. Vino de casa was 100 pesetas (96¢). The menú del día is 550 pesetas ($5.28) and includes a wide variety of main dishes, with soup, bread, wine, and flan. An average meal will cost between 700 pesetas ($6.72) and 1000 pesetas ($9.60)" (Robert and Nadia Price, North Hollywood, Calif.).

READER'S HOTEL SELECTION AT CARTAGENA: "At the **Hotel los Habañeros**, 52 Calle San Diego (tel. 50-25-50), a double room with full bath is only 1800 pesetas ($17.28), with a continental breakfast costing an additional 150 pesetas ($1.44) per person. The hotel also has a restaurant where the meals are good and cheap. We traveled by car, and this was a pleasant break in our trip from Valencia to Málaga" (M. E. Lowey, Altoona, Pa.).

READER'S SIGHTSEEING TIPS: "On our way from Murcia to Granada, we turned in Velez Rubio to **Velez Blanco,** which is about eight kilometers off the highway. It is a lovely 'white town,' and the castle there is very interesting. A guide has the keys to the castle, and he also took us to see the prehistoric drawings at the **Cueva de los Letreros.** In **Guadix** we stayed at the **Hotel Comercio** (one-star), 3 Mira de Amezcua (tel. 66-05-00), which is clean, pleasant, and reasonable. Doubles with bath rent for 1760 pesetas ($16.90), dropping to just 1450 pesetas ($13.92) if bathless. A continental breakfast is an extra 125 pesetas ($1.20) per person, and a lunch or dinner costs around 525 pesetas ($5.04). Around 10 o'clock in the evening, we went to visit the cave quarter of Guadix, a much nicer, cleaner, and safer place than Sacro-Monte in Granada" (Dr. D. Almagor, Tel Aviv, Israel).

Chapter IX

SETTLING INTO BARCELONA

1. Finding a Room
2. The Catalán Cuisine
3. The Top Sights
4. The City After Dark

BARCELONA IS the most European of Spanish cities. The largest of Mediterranean ports, a formidable rival of Madrid, it lies between two hills, Tibidabo and Montjuich. Staunchly independent, Barcelona is the reluctant bride of Spain. It has a separate language, Catalán, once outlawed, but now spoken as an assertion of independent pride.

This port is big, bustling, commercial, residential, cultural, artistic, new, and old. Sometimes these elements are at cross purposes. Barcelona has attained its present power and importance by the sheer work and determination of its middle class. But the Spanish bourgeois stamp doesn't blot out the city completely, for the simple reason that there are too many French people, Britons, Germans, and Americans who flock to Barcelona to have fun. It's a rocking city.

It is also a capital of contrasts. The narrow streets of the Gothic quarter are little changed since the Middle Ages, yet the wide boulevards and splashing fountains of the more commercial 19th-century town could be found in any number of Western European cities.

On the labyrinthine narrow streets branching off from the south of the Ramblas (near the Puerta de la Paz) walk Jean Genet's "whores, thieves, pimps, and beggars" ripped from the pages of *The Thief's Journal.* Also through the maze wander the sailors and foreigners in search of adventure. Yet it seems that great numbers of the Cataláns are puritans who are disdainful of the "riff-raff" attracted to the big harbor city of the Mediterranean.

Further evidence of Barcelona's contrasts is to be found in the burgeoning number of apartment houses that look as if they've been transplanted from the Bronx. These cold, impersonal structures exist in a city that was uniquely stamped with the work of Gaudí, the architect who "outrococoed rococo" with his architectural wonders that look like melted fudge dripped over a child's erector set.

Barcelona is a city of colorful restaurants and moderately priced hotels, reviewed in this chapter. Its winters are mild (palm trees flutter in the cool wind); its springs and autumns are ideal; its hot summers are almost bearable. And it has a beach.

The **Plaza de Cataluña** is the city's heart; the **Ramblas** with their evening promenades are its arteries. The Ramblas begin at the **Puerta de la Paz,** with its 200-foot-high-monument to Columbus, and stretch all the way to the Plaza de Cataluña. Along the way you'll find chairs for sitting and viewing the parade, book shops and newsstands, and stalls selling birds and flowers. Both the feathers and flowers, in particular, greatly color the charm of the Ramblas.

The major wide boulevards are the **Avenida Diagonál,** the **Paseo de Colón,** the **Calle del Marqués del Duero,** and the elegant shopping street—the **Paseo de Gracia.**

By all means, visit this capital of Catalonia. Its attractions are many. It's also an important center from which you can branch out on a number of excursions: to the Costa Brava, the principality of Andorra, the old Roman city of Tarragona, and the Monastery of Montserrat. The port is, finally, a jumping-off point—either by plane or boat—to the Balearic Islands.

GETTING AROUND BARCELONA: The city offers several adequate means of transportation: taxis, buses, subways.

Taxis: When you get into a taxi in Barcelona, a rate of 30 pesetas (29¢) will (or should) be shown on the meter. However, you must add 20 pesetas (19¢) to all fares. For each kilometer you travel in the city, you'll have to pay another 20 pesetas (19¢). As taxi rates go, these are low, and you'll find this means of transportation most efficient. You will have to pay 60 pesetas (58¢) extra if the taxi takes you to the bullring and 250 pesetas ($2.40) if you go to the airport. You'll also have to pay extra for big pieces of luggage. *Warning:* Make sure that the flag is turned down when you enter the taxi.

Subway: The "Metro" is a low fare of 30 pesetas (29¢) on most rides. The Gran Metro cuts across Barcelona from north to south, and the Transversal heads east to west. The best connecting station for subways in all directions is the Plaza de Cataluña.

Motorbuses: Barcelona has a system of motorbuses—30 pesetas (29¢) for most fares—but unless you know the complicated routes, or have some facility with the language, you'll find this a confusing means of travel. Buses on Sunday costs 35 pesetas (34¢).

Railroad: The terminal where most visitors arrive is the Estación de Francia, next to the Ciudadela Park, on Avenida del Marqués de la Argentera. Trains pull in here for Madrid, Zaragoza, Valencia, and Tarragona.

1. Finding a Room

Hotels in Barcelona are plentiful, and are some of the most reasonable in Spain. However, the picture is not totally rosy. For some reason, Barcelona lags behind many Spanish cities in top-notch modern offerings in our price range (with a handful of exceptions). The top-rated hotels possible on our budget are a bit tarnished, but comfortable and adequate. Without question, they offer good value for the money they charge.

Hotel Gaudí, 12 Conde de Asalto (tel. 317-90-32), is one of my most preferred choices: it is modern and just off Nou de la Rambla on a bustling, colorful street. The rooms are tastefully decorated, spacious, and offer telephones and steam heat in the winter. This comfortable hotel charges from 2500 pesetas ($24) to 3000 pesetas ($28.80) in a double room with private bath. Singles with shower rent from 1800 pesetas ($17.28).

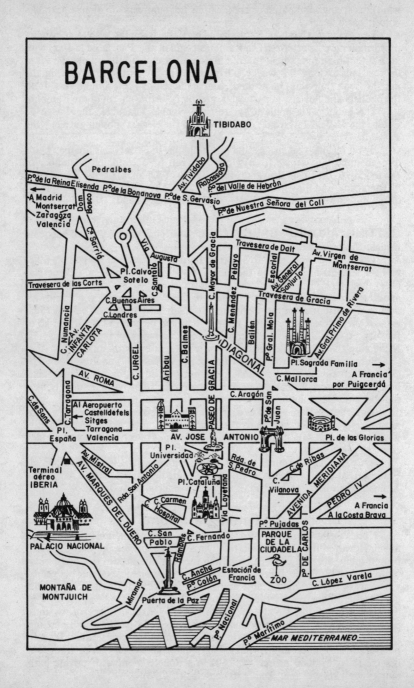

The lounge has a curving staircase, walls of stone, paneling, and cozy seating arrangements. There is a large dining room, as well as a lounge-bar combination. This hotel was named after the architect Gaudí, and it is opposite the Gaudí Palace, housing the city's Theater Museum.

Gran Vía, 642 Gran Vía (tel. 318-19-00), provides old-style living in a great old city. On one of the most fashionable boulevards in the city, the hotel preserves accoutrements evoking another era. For example, the drawing room glitters with gilt furniture, mirrors, inlaid pieces, tables, and high-backed chairs. The long dining room is done in Wedgwood blue and white, with a row of crystal chandeliers, and French provincial chairs. Typical of the faded grandeur of the hotel, the elevator is also antiquated. Cacophonous sounds rising from the street below might disturb the light sleeper.

In the two-story-high reception lounge is a grand balustraded stairway (worthy of *Sunset Boulevard*), leading to the arched balcony. In the Andalusian style, the courtyard is set with tables for al fresco drinks in the midst of palm trees and fountains. Behind the arches is a garden room serving continental breakfasts.

The bedrooms are traditional, often featuring interesting reproductions of antiques—you might find an elaborate carving or painting in yours. It's not luxury, but good comfort. Rooms rent for $18 (U.S.) in a single to $30 in a double nightly. All of the bedrooms contain private baths, and there is central heating as well.

Hotel Principál, 8 Junta de Comercio (tel. 318-89-74), is a good class hotel, lying within walking distance of the heartbeat Plaza de Cataluña. An attractive hotel with lots of Spanish character, it has an old-fashioned ambience in parts, although there has been much modernization. The highest prices are charged in July and August, when singles rent for 1400 pesetas ($13.44) and doubles go for 2200 pesetas ($21.12). All the comfortably furnished units contain private baths or showers. Since the food is quite good, you might want to request half-board terms at a rate of 1900 pesetas ($18.24) in a single, 3200 pesetas ($30.72) in a double. Motorists will welcome the hotel's private parking arrangements.

Montecarlo, 124 Rambla de los Estudios (tel. 317-58-00). The main lounge here features an elaborate carved ceiling, stylized carved doors, a crystal chandelier, and a baronial fireplace. The furniture has been renewed in the hall and in the rooms. Doubles with private baths cost 2900 pesetas ($27.84); singles, also with bath, go for 2000 pesetas ($19.20). There is a large covered garage in the same building, plus a coffeeshop on the premises. A continental breakfast costs an extra 175 pesetas ($1.68).

Hostal Levante, 2 Bajada de San Miguel (tel. 317-95-65), is one of the nicest and most reasonable places to stay in Barcelona. It's housed in an imposing building, more than two centuries old, and it lies just a short distance from Plaza San Jaime, directly in the center of the Gothic Quarter. For 450 pesetas ($4.32) you're given a single room, or else you'll pay 800 pesetas ($7.68) in a double. Units are clean and comfortable. There is central heating, and use of the hot showers in the corridors is included in the tariff. The hostal is removed from the noise of the streets. This 38-room establishment is run by a hard-working, helpful couple, Mr. and Mrs. Manuel Ibáñez, who speak English.

Hotel Residencia Habaña, 647 Avenida de las Cortés Catalanes (tel. 301-07-50), has a gentility to it, an old-fashioned touch. It is a well-run hotel on an important street that is likely to be noisy and therefore can't be recommended to light sleepers. There is a modern reception room downstairs, and an elevator will take you up to the pleasantly appointed rooms. The Habaña, incidentally, has rooms in several price ranges. Doubles with bath go for 2900 pesetas ($27.84). The most expensive singles, those with bath, rent for 2000 pesetas ($19.20). A continental breakfast at 175 pesetas ($1.68) is the only meal served.

Hotel Inglés, 17 Calle Boquería (tel. 317-37-70), is a small hotel in the old quarter, along a narrow street off the Ramblas. Because of its isolated position, this modest place is off the heavily trodden tourist trail, but a few minutes' walk will take you to the heart of the city. The management is helpful, and has set a moderate rate schedule: 2000 pesetas ($19.20) for a double room with private bath. Singles with shower rent for 1400 pesetas ($13.44), and a continental breakfast is an extra 150 pesetas ($1.44). The rooms are fair, each with its own telephone. The level of cleanliness is adequate, and the Inglés can make for a pleasant stopover if your expectations aren't too high.

Hotel Alicante, 4 Ronda de la Universidad (tel. 318-31-70), is a bargain. Frankly, it's a marginal establishment—somewhat rundown, attracting mostly a Spanish clientele who know they can get some of the cheapest hotel rooms (and some of the noisiest) in the city. A few of the doubles have private bath, and these rent for 1800 pesetas ($17.28) nightly. However, the bathless doubles drop to only 1400 pesetas ($13.44). The single rooms—some with shower, others with water basin—are 900 pesetas ($8.64) to 1200 pesetas ($11.52). A continental breakfast is an extra 150 pesetas ($1.44) per person. A night watchman (the *sereno*) patrolling the street with a large ring of keys will let you in after midnight.

Residencia Jardín, 1 Plaza San José Oriol (tel. 301-59-00), truthfully calls for a painter's smock, as its prices are designed to please the struggling artist. A turn-of-the-century double bedroom with bath—small, quite clean, fairly comfortable—rents for 1200 pesetas ($11.52). Doubles with water basins only go for 1300 pesetas ($12.48); singles in that bathless bracket cost only 900 pesetas ($8.64). No meals, other than a continental breakfast at 125 pesetas ($1.20), are served. The situation of the Jardín is ideal: near the Ramblas, where two tiny plazas (Plaza del Piño and Plaza San José Oriol) converge in Siamese fashion. From most of the windows of the Jardín, you can see the local life and the old church of Santa María del Pinto. This section is the Montmartre of Barcelona.

Hostal Roma, 11 Plaza Real (tel. 302-03-66), is on one of the most attractive squares in Barcelona, the center of much nightlife and a plaza filled with students of all nations. A third-class hotel, the hostal is basic and simply furnished, but clean. Singles rent for 500 pesetas ($4.80); doubles for 800 pesetas ($7.68), and triples for 1200 pesetas ($11.52). Each unit is equipped with showers.

Suizo, 12 Plaza del Angel (tel. 317-83-99), is a little gem. The rooms with complete bath are good—both spacious and cheerful. The man at the desk, Philip, is a treasure, always helpful and a fountain of knowledge. The charge is 1800 pesetas ($17.28) in a double, dropping to only 1125 pesetas ($10.80) in a single.

THE PICK OF THE PENSIONS: Hostal Turín, 9 Pintor Fortuní (tel. 302-48-12), given two stars by the government, is just off the Ramblas de los Estudios. The Turín is easily identifiable by its terracotta grillwork front. It's housed in a balconied, elevator building. Neat and simple, it is a good choice because of its streamlined bedrooms—small but comfortable. Most doubles are bathless, but contain water basins, and cost only 1400 pesetas ($13.44) a night.

In one of the 18 doubles with private bath, the rate is 2000 pesetas ($19.20). Bathless singles go for only 900 pesetas ($8.64).

Hostal Basilea, 17 Plaza Real (tel. 318-51-90), has been renovated and much improved, and now offers fair and better decorated rooms. The location is just a whisper away from the Ramblas, and the Basilea is frequented by young people from many countries. It is conveniently situated next door to a flamenco club. The price of the double accommodations with private bath is 2400 pesetas ($23.04). Singles with the same plumbing rent for 1600 pesetas ($15.36). For half board you pay 900 pesetas ($8.64) per person extra.

The **Hotel Universidad,** 10 Ronda de la Universidad (tel. 317-14-41), is a postwar boarding house that has fewer amenities than some of the more preferred pensions previously recommended, but it's quite a bargain. Right in the heart of the city, the Universidad rates at least a bachelor's degree for running an efficient, well-kept, spotless, and friendly accommodation. The way the maids polish around here, you'd think you were in Amsterdam. The moderately attractive, but basic, double rooms with bath rent for 1750 pesetas ($16.80) nightly dropping to 1300 pesetas ($12.48) if bathless. Singles, on the other hand, are equipped only with wash basins, and cost 1000 pesetas ($9.60). Full board, incidentally, is an additional 1200 pesetas ($11.52) per person daily.

Hostal Neutral, 42 Rambla de Cataluña (tel. 318-73-70) is just that—a neutral but very recommendable place, known to a select group of Spaniards attracted here by its cleanliness and efficiency. Like the Universidad, this is a postwar pension, but this time I'm referring to World War I. Still, its quite good doubles rent for only 1540 pesetas ($14.78), and these have private baths. But you may be assigned to a double with only a water basin for 1190 pesetas ($11.42). The single rooms rent for 750 pesetas ($7.20) nightly. A continental breakfast is included. The dining room is pleasant, homey in fact, and the waitress brings in well-cooked lunches or dinners. English is spoken.

Hostal Residencia Nilo, 17 José Anselmo Clavé (tel. 317-90-44), although modest, attracts a steady clientele of travelers from English-speaking countries. In the center of the city by the port, railway station, and Ramblas, the hostal is clean, and there is always hot water, fresh linen, and good friendly service. For 650 pesetas ($6.24) a bathless single is offered, increasing to 950 pesetas ($9.12) in a double. However, the super-economy special is a triple room, sleeping three at a cost of 1200 pesetas ($11.52). A continental breakfast is served for 110 pesetas ($1.06). The hostal remains open all night.

Pension Francia, 4 Detras Palacio (tel. 319-03-76), is a simple little place which has found favor with some readers on a low budget. In modestly furnished units, guests pay only 750 pesetas ($7.20) per night for a bed with a continental breakfast. With shower, the rate rises to 950 pesetas ($9.12) per person. The food is good and the portions generous, so most guests request full board for an extra 1200 pesetas ($11.52).

READERS' HOTEL SELECTIONS: "We stayed at the **Hostal Residencia Montserrat,** Plaza Victoria (tel. 317-27-00), at the top end of Paseo de Gracia. They charge 1550 pesetas ($14.88) for a double with complete bathroom. A continental breakfast costs 125 pesetas ($1.20). We even had a large balcony adjoining our room. It was so quiet that we couldn't believe we were in Barcelona. More important, we were able to park our car in a garage practically below the hotel. Parking is next to impossible at the hostals off the Ramblas. The subway also was at our doorstep, and it was easy to go downtown" (Mrs. Anne Bachusky, Guelph, Ontario, Canada). . . . "The best place to stay is **Australia Guest House,** 11 Ronda Universidad, fourth floor (tel. 317-41-77). It is small (only two singles and two doubles) and warm, clean, and friendly. My family's experience over a period of a year proved the prices here to be consistently the lowest available for the quality of the place. Although the building is old and centrally located (two blocks from the Plaza de Cataluña), all rooms and bathrooms have been redecorated and are quite modern. All members of the charming Spanish family which operates this guesthouse speak English, as they lived in Australia for 18 years. Mrs. Lorenzo is a warm woman who loves helping people and taking care of them. She is an excellent cook and prepares whatever breakfast you order, from continental to eggs and bacon, as a nominal extra charge. Other meals can also be arranged for, but you'd better be hungry, as they are enormous" (Ruth Cory, Durango, Colo.).

2. The Catalán Cuisine

From the top of Montjuich to the lowliest dive, Barcelona offers a wide variety of places at which to eat. If the Cataláns aren't always gourmets, they make up for it in the huge, filling portions they serve. The hotels and pensions offer good Catalán cooking, but it would seem that large numbers of the visitors to Barcelona like to get out on the lively streets at night and search for a restaurant. Keep in mind that the city enjoys a large cult of midnight diners; if possible, have a late, late lunch.

THE BEST BARGAINS: The **Casa José,** 10 Plaza San José Oriol (tel. 302-40-20), wins, forks down, as the best all-around spot for rock-bottom economy dining in Barcelona. Placed on a medieval plaza, the restaurant draws an intriguing clientele—the local habitués, the mainstay, bending elbows with the transient foreigners. An occasional frugal Catalán artist, with a trimmed Van Dyck beard, may be seen carefully ordering a well prepared cubierto for 125 pesetas ($1.20), featuring, say, spaghetti, lamb stew, plus bread and dessert. For a big 160 pesetas ($1.54), you get roast chicken, french fries, salad, bread, and dessert. Paella is available for 140 pesetas ($1.34), although you must wait about half an hour for it to be prepared. A quarter bottle of wine costs 25 pesetas (24¢). This corner bistro overlooks the back of the old Church of Santa María del Piño. From the Rambla San José, it's only a three-minute walk up the Cardenal Casañas and Calle Boquería. Closed Saturday.

C'an Tripas, 16 Calle Sagues, is a good find, and is well known in Barcelona as a top budget restaurant. It has no frills, but still there's a certain charm about the place. The tables are laid out with oilcloth, and there are small chairs, arc lights, bottles standing on racks along the walls, sawdust on the floor, a televison set, an open refrigerator, and a freezer in the small dining room. The walls are decorated with posters and coats hanging on hooks. You may select from a wide range of dishes, including, for example, fish soup, beef with brussels sprouts, brook trout, and Spanish melon. Most hot plates cost from 90 pesetas (86¢) to 250 pesetas ($2.40), and the tourist menu is offered at 375 pesetas ($3.60).

La Oca, next to Sears at 10 Plaza Calvo Sotelo (tel. 321-10-19), is a popular spot with young people for quick snacks and light meals. There's a ground floor and a downstairs dining area, both of them jammed in the evenings. Best here are the pastries and the club sandwiches. Also good are the hamburgers and hot dogs. Cubiertos range from 250 pesetas ($2.40) to 600 pesetas ($5.76). You can also sit outdoors at a spacious cafe.

Restaurant Canaletas, 135 Rambla Canaletas, right off the Plaza de Cataluña, is my star choice in the heartland of Barcelona. This turn-of-the-century bar-restaurant smugly retains its old Catalonian trappings of brass and mahogany. An oval-shaped central bar of marble is for tapa nibblers, while the mezzanine draws the "proper" diners. Small tables hug the open front, over-flowing onto the sidewalk. Although there are several higher meals here, the best one is a 375-peseta ($3.60) cubierto—a rápido meal featuring (1) soup or salad; (2) spaghetti or potato omelet; (3) hake or stew; finished off by (4) flan or ice cream, plus wine. A simpler meal costs only 250 pesetas ($2.40). This is served from 1 to 3:30 p.m. and from 8 to 10:30 p.m. The Canaletas is just right for a quickie lunch or a night-owl snack, as it offers ready-made sand- wiches and pastries.

Restaurant Aquarium, 15 Calle del Cardenal Casañas, off las Ramblas de las Flores, is as small as a sardine can, as undistinguished as unseasoned potatoes, and overly lit by neon—but if you can cross these hurdles, you'll find one of the biggest and best cubiertos offered by a Barcelona bistro. For 480 pesetas ($4.61), a typical repast features (1) fish soup, típico of the region; (2) veal filet and tomatoes, hearty and filling; followed by (3) a dessert (nothing special in this department), plus bread, wine, and service. Closed Sunday night.

Restaurante Roma, Plaza Real, is another budget eatery, featuring a tourist menu for 450 pesetas ($4.32), which might include a soup or salad, cannelloni, omelet or eggs, then hake, breaded veal cutlet or chicken, plus bread and a dessert. The place is clean and otherwise pleasant.

Pimpollo, 11 Calle Pintor Fortuni (tel. 318-22-97), near the Rambla de los Estudios, in the Hotel Sorvi building, features golden-brown, spit-roasted chickens at prices to cluck about. In this narrow, modern "henhouse," diners roost on stools. For 500 pesetas ($4.80), diners can order a complete dinner. Open from 8 a.m. to midnight, the Pimpollo is a good way to keep food costs down in Barcelona without compromising your taste buds.

AT BARCELONETA: Bar Hispaño, 19 Paseo Nacional, looks as if it belongs in St.-Germain-des-Prés, but it's near the harbor in Playa de la Barceloneta, a favorite haunt of both the Cataláns and the foreign invaders during the summer months. Gravitate to the sidewalk tables, where you will have what one lovely Barcelona lady termed "a distinguished banquet." The chef special- izes in seafood. Try, in particular, the gambas (shrimp), which is prepared here in a variety of ways. Most of the fish plates offered range in price from 150 pesetas ($1.44) to 450 pesetas ($4.32).

Restaurant Peru, 9 Paseo Nacional, is the Bargain Bella on this restau- rant-lined boulevard, although it dishes up savory viands in less than savory surroundings. Nevertheless, a good meal is a good meal. A 500-peseta ($4.80) cubierto is wheeled out. You get four courses: salad or soup; paella or cannel- loni; roast veal; and dessert, plus a Catalán wine and service. The portions and the courses are large. Hearty, vigorous Spanish fare is served.

Ramonet (known as **Bon Xarello**), 17 Calle Maquinista, is a charming old tavern. You eat standing up, with your plate resting on large wine barrels. Typical fare here is the *pan i oli* (a large slice of regional bread with tomato and oil on it), costing 40 pesetas (38¢). Tops are the tapas (hors d'oeuvres) such as snails, mussels, small clams, and grilled squid. Also good here is the shish kebab and the mushrooms (setas) which are in season in October. Most tapas range in price from 90 pesetas (86¢) to 175 pesetas ($1.68). The place has a beamed ceiling from which hang hundreds of hams, red peppers, loaves of bread, and garlic pigtails.

THE BIG SPLURGE: Los Caracoles, 14 Escudillers (tel. 302-31-85), flourishes in the labyrinth of the narrow, cobblestone streets of old Barcelona. Most visitors to this Catalán capital write a memo to themselves: "See Gaudí's cathedral and dine at Caracoles." It's that popular. One of the port's most colorful restaurants, Los Caracoles is acclaimed for its spit-roasted chickens and for its namesake, snails.

The spit is outside on the alleyway-like street, tempting the milling crowd of sailors, strollers, and Mr. and Mrs. Smith of Topeka with its wafting aromas. A long angular bar, filled with all the típico claptrap, is in front. This leads to a restaurant in back, with an upper level. You can look in at the busy preparations going on in the kitchen, dried spices, smoked ham shanks, and garlic bouquets hanging from the ceiling. In summer, tables are placed outside in the "cat alley." To dine here is a complete experience . . . but you'll be so close to the passersby they can inspect your chompers.

The food at the restaurant is excellent, with all sorts of Catalán specialties, but the caracoles and the chicken walk off with top honors. A typical repast will cost from 1000 pesetas ($9.60) to about 1200 pesetas ($11.52), although your final tab could run much more.

El Caballo Blanco, 197 Calle Mallorca, is an old Barcelona standby, long popular with local gastronomes. The "White Horse," in the Paseo de Gracia area, is famous for its seafood, and features a huge selection. You can order rape (a white fish) or else mussels marinara, plus a wide selection of other fish platters, at prices beginning at 300 pesetas ($2.88) and going up to 600 pesetas ($4.80). There's also a tourist menu for 450 pesetas ($4.32). On the left is a bar, with tables set in an elongated room lit by fluorescent bulbs. In lieu of decor, you'll find good food at medium prices.

El Bodegón, 197 Calle Mallorca, is across the street and features similar fare at similar prices, but it's a bit cozier, with indirect lighting and a bistro atmosphere. Best here are the tapas and the seafood. The tourist menu is 600 pesetas ($5.76). Sometimes a guitar player comes around to entertain while you're dining. There are two dining rooms, with plastic chairs, paper tablecloths, paintings on the walls, and a low ceiling. The à la carte choice is particularly appealing, as it usually includes such selections as besugo (sea bream), kidneys in sherry, partridges (in season) served with fresh mushrooms that are on the market only in the autumn, and a civette of boar, again a seasonal dish. Most of these unusual specialties range in price from 500 pesetas ($4.80) to 600 pesetas ($5.76).

Restaurante d'España, in the hotel of the same name at 11 Calle San Pablo (tel. 318-17-58), just off the Ramblas, has a large medieval-type dining room with huge chandeliers, bentwood chairs, and tiled walls. It serves a tourist menu for 600 pesetas ($5.76) that'll include hors d'oeuvres or salad, paella or hake, followed by a grilled veal steak. The meal ends with ice cream, fruit, or flan.

THE STARVATION BUDGET: Those on a starvation budget might try the **Tamoyo,** 16 Arco del Teatro (also near the Ramblas), where you can get a meal for only 300 pesetas ($2.88). Although the decor is a bit smudgy, this place is much patronized by shoestring travelers and impecunious locals.

THE "DRUGSTORES": The **Drugstore,** 71 Paseo de Gracia (tel. 215-38-41), is an elegant sibling of similar establishments in Paris and Madrid. It features the usual "Drugstore" trappings: a snack-cafeteria, boutiques, toys, records, books, magazines, tobacco shop, and shoeshine stand. At the snack delicatessen, combination dishes cost from 350 pesetas ($3.36). The tourist dish of the day goes for 250 pesetas ($2.40), and includes butifarra, a fried egg, mashed potatoes, tomato, bread, wine, and ice cream or coffee. There's a small dining area downstairs, plus a balcony. This Drugstore also has a pleasant sidewalk café, with white garden-type tables and chairs, pleasant for summer sitting. It's open till 5 a.m.

More in fashion, at least at the last time I was there, is another drugstore on Tuset Street, off the Avenida Diagonal. It's called **Drugstore David.** You can enter directly from Calle Tuset or from Calle Aribau (you then have to go through a garage). The decor here consists of a maze of yellow walls and glass. For 300 pesetas ($2.88) you can order a hamburger with mushrooms.

OMELETS: Also in the Tuset area, at 25 Calle de la Granada, is a unique restaurant called **Flash Flash,** Tortillería (tel. 228-55-67), which specializes in omelets. In fact, it has about a hundred different kinds, including those made with beans, mushrooms, macaroni, kidneys, potatoes, peas, corn, eggplant, and fish—you name it! They cost anywhere from 150 pesetas ($1.44) to 400 pesetas ($3.84), the latter with truffles. Should you prefer something else, have a hamburger with french fries for 300 pesetas ($2.88). A half bottle of Marfil wine goes for 300 pesetas also.

This place is decorated on the outside with drawings of photographers flashing bulbs (they actually go on and off). The theme is carried on inside, with black cameramen painted on the white walls all around. You can sit at a table, but most clients seem to prefer the counter.

SOME GOOD FINDS: **Casa Culleretes,** 5 Calle Quintana (tel. 317-30-22), off the Ramblas, has a rightful claim as Barcelona's oldest restaurant. Founded in 1786, it still retains many of its original architectural features: all three dining rooms are decorated in a Catalán style, with tiled dado and wrought-iron chandeliers. When you taste the food here, you'll know that someone has been at the stove long enough to perfect his or her craft. Today, as you could "back then," you can get spit-roasted chicken, tender inside, crisp outside, and flavored with charcoal. Specialties include sole, Roman style, zarzuela à la marinara, cannelloni, and paella. Complete meals start at 850 pesetas ($8.16). From October to January, special game dishes are featured, including partridges (perdices). Celebrities, flamenco artists, bullfighters, have frequented this casa for its authentic dishes of northeastern Spain. They have left signed photographs on the walls to testify to their good times and meals here. The restaurant is closed Sunday night and Monday and July 1 to 20. Metro: Liceo-Ramblas.

Another real find is the **Restaurante Blanch,** off the Paseo de Gracia, 269 Diputación (tel. 302-40-24). Go through a bar area and enter a cozy, low-vaulted dining room where a good lunch is served for 600 pesetas ($5.76). It includes a big bowl of soup (brought in a tureen) or a mixed salad; paella, ravioli, sardines, or hors d'oeuvres; wienerschnitzel, a quarter chicken, or a steak. You end with dessert, and a half bottle of wine or beer is included. Portions are so large you can hardly finish them. It's closed Sunday.

A VISIT TO SOME TASCAS: The **Parrilla Grill Room,** 8 Calle Escudillers (tel. 231-61-13), off the Ramblas Capuchinos, is perfect for a before-dinner glass of wine. On this teeming street, it captures the spirit of old Barcelona, and the Gaudí-inspired art nouveau decor is a harmonious backdrop. Served until midnight, a cubierto goes for 600 pesetas ($5.76) to 900 pesetas ($8.64).

Taverna Kit Kat, 10 Escudillers (tel. 318-87-29), near the above recommendation, is another way to pacify your stomach while waiting for the late dinner hour. The tasca is usually crowded at sundown with drinkers and munchers. It displays its wares under glass, and you can actually get real Mexican tortillas here. At a table lining the window, you can watch your fellow tasca hoppers eating and drinking as if both were going out of style. Cubiertos begin at 425 pesetas ($4.08).

READERS' RESTAURANT SELECTIONS: "My own favorite restaurant for a cheap lunch which budget travelers will be glad to hear of is **L'Espigó**, 20 Ripoll/2 Copons, on the corner of two side streets behind the Residencia Colón in the Gothic quarter. To look for it, you start at the square in front of the cathedral, remembering that the Residencia Colón is behind the Hotel Colón . . . and keep your eyes open! L'Espigó serves a four-course lunch, including bread, wine, and coffee for 570 pesetas ($5.47). On fiestas and Sunday, the lunch is 650 pesetas ($6.24), but it is a little more luxurious. In the evening, it only serves à la carte and is worth a splurge. A sample evening banquet, which I have tried, is: lush shrimp cocktail in a super-duper-yummy-tummy sauce, chateaubriand (a minimum of two persons), crêpes à L'Espigó (pancakes cooked in burning liqueurs), sangría, and coffee, all adding up to 1250 pesetas ($12) per head and worth every peseta. Solitary diners can try the filete al whisky (only Vat 69) or entrecôte al pimiento. The atmosphere is simple: at lunchtime it's crowded, but not in the evening when it's quite romantic. Another budget restaurant in another part of town, near Plaza Calvo Sotelo, is **La Cova**, which as its name implies is in a basement with entrances on two parallel streets (9 Sagues and 14 Calvet). This restaurant has the advantage that, although there is a daily menú of 450 pesetas ($4.32), the customer is at liberty to eat à la carte however much or however little he wants. You can see the typical dishes being prepared behind the bar at one end. This is still very much a restaurant for Spaniards and as yet not a mecca for tourists. It's a happy place and gets crowded, so you may have to wait a while for a seat" (Jonathan Gall, Barcelona, Spain).

"The **Restaurante Vegetariano**, 41 Calle de Canuda (tel. 302-10-52), near the Gothic quarter, is a few blocks off the Ramblas, clean, modern, fairly new, with low prices. Arroz paella is almost a complete meal, with rice, beans, artichokes, peas, cauliflower, and a delicious sauce. Nine fresh fruit drinks as well as carrot juice are available. The menu of the day for 425 pesetas ($4.08) included fried eggplant à la Romana. Lots of eggs and cheese dishes are offered at cheap prices. The whole-wheat rolls are marvelous. It's affiliated with the Vegetarian Society of Barcelona. Hours are unusual—that is, 8:30 a.m. to 6 p.m. It's closed on holidays and Sunday. Incidentally, no tipping is the policy" (David Fitch, Las Vegas, Nev.). . . . "In Barcelona we ate at **Restaurante Balear O Casa del Couscous**, 6 Calle Quintana (tel. 302-50-60). It's within walking distance of the Hotel Ingles. The meal of the day was 400 pesetas ($3.84). The restaurant is operated by a Catalán woman, and the food was quite good" (Wayne and Barbara Morley, Edmonton, Alberta, Canada). . . . "By the time we got to Barcelona, we were frankly a little tired of the food, which was quite similar wherever we went, and not spicy enough for us. We stumbled onto a great Chinese restaurant, which compares favorably with several Cantonese restaurants in San Francisco or Los Angeles: Restaurant **Chino Nanking**, 124 Rambla de los Estudios (tel. 257-50-55). The menú del día, for only 450 pesetas ($4.32), was excellent in quality and generous in quantity. It was a fascinating change to find personnel speaking Chinese, Spanish, and English all intertwined" (Bette Myerson, Bakersfield, Calif.). . . . "At **Diagonal**, a very nice restaurant near the intersection of Calle Majorca and Avenida Diagonal, the set meal costs 375 pesetas ($3.60) for three courses, wine or mineral water included. One may dine inside or in the open air. The restaurant is just a short distance from the Holy Family Church" (Judith D. Mammon, San Mateo, Calif.). . . . "**Topics**, 474 Avenida Diagonal (tel. 218-11-96), is a self-service cafetería (auto-service) which specializes in menu-of-the-day meals of four courses for only 450 pesetas ($4.32) and is open from 12:30 to 4 p.m. and 8:30 to 11:30 p.m. No language problem arises: what you see and pick is what you get, and you get good value" (Edward H. Pietraszek, Chicago, Ill.).

"A confection-lover's dream come true is **La Pallaresa**, 11 Petrixol, half a block east of Ramblas, between Ramblas and the Plaza José Oriol—location of the legendary Casa José restaurant. This is a dairy bar and choclatería that boggles the mind with its array of sweet, creamy, milky, etc., goodies, including crème de Cataluña, a special Cataluñan version of flan which makes French crème de caramel look bland. The summertime standard is horchata, not a milk drink but a milky almond beverage" (Charles E. Colson, Oak Brook, Ill.). . . . **The Normandie**, La Petite Auberge, 23 Calle Magdalenas, has only eight tables. It is run by a French couple. Monsieur is the chef, Madame the maître d', waitress, and salad chef. We had onion soup, veal Cordon Bleu, and a mixed salad which was fresh, crisp, beautiful, and perfectly seasoned. The prices are from 600 pesetas ($5.76) to 900 pesetas ($8.64) for a complete meal. The restaurant is near the cathedral. We found it as we cut off from Layetana onto Magdalenas on our way there" (Mrs. L. J. Lurie, Wheaton, Md.).

"We found one outstanding bargain, the **Restaurant El Puma,** 40 Calle de Ariba. It is near Calle de Aragón and convenient to the Hospital Clinico metro stop. This clean, friendly, and modern restaurant offers a 25-item buffet for 500 pesetas ($4.80). The buffet consists of meat, fish, egg dishes, salads, and other vegetables common to Barcelona, and you can have all you can eat. Drinks are not included but are reasonably priced. Ramon, the owner, who speaks no English, is very proud of this buffet and rightfully so. Both hot and cold dishes are served. North Americans will appreciate the cleanliness of this restaurant as much as the food" (Peter L. Smith, Canton, Ohio). . . . "Dinner at **Vía Beneto,** 8–10 Calle Ganduxes, will be in the big-splurge category. This extremely elegant restaurant is a fine choice for a special occasion. We celebrated our fifth anniversary there. You are greeted at the door by a uniformed doorman, then escorted to your table by a tuxedo-clad waiter. A large cushion is immediately placed beneath your feet in case they do not reach the floor. The sommelier is dressed in his traditional apron with a taster's cup at hand. Glasses are cooled with crushed ice before the cascading froth of a chilled Cordoniú, for example, is allowed to bubble against their rims. Amid the impeccable service and luxurious surroundings, it is easy to imagine that one is dining at the Spanish equivalent of Maxim's, without the French prices. The food, beginning with complimentary hot hors d'oeuvres, is outstanding. We sampled a creamy vichyssoise and an ensalada quatro estaciones (hearts of palm, avocado, tomatoes, and endive) for an appetizer. My husband's main dish, roast duck with fresh Valencia oranges, was the finest we have tasted anywhere. I also enjoyed the roast pork with apple, a Catalán specialty. Count on spending approximately $75 (U.S.) a couple, including wine and the tip. While not inexpensive, a similar meal in North America in this type of restaurant would cost twice as much. You can have a very special evening here" (Rosemary Doyle-Morier, Ottawa, Canada).

3. The Top Sights

From the top of Montjuich to the top of Tibidabo, there is much to see and do in Barcelona. The eccentric Tarragona-born architect, Gaudí, has left numerous art nouveau edifices to render us speechless; the Gothic quarter is fascinating, as are the Ramblas; some art museums (medieval to Picasso), an entire village (an architectural melting pot of Spanish styles), and a surrealist park are only a few of the sights awaiting you. Give yourself at least three days, if you can spare them, to get acquainted with the city.

Incidentally, at some point during the day, you may want to pay a visit to the **Paseo de Colón** at the Barcelona harbor, dominated by a statue of Christopher Columbus. While here, you can see a good reproduction (go aboard if you wish) of the *Santa María* for 50 pesetas (48¢).

Since Barcelona is likely to be confusing to the first-time visitor, you may need a good orientation point first. The **Torre San Sebastián,** a sky-high restaurant, houses an observation room giving visitors a seagull's view of the Mediterranean port. The Eiffel Tower–like iron-grill structure is out on the Paseo Nacional at the harbor. For 25 pesetas (24¢), you can use the elevator to ascend the tower. A cable car operates from this tower from 10 a.m. to 9 p.m., swinging out over the harbor to Montjuich. A round-trip ticket costs 75 pesetas (72¢).

THE TEMPLE OF THE SACRED FAMILY: This uncompleted work by the irrepressible Gaudí, who died in 1926, is a symbol of the defiant spirit of Barcelona. If you have time to see only one Catalán landmark, make it this cathedral. It is at Calle Mallorca and Provenza y Marina-Cerdaña. Begun in 1882, this incredible cathedral is one of the bizarre wonders of Spain. Its appearance is so odd that it's difficult to describe and must be seen to be

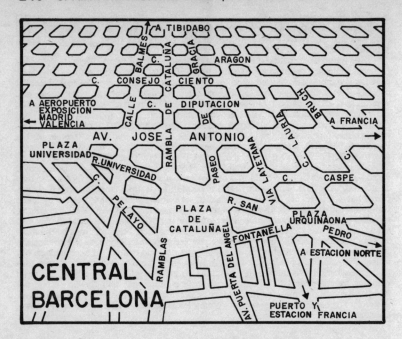

CENTRAL BARCELONA

appreciated, but this may give you a clue: spatial looseness à la art nouveau, ornamental figures, eight principal wall-ventilated tapering towers with celestially orbed peaks fringed with balls, and lots and lots of melting gingerbread draped in a majestic batter-like ooze over a forest of stalagmites and jutting brown icicles.

You'll have to pay 60 pesetas (58¢) to go inside the grounds, and then an elevator in one of the towers will take you to the top (about 200 feet) for 15 pesetas (14¢). It is open from 9:30 a.m. to 2 p.m. and 3 to 5:30 p.m.; from 9 a.m. to 2 p.m. and 3 to 8:30 p.m. in summer.

THE CATHEDRAL: At the Plaza de la Catedral, the **Cathedral of Barcelona** is a celebrated example of Catalán Gothic. Except for the west facade (built in the 19th century), the basilica was in the works from the end of the 13th century until the mid-15th century. Inside, the three naves, formerly dimly lighted, have now been cleaned and artistically illuminated, revealing their splendid Gothic details. This impressive cathedral is the grand old lady of the Barrio Góthico of Barcelona. With its large bell towers, its blending of medieval and Renaissance styles, its beautiful cloister, high altar, side chapels, sculptured choir, and Gothic-style arches, it is one of the most important cathedrals in Spain. In the cloister—artistically illuminated on Saturday and fiesta days—is a museum filled with medieval art. Open from 11 a.m. to 1 p.m., it may be inspected for only 20 pesetas (19¢). The cathedral is free.

At noon on Sunday, the best time to visit, you can see a sardana spontaneously danced in front of the cathedral. This is the most typical folk dance of Catalonia.

THE GOTHIC QUARTER: This is the old aristocratic quarter of Barcelona that recalls to mind the days of the legendary counts. Spend at least two or three hours walking through its narrow streets and squares, elegantly preserved from the Middle Ages. A nighttime stroll takes on an added drama. The buildings, for the most part, are austere and sober. The cathedral is the crowning achievement, but the colonnaded, 18th-century **Bishop's Palace,** 5 Calle del Obispo Irurita, is also worth a visit. In addition, you'll find Roman ruins and the remains of the third-century walls. The Gothic Quarter lies east of the Ramblas (the Calle del Carmen leads to it).

THE PICASSO MUSEUM: Three old converted palaces at 15, 17, and 19 Calle de Moncada have been turned into a museum, housing works by Pablo Picasso, the Málaga-born artist. Once belonging to one of the nobles of Barcelona, the splendid museum sits on a street left over from the Middle Ages.

In the winter of 1970, the artist donated some 2500 of his works to the museum of Barcelona. Although other museums—certainly those in France—were hoping to receive the bequest, he favored Barcelona. Perhaps he remembered much of his youth spent there, during what biographers call his "formative years." The multi-million-dollar collection consists of engravings, paintings, and drawings. Richard Eder, in a press comment, called the collection "the extraordinary trail of Picasso's early assertions, disguises, concealments, reappearances, and transformations."

Some of the exhibit dates back to when Picasso was nine years old. Painted in 1891, one portrait depicts his stern aunt. Another, completed at the turn of the century and called *Science and Charity,* was painted by Picasso when he was 16 years old (his father was the model for the doctor).

Many of the works, especially the early paintings, show Picasso's debt to such artists as Van Gogh, El Greco, and Rembrandt. The so-called "academic paintings" reveal nude, bearded men. The famous series, the *Menines* (1958), are said to "impersonate" those of Velázquez. From his blue period, the *La Vie* drawings are perhaps the most interesting. Many sketches of scenes in Barcelona are in his notebooks.

The museum is open daily from 9:30 a.m. to 1:30 p.m. and 4:30 to 8:30 p.m. It is closed Sunday afternoon and Monday morning. The charge is 60 pesetas (58¢).

PARQUE GÜELL: At the slope of Tibidabo, overlooking the city from the north, is the park (free entrance), where Gaudí's imagination went to work again, this time for a wealthy count by the name of Güell. Gaudí created a surrealist's Disneyland with a mosaic pagoda, popular with children of all ages. The central architectural attraction looks like some ancient tomb of a lost civilization, what with its deliberately crooked columns and all. One sculptured piece resembles a prehistoric monster spitting water. Have a seat on the curvy mosaic bench, and contemplate what a schizoid dream must be like. Gaudí must have wanted to make his comment on the hanging gardens of Babylon. To "take a trip," catch bus 24 at the Plaza de Cataluña.

PUEBLO ESPAÑOL: This Spanish Village in Montjuich Park was built in 1929 for a world's fair. Even though that "bust" year wasn't a good one for a fair, somebody had the good sense to preserve this beautiful village, pieced together with the various types of architecture represented in the provinces of Spain, from the Levante to Galicia. At the entranceway, for example, is a facsimile of the gateway to the walled city of Ávila. On the Plaza Mayor, in the center of the village, you can sit outside and have drinks. Also, you can buy any number of handicraft and souvenir items from all of the provinces, and, in some of the shops, you can see craftspeople at work, printing fabric, blowing glass. Open all day, the village, with its more than 70 shops, charges 25 pesetas (24¢) admission; 20 pesetas (19¢) on Sunday. You can spend an entire afternoon here and still not see everything.

TIBIDABO MOUNTAIN: After seeing Gaudí's park, you can continue up the mountain to the top of Tibidabo, with its spectacular view of Barcelona. The ideal time to visit this hill, north of the port, is at sunset, when the city lights are being turned on. Quite a sight—and it should be. For as legend has it, Satan took Christ up here and tempted him with the world. Come here for the views of nature; the man-made attractions run a poor second. Tibidabo has been turned into a Coney Island of the sky; ferris wheels swing over Barcelona, some 1600 feet above sea level. Being Spanish, the Cataláns also had to crowd a church into this carnival-like setting; it's called Sacred Heart. There are also restaurants and mountaintop hotels. From the Plaza de Cataluña, take a bus to the Avenida del Tibidabo, where you can board a special bus that will transport you to the funicular. You can hop aboard and scale the mountain and return for 25 pesetas (24¢).

MONTJUICH PARK: At the south of the city, Montjuich is an all-year delight. With its splashing fountains, gardens, outdoor restaurants, and museums, it makes for quite an outing. There are many walks you can take and places where you can peer out over the skyline of Barcelona. The park also contains the Pueblo Español, dealt with separately as an attraction. To reach Montjuich, take tram 33 to the Plaza de España. If you wish, you can walk up to the Catalán Art Museum first, then hop bus 1 to the Spanish Village. But the most exciting way to go to Montjuich is to take the funicular on the Calle del Marqués del Duero. On weekend nights, particularly Saturday, there is an illuminated fountain display—with dazzling color—near Plaza de España, lasting from around 9:30 to 11 p.m. In summer, the display is also staged on Thursday night.

MUSEUM OF ART OF CATALONIA: At some point during your visit to Montjuich Park, you may want to visit this museum at the National Palace, which has been turned into a treasure house of medieval art. Here is displayed a collection of Catalán Gothic retables, woodcarvings, medieval murals—endless Spanish and European baroque works, most of them religious in nature. The museum also houses an impressive collection of Romanesque murals.

In Sala V is a 12th-century painted front altarpiece (no. 13809) depicting a saint being tortured and other Bosch-like scenes of horror, including victims boiled in a pot. In Sala VI we see fragments of 12th-century decorative murals from the Church of Santa María de Tahull (Lérida). But the pinnacle of the 12th-century works is reached in Sala VIII in the *Pantocrátor* (God the Majesty), a concave fresco removed from San Clemente de Tahull. Although it owes a heavy debt to the Byzantine influence, the fresco is a creative breakthrough in that it represents the attempt of a Spanish artist to make his personal statement.

In Sala XI are to be found woodcarvings and paintings from the Church of Esterri de Cardós, representing work from the 11th and 12th centuries. In

Sala XVIII are Gothic works of the 14th century—notably no. 26, a retable dedicated to St. Vicente. In Sala XIX is a 15th-century Virgin of alabaster. Also displayed here are two especially outstanding retables—one (no. 38) by the Serra brothers from the Monastery of Gaulter in the province of Lérida; another (no. 35) by Jaume Serra, this latter one dedicated to the Virgin. No. 13, a 14th-century retable dedicated to Santa Catalina, is interesting in that it depicts death, demons, and decapitation.

Sala XX displays a notable collection of Gothic paintings, such as a Virgin nursing her child and an especially good *Resurrection.* In Sala XXI (no. 15814) is another exceptional retable, this one a 14th-century work dedicated to San Juan Bautista, Santa Eulalia, and San Sebastian. See, in particular, a 15th-century triptych to Saint Estebán, and a well-known painting by Jaume Cireca, showing *Angels and Demons* in the mouth of hell, dating from 1433.

In Sala XXII is another important work, this one entitled *The Virgin of the Consellers,* by Lluis Dalmau.

In Sala XVII are works by Jaume Hugnet, a 15th-century Tarragona-born artist, known for his realistic faces (see his *Virgin and Child with the Angels*). In Sala XXXII is a work by an artist a bit better known than those previously mentioned—El Greco's *Sts. Peter and Paul.*

The museum is open from 9:30 a.m. to 1:30 p.m. and charges 30 pesetas (29¢) admission. Closed Monday.

READERS' SIGHTSEEING TIPS: "Spain's top zoo is still probably the one in the Ciudadela Park in Barcelona, near the Estación de Francia. This one is decidedly modern, with lots of barless enclosures, both indoor and outdoor dolphin shows, and quite a number of animals from the Spanish colonies in Africa that one doesn't normally see elsewhere. And above all, there's Snowflake, the only albino gorilla ever recorded. Next to a few giant pandas, he's probably the most famous individual zoo animal anywhere, although he seems to have been relatively little publicized in the English-speaking world. A combination ticket for 125 pesetas ($1.20) entitles you to visit all areas of the zoo. It costs an additional 50 pesetas (38¢) to see the dolphins' show" (Dennis R. H. Levy, Bournemouth, England). . . . "For only subway fees in Barcelona one may enjoy the treat of viewing certain Gaudí buildings other than La Sagrada Familia. An especially enjoyable one is the **Casa Batllo,** 43 Paseo de Gracia, at the corner of Gracia and Aragón, a subway stop. We recommend taking the elevator up to the top floor (one can see out during the ride) and then walking down the steps. After that, going along Gracia for a few blocks one can hardly fail to notice another Gaudí creation, **La Pedrera,** 92 Paseo de Gracia. It is most enjoyable to view the sculpted stone outside, its inner courtyard, and, at a distance, the unique rooftop decorations" (Robert and Janice Titiev, Detroit, Mich.). . . . "You should mention the **Joan Miró Foundation** in Montjuich Park, open 11 a.m. to 8 p.m. every day. The beautiful white contemporary building was designed by Juan Luís Sert. It contains a collection of Miró graphics, some paintings, a few sculptures, and a large woven wall tapestry (about 14 feet high). The museum is reached by the no. 1 bus on María Christina near the entrance to the park closest to Plaza de España" (Sharlene P. Hirsch, San Francisco, Calif.).

A SHOPPING NOTE: Casa Arpi, 40 Rambla de los Capuchinos (tel. 301-74-04), although you wouldn't know to judge by its unprepossessing entrance, is one of the most famous camera shops in Europe. A multilingual staff will guide you to the best buys in both new and used cameras, including products manufactured by such names as Minolta, Nikon, Hasselblad, and Pentax. The "backup" equipment sold here is extensive, ranging from macro lenses to flash units. They even sell equipment to take care of the problems confronted by near- or far-sighted photographers. All the familiar names in film, Kodak or Fuji, are sold here, along with brands that you may never have heard of, particularly those imports from Eastern Europe. The firm also does quality processing, and the finished work should be ready within 24 to 48 hours after you drop it off.

4. The City After Dark

Barcelona comes alive at night. Especially popular with the evening crowds is the funicular ride to Tibidabo or the waterworks of Montjuich. The center of the club life is the cabaret-packed district at the south of the Ramblas.

The Ramblas teem with excitement in the early evening: a wide segment of the populace converges on this boulevard of cafés and bars. Later in the evening, you may want to walk east down the **Calle Escudillers** (off the Plaza del Teatro, at the Ramblas Capuchinos). In the maze of narrow streets branching off from here are to be found out-of-the-way cabarets, some very good and some very bad restaurants, bars, and assorted nightlife catering to all tastes. It's safe to go walking here, although women alone may feel intimidated and men alone will get occasional offers from prostitutes.

Barcelona's nightlife is far more liberated than that of Madrid, a subject that brings us to . . .

A Word About Vice: Tourists, notably American sailors, who once visited the **Barrio Chino** (Chinese Quarter), have spread the word about what a "wild" place Barcelona is. As Spanish cities go, it still is. Its reputation for depravity has been exaggerated, but do be careful.

If you visit one of the dives in the old quarter, don't carry too much cash, because dimly lit, crowded cabarets are a haven for pickpockets. Many of the questionable establishments and gypsy joints are unabashed tourist traps for sailors and their pickups. Proceed with caution in selecting your slumming adventure for the evening, keep a healthy tongue-in-cheek attitude—and you're likely to have a good time.

My lead-off entertainment choice is a unique experiment.

AN EVENING WITH THE RED-HOT MAMMAS OF YESTERYEAR:

The incomparable **Bodega Bohemia,** 2 Lancaster (tel. 302-50-61), off the Ramblas, is a Barcelona institution. In medieval-esque surroundings, the fading swan-like chansonniers and dying refugees from the cloak-and-dagger plays of Lope de Vega entertain you with their wit, irony, and satire—and what roughly might be called singing.

The bodega is a cabaret extraordinaire. Everybody from Marcello Mastroianni to Tennessee Williams to American collegiates to playgirls frequents this place, which answers the question: *Whatever Happened to Baby Jane?* The Spanish Baby Janes are still belting one out for the boys in the back room.

As you may have gathered, the Bodega Bohemia is a talent showcase for theatrical personalities whose bones aren't so bouncy, but whose spirits are undimmed by rheumatism. It's not a freak show. Not at all, but more in the tragicomedy vein of the old Shakespearian actor in the long-running off-Broadway show *The Fantasticks.*

The woman who sits next to you may look like Count Dracula's great-grandmother, but when she gets up to perform, chances are she'll sound more like Florence Foster Jenkins. She's likely to sing "Granada," much to the delight of the rocking audience. Then the pinup queen of the boys who fought our boys in the Spanish-American War is likely to be followed by another love goddess of the octogenarians—this one a dead ringer for a drag version of Bela Lugosi. She'll probably play the accordion and do a few bumps and grinds that would have caused her to be arrested if she were only 30 years younger.

Curiously, most audiences fill up with young people, who cheer, boo, cat-call, and scream with laughter—and the oldtimers on the stage love it. The show stretches on forever.

The cost? Only 300 pesetas ($2.88) for your first drink (no cover). In all, an incredible entertainment bargain if your tastes dip slightly into the bizarre.

Also typical of Old Barcelona are shows at that octogenarian institution, the **Molino,** 99 Vila Vila. The Molino is a regular theater, featuring variety shows and girlie acts, most of them pretty bad, but fun to watch nonetheless. Especially delectable are the give-and-take between audiences (often sailors and locals) and performers. You sit in regular theater chairs, and place your drink (a Coca-Cola, for example) on a ledge in back of the seat in front of yours. The 5:30 p.m. show costs 350 pesetas ($3.36), although the 10:30 one is raised to 500 pesetas ($4.80). On Sunday, the shows are tabbed at 600 pesetas ($5.76).

For more typical Spanish night-owl fare, sample:

FLAMENCO: Los Tarantos, 17 Plaza Real (tel. 317-80-98), offers some of the best flamenco in town. Its *tablao* is presented daily from 10 p.m. to 3 a.m. Featured on my latest rounds was that well-known star Maruja Garrido. The price of admission is 1200 pesetas ($11.52) which includes the cost of your first drink.

NIGHTCLUBS WITH SHOWS: La Buena Sombra, 3 Ginjol (tel. 302-00-87), offers a wide range of ever-changing international shows, including dancing to a band. On one recent occasion, a statuesque fraülein greeted the audience in four languages, then proceeded to sing "I Write the Songs" in English. The oldest cabaret in Barcelona, La Buena Sombra has reached its 90th birthday. It's a place for single men or men with dates, but the hookers are likely to resent the competition of unescorted women. On some nights, the club presents nude shows. The Sombra is off the Ramblas, near the Plaza del Teatro. There's no cover, although the first drink costs a high 750 pesetas ($7.20)—but you can make an evening of it. The establishment, incidentally, is strictly for night owls. There's an "early" show around midnight, but the best show begins at 2 a.m.

Those interested in a supper-club type of affair should head to the **Scala,** 49 Paseo de San Juan (formerly the site of the **2001**), a huge, rambling place which takes up a whole corner of two streets. The dinner, dance, and show starts at 8:30 p.m. and costs 2500 pesetas ($24). Another session starts at 12:30 a.m., only for drink, show, and dancing, at 1800 pesetas ($17.28). On Sunday, the club also has a special session at 5 p.m. (dancing, drink, and show).

DISCOS: When a young man of Barcelona wants to take his girl to a special place, he might head for the elegant disco known as **Bocaccio** (tel. 247-31-36). Unlike the *Decameron,* this spot is more romantic than racy. Bocaccio has steadily gained in fame since its opening in 1967. The elaborate door is unmarked—so search carefully. Actually, the club is at 505 Muntaner (take autobus 23 or 64), and is open between 6 p.m. and 4 a.m., reaching its chromatic crescendo around 2 a.m.

A stylized, free-form atmosphere is in evidence everywhere. The setting, in part, is art nouveau, with hanging glass light fixtures. The open half-swinging doors lead to booths on raised platforms. Add to that opera-red, plush wall coverings, the long drinking bar, and crescent-shaped banquettes. Helping make the setting what one client called "lavishly decadent" are the tufted red stools with art nouveau legs, the fringed red silk lamp shades, and the Turkish beaded portieres. A first drink costs from 350 pesetas ($3.36) to 500 pesetas

($4.80); a second (or any subsequent libation) for 250 pesetas ($2.40) to 350 pesetas ($3.36).

As in most big cities, the fashionable discos change every couple of years, or less. Real trend setters are *off* the **Bocaccio** and have veered toward the **Metamorfosis** and the **Don Chufo**, the former at 9 Calle Beethoven and the latter across the street, both behind a huge new building development on the Avenida Diagonal, past the Calvo Sotelo.

The **Metamorfosis** has no sign whatsoever outside (everyone should simply know where it is, of course), and the entrance prices are as spectacular as the goings on. Although you can get into the afternoon sessions (6:30 to 9:30 p.m.) for 400 pesetas ($3.84), the nighttime marathons (11:15 p.m. to 4 a.m.) cost a steep 800 pesetas ($7.68). The Metamorfosis is a fairly smallish place inside. A circular staircase leads downstairs to an elegant bar, dance floor, dim lighting, and the usual secretive nooks. The Don Chufo, with similar amenities, charges the same prices.

BEER AND FOLK SINGING: For a more leisurely pace, head to the **A Cova Dei Drac**, 30 Calle Tuset, which is a Greenwich Village–type café where you can sit for hours over a beer, at 50 pesetas (48¢), or a coffee, at 40 pesetas (38¢), and gab with the young Cataláns. Sometimes the Drac also has folk singing.

AN ELEGANT PUB: Those liking more intimate entertainment should go to **Pub 240**, 240 Aribau (near the Tuset area). Currently the most fashionable place for the young, the elegant Pub (which has absolutely nothing to do with the English concept of a pub) features nightly guitar playing and folk music. There are three sections, one consisting of a bar, another a small theater, yet another a lounge for talking and listening. It's all elegant and chic and is jammed every night. The action lasts till about 3 a.m. The average drinks go for 250 pesetas ($2.40) and up.

Coming up, a description of the several one- and two-day trips from Barcelona.

Chapter X

BRANCHING OUT FROM BARCELONA

1. Montserrat
2. Tarragona
3. Sitges
4. Andorra
5. Lloret de Mar
6. Tossá de Mar
7. Cadaqués
8. Figueras
9. Cardona
10. Gerona

AFTER YOU HAVE seen the sights and smelled the smells of Barcelona, it will be time to branch out for a series of one- and two-day excursions in all directions from this capital of Catalonia. Barcelona is like the hub of a wheel of a number of widely varied adventures. For example, about 28 miles northwest of Barcelona lies the most popular excursion from the capital, the Benedictine monastery of **Montserrat.** But there are others equally as enticing.

South of Barcelona is the too-long-neglected Roman city of **Tarragona,** of particular interest to those who appreciate history.

But lest we become too monastic or too steeped in the past, the beach resort of **Sitges,** a nugget on the "Gold Coast" south of Barcelona, returns us to today.

A final tour takes us to **Andorra,** a principality in the Pyrenees that is ever growing in popularity. Andorra can be reached in a day from Barcelona, but you should definitely count on spending the night before heading back.

1. Montserrat

The **monastery** at Montserrat is one of the important pilgrimage spots in Spain, ranking with Zaragoza and Santiago de Compostela. Built on ground approximately 3000 feet up, the monastery is not so spectacular, but the mountain on which it sits is—and should be of interest to Catholics and non-Catholics alike. Mother Nature must have created the mountain in a frivolous moment; it suddenly springs up from an otherwise unimpressive landscape.

The church contains a 12th-century statue of *The Black Virgin,* the patron saint of Catalonia. Thousands of the faithful touch her every year, hoping to be blessed. So many newly married couples flock here for her blessings that Montserrat has become a honeymoon center, the Niagara Falls of Spain.

The renowned boys' choir here is one of the oldest in Europe. At 1 p.m., you can usually hear choral singing in the basilica.

While at Montserrat, one of the most exciting things to do is to take the funicular to the peak, Sant Jeróni. The cost is 125 pesetas ($1.20). The aerial ropeway goes to the summit of the mountain, at 4119 feet, in only nine minutes. From there, one of the most extensive panoramic views in Spain can be seen. Passengers can see not only the whole of Catalonia, but the Pyrenees and all the way to Majorca and Ibiza.

Montserrat is easily reached from Barcelona, and the **Empresa Juliá** company operates regular buses to the monastery, leaving from 5 Ronda Universidad from 9 a.m. till 4:30 p.m.

But the best and most exciting way to go is via the Catalán railway, **Ferrocarrils de la Generalitat de Cataluyna,** leaving from the Plaza de España at 9:10 a.m. and 11:10 a.m. The central office is at 1 Plaça Cataluyna (tel. 302-48-16). The train connects with an aerial cableway.

WHERE TO STAY AND EAT: Montserrat has both a three- and a two-star hotel to greet the constantly arriving pilgrims. Few of us will be spending the night, but most visitors will want at least one meal. If you don't care to pay a fat tab for lunch, either ask your hotel to pack your meal or do it yourself from the makings easily obtainable at one of the cafeterías in Barcelona.

Living in a Monastery

You don't have to take the sacred vows to stay in this sky-top monastery. After about 800 years, the monks have gotten used to single and group pilgrimages to their retreat. As the years have passed, more comfortable quarters have been built for them, to replace the straw mats formerly handed out. Montserrat now boasts two hotels, run by the same management. The more expensive one is the **Hotel Abat Cisneros** (tel. 835-02-01), and the less costly is the **Residencia El Monasterio** (tel. 835-02-01). Both are at the Plaza del Montserrat.

At Abat Cisneros, the price of the excellent, attractively furnished doubles with private baths is 3000 pesetas ($28.80), not bad for this so-called "Hilton of the monasteries." Even cheaper are the doubles with shower, at 2400 pesetas ($23.04). The best singles—those with private shower—cost 2000 pesetas ($19.20), and the cheaper "monk's cells," with shower baths, are priced at 1800 pesetas ($17.28). A continental breakfast is another 230 pesetas ($2.21). The three-star hotel has a lounge that is only a whisper away in style from one of the newly built museums springing up in America. Comfortable couches, simple lines, paintings, and plants—all these elements blend together to make it worthy of . . . a honeymoon at least.

In a similar manner, the more vintage **El Monasterio** is nothing to complain to the monks about. Its pre-World War II rooms are simpler, but still modern. The prices are even more to our liking: 1600 pesetas ($15.36) for a double room with private bath. No singles are offered. The residencia (no meals served) is open from April 1 to October 31.

After leaving Montserrat and returning to Barcelona, we strike out south the next day for:

2. Tarragona

About 60 miles south of Barcelona lies the ancient Roman city of Tarragona, a Mediterranean port that is one of the grandest, but most neglected, sightseeing centers in Spain. Its Roman and medieval remains make it the principal city of historic interest on the Spanish Mediterranean coast.

Its population today is approximately 100,000, but under the Romans, it is believed the city sheltered one million persons behind its nearly 40 miles of city walls. Its architecture is fascinating, particularly the part lying inside the wall-enclosed old quarter. Many of the houses have connecting balconies.

One of the four capitals of Catalonia when it was an ancient principality, Tarragona today consists of a new town in addition to its old quarter. At some point, you want to walk along the **Rambla Nova,** a wide and fashionable boulevard, the main artery of life in modern Tarragona.

The Iberians settled in Tarragona; it was captured in 218 B.C. by the Romans, and was thus embarked on the period of its greatest glory. But wars, sieges, neglect, and plunder caused Tarragona to experience decline. Today it seems to be thriving again. The sprucing up of its historical monuments has begun. The city has a bullring, good hotels, a mild climate, and beaches, and is the center for some interesting excursions. Primarily, it is visited for the day. In a sense, it has the same kind of older sister relationship with Barcelona that Toledo has with Madrid.

You can reach Tarragona easily by either bus, train, or car.

THE SIGHTS: The City Walls: This is the top attraction, partially enclosing the old quarter. The base of the walls is called "Cyclopean," because of the enormous size of the blocks (this part of the wall was erected by primitive people). The Romans later built on top of this earlier foundation. It's possible to take a stroll on top of the ancient walls from 9 a.m. to sunset for 15 pesetas (14¢).

The Cathedral: This 12th-century cathedral represents the transition from Romanesque to Gothic. It has an enormous vaulted entranceway, stained glass that sparkles like jewels. Romanesque-style cloisters, and an open choir. It is at the loftiest point in Tarragona. The main part of the cathedral may be visited free, but it costs 40 pesetas (38¢) extra to visit the museum, with its collection of Catalán art. Hours are 10 a.m. to 1 p.m. and 3:30 to 7 p.m.

Roman Amphitheater: On the side of a cliff, the tides of the Mediterranean washing up on it, is this gallery, the remains of an ancient amphitheater where thousands of Romans went in the third century for amusement. Carved out of the side of a cliff, it lies near the grounds of Milagro Park.

Necropolis and Paleocristiano Museum: This is one of the most important burial grounds in Spain, having been used by the Christians from the third to the fifth centuries. It is along the Avenida de Ramón y Cajal, outside of town, next to a tobacco factory. On the grounds you'll find a museum that contains a number of sarcophagi and other objects discovered in excavations. It may be visited from 10 a.m. to 1:30 p.m. and from 4 to 7 p.m. (in summer, 4:30 to 8 p.m.). The admission charge of 100 pesetas (96¢) also includes the Archeological Museum.

Archeological Museum: This museum, at the Plaza del Rey, houses a collection of relics from the Roman epoch in Tarragona. You'll discover such items as mosaics, ceramics, coins, silver, and countless other objects. This rebuilt stone building overlooks the sea. It may be visited from 10 a.m. to 1:30 p.m. and 4 to 7 p.m. In summer, hours are 10 a.m. to 1 p.m. and 4:30 to 8 p.m., and the cost is 100 pesetas (96¢).

Finally, to cap your day's sightseeing, I'd suggest a stroll around sunset along the **Balcón del Mediteranéo**—not only for its beautiful vista of turquoise-blue water but the rich vegetation in the region.

WHERE TO STAY: The **Hotel Astari**, 97 Vía Augusta (tel. 20-38-40), is a resort-type establishment near the sea on the road to Barcelona. Its rather plain doubles are fresh and airy, ranging from 2000 pesetas ($19.20) to 2500 pesetas ($24) each with a private bath. Only six singles are available, each one quite good, and costing 1500 pesetas ($14.40) with a private shower. A continental breakfast is another 150 pesetas ($1.44).

The Astari rises five floors; its long balconies and terraces provide both in- and outdoor living for its guests. It also has a swimming pool, as well as a solarium and modern cafetería.

The low-level dining room has wide and tall windows; the food here is praised. A complete meal—served in a friendly manner—costs 700 pesetas ($6.72). The favorite spot of most guests seems to be the outer flagstone terrace —willows, umbrella tables, orange trees, and geranium bushes. At dusk one can have drinks in the cocktail lounge, also with high windows. The hotel is open from April through October. In-the-know travelers who want to languish peacefully at a Mediterranean resort come here and let the crowds fight it out for the beachfront hotel in Sitges.

Nuria, 217 Vía Augusta (tel. 20-28-40), was built near the beach in 1967; it's a five-floor modern building, honeycombed with balconies in saffron yellow and white. It's hardly for those seeking distinguished contemporary design or super-smart furnishings. Rather, its appeal lies in its neat, pleasant rooms— each with a private bath (sometimes showers instead of tubs) and most with balcony. A double rents for 1800 pesetas ($17.28), singles for 1500 pesetas ($1.44), plus another 150 pesetas ($1.44) for a continental breakfast. You can dine in the sunny restaurant, where a meal featuring a plate of the day goes for 700 pesetas ($6.72). The Nuria's specialty is a romesco, a kind of zarzuela, a seafood blend.

WHERE TO EAT: The **Restaurant España** is in a somewhat unusual building next door to the Banco de Vizcaya, at 49 Rambla Nova. It makes a good stopover at some point during your day if you want only light, luncheon-type fare. It serves mainly ice cream, coffee, soft drinks, and sandwiches from 60 pesetas (58¢) and up.

For a real economy find, head for the **Restaurant Delicias,** 8 Calle de Augusto, one block from the Rambla Nova (walk to the Plaza de Jacinto Verdaguer, then turn left). Here is dished up an aromatic cubierto for 400 pesetas ($3.84). A meal might include soup or eggs, and a choice of hake, veal filet, or pork. The regular menu costs 650 pesetas ($6.24), and you could have a paella, macaroni or cannelloni, then hake, a veal filet, fruit, and, of course, bread and wine. Bring along a healthy appetite as the portions are large.

Those with a bit more cash might head to **Els Arcs,** 1 Cartagena. This used to be a huge wine cellar, but has been converted into a rustic and comfortable restaurant with indirect lighting, tiled floors, and large stone arches. This two-fork eatery serves a good meal in fairly elegant surroundings for 550 pesetas ($5.28).

READERS' RESTAURANT SUGGESTIONS: "**El Tiberi,** 5 Martí Ardeña (tel. 20-32-05), is 2½ blocks southwest of Rambla Nova. It is run by a family; it does not provide the usual type of menu but rather a fantastic buffet which includes any sort of Catalán dish you can name. For this, you don't need a menu. Just pick what you want. You won't know when to stop. There are hot and cold dishes, soup, desserts, salads, the whole works, served in a perfect Catalán setting in good taste and cleanliness. The price is 750 pesetas ($7.20) per person" (James L. Busey, Manitou Springs, Colo.). . . . "At the **Arimany,** 43–45 Rambla Nova (tel. 20-57-16), we enjoyed one of our best meals in Spain. Although from the outside, the building is rather unprepossessing, it boasts an attractive, hotel-style dining room. Its shrimp in garlic oil at 500 pesetas ($4.80) is outstanding" (Rosemary Doyle-Morier).

TARRAGONA NIGHTLIFE: You might first head for **La Boîte,** a disco at the Hotel Lauria, 4 Lauria (right off Rambla Nova). To accommodate the increasing upsurge of European youth descending on the old Roman town in summer, La Boîte gets into the swing of things with records going full blast. Admission is 300 pesetas ($2.88). This is a nice place for a rendezvous if you dance more than you drink. It's open only from 6:30 to 10 p.m. Then activity shifts to the nearby **Imperial Tarraco Boîte** (tel. 20-30-40), under the same management.

Those who want a lively disco with a slightly older crowd should head for the **Whiskey Club,** 17 San Francisco, where drinks begin at 300 pesetas ($2.88).

EXCURSIONS: If you have a car, you can visit two star sightseeing attractions, a 30- to 45-minute drive from Tarragona. The first stop is the **Monastery of Poblet,** 29 miles northwest of Tarragona, one of the most intriguing monasteries in Spain. A mixture of Romanesque and Gothic, it has cloisters that are somewhat reminiscent of those at Westminster Abbey. Constructed in the 12th and 13th centuries, the monastery is still in use. The monks of the Cistercian order of the common observance live here and they pass their days writing, studying, farming, working with a printing press, and helping with the restoration of the building, which suffered heavy damage in the 1835 revolution. After 100 years of emptiness, a new foundation was started in 1940 by Italian monks. The most exciting feature is the oddly designed tombs of the old kings of Aragón and Catalonia. The monastery may be visited from 10 a.m. to 12:30 p.m. and 3 to 6 p.m. for an admission of 100 pesetas (96¢).

The monks dine frugally in the stark refectory, but you can enjoy lunch at **Fonoll,** near the cloister, l'Espluga de Francoli (tel. 87-03-33), a country inn where a large, filling menu costs from 750 pesetas ($7.20). The restaurant is closed on Thursday, however, and from November to March. If you'd like to stay over in this enchanting part of Spain, you'll find that the innkeeper offers 17 simply furnished rooms, costing from 500 pesetas ($4.80) in a single, from 850 pesetas ($8.16) in a double. All the accommodations are bathless, and a continental breakfast goes for another 100 pesetas (96¢).

About three miles away is one of the most fascinating of Spanish towns, **Montblanch,** a living museum of the Middle Ages. At the entrance to this town, you'll see a map outlining the principal artistic and architectural treasures—and there are many of these. The town is unspoiled. The crumbling facade of its once-elegant baroque church fills one with awe. Taking a car along these narrow, winding streets is somewhat risky. Walking is much preferred.

3. Sitges

Lying some 25 miles south of Barcelona, Sitges is one of the most frequented resorts of southern Europe, easily reached by bus or train from Barcelona. The resort is the brightest spot on the Golden Beach, the **Costa Dorada.**

The sands of Sitges are thronged in summer by a rising, affluent crowd of young moderns from northern Europe—girls who are dead-ringers for Marimekko models, boys who look as if they could call Greta Garbo mom. For years, the resort was patronized largely by prosperous middle-class industrialists from Barcelona and Catalán artists such as Dali, Russiñol, Casas, Nonell. But those rather staid days have gone; Sitges rocks today like its sisters down the coast (Benidorm and Torremolinos).

Reminiscent of the resorts on the Costa Brava, Sitges has whitewashed houses, horse-and-buggy streets, and flower-draped balconies. Some good and some regrettable modern envelops it. In spite of the building spree, the tides of tourists washing up on Sitges's shores have found the little resort shamefully unprepared. Its accommodations—strained in a corset squeeze in July and August—can't tuck in all the bulge. Furthermore, Sitges is caught in a spiral of rising prices that place many of its major hotels beyond the means of the average budget traveler. But I have managed to scare up a number of bargains for those willing to nail them down with reservations. By mid-October just about everything, including virtually all hotels, restaurants, and bars, is closed.

WHERE TO STAY: The sea and the sand are the big attractions during the day. The crescent-shaped, white sandy beach stretches along the azure bay for about 1½ miles. With that in mind, I've sought to find establishments within wasy walking of the shore.

El Galeón, 44 San Francisco (tel. 894-06-12), is a leading three-star hotel, only a short hop from the sands. It's a well-styled hostelry, blending Old Spain with modern. The public rooms, although small in size, have suitable furnishings and a cozy overall feel, while the bedrooms are good-size and streamlined with wood-grain. The baths, like the public rooms, are dwarfish. Open April through October, the hotel charges 2000 pesetas ($19.20) for its doubles with private baths. Singles with private bath rent for 1400 pesetas ($13.44). A continental breakfast is 125 pesetas ($1.20) extra. A complete luncheon or dinner goes for 660 pesetas ($6.34). An attraction is the small swimming pool in the rear patio. Advance reservations are usually necessary.

Hotel Montserrat, 11 Espalter (tel. 894-03-00), does not put its best foot forward. Its exterior is too neutral, its position among shops and restaurants too unchic. But the Montserrat is best inside. The bedrooms, although impersonal, are spacious enough and reasonably comfortable. Many of the doubles have private shower baths and rent for 1750 pesetas ($16.80) to 2000 pesetas ($19.20) nightly. The bathless singles are a bargain at 900 pesetas ($8.64) each. For around 900 pesetas also per person extra, you can take half board here. In fair weather, diners enjoy the rooftop. Open April through October, the Montserrat is about three blocks from the beach.

Hotel Don Pancho, 2 Calle San José (tel. 894-16-62), is a modern white stucco corner hotel, with wrap-around balconies. Inside, it's been given the Scandinavian treatment—natural woods, a raised fireplace, rush-seated dining chairs. From its rather cacophonous location, Don Pancho offers fair-size and recently renovated doubles with bath for 2200 pesetas ($21.12), only 2000 pesetas ($19.20) in rooms with shower baths. Singles are 1400 pesetas ($13.44) with private baths. A continental breakfast, at 160 pesetas ($1.54) extra, is the only meal served. The Don Pancho is open only from April 1 to October 31.

Hotel Florida, 6 Espalter (tel. 894-02-21), is the successful remake of an old hotel. It's centered around a large dining patio, which is surrounded by 25-foot-high walls covered with ivy and shaded by purple flowering trees—a separate little world, only a few blocks from the sea. All of its rooms lack decorative flair, but they make up for this by their good, simple comfort. Open from April through October, the Florida charges un-Miami prices of 2000 pesetas ($19.20) to 2400 pesetas ($23.04) for a double with private bath, 1600 pesetas ($15.36) for a single with shower. Full board is required in July and August at an extra cost of 1600 pesetas ($15.36) per person.

Hotel El Cid, 19 Calle San José (tel. 894-18-42), combines the Spain of yesteryear with that of today. Its facade suggests the 16th-century world of Segovia. Inside are beamed ceilings, a wall of natural stone, heavy wrought-iron chandeliers, and leather chairs. The same theme is carried out in the rear dining room, and even in the pleasantly furnished bedrooms. The best doubles have private shower baths, yet rent for 1800 pesetas ($17.28). A single with bath goes for 1100 pesetas ($10.56). The price for three fine repasts a day is 1200 pesetas ($11.52) extra. Board is required in summer. El Cid lets down the drawbridge from May 1 through October 31. In summer, it's a beehive of activity, attracting a handsome crowd of young Europeans with lots of Nordic joie de vivre.

Hotel Residencia Alexandra, 1 Pasaje Termes (tel. 894-15-58), is hidden on a narrow and unfashionable street, a short stroll from the beach. It's all brick built, given added flair by its canopied balconies. The Alexandra charges prices low for Sitges: 1680 pesetas ($16.13) for a double room with private bath, 1100 pesetas ($10.56) in a single with bath. The rooms are compact, with a complete streamlined look reflected in the wood-grained headboards and up-to-date bathrooms. A continental breakfast at 190 pesetas ($1.82) extra is the only meal served. Open March through October, Alexandra hosts an attractive "house party," with northern European sunbathing on the roof terrace, or else meeting evenings in the bar.

Residencia Sitges, 5 San Gaudencio (tel. 894-00-72), is open May through October. The bedrooms rely on "Korean War modern." Doubles run the gamut from private bath to lonely lavatory. At this little one-star residencia, a single room with wash basin rents for 1025 pesetas ($9.84). Depending on the plumbing, one person sharing a double room is charged from 900 pesetas ($8.64) to 1150 pesetas ($11.04) nightly. A continental breakfast is included in these tariffs. Full meals aren't served here, but Sitges maintains a snack service if you don't want to leave the premises.

One of the pleasantest bargains in town is the **Sitges Park Hotel,** 12 Jesus (tel. 894-02-50). More centrally located than most of the above, its outside is unprepossessing; but once past the desk you come into a beautiful garden with palm trees and a swimming pool. A twin with bath looking down on this peaceful scene costs 2000 pesetas ($19.20). Singles with bath go for 1300 pesetas ($12.48). There is a pleasant restaurant downstairs, and you can have your coffee or drinks indoors or outdoors at the hotel's café-bar. A complete lunch or dinner costs 500 pesetas ($4.80). Service is friendly and efficient. The Sitges Park is open from April 15 to October 15.

Terminus Hotel, 7 Avenida de las Flores (tel. 894-02-93), in spite of its dull-sounding name, is a very pleasant place at which to stay—and it's quite reasonable: from 400 pesetas ($3.84) per person nightly in a unit with shower. Most of the young people who pass through Sitges seem to stay here—if they can get in. It's that popular. It is not only clean, but friendly. The owner is Canadian and his wife Catalán. Their gracious welcome and personalities are the reasons behind the success of this place.

WHERE TO EAT: Sitges offers a number of commendable dining spots. Only trouble is, with all those full-board requirements at the hotels, you'll rarely get a chance to sample them. But if you do decide to sneak out, head for . . .

The **Restaurant Vilalta,** 22 General Sanjurjo (tel. 894-32-43), opposite the railroad station, has a good set menu for 550 pesetas ($5.28) that might include hors d'oeuvres or salad; cannelloni or eggs; squid, chicken, or fish; then flan or ice cream, plus bread and wine. There are no frills here. In winter the outdoor dining area is closed off with glass plates in the French manner.

Other good budget restaurants are:

Pizzería Ariston, in the Galeón Hotel, 42 Calle San Fernándo, offering a set menu for 500 pesetas ($4.80) that includes gazpacho, paella, a breaded veal cutlet, bread, and dessert. There are checkered tablecloths, a bistro atmosphere, and a pleasant garden in the rear for outdoor dining.

Els 4 Gats, 11 Calle San Pablo (tel. 894-19-15), is named after a famous old Sitges café where such painters as Picasso, Nonell, Casas, and others used to congregate at the beginning of the century. This intimate, auberge-type restaurant is decorated with paintings on the walls and a paneled wood ceiling, a raised corner fireplace, and crudely styled wooden chairs. Set meals range in price from 550 pesetas ($5.28) to 750 pesetas ($7.20). Specialties include sole meunière, red mullet "à la Diana," veal Cordon Bleu, and shrimp cocktail, although these items are priced à la carte. If you order form the à la carte menu, chances are you'll pay from 850 pesetas ($8.16) to 1500 pesetas ($14.40).

READERS' RESTAURANT SUGGESTIONS: "If you are looking for atmosphere, great food, and moderate prices, be sure to stop for dinner at **Hotel Platjador,** 35 Paseo de Rivers (tel. 894-03-12), facing the beach. It features white-gloved waiters serving good food attractively prepared. Especially recommended are the gazpacho, paella, pescado, and for dessert, flan. For 700 pesetas ($6.72), a set menu, featuring some of the specialties mentioned, is offered daily. . . . When your appetite is larger than your budget, stop at **El Superpollo,** 6 San José. The restaurant is actually a fast-food counter-type establishment with large racks of chickens barbecued in the front. The chickens taste as good as they smell (you can catch the aroma of the roasting from several streets away). Prices are low: a half chicken, 200 pesetas ($1.92); potatoes, 60 pesetas (58¢); a glass of wine, 50 pesetas (48¢); and beer or Coke, 60 pesetas (58¢)" (Ken and Lois Popler, New York, N.Y.).

SITGES NIGHTLIFE: When the sun goes down over Sitges, people seem to head for **Juan Ramón,** 9 Calle San Francisco (tel. 894-05-53), a unique bodega with hundreds upon hundreds of sherry and wine bottles stacked floor to ceiling. Near the Galeón Hotel, the bodega charges low prices. Most drinks begin at 75 pesetas (72¢), although sangría is priced at only 45 pesetas (43¢) per glass.

Club 24, 24 Rambla José Antonio, in the neighboring village of Villanueva y Geltrú, is more of a social center than a nightspot. Holiday makers from miles around make it their headquarters. In a country-tavern style, the front lounge contains a red-brick floor and beamed ceiling, a raised corner fireplace, crudely styled wooden chairs, a collection of old guns and powder horns hung decoratively. Beside the bar-lounge is a large patio with round stone tables, on which barbecues such as baby pigs and chickens are served. In the bar, your first drink—depending on what you select—is priced anywhere from 300 pesetas ($2.88) to 500 pesetas ($4.80). The disco portion gets under way late in the evening, as international records are played (occasionally, there's a live group).

For dancing and flamenco, your best bet is the **Jardines Casino Prado,** a block from the railway station. The gardens feature flamenco acts preceded and followed by dancing to an orchestra. The price of a drink? It's 600 pesetas ($5.76) and up.

For our next trip, we head deep into the Pyrenees to:

4. Andorra

Once upon a time, when feudal kingdoms existed throughout Europe, Andorra was commonplace. But perhaps because of its isolation—sandwiched between France and Spain high in the eastern Pyrenees—no one got around to telling Andorra that feudal kingdoms had gone out of style. Consequently, it's a tiny but flourishing little country that is experiencing a minor tourist boom sans gambling casinos but avec duty-free goods.

The father of Andorra, according to Andorrans, is none other than Charlemagne, who gave the "country" its independence in 784. That it survived at all in the ensuing centuries is something of a miracle. With a rather amused condescension, Napoleon let Andorra keep its autonomy. Napoleon, of course, could afford to be benevolent to principalities, such as pint-size San Marino in Italy.

Andorra's a storybook country—ruled by two co-princes—a land of cavernous valleys and snow-capped peaks, rugged countryside, pastureland, deep gorges, and breathtaking scenery. It's a highly popular summer excursion center, and recently has been gaining as a winter ski resort as well.

For centuries, Andorra lay hidden from the world, one of the most insular peasant cultures in Europe. But since the late '50s tourists have increased from a trickle to a flood. That this has created havoc with Andorra's economy is an obvious fact. What the deluge has done to Andorra is a matter of a sharp division of opinion.

There are those who have suggested that Andorra has ruined its mountain setting with urban sprawl, as taxis, crowds, and advertising have transformed the once-rustic principality into a beehive center of trading and commerce.

At first glance, the route into the country from Spain looks like a used-car lot. Virtually every Andorran at the age of 2½ gets his own automobile. When the local cars converge at the junction with the French and Spanish motorists crossing into Andorra for the day, it's bedlam. A typical sight in summer is to see, say, a Spaniard crash into a Frenchman's vehicle. While the helpless husbands stand in the background, the Latin ladies from different sides of the Pyrenees shout the blame and assess the damage. On one recent occasion, a parked car filled with a French family was rammed by a bus. The French housewife, wearing only her black underwear, had been discreetly hiding behind a towel in the August heat. But the volatile woman jumped out of the car, forgetting about the protective towel, and gave the poor Catalán bus driver a taste of her pretty Gallic tongue. The spectators, meanwhile, got a taste of French striptease.

New hotels and hundreds of shops have opened in the past decade to accommodate the French and Spanish pouring across the frontiers to buy such duty-free merchandise as Japanese transistor radios, cultured pearls, suede jackets, and enough liquor to sink the *Titanic*. A magazine once called Andorra "Europe's Feudal Discount Shopping Center." In addition, because of cheap gasoline prices in Andorra, there are enough pumps to have kept all the tanks of the Allies and the Third Reich rolling in World War II.

The little principality has long been known as a smugglers' haven. But today's smugglers are the French and Spanish visitors. Once it was possible for a North American to visit Andorra, flash a passport, and be waved on. A traveler can still whiz across the border in a jiffy, but on the road to the next stopover, he or she is likely to be swooped down upon by Napoleonic policemen who check every denture for undeclared goods.

Andorra is less than 200 square miles in size. Its language is Catalán. The base for most is the small capital, **Andorra-la-Vella,** and the adjoining town,

Les Escaldes, another prime target, with plenty of shops, bars, and hotels. Little shuttles run back and forth between the towns, but most shoppers like to walk the distance. Most of the major hotels and restaurants are either on the main street (**Avenida Meritxell**) in Andorra-la-Vella, or the main street of Les Escaldes (**Avenida Carlemany**). French francs and Spanish pesetas may be used interchangeably. Often, hotel, restaurant, and shop prices are quoted in both currencies.

In spite of its super-abundance of hotels, shops, automobiles, and gasoline tanks, Andorra is still a bit preposterous . . . like an old Peter Sellers movie.

GETTING THERE: The ideal way to go, of course, is by car through what must surely qualify as some of the finest mountain scenery—peaks, vineyards, rushing brooks—in Europe. The tiny country may be approached from Spain, via Puigcerdá to Seo de Urgel on a passable road from Barcelona.

Another way to go is on one of the buses run by the **Alsina Graells** line in Barcelona. It's about a six-hour ride across a distance of 143 miles. The bus leaves from 4 Ronda Universidad in Barcelona (tel. 222-11-63 for time of departure). It's also possible to return to Barcelona on the same line. A one-way trip costs 600 pesetas ($5.76).

If you're driving to Andorra from Barcelona, the following short detour is suggested:

On the Way—a Spanish Town in France

Llivia is a geographic freak, the Little Orphan Annie of Spanish towns. It is a man-made island, lying about four miles inside French territory and completely surrounded by France, except for a route of access that crosses French territory. If at any point you leave this road, you'll have to clear French customs.

This mongrel town has little architectural interest; in fact, it's quite poor, having experienced greater and better days (it was known to the Romans). The only reason for visiting it is because of its ironic position.

The town is approached from the Spanish border at Puigcerdá. Its curious status dates back to a long-ago border dispute between France and Spain; Llivia became a pièce de résistance to the Spanish monarchy, and France allowed Spain to retain the town, since it was grabbing up so many other Spanish villages.

A quick tour of this town will suffice, and then it's on to Andorra.

WHERE TO STAY IN LES ESCALDES: Hotel Pla, near the top of the Avenida Carlemany (tel. 21-432), is an old típico inn, founded as long ago as the American Civil War, believed to be the oldest inn in the country. The Pla is in the friendly hands of X. Pla Pujol, who speaks English. Its location is alongside a mountain stream and stone bridge and just apart from the commercialized center of Andorra. The hotel is built of stone, and the wrought-iron balconies have French doors, permitting you to step out and look at the dramatic scenery. A basic, simply furnished double room with a good view and a private bath costs 2800 pesetas ($26.88). Depending on the plumbing, singles range in price from 1600 pesetas ($15.36) to 2000 pesetas ($19.20). The hotel has an elevator.

Dining is in the old banqueting room, with its large arches, beamed ceiling, and terrace overlooking the mountain and river. The country-crude reed chairs are appropriate for the home-cooked meals served here. Lunch or dinner usually costs 800 pesetas ($7.68). Mountain trout is featured on the menu. Sometimes in summer there are folk-dancing exhibitions (in regional dress) on the little plaza opposite the Pla.

Hotel Cornella, 61 Avenida Meritxell (tel. 21-480), is close to the bridge that separates the towns of Andorra-la-Vella and Les Escaldes. There is central heating in addition to good elevator service. Garage space for your car is provided. The lounge is tasteful, as is the dining room—and there's a bar. The double rooms are simply furnished but perhaps not as well maintained as they could be. The Cornella has 130 rooms in all, and charges from 2100 pesetas ($20.16) for its doubles. Singles cost 1500 pesetas ($14.40). A continental breakfast is another 150 pesetas ($1.44).

Hotel Marfany, 99 Avenida Carlemany (tel. 20-856), is a little budget find in the swing of things on this principal street in Les Escaldes, but it's more like a comfortable, well-run French pension than a hotel. Its chief attraction seems to be the popular restaurant downstairs. Open all year, the Marfany offers quite adequate rooms upstairs. None of the rooms contains a bath, and a double costs 1500 pesetas ($14.40) nightly; a single, 1000 pesetas ($9.60). Complete board is required in summer at a cost of 1500 pesetas ($14.40), including three meals and the price of a room.

WHERE TO EAT IN LES ESCALDES: Restaurant Marfany, 99 Avenida Carlemany in Les Escaldes (tel. 20-856), is a large and pleasant French restaurant, connected with the Hotel Marfany. This is not exactly the Maxim's of Andorra, but the French tourists who flock here dine festively and well. For 600 pesetas ($5.76), you can have hors d'oeuvres made by the people who know what their purpose is, a ham omelet (magnifique), roast pork (quite respectable), and a simple dessert. The price includes service and wine.

THE COSTA BRAVA

It is with mixed emotion that I report on the Costa Brava, that rugged stretch of coastline that begins about 43 miles north of Barcelona in the fishing village of Blanes, and stretches like a python toward the French frontier. The happy news is that this 95-mile stretch of shore and beach dotted with fishing villages is beautiful. The azure Mediterranean contrasts with the verdure on the hills, which often are peppered with pine and cork trees.

But now the sad part. The Costa Brava ranks next to the Costa del Sol in phenomenal growth. It is amazing how a relatively unvisited coastline, almost completely unknown to Americans, within 15 years has moved into the foreground of the most-frequented spots in Europe.

Hotels are booked from spring through fall, often months in advance. It is virtually impossible to secure an accommodation during the peak months without way-in-advance reservations. Occasionally, someone secures a room, perhaps by default, in mid-August, and then reports that all those stories about overcrowding on the Costa Brava are exaggerated. Not so. The passing parade of tourists to the Spanish Riviera is in the millions. It is also a paradise for the charter-tour crowd, and that further swells the bikini-clad bodies on the overburdened sands.

Numerous stories have been circulating that foreign visitors have to pass a little money under the table to get hotel managers to remove the no-vacancy sign. Although the Spanish government regulates the price that hotels may charge for accommodations, abuses of the latter kind are hard to discover or stop.

Hotel construction on the Costa Brava has been booming. Little villages that hardly had a decent pension a few years back are now resort towns. The best spot on the Costa Brava for the average North American visitor is the attractive little town of **Tossá de Mar.** Lloret de Mar enjoys immense popularity, too, but somehow it seems commercial, too loaded down with hastily assembled hotels. In a poor third position is **San Feliú de Guixols,** the largest town on the coast, but old-fashioned and dated in its appeal. The most unspoiled and remote village is **Cadaqués.**

The roads between the fishing villages have not been marred with cheap commercial advertisements. However, most skirt dangerously close to the edge of cliffs—and great care should be taken if you're driving. Many of these smaller villages are excellent for stopovers, but not suitable as bases.

If you want to visit the Costa Brava, but simply cannot secure space in high season, you can either drive the distance or book one of the daily organized tours that leave from Barcelona. Allow plenty of time, however, for motoring. In summer, the traffic tie-ups can be fierce. If you visit the coast in summer (without hotel reservation), you might—in an emergency—spend the night in inland **Gerona,** the capital of the province, where you stand a far better chance of getting a room. If you visit the Costa Brava in the early spring or late fall, your prospects improve tremendously. And if you arrive during the winter months, you can have your pick of the few hotels that remain open, hungrily awaiting the arrival of a trickle of tourists. The season here is short, in all, compared to the Costa del Sol in Andalusia, and runs from mid-June to mid-September.

5. Lloret de Mar

Lying some 62 miles from the French frontier, Lloret de Mar, like Topsy, just grew and grew. On my first visit, when Eisenhower was in office, there weren't more than a dozen hotels. But at last check, it was impossible to count them at all. By the time you finish tallying them up, some orangepicker has rounded up a few army cots and opened up another less-than-scrumptious pension.

The half-moon-shaped sandy beach bordering the sea is good, as the overcrowded sands will testify. Lloret is neither chic nor sophisticated, drawing its chief clientele from low-waged Europeans—with the French, Germans, Scandinavians, and British in ascendancy. The competition for cheap rooms is fierce.

Typical of the Costa Brava towns, Lloret de Mar skips from the most impersonal of the modern box-type structures to the vintage charm of its whitewashed, flowerpot-adorned buildings on the narrow streets of the old town. Rich vegetation and a mild climate tend to give Lloret de Mar a scenic advantage, regardless of how hard Señor Hotelier tries to blot out that asset.

From Barcelona, it's possible to take a train to the nearest railway station at Blanes (lying about five miles from Lloret by easy bus connections). Or—and this may be preferred—you can take a bus operated by **Empresa Sarfa,** leaving from the post office in Barcelona (tel. 231-79-46 for departure time). The bus goes direct to Lloret.

WHERE TO STAY: Besides the overcrowding already noted, the accommodations of Lloret present still another hurdle to the innocent pilgrim seeking a room. Many of the hotels—particularly the three-star ones—are booked almost solidly by tour groups. Those you needn't bother with, but here are some bargains if you snare a reservation:

The **Hotel Excelsior,** 16 Jacinto Verdaguer (tel. 36-41-37), is more or less a glorified beach clubhouse. Its six floors of 45 rooms are right on the beach esplanade, making it possible to go for an early-morning dip before facing your Spanish coffee and continental roll. The Excelsior, open from April 1 to October 30, can get you in easily off-season—although the chances are nearly nil in July and August. The hotel charges 2400 pesetas ($23.04) for a pleasant, clean double room with a private bath; 1400 pesetas ($13.44) in a single with bath. Although uninspired, the furnishings are modern (from the '60s anyway), and the rooms are compact and convenient. A complete luncheon or dinner is 700 pesetas ($6.72) extra. Pension, costing 2500 pesetas ($24) per person daily, is obligatory from July to September.

The **Hotel Reina Isabel,** 11 Venecia (tel. 36-41-21), is to be congratulated for trying to break the monotony of the icy-cold (in decor only) bedchambers of Lloret. A throwback to the more típico Spanish style, this corner hotel attracts with its wrought-iron balconies and tall shutter doors. A certain style and flair exist inside, even in the bedrooms, which have some ornate touches— painted and gilt furnishings, baroque wall fixtures, and paintings that coexist with a few contemporary pieces. The bedrooms are large enough for long stays. Doubles with private baths cost 1400 pesetas ($13.44), dropping to just 1100 pesetas ($10.56) if bathless. Singles pay 900 pesetas ($8.64) in rooms with shower baths, only 800 pesetas ($7.68) in the bathless accommodations. A continental breakfast at 135 pesetas ($1.30) extra is the only meal served. An attractive feature of the hotel is the rear dining patio, with its tree-shaded tables. Open from April to October, the Reina Isabel lies only a short walk from the beach.

Tropicana Hotel, 19 Juan Llaverías (tel. 33-41-30), is only 75 feet from the sands—a fairly appealing six-story hotel, featuring a restaurant with its feet on the ground and rooms and balconies higher up. Catering primarily to low-income English groups, the Tropicana, open from June through October, charges 1800 pesetas ($17.28) in a double room with private bath, 1500 pesetas ($14.40) in a room with shower (no toilet). The singles—shower, no toilets— cost only 1200 pesetas ($11.52) nightly. A continental breakfast is another 125 pesetas ($1.20). The rooms, although lackluster, are genuinely comfortable.

The **Metropol,** 2 Plaza de la Torre (tel. 36-41-62), is a simple, clean, modern place near the beach, in the center of town. It has 86 rooms, and a comfortable double with bath costs 2600 pesetas ($24.96) with breakfast, 4600 pesetas ($44.16) with full board, for two persons. Singles with shower run 1400 pesetas ($13.44) with breakfast, 2500 pesetas ($24) with full board. The Metropol is open from May until October.

Xaine Hotel, 45 Via del Caudillo (tel. 36-50-08), is a deceivingly large hotel (accommodating 86) that appears small and compact. Although right in the noisy center of town activity, it is only a short walk from the beach. Crisply modern, it offers above-average bedrooms, many with their own balconies and private shower baths. The most expensive doubles peak at 1750 pesetas ($16.80), dropping to 1400 pesetas ($13.44) if bathless. Full board is required in July and August, costing an additional 1400 pesetas ($13.44) per person. The Xaine does business from May to October 16.

WHERE TO EAT: Bacochtala de Xaine Hotel, 47 Vía del Caudillo, is at least four forks ahead of the usual hotel dining fare. From its ground-floor nest, this restaurant catches the eye with its 550-peseta ($5.28) repast. It doesn't disappoint the taste buds either, offering this typical menu—cream of mushroom soup, York ham with mashed potatoes, a French omelet, and dessert (the drink's extra). The view of the passing parade is worthy of a top Nielsen rating.

Buenos Ayres, 17 Paseo Marítimo, is a beachside snackery, ensconced in glass, with an al fresco section for nibbling burgers on the beach. Combined hot dishes are offered for 325 pesetas ($3.12) to 800 pesetas ($7.68), but most of the young set seem to gravitate to the old reliables—a hamburger with french fries, 150 pesetas ($1.44); paella, 375 pesetas ($3.60); chicken with french fries, 250 pesetas ($2.40); and ham and eggs, 150 pesetas ($1.44).

About the cheapest restaurant in town, popular with Spanish workpeople, is **La Estrella,** 44 Calle de la Fábrica, where you can actually get a complete meal for 375 pesetas ($3.60). There are small plastic tables, and, of course, no frills.

LLORET NIGHTLIFE: **El Relicario** holds first place among the temples of flamenco in town. Near the edge of town, it offers an Andalusian courtyard, open to the moon and stars. There's an entrance fee of 500 pesetas ($4.80), then your bill will vary according to what you drink—250 pesetas ($2.40) for local whisky, 150 pesetas ($1.44) for soft drinks. Brightly colored chairs and tables are set around and inside the quadrangle of arches, leaving space in the court-yard for the big-time floor show held nightly after 10. The show may feature as many as six acts, including flamenco singers and dancers, classic and country dancers, plus folk music.

Also on the premises is **L'Ast Celler,** 34 Carmen, which has successfully captured the spirit of an old Spanish bodega, with its wooden beamed ceiling, regional chairs, and brick walls. Chickens are grilled on the spit and cost from 300 pesetas ($2.88). You can dance and eat till 4:30 a.m.

The **Western Saloon,** Calle Santa Cristina, fashioned in the style of an American western bar, features country and western music—either records or live groups. One of its more faithful habitués claims that "it has the best atmosphere on the Costa Brava." Most Yanks eventually find their way here. Drinks range from 90 pesetas (86¢) to 150 pesetas ($1.44) for a Cuba libre.

The **Londoner,** 14 Calle Santa Cristina, next to the Western Saloon and in the heart of the resort, was inspired by an English pub. It offers live entertain-ment, plus records. Drinks range in price from a local cognac at 75 pesetas (72¢) to a Cuba libre at 125 pesetas ($1.20). It's open until 2:30 a.m.

Above the Londoner is **La Cala Disc-O-Tec,** 14 Calle Santa Cristina, which offers dancing to international records until 4:30 a.m. The entrance fee is 125 pesetas ($1.20) and drinks range from a martini at 75 pesetas (72¢) to scotch at 150 pesetas ($1.44). It closes from September 30 to May 30.

Finally, you may want to pay a call at the **Duke of York,** 2 Calle Arenys, in the back streets of old Lloret. The cozy atmosphere attracts those seeking a quiet drink—perhaps a game of darts. The best draft English bitter is 90 pesetas (86¢) a pint; Spanish champagne is 275 pesetas ($2.64) a bottle.

From Lloret de Mar, we head up the winding coast to:

6. Tossá de Mar

This gleaming white town, with its 12th-century walls and a labyrinthine old quarter, fishing boats, and fairly good sands, is the most attractive center for a holiday on the Costa Brava. In a setting reminiscent of the old Ava Gardner movie, *Pandora and the Flying Dutchman,* Tossá seems to have more joie de vivre than its competitors.

The little town is 56 miles north of Barcelona, eight north of Lloret de Mar. It has direct bus service from Blanes (the gateway village), as well as from Lloret. In addition, it is on the main Barcelona–Palafruggel autobus run. From Barcelona, buses leave for Tossá from the Empresa Sarfa terminal, 3 Paseo de Colón. Departures are fairly frequent, and the service is good.

Tossá is one of few resorts that has withstood exploitation and retained most of its charms. No longer an outpost of British sun-seekers, Tossá enjoys a broad base of international visitors—so many, in fact, that it can no longer shelter the influx. In spring and fall finding a room may be a lark, but in summer the no-vacancy sign may make you eat crow.

WHERE TO STAY: Hotel Diana, 10 Plaza de España (tel. 34-03-04), is right on the waterfront, but set back from the esplanade. A former seaside villa, it has been converted into a two-star hotel. All its modernized bedrooms have private baths, and many open onto their own balconies. The rooms are spacious, containing many fine furnishings. Two persons pay 3500 pesetas ($33.60) in a double with bath for full board. Only couples or trios are accommodated. The inner patio—with its towering palms, vines and flowers, and fountains—is almost as popular with guests as the sandy "frontyard" beach. In front of the hotel is the promenade, the best place for people-watching. The Diana receives visitors from May 1 through October 31.

Hotel Corisco, Paseo del Mar (tel. 34-01-74), is a modern little hotel catering to an international clientele. It opens right onto the sea; you couldn't get closer to the water if you tried. Its decor is bright and airy, with an all-glass front dining room. Spanish tiles are used in the reception lounge—all pleasant and cheerful. The traditionally styled bedrooms are comfortable and tasteful, and price reasonably: 2400 pesetas ($23.04) in a double with bath. Singles pay 1500 pesetas ($14.40) in rooms with showers. A continental breakfast at 175 pesetas ($1.68) is the only meal served. The Corisco is open from April to mid-October.

Hotel Cap d'Or, Paseo del Mar (tel. 34-00-81), is perched on the waterfront, at the edge of the village away from the turmoil. It nestles against the stone walls and towers of the village castle. Built of rugged stone, the Cap d'Or is like an old country inn and seaside hotel combined. It is well run and neat, and attracts a stream of visitors with its scrubbed and polished bedrooms.

All of the doubles have private baths, and only three singles are available. You can stay here for about 1850 pesetas ($17.76) per person daily, including both room and board. The food served here is good—far above the usual. The dining room—ceiling beams and ladderback chairs—is a bit old-world, and the view of the sea is pleasant. Outsiders are welcome to come in for a complete meal. The hotel is open April 1 to October 31.

Sant March, 9 Calle Nueva (tel. 34-00-78), on a busy shopping street inside town, is entered through a covered passageway. The modern hotel opens toward its rear grassy patio, with its graceful eucalyptus trees and potted flowers. The hotel (open May through September) charges 650 pesetas ($6.24) for a double with shower used by one person, 1300 pesetas ($12.48) for two, including a continental breakfast. The staff is friendly and skilled at providing the little extras to make a holiday at Tossá more enjoyable. The Sant March is about 2½ blocks from the beach, and it even has parking space.

Ramos Hotel, Avenida de la Costa Brava (tel. 34-03-50), is a streamlined, three-story hotel built motel-style right on a main shopping and commercial street. All of the 74 rooms—both the singles and doubles—have balconies and private baths (but in some you'll get a shower instead of tub), and yet the cost of staying here is low. A double ranges from 1400 pesetas ($13.44) to 1750 pesetas ($16.80); a single, 900 pesetas ($8.64) to 1200 pesetas ($11.52). Three meals go for an additional 1500 pesetas ($14.40) per person. In July and August, board is required. In the rear is a garden with an arbor, an ideal spot for a before-dinner sherry. The hotel is open from May to September.

Hotel Tonet, Plaza de la Iglesia (tel. 34-02-37), is on a plaza inside the town, only a three-minute walk from the sea, through the narrow streets. The hotel has the atmosphere of a country inn. It is built with set-back terraces on its upper floor, and as you look up, you can see potted vines and plants, and sun umbrellas where guests relax. The hotel is classified as one-star by some bureaucrat—but what does he know? The classifier is probably a relative of one of the men who said no to Columbus. In the morning, if you have your breakfast tray brought up to the terrace, you can watch the town come alive, observing the village people entering the little church, or going out for freshly baked bread. All of the Tonet's 36 rooms have private baths. The rooms are country simple, with natural Spanish-style wooden headboards and rush-seated chairs. The hotel is open from May through September. The price for a double room with bath and two continental breakfasts is 2000 pesetas ($19.20) per day, dropping to just 1500 pesetas ($14.40) in a single.

L'Hostalet, 4 Plaza de la Iglesia (tel. 34-00-88), is placed on the same plaza as the Tonet. It is a modern-looking hostelry that doesn't overlook the romantic style. The architect took full advantage of L'Hostalet's position by creating an open garden terrace on the front—simple but in good taste. This patio is shaded by lemon trees. All of the rooms are fresh and comfortable, basic in their appeal and most inviting—as is the price.

The most expensive doubles, those with private baths, rent for 1750 pesetas ($16.80), but doubles with showers go for 1500 pesetas ($14.40). Only a continental breakfast is offered at an additional 150 pesetas ($1.44). Open May 1 through September 30, the hostal is sometimes known as "The House of the American Student," because of the number of Yanks who slumber here.

Hotel Mar Blau, 12 Avenida de la Costa Brava (tel. 34-02-82), built two stories high in the motel style, has tried a little harder to jazz up the scenery. The verdict: just plain but more than passable. Still, it features large, well-furnished rooms with private baths. Doubles with bath or shower range from 1100 pesetas ($10.56) to 1800 pesetas ($17.28), and singles with showers cost 650 pesetas ($6.24) to 950 pesetas ($9.12). Well-prepared food is served in an attractive dining room, and the price of three meals a day comes to 1000 pesetas ($9.60) per person extra. An American bar is also on the premises. All in all, the Mar Blau is a good candidate for a Costa Brava holiday any time between May 1 and September 30.

READERS' HOTEL SELECTIONS: "The **Hotel La Palmera,** 29 Flechas Azules (tel. 34-02-49), was the greatest find during our two months in Europe. It's in the center of town, about 160 yards from the beach, and is one of the most modern hotels in Tossá. All rooms are with private baths and terraces. There is, as well, a beautiful swimming pool, solarium, and bar. The hotel is also equipped with an elevator (what a blessing!). Also included were three mammoth meals in the Spanish-continental manner. By the way, the cost of a room, all meals, and the most friendly and hospitable service and atmosphere was 3000 pesetas ($28.80) for two persons. While sunning by the pool, we were served huge mugs of beer" (Mr. and Mrs. Bob Martin, Brooklyn, N.Y.).

READER'S RESTAURANT SUGGESTION: "Try at least once paella Valenciana, while staying at Tossá de Mar. I suggest you enjoy one of the best paellas of Spain at the **Snack Bar El Ruedo** (tel. 34-00-01). This is actually a fine budget restaurant, only a few minutes away from the seafront. Starting at the Paseo de Mar, follow the colorful Avenida de la Costa Brava till the end. Here, at the crossing of the roads to San Feliú and Llagostera, the paella is waiting for you. The portions are generous and it's very filling. Don't order anything else before you've finished it. The bill? Only 550 pesetas ($5.28) per person" (R. Depreitere, Kortrijk, Belgium).

TOSSÁ NIGHTLIFE: El Ruedo (tel. 34-00-19) is the brightest star in the Tossá nighttime galaxy. On the edge of town, near the camping grounds, the club books a varied group of Spanish entertainers, usually flamenco dancers and guitarists. Between entertainment numbers, you can dance to a live band. For 800 pesetas ($7.68), you may see the show and have your first drink.

Rocamar, 7 Calle Codolar (tel. 34-10-47), is a bodega-restaurant reached by a five-minute walk along the Calle Puente Viejo (from the beach promenade). Built on several levels, it has a Catalán-style wine cellar, with racks of old kegs, rattan stools, and drippy candles. From the deeply recessed windows are views of the rugged coast. It's open from April 1 to October 15. A menú turístico costs 850 pesetas ($8.16). However, if you're feeling extravagant, you may want to order the special menú of the house for 1400 pesetas ($13.44). You won't need to eat until tomorrow night. Specialties include fisherman's soup, grilled rabbit, and a wide range of seafood dishes, including sole with almond sauce, and sea bass with fennel. Another specialty is the filet Café de París. The bodega, featuring music, stays open until 3 a.m.

7. Cadaqués

The little village of Cadaqués, despite the publicity it has received because of painter Salvador Dali, is still amazingly unspoiled and remote. There are, as yet, no high-rise apartment blocks nor garish hamburger joints, nor even shops that make "tea like your mother." The village, the last resort on the Costa Brava before reaching the French border, is reached by a small winding road, twisting over the mountains from Rosas, the nearest major center. When you get to Cadaqués, you really feel you're off the beaten path.

The village twists around a half dozen small coves, with a narrow side-walkless street leading along the water's edge. It has no railing, so many a drunk must plummet into the water on fine summer nights.

Scenically, Cadaqués is a knockout, with its crystal-blue water, its fishermen's boats pulled up on the tiny sandy beaches, its old, whitewashed houses, it's narrow, twisting streets, and its 16th-century parish up on a hill. At times, the place is reminiscent of Venice, and proves equally difficult to park in when the visitor crush hits it in the summer. There is simply no place to park within the village.

Dali, who is in his late 70s, lives next door to Cadaqués in the tiny village of Port Lligat, opposite Port Lligat Hotel.

WHERE TO STAY: The **Playa-Sol,** Playa Pianch (tel. 25-81-00), offers 50 doubles with bath, costing 3800 pesetas ($36.48) to 4700 pesetas ($45.12), a continental breakfast included. Singles run 2000 pesetas ($19.20) to 2600 pesetas ($24.96), also with breakfast. The Playa-Sol is a modern, comfortable hotel, right on one of the coves. Twenty-eight of the accommodations have terraces with views of the harbor and the village. Another asset here, and an important one, is that the hotel has its own garage. Also, there is a spacious swimming pool and lawn area, with a poolside bar. In winter the central heating is welcome.

In the budget range, there's the older **Port Lligat Hotel** (tel. 25-81-62), perched on top of a hill, one kilometer up from the village. The views are splendid. The most expensive doubles with baths cost 1825 pesetas ($17.52); those with showers go for 1525 pesetas ($14.64). Singles rent from 1000 pesetas ($9.60) and you can have a meal here for 710 pesetas ($6.82). The place is open from April until the end of September.

WHERE TO DINE: Don Quijote, 6 Avenida Caridad Serinana (tel. 25-81-41), on the road leading into the village, is a pleasant, intimate, bistro-type place, with a large, vine-covered garden in front. Its à la carte specialties include paella, rape (a whitefish), and hake. The Don Quijote cup, a mixed dessert, is the best way to end a meal. The menú del día costs 610 pesetas ($5.86), and most à la carte meals range in price from 900 pesetas ($8.64) to 1600 pesetas ($15.36).

Sa Gambina, Tomás Carreras Corsellas (tel. 25-81-27), on the waterfront, serves reasonably good food at medium prices. A Catalán salad (tomato, lettuce, peppers, butifarra, onions, and olives) is a good choice, as is the paella or the fish soup. The shrimp (gambas), for which the place was named, are always reliable. A complete meal goes for 500 pesetas ($4.80). The ambience is típico, with a cave-like back dining room.

The cheapest restaurant in Cadaqués, where local workmen and fishermen eat, is **Casa Juan,** on Calle Guillermo Bruguera. There's no sign outside—just walk up toward the church from the Placa del Doctor Pont and you'll come to it. This no-frill eatery serves a complete meal for only 500 pesetas ($4.80).

The only public transportation to Cadaqués is a bus that leaves twice a day from Figueras, 14 Mendez Nuñez (at 12:30 and 6:45 p.m.), and costs 150 pesetas ($1.44). It returns to Figueras at 7:30 a.m. and 5 p.m. On Sunday there's an added bus leaving from Figueras at 12:30 and 9:15 p.m. To get to Figueras, take the train.

AFTER DARK: L'Hostal, 8 Plaza del Generalísimo (tel. 25-80-00), is a Dixieland bar par excellence, run by a charming couple, Veronica and Marci Pogany. If you like not only Dixieland, but flamenco, rock, and Catalán songs as well, go here from 8 p.m. to 3 a.m. One prestigious music magazine called L'Hostal the second best jazz and rock club in Europe. Once it was Salvador Dali's favorite bar, and he designed the sign of the club (for free). The club is very popular with artists, and you might occasionally see a movie star dropping in for a drink.

The ambience is especially nice because of the beauty of the Spanish furniture. Illumination is by candlelight. A beer goes for 130 pesetas ($1.25); gin and tonic, 195 pesetas ($1.87); and whisky, 375 pesetas ($3.60).

8. Figueras

A 40-minute drive from Cadaqués delivers you to Figueras, which you may want to visit for two reasons—it has one of the best places to eat in Spain as well as a museum which is Spain's second-most-visited museum (ranking just after the Prado).

First, the museum is called **Teatro Museu Dali,** and it is filled with works by the ailing surrealist artist Salvador Dali, who makes his home in the small village of Port Lligat (Cadaqués).

Dali, of course, hardly needs an introduction. Born in 1904 in Figueras, the Spanish painter is a leading exponent of surrealism, depicting irrational imagery of dreams and delirium in a meticulously detailed style. He's known throughout the world for his uninhibited exhibitionism. His twirling waxed mustache has perked up many a Sunday supplement.

Dali's world is often an erotic one. Chances are you'll see, say, five nude blondes swathed in polyethelene or entangled with a Bardot reptile. Often you'll see the maestro's presence, his cane hooking onto a nymph's arms or his dark beady eyes lusting from one corner.

At the Figueras museum, you'll view much rich Daliania. Dali's oeuvre includes watercolors, gouaches, charcoals, and pastels, along with graphics and sculpture. Much is rendered with seductive and realistic imagery. He is wide ranging in subject matter, as his works are likely to depict everything from putrefaction to castration.

You enter into a central domed hall, and can explore at your leisure, viewing such works as *The Happy Horse,* a grotesque and lurid purple beast, recumbent, which the artist painted during one of his long exiles at Port Lligat.

An adjoining building was purchased to permit the expansion of the museum. A catalogue is being prepared, which Dali says is most important. With a perfectly straight face, he claims, "It is necessary that all of the people who come out of the museum have false information."

The museum is open daily in the morning, shutting down around 2 p.m. for a siesta, and not opening again until 4:30, when it's likely to stay open until 8 p.m. But check these hours, as well as the admission price—unconfirmed at press time.

For dining, my preferred choice is the **Ampurdán,** 1½ kilometers outside of town on the old road to France (tel. 50-05-62). The daughter of the founder, Ana María, and her husband, Jaume Subiros i Jorda, welcome you to the finest meal you're likely to be served in Catalonia. Don't judge it by its appearance, which is ordinary. The look, in fact, is institutional. But not the cuisine, as all the food-loving French who cross the border to dine here will tell you.

The family-run restaurant was founded by Josep Mercader in 1961, and he early established a reputation among U.S. servicemen in the area for his subtlety with game and fish dishes.

My favorite, if the catch has been good, is called molla, which is a rare whitefish, smooth in texture. Since it needs no adornment, such as fancy sauces or whatever, it is fried in a pan—it's that good.

I'd also suggest a cold bean salad, which is superb. It's called ensalada de habas frías a la menta. Meat is prepared well too, especially the solomillio de ternera à la crème sanfaina, a veal steak served with a delicately light cream sauce. Another exquisite dish is dorada al horno, a baked fish dish. For dessert, you're faced with crema Catalána, a burnt-caramel custard, or a selection of sorbets.

Expect to spend from 1600 pesetas ($15.36) to 2200 pesetas ($21.12) for a memorable meal.

The other preferred place in town is **Durán,** 5 Lasauca (tel. 50-12-50). It's best to start here with the salad Catalán made with radishes, boiled egg, a ham pâté, tuna fish, tomato, and fresh crisp salad greens. Other specialties include steak al Roquefort, a zarzuela (a Catalán fish stew), filetes de lenguado à la naranja (sole in orange sauce), and crépinette de sepiones à la col. Like the Ampurdán, Durán also specializes in game. Try, if featured, the grilled rabbit on a plank, served with white wine. The french fries here, unlike those served in most of Spain, are crisp and excellent, prepared just right. Finish off with a rich dessert or at least an espresso. Expect to spend from 1200 pesetas ($11.52) to 2000 pesetas ($19.20) for one of the top-notch meals in the provinces.

9. Cardona

On the Carretera 1410, about 50 miles to the northwest of Barcelona, the busy town of Cardona doesn't present any particular tourist interest, except for its fortified convent and castle perched high on a steep hill and dominating the town and the roads which converge there. This castle was the home of the dukes of Cardona. It has been turned into a national parador by the Spanish Ministry of Information and Tourism.

Parador Nacional Duques de Cardona (tel. 869-12-75). The castle was begun in 789 by Ludovico Pio to help secure lands conquered from the Moors. It became the property of Ramón Folch, the nephew of Charlemagne. In the Middle Ages its walls withstood many sieges. Today it's been converted into a parador of 65 rooms, all with private baths. The charge for a double is 3800 pesetas ($36.48). In a single, the rate is 3000 pesetas ($28.80). A continental breakfast is an extra 250 pesetas ($2.40). Six floors are reached by a very welcome elevator. The furnishings contain many Catalán antiques and reproductions.

Dining is in the main room of the old castle. To reach the lounge, you cross the inside courtyard where genuine wells open onto the tanks below which were used by the dukes of Cardona when enemies were surrounding the château. A luncheon or a dinner costs 950 pesetas ($9.12). On my most recent visit, I enjoyed a selection of regional hors d'oeuvres, at least a dozen, followed by spaghetti in a cheese sauce, then cod à la verde with fresh garden vegetables and a tart.

A Gothic court and chapel, part of the original structure, have been converted into a museum.

10. Gerona

Split by the Onar River, this sleepy city with an ancient history is beginning to feel the impact of tourism, as excursion crowds from the Costa Brava dart inland for the day. One of the most besieged cities in Spanish history, Gerona has preserved parts of its old city walls, and its old quarter is from the Middle Ages.

Although Gerona is not a major tourist mecca, it can be a lifesaver for the night, particularly when hotel bookings are impossible on the Costa Brava for those who didn't make reservations. Gerona is also a good stopover station on the way to and from the principality of Andorra if you have a car; it is not recommended that you cope with the difficult bus connections to Gerona.

The major attraction of Gerona is its magnificent **cathedral,** reached by a climb up 90 steps that are centuries old and as steep as ever. The 14th-century cathedral represents many architectural styles, notably Gothic and Romanesque. It may be visited from 9 a.m. to 1:30 p.m. and 4 to 7 p.m. (10 a.m. to 1:30 p.m. only in winter). The price of admission is 30 pesetas (29¢).

The **Museu d'Art** is in the former episcopal palace next to the cathedral, displaying artworks from the 12th to the 19th centuries. The museum is open from 10 a.m. to 1 p.m. and 4 to 7 p.m. (10 a.m. to 1 p.m. in winter). Admission is 75 pesetas (72¢).

While in this old quarter of the city, you might also seek out the 12th-century **Arab baths,** from 10 a.m. to 1 p.m. and 4 to 7 p.m. (10 a.m. to 1:30 p.m. in winter). The admission is 75 pesetas (72¢).

Two minutes' walk from the Arab baths is the **Sant Père de Galligants Archeological Museum** in a Romanesque church and cloisters from the 11th and 12th centuries. Hours are from 10 a.m. to 1 p.m. and 4 to 7 p.m. (10 a.m. to 1 p.m. in winter). It's closed on Monday.

There is a special rate of 150 pesetas ($1.44) for all three museums.

OVERNIGHT LODGINGS: Hotel Peninsular, 3 General Primo de Rivera (tel. 20-38-00), is the leading second-class hotel in Gerona, a comfortable but characterless structure near the old quarter and the river. Open all year, this good-size commercial hotel charges from 1950 pesetas ($18.72) in a double room, from 1430 pesetas ($13.73) in a single. Its rooms are traditionally styled and most of them contain private baths. The Peninsular is more suited for stopovers than for longer stays. It has no restaurant, and serves only a continental breakfast.

Condal, 10 Juan Maragall (tel. 20-44-62), is a bargain. It's rated third class, yet it is modern and pristine. However, its lounge is meager, the reception desk is tiny, there is no service elevator—and no meals other than breakfast are served. But these are minor concerns. The bedrooms are good and comfortable —and that's more important. Singles rent for 800 pesetas ($7.68), doubles for 1400 pesetas ($13.44) with complete bath. If bathless, a double room goes for only 750 pesetas ($7.12), a real bargain. The bedrooms are compact, some opening onto a view of a square. On the ground floor is a restaurant-snackbar, which is a popular gathering place in the evening. On the second floor is a tiny breakfast room, serving up continental fare in the morning, which is included in the tariffs quoted.

WHERE TO DINE: Bronsoms, 7 Avenida San Francisco (tel. 21-24-93), is a bustling restaurant in the heart of Gerona, which was founded in 1882 by the grandfather of the present owner, English-speaking Joe Bronsoms. Bronsoms has a nicely integrated crowd of locals mixed with visitors, mostly European. You can get some of the best food in town here, although this is a modest restaurant. The chef knows how to make those close-to-the-hearth vegetable soups, served in good-size bowls. Another favorite choice is veal with mushrooms, a hearty dish that might fortify you for your climb up the 90 steps to Gerona cathedral. Other specialties include canelonis, typical fish dishes, a steamed beef ragoût, and roast leg of lamb. There's also a bar if you need stronger fortification. Meals run from 1000 pesetas ($9.60). The restaurant is closed on Sunday.

Chapter XI

ZARAGOZA AND PAMPLONA

1. Zaragoza
2. Pamplona

ARAGÓN AND NAVARRE, two districts of the northeast, are the wallflowers of Spain from the standpoint of the tourist. The ever-fickle sightseer, seduced by Andalusia, lured by the shapely resorts along the coastal regions, tends to neglect both these forgotten daughters. Admittedly, they don't walk off with the top prizes in the beauty contests. But those preferring the stark and rugged will pay a call on these Amazons.

Aragón, of course, was the old kingdom that united with Castile after the marriage of native son Ferdinand to Isabella. Today, the term Aragón refers to the provinces of **Heusca, Teruel,** and **Zaragoza** (Saragossa in English). The pilgrimage city of Zaragoza, the largest population center in Aragón, is the major stopover in the district—for the simple reason that it lies on the most frequented route between Madrid and Barcelona.

Navarre, on the other hand, is more remote. It nestles to the east of the Basque provinces and grabs up some of the Pyreneean landscape. The province is less populated. **Pamplona** is its biggest city, and it becomes even denser with aficionados during the San Fermín fería in July, when the bulls are run through the streets. If the bulls aren't trampling you underfoot, then you may be run down by gringos—noisy, and drunk on vino. Frankly, the festival is Pamplona's big drawing card, but I like the city best at other times, when it's soft and subdued, and you can take time to appreciate the dramatic scenery surrounding it that loomed so large in the pages of *The Sun Also Rises.*

READER'S SIGHTSEEING TIP: "On the way to Zaragoza, be sure to go off the road to **Medinaceli.** It's a fascinating town, with Roman walls and a unique Roman arch high on a cliff commanding marvelous views. For lunch, try the attractive two-fork **Mesón del Arco Romano,** 1 Portillo (tel. 53)" (Joseph W. Zdenek, Rock Hill, S.C.).

We'll begin our look at:

1. Zaragoza (Saragossa)

Halfway between Madrid (215 "rail" miles) and Barcelona is the big provincial capital of Zaragoza, the seat of the ancient kingdom of Aragón. This main terminus of road and rail travel has a population of more than 300,000. It's a bustling, commercial city of wide boulevards, arcades, and of the newly prosperous Aragonese, who pronounce the name of their city, Zaragoza, with each "z" sounding like a lisping "th" ("Tha-ra-go-tha").

It definitely rates a stopover, although A. E. Hotchner, writing in *Papa Hemingway*, called it "... an unattractive, crowded, industrial city, with what must surely be the homeliest cathedral in Christendom—a cavernous, square, fortlike structure, which at night glows with neon trim that runs all around it, and an interior that resembles the waiting room of a suburban-Chicago railroad station."

Hotchner may not have known that Zaragoza has not one but two cathedrals. And his words are certainly heretical to the devout, as the city ranks with Santiago de Compostela in Galicia (the northwest) as a pilgrimage center. According to legend, the Virgin Mary appeared to St. James, the patron saint of Spain, on the banks of the Ebro, and ordered him to erect a church on that spot. The city's big festivities take place the week of October 12, with top-name bullfights, religious processions, and general merriment.

While in Zaragoza to watch the matador Antonio Ordoñez, Hotchner and Hemingway stayed at the Gran. But with our budget, we'd best consider overnighting in one of the following:

WHERE TO STAY: For all-around value, the champion is the **Hotel Goya,** 5 Cinco de Marzo (tel. 22-93-31), a modern (1965) building with excellent bedrooms that, in some respects, equal the much more expensive chambers at the Gran. It is easy to find, just off the Avenida Independencia, near the Plaza de España (heartbeat of the city). The well-furnished and sufficient doubles with private baths are 3400 pesetas ($32.64); the doubles with private showers cost 2800 pesetas ($26.88). Singles with private showers rent for 2000 pesetas ($19.20). A hulking giant for Zaragoza, the Goya can accommodate 290 overnighters. The hotel is tucked away on a fairly quiet street, away from much of the traffic noises. There is a garage for your car.

Hotel Lafuente, 7 Valenzuela (tel. 22-48-06), is a neat, four-story hotel that attracts a stream of economy-minded clients. The management resists the popular urge to toss out traditional furnishings and replace them with cold modern. Many of the old-fashioned appurtenances have been kept, including the crystal chandeliers. Some of the high-ceilinged bedrooms are big enough to be converted hastily into dormitories. A number of the bathrooms are the size of most bedrooms in any number of hotels. Still, Lafuente's a bit creaky. The best and biggest doubles rent for 1850 pesetas ($17.76); the bathless doubles go for 1400 pesetas ($13.44). Most singles are bathless, going for only 900 pesetas ($8.64). The hotel doesn't have a restaurant, but it shelters an American bar.

Hotel Oriente, 11 Coso (tel. 22-19-60), was completely overhauled and given three stars by the government. The lobby has been modernized, and its fairly attractive and reasonably comfortable bedrooms considerably upgraded. The most expensive doubles with private baths peak at 3200 pesetas ($30.72), and singles with bath pay 2200 pesetas ($21.12). A continental breakfast is an extra 210 pesetas ($2.02). Occupying a good location, the Oriente is about a block from the Plaza de España and the Plaza de Salamero.

READER'S HOTEL SELECTION: "The **Hotel Patria,** 8 Hermanos Ibarra (tel. 22-49-55), is an excellent and reasonable place to stay. On our tour of Spain, we found it to be the nicest. Depending on the plumbing, doubles range from 1800 pesetas ($17.28) to 2100 pesetas ($20.16). Singles are priced from 1200 pesetas ($11.52) to 1500 pesetas ($14.40). A continental breakfast is another 150 pesetas ($1.44). The meals at 600 pesetas ($5.76) are good, and served in the provincial style. A selection of entrees included a special surprise every day that was a delight and a credit to the chef. The hotel is within the center of the city, near the church of St. Miguel" (Hilario Luna, Anaheim, Calif.).

WHERE TO EAT: First, a splurge, then two low-budget choices.

The **Mesón del Carmen**, 4 Calle de Hernán Cortés (tel. 21-11-51), is an unusually fine Spanish restaurant. This L-shaped popular dining place has beamed ceilings, walls of inlaid tiles, and a long shelf of Aragonese pottery, brass, and copper. It all makes a fit background for some of the fine cooking of this region. The smooth and creamy soups (particularly the mushroom) and the grilled trout (ask for it to be done in butter, mantequilla), a gourmet's delight, are recommended. The menú del día goes for 750 pesetas ($7.20). However, if you order à la carte, expect to spend from 800 pesetas ($7.68) to 1800 pesetas ($17.28).

Taberna Aragonesas, 8 Hernán Cortés (tel. 22-52-50), is a place to eat and dine where the atmosphere is ethnic. On two levels, this has all the flavor of an Aragonese wine cellar: bunches of garlic and peppers as well as gourds hang from the ceiling. It's crude, provincial—dark and cool in the summer. You may want to start your meal by stopping at the little bar in front for a drink. The waiter will serve you hors d'oeuvres. Later, you might want to try the crisp, fresh, antipasto-like salad, a second course of eggs and Majorcan ham, followed by a tender veal stew. The bill? 575 pesetas ($5.52), and this includes bread, wine, and service. If you order à la carte, expect to spend from 700 pesetas ($6.72) to 1200 pesetas ($11.52).

An oldtime restaurant oozing with atmosphere and low prices is **Rieva**, 12 Martires, in the oldest part of the city where the streets are so narrow they're closed to traffic. This budgeteer's dream come true charges 425 pesetas ($4.08) for a menú del día. On my last visit I had paella, boiled eggs with mushroom sauce, a steak with lettuce, ice cream, and half a bottle of red wine. Upstairs is a beautiful dining room—beamed ceiling, wood paneling—where you can eat well for low prices. Downstairs is an old-fashioned pastry shop.

THE SIGHTS: Zaragoza has three principal sights, conveniently near each other and easy to cover in a morning.

Church of El Pilar

This 17th- and 18th-century basilica, on the banks of the Ebro River, contains the tiny statue of the *Virgin del Pilar* in the Holy Chapel. Thousands of the faithful travel hundreds of miles each year to pay homage at this important Catholic shrine. The name of the cathedral, El Pilar, comes from the pillar upon which the Virgin, according to tradition, is supposed to have stood as she made her request to Santiago (St. James). Some of the frescoes inside were painted by Francisco Goya. In the second week of October, the structure serves as the backdrop for an important festival devoted to Our Lady of the Pillar, but the ceremonies merge into parades, bullfights, fireworks, flower offerings, and street dancing. The almost Oriental-looking basilica, designed by Herrera, may be visited from 8 a.m. to 2 p.m. and 4 to 7 p.m. in summer (from 9 a.m. to 2 p.m. and from 4 to 6 p.m. in winter).

La Seo

This Gothic-mudéjar church, built between 1380 and 1550, is more impressive than El Pilar, but somehow seems sadly neglected. Still, in a rich baroque and plateresque setting, it manages to come off as more than a poor sister, and contains numerous artistic treasures and interesting architectural features, the most important of which is the main altar. It is a particularly fine representation of the Aragón style of Gothic architecture. In the museum is a collection of Franco and Flemish tapestries from the 15th to the 17th centuries. In the Temple of Pilar, constructed in the baroque style, the cupolas were decorated by Goya and Bayeu. Hours are from 7 a.m. to 2 p.m. and 4 to 7 p.m.

Aljafería

This most unusual sight, a Moorish palace in Aragón, has been restored by the government and preserved as a National Monument. Long neglected, it is reminiscent of some of the architecture of Córdoba. The palace was originally built in the 11th century for Moorish kings, but it has seen considerable alterations and additions since, particularly when those itinerant monarchs, Ferdinand and Isabella (who carried their kingdom with them), lived here. The palace may be visited from 11 a.m. to 1:30 p.m. and 4 to 5 p.m. weekdays; on Sunday, from 11 a.m. to 1:30 p.m. Admission is 25 pesetas (24¢).

AFTER DARK: Zaragoza offers at least one offbeat attraction. In the **Bar Plata,** Calle 4 de Agosto (opposite the Rieva), you can see one of the last café-cantantes left in Spain. This is a good-size café, with a bar at the entrance, and an old, musty stage at the other end of the room. The café is filled with unshaven men wearing berets, farmers, and other locals, almost all of them men. There's a wooden planked floor, pillars covered with tiny bits of mirror, and a small balcony with more tables and chairs. Four times a day (from 3:15 to 4:15; 5 to 6; 7:50 to 8:45; and 10:30 to midnight) there's a kind of oldtime girlie show. A wobbly three-piece orchestra whoops up the tunes, and a scantily dressed girl comes out to warble a love song and do a couple of bumps. It's all hilariously simple and authentic. The cost? Only 75 pesetas (72¢) for a coffee.

If you're motoring to Madrid after leaving Zaragoza, you'll have a rare opportunity to sample the following:

ON THE ROAD—STAYING IN A MONASTERY: Founded in 1195 at Nuevalos, the **Monasterio de Piedra** (tel. 84-90-11) is a three-star hotel open year round. It lies 136 miles from Madrid, 67 miles from Zaragoza, and was originally built as a spiritual retreat in an area known for its good climate and mineral waters. At some point, an impressive wing with comfortable rooms was added, and it is this three-story addition, with its three tiers of arches reminiscent of a Roman aqueduct, which contains the excellent bedrooms. A couple can stay here, in a room with balcony and private bath, for 2200 pesetas ($21.12) nightly. Eight singles, also with private bath, are available for 1500 pesetas ($14.40). A continental breakfast is an extra 150 pesetas ($1.44).

Walk through the woods and grounds to get the best of nature: a waterfall emptying into a small river, little log bridges, masses of flowering plants and trees. Dining in the great hall is a colorful, medieval event. The room has been tastefully decorated, and is a perfect background for the good Spanish meals—served for 850 pesetas ($8.16).

The monastery is about ten miles off the main Madrid–Zaragoza road. If you're coming from Madrid, turn east at Alhama de Aragón. From Zaragoza, turn left at Calatayud, and it'll be 14 miles from there. By train, go to Alhama de Aragón from Madrid, and from there take a taxi to the monastery. It is open from April until the end of October.

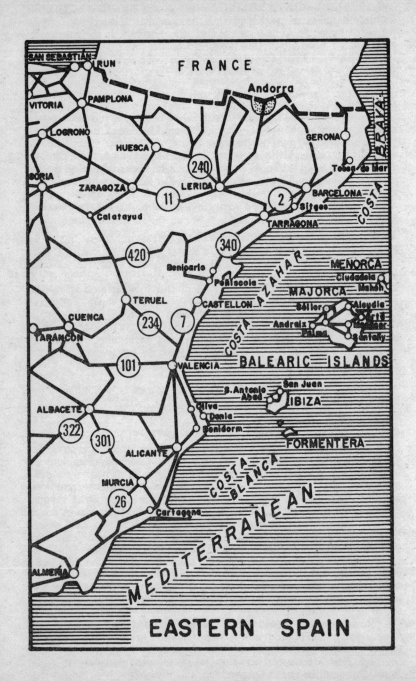

EASTERN SPAIN

From Aragón, we move to the province of Navarre and to:

2. Pamplona

More than half a century has passed since Ernest Hemingway wrote *The Sun Also Rises* (*Fiesta,* if you read the British edition). But the book's glamor remains undiminished for the American youths who read the novel, then rush off to Pamplona to see the running (*encierro*) of the bulls through the streets. Attempts to outlaw this world-famed ceremony have failed so far, and it remains a superstar attraction, particularly among Spanish aficionados. The festival of **San Fermín,** during which the *encierro* takes place, usually begins on July 6 and lasts through the 20th.

Nobody sleeps, which is just as well—as accommodations are virtually impossible to find, unless you have a notarized letter from Angel Gabriel. Fireworks and Basque flute concerts are only some of the spectacles that give added color to the fiesta.

With or without Papa's book, you can bed down in sleeping bags in an emergency, or stay up carousing around the clock (by far the prevalent custom). Those who have grown weak and spoiled by capitalistic society—and who want to know they'll have a bed after watching the *encierro*—should reserve a millennium in advance at one of the city's handful of hotels or pensions. Or they can base in San Sebastián and visit Pamplona during the day. After all, chances are that one visit to Pamplona will be enough to satisfy all but the insatiably bloodthirsty.

Hemingway, incidentally, used to give an old down-on-his-luck pal a regular yearly stipend to acquire accommodations and bullfight tickets for him. The ring at Pamplona is simply too small to accommodate the demand for tickets—so the scalpers make enough in July to get them through the winter. It helps to have a friend fending for you in Pamplona.

Actually, the bullring has recently been somewhat enlarged and tickets are now easier to obtain. Those wishing to see the running of the bulls through the streets should get downstairs by 6 a.m. Tickets for a seat in the ring cost about 300 pesetas ($2.88) to 500 pesetas ($4.80) and go on sale at 8 p.m. the night before the corrida. Tickets for standing room are on sale at 4 p.m. the day of the bullfight.

Pamplona, like the Roman god Janus, has two faces. One it presents only at fiesta time; the other is around for the rest of the year, when Pamplona is just a sleepy provincial capital.

Hot in summer, fiercely cold in winter, Pamplona converges at the **Plaza del Castillo,** the heartbeat of the city. Head here to check the pulse of the old kingdom of Navarre. And don't fail to spend as much time as you can exploring the nearby streets of the old town. The single most important sight is the cathedral, lying within walking distance from the Plaza del Castillo. But, first:

WHERE TO STAY: Residencia Eslava, Plaza Virgen de la O, right off the Plaza del Cardenal Ilundain (tel. 22-22-70), is a honey. Built within the shell of an old building, it captures the spirit of old and new Spain. Its smallish living room is more like the drawing room of a distinguished Spanish family—as indeed it is. Doña María Vidaurreta, the owner, has created a congenial atmosphere at low prices. For a double with private bath, the rate is 2400 pesetas ($23.04) nightly. Singles with shower bath are 1800 pesetas ($17.28). A continental breakfast is yet another 150 pesetas ($1.44). The rooms, a few with balconies, are medium-size, employing the same imaginative taste reflected in the public rooms. The baths are shiny clean and compact. You sip your breakfast coffee while perched on three-legged stools, and later in the day you can drink in the lounge cellar.

Hostal Valerio, 5 Avenida de Zaragoza (tel. 24-54-66), is the leading pension of Pamplona, my economy choice. On the second floor of an old elevator building, this hostal is family run, friendly, and intimate. It is hosted by Don José Romero Aranguren, who speaks English, and who doesn't want too many changes made. He likes the hand-carved ladder-back chairs, the old pieces of furniture—everything blending to create a homey and personal atmosphere. Especially cordial to U.S. students, Don José charges 1000 pesetas ($9.60) for singles with water basins, 1700 pesetas ($16.32) in doubles. The functional rooms are basic, clean, and pleasant—in all, sound comfort. A continental breakfast at 160 pesetas ($1.54) per person is the only meal served.

Note: During the San Fermín festivities, when the town is packed, you can sometimes get rooms in private homes. Inquire at the Tourist Office.

READER'S HOTEL SELECTION: "A most satisfactory accommodation is **Hostal Artazcoz,** 9 Tudela (second floor; tel. 22-51-64). Once reached, this second-story hostal is bright and clean, with good beds and a gracious hostess. Do not let the beat-up entranceway and stairs dampen your spirits. Forge ahead, and you will be amply rewarded. The price is 1200 pesetas ($11.52) double, with wash basin. A continental breakfast costs an extra 100 pesetas (96¢). There is a 'two-fork' restaurant on the street floor" (L. A. Reese, Mason, Mich.).

WHERE TO EAT: Quite a problem in Pamplona, where fishing for a good restaurant is easy enough, but "angling" for an inexpensive one is sometimes hard. Exceptions include the following:

The **Bodega Señorio Sarria,** 50 Calle de Estafeta (right off the Plaza del Castillo), is a medieval-type tavern, suitable for light meals, but dark enough for intimate rendezvousing. In this cozy atmosphere, drinkers and lovers sample the wines from the kegs for only 30 pesetas (29¢). Those whose bodies need more than romance for sustenance can order gazpacho, half a roast chicken, fruit or the local cheese of Navarre, plus a glass of wine—a complete meal for about 480 pesetas ($4.61).

READER'S RESTAURANT SUGGESTIONS: "Just off the Plaza del Castillo on a backstreet corner is the **Bar Casa Sixto.** If you sit at the counter (in the kitchen), you are served whatever you point to for very low prices. The address is 81 Estafeta. It is a bit hard to find, as there is a bar in front of the building, and you have to walk through to the back. It is clean, and all the typical Basque dishes are served during the week. There are tables, too, and a few bench seats on a balcony overlooking the kitchen where business people eat at noon. You can dine for less than 500 pesetas ($4.80), wine included. Highly recommended for down-and-outers. Servings are big, and the cooks are friendly. If you have money and want a good chop or steak, go to the **Asador Olaverri,** 4 Santa María. This is a little-known place a good way from the main square, but well worth the really short trip. All the times we went there I saw perhaps two tourists. The management only serves roast meat, and you see it barbecued on an open grill at the rear of the big, country restaurant. The choice is between steaks or chops, and red or white wine. On the expensive side, it charges 750 pesetas ($7.20) for a steak or a barbecue. The best típico place is the **Restaurante Marceliano,** near the market (7–9 Calle Mercado), where you can sit in one of the four large dining rooms on either of two floors and order from a large menu. Very popular are the mussels in garlic broth. The 'ponchas con chunga' (shelled green beans with ham) are a favorite when they're in season. There's a wine bar downstairs. Plates go from 150 pesetas ($1.44) to 400 pesetas ($3.84), and servings are very large. Go early. This is a good place to eat in the mornings during the fería" (Roderic Cossey, Almería, Spain).

THE CHIEF SIGHT: The **Cathedral of Pamplona** is Gothic, begun near the end of the 14th century on the site of an early Romanesque basilica which caved in. The final facade is in the neoclassical style of the 18th century, and is flanked by two towers. Inside, the interior reverts to a somber Gothic style, with lots of fan vaulting. In the center of the cathedral is the tomb of Charles III (note the deftly carved figurines on his alabaster sepulchre) and his Castilian wife. From the architectural point of view, the chief interest centers on the magnificent Gothic cloisters. For 50 pesetas (48¢), you can visit the Gothic Barbazan "capilla," as well as the Diocesano Museum, filled with medieval sculpture, much of which is interesting.

Pamplona has both train and bus connections to our next stop, San Sebastián, 56 miles away on the Basque Coast of Spain.

Chapter XII

ALONG THE ATLANTIC

1. San Sebastián
2. Guernica
3. Santander
4. Santillana del Mar and the Caves of Altamira
5. Oviedo
6. La Coruña
7. Santiago de Compostela
8. Pontevedra
9. Vigo
10. Tuy

SAN SEBASTIÁN AND SANTANDER have much in common; both are Atlantic Coast beach resorts frequented predominantly by Spaniards. San Sebastián, closer to France, of course is more international. Both are modern, with good hotels and restaurants, and both are noted for their excellent beaches. In addition, they are capitals of two of the most beautiful provinces in Spain. But San Sebastián is the queen of the Basque country, while Santander is in Old Castile, the only part of that ancient kingdom that has a coastline.

From the snow-capped **Picos de Europa** to the streets of **Laredo,** from the medieval village of **Santillana del Mar** to the nearby subterranean grottoes of **Altamira** with prehistoric paintings, the province of **Santander** offers much to see and do. Similarly attractive is Spain's smallest province, **Guipúzcoa** (capital: **San Sebastián**), which is one of the most heavily visited regions in Spain.

San Sebastián lies about 13 miles from the French border, and North Americans, among others, by the car and busload, pour over from Biarritz for a glimpse of Spain. It is safe to assume that what they see often surprises them. These Atlantic Coast provinces are not the Spain of legend, as reflected in Granada and Seville. But they form a land of unspoiled fishing villages, snug harbors, inland spas, ancient ruins, towering mountains, rivers, fertile valleys, pine trees, and bays with sandy beaches.

Even farther along the coast you reach **Galicia,** which embraces the provinces of La Coruña, Pontevedra, Lugo, and Orense. It occupies northwestern Spain with **Asturias,** once the only stronghold of Christian Spain and later a principality.

A native of Galicia is known as a *gallego.* These farmers and fishermen have a reputation as a somber, hard-working people, who have had to contend with many hardships inflicted by nature. Generalísimo Franco came from El Ferrol, the most important navy base in Spain, north of La Coruña.

In the province of La Coruña, visitors can explore the *rías* country. *Rías* are what the Spanish call the lochs that cut inland from the sea, providing some of the most dramatic scenery in the country. Galicia has much to offer: stone-gray medieval villages and towns, a rugged coastline, fishing harbors, fertile valleys, mountains, a unique cuisine, sandy beaches, and some of the most colorful festivals in Spain.

The capital, **La Coruña,** is one of the legendary cities founded by Hercules. It lies some 375 miles from Madrid, and is distinguished by its *miradores,* glass-enclosed balconies on buildings facing the sea. Rows and rows of this glazed and glistening glass make for a stunning sight. The *gallegos* can sit behind them, absorb the sun, and remain sheltered from the windy Atlantic.

Interesting as La Coruña is, it must take second place to **Santiago de Compostela,** that goal of the medieval pilgrim.

Our exploration will begin, however, near the French border at:

1. San Sebastián

San Sebastián is the summer capital of Spain—hundreds of Spanish bureaucrats escape to this coastal city when the Madrid sun becomes too hot. San Sebastián is a tasteful resort, and has none of the tawdry trappings associated with major beachfront cities. It is also an ideal excursion center for trips to some of Spain's most fascinating little villages.

San Sebastián contains an old quarter—narrow streets, hidden-away plazas, medieval houses—but is primarily a modern city of elegant shops, wide boulevards, sidewalk cafés, and restaurants. Its most celebrated feature is its **La Concha Beach** where, it would appear, half the denizens of Spain and France spend their days under striped canopies when they're not dashing into the refreshingly cool, sky-blue waters of the bay. La Concha is half-encircled by a promenade, where the crowds parade in the evening. The adjoining beach is called **Playa de Ondarreta.**

For the best view of the city, take the funicular to the top of **Mount Igueldo.** It's also possible to drive up for a cost of 25 pesetas (24¢). In spring, the air is scented with honeysuckle. At the top, a cliff-hanging belvedere has been built, affording a fabulous view of the sheltered bay and the Cantabrian coastline.

San Sebastián, nestled ideally on a choice spot on the Bay of Biscay, is surrounded by green mountains. Its population swells enormously from June to September. It has a good, but inadequate, choice of hotels, and an excellent number of Basque restaurants that are mostly expensive. Its chief drawback—overcrowding in July, no space at all in August.

To the Spaniards, and to the civil servant in particular, San Sebastián is the most fashionable resort in Spain.

What with its bullfights, art and film festivals, sporting events, and cultural activities, San Sebastián in the peak summer months is a hub of constant activity. But since gambling was abolished with the fall of the old monarchy, neighboring Biarritz, across the border, draws the casino devotees.

San Sebastián is principally reached by rail or car, although it has both bus and airplane service. From Madrid, the TALGO departs for here from the North Station. But, for approximately the same amount of pesetas, it's possible to fly, and Aviaco maintains services between Madrid and San Sebastián. There's also train service from Barcelona, although it's a difficult run. In summer, there is also some bus service from Madrid to San Sebastián, a distance of approximately 300 miles, but the ride is long and hard.

WHERE TO STAY: The key to hotel bargains in San Sebastián is to reserve in advance. As mentioned before, that vacancy sign in July and August is rare. But the visitor who does book space in advance will find an array of good hotel values, surprising for a resort of such international status. Assuming you do get a room at that busy time, most hoteliers will insist that you take full pension, or at least half board (breakfast, plus one main meal).

Niaz, 56 Zubieta (tel. 42-66-63), is a little 41-room hotel with character. Savored by those who like to be near the beach and esplanade, it is well appointed, combining a selection of Scandinavian modern in its bedrooms with antiques in its public lounges. The petit salon, for example, is furnished as a drawing room, with an Oriental mauve rug, Directoire chairs, a tall grandfather clock, a rosewood breakfront. In direct contrast are the basic rooms, with wooden headboards, white walls—usually wall-to-wall scarlet carpeting. A double room with bath costs 3800 pesetas ($36.48). A single with bath is 2200 pesetas ($21.12) nightly. Only a continental breakfast is served, at 75 pesetas (72¢).

Arana, 7 Vergara (tel. 42-69-46), attracts middle-class Spanish families who have come to stake their claim for a few feet of sand on Playa de la Concha. The Arana is on a commercial street in the shopping section, but only a block or so from the river (a five-minute walk to the beach). This year-round hotel is your best bet for an off-season visit to San Sebastián. It offers doubles with every conceivable kind of plumbing—ranging from water basins at 1800 pesetas ($17.28), to private baths at 2800 pesetas ($26.88). Singles are available with showers (no toilets) for 1600 pesetas ($15.36). The best rooms face the street and have private "Miss Muffet" sitting rooms opening onto glassed-in bay windows. The furniture is comfortably stuffy, and each bed has enough pillows to help stop a Mississippi flood. A continental breakfast, costing 160 pesetas ($1.54), is the only meal served.

Avenida, Carretera Subida a Igueldo (tel. 21-20-00), is of recent vintage, nestling on the fringe of San Sebastián on the road up to Mount Igueldo. The Avenida, graced with terraces and a swimming pool, charges 3000 pesetas ($28.80) for its doubles with private bath and 2100 pesetas ($26.88) in its singles, also with private bath. In addition, you pay 2000 pesetas ($19.20) extra should you take all three meals. Accommodations are tasteful, offering a good standard of comfort. The lounge, with its French provincial pieces, has a view of the hills beyond. A guest can sit here, watching sunrises and sunsets from April through October.

Hispano Americano, 1 Prim (tel. 42-42-06), looks like an old Basque mansion, painted in white and oozing Victorian charm. It's near the river on a tree-lined street. This pretty, old-world hotel provides top value room and board: the best doubles with baths go for 2200 pesetas ($21.12); the ones with showers are 2000 pesetas ($19.20). Singles with baths range from 1500 pesetas ($14.40) to 1800 pesetas ($17.28). The 75 rooms are simple, with phones, good modern baths, although some have balconies and carpeted floors. Everything is spotless. The dining room has picture windows, Muzak, a large mural of Indians on one wall, Greek statues in niches, fluorescent lighting, old wood paneling, and white-and-black-clad waitresses to serve you. There's a modern bar downstairs, plus a small terrace for al fresco sipping.

Monte Igueldo, Placa de Plata (tel. 21-02-11), is a contemporary hotel "fortress" perched like a castle on the crown of Monte Igueldo, at the edge of

San Sebastián. From its windows a panoramic view of the Cantabrique Coast unfolds. Both the public rooms and the bedrooms have spacious windows to capture this view. The swimming pool terrace also juts out into space for a coastal view. This first-class "super-splurge" hotel is for festive occasions only. All of its 120 rooms contain private baths and showers, with private balconies as well. Tariffs vary according to view, season, and room size. Doubles range from 3850 pesetas ($35.04) to 4300 pesetas ($41.28) and singles pay from 2100 pesetas ($20.16) to 2600 pesetas ($24.96). A continental breakfast is an extra 275 pesetas ($2.64), a lunch or dinner going for 800 pesetas ($7.68). All bedrooms are streamlined, with semi-modern furnishings. The atmosphere is comfortable.

The **Codina,** 21 Zumalacárregui (tel. 21-22-00), is a modern structure built in a free-form style so that nearly all of its bedrooms have a view of the bay. It's a real Spanish hotel—guests often hang their laundry to dry from the windows. The compact bedrooms are simply furnished, the baths slick and efficient (sometimes). The doors to the bedrooms have panels with frosted glass inserts, just enough to protect your privacy. From July to September, only guests taking half board are accepted. Full board in the summer costs 3000 pesetas ($28.80) per person based on double occupancy; it's 2300 pesetas ($22.08) per person for half board. The doubles come in all price ranges, those with private baths renting for 2000 pesetas ($19.20) to 2800 pesetas ($26.88), without baths for 1400 pesetas ($13.44) to 1800 pesetas ($17.28), plus a continental breakfast for another 200 pesetas ($1.92). You can order a complete luncheon or dinner for 750 pesetas ($7.20). On the wide, busy boulevard is a popular café and bar. Open all year, except in February, the hotel is near an attractive residential district and close to a strip of beach.

Hostal Bahía, 54 San Martín (tel. 46-10-83), open all year, is a top-notch little pension just one short block from the beach and near a string of hotels. It charges 2100 pesetas ($20.16) for the most expensive double with private bath. However, bathless doubles cost only 1495 pesetas ($14.35). A single without bath rents for 1050 pesetas ($10.08), rising to 1400 pesetas ($13.44) with bath. Breakfast is not included. The boarding house is family operated by Mr. and Mrs. Jesus Fernández Garate, both of whom speak English. They keep their domain well, although seeing to it that it always remains informal. Some of the Bahía's bedrooms are large enough to contain sofas and armchairs; others fall more into the cubicle classification. Many North Americans stay at the hostal and "commute" to Pamplona for the running of the bulls.

Residencia Parma, 11 General Jauregui (tel. 42-88-93), has seven of its rooms with beautiful views of the ocean. It is a modern, clean hotel, featuring a snackbar downstairs. There's also a pleasant TV lobby, with armchairs and sofas. The rooms are up-to-date and cozily furnished in wood. Bathrooms are as in a luxury hotel. The best doubles with bath go for 3200 pesetas ($30.72), but cheaper ones with showers cost only 2500 pesetas ($24). Singles peak at 1800 pesetas ($17.28). A continental breakfast costs 175 pesetas ($1.68).

At Fuenterrabia

Parador Nacional El Emperador, Plaza Armas del Castillo (tel. 64-21-40), is in a tenth-century castle. Emperor Charles V reinforced it to guard the river border with France. It is an impressive bunker which has been restored, as have most other national paradors, with a lot of taste and imagination. Many antiques, old weapons, and standards hang from the high vault. Corridors lead to rooms of great comfort. Prices are moderate, considering the amenities. For 2400 pesetas ($23.04) a single with bath is rented. Doubles, on the other hand, pay a maximum of 3000 pesetas ($28.80). To this price 250 pesetas ($2.40) per person for a continental breakfast are added. In every accommodation is a mini-bar, from which you may select your apéritif before facing a copious dinner served in the old armor room. The price of a complete luncheon or dinner is 950 pesetas ($9.12), a pitcher of the local wine going for an extra 150 pesetas ($1.44). It's best to reserve in advance, as El Emperador has only 18 rooms.

READER'S HOTEL SELECTION: "We stayed at the **Hotel Isla,** 17 Miraconcha (tel. 46-48-97), run by Angel and June Alonso, who are very friendly and helpful and speak English well. The charge is 2300 pesetas ($22.08) for a double room with full bath. Singles with bath are 1200 pesetas ($11.52). A continental breakfast is an extra 175 pesetas ($1.68) per person. Closed from October 16 till Easter" (M. E. Lowey, Altoona, Pa.)

THE BASQUE CUISINE . . . AND WHERE TO EAT IT: The Basques are considered the best cooks in Spain—and not just by fellow Basques. Both visitors and other Spaniards praise the native cuisine of these northeastern provinces. Many of the dishes, of course, would put hair on your chest—and are to be recommended only for the most adventurous stomachs. But the average diner will usually find a large and safe array of well-prepared and attractively served dishes, platters of tempting hors d'oeuvres (mainly "creatures from the sea")—and lots more. The Basques also take special care to prepare their vegetables in unusual ways. Here is a selection of the best and most inexpensive of the típico restaurants, most of them in the old quarter of San Sebastián.

Gandarias, 25 San Jerónimo, in the old town, is the preferred choice for the best of the platos típicos of the Basque country. This regional-style restaurant—two adjoining ones, in fact—is where the natives of San Sebastián go for abundant and rich-tasting meals. This casa affords an opportunity to sample the cuisine of the Basque women, who have not varied their recipes in decades. The staunch women who work here scurry back and forth, chattering away informally, bringing one good platter after another. A favorite dish here is hearts of artichokes. A treat is the platter of baby stuffed squid, cooked in its own ink (don't knock it till you've tried it). Less adventurous readers may prefer the fish soup, then the veal escalope. The tourist menu costs 600 pesetas ($5.76), and most of the fish plates range in cost from 250 pesetas ($2.40) to 600 pesetas ($5.76).

Basarri, 17 Fermín Calbetón, is a little two-fork restaurant frequented for years by the fishermen of San Sebastián. Up front is a tavern, where the sherry drinkers are nonchalant about dropping napkins and shellfish hulls on the floor, in the true Spanish tradition. Trays of tapas rest on the counter to stimulate the wine drinking. Past a view of the cluttered kitchen is a big family-style dining room in the rear (the pace is frenetic at meal times). A special set menu is offered for 550 pesetas ($5.28), including, on my most recent rounds, a choice of mushroom omelet or a bowl of fish soup, followed by a steak with a salad, plus dessert, bread, wine, and service. The best entrees are the fish specialties, including rape (a sweet whitefish) in a classic green sauce, marinated clams, and grilled prawns.

La Cueva, Plaza de la Trinidad, is a relatively undiscovered two-fork restaurant—a tavern on a little square, set against a hillside of stone terraces and trees. Depending on the weather, you can dine inside or out on a terrace under a large canopy. La Cueva is on the lower level of an old timbered and brick building, and there's a small bar on your left when you enter. The atmosphere couldn't be more típico—with beams, brass pots, and bright plaid tablecloths. The intimate dining room is on several levels.

The set luncheon or dinner is 525 pesetas ($5.04). The bill of fare is likely to include sopa de pescado (a potpourri of the sea), followed by a selection of dishes such as caracoles (snails), prawns, or tasty mussels grilled in butter. The specialty is hake, which pops up in nearly every inland and seaside town in Spain, but is one of the staple foods of the Basque country. The way of preparing it here is in pungent green sauce, most appetizing. Desserts include the standard caramel custard, fruit, or ice cream.

Casa Bartolo, 38 Fermín Calbetón, in the fisherman sector of the old quarter, is a warm tribute to Basque cooking. The restaurant has been completely modernized, with wood paneling, natural brick walls, Spanish-colonial chairs, pine tables. You choose a seat either in the front dining room or in the rear. Two different menus are featured, the cheaper one offering excellent value at 525 pesetas ($5.04)—hors d'oeuvres or fish soup, paella or chicken, followed by ice cream, bread, and wine. A more elaborate menu goes for 850 pesetas ($8.16). The composer Raimundo Sarriegui (1838–1913) once lived in the casa.

Juanito Kojua, 14 Puerto (tel. 42-01-80), in the old part of town, is a little fish restaurant which has become famous throughout Spain. There is no decor to speak of, the tables are few, and there's a wait, but it's worth it. The atmosphere consists of beamed ceilings, wood-paneled walls, and stone floors. There are two dining areas on the main floor, after you pass along a narrow bar (perfect for an appetizer while you're waiting for your table), plus one downstairs—all of them air-conditioned in summer. The standard menu costs 650 pesetas ($6.24) and might include fish soup, chicken, and fruit. But you're better off ordering the à la carte specialties. Each one of the dishes is virtually a meal in itself: paella, pisto, half a besugo (sea bream), rape (a whitefish) l'americana, and lubina. Meats are good, too, but it's best to stick to the fresh fish dishes. Most fish plates range in price from 250 pesetas ($2.40) to 700 pesetas ($6.72). If you order à la carte, you can escape for 900 pesetas ($8.64), although your tab could run as high as 2000 pesetas ($19.20).

Sardines Along the Harbor

In the summer, the thing to do is to walk along the Fishermen's Harbor in San Sebastián and order a plate of charcoal-broiled sardines. At several bistros, rustic wooden tables and chairs have been placed outside rough-and-tumble restaurants that offer good food. One of the best is **Casa Panchica,** 16 Muelle, a typical dockside fish restaurant facing the harbor, where for 450 pesetas ($4.32) you can order soup, a half-dozen grilled sardines, dessert, and wine. The repast would put a twinkle in the eye of an old sea captain. One American woman reports that after having a meal of sardines here, she was stalked by two cats when she visited the old quarter.

Restaurante Anastasio, 19 Victor Pradera (tel. 45-35-01), has very good Basque cookery at moderate prices, an unbeatable combination. The English-speaking owner, Placido Eceiza, will welcome you graciously and feed you well. His least expensive dinner costs 350 pesetas ($3.36), with both a first and a second course, plus dessert. However, you may want to roam the à la carte menu which is in English. A good appetizer might be a selection of cold cuts, followed by an omelet with fresh asparagus. Rabbit is cooked in a savory sauce, and the fish dishes are excellent. Try "cocochas," a typical fish of the Basque country, costing 450 pesetas ($4.32). Most other fish plates range in price from 150 pesetas ($1.44) to 350 pesetas ($3.36). On my latest visit, I counted 40 different desserts, ranging from apple pie to "pie whisky ice."

SAN SEBASTIÁN NIGHTLIFE: When the lights illuminating the bay go on, the visitor to San Sebastián begins to map out plans for the evening. **La Perla,** a big dance parlor on the beach (Paseo de la Concha), is the favorite spot. It features dancing to orchestra music, as well as an international floor show presenting performers with such names as Isa Esmeralda. The price of entrance, including your first drink, is 600 pesetas ($5.76).

But for those who want more intimate fare (and a younger crowd), there is a "sala de fiestas," **Zorongo 66,** 66 Calle de San Martín (tel. 46-35-93). Prices, hours, and entertainment vary. The price of admission and your first drink ranges between 300 pesetas ($2.88) and 700 pesetas ($6.72), depending on the time of day and whether you're a man or woman.

SIDE TRIPS FROM SAN SEBASTIÁN: One of the reasons for coming to San Sebastián is to use it as a base for branching out to the sight-filled environs. Readers with cars are fortunate, as buses connect some of the more important sights, but are awkward or nonexistent for others. Our first and easiest trip is to:

Pasajes de San Juan

On the east bank of a natural harbor 6½ miles from San Sebastián is one of the most typical Basque fishing villages, Pasajes de San Juan. Visitors like to come here to dine. The village, with its codfish factories, huddles close to its sheltered harbor; little fishing boats are tied up at the wharf. The architecture is appealing: five- and sometimes six-story balconied tenement-like buildings spring up from the precious land space. Many of them are in different colors, and the flamboyant laundry sailing from the porches makes Pasajes de San Juan look like the melting pot that paints the rainbow.

It is understandable why Victor Hugo lived here in the 19th century (it hasn't changed since) at building no. 59 on the narrow main street.

For a sumptuous repast, try **Txulotxo,** 71 Calle San Juan, Pasajes de San Juan (tel. 35-66-09), one of the most authentic and typical of Basque restaurants. Right on the waterside, the restaurant is in an old stone building, part of it under an arch. The kitchen is on the main street (you can peer in and inspect it). Two sides of windows encase most of the dining room, which juts out onto the harbor. A two-fork restaurant, the Txulotxo charges 550 pesetas ($5.28) for its menú del día. Otherwise, you'll pay from 800 pesetas ($7.68) to 2000 pesetas ($19.20) on the à la carte menu. The specialties of the casa are made from fish which is delivered at the doorstep each day fresh. On any given day you may share the restaurant with local fishermen and their families and other Basques who always break into song at the finish of their meal. Closed Tuesday.

Taking a car into the village in summer is not advised as parking space is at a premium. The medieval street accommodates one-way traffic only, and Pasajes de San Juan has the longest traffic signals known. All the south-moving traffic has to clear the street before north-bound motorists have the right of way.

A bus leaves every 15 minutes from Calle Aldamar in San Sebastián for **Pasajes de San Pedro,** San Juan's sister fishing village. It's possible to walk over from the neighboring village. Buses head back to San Sebastián from Pasajes de San Pedro at a quarter to the hour all day long. A one-way trip costs 60 pesetas (58¢).

After a visit to Pasajes de San Juan, you may be in the mood for a much longer pilgrimage—one to:

Loyola

This sanctuary, lying about 34 miles southwest of San Sebastián, is the most-visited attraction outside the city. Surrounded by mountain scenery, Loyola is where St. Ignatius, the founder of the Jesuits, was born. The sanctuary has an enormous regal dome, and subtle muted coloring. The **Santa Casa** (Holy House) may be visited free throughout the day.

Buses going by way of Loyola leave from 2 Plaza Guipúzcoa in San Sebastián. There are six buses a day, the first departing at 8:30 a.m. and the last at 8 p.m. The return trips run about every two hours.

Those with a car can continue northwest toward Bilbao for a visit to:

2. Guernica

This town that became the subject of Picasso's most famous painting, now returned to Spain, was destroyed by bombs in an air raid on April 26, 1937. Guernica is the spiritual home of the Basques and of Basque nationalism. It was the site of a revered oak tree, under whose branches Basques had elected their officials since medieval times. No one knows how many died during the 3½-hour pounding—estimates range from 200 to as many as 1600 persons. After the bombers departed, the town had been reduced to rubble, but a mighty symbol of independence had been born.

Controversy still swirls around Guernica. The town has been attractively rebuilt, somewhat in its former style. Today it looks as if it had never seen a bomb. The quiet life goes on—old men lead heavily laden donkeys through the street. Women gossip over the fence. The chimes of a church ring softly, and happy children play in the street. Suddenly, you'll come upon a sign: "Souvenirs . . . Remember" (in Spanish). And you will.

At the **Casa de Juntas,** the principal attraction in the town is a display of the history of Guernica, but no exhibits of the Civil War destruction. Outside are the remains of the ancient tree, around which the Basque rulers gathered for centuries for their communal meetings. The specific symbol of Basque independence was not uprooted by the bombs.

If you are there for lunch, I'd recommend **Arrien,** 2 El Ferial (tel. 685-10-07), which was bombed out and subsequently rebuilt. Even today, the old guard, some of whom wear Gudari emblems in their lapels, symbol of the Basque republic, play cards and drink wine in the place before lunch or dinner tables fill up with hungry guests drawn to its Basque cookery. Full, hearty meals range in price from 750 pesetas ($7.20) to 1400 pesetas ($13.44).

On the way back to San Sebastián, try to make this stopover on the Cantabrian coast:

Ondarroa

This little fishing village is considered by some to be one of the most attractive in Spain. Although there are many contenders for that title, Ondarroa is certainly in the final competition. It has a snug harbor, a fishing fleet, balconied houses draped with hanging plants and vivid laundry. The people look as if they are waiting for the movie cameras to roll.

After San Sebastián, we leave the Basque country and head west for Old Castile.

3. Santander

This Atlantic Coast capital is a summer festival. It is not only one of the most popular resort cities in Spain, but one of the most modern. Yet Santander is ancient. In the early '40s a fire swept over the city, destroying its old quarter and most of its colorful dwellings. The industrious people rebuilt along sane lines, and what greets the visitor is a sparkling area of wide boulevards, a promenade along the waterfront, sidewalk cafés, new buildings, shops, restaurants, and good hotels.

Santander plays host to an international **Music and Dance Festival** in August that is considered one of the most important artistic events in Spain (hotel bookings are most difficult then). At times this festival coincides with religious celebrations honoring Santiago, the patron saint of Spain.

Santander is an education center in summer, as well. Courses are presented at the once-royal palace, now the Menéndez Pelayo International University. Students and teachers from all over America, Canada, and Europe come here to study and visit.

In addition, Santander is a fit base for the sportsman. There's wild game up in the surrounding hills, and the fishing is good.

On the Cantabrian bay, this Castilian city is an important seaport, and has a prosperous commercial and industrial section.

But most visitors head for **El Sardinero,** less than a mile and a half from the city. This resort section resembles many East Coast, U.S.A., beach towns that grew up in the '20s. Besides its hotels and restaurants, Santander has three beaches, **Playa de Castañeda, Playa del Sardinero,** and **Playa de la Concha.** Under candy-striped umbrellas, you'll find the beauties and the beasts. Buses and trolleys make the short run between the heart of Santander and El Sardinero both day and night.

If these beaches get too crowded, you can take a little boat to **El Puntal** beach. The trip lasts about 15 minutes. El Puntal is a beautiful beach and is not crowded, even in August.

Those who don't like crowds *and* beaches should go up to the lighthouse, about two kilometers from El Sardinero beach. Views are spectacular, and there's a restaurant serving indoor and outdoor snacks. Here you can take a walk along the tops of the green cliffs, or loll in the lush grass.

WHERE TO STAY: Santander is loaded with bargains, ranging from its year-round hotels in the city itself to summer villas at El Sardinero. But the early bird who writes in advance gets the room.

In the Town

Hotel Rex, 9 Avenida de Calvo Sotelo (tel. 21-02-00), is considered one of the best hotels in Santander. This seven-story, most respectable establishment was built at the turn of the century when hotels were known for their lavish comfort. Its large, recently modernized doubles with private baths rent for 2400 pesetas ($23.04) to 3200 pesetas ($30.72), singles with bath peak at 2400 pesetas ($23.04), and rooms with showers rent for even less. A continental breakfast is an extra 200 pesetas ($1.92). The pleasant, oak-paneled lounge has comfortable groups of armchairs and couches—and Victorians will like those special antimacassars. The Rex is a year-round favorite.

At El Sardinero

Hotel Roma, 5 Avenida de los Hoteles (tel. 27-27-00), stands in the heart of El Sardinero; it's an old mansion in the shadow of the once-grand Casino. This turn-of-the-century hotel, open from June through September, was built when life at Santander was lived on a much grander scale. Many of the classic features remain—the crystal chandeliers, the great central staircase. But when we look closely at this "birthday cake," we see that the Roma has skimped on the icing. The room furnishings are strictly utilitarian, although clean and comfortable. The most expensive doubles—with private baths—cost from 2800 pesetas ($26.88). However, a number of the doubles contain showers (no toilets) and rent for 2400 pesetas ($23.04). Only a few singles are available, at a top price of 2000 pesetas ($19.20). Breakfast is the only meal. Guests can play tennis and enjoy the garden.

The **Hotel París,** 6 Avenida de los Hoteles (tel. 27-23-50), is a soul sister to the Roma. Sitting side-by-side on this hotel street, both were built at the same time and both have old-fashioned appurtenances, the Paris a bit more so than the Roma. But the summer mansion, despite its clutter, has many once-opulent bedrooms. The best have front windows overlooking the Plaza de Italia. The hotel is open from June through September. The most expensive doubles—those with private baths—rent for 2000 pesetas ($19.20). Most doubles, however, contain showers (no toilets), and cost 1500 pesetas ($14.40) a night. A continental breakfast is an additional 150 pesetas ($1.44).

WHERE TO EAT: For the most part, visitors to Santander eat at their hotels or pensions, which—without a doubt—give better value for the money, and often more efficient service than any of the city's restaurants. However, to vary the hotel dining, a group of budget restaurants has been found in modern Santander, the best of which follow:

The **Bodega Cigaleña,** 19 Daoiz y Velarde (tel. 21-30-62), is a Castilian taverna in the center of the city that dishes up the most typical of regional cuisine in a rustic backdrop—hanging hams, large wine kegs, provincial tables. What more could you ask? Popular with the young set of Santander, it serves a special 800-peseta ($7.68) menú del día from noon to 4 p.m. and from 7 p.m. till midnight. The bodega changes its set menu every day so you can come often. A sample meal: sopa de pescado (fish soup), followed by shellfish paella, the fruit of the season, bread, and wine. The Cigaleña is also an ideal stopover on your bodega-hopping circuit, offering a good choice of wines from an old Castilian town near Valladolid. Ask to see its Museo de Vino.

Jauja, 3 Medio, is one of the best bargains in town. In a simple dining room you can order a set menu for 425 pesetas ($4.08), or a large portion of paella for 225 pesetas ($2.16). The paella is brought in a steaming dish, and there's almost enough for two. Salads and meats here are okay, and the service is friendly and efficient. Patronized mostly by local families, the Jauja still serves food in the traditional unhurried manner.

In the evening, for a change of pace, walk or take a taxi to the fishing port, where three or four outdoor restaurants specialize in grilled sardines and other freshly caught seafood. Across the street fishermen are mending their nets. It's all part of the local color. On my last visit I had an excellent meal in **Los Peñucas,** Barrio Pesquero, where a set menu costs 450 pesetas ($4.32); special paella, 325 pesetas ($3.12); sardines, 150 pesetas ($1.44). Service is slow, but then who's in a hurry?

El Recreo, 2 Somorrostro, is right behind the main post office. The decor is simple, and you can get a fairly good meal for 500 pesetas ($4.80), featuring a fish soup, hake, or veal steak with potatoes, fruit, bread, and wine.

Those content with a snack or a triple-decker club sandwich should head for the Paseo de Pareda lined with cafeterías, most of which place chairs and tables outdoors in the summer months. At the **Cafetería Taverna Dover,** 13 Paseo de Pareda (tel. 22-20-20), for example, you can order combination dishes at the counter for 325 pesetas ($3.12) to 450 pesetas ($4.32). The special Dover sandwich, a triple-decker containing ham, egg, bacon, tomato, lettuce, and mayonnaise, costs 250 pesetas ($2.40) at the counter.

EL SARDINERO NIGHTLIFE: **Beneales, Club 501,** 43 Avenida Los Castros, is for rock. It is the smartest club in El Sardinero. Nighttimers, a young crowd usually, dance to the latest international records, but during high season a live combo is imported—occasionally from the New World. The club is open from 7 p.m. till 2 a.m., and charges an entrance fee of 450 pesetas ($4.32) for men, 250 pesetas ($2.40) for women. Once inside, the price of a local whisky is 275 pesetas ($2.64).

4. Santillana del Mar and the Caves of Altamira

This medieval village, considered by some to be the most perfectly preserved in Europe, lies about 18 miles southwest of Santander. Santillana is the home of one of the best known of the government-run paradors, the mansion of Gil Blas, named after the legendary rogue dear to the Spanish heart.

This sleepy little village of aristocratic mansions is a National Monument. That means that nothing can be changed, and who would want to?

If you have at least a night for Santillana, walk through its moonlit, rough, cobblestone streets, strolling back to a time when people concerned themselves with such phenomena as heretics and infidels—and Hell, Purgatory, and Paradise were more than just a poem to the villagers.

In the morning, you may see men hitching up oxen to their carts, or women washing their clothes in the stream, just as their ancestors did generations before them. But if you start to photograph them, you'll find that they are more sophisticated than their great-grandmothers. They'll usually stop scrubbing and start adjusting their dishevelled coiffures.

Even the most confirmed atheist can usually find a good word to say about the splendidly designed Romanesque **Collegiate Church,** with its decaying but lovely cloisters. In the center is the tomb of the patron saint of the village, **Juliana.** The 800-year-old cathedral holds the same rank as Westminster Abbey, and contains 1000-year-old documents and such gems as a 17th-century Mexican silver altarpiece.

In addition, I'd suggest a visit to the rich art collection gathered in the **Convent of the Poor Clares,** a restored 400-year-old monastery. A Madrid art professor inspired some two dozen nuns to collect and restore religious paintings and statues either damaged or abandoned during the Spanish Civil War. The collection is constantly growing.

Santillana Zoo is about one kilometer on the road to the Altamira Caves. So far it has limited itself solely to fauna found in Spain (wolves, foxes, reptiles, and birds). It's open from June to September. Entrance is 100 pesetas (96¢) for adults, 60 pesetas (58¢) for children 5 to 12 years old. Movie cameras are assessed an extra 25 pesetas (24¢); parking is 25 pesetas also; and the "Museum of Zoology" is another 25 pesetas. Daily hours are from 10 a.m. to 8 p.m.

LIVING IN A PALACE: The **Parador Nacional Gil Blas,** 11 Plaza de Ramón Pelayo (tel. 81-80-00). The Middle Ages are revived in this 400-year-old palace. A heavy nail-studded doorway opens onto a front gallery lounge, elegantly informal. Guests are assigned rooms here (some with views of the garden), then they are taken up an ancient stairway to the timber-ceilinged upper hall. Large pictures of knights in armor hang in this gallery. The hand-hewn plank floor, the time-aged brass chandeliers, the two refectory tables with bowls of fresh flowers, do their part to create the mood.

Large iron keys are used to open the doors leading to the suites. Most of the bedrooms are unusually large, and most have windows on two sides. Old furniture, dark with centuries of use, is combined with comfortable twin beds that have been reproduced in the old style. When the shutters are closed and the red velvet draperies are drawn, this medieval masquerade is complete. The cost? 3900 pesetas ($37.44) for two persons, 3120 pesetas ($29.95) for the most expensive single. In addition, 18 bathless doubles are offered in the annex at a cost of 1850 pesetas ($17.76). The baths are half the size of the bedrooms, it seems, and they contain all sorts of built-in conveniences. White, freshly laundered terry-cloth dressing robes are provided. *Note:* The third-floor rooms get thumbs down from readers. One wrote that they "must have been for the servants originally, as they are the smallest double rooms possible."

Four-course evening meals and luncheons are served in the great dining hall. The price? A set meal for 950 pesetas ($9.12). The palace is "fit for a king." Juan Carlos was known to stop here before he became king.

Alternate Choices

Hotel Altamira, 1 Cantón (tel. 81-80-25), is a two-star hotel, managed by David Oceja Bujan near the Gil Blas that offers another opportunity for a visitor to meet the past. This small palace, built about 400 years ago, is not as great as the government-run parador, but it holds its own, picking up the overflow. Open from March through December, the Altamira charges low rates for its double rooms with private baths—1950 pesetas ($18.72). You can get a complete meal here for 1000 pesetas ($9.60) even if you aren't staying over. The hotel's restaurant, seating 300 persons, is decorated in the Castilian style. A continental breakfast at 150 pesetas ($1.44) is obligatory. Lunch or dinner costs 500 pesetas ($4.80). The Altamira is in the center of the village. It is entered through a front garden and is enclosed behind a high stone wall, locked away in the past.

Not quite so charming as the Altamira, but more modern and comfortable, is the nearby **Los Infantes,** Avenida Le Dorat, on the main road leading into the village (tel. 81-81-00). This three-star hotel, opened in 1974, features 17 doubles, plus three singles. The Infantes has successfully kept the old flavor of Santillana in its interior decorations. There are beamed ceilings, pretty lounges, tapestries, antiques, clocks, and paintings. The rooms are pleasant and simple, with wall-to-wall carpeting, telephones, and Muzak. Two have small balconies. Doubles with baths cost 2400 pesetas ($23.04) to 3000 pesetas ($28.80); singles with baths, 2200 pesetas ($21.12). A continental breakfast is an extra 200 pesetas ($1.92) per person.

About the only other accommodations are two small hostals off the main road leading into the village, both of them private, two-story houses. The **Hostal-Residencia Emperador,** 12 Avenida Le Dorat (tel. 81-80-54), has only three rooms, all of them simply furnished doubles. The staff is courteous and polite, and the hospitality, for such a modest place, is gracious. The highest tariffs are charged from June 15 to September 1. At those times, the double rooms rent for 1950 pesetas ($18.72) per day, dropping to just 1600 pesetas ($15.36) during the rest of the year.

The **Hostal Le Dorat,** 28 Avenida Le Dorat (tel. 81-81-74), has six doubles, without baths, which go for 1400 pesetas ($13.44) to 1600 pesetas ($15.36). A continental breakfast is an extra 125 pesetas ($1.20). Both hostals are a five-minute walk from the center of the village.

WHERE TO EAT: Aside from eating in the parador or the Altamira Hotel, you can opt for the budget **Hostal Santillana** (now a restaurant only), on the main road on the corner El Cruce (tel. 81-80-11), which has a set meal for 525 pesetas ($5.04), including a soup or salad, ham or asparagus omelet, roast veal or pork, dessert, and bread. Items that appear on most Spanish menus are prominently featured here. Specialties such as paella, hake, and roast lamb range in price from 250 pesetas ($2.40) to 600 pesetas ($5.76).

Santillana is tiny, yet it has long had a "whisky club," called **Los Blasones,** Plaza de la Gandara (tel. 81-80-70), a kind of bar-cum-restaurant where some of the local youths hang out. There's a dimly lit ambience in winter months. In summer the two-fork restaurant offers a set meal for 750 pesetas ($7.20). Barbecue specialties from the grill are also featured. Los Blasones is off the Calle del Cantón. The same establishment runs a disco, open from about 5 till 11:30 p.m. (in summer till 1 a.m.), where drinks cost 300 pesetas ($2.88).

Near Blasones is a newly constructed teashop, **El Jardín,** where you can order coffee, tea, or snacks, while enjoying recorded classical music.

If you want a small snack, go down to the Collegiate Church. Outside, two women have been selling fresh milk and biscuits for the last 16 years (at least). They are always extremely friendly.

You can get to Santillana from Santander by a direct bus that leaves the Plaza Estaciones in Santander at 11:50 a.m. and 7 p.m. and returns from Santillana at 8:30 a.m. and 3:30 p.m.

Another way to go is to take the train from Santander to Torrelavega (about six trains a day), and then catch the bus from Torrelavega to Santillana. It leaves about every half hour.

From Santillana del Mar, be sure to make an important side trip to:

THE CAVES OF ALTAMIRA: About a mile and a half from Santillana del Mar are the subterranean caves of Altamira (now closed to the public), whose prehistoric paintings go back to the twilight when men clad in animal skins were emerging from the Ice Age. These drawings are one of Spain's greatest artistic treasures. They have been called the "Sistine Chapel" of prehistoric art.

Here on the ceiling of a cave, undetected by the world until the latter part of the 19th century, bisons, boars, and horses are captured in the most vivid of reds, the darkest of blacks—the colors of Spain itself.

It took a long time for the world to accept the authenticity of the Altamira drawings, but once that was done, scholars, laymen, and the idly curious flocked to these grottoes, which provide a fragile link to our remote ancestors.

In fact, they flocked in such great numbers that the public caused severe damage to these long-hidden caves. Modern bacteria are the culprit. Like the celebrated Lascaux grotto in France, Altamira is still viewed by only about a dozen visitors a day, and these are by invitation only (archeologists and such).

If you're in the area, you'll have to settle for going through a little museum at the site. There you can see reproductions of the artwork in the caves and buy color slides which show the subtleties in some of the caveman colors—rich vermillion, magenta, ochre. You'll also see pictures of what that bacteria did to these priceless paintings.

5. Oviedo

Oviedo is the capital of the province of Asturias on the north coast of Spain, a land with the largest coalfields in the country. Bathed by the Bay of Biscay, the old kingdom of Asturias—later a principality—is officially tabbed the province of Oviedo today. It is the Wales of Spain. Yet Oviedo, in spite of its concentrated industry and mining areas, contains some of the most unspoiled scenery in "Green Spain."

Asturias, as you may remember, was the Christian resistance to the Moslem invaders who took Andalusia. The Cantabrian mountains run right through Asturias, and, while based at the capital of Oviedo, you can strike out for excursions in many directions, although you are likely to get rained on. Oviedo lies 16 miles from the coast, and is very pleasant in summer when much of Spain is unbearably hot.

Damaged heavily in the Civil War, Oviedo is a modern city, but it contains sections with historical and artistic monuments. Chief of these is the **cathedral,** a Gothic building begun in 1348 and completed at the end of the 15th century. Its one spire dates from 1556. Inside is an altarpiece in the florid Gothic style, as are the cloisters which date from the 14th and 15th centuries. Hours are from 9 a.m. to 1 p.m. and 3:30 to 6 p.m.

The cathedral's **La Camara Santa** (Holy Chamber) is famous, dating from the 12th century, although much restored. Containing two chapels, the Holy Chamber possesses the celebrated cross of Don Pelayo, the cross of the victory, and that of the angels, the finest specimens of Asturian art in the world. Its hours are from 9:30 to 10:30 a.m., from 11 a.m. to noon, and from 4 to 6 p.m., charging 50 pesetas (48¢) for admission.

The **Museum and Cloister of San Vicente,** on Calle San Vicente, belongs to a former Benedictine convent. Most of it is from the 18th century, although sections date from the 16th century. Today it houses a fine arts museum, with several interesting exhibitions of archeological interest. See, in particular, the series of Romanesque and Gothic sepulchres. Hours are from 9 a.m. to noon and 4 to 6 p.m. (on Sunday noon to 2 p.m.). No admission is charged.

In hotels, I'd suggest the **España,** 2 Jovellanos (tel. 22-05-96), which stands in the center of town, right near the cathedral. A good-size commercial hotel, with 106 well-furnished bedrooms, it rents out singles for 2000 pesetas ($19.20), doubles for 2500 pesetas ($24). A continental breakfast at 160 pesetas ($1.54) is the only meal served here.

For real Asturian cookery, I'd recommend **Casa Fermín,** 23 Avenida del Cristo (tel. 23-99-50). The chef here is the best in town. To order the most classic dish of the former principality, ask for fabada asturiana, which is a bean dish with Asturian black pudding and Áviles ham. He also prepares a tasty hake cooked in cider, the most characteristic drink of the province. In season (from October to March) venison is the specialty. Try also the traditional Cabrales cheese of the province. Expect to pay from 1400 pesetas ($13.44) to 2000 pesetas ($19.20) for one of the finest regional repasts in the province.

Motorists going on to La Coruña and Santiago de Compostela may want to anchor for the night in a little town, Cornellana (Salas), 24 miles from Orviedo. There the **Hostal La Fuente** (tel. 83-40-35) welcomes you to a nice little inn with more than a dozen rooms. As a thoughtful touch, the sheets and pillow cases are trimmed with embroidery. One person pays 650 pesetas ($6.24), a double going for 750 pesetas ($7.20). There's a sitting room on each floor, as well as a bath. Attached is a dining room overlooking a garden, serving a menú del día for 500 pesetas ($4.80). For that, you get three courses of attractively served good food, along with bread and wine. The place is family operated.

6. La Coruña

La Coruña, jutting out on a peninsula, is the Neptune of Spain. This capital of an Atlantic maritime province looks to the sea for much of its livelihood. Yachts, fishing boats, and transatlantic liners vie for space in the harbor. But that's not all that makes the god of the sea claim La Coruña. The government tourist pamphlet, in trying to apologize for the amount of rainfall, says that the port experiences "many days of cloudless skies." That's true, of course.

This city, with its excellent beaches, is expanding rapidly as a summer tourist resort. In July and August, its population swells tremendously. **Riazor,** a good, fairly wide beach, is right in town, but the best one is called **Santa Cristina,** which is about three miles on the outskirts. There is regular bus service to and from it (the ideal way to go is on a little steamer plying across the bay).

La Coruña (known as Corunna to the English) goes back into ancient history, but, surprisingly, does not have a wealth of historical and architectural monuments, as Santiago de Compostela does. The port was known to the Celts and Phoenicians, and was conquered by the Romans.

It is, as mentioned, another of the legendary cities that points to Hercules as its founder. The city's major monument is the **Tower of Hercules,** a lighthouse more than a mile from the center of La Coruña. It overlooks the city and the sea, and was believed to have been built by the emperor Trajan (restored in the 1700s). But the great event in the history of La Coruña occurred in 1588 when the not-so "Invincible Armada" sailed from here to England. The following year, Sir Francis Drake and his ships attacked the port in reprisal.

About 375 miles from Madrid, La Coruña consists of an old and new town, in addition to some fast-developing modern outskirts. The old town is ideal for walks. It has a number of historic churches and mansions. Dividing these two towns is the Plaza de María Pita. This landmark was named after the 16th-century Spanish heroine who is probably unknown to many foreigners, but to the gallegos she is Joan of Arc. María Pita is famous for her courage and bravery during Drake's reprisal attack against her city.

From Madrid, La Coruña is best reached by rail, a distance of 467 miles on the tracks (via Orense and Zamora). There is daily express service from Madrid.

If a visitor is going on to La Coruña after a stopover in Santiago de Compostela, there is a daily bus service leaving Santiago, traveling the 46-mile run.

FOOD AND LODGING: You might as well stay on the beach. **Residencia Riazor,** Andeen de Riazor (tel. 25-34-00), has been known to me since it first opened its doors in 1963. At that time it started a trend in hotel building of leaving the heart of town and going to the beach, making it possible for guests to arrive, check into their streamlined bedrooms, change into their swimsuits, and hit the beach—all in 20 minutes. The tall, modern establishment charges 2500 pesetas ($24) to 2900 pesetas ($27.84) in a spacious double with private bath, 1700 pesetas ($16.32) in a single, also with private bath. A continental breakfast is an extra 200 pesetas ($1.92). The residencia rises 12 stories, with an all-glass living lounge on the second floor. It perhaps takes spacious modern a bit too seriously. The lounge seems half furnished, but the existing fixtures are comfortable. The bedroom decor and equipment are a bit reminiscent of Florida early-motel design. There is a snackbar-cafetería on the premises, but no major restaurant. The friendly employees speak a lilting Spanish with a Galician accent.

In the very heart of La Coruña, two or three blocks from the water, are several restaurants specializing in the Galician cuisine. It is customary to go window shopping for food here. The restaurants along two of the principal streets—**Calle de la Estrella** and **Calle de los Olmos**—have display counters in front of their establishments. Most of them charge comparable prices.

My favorite is **El Coral**, 15 Calle de la Estrella (tel. 22-10-82), one of the most popular restaurants at the port. Cesar Gallego Pita has been around running the place since it opened back in 1954. Galician cookery is prepared with distinction here. A two-fork restaurant, El Coral specializes in shellfish, fish, meats, and Galician wines. The chef's specialty is turbante de mariscos (shellfish). Try also the stuffed squid (calamares rellenos). My favorite main course is lubina (a large, boneless fish) al horno straight from the oven. The dessert specialty is a rich and fattening "filloas." A pitcher (one liter) of Ribero wine goes for 195 pesetas ($1.87), and you can also order Condados and Riojas wines. For a full dinner, expect to spend from 1500 pesetas ($14.40), especially if you order the more expensive shellfish dishes. The service is polite and friendly, and the standard of cleanliness is high. The restaurant is closed on Sunday night (except in summer), and it's suggested that you reserve a table.

In the center of town, within an easy walk of the Playa del Orzan, **Naveiro**, 129 San Andre (tel. 22-90-24), is perhaps the most typically Galician restaurant in the port. In a regional, rustic setting, this well-patronized restaurant offers inexpensive but tasty Galician specialties. It serves the classic green and white soup of the northwest, known as caldo gallego (potatoes and greens). But hake, that good-tasting old standby, is prepared differently in La Coruña. Here it's usually served with peppers and potatoes. Spider crabs and oysters are other popular dishes, and octopus is occasionally featured, but if that's too exotic, you can order red mullet. A small beefsteak is offered to those who've had their fill of the sea. Dinners range from 1000 pesetas ($9.60) to 1800 pesetas ($17.28). The restaurant is closed on Sunday.

7. Santiago de Compostela

All roads in Spain used to lead to this northwestern granite city that has survived intact from the Middle Ages. The tomb of the beheaded apostle, St. James, was the end of the Milky Way for the faithful medieval pilgrim—both peasant and prince—who journeyed here from all over Europe, often under the most adverse of conditions.

These wanderers risked their lives, their money, and often their virginity, to pay homage to Santiago, the patron saint of Spain. At the same time, these pilgrims brought culture and learning, especially in the area of architecture, where their Romanesque influence has had a profound effect on the skylines of Spain.

Along the pilgrims' way, hospitals, hospices, and sanctuaries—many of which are still preserved—were established. Across the Pyrenees, through Navarre and León, came this never-ending stream. The pilgrimages grew so important that a guidebook, the first of the Middle Ages, was written, giving sage advice. Bits of advice: (1) The water in Solares, it seemed, was clear and sparkling—perfectly safe to drink. (2) Beware of the robbers in Asturias.

Santiago de Compostela's link with legend began in A.D. 813 when an urn was discovered mystically one starlit night. It contained what was believed to be the remains of St. James. A temple was erected over the spot, but the poor saint wasn't allowed to remain in peace. Wars, and specifically the arrival of vengeance-seeking Drake from England, necessitated removal. After a long and mysterious disappearance, the remains were later "rediscovered" and transferred back to Santiago, where whatever is resting in that silver box in the crypt of the cathedral has been "authenticated."

In addition to being the third Holy City of the Christian world, Santiago de Compostela is a university town and marketplace for gallego farmers.

It has the dubious distinction of being the rainiest city in Spain. But one can always slip under a pillared arcade—that is, unless a victim happens to be caught standing in a large plaza. The rainfalls arrive uninvited and unannounced, then take sudden leave. But they leave the ancient buildings glistening like silver. The fading sun comes out, cutting through the slight steaming mist with orange spears—and Santiago is bathed in an enchantment that must have inspired Isabella or perhaps Philip II centuries ago.

Santiago de Compostela, with its flagstone streets, churches, and shrines, is one of the most romantic and historical of Spain's great cities. The government has declared it a sacred cow architecturally, so the chances are that it will remain this way. By all means, see Santiago at dusk. The rusty-colored roofs of its moss-patched stone buildings contrast dramatically with the rich Celtic greens of the surrounding valleys and mountains. In all, the town is a Romanesque and baroque fantasy.

Santiago can be reached from Madrid by air, car, or rail. It lies about 391 miles from the Spanish capital.

Iberia has daily flights between Madrid and Santiago, as well as daily return flights from Santiago to Madrid. Santiago is easily reached from La Coruña, 39 miles away. There are daily trains from La Coruña to Santiago.

THE SIGHTS: When most visitors arrive, they head first for:

The Cathedral

This great structure, begun in the 11th century, is considered by some to be the crowning achievement of Spanish Romanesque, the heart and soul of the Jerusalem of the West for the faithful pilgrim. Today, it is still the most revered architectural site in all of northwestern Spain.

In the center of Santiago, opening onto a great plaza, the cathedral has seen a number of architects since the 11th century. Each new designer brought his own interpretation to the facades, the retables, the chapels, as well as the style of his age. Consequently, plateresque and Renaissance waltz with Gothic, Galician baroque plays leapfrog with Romanesque.

As mentioned, a silver urn in the crypt, which may be visited, contains what is believed to be the remains of the Apostle St. James. However, the glory of the cathedral does not rest on even so illustrious a tenant.

The cathedral has a number of spectacular architectural features, the most notable of which is called the Pórtico de la Gloria. Carved by Mateo in the late 12th century, this portico houses brilliantly conceived and characterized sculpture, considered the finest produced in Europe during the entire 1100s. The floor plan of the cathedral resembles a cross; it has three naves, as well as an abundance of chapels and cloisters. In the 1700s, the cathedral acquired one of its most splendid facades, known as Obradoiro.

This Santiago landmark has the most extraordinary altar of all the major cathedrals of Spain, harmoniously blending Gothic simplicity with a baroque decor.

Don't be surprised to encounter pilgrims embracing a statue and asking for help, or inserting their fingers into openings in the "Tree of Life" for protection, or touching their heads against a stone figure three times for intelligence.

The cathedral may be visited all day. However, to see the tapestries and archeological remains in the museum, a charge of 75 pesetas (72¢) is assessed; the museum is open from 10 a.m. to 1:30 p.m. and 3:30 to 7:30 p.m.

Adjoining the cathedral is the **Palacio de Gelmírez,** an archbishop's palace built in the 12th century, a most outstanding example of Romanesque. It may be visited from 10 a.m. to 1:30 p.m. and 3:30 to 7:30 p.m. for a 25-peseta (24¢) admission fee.

Hostal de los Reyes Católicos

Founded by Ferdinand and Isabella at the dawn of the 16th century, this former hospital has been turned into one of the most spectacular hotels of Europe. Once it was a refuge for pilgrims visiting the tomb of St. James.

This hotel on the Plaza de España (tel. 58-22-00) is seen at some point by most visitors to Santiago who pass through its dazzling Renaissance entranceway, seeking accommodations, meals, or drinks. Casual sightseers should announce themselves at the desk.

The hotel has four huge open-air courtyards, each with its own covered walk, trees, gardens, or fountain. In addition, there are chapels, libraries, great halls, grillwork from France, and paintings (Goya, El Greco). Antiques greet the visitor at every turn. The Gothic chapel has been adapted to form the setting for weekly concerts. Imagine going in after dinner to hear the artistry of Montoya.

There is a full range of accommodations, everything from Franco's former suite to monk-like dormitories. The suites, done in original styles, often have canopied beds with ornate crests, draped in embroidered red velvet. Hand-carved chests, gilt mirrors, and oil paintings enhance the luxury. The sumptuous, palace-like double rooms with private baths start at 6500 pesetas ($62.40). Singles with bath go for 3000 pesetas ($28.80). Each meal here runs to 1700 pesetas ($16.32).

STAYING OVER: It would be ideal if one could afford the luxury of the 16th-century former hospital, but if that's not possible, Santiago has other comfortable, but less expensive establishments. In descending scale, they are:

Hotel Compostela, 1 Calvo Sotelo (tel. 58-57-00), has long been considered the grand old lady of hotels in this section. Built of native gray stone, this corner hotel has been the center for many of the elegant social events for years. It charges 3100 pesetas ($29.76) for the best doubles with private baths. Singles with baths cost 2200 pesetas ($21.12). The Compostela was recently enlarged, so that it now has a total of 96 rooms. Inside you'll find a carved oak staircase in the central hall, with its hand-woven carpet, as well as many salons with old-style furniture. Everywhere are huge chandeliers, oil paintings, and tapestries, and a central glass-covered patio with arches that make it reminiscent of a monastery courtyard. The formal banquet room, with its French mahogany chairs and rows of Corinthian columns, makes an impressive background for meals.

Hotel del Peregrino, Avenida de Rosalía de Castro (tel. 59-18-50), a three-star hotel, is at the edge of town, off the main road, and, although not a budget hotel, is still preferred by many readers traveling to this remote part of Spain. It has a long gallery lounge opening onto its rear garden, with centered swimming pool. Restrained furnishings and textured upholstery—all has been tastefully selected. The fresh, modern, and well-furnished double accommodations with private baths rent for 3500 pesetas ($33.60) nightly for those who can afford to spend this much. Singles with bath cost 2100 pesetas ($20.16). A continental breakfast is another 250 pesetas ($2.40) per person.

Gelmírez, 92 Calvo Sotelo (tel. 59-11-00), is a modern, central hotel which rents double rooms with baths for 2500 pesetas ($24), and singles with showers for 1700 pesetas ($16.32). No meals are served here except a continental breakfast costing 175 pesetas ($1.68).

Hostal La Senra, 1 General Mola (tel. 59-29-46), is a spotlessly clean, little seven-bedroom boarding house that is very comfortable. It's nicely situated, lying about a five-minute walk from the cathedral and near several main streets of sightseeing interest. The rate charged is about 800 pesetas ($7.68) per person in a room with hot and cold running water.

WHERE TO EAT: The **Restaurant Alameda,** 15 Avenida de Figuero (tel. 58-47-96), is a second-story, two-fork restaurant, at the beginning of a tree-lined avenue. The constant stream of diners, both foreign and domestic, attest to its continued popularity. For 950 pesetas ($9.12), a complete meal is served, including many of the specialties for which Galicia is well known. The caldo gallego is a Galician broth that starts most meals. Americans, from the southern states in particular, may be lured by lacón con grelos, one of the most popular regional dishes of the northwest—hamhock cooked with greens. If more elegant fare is the order of the day, then the fresh fish dishes are reliable. Try the necoras (spider crabs), a real gourmet's delight. There is a cafetería-snackbar on the ground floor, handy for light meals and drinks. Guests sit at sidewalk tables.

Restaurante "El Caserío," 13 Bautizados (tel. 58-59-80), is one of the best of the seafood restaurants of Santiago, but it's expensive. The decor is modern, and the location is near the Alameda. The main seafood specialties are usually sold by weight. Featured are spiny lobsters, spider crabs, barnacles, shrimps, prawns, and scallops. Galician soup starts most meals, followed by Galician hake, or perhaps the already mentioned lacón with grelos. Desserts include natural yogurt. If you order à la carte, your tab is likely to range from 1200 pesetas ($11.52) to 1800 pesetas ($17.28). Service is until midnight.

8. Pontevedra

This is an old aristocratic Spanish city, on the Lérez River. The capital of a province by the same name, Pontevedra makes for an interesting stopover, as the government has installed a parador in one of the city's oldest palaces. Visitors can see the remains of the wall that once encircled the town.

Santa María Church, in plateresque, with its avocado-green patina, is the most visited architectural sight. But try to see the beautiful Town Hall Square as well. In the old quarter of Pontevedra, you will discover many stone buildings with green trim.

This provincial Galician town is some 36 miles from Santiago de Compostela, and 521 miles from Madrid. It is often visited by the Portuguese, who cross over the nearby border for short excursions.

LIVING IN A 16TH-CENTURY PALACE: The **Parador Nacional,** Casa del Barón (tel. 85-58-80), is a well-kept 16th-century palace, which the Spanish government has preserved and transformed into an excellent parador. Guests are offered an opportunity to live like landed barons, even better, as modern plumbing and central heating have been installed. The hotel contains 27 rooms which accommodate a total of 51 guests.

Off the entrance hallway is a courtyard dominated by a large old stone staircase, leading to the rooms upstairs. The inside has been maintained very much as the old *pazo* (manor house) must have looked. It includes a quaint old kitchen or *lar* (literally "hearth"), which is typical of Galician country houses, furnished and decorated with characteristic items. The accommodations are large enough to have sitting arrangements; the beds are comfortable; and the furnishings attractive. Many of the rooms have views of the walled-in, formal garden. The cost is 3900 pesetas ($37.44) for a double with private bath, 3100 pesetas ($29.76) for a single with private bath. Both luncheons and dinners are 950 pesetas ($9.12). And almost any appetizer, such as a casserole of shrimp with tomato sauce, is delicious. The cake of the day is usually moist and delicate. The cooking is good, and the waitresses are friendly. The parador is in the old quarter of Pontevedra, ideal for exploring.

9. Vigo

If you continue south from Pontevedra (there are numerous buses every day), you arrive at Vigo, a distance of only 17 miles.

Vigo is a modern city, its harbor one of the most important in Spain, forming a natural amphitheater. The harbor is known for its sardine fishing fleet, and many of Vigo's inhabitants who live in white granite houses are employed in the canned-food industry.

The setting is outstandingly beautiful, the harbor surrounded by ridges, two of which are crowned by obsolete fortresses. From one of these pinnacles, the **Castillo del Castro** at 400 feet, a magnificent view of the city and the estuary unfolds before you.

The **Isles de Cies** (the ancient Insulae Siccae), a rocky archipelago at the entrance of the bay, act as a breakwater to the Atlantic, providing shelter and a handsome background for Vigo, particularly at sunset. You can take a boat tour to these islands. Sir Francis Drake did when he captured Vigo—once in 1585, again in 1589. In 1719 Vigo was once again captured by the British.

The old fishing village, the **Berbes Quarter,** bordering the bight of San Francisco, is unusual and makes for a pleasant stroll along with milling sailors, who are likely to be in town for the night while stationed on a Dutch, French, German, or British vessel.

The fish is unloaded at 11 p.m., and the bustling activity is best viewed then; however, if you're an early riser, you can go there at 7 a.m. when the wholesale merchants come down to purchase the catch from the night before.

The **Samil and Canido beaches** are easily reached by bus, about a 15-minute ride from the city.

FOOD AND LODGING: One of the most recommendable establishments in port, in terms of a bargain, is the **Estoril,** 12 Lepanto (tel. 21-56-28), which provides 48 beds for peseta-watching visitors. It is pleasant and central, and in spite of its elegant name, relatively modest in appointments. However, it is well kept and clean, and the welcome is friendly. Expect a bill of 750 pesetas ($7.20) per person in a room with hot and cold running water.

On the same street, you can dine at the **Restaurante Celta,** 22 Lepanto, which is most reasonable. Of course, seafood dominates on the menu, and it was probably bought fresh that morning. Expect to spend from 500 pesetas ($4.80) for a complete meal, more if you order the expensive shellfish.

READER'S TOURING TIPS: "About 17 miles from Vigo lies the town of **Puenteáreas.** For the Festival of Corpus Christi, the streets of the town are carpeted with flower petals in beautiful designs. Buses from Vigo leave at 7 a.m., and the drive gives you a chance to see the beautiful landscape of Galicia, even if there's no festival going on there when you arrive.

"Along the Ría de Pontevedra there are many lovely beaches and charming villages. **Sangenjo,** which reportedly has one of the best climates in Galicia, is a pleasant town with a good beach. I stayed at the **Hostal Venezuela,** 6 Carlos Casas (tel. 72-00-86), which is about three minutes from the beach. I paid 450 pesetas ($4.32) for a single room with hot and cold running water.

"About a 15-minute walk over a hill (from which you have an impressive view of Sangenjo), you arrive at **Portonovo,** another colorful fishing village with an excellent beach.

"You can continue along the coast road enjoying the scenery, passing by the magnificent beach of **La Lanzada,** five miles in length. You'll arrive at **El Grove,** a summer resort and fishing village renowned for its fine cuisine. There is a shellfish festival held every October.

"The island of **La Toja** has now been joined to the mainland by El Grove. The island is known for its spa waters, and is covered with pine trees and surrounded by some of the finest scenery imaginable in Spain. It is a center for golf, tennis, and water sports. It also has a gambling casino" (Cecily C. Kennedy, Tuam, County Galway, Ireland).

10. Tuy

A frontier town, Tuy stands only a short distance from the historic bridge over the Minho River, linking Spain with Portugal. For motorists coming from Portugal's Valença do Minho, Tuy will be their introduction to Spain.

Its age-old, winding and sloping streets lead up to the **cathedral,** a national artistic treasure dominating the *zona monumentale.* The cathedral-fortress stands like an acropolis, with its turrets and towers. It was built in 1170, although it wasn't used for religious purposes until early in the 13th century. Its principal portal, Ogival, is exceptional. If time remains, you may want to seek out the **Church of San Bartolomé,** which was built in the Romanesque style, and the **Church of Santo Domingo,** a beautiful example of the Gothic style (look for the bas reliefs in the cloister).

Walls which were built over Roman fortifications surround Tuy. In this little provincial town, you'll find one of the finest accommodations in all of the province of Galicia.

Parador Nacional de San Telmo, Avenida de Portugal (tel. 60-03-09), appears almost like a fortress-style hacienda, jutting out on a promontory from the right bank of the Minho. The inn, with its cantilevered roof, was designed to perpetuate the architectural spirit of the province, with an emphasis on local stone and natural woods. The end result is one of elegant austerity, a building which blends perfectly with its landscape. The public rooms are enhanced by brass chandeliers, paintings by well-known gallegos, and antiques interspersed with reproductions. The main living room has a large walk-in fireplace and a tall banjo-shaped grandfather clock, along with hand-knotted rugs, 18th-century paintings, hand-hewn benches, and comfortable armchairs.

The dining room, with its high wooden ceiling, has tall windows, allowing a view of the surrounding hills. You dine in dignity on leather chairs studded with brass. Even if you don't spend the night, you can enjoy the regional cuisine here. The hors d'oeuvres alone consist of almost a dozen little dishes. The fish dishes are excellent, especially (when available) the renowned lampreys, as well as salmon, shad, trout, and succulent baby eels. Homemade cakes are offered for dessert. A complete meal costs 950 pesetas ($9.12).

The bedrooms, 16 in all, are sober but comfortable, overlooking hills and river and a courtyard with a colonnade. The bedrooms are furnished with Castilian-style pieces, costing 2960 pesetas ($28.42) in a single, from 3700 pesetas ($35.52) in a double. The baths and plumbing are modern, with a lavish use of tile. Because of the limited space, reservations are essential.

Chapter XIII

THE BALEARIC ISLANDS

1. Finding a Room in Majorca
2. Sampling the Cuisine
3. Island Attractions
4. Ciudad de Ibiza
5. San Antonio Abad
6. Santa Eulalia del Río
7. Minorca

THE LARGEST OF the Balearic archipelago, **Majorca** (Mallorca in Spanish) is the most touristy of the Mediterranean islands, drawing around 3.5 million visitors yearly. Everybody from Faye Emerson and Mark Stevens to Princess Radziwill flies in to bask in the sun, relax, and enjoy life.

Majorca is boasting proud of its 185-mile coastline. The island is most beautiful, an explorer's paradise. The northern part, with its winding precipitous roads, is mountainous, but the flatlands in the south are agriculturally fertile, devoted to raising olives and almonds. The flat landscape is occasionally broken by windmills.

With its fine beaches, little harbors, hidden mountain villages, and historical sights, the island has much to offer, both to the permanent and transient visitor. The English and Americans alike have settled in, and more are buying either homes or apartments.

But the "Chopin Heights Real Estate Development" is a bit much! (Chopin and his mistress, George Sand, were the legendary vanguard of the tourists to Majorca. They spent a few months on the island in 1838.)

The natives weren't too receptive to foreigners in those days, but with the steady flow of gold into their pockets, they have become tolerant of strange new ways, such as bathing suits that don't tax the imagination.

MAJORCA

PALMA DE MAJORCA: Palma, on the southern part of the island, is the capital of Majorca, and the bustling, boom-town center of most of the hotels, restaurants, and nightlife. It has an interesting old quarter that is encircled by a flood of modern hotels. The ever-increasing new city of wide boulevards, shops, and restaurants is pushing out as its seams.

Palma's prices have been on the upsurge, but dozens of its hotels, restaurants, and pensions are possible on our budget. On a hot day in August, it would

appear that half of the economy-minded Europeans—from Liverpool to Lü-
beck, from Manchester to Munich—have anchored their sun-parched bodies
on the white Majorcan sands.

Swimming is possible from late April through October, when the last of
the Stockholm-Hamburg-London set departs for the cold north and fast-fading
tans. Don't believe the promoters selling that mild weather label in January and
February. It can get downright cold, and you might catch galloping pneumonia
if you plunged into the Mediterranean without a wet suit. Spring and fall can
be heaven-sent, however; and, in summer, the coastal areas are pleasantly
cooled by sea breezes.

The capital city is about 130 miles from Barcelona, and 90 miles from
Valencia. The natives speak Spanish and a language of their own, a dialect of
Catalán called Mallorquín that dates back to the days of the Christian king
Jaime I, who drove out the Moslems in 1229. Majorca has often been the target
of invasions (the Greeks and later the Romans left their calling cards in the old
days). But in spite of its many conquerors, Palma has never seen anything like
the present onslaught.

GETTING THERE: Most visitors head over from either Valencia or Barcelona (the preferred choice) on the mainland. The easiest, most efficient, and
most expensive way to go is by airplane. A slower and cheaper method is by
boat. At certain times of the year, the trip by boat or plane can be pleasant.
But in August, the routes to Palma must surely qualify as the major bottleneck
in Europe. Without advance space already booked, they're murderous, particularly the planes. Be sure you have a return plane ticket if you come in August—
otherwise you may not get off the island till September.

By Boat

The **Compañía Transmediterránea** offers regular ship services between Palma and Barcelona. The booking office in Barcelona is at the headquarter's of the company's agent, Aucona Company, 2 Vía Layetana (tel. 319-82-12). In Palma, the agent is at 5 Muelle Viejo (tel. 22-67-40). Schedules and times of departure must be checked in advance. What appears below is only valid at the time of research and could change dramatically before your actual visit.

The boat usually leaves Barcelona at midnight. There are no sailings on Tuesday. It's a long run, usually arriving in Majorca at 8 a.m. Second-class cabin space is available for two or three persons. The one-way cost per person is 5730 pesetas ($55.01) in a cabin for two, 4400 pesetas ($42.24) in a cabin for three. A less expensive way to go is to rent a deck seat for 2670 pesetas ($25.63). The Barcelona-bound boat leaves Palma at noon. There are no departures on Wednesday. The Transmediterránea also has daily sailings to and from Ibiza and Mahón and less frequent trips to Ciudadela, Cabrera, and Alcudia. It also offers regular ship services to and from the Canary Islands and Morocco.

By Air

Both **Iberia** and **Aviaco** fly to Palma from Barcelona, Valencia, and Madrid. Daily planes are flown between Madrid and Palma, and between Valencia and Palma. But Barcelona is the major gateway to the Balearics, and it has several daily flights in summer—depending on the volume. Even so, the bookings are so tight in August that many prospective visitors to Majorca have to cool their heels at least 24 hours, sometimes more, in Barcelona, waiting for an empty seat. The fare to Palma from Barcelona is from 1800 pesetas ($17.28) to 2000 pesetas ($19.20), depending on the flight.

1. Finding a Room in Majorca

At last count, the island of Majorca had around 1400 hotels and pensions, a staggering number. But hold onto your reservation, for even that quantity is vastly inadequate to meet the demand in summer, particularly August.

If you stand at the hotel-booking desk at the airport, it's quite customary to see students, with knapsacks on their backs, come up to the clerk to inquire about a cheap room. In many instances, the only space available would be, say, at the deluxe Son Vida. I strongly advise against going to Majorca during the peak summer visiting spree without a reservation.

Of course, Majorca in spring and fall will tempt you with many inviting rooms . . . at reduced prices. The rates quoted in this chapter are for *high season* only. Off-season, you may get substantial reductions, around 20%. But that occasionally depends on personal negotiations between you and the management.

Most of my hotel recommendations are in Palma, particularly in the **El Terreno** section, the heart of the nighttime district (don't book into one of these hotels unless you like plenty of action . . . until late at night). Those who prefer more seclusion will find that possible also at my other recommendations.

Palma has long ago overflowed its boundaries—and is sprawling out into the suburbs, notably **Cala Mayor**, about 2½ miles from the center. Another satellite, **San Agustín**, about three miles from the center, is fast expanding. In the **El Arenal** area there is a huge concentration of hotels. I have a number of top pension and hotel recommendations in these suburbs for those who don't mind using public transportation. Leading off will be the pick of the hotels in

Palma in descending order of preference and prices. A survey of the other moderately priced hostelries in the suburbs will follow.

STAYING IN PALMA: Hotel Cannes, 22 Cardenal Pou (tel. 22-69-43), is a remodeled hotel with moderately priced rooms, off an old and quiet square. Open all year, the Cannes requires full pension in high season. The doubles, all with private baths (some with showers), range from 2000 pesetas ($19.20) to 2400 pesetas ($23.44). The most expensive singles, those with private baths, cost 1500 pesetas ($14.40). In high season, full board is obligatory, costing 1250 pesetas ($12) per person extra. The bedrooms have the bare essentials, and the public lounges are decorated with modern furnishings. Guests gather around the fireplace in winter, enjoy the air conditioning in summer.

Hotel Residencia Nácar, 21 Avenida Rey Jaime III (tel. 22-26-41), is small and intimate, a typically Spanish hotel of 60 well-furnished bedrooms, all with private baths and phones. Most of them contain private terraces as well, and half a dozen also boast sitting lounges with television. The style is modern, perhaps a little too commercial for many tastes. A twin-bedded room rents for 2000 pesetas ($19.20) per person, although singles cost 1800 pesetas ($17.28). The hotel lies right in the center of town. The Nácar doesn't have a restaurant, but it does offer a first-class, air-conditioned cafetería. A continental breakfast is served for an extra 150 pesetas ($1.44).

Hotel Rosamar, 74 Joan Miró (tel. 23-27-23), is one of the newer hotels sprouting up in the boomtown El Terreno district. Right on the main road, within an easy walk of the Plaza Gomila, the hostelry is built around a front patio with a tall palm tree. The fresh and clean bedrooms open onto balconies overlooking the patio. Most of the well-furnished double and single rooms have private baths, and rent for 1200 pesetas ($11.52) per person. The social life of the young and lively crowd attracted to Rosamar centers on the front terrace, although the living room with its good-size armchairs gets its share.

Hotel Britania, 21 Son Catleret (tel. 23-24-40), lies only a five-minute walk from the Plaza Gomila (two to the water), but most of its guests seem to stay beside the hotel's free-form swimming pool. For reasonable prices, this modern (1965) hotel will feed, shelter, and sun a pilgrim at the height of high season. Furthermore, all of its rooms have private baths. Doubles rent for 1400 pesetas ($13.44), singles for 900 pesetas ($8.64). A continental breakfast is an extra 125 pesetas ($1.20). For some unexplained reasons, the government awards the Britania only one star—hence, its prices remain reasonable. The bedrooms are compact with built-in, wood-grained headboards. The rooms on the sea side have terraces. The immaculate, streamlined dining room and lounges on the lower level open onto a wide terrace. Granted, the architecture and the furniture aren't avant-garde, but for basic amenities it's a winner.

El Valle, 112 Calvo Sotelo (tel. 23-12-43), is a modern temple for sun worshippers. Encircling balconies of bedrooms with picture windows overlook a swimming pool. You can get a double with a private bath and terrace for only 1850 pesetas ($17.76), plus 1150 pesetas ($11.04) per person extra for three meals a day. A single goes for 1200 pesetas ($11.52). The bedrooms are Danish style, with streamlined wooden pieces and built-in headboards. There's even central heating should you be there during those nippy winter days. In a commodious lounge, sofas and armchairs are arranged for conversation. There's also a wood-paneled drinking lounge with stools for loners, Windsor chairs for groups. Three picture windows in the dining room let in the light, revealing a display table of prepared hors d'oeuvres, salads, and desserts. The Plaza Gomila is only a short walk away.

Borenco, 61 Joan Miró (tel. 23-23-47), is a favorite two-star hotel with Europeans who like its "touristic" location, right off the Plaza Gomila. From your little terrace you are likely to have a view of Bellver Castle and the Paseo Marítimo. Rooms are clean, comfortable, and modestly furnished, costing 1200 pesetas ($11.52) per person daily for half board, based on double occupancy. For a single room, there's a supplement of 400 pesetas ($3.84) per day. All units have private baths, as well as terraces, plus phones, central heating, and music. The magnet is the rooftop pool and solarium. There's also a bar there. Spanish and international cookery is served in the air-conditioned dining room.

Hotel Infanta, 10 Teniente Mulet (tel. 23-24-43), sits right in the midst of nightclub alley in El Terreno district, overlooking the Plaza Gomila. It charges reasonable prices, considering that it is a well-designed, Korean War structure. Its 51 rooms come with every sort of plumbing—water basin, shower only, shower baths, complete private baths. It charges 1400 pesetas ($13.44) for a double with bath, this price dropping to 1000 pesetas ($9.60) if bathless. Singles are rented for 850 pesetas ($8.16) without private bath. A continental breakfast is an extra 100 pesetas (96¢). The rooms, some of which have balconies, are comfortably furnished and well kept. The lounge is inviting, the staff and management friendly, and the breakfast room a pleasant spot. Closed in winter.

El Paso, 11 Alvaro Bazán (tel. 23-76-02), is one of the best bargains in the Terreno district. It's a complete resort, containing an array of public facilities, including a heated swimming pool, three bars, three lounges, one restaurant, and a grill room. In addition, this well-kept modern building offers a total of 300 bedrooms, each with private bath and private terrace. In a double the cost is 1850 pesetas ($17.76) per person daily, including a continental breakfast. For single occupancy, you must pay a supplement of 300 pesetas ($2.88). On the half-board plan, the charge is from 2200 pesetas ($21.12) per person daily, based on double occupancy. Good meals are served in the large dining room with its white chairs.

Villa Río, 333 Avenida Calvo Sotelo (tel. 23-33-46), is a modern building in a choice position, whose rooms have balconies overlooking the bay. The location is between the heartbeat Plaza Gomila and the Club de Mar, which juts out into the water. A two-star choice, the hotel is furnished in part with reproductions of traditional Spanish pieces. The rooms, immaculately kept, are uncluttered and of suitable comfort for a long stay. Highest tariffs are in effect in July and August when it's best to stay here on the half-board plan—from 2200 pesetas ($21.12) in a single, from 3400 pesetas ($32.64) for two persons sharing the same twin-bedded room. The hotel also has a bar, with plenty of chairs for relaxing, and a good restaurant. At midday you'll find most of the guests lounging around the swimming pool.

Hotel-Residencia Capitol, 5 Plaza Rosario (tel. 22-25-04), is one of the better two-star hotels lying within the city. It appeals especially to those who don't want to cope with public transportation. The location is just a short walk from the Mediterranean-Gothic cathedral of Majorca. Rooms are pleasantly and adequately furnished, and a welcome is provided by English-speaking Federico Bringas. The rate for a double room with private bath and with continental breakfast included is 2200 pesetas ($21.12), dropping to just 1400 pesetas ($13.44) in a single with shower.

Pensions in Palma

Hostal Tirol, 19 Calle Apuntadores (tel. 21-18-08), can't be beat if you're under 30. Nestled on an alleyway lined with restaurants, bars, and nightclubs, the Tirol is entered through an open patio that leads to an old staircase winding up to the second floor. It charges 750 pesetas ($7.20) per person daily for a room with bath. A continental breakfast is an extra 100 pesetas (96¢). Inside, the main lounge and dining room are decorated with flourish. The bedrooms haven't been neglected either, as both the old and new in furnishings have been combined. Some of the doubles have private baths (these rooms awarded on a first-come, first-served basis), but most doubles—as well as the singles—have water basins only. The Tirol is only a minute's walk from the Plaza de la Reina.

Hotel Bonanova, 5 Francisco Vidal, in El Terreno, up the hill on the road to Genova (tel. 23-59-48), is a large hotel (two stars), ideal for budgeteers. The furnishings are modern, and many rooms have balconies with views of the ocean. There's a swimming pool, plus a bar and several pleasant lounges. Doubles with baths cost 1600 pesetas ($15.36); singles with baths, 1250 pesetas ($12). Breakfast is an additional 150 pesetas ($1.44), and other meals are 500 pesetas ($5.28) each.

Hostal Borne, 21 San Jaime (tel. 21-29-42), back in town, used to be the home of Spanish nobility, but is now a large, rambling, comfortable, and homey hostal. You come in through a large, palatial entrance opening up to a pretty garden. The rooms are simple and functional. Doubles with wash basin are rented at a charge of 1000 pesetas ($9.60) a night, with a continental breakfast costing an extra 110 pesetas ($1.06). The hostal's 48 rooms are available all year.

STAYING IN SAN AGUSTÍN: Hotel Atalaya, 14 Cabo Martorell Roca (tel. 23-06-40), has wedded an older hillside villa to a modern addition—and the liaison is proving compatible. The Atalaya was built between the lower coastal road and a hillside-climbing upper street. The lower terrace features a free-form swimming pool, with a flagstone terrace for sunbathing. Bedrooms in the newer wing are Cadillac-size, roomy enough to have sitting-room sections in addition to twin beds, lots of wardrobe space, and a private balcony. Spanish furniture reproductions are used liberally.

A double room with private bath rents for 1800 pesetas ($17.28). Only six singles, with bath, are offered, peaking at 1250 pesetas ($12). A continental breakfast is an additional 150 pesetas ($1.44). The hotel has a good kitchen, and the dining room offers a wide window view of the sea. On summer weekends, a small band plays for dancing.

ALONG PLAYA DE PALMA: Hotel Amazona, 4 Calle San Bartolomé (tel. 26-36-50). So many guests run around this hotel in their bikinis, it looks like a beach club, and, in a way, it is. At El Arenal, the Amazona is one of a string of beachfront hotels along this strip. Its rooms with views are often done in reproductions of traditional Spanish pieces, and each unit is complete with bath, phone, and terrace. In a double room, with a continental breakfast included, the tariff is 1400 pesetas ($13.44) per person, rising to 1800 pesetas ($17.28) in a single. The hotel has a good-size swimming pool, although the location is just 100 meters from the beach. A joie de vivre prevails in the bar, and the restaurant serves good food, a lunch or dinner costing from 750 pesetas ($7.20). The hotel is open all year.

Hotel Luxor, 23 Avenida Son Rigo (tel. 26-05-12), is strikingly modern with an Egyptian motif on its facade in honor of the hotel's namesake. Attracting a large number of European guests, it lies about 200 meters from the beach of Palma. In typically Spanish contemporary—no surprises—styling, it rents out 52 bedrooms, each with private bath, phone, and terrace. In a double, the half-board rate is 2400 pesetas* ($23.04) per person, rising to 2900 pesetas ($27.84) in a single. The hotel has its own heated swimming pool, plus a garden and solarium as well. In cooler months, there is central heating. Sundowners are served in the American bar.

Hotel Oasis, 24 Bartolomé Riutort, Ca'n Pastilla (tel. 26-01-50), has been recently renovated, emerging as one of the better bets strung along the beach of Palma, about seven kilometers from the capital. The hotel is tastefully decorated, with a quiet, subdued atmosphere. Facing the sea, its rooms are well kept and maintained. Highest tariffs are charged from July 15 to September 15. At that time, a twin-bedded room with bath goes for 3000 pesetas ($28.80), a single room, also with bath for 1700 pesetas ($16.32), these tariffs including a continental breakfast. Full board costs an extra 2200 pesetas ($21.12) per person, based on double occupancy, and a lunch or dinner, ordered separately, goes for 850 pesetas ($8.16). The Oasis is just that, surrounded by gardens and terraces, and its facilities include a bar and garage.

Neptuno, El Arenal (tel. 26-00-00), stands right on Playa de Palma beach, its nicest feature. It might be suitable if other more attractive hotels along the strip are rented. Some rooms are pleasantly furnished, although others are quite plain and disappointing to readers. Try to get one with a private terrace overlooking the beach. The hotel's public terraces are large, and guests also enjoy the solarium. Only breakfast is served at this spacious, modern beachfront choice. A double room with continental breakfasts included costs 2400 pesetas ($26.88) a day, while singles go for 1500 pesetas ($14.40). There is bar service both day and night, and a big private pool in the center of the complex.

Lotus Playa, Maestro Ekitai Ahn, Ca'n Pastilla (tel. 26-21-00), stands on the beach of Ca'n Pastilla, opening onto the bay of Palma, about 6½ miles to the east of the capital, next to the Marina and Yacht Club. Done in modern Spanish styling, it invites guests to enjoy its large, spacious rooms which have private baths and terraces overlooking the sea. A single costs 1500 pesetas ($14.40), the price rising to 2200 pesetas ($21.12) in a twin-bedded room. For three obligatory meals a day, served in the hotel's big restaurant, the cost is yet another 1500 pesetas ($14.40) per person. Facilities include a lounge, a bar, a solarium, a terrace restaurant, and a heated swimming pool.

STAYING AT LA BONANOVA: Hotel Constelación, 27 Corp Mari (tel. 40-05-01), is completely up-to-date, with an illuminated swimming pool, a flower garden, a large bar with a disco, and well-furnished rooms which open onto views of the water. In the high season, guests are accepted who take full board—from 2500 pesetas ($24) per person based on double occupancy, from 2800 pesetas ($26.88) in a single. At other times of the year you can rent a room only, paying 1400 pesetas ($13.44) in a single, from 2400 pesetas ($23.04) in a double. A continental breakfast is another 250 pesetas ($2.40).

READERS' HOTEL SELECTIONS: "**Hostal Castilla,** 19 San Jaime (tel. 22-40-92), is right next to Woolworth's. We enjoyed it because of the location. A double room costs 1200 pesetas ($11.52). Our room was spacious, in excellent shape, with hot and cold water. The toilet, bidet, and shower/bath was just across the hall, and there is no extra charge for the showers. Our room at the Castilla faced an inner courtyard and was quiet. The manager speaks some English, but the chambermaid was a lost cause!" (S. Scott Lucas, New York, N.Y.). . . . "At the **S'aigo Dolca Hotel,** 210 Habitación, Calle 297 s/n (tel. 23-47-47), I had a very clean, well-furnished room, a private bath across the hall with my own room number on it (and a very complete bathroom it was), a step-out private balcony that was larger than the room and furnished with table and chairs, too, and three meals a day. There is a free phone in every room and a huge, well-appointed

TV lounge and bar downstairs. It is within walking distance of every important Palma site. For all of this, the charge is 2000 pesetas ($19.20) per person, based on double occupancy. The pension requirement is obligatory, but the meals are very good" (Constance Maxon, Palma de Majorca, Spain). . . . "We drove along the southwest coast from Palma to a little fishing village called **San Telmo**, and there inquired at a neat and clean-looking hotel which commanded a view of the protected cove and island nearby. At the **Hotel Aquamarin**, Playa de San Telmo s/n (tel. 67-10-75), we were amazed to be offered a double room with front seaside balcony, a private bath, and full pension for 2400 pesetas ($23.04) per person based on double occupancy, including tax and service. This rate is for April, May, June, September, and October—the loveliest months" (Mr. and Mrs. Douglas Cameron, Bellevue, Wash.).

"**Hotel Horizonte**, 5 Vista Alegre (tel. 40-06-61), is only one block from the water. This modern hotel gave us large rooms with private baths and full balconies with a beautiful view of the bay for 2000 pesetas ($19.20). The director, Sr. Marimon speaks English, as does the desk clerk. Both were helpful during our five-day stay. The hotel has two pools, one kiddie and one full size, surrounded by a patio having a panoramic view of the bay, two lounges, a full bar, TV, and a pool table. For full pension, one pays an additional 1400 pesetas ($13.44) per person daily. Although the food wasn't exactly an epicurean delight, the meals were hearty and sustaining, and no one suffered the 'El Cid quick step' as a result of them. Horizonte is a fine establishment run by fine people" (J. Anthony Crawford, Garden City Park, N.Y.). . . . "**Hotel Flamingo**, El Arenal (tel. 26-05-00), is a modern beachfront hotel offering guests pleasantly furnished rooms with large balconies overlooking the Mediterranean. Facilities include a lounge, a bar, and a private pool. A special feature of the Flamingo is the nightly entertainment provided, e.g., a flamenco dancer, an accordionist, and other acts. Accommodation in a double room with bath and balcony, in addition to two meals per day, costs 1600 pesetas ($15.36) per person. The managment is helpful and the atmosphere relaxed and friendly. A special note to those who enjoy something more substantial in the morning than a continental breakfast: Breakfast at the Flamingo includes fruit juice, cereal, cheese, and one hot dish such as eggs or sausage, as well as rolls or croissants. While the main course served at lunch or dinner is rather ordinary, there is an excellent bar which precedes it. One day the salad bar included sardines, a huge bowl of artichokes, potato salad, eggs, and a variety of garden salad greens—more than a meal" (Rosemary Doyle-Morier, Ottawa, Canada).

2. Sampling the Cuisine

That any eating establishments exist at all in Palma—and haven't been nailed tight by the hoteliers—is surprising. But in spite of the octopus-grip of the full-board requirement, the restaurants are thriving—featuring a bastardized old island cuisine blended with continental fare. Here is the pick of the budget restaurants:

There are three members of a popular Majorcan chain restaurant, standing side by side. One is called simply **Click I**, 8 Paseo Mallorca (tel. 22-40-26); another **Click II**, 8a Paseo Mallorca (tel. 22-40-26), and a third, **Click El Griego** ("The Greek"), at 8c Paseo Mallorca (tel. 21-44-15).

Click I serves some of the best hamburgers on the island, a simple one costing 250 pesetas ($2.40), although they come with a wide variety of accompaniments. One of the more daring burgers is called "Towering Inferno," and it's very, very hot. Another, which I always avoid, is El Golpe—that is, banana and egg.

In addition, the restaurant has a large number of sandwiches, ranging from "Oh! Calcutta" to "Hair," the latter the most unappetizing-sounding name for a sandwich I've ever seen on any menu, although it tastes very good. Prices begin at 175 pesetas ($1.68) for the "Shaft," going up to 250 pesetas ($2.40). Rib steaks are also featured, costing from 525 pesetas ($5.04).

At Click II you get some very good pizzas, starting from 200 pesetas ($1.92) and going up to 250 pesetas ($2.40). Many diners like to drop in here just for the chef's wide selection of cheeses, including La Bohème, a selection of French cheeses which is a meal in itself, 450 pesetas ($4.32). The pastas are also tempting, beginning at 175 pesetas ($1.68).

El Griego lives up to its name, specializing in Greek shish kebabs, beginning at 350 pesetas ($3.36) and going up to 500 pesetas ($4.80). Brains, prepared in three different ways, is another one of the chef's specialties, costing from 350 pesetas ($3.36). Some of the best ice cream concoctions in the city are served here. One, for example, is called Copa El Griego, consisting of chocolate, hazelnut, lemon, and almonds, with nuts, pineapple, orange, honey, Grand Marnier, and whipped cream, going for 250 pesetas ($2.40).

El Siglo, 7 Plaza Mayor (tel. 22-60-62), in the heart of old Palma, under the Calso pension, is a good, solid, unchic budget choice on this ancient square. Come here for hearty meals high on flavor, low on your pocketbook. Diners order a 350-peseta ($3.36) cubierto—say, macaroni and cheese, followed by pot roast, fresh fruit, and a quarter liter of wine. On the à la carte menu, specialties include chicken villaroy, kidneys in sherry sauce, sole meunière. The chef is proud of his brandy soufflé, but you may be too stuffed to try it. Most à la carte main dishes range in price from 250 pesetas ($2.40) to 350 pesetas ($3.36).

Restaurant Sud-Americano, 7 Calle de San Juan (tel. 21-78-31), is a central, neon-lit bistro, usually crowded with young people drawn here by its 450-peseta ($4.32) fixed-price meal. My most recent meal included a choice of Russian salad, followed by a breaded veal cutlet and a fresh fruit salad, along with the regional wine. Most diners, however, order the house specialty, an entrecôte—charcoal-grilled at 500 pesetas ($4.80). If you're ordering à la carte, try one of the platos del día (plates prepared specially that day). There's also a 650-peseta ($6.24) menu: asparagus; hors d'oeuvres or soup; then entrecôte with potatoes or pork; followed by flan or fruit; bread, and wine. To reach the "South American" from the Plaza de la Reina, walk up the Apuntadores one block, then turn left.

At the **Celler Sa Prema,** 33 Calle Calvo Sotelo (tel. 23-17-39), and at the same-name subsidiary at Plaza Obispo Berenguer de Palou, the typically Majorcan cuisine is served against a backdrop of wine casks, strings of garlic, log benches, beamed ceilings, tavern tables, and hanging gourds.

The tavern on Calvo Sotelo is in the El Terreno district, right off the Plaza Gomila. The cellar is the choice of many matadors during the summer bullfight season. My most recent meal included sopa de Mallorquinan, roast suckling pig (crackly crisp on the outside, moist and sweet inside), and dessert. Most main dishes range in price from 175 pesetas ($1.68) to 450 pesetas ($4.32), and a complete meal will cost from 450 pesetas ($4.32) to 850 pesetas ($8.16). Closed Tuesday and from January 11 to March 20.

The flamboyant branch on the Plaza Obispo Berenguer de Palou wins the award for "Spanishery." It's only a one-fork restaurant, but the atmosphere's worth ten forks. Specialties at this one include Majorcan soup or garbanzos (chick peas), main dishes such as mejillones (mussels), spit-roasted chicken, or succulent roast lamb. Closed Sunday.

Svarta Pannan, 5 Calle Brondo (tel. 22-10-39), in the heart of Palma, right off the Plaza Pio XII, satisfies the needs of the Swede who gets as hungry for his frikadeller (meatballs) as the Yank does for his burger. Herring with onion and potatoes is 225 pesetas ($2.16); a *svarta pannan* (black pan) salad costs 185 pesetas ($1.78); and meatballs, 285 pesetas ($2.74), with salad and potatoes included. Decorated in the rustic style, this tavern is as refreshing as a Nordic breeze.

Celler Payes, 4 Calle Felipe Bauza (tel. 22-60-36), has a set menu for 550 pesetas ($5.28) that includes soup, noodles, or gazpacho; steak or fish; plus dessert, bread, and wine. From the à la carte menu, you can select the fish of the day which most guests prefer to have grilled. Other dishes include the classic kidneys in sherry or a simple roast chicken. Most à la carte orders will mean a tab ranging from 600 pesetas ($5.76) to 1000 pesetas ($9.60) for a complete meal.

La Paloma, 24 Calle Apuntadores, has a set menu for 450 pesetas ($4.32) for which you get spaghetti, soup, or rice; a meat or fish dish; and dessert. Wine and bread are included. There are no frills here, but the food is good value.

Texas Jack's, 12 Calle San Felio, in the heart of Palma, is something really out of the ordinary. Run by Mr. and Mrs. Jack Osborne, this place has become a favorite spot for Yankee sailors, expatriates, tourists, even local Majorcans. Outside, you'll see such homespun signs as: "Prices are so cheap, we can't afford waiters," "We speak Texan," and "If we are closed, just slip the money under the door." The biggest sign in front says "If you haven't been to the Cathedral *and* Texas Jack's you haven't been to Majorca." Opened in 1973, Jack's has a large, barn-like room with two big, round ten-seater tables. In the evening, visitors sit, drink, eat, and gab either in the dining room or at the bar. Jack's specializes in barbecue, sandwiches, and Texas chili. A sandwich plate is 175 pesetas ($1.68). A large mug of draft beer is 125 pesetas ($1.20), and a pitcher goes for 350 pesetas ($3.36). Country and western music is played.

Yate-Rizz, 18 Generalísimo, is anything but ritzy in decor, but offers a top budget meal for 450 pesetas ($4.32), including hors d'oeuvres, followed by a thin steak with potatoes, plus fruit, bread, and wine. There's a pleasant, low-ceilinged dining room upstairs, with 12 tables and nautical decorations consisting of fake porthole windows and captains' steering wheels. Closed Sunday.

La Casita, 68 Juan Mira (tel. 23-75-57), in El Terreno area, is an old standby featuring Franco-American specialties. The food is unbeatable for the price. The ambience is much improved by artworks decorating the walls of the dining room. These are the latest paintings of John Winn-Morgan, a well-known English artist. On my last visit I had roast chicken with stuffing, gravy, and potatoes, accompanied by fresh green vegetables, for 295 pesetas ($2.83). À la carte specialties include French onion soup, chopped chicken livers, peppered tenderloin steak, tournedos with mushroom sauce, trout with almond sauce, and homemade apple pie. Most of the dishes offered range in price from 150 pesetas ($1.44) to 695 pesetas ($6.67). Closed Monday lunch and Tuesday.

Gina's, 1 Plaza de la Lonja (tel. 21-72-06), is one of the top medium-priced restaurants in Palma. There's soft lighting, tablecloths, and paintings hung on a white brick wall. A paella goes for 350 pesetas ($3.36); zarzuela, 500 pesetas ($4.80); chicken Kiev, 275 pesetas ($2.64); bouillabaisse, 625 pesetas ($6); steak with potatoes, 250 pesetas ($2.40); flan with rum, 120 pesetas ($1.15); or a soufflé for two, 275 pesetas ($2.64). Expect to spend from 800 pesetas ($7.68) to 1400 pesetas ($13.44) for a complete meal.

Snacks in Cala Mayor

Bar Torres, 290 Calvo Sotelo, Cala Mayor, is run by Virginia Morse, an American, and her husband, Miguel Angel Fueutes, who give you a friendly welcome. It's a good place to visit for a hamburger at 110 pesetas ($1.06), or perhaps a hot dog or a ham-and-cheese sandwich. In addition, they sell a few tapas or hors d'oeuvres along with draft beer at 60 pesetas (58¢) a mug. They also offer many other selections of canned and bottled beer. The bar is known as the last one to close at night, so many revelers like to drop in here quite late for a snack of something. Dart tournaments are staged throughout the year, and the jukebox plays the latest hits.

READERS' RESTAURANT SELECTIONS: "For an inexpensive dinner or snack, **San Felio Chips** is quite a spot, frequented by locals. We were the only Americans we ever saw there. It's on San Felio, just a block off the Borne, and specialized in American-type sandwich items—hot dogs, hamburgers, ham sandwiches, chips (french fries), soft drinks, and beer. It's a stand-up place only, but the food is good, the prices very cheap, and the English-speaking manager is quite a character to watch at work. Some prices are: hamburger, 90 pesetas (86¢); chips, 45 pesetas (43¢); hot dogs, 75 pesetas (72¢); soft drinks and bottled beer, 60 pesetas (58¢). Considering what the two of us could eat there for, we stopped in often. Open at 5 p.m. . . . Another reasonably priced place is away from the center of town, out by the train station and Plaza España. The bar/restaurant **Casa Miguel**, 4 Enrique Alzamora (tel. 22-61-48), runs a daily special consisting of bread and butter, a large plate of spaghetti, beefsteak, and french fries, all for 400 pesetas ($3.84). The food is really good, too" (S. Scott Lucas, New York, N.Y.). . . . "The **Portixol** at El Arenal offers tourists a welcome change from the fast-food outlets and beer gardens which have proliferated here. Overlooking a marina, this elegant restaurant sports a nautical air. Platters of appetizing crustaceans are displayed from a small rowboat moored in the center of the restaurant. While the seafood prices are high, the Portixol offers an excellent paella for 500 pesetas ($4.80). The house wine sells for only 150 pesetas ($1.44) a bottle. To reach the Portixol, board a Palma-bound bus, and get off when the marina first comes into view" (Rosemary Doyle-Morier, Ottawa, Canada).

3. Island Attractions

Majorca is more than sun and surf. Visitors are often surprised at the wide range of activities with which they can occupy their days. Palma has a number of things to do (you can test your skill against a bull in the ring, and dance all night on a terrace overlooking the ocean), but the island itself is the big attraction, offering sights that range from caves with subterranean lakes to easily reached villages in the hills.

SIGHTSEEING IN PALMA: Most visitors don't get around to exploring the historical sights in Palma, but there are a number of places to see if you wish to break the monotony of going to the beach every day. The three most important attractions are:

The Cathedral

Founded by James I (called "The Conqueror"), this Mediterranean-Gothic cathedral took several centuries to build. Construction actually started during the reign (1276–1311) of James II, and lasted until the 17th century. Overlooking the seaside, the building stands in the old part of town. The main feature of the church is its gracefulness. Its central vault is about 160 feet, its columns rising 65 feet. Displayed in the Chapter House museum are panels and Gothic statues, and examples of craftsmanship in precious metals, tapestries, and liturgical ornaments. The cathedral is open from 10 a.m. to 1 p.m. and 3:30 to 6 p.m., charging an entrance fee of 50 pesetas (48¢).

Bellver Castle

Erected in the 14th century, this hilltop moated castle was once the home of the kings of Majorca—during the short period when there were kings of Majorca. The castle is well preserved and has some interesting treasures. It houses the **Municipal Museum** devoted to archeological relics and old coins. It's open from 9:30 a.m. to 1:30 p.m. and 3:30 p.m. to sunset; admission is 50 pesetas (48¢). It is really the view from here that is the chief attraction.

La Lonja

This 15th-century structure is left over from the wealthy mercantile days of Majorca. La Lonja was, roughly, an exchange or guild, and represents an original interpretation of Gothic architecture. It houses the **Provincial Museum of Fine Arts,** featuring an exhibit of paintings and archeological relics. For 100 pesetas (96¢), you can visit the museum. The exchange is open from 9:30 a.m. to 12:30 p.m. and 4:30 to 7:30 p.m.

Finally, for variety, you can attend:

A School for Bullfighters

The **Cortijo Vista Verde,** at Ca'n Pastilla (tel. 26-02-12), is a farm where you can see the El Cordobés of tomorrow execute a *verónica* or a *farol.* But the surprise of the school is that it allows a neophyte matador, such as yourself, to test your skill (or lack of it), against a year-old "bull." In summer, you can visit the school on Thursday, from 4 to 6:30 p.m. The entire event costs 800 pesetas ($7.68). Bus transportation from Palma costs 30 pesetas (29¢). Usually, your hotel can make all the arrangements; if not, any travel agent in Palma will book you a seat. After the bull "fight," you'll be invited into the garden to sample the regional wine and a presentation of flamenco.

READER'S SIGHTSEEING TIP: "The **Almudaina,** a former Moorish fortress with lovely gardens and fountains, was converted by the kings of Majorca into a royal palace. Somewhat reminiscent of the Alcázar in Málaga, it rewards its visitors with a profusion of colorful roses and bougainvillea as well as a spectacular view of the harbor" (Rosemary Doyle-Morier, Ottawa, Canada).

ONE-DAY EXCURSIONS: Not all the sights are confined to Palma. Majorca has several interesting caves, a legendary shrine, an artificial pearl industry— and countless other offerings. In a personal selection, I've narrowed the excursions down to two. First, we'll head east from Palma to:

Pearl Factories and Underground Music

A good road splits the island in two in its eastward dash from Palma to the sea. A 31-mile trip will take us to the prosperous little town of **Manacor,** where Majorcan pearls (artificial) are made. At cathedral square, the factory welcomes visitors, who are shown through the establishment, and can actually watch the various processes necessary for the making of a pearl (if one can stand the odor). The trade name for the world-famous pearls is **Majorica,** and visitors should be careful to avoid imitations. Across the street from the factory is a shop selling these artificial pearls in many price ranges, along with gifts and necklaces for the souvenir collector or random shopper.

From Manacor, we take the road southeast to the sea (about 7½ miles) and the beige-colored town of **Porto Cristo.** Outside this town is **Las Cuevas del Drach,** an underground forest of stalactites and stalagmites. In this icicle-like world of many shapes, you can attribute various identities to the freakish formations: hooded monks, whatever. The guide suggests a virgin, but who can be sure of that. The most exciting aspect of the cave is its subterranean lake, where you can listen to a concert and later go boating à la Jules Verne. Beyond the steep abysses are five subterranean lakes, Martel being considered "the largest underground lake in the world." Every day at noon, a concert (great acoustics) is given in the cave. Try to schedule your visit to coincide with a presentation of a musical performance. Price of admission: 125 pesetas ($1.20).

The least expensive way to go is to take one of the four daily buses that leaves from the railroad station in Palma (inquire at the Tourist Bureau for exact times of departure). The buses pass through Manacor on the way to Porto Cristo. The price of a round-trip ticket is about 300 pesetas ($2.88). It's also possible to book an organized excursion at **Viajes Iberia**—leaving at 9 a.m. on Wednesday, Friday, and Saturday. This tour visits Manacor, Drach, and Ham, and costs 800 pesetas ($7.68). This fee includes admission to the caves of both Drach and Ham. Lunch is 600 pesetas ($5.76) extra.

READER'S SIGHTSEEING TIP: "There is a very ancient, narrow-gauge railway going from Palma to **Soller** at 8 and 10:30 a.m. and 1, 4, and 7:30 p.m. from Plaza España, returning at 6:45, 9:30, and 11:30 a.m. and 2:15 and 6 p.m. In Soller a connection is made with an equally ancient tram for **Puerto de Soller**, a most attractive small village. The round-trip fare is 125 pesetas ($1.20) second class or 175 pesetas ($1.68) first class. The trip affords an interesting panorama of the Majorcan countryside and a ride through the mountains" (Brook Hill Snow, Orlando, Fla.).

Valldemosa and Deyá

For a second tour, we head north to the mountains along a twisting, narrow road, for 11 miles. First stop: Valldemosa, the legendary rendezvous of Chopin and George Sand. It shows little change; the olive pickers still return from the fields at sundown the way they have been doing for generations.

Valldemosa is the site of the **Royal Carthusian Monastery,** which contains relics of what the townspeople regard as the illicit lovebirds. It may be visited from 9:30 a.m. to 1:30 p.m. and from 3 to 7 p.m. for 100 pesetas ($9.60) admission. Off-season it shuts down an hour earlier and is always closed on Sunday. It seems ironic that the unconventional couple the villagers could hardly tolerate more than a century ago should later be deified, in a manner of speaking. These latter-day relatives of the old contemptuous villagers know how to prosper off the romance of the Polish composer-pianist and the novelist.

In Palma, Valldemosa-bound buses leave from 16 Avenida Juan March Ordinas. Departures on weekdays and Saturday are at 9:30 a.m., 2:30 and 8 p.m. On Sunday and holidays at 9 a.m., 3, 8, and 10:30 p.m. Tours are also run by **Viajes Iberia,** which leave on Monday and Thursday at 9 a.m.

From Valldemosa, we continue through the mountains for 6½ miles to Deyá.

Set against a backdrop of olive-green mountains, Deyá is peaceful and serene, with its stone houses and creeping bougainvillea. It has long had a special meaning for artists, notably Robert Graves, the English poet and novelist, author of such historical novels as *I, Claudius,* and *Claudius the God.*

After walking through the old streets, you can stand on a rock overlooking the sea and watch a fire-red sun set over a field of silvery olive trees and orange and lemon groves. Then you'll know why painters go to Deyá and why Robert Graves found his Shangri-La here.

To reach Deyá by public transportation, just stay on the bus that stops off in Valldemosa. Those with cars may want to consider one of the idyllic, and attractively priced, accommodations offered in this little Majorcan village.

READER'S SIGHTSEEING TIP: "Many visitors are not aware that included in the price of the ticket required to visit the Royal Carthusian Monastery is admission to the **palace** built by one of the four kings of Majorca. A short guided tour of the palace by a woman dressed in traditional Majorcan costume is provided. Regional dances are performed daily at 11 a.m. in the palace" (Rosemary Doyle-Morier, Ottawa, Canada).

Staying in Deyá

Mundial Ca'n Quet, Costa Topa (tel. 63-90-10), is a family-run pension owned by Francisco Arbona Puig. He has taken this farmhouse-style villa, built a short walk from the village, and turned it into a choice little pension. Guests are accepted April through October at a rate of 2000 pesetas ($19.20) in a double room with private bath. This charge drops to only 1500 pesetas ($14.40) if bathless. Singles are rented for 1200 pesetas ($11.52). You can also stay here on the full-board plan, enjoying home-cooked meals, for a charge of 1700 pesetas ($16.32) per person daily. The bedrooms vary in size. Many generations of life have led to an accumulation of matrimonial beds, as it is a Majorcan custom for the bride to bring a bed as part of her trousseau. Dining is often on the outer terrace, under the almond and orange trees, next to an old well. A nightly barbecue is held here. It's a 20-minute walk (for goats) through the olive groves to the beach. In spring, the nightingales keep you awake . . . all night long. The pension is open one week before Easter until October 31.

Hostal Costa d'Or, Lluch Alcari (tel. 63-90-25), outside the village proper, is a former villa, situated strategically so as to have the best possible view of the vine-covered hills and the rugged coast beyond. Surrounded by private gardens, filled with a swimming pool, fig trees, date palms, and orange groves, the old-fashioned estate is rather large (42 private bedrooms), and furnished with oddsy-endsy type pieces in the rooms. But it's clean and comfortable, and the price is just fine: from 1250 pesetas ($12) to 1800 pesetas ($17.28) in a double, depending on the plumbing. Bathless singles cost only 750 pesetas ($7.20). The bedrooms are divided between the villa and an annex, but most of the rooms have good views. From April 1 to October 31, guests can stay here, enjoying one of the good, home-cooked meals at a cost of 550 pesetas ($5.28). A continental breakfast is another 125 pesetas ($1.20).

PALMA NIGHTLIFE: Long after the sun sets over Majorca, the night birds of Palma start flying, after something of a late start. If visitors are just filing into their hotel dining rooms at 10:30, it's going to be after midnight before they get into the after-dark world.

The bars and bodegas are popular, but much of the more organized nightlife is likely to be expensive.

Discos and international floor shows are the biggest attractions on the nighttime circuit. For a club that's the best of its kind in Spain, we'll call on:

Tito's, 3 Plaza Gomila (tel. 23-76-42), is one of the finest nightclubs in Europe. For floor shows (11 p.m. and 12:30 a.m.) it beats every other club in town by 20 fathoms. But it charges a steep 1400 pesetas ($13.92) per person, although this includes your first drink. A second drink goes for 400 pesetas ($3.84). The shows feature occasional Spanish ballet, crooning, and folk dancing, along with other specialty acts. Tito's is sophisticated, charmingly modern (outdoor theater), and the shows often star a headliner. After the numbers, an orchestra plays for dancing. It is open from 9:30 p.m. Closed from November through February.

Much more for a younger crowd is **Zhivago,** 34 Teniente Mulet, right off the Plaza Gomila in El Terreno, the liveliest disco in Majorca, packing them in at 450 pesetas ($4.32). Frenetic dancing and live combo sounds are the rule here. The price of admission, incidentally, includes the first drink. On one recent inspection, a little old woman dressed in black sat on the curb nearby. As each of the scantily attired northern European girls crossed the threshold, the aging dueña crossed herself.

The Guitar Center (El Centro de la Guittarra), 8 Calle Montenegro (tel. 21-31-40), is a unique club cum performing center cum guitar shop run by an American, Peter Burr, from San Franciso. Housed in what was formerly a palace, the center has a kind of baroque lounge furnished in red plush, with antique guitars, Victorian knickknacks, a fireplace, and old hats. Guitar recitals are given every night, except Sunday and Monday, from 10 p.m. to 12:30 a.m. The music can be anything from classical to jazz. There are also special programs a couple of times a month, when name guitarists are invited to perform. In an adjacent room is a comfortable bar, such as one might have found in an old English Pall Mall club, which used to be the family chapel, and is now for chatting and playing chess. There's a shop for buying guitars, and guitar lessons are given as well during the day. The 300-peseta ($2.88) entrance fee includes a first drink. A second drink costs 150 pesetas ($1.44) if it's beer, wine, or a soft drink, and 250 pesetas ($2.40) for, say, a gin and tonic or rum and Coke. The same price is charged for special concerts. This low-key place has been open for more than a decade, drawing music lovers from many different countries.

The Formentor Bar, opposite the post office, at 1 Avenida José Antonio (tel. 22-10-18), is the central meeting place for foreign expatriates in Palma, especially those involved in the arts. There are tables placed outside on the sidewalk with wicker chairs. Inside it's a kind of tearoom complete with gilded mirrors and Corinthian pillars, where many an elderly lady has sat. Coffee costs 60 pesetas (58¢); a ham sandwich, 175 pesetas ($1.68); an omelet, 150 pesetas ($1.44); a melba ice cream cup, 125 pesetas ($1.20). But pass through the tea parlor and you come to a small bar which is still *the* meeting place in town, but which closes at 10 p.m.

The best bars, nightclubs, and discos are in El Terreno. Perhaps you'll choose Barbarela, on Calvo Sotelo, just before Plaza Gomila coming from Palma. This place is the supreme definition of a disco with settees, psychedelic lights, and two live combos playing nightly. The charge for admission is 350 pesetas ($3.36), which includes your first drink. The club is open till 4 a.m.

Across the street is the Crazy Daisy, Calvo Sotelo, charging 350 pesetas ($3.36) as an entrance fee, with disco facilities and a large dance floor.

Next door, and for 300 pesetas ($2.88), you can go into the Bavaria, a fun place in the Bavarian style. It attracts not only homesick German visitors but also its share of young people who dance or munch to the stomping Tyrolese band. Sauerkraut costs 150 pesetas ($1.44); a leg of pork, 350 pesetas ($3.36); chicken and bread, 250 pesetas ($2.40); and goulash soup, 100 pesetas (96¢). The Bavaria is open till 3 a.m.

If you want a place purely for drinks, there are two good ones: Don Gomilo, right off Plaza Gomila, run by Juanito—catering to a good, expatriate crowd. You pay 175 pesetas ($1.68) for a local whisky or cognac and 300 pesetas ($2.88) for imported brands. Even more fashionable is Riki's My Own Place, 14 Calle 11 at El Jonquet (don't try to find it by yourself at night—take a taxi), owned and run by Riki "Lash" Lazaar, an expatriate Yank from the West Coast who has a radio program in Palma as well as a gossip column in the local English-language newspaper, the *Majorca Daily Bulletin*. Riki's MOP is spectacularly perched atop a cliff, and its picture windows provide a view of the coast and the ocean. A whisky in the comfortable, posh cocktail lounge costs 300 pesetas ($2.88); a local cognac, 100 pesetas (96¢). Other drinks average 175 pesetas ($1.68). Mostly an Anglo-American clientele patronizes the establishment. For the price of a drink, one may watch Riki broadcast over Radio Majorca from 7 p.m. till midnight, enjoying one of the most fabulous views on the island. Riki opens at 7 p.m., closing at 3 a.m. in summer, 2 a.m. in winter.

Jaguar Discotheque is on the Calle Gaviota in Cala Mayor. Its 600-peseta ($5.76) entrance fee includes the price of your first drink. Completely renovated, the disco features the finest Altec sound system, multilight and projector effects, and comfortable red plush seats. The Canadian disc jockey, Bob Gourlay, speaks six languages and plays a wide variety of music (even special requests).

READERS' SIGHTSEEING SUGGESTIONS: "The place of most interest to Americans is **Petra,** the birthplace of Father Junipero Serra, founder of the California missions. In Petra is the house where Father Serra was born, which now belongs to the city of San Francisco (California). It was presented to the people of California as a gift from the people of Majorca. Here, too, is the **Father Serra Missions Museum** (entrance free), and one can also see the **Convent of the Franciscan Fathers.** It was from the altars here that Father Serra was inspired to name the new missions: San Juan Capistrano, San Fernándo, and San Gabriel. In our opinion, Petra is the most interesting link between Spain and the United States" (Ms. Francisca A. Pomar, Cala Gamba, Palma). . . . "Along the Paseo Marítimo is the **Flipper II,** a small boat with sailings at 10:30 a.m. and 3:15 p.m., featuring a two-hour cruise along the waters off the coast. Spanish champagne is served. The cost is from 600 pesetas ($5.76) to 1000 pesetas ($9.60) per person, depending on the length of the cruise. It's a five-minute walk from Hotel Bellver" (Patricia and Maurice Wade, Rockaway Point, N.Y.).

IBIZA

A New York art student wrote, "Even those who come to Ibiza (pronounced 'Ee-bee-tha') for the 'wrong' reason (to work!) eventually are seduced by the island's easy life. Little chores like picking up the mail from the post office stretch into day-long missions."

It is presently estimated that some 1000 U.S. expatriates live in **Ibiza.** Some 200 of these persons introduce themselves as writers (one columnist reported that no more than "half a dozen have ever been published").

To those who may never have heard of Ibiza (if such a traveler still exists), it is the third largest of the Balearic Islands. It can be reached by both boat and air. The island is more than 225 square miles in size.

Physically, it has a jagged coastline, some fine beaches, fig and olive trees, whitewashed houses, secluded bays, cliffs, and an essentially hilly terrain. Ibiza has a warmer climate than Majorca, which makes it a better choice for a winter holiday—but it can be sweltering in July and August. Thousands upon thousands of scrubbing tourists in summer greatly tax the island's limited water supply. But some of the pedestrians who roam the streets of **Ciudad de Ibiza** don't drain one drop from the reservoir.

Once Ibiza was virtually an unknown and relatively unvisited island, frequented only by the most esoteric of travelers. Majorca, its bigger sister, got all the business. But in the '50s, when a rising new liberated group began to chart a course through unknown waters to undiscovered lands, Ibiza was singled out. One of the more famous of these visitors was Jan Cremer, the Dutch artist who wrote the controversial bestseller (in the Netherlands), *I, Jan Cremer.* But by the time Jan-come-lately Cremer arrived, Ibiza already had the nucleus of an art colony. In fact, the artist was to have his first show here—or, to put it in his own words, "Jan Cremer came, saw and conquered."

Reputations take a long time to build . . . and to die. Many of the Jan Cremers are still arriving, dreaming of soft drugs and hard sex. Both exist in great abundance. But there are dangers. It's common to pick up the local paper and read the list of the latest group of people deported because of *irrespon-*

sibilidad económica (no pesetas) or *conducta antisocial*. A Brooklyn school-teacher was sentenced to six years in a Spanish jail for possession of a small amount of hash. Many young travelers, frankly, are deserting Ibiza, taking a ferry 40 minutes away to the south to the island of **Formentera** where they find less harassment (although anyone looking suspicious is likely to be checked out here, too). In Ibiza, the Guardia Civil (watch out for these guys) is known to take your passport until you can show them a one-way ticket—that is, out of the country.

Back in the '60s—the heyday of Ibiza's "in" position—one writer made the claim that "time of residence on the island is a better passport to the 'in-hip' scene than having a novel published, or a successful art show." Today, having that art show or that novel published is a better passport. Ibiza today is virtually overrun by middle-class tourists from England, France, Germany, and Scandinavia. Some of the English residents have organized vigilante groups to protect their winter villas from squatters.

THE HOTEL OUTLOOK: The chances of finding space in peak summer months are dismal, the worst of any Mediterranean resort in Spain. At other overcrowded resorts, such as those on the Costa Brava and the Costa del Sol, a visitor—faced with the no-vacancy sign—can always press on, even go inland to find a room for the night. But in Ibiza, because of infrequent transportation, a visitor without a reservation in July and August can land in a trap. Cremer relates that he slept in caves when he first visited the island. But that was for financial reasons. You may end up sleeping on the beach on an air mattress (if the police let you; there are camping areas), even though your pockets are bulging with pesetas.

The island of Ibiza is not always prepared for its hordes of international tourists. The hotels can't be built fast enough. Many of the hastily erected ones sprouting up in San Antonio Abad, Santa Eulalia del Río—even on the out-skirts of Ciudad de Ibiza—are more frame than picture.

At most resorts, you can write ahead to make a reservation. But at hotel after hotel on the island of Ibiza, you can't do this. Individual bookings in most establishments range from horrifically difficult to impossible. In many cases, hoteliers don't bother to answer requests for space in summer. Armed with a nice fat contract from a Midlands tour group, they're not interested in the plight of the stranded pilgrim.

Don't—repeat don't—go to Ibiza in summer without an iron-clad reservation, unless you're reasonably attractive, at least a good enough looker to assure yourself that you'll get an invitation to share someone's pad in the old town.

GETTING THERE: The easiest way to reach Ibiza is by an **Iberia** or **Aviaco** flight from Palma, Barcelona, or Valencia. From Palma, the one-way economy-class fare is 1800 pesetas ($17.28), rising to 3400 pesetas ($23.04) from Valencia, peaking at 4200 pesetas ($40.32) from Barcelona. At the airport in Ibiza, taxis transfer four people at one time to one of the resorts. From the airport into town costs 350 pesetas ($3.36) in a taxi, but only 23 pesetas (22¢) on a bus to the terminal.

The shipping line **Compañía Trasmediterránea** maintains services between Ibiza and Barcelona, Palma and Ibiza, as well as Valencia and Ibiza. Of course, these runs are limited in winter, increasing in summer to meet the capacity. Even so, space is sometimes at a premium. Generally, you can catch a boat in Barcelona, in summer, at 10 p.m. daily, which makes a stop in Palma and gets into Ibiza the next day. Second-class or third-class tickets appeal to those, such as readers of this book, who are economizing. Deck space is 1400 pesetas ($13.44). To purchase tickets in Barcelona, go to 2 Via Layetana.

In Palma the booking office is at 5 Muelle Viejo. In Ibiza, the booking office is on Avenida Bartolomé Vicente Ramón.

Again, as with Palma, if you come in August be sure you have a return ticket (boats are easier) reservation. Otherwise you may be stranded for days until a seat opens up.

4. Ciudad de Ibiza

Ibiza, with more than 15,000 residents, is the capital of the island. Founded by the Carthaginians 2500 years ago, it is graced with a harbor filled with boats and yachts. The town is not a resort, consisting of a lively, scruffy **Marina** district around the harbor, and an old town **(Vila)** with narrow, cobblestone streets, and flat-roofed, whitewashed houses that climb a steep hill.

The Marina quarter physically is drab, especially along its mainstreet paseo, **Vara del Rey,** but it has a distinctive personality. It is the people—the skeptical natives and the expatriates—who provide the evercontinuing spectacle. It is a study in contrast. The old fishermen, long accustomed to Ibizan women swathed in black, are treated to sights that pop their eyes, as the fair-skinned American and northern European Mary Janes parade around in bikinis and halter tops. In addition to the people, the Marina quarter is intriguing for a stroll because of its art galleries, discos, boutiques, and foreign-operated bars and restaurants.

WHERE TO STAY: The hostelries in the town are limited and often lack style and amenities. Some suitable candidates follow.

Hotel Montesol, 2 Vara del Rey (tel. 30-11-04), was once the leading social center of town for the old islanders. Now, after renovation, it is making a bid for tourism. Designed as a neoclassic building with Ionic inset, it lies on the main street, a short walk from the harbor. All rooms contain private baths or showers. Singles with showers cost 1200 pesetas ($11.52); doubles with showers, 2000 pesetas ($19.20), peaking at 2600 pesetas ($24.96) for doubles with complete private baths. A continental breakfast is the only meal served, at 200 pesetas ($1.92) per person.

Residencia Parque, 1 Cayetano Soler (tel. 30-13-58), on a satellite square off the main plaza, is somewhat drab. Still, in hotel-scarce Ibiza, no one can afford to overlook any possibility. Open all year, it decks out its single and double units with water basins. Singles in that category rent for 1000 pesetas ($9.60) to 1200 pesetas ($11.52), doubles for 1800 pesetas ($17.28). Some doubles contain private baths, and they go for 2000 pesetas ($19.20). A continental breakfast is 150 pesetas ($1.44). The reception cubicle is small, and the Formica-outfitted bar provides a clue to the utterly impersonal, functional bedrooms upstairs.

Playa de Figueretes

On the edge of town, around some fair sands, a number of modern beach hotels are sprouting up, far superior to the ones in the city. With few exceptions, most of these are booked solidly in summer by tour groups.

Hotel Cenit, Luís Salvador (tel. 30-14-04), is your best choice along this playa. Circular shaped, it looks like a quartered wedding cake. In the pueblo fashion, each floor has been staggered so as to provide a terrace for the rooms above. In high season, a person can stay here in a double with bath for 2200 pesetas ($21.12), but only 1600 pesetas ($15.36) in a comparable single. The rooms are routine, but not so bare boned that they lack comfort. All of the 62 accommodations contain private baths (some with showers, but not toilets). The curved dining room, with its picture windows, is a pleasant, tasteful place to enjoy a continental breakfast at an extra 175 pesetas ($1.68). The Cenit is perched on a hillside, a short walk down the beach. It's open all year.

Hotel Palaú, 12 Galicia (tel. 30-23-50), is one of the more laudable contenders near the beach, having been built in 1965 to house the northern invaders. You can book a fairly pleasant and well-equipped double room (all with private bath) for 2000 pesetas ($19.20), 1500 pesetas ($14.40) single. The rooms have picture windows opening onto views of the sea and mountains. A continental breakfast, costing 175 pesetas ($1.68) extra, is the only meal served. In sum, it's an agreeable spot to stop, only a short block from the beach. The hotel is open from April 1 until the end of October.

Hotel Marigna, 18 Al Sabini (tel. 30-14-50), is an inexpensive, relatively new hotel that's a sure-fire bet. Like nearly every other hotel around here, it's hooked up to the umbilical group cord—notably English and German—but it will accept those who write in advance. Its bedrooms are efficient, good size; nearly all of them have compactly modern baths and balconies. As for the decor, someone tried, making for a welcome relief from the utter vacuousness of many of its competitors. Doubles with bath cost from 1800 pesetas ($17.28) to 2100 pesetas ($20.16), dropping to 1600 pesetas ($15.36) if bathless. Singles, depending on the plumbing, range in price from 1100 pesetas ($10.56) to 1500 pesetas ($14.40). A continental breakfast at 125 pesetas ($1.20) is the only meal served. The hotel is open all year.

WHERE TO EAT: Be warned: Most restaurants in the port section of Ibiza could afford to hire the scrubwoman in the Old Dutch Cleanser ad.

Los Pasajeros, 6 Calle de Vicente Soler, is a proven favorite with barefoot boys and girls drawn here by its good food and a 175-peseta ($1.68) tourist menu. You can dine inside or out, selecting from a limited but good bill of fare. Usually you have a choice of soup or salad, then paella (a house specialty), or roast pork. The grilled sole is a perennial favorite, as is the excellent grilled trout.

Alfredo, St. Anthony and Paseo Vara del Rey (tel. 30-10-00), is where you can order a belt-loosening meal for 600 pesetas ($5.76). The first course might begin with a homemade fish soup, then follow with a plate of freshly caught fish, plus a good steak with fried potatoes, finishing off with fruit or caramel custard, not to mention freshly baked bread and a regional wine. The waiters in their tidy white jackets are attentive. After the dessert, you can have your coffee on the terrace.

Sam's Hamburguesa, 4 Calle de Vicente Soler, on an alleyway between Calle Mayor and the harbor, fills that insatiable expatriate need for a hamburger and hot dog. A hamburger special—"with everything we can get on it"—is the reason most people go here, but Sam also serves hot dogs and other sandwiches as well as milkshakes. Most orders range in price from 75 pesetas (72¢) to 200 pesetas ($1.92). Its handful of sidewalk tables are staked out early. Most nibblers stand around talking, or perch on the doorsteps of the Ibizans who have either the misfortune or blessing to live on this jam-packed street. Sam's is open from February through November.

The **Pizzería Pinocchio,** 16 Calle Mayor (tel. 30-38-17), is a simple eatery featuring lasagne for 225 pesetas ($2.16), pizzas for 150 pesetas ($1.44) to 300 pesetas ($2.88), and beer for 50 pesetas (48¢). It is open from noon to 1 a.m. from March to October.

The **Restaurante Victoria,** 1 Calle Riambau, is a pleasant little bistro with a set tourist menu for 475 pesetas ($4.56), consisting of paella, meatball stew, bread, wine, and dessert. Otherwise, you can have chicken or hake for 225 pesetas ($2.16).

Celler Balear, 18 Avenida Ignacio Wallis (tel. 30-10-31), is unpretentious in its decor. There's a large, vaulted dining room, and you enter the place by going past huge wine barrels. The prices are medium, but food quality is tops. The tourist menu costs 550 pesetas ($5.28). À la carte specialties include an Ibizan salad, cream soup, cannelloni, rape (a whitefish) seaman's style, and a zarzuela de mariscos (highly recommended). Most dishes range in price from 125 pesetas ($1.20) to 600 pesetas ($5.76).

The **Restaurant Pages** at the port is a cozy little place run by three Majorcans. Open 8 to 11 p.m. and closed on Sunday, it serves fresh vegetable soup, chicken with gravy, rabbit with onions, and stuffed squid, at prices that range from 150 pesetas ($1.44) to 450 pesetas ($4.32).

For the big splurge, head to **El Bistro,** 15 Avenida General Franco, in the Alt Vila. Run by a Frenchman who has a French cook, this veritable bit of France in Ibiza serves up stuffed noodles, mushrooms Greek style, leg of lamb, and a lemon tart, among other offerings. An average repast here will range in price from 450 pesetas ($4.32) to 900 pesetas ($8.64). The food and service are top-notch.

Nearby, is a delightful tearoom called the **Samovar.** At 4 Plaza Desamparados, it is a small, cozy place decorated with paintings, wooden sculptures, and, of course, a samovar. It used to be an antique shop, but, when taxes got too high, the owner decided to make a tea shop out of it instead. There are about a half dozen tables where you can sit, talk, read, or write. It is open only from 5 to 11 p.m. The items to order are the homemade apple cake with whisky, 250 pesetas ($2.40), and the sachertorte, 225 pesetas ($2.16). A cup of cappuccino, made with fresh cream flown in from Palma and served in quaint old cups, costs 100 pesetas (96¢). The owner serves the tables herself. You usually hear several languages being spoken, and the feel of the place is like a White Russian Parisian café in the 1920s.

THE CHIEF SIGHT: Ibiza is an island to strike out for if you're seeking sun and fun. But there's one sightseeing attraction worth a special visit. It's the **Archeological Museum,** containing what is considered by some to be one of the finest collections of Punic relics in Europe. The museum is housed in a large, modern building at Puig des Molins, the site of the Carthaginian and Roman necropolis from which many of the museum's displays were excavated. The site and museum are just a short walk along a well-marked route from the center of town.

See in particular the collection of Carthaginian amulets and the rose-painted Punic vases. Another display consists of a group of intriguing terracotta figurines as well as two Hellenistic busts from the second century B.C. Another section of the museum is devoted to a collection of vases and urns, some as old as the third or fourth century B.C., along with many fragments of ceramics, glassware, and artifacts from the imperial Roman period. A numismatic exhibit reflects the changes in monetary currency over the centuries, ranging from coins of ancient Carthage to 16th-century Spain.

The museum is open from 10 a.m. to 1 p.m. and 4 to 7 p.m. Closed Sunday. Admission is 50 pesetas (48¢). After visiting the museum, your ticket is also good for a guided tour to the nearby excavations (declared a National Monument) where you can view gravesites containing ancient stone sarcophagi.

THE BAR SCENE: To make the rounds at night is fun here. A good place to start might be **Wauna's** on the Calle Mayor. You can listen to Nana Mouskouri's favorite Greek songs, sip tall Cuba libres, pound the piano keys—or stare at fellow drinkers—the latter custom is by far the more intriguing. Mixed drinks are 125 pesetas ($1.20).

Another favorite bodega, especially with young people, is **La Tierra,** in the Callejón Trinidad. Here globe-trotters get a friendly welcome from Giorgio, who charges 100 pesetas (96¢) for simple drinks and stays open from seven "until we can't take any more."

Around the corner from La Tierra is one of the best discos on the island, **Sirena Gorda.** At 8 Olozaga, it is open from 6 in the evening till 3 a.m., and charges 150 pesetas ($1.44) for ordinary drinks, 200 pesetas ($1.92) for mixed drinks. The patrons dance to recorded music, mostly American and English. The proprietor is Swiss.

The **Bar Alhambra,** Paseo Vara de Rey, in the main part of town, is where the old guard meets the new invaders. It enjoys continuing popularity (there's a pool room in back). Spanish army officers, their chests covered with medals, sit side by side with languid Norse boys and pig-tailed Brünnhildes from Germany. In all, the bar proves that a widely diversified segment of humanity can sip together. Drinks are from 90 pesetas (86¢) for a beer and up. It's popular, international, yet typically Spanish.

For another recommendation try **Lord Nelson,** at the nearest beach, 1½ miles from the center of town. Owned appropriately enough by an Englishman, Peter Ross, and run efficiently by Roy Booth, it is another English pub. The interior is a replica of H.M.S. *Victory,* Nelson's flagship, complete with a talking parrot, ship's wheel, upper deck, and an antique ship's compass. The prices are about 125 pesetas ($1.20) for most simple drinks. Guinness stout and Courage are sold, along with such English concoctions as salmon-and-cucumber sandwiches, roast beef, and homemade chicken-and-savory pies. If you don't have a car, you can walk to the Lord Nelson in about 15 minutes.

For nightspots, head for the **Mar Blau,** just outside of town, which has flamenco, combos, and shows each night that run from 10 p.m. to 3 a.m. Built high on the rocks, it is an unusual structure, with a bamboo roof, a small dance floor, and tables on several levels, some in grotto-like niches. From some of the tables there's a magnificent vista of the sea. Entrance and your first drink cost 750 pesetas ($7.20).

About the best disco on the island is at Talamanca beach and is called **Pasha's.** Actually, it's a converted old farmhouse. There's no show, only music, and you sit in inflated leather-balloon chairs. Once a week there are live bands, and it's always packed full in the summer. Admission to this super-modernistic disco is 600 pesetas ($5.76).

READER'S BODEGA SELECTION: "**La Bodega,** across from the Hotel Parque, on the Plaza Cayetano Soler, is our favorite hangout in Ibiza Town. The prices are Spanish, not tourist, and you can sit at the bar or in front with the wine barrels. There is even a patio with greenery and a little fountain where you can take your pick of the current English-language magazines for a quiet hour or so. This is an old guard hangout about noon, but a pleasant place to have a drink any time and just off the beaten path. Simple drinks go from 100 pesetas (96¢) and up" (Roderic Cossey, Almería, Spain).

5. San Antonio Abad

Known as Portus Magnus to the Romans, this small hamlet is the chief resort of Ibiza. Lying ten miles from Ciudad de Ibiza, San Antonio Abad as a resort was discovered largely in the '50s.

In summer you have as much chance of finding a room here as you would of booking a reservation on the last flight to the moon if the earth were on fire. Virtually all of the hotels have a direct pipeline to tour-group agencies in northern Europe, which feed constant plasma directly into the bloodstream of San Antonio. The individual probably won't get the time of day. The hotel clerk will be too busy rerouting army cots, as he's already overcrowded on his tour clientele.

The resort is built on an attractive bay. A four-minute ferry ride takes you across the bay to the popular beaches. With all its influx, San Antonio does have a joie de vivre, plus lots of mildly entertaining nightlife. Even if you're staying in Ibiza or Santa Eulalia, you may want to hop over for the day or evening. A bus leaves every half hour from Ciudad de Ibiza to San Antonio and vice versa, costing 60 pesetas (58¢).

First, I'll survey a handful of the budget hotels for the off-season visitor. Some might possibly grant you a reservation in summer if you give them plenty of notice.

WHERE TO STAY: Arenal Hotel, Avenida Doctor Fleming (tel. 34-01-12), built in 1966, ranks among the top hotels in San Antonio Abad, offering comparable value to its more expensive neighbor, the Hotel Palmyra. During high season the groups take over, but in October and from April to mid-May you can generally get a reservation if you write two weeks in advance. Off-season, all you need do is arrive. At the edge of town, on its own beach, the Arenal is a long, four-floor establishment with a swimming pool. Contemporary architecture and furnishings are used throughout. Simple and attractive, the rooms offer comfortable beds. All of the units contain private baths and balconies opening either onto the sea or the little front garden lawn with palm trees. A double costs 2400 pesetas ($23.04); a single, 1800 pesetas ($17.28). For three meals a day, expect to pay 1700 pesetas ($16.32) per person extra. *Off-season note:* One living room has a circular raised fireplace with surrounding banquettes.

Hotel Portmany, 18 Balanzat (tel. 34-05-33), is one of the oldest hotels in San Antonio, built back in the '30s when a three-fingered man could count the hostelries here on one hand. But age has given it character, and it's a happy choice for those seeking an old Spanish atmosphere—rooms with deep-arched recesses, provincial chairs, furnishings that are antiques. The hotel is open from May to October 31. If you write in advance, you stand a chance of securing space at the beginning and near the end of the season.

In a single the rate is 1200 pesetas ($11.52) to 1500 pesetas ($14.40). The most expensive doubles, those with private baths, rent for 2100 pesetas ($20.16), although the bathless doubles are priced at only 1700 pesetas ($16.32). A continental breakfast is an extra 175 pesetas ($1.68). On its front colonnade pergola, you can nurse your drink for hours, watching the passing parade.

Galfi Hotel, Avenida Doctor Fleming (tel. 34-09-12), is a small hotel outside of town, near the beach. Miracle of miracles, it will consider individual bookings in summer, provided the prospective guest writes two weeks in advance. Owned and run by a friendly English-speaking owner, Luís Hormigo Escandell, and his attractive Bavarian wife, the hotel offers doubles and singles with private bath. The bedrooms are good, although simple, and all are well maintained. Based on double occupancy, the rate is 1400 pesetas ($13.44) per person daily for bed, breakfast, and an evening meal. The hotel also provides cafetería-bar-restaurant service at reasonable prices, with a wide selection of local dishes as well as traditional. The hotel is open from April 1 to October 31.

The food is home-cooked and quite good (the hotel caters to northern European tastes: for example, a strawberry cream "high tea" is often held in the summer afternoon). After-dinner drinks and coffee are served on the rear terrace under the olive trees. A swimming pool is in the garden. The living and dining rooms have a warm, homelike touch to them. It's a choice spot for the budgeteer to anchor.

Hotel Coves Blanques, Playa de Coves Blanques (tel. 34-11-12), is a small hotel (26 doubles) built at the water's edge in 1965. Well styled, its lounges are restful and pleasant, using simple leather and natural wood furniture. The rooms open onto a terrace facing the sea. Every bedroom has a private bath, is good-size, contains up-to-date, comfortable furnishings. An added bonus is the private sun balconies. The cost of a double room is 1800 pesetas ($17.28) nightly, 1200 pesetas ($11.52) in a single. A continental breakfast is an additional 160 pesetas ($1.54), and a lunch or dinner goes for yet another 600 pesetas ($5.76). The hotel is open only from April 1 to October 31.

WHERE TO EAT: Ferrer, 5 Calle Obispo Ferrer, opposite the Cine Torres, is a real budget find. You can order spaghetti or cannelloni, or a heaping plate of macaroni with meat sauce and cheese, followed by roast veal or chicken. On my last visit I had three huge slices of pot roast with french fries and vegetables, and on another occasion an equally huge portion of pork chops. Most of the main dishes range in price from 175 pesetas ($1.68) to 450 pesetas ($4.32). The decor is nothing to speak of: a simple, white-walled dining room with tablecloths, a bar on one side. But the service is friendly and fast, there's an English menu, and the location is just a block away from the main street.

Restaurant El Pescado has fish 'n' chips for 175 pesetas ($1.68), a quarter chicken and chips for 250 pesetas ($2.40), and a mixed salad for 100 pesetas (96¢). This is a small, unpretentious snackery, and you'll find it on a nameless street by going up the Calle Ramón one block and turning left.

Other budget delights are: **S'Olivar,** Calle San Mateo (tel. 34-00-10), a bistro-type place with two small adjoining gardens, one of them with an olive tree and the other with grape vines. Tables are covered with checkered cloths, and there's a friendly bar. Tourist menu costs 550 pesetas ($5.28). On the à la carte menu, you'll find an array of Spanish and continental dishes, including onion soup au gratin, mero (a whitefish), rabbit ayoli, and crêpes suzette. If you order from this menu, expect a bill beginning at 700 pesetas ($6.72) for a complete meal.

Bar El Pescador (Fisherman's Bar), 29 Vara de Rey, run by Vilma and Frank Ventris, is a favorite hangout for expatriates. On the edge of town (turn right at the Bodega del Mar liquor shop and follow the signs), it serves a meal of pork chop, chips, and a salad for 350 pesetas ($3.36). Steaks with the same extras cost 450 pesetas ($4.32), and hamburgers go for 125 pesetas ($1.20). The hot Indian curry is 400 pesetas ($3.84). The bar is open from 6 p.m. to 3 a.m. every day from March 1 to October 31.

Nearby, on an unnamed street, is the **Pitango Restaurant,** serving good meals for a tourist price of 300 pesetas ($2.88). There's no decor to speak of, but it's clean and the food is recommended. Paella costs 350 pesetas ($3.36). Other recommendable dishes include fish soup, squid, meatballs, and roast veal.

Most of these dishes range in price from 125 pesetas ($1.20) to 350 pesetas ($3.36).

NIGHTLIFE: The **Capri Playboy Club,** Avenida Doctor Fleming, on the water at the edge of town, is a pop dance house, the best and most popular spot on the island for rock sounds. Drawn to the deafening cacophonies is an attractive set of young people who pay 300 pesetas ($2.88) entry fee, then 250 pesetas ($2.40) for the first drink (about half that for the next libation). The orchestra's live, and so's the audience.

For different decibels, head for **La Reja Piano Club,** right off the Calle B. V. Ramón, around the corner from the Celler El Refugio. Occasional jazz combos enliven the atmosphere. It's a good way to spend an hour or so—just for the price of a drink. A local vodka goes for 150 pesetas ($1.44); imported whisky, 300 pesetas ($2.88). The club is decked out in the typical Spanish style (hand-hewn beams, candlelight, a wrought-iron grill).

Also stirring up the air waves is the cueva (cave) of the **Celler El Refugio,** on the Calle B. V. Ramón. A colorful tavern, it often features Spanish guitarists. There's no cover, but local vodka costs 150 pesetas ($1.44); local whisky, 200 pesetas ($1.92); imported whisky, 300 pesetas ($2.88). An intimate atmosphere prevails, and the bartenders aren't pushy about drinks.

6. Santa Eulalia del Río

Five miles north of the Ciudad de Ibiza, on the estuary of the only river in the Balearic Islands, is Santa Eulalia. Formerly patronized by expatriate artists from the capital, it presently draws a broader base of tourism—largely middle-class northern Europeans.

Santa Eulalia nestles at the foot of the Puig de Missa, crowned by an ecclesiastical compound gleaming white in the Ibizan sun. The church dates from the 16th century. The hill lies between the river and the resort. The best beach is El Caná, rapidly becoming cosmopolitan in character.

Santa Eulalia is suitable if you're in the market for a cheap retreat, a relatively quiet and secluded spot free of the plastic quality of San Antonio Abad. Sometimes a visitor has a better chance of finding an accommodation here, despite its location and limited choice of lodgings, than in the other two major towns.

WHERE TO STAY: **Hotel Riomar,** Playa del Pins (tel. 33-03-27), brings a host of modern comforts to service the needs and whims of the guests it welcomes from May through October. Built smack on the beach, it is graced with six floors of good-size, nicely furnished bedrooms, each with a wall of glass opening onto a pigmy balcony. But try to garner one of the sea-view rooms, or you may gaze into the wide eyes of Elsie in the pasture beyond. The 88 double rooms have either private tub or shower baths. The cost for a double is 2200 pesetas ($21.12), 1500 pesetas ($14.40) in a single. For three uncomplicated meals a day, you pay 1700 pesetas ($16.32) per person extra. From the living room lounge, you can make a quick dash for a plunge into the waters of the Mediterranean. The best for the value in Santa Eulalia del Río, the Riomar usually draws a congenial crowd.

Hotel Ses Roques, Calle del Mar (tel. 33-01-00), is modern but basic. It provides year-round accommodations right beside the sea, three floors of 35 rooms—all with private bath (either shower or tub), plus a private balcony. The furnishings are contemporary, and everything's scrubbed and polished daily.

In the cold of an Ibizan winter, the central heating is welcome. The meals are served near the water. Doubles range in price from 1600 pesetas ($15.36) to 2000 pesetas ($19.20), singles from 1200 pesetas ($11.52). A continental breakfast is an extra 150 pesetas ($1.44).

WHERE TO EAT: La Bota, 47 Calle San Vicente (tel. 33-02-06), is a simple little restaurant, with a bar in front and open-air dining in the rear. The menu aims to please with its wide selection. For 550 pesetas ($5.28), you can order the special menú del día, including a bowl of soup, grilled pork chops or fried fish filets, fresh fruit, wine, and good-tasting bread. It's a bargain. The place is open every day till 11 p.m., but closed in December and January.

NIGHTLIFE: Ses Parres, Avenida San Lorenzo (tel. 33-00-32), is a modest little place that tries to stir up a storm in the low night tide of Santa Eulalia. It's good on a summer night if you've exhausted all the gossip on the veranda. The action commences after 10:30 p.m. Men pay 500 pesetas ($4.80) entrance fee, that tab including their first drink. However, women are charged only 400 pesetas ($3.84), but that doesn't include a drink. Guests dance to live music, watching an occasional flamenco or Spanish night show. The club is open every night till 3 a.m.

7. Minorca

[*This section was compiled by Walter Logan, former foreign editor of United Press International who is a summertime resident of Minorca.*]

Minorca, still unspoiled after 7000 years of visitors, is one of the most beautiful islands in the Mediterranean, with miles of sunswept beaches. It is relatively unknown to Americans, but has long been a favorite vacation spot for the English, Germans, French, and Scandinavians.

After Majorca, it is the second largest of the Spanish Balearic islands, but it has more beaches than Majorca, Ibiza, and Formentera combined. These beaches range from miles-long silver or golden crescents of sand to tiny beaches inside great rocky coves, or *calas* as they are called here. These calas are reminiscent of the fjords of Norway.

Minorca, barely 9 miles wide and less than 32 miles long, lies 130 miles off the coast of Spain and 27 miles northeast of Majorca. Its principal city is Mahón, a city of 25,000 people on a rocky bluff overlooking the great port which was fought over for centuries by the British, French, and Spanish.

Minorcans are friendly and prosperous—unemployment is virtually unknown here—and it has not had to depend on tourism, a fact which has kept it so unspoiled. Minorca has only 30 hotels whereas smaller Ibiza has more than 1200. The Minorcans have yet to discover tourist traps and double pricing.

The beaches are the island's greatest attraction, and there is nude bathing at many, although the practice is frowned upon by Spanish law. There are many items of interest for those interested in history, archeology, music, and art. Everywhere you look there is also a restaurant or disco.

A BIT OF HISTORY: The island has been occupied over the centuries by the Phoenicians, Greeks, Romans, Vandals, Byzantines, Moors, Normans, and finally the Spanish. It was occupied for almost all of the 18th century by the British, with one interruption by the French who used the occasion to discover *salsa Mahonesa,* mayonnaise.

The first American midshipmen were trained in the port of Mahón by Admiral James G. Farragut until the U.S. Naval Academy opened at Annapolis in 1845. There is a small American cemetery in the harbor, with graves of young men who died in the service of their country more than a century ago.

Archeologists say Minorca was first occupied as much as 7000 years ago by a strong, athletic race of tribesmen who emerged from their caves to build underground villages, the oldest housing in Europe. The island is dotted with prehistoric monuments still a mystery to scientists. The most spectacular are the *taulas,* Stonehenge-type structures made of a great slab of rock lying atop a vertical slab to form the letter "T." There are also *talayots,* huge circular stone towers. Their purpose is also a mystery.

A PREVIEW OF THE ISLAND: Mahón and neighboring **Villacarlos** still show traces of the long British occupation—casement windows that slide up and down, the only place in Spain where they don't swing out; beautiful Georgian architecture including Golden Farm, the magnificent Georgian mansion overlooking Mahón harbor and where (according to local legend) Admiral Lord Nelson and Lady Hamilton lived in sin.

Ciudadela, on the opposite end of the island, is pure Spanish with its heavy Moorish accents. It is the ecclesiastical capital of Minorca and contains many beautiful palaces and churches. The streets are narrow, flanked by vaulted passages and Arabian-style arches whitewashed and gleaming in the sun. It is noted for its manufacture of women's fine-quality shoes, one of the great bargains of the island. Bargains in men's shoes can be found in Alayor, farther east.

Many artists live in Minorca, and there are frequent exhibitions, listed in the local paper. The **Cathedral of Santa María** in Mahón has one of the great pipe organs of Europe, and world-famous organists give frequent free concerts.

Golf, tennis, and sailing are available to the tourist at comparatively small fees, and details on these can be obtained from your hotel or the Oficina de Turismo in Mahón or Ciudadela—there are signs all over both towns pointing to these offices. Windsurfing is available at every major beach.

GETTING THERE: The high season is, of course, the most delightful time to visit Minorca, but one can swim as early as May (cool evenings) and as late as October (cool evenings and occasional rain).

One-way airfare from Madrid to Mahón is $78 (U.S.), only $40 from Barcelona. One can also take the fast TALGO Rapido express train from Madrid to Barcelona for about the same price as air passage. There is ferry-boat service from Barcelona to Mahón, a trip of nine hours aboard a fairly luxurious liner. Lowest fare is $30 (U.S.) for a deck seat (similar to the seating on a 747). Highest is $65 for a double cabin with bath. Cars cost about $70.

If you're already in Europe, you can get extremely low-price charter flights to Mahón. There's a large British colony in Minorca, and round-trip flights from London can be arranged for as low as £45 ($87.75) (handled through Thomas Cook).

TRANSPORT ON THE ISLAND: The best way to travel around Minorca is by car. Rentals run from about $100 (U.S.) a week for a small Seat (Spanish-made Fiat) to nearly $200 for a large French Renault 12. Motorbikes rent for around $10 a day. Taxis are fairly expensive—$15 from Mahón to the big beach at Son Bou on the south coast. Bus service is excellent and cheap, and the fare from Mahón to Son Bou runs around $1. To Ciudadela, a distance of 25 miles, it's about $2. Bicycles are comparatively cheap but impractical because of the distance to the beaches and the hills en route. The Fomento de Turismo and the Ofcina de Turismo in both Mahón and Ciudadela have complete information about how to arrange transportation in Minorca.

ACCOMMODATIONS: Hotels are generally booked solid through the favorite vacation months of July and August, and it is well to make reservations far in advance.

You can also rent British villas in Minorca through a company called **Broxbourne,** whose address is Hertfordshire, England (tel. 09-02/87211; Telex 267039). A fully furnished villa for six persons, offering swimming, tennis, and golf facilities, can run as low as £202 ($393.90) per person for two weeks, including round-trip airfare from Gatwick.

In hotels, facilities range from the luxurious and expensive four-star Hotel Port Mahón overlooking the beautiful harbor to small residencias with communal showers. Some of these small residencias have double rooms for as little as 800 pesetas ($7.68) a day.

In Mahón

Hotel Port Mahón, Paseo Marítimo (tel. 36-26-00), is a four-star hotel of substance and comfort, considered the best on the island. Those who want to splurge can obtain bookings at this charming, up-to-date hotel which has many traditional features, such as its fine furnishings. The location on the cliffs opens onto what many visitors have considered one of the best views in the Mediterranean.

Rooms are handsomely equipped, containing private plumbing. A double room with bath and balcony overlooking the harbor is 6700 pesetas ($64.32), including breakfast and one other meal, either lunch or dinner. With all three meals, the cost is 8110 pesetas ($77.86) for two persons.

The hotel has a fine restaurant at which you can dine even if you aren't a guest of the hotel. Guests walk through the gardens by day, enjoying the sunny terraces and the private swimming pool, then retreat to the hotel's nightclub after dinner.

If this luxury retreat is far too much for your budget, you can descend to **Sa Roqueta,** 122 Virgin del Carmen (tel. 36-43-35), a one-star hostal-residencia. At this simple place, a double room with private bath rents for 900 pesetas ($8.64); a single, also with bath, goes for 740 pesetas ($7.10).

The one-star **Reynés,** 26 Comercio (tel. 36-40-59), has uncluttered, well-maintained, basic rooms, which cost 1012 pesetas ($9.72) per person, with a bath down the hall. The food is acceptable, and you might want to stay here on the full-board plan at 1086 pesetas ($10.43) per person. Half board (*media pension*) is only 599 pesetas ($5.75) per person daily if you'd like to be away during the lunch hour, returning in time for dinner.

A typical two-star hostale in Mahón is **El Paso,** 157B Cos de Gracia. The entrance is somewhat depressing, but the big rooms inside have a fine view of the city. A double with bath costs two persons only 1351 pesetas ($12.97) per day. An inexpensive bar and restaurant is in the same building.

At Villacarlos

The leading hotel in Villacarlos is the **Hotel Agamenón,** Paraje Fontanillas (tel. 36-21-50), a gleaming, white, six-story hotel overlooking the harbor at a point which, according to local legend, receives the first morning sun in Spain. It has everything from a swimming pool to its own disco. There are plenty of terraces for soaking up the sun. Rooms are attractively, but simply, furnished, and guests can book in here any time between March and October. Rates run from 3170 pesetas ($30.43) for two persons in a double room. Half board—breakfast and either lunch or dinner—runs the bill up to 5260 pesetas ($50.50) for two persons daily. Or you can have full board—all three meals—for 6350 pesetas ($60.96) in a double.

There are some real bargains in Villacarlos. In Horizonte (horizons), a housing development on the edge of the city, there is the one-star hostal, **Horizonte,** a small and immaculately clean hotel where double rooms with bath are 1400 pesetas ($13.44) per day. A room with lavatory (shower down the hall) goes for only 800 pesetas ($7.68). Full pension is 1050 pesetas ($10.08) per person daily, and half board goes for just 700 pesetas ($6.72) per person.

On the Outskirts

On the highway between Villacarlos and Mahón is the small **Hotel del Almirante,** Fonduco, Puerto de Mahón, Villacarlos (tel. 36-27-00), one of the most beautiful on the island. It was originally the home of Admiral Collingwood, Nelson's flag officer, and has a spectacular view of the port, directly across from Nelson's huge villa. A double, including breakfast and either lunch or dinner, is 1750 pesetas ($16.80) per person daily. Full board is 2000 pesetas ($19.20) per person daily. The hotel, a red and white Georgian mansion, with a pool and tennis court, is tucked into a setting of bougainvillea, orange nasturtiums, and pine trees.

Cala Galdana Beach

Every major beach in Minorca has a large resort hotel, as fully equipped as a cruise ship, with swimming pools, discos, restaurants, and bars. A typical one is **Hotel Los Gavilanes,** one of the more beautiful on the island. The big (357 rooms) hotel with a magnificent view of the Mediterranean runs 3000 pesetas ($28.80) for two persons in a room with bath. With all three meals, the charge comes to 3365 pesetas ($32.30) per person daily.

Ciudadela

A typical fonda is the **España,** 13 Calvo Sotelo (tel. 38-02-88), where a double room rents for only 950 pesetas ($9.12), a single for 700 pesetas ($6.72). The shower is down the hall.

There are also dozens of *casas de huespedes,* usually private homes that take in roomers. A typical one is **Validemosa,** 84 República Argentina (tel. 38-15-36), where a double room—simple, basic, uncluttered—rents for only 600 pesetas ($5.76) a day, a single costing 300 pesetas ($2.88). There is a communal shower. This is one of the best bargains on the island.

WHERE TO DINE: As some wit said, the British landed in 1708, and Minorca is still studded with fish and chips places. There are also pizza parlors and a few hamburger joints. Restaurants come and go on Minorca almost as often as the tourists, but a few landmarks remain.

The best buys for lunch are the innumerable beach restaurants, where you traipse in barefoot in your swimming togs. Most specialize in freshly caught seafood. The menus are in Spanish, English, French, and German, and the prices are low. A typical one is **Es Bruc** restaurant, at the western end of Santo Tomás beach, where you get a magnificent view of the sunset, plus dinner for two, including a bottle of wine, for 1280 pesetas ($12.29).

You can eat for very little at some of the fast-food restaurants now found throughout much of Minorca. There are literally hundreds of restaurants in Minorca, and it is better to avoid the complete "pension" at your hotel so you can sample them.

At Mahón

One of those landmarks referred to is **Rocamar,** on the Mahón harbor (tel. 36-56-01). Here a dinner for one with wine will run about $12 (U.S.). Some prize varieties of fish can be expensive, but not the small rougets or red mullet which are not only moderately priced, but delicate in flavor. Often the fish of the day is prepared with wild fennel which is then flamed under the catch.

A very good island restaurant with typical Minorcan food is **Pilar's,** 61 Cardona y Orfila (tel. 36-68-17). Appetizers run around 400 pesetas ($3.84), and seafood plates average around 780 pesetas ($7.49). Desserts from the buffet cost from 150 pesetas ($1.44) to 250 pesetas ($2.40). The four best tables are in the patio at the rear and must be reserved in advance.

At Fornells

This north coast fishing village, overlooking a yacht harbor, lies about 18½ miles from Mahón. If you have a car, you might want to drive there to sample the food at the following well-recommended place:

Es Plá, Passaje d'Es Plá (tel. 37-50-75), is another classic Minorcan restaurant, a favorite of King Juan Carlos. It does a number of fish dishes. Try, if featured on the menu, such specialties as mero (brill) which is grilled and served with a mayonnaise sauce, and calamares (squid) which is also grilled. With wine, salad, and dessert, your dinner should run as low as $15 (U.S.) per person. However, Es Plá is known for its local specialty, caldereta de langosta, a peppery soup which contains chunks of spiny lobster. But lobster now runs as much as $25 a pound.

At Ciudadela

Like Rocamar at Mahón and Es Plá at Fornells, the third "classic" restaurant is **Casa Manola,** 105 Marina (tel. 38-17-28), in the yacht basin at Ciudadela. It is also a favorite with the king of Spain. The specialty, as in most Minorcan restaurants, is seafood. Dinners run around $15 (U.S.) per person, and reservations are necessary.

On the Outskirts

A typical British restaurant is **El Picadero** (tel. 36-32-68), on the road between Mahón and San Luís. Fresh fish will run around 900 pesetas ($8.64) per person, and owner Terence Hazzard will let you mix your own dry martini at the bar.

A brilliant country restaurant is **Biniali** (tel. 36-17-24), just outside San Luís, on the road to Binibeca. Biniali is an exquisite small hotel furnished with Spanish antiques. Incidentally, it rents a double room with bath for 3500 pesetas ($33.60) in case you'd like to stay here.

Again, the specialty is seafood, served by waitresses wearing such modern fashions as Nancy Reagan–type bloomers. Dinner for two with wine will run around 2500 pesetas ($24).

AFTER DARK: Cala'n Porter has the most spectacular disco, **Cova d'en Xoroi,** a vast cave overlooking the sea 100 feet below. Dancing is usually to recorded music, often American. The first drink costs 600 pesetas ($5.76).

Chapter XIV

GIBRALTAR

1. **Where to Stay**
2. **Where to Eat**
3. **What to See and Do**
4. **The Rock After Dark**

WHERE ELSE WOULD you find a town which is also a country? Gibraltar is only 2¼ square miles in size, with a population of 30,000, but it has its own airport, currency, postage stamps, naval and military garrisons, two cathedrals, its own newspapers, radio, and TV—and a casino. "The Rock" enjoys a healthy climate and has a recorded history dating from A.D. 711 and traces of cave occupation 40,000 years ago.

The Rock of Gibraltar is a massive limestone rock rising out of the sea to a height of 1396 feet, often referred to as the Gateway to the Mediterranean. It was originally a Phoenician trading post called Calpe. In Greek mythology it was the northern bastion of the Pillars of Hercules. Abyla (now Jebel Musa at Ceuta) was the southern bastion. Hercules is said to have stood with a foot on each "pillar," pushed them apart, and formed a bridge across the straits. During Phoenician domination of the Mediterranean, it was also recorded that Calpe was the end of the world, the point beyond which no trader should venture.

In 711, a Berber called Tarik Ibn Zeyad landed and named the rock Begel Tarik (mountain of Tarik), from which the name of Gibraltar is derived. The rock was captured from the Moors in 1309 by the marauding El Bueno, then recaptured by the Moors in 1333. In 1462 Spain seized and fortified the prestigious rock against further attack but, in 1704, during the Spanish War of Succession, the British made a surprise attack, capturing the fortress with little opposition.

The Spanish and the French have since made attempts to conquer the rock by siege, bombardment, tunneling, and, finally, with specially reinforced ships, upon which the British rained red-hot cannon balls which set the ships afire.

There have been three treaties confirming Gibraltar as a British possession —Utrecht, 1715; Seville, 1729; and Versailles, 1783. In two world wars, the rock was invaluable in keeping the Mediterranean open in spite of aerial bombardment. Its only land frontier—referred to by many Gibraltarians as the Garlic Wall—was closed by the Spaniards in 1966, in an attempt to enforce Spanish sovereignty on the people. The Spanish finally banned all trade to Gibraltar in 1969 in an attempt to bring further pressure to bear. But the Gibraltarians, in a free vote, decided by 12,000 to 44 to remain under British rule.

Spain's frontier restrictions against Gibraltar were to have been lifted on April 20, 1982, but tension over the British invasion of the Falklands forced a postponement. Check with local tourist offices for the latest news about the frontier before heading there. If entry from Spain is not possible by the time of your visit, you'll have to fly there or take a boat from Tangier.

Two languages are spoken, English and Spanish. The community is made up of Gibraltarians, Britons, Spaniards, and a few Italians and Indians. More recently, Moroccans have taken over the jobs of the Spanish workers who used to flock daily on to the rock until the frontier was closed.

The town of Gibraltar lies on the west side of the rock around the harbors.

GETTING THERE: Gibraltar can be reached by air or sea, and, perhaps by the time you read this, the frontier with Spain at La Línea will have been reopened, at least to foot passengers and hopefully to vehicles as well.

Because it is under the British Crown, Gibraltar benefits from advantageous airfares from London, and you may find this an ideal gateway for your subsequent tour of southern Spain or North Africa. The advance-purchase one-way airfare from London is £175 ($341.25), and a round-trip exclusion fare goes for £224 ($436.80). Services are operated by **British Airways** and **Gibair** which also provide the service to Tangier. If you are already in Morocco, then Gibair charges £22 ($42.90) each way. Don't be surprised if you hear the plane referred to as Yogi Bear, as this is the affectionate name Gibraltarians have for their air link with Morocco.

Their affection also extends to **Mons Calpe,** the ferry which has been covering the crossing of the straits for the last 30-odd years. Now that the Spanish workers have been replaced by Moroccans, the ferry has gained a new lease on life. Under the command of Bob Thornton, the second captain, the trip takes three hours. A one-way ticket costs £13 ($25.35), a same-day round trip the same price. On some days she stays long enough for you to visit the Casbah and walk back to the harbor through the Medina. In addition to the ferry, there is a hydrofoil service to Tangier and Mdiq, with a one-way journey costing £10 ($19.50) or £8.50 ($16.58) to Mdiq. The hydrofoil service only sells tickets on the day before you wish to travel, as the weather often makes the crossing impossible.

From Tangier, it is possible to link up with the ferry to Algeciras, only five miles across the bay from Gibraltar (this crossing only costs about £5 ($9.75) in steerage, £8 ($15.60) to travel in comparative style). Of course, if the frontier is open, it should be possible to pass at will into Spain at **La Línea,** now almost a forgotten town but sure to prosper again.

1. Where to Stay

Accommodations in Gibraltar are limited, and tend to be more expensive in general than those in Morocco or along the Costa del Sol in Spain. During the summer, the British book most of the rooms, so reservations are strongly recommended. I've included the following listing of hotels, many of which are, frankly, over our budget, but could be handy to know about if you find yourself staying over in Gibraltar.

Montarik Hotel, Main Street (tel. 4662), is a charming collection of awnings and balconies above the shops of this major artery. The entrance is down Bedlam Court, opening into a bare lobby with an Elizabethan Room for candlelit dinners or substantial lunches. A cheerful, friendly bar makes up the ground floor. Rooms are neat with good beds, and all have a bathroom or shower as well as a phone. On the roof the sun terrace offers a certain amount of privacy among the rooftops of the town. It is open only in July, August, and September. There is also a coffeeshop for quick snacks and breakfast, plus a hairdressing salon and laundry service.

A single room with shower goes from £12 ($23.40) and a double with shower for £16 ($31.20), increasing to £17 ($33.15) with private bath. There are some three-bedded rooms at £23 ($44.85). Tariffs include a continental breakfast. Tea, coffee, and basic supplies can be made ready for your arrival, and the shops of Main Street and the market are just outside.

Major (retired) A. L. Casciaro rules the hotel with a steady hand, seeing that the place is kept spotless. A three-course table d'hôte meal costs £4.50 ($8.78). The à la carte menu includes appetizers of prawns or mushrooms in cheese sauce, mussels (in season), pâté and fruit cocktails; main dishes of fresh fish, sole, swordfish and hake, chicken and steaks, all served with potatoes and fresh vegetables or a mixed salad. Three courses will cost about £7 ($13.65) unless you order smoked salmon and the chef's special filet steak which are more expensive.

Bristol Hotel, Cathedral Square (tel. 2992), is a bright white building on a pretty square opposite the Anglican cathedral and across from the Tourist Board. There is a large lounge and bar, and the restaurant is reached by a covered bridge across a narrow side street and down into the hotel's garden. As all catering is done on this side, room service can only be provided when you are ill or otherwise confined to your room. There is a charming leafy garden surrounding a small swimming pool and a sauna. Rooms have been recently refurnished. A single without bath goes for £10.50 ($20.48); with bath, £14.50 ($28.28). Doubles are from £16 ($31.20) to £23 ($44.85). A 12½% service charge is added to all bills. A table d'hôte meal costs around £3.40 ($6.63).

Mr. Patron, the manager, is very eager to update and improve the service offered to all guests. All units have radio and color TV (the only hotel to offer color TV in each room). An English-language program is broadcast nightly from 7 p.m. to midnight. Meals in the Garden Club are simple but tasty, and if you don't want the set menu, there's a reasonable à la carte choice. Picnic lunches at £2 ($3.90) each are available if you give the staff time enough to prepare. All in all, the Bristol is a very reasonable and central place.

Queens Hotel, Boyd Street (tel. 74000), lies close to the bottom station of the cable car that travels to the top of the rock. It's a rather plain, tall building surrounded by busy streets. The furnishings are very Spanish with roughcast walls and dark wood beams in the bar and lounge. There is an elegant dining room with a terrace for coffee or dancing after dinner in summertime. Bedrooms are large, and many have communicating rooms for family occupancy. Most have balconies and private baths or showers. A bathless single rents for £8 ($15.60), going up to £10 ($19.50) with private shower or bath. Without bath, a double or twin ranges from £10 ($19.50), going up to £20 ($39) in a twin with bath and sea view, plus 12% added for service. There is a friendly atmosphere and the chef is known for his good French cuisine. A continental breakfast costs £1.50 ($2.93), but most guests seem to order the English one at £2.50 ($4.88). No lunch is served, and dinner costs from £5 ($9.75).

The two super-splurge hotels in the town are as follows:

Holiday Inn, Governor's Parade (tel. 70500), stands on a delightful tree-lined square in the old and interesting part of town, within steps of Main Street. A friendly, pleasant place, it has a large and cheerful bar, lively with talk and chatter, which is furnished with deep leather chairs. In the basement, the coffeeshop serves hamburgers, fried fish, calamares, omelets, salads, and other light meals for about £3 ($5.85) a dish. Breakfast is a help-yourself affair costing

£5 ($9.75) for a selection of fruits, yogurts, bacon, and eggs. A set lunch or dinner costs around £8 ($15.60). On the roof, the eighth floor, is a glass-walled patio and swimming pool. Here, too, guests of the Oasis Night Club can dance into the night to disco and live groups, while enjoying views over the harbor and bay. Singles are £33 ($64.35); doubles and twins, £36 ($70.20). All units have bathrooms, television sets, and telephones.

Rock Hotel, Europa Road (tel. 73000), lies quite a steep walk up from sea level, with panoramic views over the Alameda Gardens and the Naval Dockyard to Algeciras across the bay. This is *the* place for the traditionalist. There are gentle walks through the geranium-bright gardens, as well as a wisteria-covered terrace for a sundowner. The bar is sober with leather armchairs and naval battle scenes on the walls. There is TV in the lounge and dancing nightly in the soundproof disco. The large, airy dining room has a small dance floor with dancing to a small group. A set dinner or lunch costs about £9.50 ($18.53), and there is a wide à la carte menu. A single room facing the Rock costs £23 ($44.85), a sea-facing single with bathroom and balcony at £25 ($48.75). Doubles, all with bathroom, go from £25 ($48.75), rising to £30 ($58.50) if facing the sea. Breakfast is extra, although service is included. The swimming pool in the garden has a restaurant and bar. Towels are provided, and it is open to nonresidents for a small admission charge.

Caleta Palace Hotel, Catalán Bay (tel. 4632), lies at the end of Catalán Bay, on the east side of the rock. A holiday hotel, it was built out on rocks over the sea with sun terraces and a swimming pool with steps down to the water. In all, it's an easy place to stay and relax in. Most rooms have balconies and overlook the sea. There are several bars, and guests dance in the Catalán Room to the music of the resident trio. The Arcadia Bar stays open until near dawn when the night ends with bacon and eggs for breakfast. There are quiet lounges or the more boisterous games room. Temporary membership at nearby tennis and squash clubs can be arranged. There is a hairdressing salon, and the hotel shops stock a wide selection of useful souvenirs and beach clothes. A single with a bath and a Rock view rents for £15 ($29.25), the tab rising to £17 ($33.15) with a sea view. An inland twin with bath costs £26.50 ($51.68), the price jumping to £29.50 ($57.53) with a sea view. All units have private bathrooms, and a continental breakfast is included in the room rate, although service is added. Snacks in the coffeeshop start at 55p ($1.07), and a meal in the Grill Room will average about £8 ($15.60).

Your Own Apartment

Both Worlds, Sandy Bay (tel. 6191), is a long, low, four-storied apartment complex stretching along the length of Sandy Bay. The units have direct access to the sands and the crystal-clear Mediterranean; each has one or two twin-bedded bedrooms, baths with shower, and well-equipped kitchens, plus a patio-balcony overlooking the bay. There is daily maid service, and, if you decide not to cook dinner, the hotel's restaurant will serve an al fresco meal. In the complex is a bar and a supermarket, and, in summer, a beach grill. TV, table tennis, bars, and weekly discos save you from having to go around the Rock for your entertainment. In addition to the sea, there is a swimming pool. In summer an excellent babysitting service is provided as well as a supervised playroom for children. A two-bedded apartment rents for £11 ($21.45) per person per day; a four-bedded apartment, £9.70 ($18.92) per person. Sole occupancy of an apartment costs 50% on top of the room rate.

Both Worlds also has the Battle of Trafalgar Coffee Shop and Grill and Nelson Bar. On Sunday they serve a traditional three-course lunch. At other times, the menu includes baked potato with crispy bacon, sour cream, and chives; smoked mackerel and Gibraltar Rocks (that is, mushrooms deep-fried and served with tartar sauce); chili con carne; spare ribs; sirloin and filet steaks; stewed beef and vegetables; spaghetti; and fried chicken. Desserts feature ice cream and sundaes. The average meal costs from £4 ($7.80). If you're here for lunch, you can order hamburgers with bacon, cheese, or chili sauce, ranging from £1.20 ($2.34) to £2.20 ($4.29). Sandwiches, such as roast beef with cole slaw and horseradish, cost from £1.75 ($3.41). For dessert, averaging around 75p ($1.46), you are served apple pie, cheesecake, or crêpes. They also do a "take-away" service in case you want to bring food back to eat inside your apartment.

Ocean Heights, Montagu Place (tel. 5548), is back in town, two minutes from Main Street and close to the harbor, within easy reach of the fish and general markets for those who really want to integrate and shop alongside the Gibraltarian housewives where the produce is fresher. In fact, it's only about a two-minute walk from the center of Gibraltar life—stores, shops, banks, restaurants, and bars. The upper floors have good views over the harbor. Apartments consist of studios, or one-, two-, or three-bedroom units, simply but well-furnished with bathroom or shower room, kitchen with stove, refrigerator, and waste disposal. There is a cleaning service and also a launderette with ironing facilities. Apartments sleep two to six persons and range from £7 ($13.65) to £14.50 ($28.28) per person per night. On the roof is a swimming pool plus an open sun terrace. Below the block is Romano's restaurant and bar, separately owned and run, offering grills and more complicated dishes, flambé grills, and crêpes. Light lunches are served daily on the terrace, and on Friday and Saturday nights a dinner dance is held. The complex contains three elevators. Its Romano's restaurant and bar offers a wide choice of à la carte and table d'hôte meals with dinner dances every Friday and Saturday. The Ocean Heights Health Club has recently opened, featuring a range of fully equipped facilities, including saunas.

2. Where to Eat

In town, Main Street and Irish Town, which run parallel from Close to Casemates Gate, contain many of the most popular restaurants. This is where you'll find a multitude of English-sounding pubs, such as the Bull and Bush, the Captain's Cabin, the Royal Oak, or the Mason's Arms.

La Trattoria Del Pescatore, 79 Irish Town (tel. 5566), is a large bare room reached through a bar where seafood snacks, samosas, and other Indian delicacies are served. The walls are decorated with pictures of the sea, fish nets, floats, and wine bottles. Fish, of course, is the specialty and, unless you are a curry-lover, you should try the bouillabaisse, octopus salad, or mussels. Frito misto or bream Trattoria is the chef's specialty, as is grilled swordfish, served Catalán style. Bass and sole are among the most popular items. The day's prices for fresh fish are shown on the blackboard which usually lists some 15 different types. Those who don't want fish might prefer the beef Stroganoff or tournedos Rossini au poivre. You won't really need a dessert, the choice of which consists mainly of flan and ice cream. Coffee is a good way to finish. A meal for two, including a bottle of light white wine and 10% service, will be about £6.50 ($12.68) per person. The restaurant is open daily from noon to 3 p.m. and from 7 p.m. to midnight.

Irish Town Fisheries, 39–41 Irish Town (tel. 74970). You can eat in style here in the York Room Restaurant where the fish overhangs the edge of the plate. But for many, the delight of this fish and chip shop is that the owners still wrap the fish and chips in newspaper after smothering them in vinegar and salt (you can have it au naturel if you wish). A large portion of cod or haddock cooked in their "secret recipe" batter costs 65p ($1.27). Fried potatoes are another 35p (68¢) per portion. The price of a meal of plaice and chips, followed by ice cream, is £3.80 ($7.41).

La Mancha, 6 Lynch's Lane, off Main Street (tel. 5300), is a simple room with high arched roof and Quixotic memorabilia decorating the walls. A tiny bar at the entrance is home base for Mrs. Santos who serves drinks, takes orders, sets tables, and generally cajoles the chef, placates the waiters, and greets customers. Alex Santos, her husband, is part of a singing group, Los Peninsulares. On Saturday evening they bring live entertainment to your table. On that night it is advisable to make a reservation.

Dishes are typically Spanish—salad with tunafish, anchovies, and hard-boiled eggs, Spanish omelet or eggs flamenco. Crêpes, a house specialty, appear as an appetizer filled with ham, cheese, and cream. Fish such as sole and swordfish is only included on the menu when it is absolutely fresh. A tournedos Rossini or a chateaubriand are among the most popular meat dishes. Paella for two, prepared only to order given 24 hours in advance, is £8 ($15.60) or you can have a pepper steak or steak Diane for £4 ($7.80). Desserts include more crêpes—stuffed with lemon, cream, and sugar, or peanuts and chocolate. A 10% service charge is added to all bills, and there is a cover charge of 25p (49¢) a person. Mohamed, the chef, manages to operate very efficiently in his tiny kitchen at the end of the room and periodically comes up for air to look around the red-checked tables and see whether his efforts are appreciated. It is open daily except Sunday from 12:30 p.m. to 2:30 p.m. and 8 p.m. to 10:30 p.m.

The Spinning Wheel, 9 Horse Barrack Lane off Main Street (tel. 6091), is owned by Norman Birch, an ex-Flying Squad policeman from London and his wife, Raqui. He claims to be general factotum in his restaurant, cleaner, potman, and washer-up, but he also manages to find time to be the chairman of the Licensed Victuallers' Association. The food has an international flavor coupled with comfortable, continental-style surroundings. Lobster cooked in a variety of ways, at £9.50 ($18.53); langoustines, at £7.45 ($14.53); and poached salmon are among the specialties, but the accent on fish includes a variety of prawn and scampi dishes at £4.40 ($8.58), or a selection of soles at £5.80 ($11.31), and swordfish steak at £3.85 ($7.51). Chicken, lamb, veal, and a variety of steaks are all in the £4 ($7.80) to £4.70 ($9.17) range. A beef Wellington or chateaubriand will cost about £9.70 ($18.92) for two persons, and a lasagne main course is £3.25 ($6.34). Vegetarian dishes go for about £3.25 also. Of course, the experienced chefs will, given time, prepare whatever suits you, as all food is cooked to order. An adjoining lounge will allow you to relax over coffee and liqueurs, in air-conditioned comfort. In the same courtyard, a grill bar is open all day, providing hot and cold snacks.

Jim's Den, 25 Prince Edward's Rd. (tel. 71289). Up the hill from the Holiday Inn, you come to the black doors and large window of an old warehouse. It's now the lair of Jim Wright and his wife Denny, who have created a pleasant, relaxed restaurant. A long bar is presided over by the tall, good-looking Mohamed. Singles are asked to eat at the stools there when the tables are filled. The wooden tables are always scrubbed clean, and rugs add color to the stone floor.

Anchors and a ship's bell provide the decor, and you can turn your entire concentration on the menu and the succulent steaks cooked at the open barbecue by Jim. Portions are huge. A T-bone, more than 16 ounces in weight, goes for £5.45 ($10.63), a rump steak for £3.10 ($6.05), and a filet for £4 ($7.80).

As a side order, try a fresh salad at 95p ($1.85), french fries or new potatoes at 55p ($1.07), or Jim's special fried onions at 55p also.

Desserts include a variety of crêpes. Jim claims to have been the first restaurant in Gibraltar to put them on the menu. Fillings range from simple—lemon and sugar—to spectacular, an alcoholic one flambeed in Grand Marnier, the cost going from 70p ($1.37) to £1.60 ($3.12).

Jim also serves more than a dozen special coffees—Gaelic, Highland, Jamaican, Calypso—costing around £1.30 ($2.54). Of course, you can also end your meal with straight coffee. A royal feast of prawn cocktail, a "small" (really three chunky pieces) filet with onions and french fries, then a crêpe will cost around £7 ($13.65) per person. The house wine goes for £3 ($5.85) a bottle. There's a cover of 30p (59¢), but no service charge.

Strings, 44 Cornwall's Lane (tel. 4800), is owned and run by Peter Wheatley who claims to be found nightly in one of two places—behind the bar with a drink in his hand, or else under the table by the door (letting his friends do his work for him). Actually, I've only seen him perfectly "sober" and behind the bar hard at work.

Strings is a converted warehouse with a wooden ceiling and a carpet-covered stone floor. Tables are in booths with high-backed bench seats and old pictures on the walls. Lighting is by candles stuck in wax-covered bottles. At a small bar built from barrels you can meet the aforementioned Peter and contemplate the blackboard with the day's specials. I always select either the day's fish catch, or fresh game when it's featured. You'll have to wait for your meal once you've ordered, as everything is prepared to order. A £3 ($5.85) bottle of wine will help you while away the time.

Appetizers include a large prawn cocktail (more prawns than greenery), a Mediterranean seafood soup with brandy, Peter's chicken liver pâté served with red currant jelly and toast. Main courses include a ten-ounce filet steak, chicken crêpes with white wine sauce, and a vegetarian platter served with jacket potatoes, "chips," and various vegetables and a salad. All desserts are homemade and succulent, enticing if you still have room. A meal will cost around £7.50 ($14.63) if you last through three courses. A 10% service charge is added to your bill. The establishment is open daily except Monday from 8 p.m. to midnight.

Among the budget places in town, the **Capri Restaurant,** 45 Main St., must be one of the best. The place hums with lively banter and laughter. The butts of much of the humor are owners John Byrne and Joe Hill, who are normally behind the bar except when Joe is away with the hockey team. Your selection is likely to include curry and rice, £1.65 ($3.22); fish and chips, calamares (squid), meatballs and chips (or else boiled potatoes), priced at £1.50 ($2.93). If you want lighter fare, order the hamburgers at 65p ($1.27) or salads at £1.20 ($2.34). Sandwiches and omelets are priced from 55p ($1.07) to 90p ($1.76), and a jacket potato with sour cream or butter goes for 45p (88¢). Hours are Monday to Saturday from noon to 2:30 p.m. and 7 to 11:30 p.m.

The **Oliver Twist Bar,** 78b Irish Town (tel. 6097), serves steak pie and chips for £1.25 ($2.44) and scampi and chips at £2 ($3.90). There is a separate room with two pool tables and loud music.

Paddington's. The Arcade, off Main Street (tel. 5387), is the domain of Brian Strange and his cat Paddy, with a recent addition, baby Charlene. Snacks and tapas are available at the bar during lunchtime, and in the evening tables are set out in the narrow alleyway between balconied houses to augment those inside the restaurant. Appetizers include fresh melon with port, harida (a rich Moroccan soup), and sweet corn for around £1 ($1.95). Main dishes feature chateaubriand with brandy sauce for two, £8 ($15.60); steak au poivre, £3.80

($7.41); and fresh swordfish au gratin, £3.50 ($6.83). Paddington Bear, that refugee from the famous railway station of the same name, is the mascot of the place.

Casa Antonio, Waterport (tel. 2069), is upstairs above what appears to be a real harbor bar. It is a large, airy room with windows the length of the place, overlooking the boats and harbor life. William Hernandez specializes in fish, and his menu has a distinctly Spanish flavor. Soups are £1.20 ($2.34), including gazpacho, shellfish, and garlic with egg. The season's salad is 90p ($1.76). Paella for two goes for £7.50 ($14.63), and fresh grilled or fried hake, bream, or swordfish ranges from £3.50 ($6.83) to £3.90 ($7.61). Steaks and chops are also available, beginning at £2.90 ($5.66) and going up to £3.95 ($7.70). Very popular with locals, the restaurant is open daily except Monday from noon to 3 p.m. and 8 p.m. to midnight.

Wesley House Restaurant, Main Street at Victualling Office Lane (tel. 4493), is run by the Methodist church in a large, plain room with a stone floor and bare tables. This must surely be the most economical place on the Rock for a square meal. From the long serving counter, the meal of the day costs just £2.50 ($4.88) for a soup, a meat dish (such as braised steak, potatoes, and a vegetable), then dessert. Rolls and sandwiches cost from 30p (59¢) to 50p (98¢); ham and chips, £1.40 ($2.73); and steak, egg, and chips, a grand £2 ($3.90). The place is open Monday to Saturday from 9 a.m. to 1:30 p.m. and 3:30 to 8 p.m.

A leading splurge restaurant is **Country Cottage,** 13–15 Giro's Passage, off Main Street across from the Roman Catholic cathedral (tel. 70084). Bob and Marg Laing from Lincolnshire, England, visited the Rock and liked the people. Bob took a year to build the restaurant from a heap of rubble on a rubbish tip. They imported a chef, Steve Shaw, from Coventry and pride themselves that everything is entirely homemade. There is a tiny bar where you pick your menu before taking one of the polished tables with flickering candles and high-backed settles. Today Bob flits between Gibraltar and Inverness, Florida, where he is part owner of a motel.

The à la carte menu includes house specials such as prawn cocktail with mushrooms and pineapple, £2.10 ($4.10), and roast baby lamb carved at your table, £11 ($21.45) for two. Other dishes include seafood pancake with cheese sauce, farmhouse beef stew, butter roasted spring chicken, and beef Wellington, each main course served with fresh vegetables, potatoes, and hot garlic bread. A blackboard menu displays specials such as fresh salmon and other seasonal dishes, including lobster and duck. Desserts from the trolley are £1 ($1.95), and unlimited coffee served with chocolate mints goes for 70p ($1.37). Bob and Marg are an enterprising young couple who deserve to go far. Their place has atmosphere, and the standard of cooking and choice of menu are excellent. The Cottage is open daily, except Monday, for dinner only from 7:30 to 11 p.m. Reservations are recommended.

English Tearooms, 9 Market Lane, is an attractive tearoom with white tables set close together. The staff is friendly, and service is from 9 a.m. to 6 p.m. Monday to Friday (from 9 a.m. to noon on Saturday). Meals start with an English breakfast at £2.10 ($4.10), consisting of juice or cereal, bacon, egg and sausage, toast and marmalade, coffee or tea. Lunch will find you ordering farmhouse soup at 45p (88¢); eggs and bacon, 80p ($1.56); omelets at 80p to £1.25 ($2.44), or a ploughman's lunch at £1.25, too. The set lunch at £2.30 ($4.49) is likely to feature soup or juice, a salad with ham or cheese, an omelet or spaghetti, ending with dessert, and tea or coffee. You can also drop in after sightseeing for an afternoon tea, British style, with sandwiches, costing around £1 ($1.95).

Over in Catalán Bay, the **Village Inn** has an excellent seafood menu of snacks and tapas, priced from 60p ($1.17), to be eaten on the patio not 30 paces from the beach. They specialize in light meals—for example, swordfish, salad, and chips for £2.75 ($5.36).

Next door, **Seawave** also has salads and seafood snacks beginning at 60p ($1.17). Both are open most of the day and until midnight.

Also at Catalán Bay is the **Bistro Piccolo,** run by Marjory Frattaroli, at 15 Sir Herbert Miles Rd. It's an open beach-café style place, with clean tables and wicker chairs. The menu is simple with soups around 65p ($1.27). Also offered are pastas, spaghetti, lasagne, grills, salads, and fried sandwiches. Steak and chips costs £2.75 ($5.36); chicken and salad, £2.20 ($4.29). The Bistro usually has something for all tastes and pockets.

3. What to See and Do

Your starting point is the frontier at **La Línea,** Spain, just beyond the friendly, informal airport, called by the Gibraltarians the **Garlic Wall.** There is little to see other than two sets of gates, a rather bored Guardia Civil in the distance, and the odd dog who knows no frontiers. Cross the airport runway with the sea on either end. On your right you see the Victoria Stadium and Sports Center.

At Sun Dial, turn left (east) and you drive straight to **Eastern Beach,** then on to **Catalán Bay** and **Sandy Bay.** Between these two bays, the major Water Catchment Area rises to your right; an enormous area of mountainside, 34 acres of sand and concrete. Thousands of tons of water are stored in caves below the catchment area, where it is purified and pumped to the town and the docks for use by naval and other vessels in the harbor. Shortly after leaving Sandy Bay, you enter one of Gib's famous tunnels, the **Dudley Ward,** some 800 meters in length. It emerges above Boathouse Cove and the Gibraltar clay-pigeon shooting club on Europa Advance Road. The shooting club is on the left, and visitors are welcomed.

Continue on south to **Europa Point,** called by many the end of Europe. The most southerly point in Europe is actually Tarifa, Spain, which can be seen in the distance from the boat crossing to Tangier. The modern word "Tariff" is derived from the ancient practice of stringing small boats across the straits from Tarifa to Morocco and extracting tolls from all who passed beyond this ancient end of the world. At Europa Point is the lighthouse built in 1841 by Trinity House, the general lighthouse and pilotage authority for Great Britain, incorporated in 1514 by Henry VIII.

Standing by the light, you can see across the straits to the west of Ceuta to Jebel Musa (formerly Mount Abyla), the other Pillar of Hercules. Here also is Lloyd's of London's only foreign spotting station, recording every merchant ship to enter or leave the Mediterranean. Some 80 to 100 ships pass by during a 24-hour period, and also many yachtsmen voluntarily report their presence and intentions. Lloyd's will, on request, without charge, notify a friend or relative through their local yacht club.

On the Europa Road, back toward the town on the east of the Rock, is the **Chapel of Our Lady of Europa.** The chapel is much venerated and often saluted by passing vessels. Before the lighthouse was built, the small chapel kept a light burning day and night to warn passersby of the treacherous rocks and the narrowness of the passage.

The chapel was pillaged by the Turks in 1540. It is said that the first time the British attempted to fire on it, the shot remained in the cannon barrel. A volunteer was called for to crawl down the barrel, and the only one to step forward was the drummer boy. Probably with a hard push from behind, he climbed down the muzzle head-first and freed the cannon ball. For his bravery, he was promoted on the spot to sergeant, and was for years the youngest to hold this rank in the British army.

You now rejoin Europa Road by way of Rosia Road, then take a sharp right beyond the filling station to Witham's Road. At St. Joseph's Church, turn left and past the hospital to the casino on Europa Road. Turn right and take Engineer Road climbing toward the top of the Rock. As you climb, notice the large iron rings set in the rock walls, which were designed to haul the old naval cannons to the top. The cannons were hauled up and placed in such strategic positions as Rooke Battery just below the summit. After Engineer Road, turn left on to Queens Road until a sharp right-hand turn takes you to—

St. Michael's Cave (tel. 73130), which is open from 10 a.m. to 7 p.m. in summer (to 5 p.m. in winter). The Lower Hall and lake are connected to the Upper Hall by five passages spanning the 50- to 150-foot difference in depth. The endless stories of adventures in the labyrinth of passages that have formed naturally in the porous rock are an attraction to speleologists, and it is possible for even an amateur to travel miles underground. For further details, get in touch with the Speleological Section of the Gibraltar Society, known as the Gibraltar Caving Society, c/o the Tourist Office, Cathedral Square, Gibraltar. If you are fortunate enough to be in Gibraltar when the **son et lumière** program is on, I can recommend it as the evening entertainment. Otherwise, just enter the caves and listen to the carefully chosen music. Admission is 90p ($1.76) for adults, 50p (98¢) for children.

On leaving the caves, rejoin Queen's Road, then take the left fork on to Old Queen's Road to visit the **Rock Apes.** Although almost universally known as Barbary Apes, they are actually tailless monkeys (macaques). Legend has it that the first apes were either brought in by the Moors or that they found their way through a tunnel that linked St. Michael's Cave with Africa and that, when Africa and Europe were joined together, there were many more monkey packs. Today there are only two packs, some 40 apes in all. Each pack has its leader and its own den halfway up the Rock. Regular mealtimes—the apes are fed daily at 8 a.m. and 4 p.m. by a member of the Gibraltar Regiment—have helped to stop their descending to the town. It was not funny to find one of these still-wild creatures in your kitchen. The apes are carefully tended and protected by the British, since the Spaniards have a saying that "when the apes leave the Rock, the British will go."

On along Old Queen's Road toward the mainland you pass beneath the cable car and then through a gap in the ruined Moorish Wall, the Wall of the Arabs. Little remains of this early fortification which ran from the sea to the summit, but you can still see its upper stages zigzagging toward the peak.

There are fine observation points along the road with views over the harbor and then toward Spain. At the end of the road you reach the **Upper Galleries,** which are open from 10 a.m. to 7 p.m. (earlier in winter). Admission is 70p ($1.37) for adults, 40p (78¢) for children (tel. 4007). These are not picture galleries, but large tunnels hewn in solid rock which are used mostly as vantage points for guns hauled up the Rock to protect it from the mainland.

St. George's Hall, the largest and best known of the galleries, was the site of a magnificent banquet given by Lord Napier in honor of U.S. Gen. Ulysses S. Grant.

The road winds back, past the waterworks, and Willis's Road takes you down to the **Tower of Homage** of the old **Moorish Castle,** which is open from 10 a.m. to 7 p.m. (closes earlier in winter). Admission is 70p ($1.37) for adults, 40p (78¢) for children (tel. 71566).

The tower is floodlit, a magnet to the eyes of visitors and ships' passengers passing through the straits. Little remains of the original castle, 12 centuries old, other than parts of the outer walls running between the castle, the harbor, and the Moorish Pier, marking the considerable area of the castle and its defenses. The rest of the sights are best seen on foot, as parking is not easy in the town.

The **Gibraltar Museum,** Bomb House Lane, is open Monday to Friday from 10 a.m. to 1 p.m. and 3 to 6 p.m., Saturday 10 a.m. to 1 p.m. Admission is 35p (68¢) for adults, 10p (20¢) for children. The museum is built over a Moorish bath in the town center, close to the Roman Catholic cathedral, just off Main Street. To anyone who has become intrigued with the history of the Rock, the exhibits are fascinating. There is a large scale model of the Rock, showing every dwelling existing in 1865, plus the land reclamations since then. Other exhibits depict the history, from prehistoric cave-dwelling days to the present. There is a mass of artifacts, cannon balls, weapons, and military uniforms.

The **Convent and King's Chapel,** Main Street, is the official residence of the governor, the Queen's representative. The Changing of the Guard takes place every Monday at 10:30 a.m.—a ceremonial occasion with full band and the governor and his family on the balcony to take the salute. The convent was so named in 1531 when a wealthy Spaniard gave the Franciscan friars land, materials, and money to build a convent and a chapel for the burial of himself and his family. There is no sign today of their graves. King's Chapel is open to view, but the convent, a private home, is not. There is a 1000-year-old Dragon Tree in the grounds which you can see if you look down from the hill behind the Roman Catholic cathedral.

Main Street runs from Casemates Square where Louis Martínez stands with his highly polished hackney carriage and patient horse waiting to take tourists around the town and past the ancient walls. He stands on the square at the corner of Cooperage Lane and Main Street. In fact, he's been driving the same carriage, a Malta carrosse, for 47 years. Along Main Street to the Trafalgar Cemetery or down to the frontier costs £8 ($15.60) for one to four passengers, the trip taking from 45 minutes to one hour. Louis is a mine of information and a proud and faithful Gibraltarian. He does all repairs and refurbishing to the carriage himself and even shoes his horse.

The street proceeds between old buildings and modern stores past the Main Post Office and on to the Piazza, a colonnaded entrance to a paved square where people drink, children play, and desultory business is conducted. There is a flower-seller as well as a newspaper kiosk, ice-cream vendor, a taxi rank, and, very important, public toilets.

Narrow lanes and streets lead into Main Street. Do wander along them, as there is so much of the past history of the Rock to see between the high walls. You come next to the square facing the Roman Catholic cathedral which is a converted mosque, an impressive structure, and one of the first buildings on the Rock. Then it's on to the Cathedral Square with the Anglican cathedral facing a green garden and the harbor. Also in this square is the **Tourist Office** (tel. 4623), where an enthusiastic staff has a vast selection of brochures on the various attractions of the Rock. They will produce information on almost any question you can think to ask.

Note: The main Information Centre of the Tourist Board is at the Piazza on Main Street (tel. 5555). Hours are 9 a.m. to 5:30 p.m. Monday to Friday, and 9:30 a.m. to 1:30 p.m. on Saturday. A team of charming and helpful young women will dispense information, maps, and other free publications. They also operate a welcome service and will meet arriving ships and aircraft if required.

Farther on you come to King's Chapel and then the convent, and the street ends at the other end of town at Southport Gates, built into the defense wall of Charles V of Spain.

Just outside the town gate, where there was once a drawbridge and a moat, is the **Trafalgar Cemetery,** a charming garden blazing with geraniums. Tombstones commemorate many who fell at the Battles of Algeciras, Trafalgar, Cádiz, and Málaga in the early years of the 19th century.

Farther on up Europa Road, the **Alameda Gardens,** now covered with subtropical trees and flowers, were once the site from which the Arabs drew water and piped it through the town to Waterport to supply their ships. The Spanish also drew water there. Nowadays there are monuments to the Duke of Wellington and to General Eliott, an open-air theater, tennis courts, and mini-golf.

On Red Sands Road just below the gardens is the Lower Station of the **cable car** which rises to the top of the Rock. The cost is £2.20 ($4.29) to the top, a round-trip charge. The one-way fare is just £1.50 ($2.93). You may prefer to walk along the path to the highest point, 1398 feet, and then down to St. Michael's Cave or along the ridge to Poca Roca Cave and down to the road near the Upper Galleries. The cable car also stops at the Apes Den halfway up the cliff. At the top is a refreshment place. A round trip to the Apes Den is £1.50 ($2.93); there is no one-way fare for this leg of the trip. For information, telephone 2151.

GETTING AROUND: There are four basic ways of getting around the places of interest on the Upper Rock—self-drive car, taxi, tour bus, or a combination of cable car, public bus, and on foot. The last, however, involves much uphill walking and is only recommended for the young and strong of heart who also have the time.

A **self-drive car** is hardly necessary for more than a day or two. A Fiat 126, including unlimited mileage and fully comprehensive insurance, costs £7 ($13.65) a day, but you have to pay £2 ($3.90) extra a day on rentals of under three days. You can also rent cars to take over to Morocco, including unlimited mileage and return ferry charges for the car, for more than £100 ($195) for one week. A collision damage waiver is available for about £1 ($1.95) per day; otherwise you are responsible for the first £50 ($97.50) or so of each or any claim.

A complete **taxi tour,** which takes about three hours and includes Europa Point, the east coast area, St. Michael's Cave, the Apes, Upper Galleries, the Moorish castle, and the Spanish frontier costs £16 ($31.20) for up to four persons. Rental charges are also available for longer periods. All taxi drivers are required to carry and display a tariff card. Tariffs are set by the government. Calls for a taxi should be made to the Gibraltar Taxi Association, 12 Cannon Lane (tel. 70027).

Gibraltar Travel Ltd., 1–5 Irish Town (tel. 73525), operates minibus tours with a driver and guide most days. A morning or afternoon tour covering the major sights, but not the whole Rock, costs £2.75 ($5.36) a person. There are also three or four bus companies running regular services from the city around the Rock and between other points on the peninsula. There is a standard fare for any journey of 17p (33¢) per person; children under 12, 9p (18¢).

Dolphins and 'Round the Rock

In Sheppard's Marina at the bottom of Glacis Road lies a fleet of yachts and cruisers of all shapes and sizes. Mary and Mike Lawrence live on **Cosmic Star,** an ocean-going sailer in which they planned to travel around the world. They got as far as Gibraltar and stayed. Mike now owns a deep-sea fishing boat with which he operates 2½- to 3-hour cruises out into the Bay of Algeciras to see the dolphins. Over the past 11 years Mike has become their friend and, on good days, great schools of more than 400 arrive to leap around the boat. Some are so friendly you can stroke their backs.

It is a photographer's paradise, and a free drink is offered to the first passenger to spot a dolphin. Afterward you cruise around Europa Point under the lighthouse and along the east coast of the Rock, past romantic cave entrances, to Sandy Bay and Catalán Bay before returning to harbor. Mike, ex-Royal Air Force, gives an amusing and factual commentary. He takes various friends and relatives as crew. Beer and Cokes are carried on board for sale at nominal prices. The trip costs £6.50 ($12.68) per person. Telephone 71914 for departure times and other information.

Deep-Sea Fishing

Although this is widely advertised, it is really only for the experienced and professional fisherman. The depth of the waters and the strength of the currents make laying out and reeling in lines a tedious business, and you will have to be very convincing to persuade Mike Lawrence or one of the other boat owners to take you out. The Tourist Office has a list of privately owned boats currently available, but you should make all arrangements with the owners. The Tourist Office can't be held responsible for any arrangements made on these private rentals.

Cruises and Crewing

At Marina Bay, just beside the end of the airport runway, lies a small boat marina, **The Yachtsman,** a yacht chandlery. The store also has a section selling duty-free liquors and stores run by Benady Barton (tel. 70252). Their notice board advertises day sailing trips with snack lunch and drinks for £14 ($27.30) a person.

Waterskiing

Out Promotions Ltd., 12 Bell Lane (tel. 72760), will provide facilities for this popular sport. A boat and skis for a party of four or five persons will cost from £60 ($117) for around four hours, including the boat ride to the ski area. Josie Richardson runs the operation where a number of freelance enthusiasts have come together. They can also arrange yacht charter and, if asked, could probably arrange for people to join a vessel going over to Spain.

Birdwatching

With the cliffs of the Bosporus, Gibraltar is one of the major staging points in Europe for migrating birds. The craggy cliffs are the breeding grounds of kestrels and Alpine swifts, peregrines, and the more exotic Sardinian warblers, blue rock thrush and Barbary partridge. Honey buzzards, booted and short-toed eagles, Egyptian vultures, and white storks, plus a multitude of seabirds, pass through each year. Warblers, chiffchaffs, redstarts, robins, and nightingales "fall" here in spring and autumn. More than 200 species have been recorded on the Rock. Take the cable car to the top and walk in the less populated areas.

There are also more than 800 species of wildflowers, some quite exotic.

Philately

There is a current set of stamps as well as three or four commemorative issues each year. A special sales counter on the first floor of the head Post Office on Main Street is open from 9 a.m. to 1 p.m. and 2:15 to 5 p.m., Monday to Friday. The Post Office also operates a mail order service. Those interested should write to Ref: TL, Gibraltar Philatelic Bureau, P.O. Box 5662, Gibraltar.

Swimming

Outside the Police Station in Irish Town, a notice states which beaches are safe to swim at that day. Most beaches have changing rooms and, for a small cost, showers at 15p (29¢) and tents at £1.50 ($2.93) can be had. Deck chairs are generally 25p (49¢) a day; umbrellas, 50p (98¢).

4. The Rock After Dark

There are four cinemas with two programs nightly and matinees on weekends. The program is changed twice weekly, so if it rains you have a selection of films to see. Admission ranges from £1 ($1.95) to £1.30 ($2.54).

DISCOS: Canes, on Boyd Street (tel. 2183), behind the Queens Hotel, is strictly for the young attracted to its flashing lights and blaring music. There are so many lookers-on that you have to fight your way to the dance floor to gyrate beneath the glare. At the bar drinks are around 60p ($1.17) for a beer, less for a Coke or fruit drink. Admission is free.

Penelope's, 8 Corral Rd. (tel. 70462), is built in one of the old defense walls, a cavern with a long friendly bar for drinks and good snacks and plenty of room just to sit and hear the music. There are several caves with low lights, low stools, and tables for intimate conversation, and another cave, brilliant with lights and vibrating with noise for freaking out. Admission is free except on Saturday when it is £1 ($1.95). But you will be refused entrance if you're wearing jeans or look untidy and/or noisy.

Cornwall's, Cornwall's Lane, is probably the only place on the Rock where you disco-dance and eat after midnight. Neil Crawford and Colin Rodken, the owners, have between them experience in catering and sailing, as well as the diplomatic field of the United Nations. They found this Moorish building and have converted it perfectly, preserving the arched vaults in the disco and an original plaque dating from 1789 in the bar.

Upstairs is the Bistro where visitors are admitted free if there's room. Open seven days a week from 8 p.m. to 4 a.m., it serves soups, tapas, stews, pâtés, chili, and grilled steaks, costing from £1 ($1.95) to £4 ($7.80) a portion. Downstairs in the old cellars is a membership-only disco, a very attractive bar with brass footrail and copper-covered tables in the split-level seating area with a wine-red carpet. The bar is beneath the arches and the old beams of this building. Through the bar leads to a mirrored dance floor with its constant pulsing beat.

Until midnight drinks are at regular bar prices, but then you're hit with an increase of 20p (39¢) a nip. Basket meals, such as chicken and scampi, are available throughout the evening downstairs. They have a 22-hour license, and, in summer, will stay open longer than ever. Membership is reasonable: £2 ($3.90) per person nightly or £2.50 ($4.88) weekly, £5 ($9.75) for two weeks.

GAMBLING: The Casino and Restaurant, Europa Road, is entered from the street, through a cave bar with trickling streams and rock pools. Guests head upstairs to the large room where slot machines clang and rattle from 10 a.m. There is a wide terrace overlooking the lights of the harbor, and bars are open all day. A large room is occupied by Bingo seven nights a week. The charge is 90p ($1.76) for ten cards. There is a £1 ($1.95) entrance charge to the gaming room, open from 8 p.m., where minimum stakes are £1 ($1.95) for roulette or blackjack.

The casino disco operates nightly from 10 p.m. to 2 a.m., charging £1.50 ($2.93) for entrance. On Saturday the management holds dinner dances in the casino restaurant with its backdrop of cliffs behind the Japanese garden. The cost of £8 ($15.60) includes a buffet dinner. On the terraces, lit with lanterns, they hold barbecue dinner dances under the stars.

Chapter XV

THE CANARY ISLANDS

1. Gran Canaria (Las Palmas)
2. Tenerife
3. Lanzarote
4. Fuerteventura

[Area researched by Peter and Caryl Barnes]

OFF THE COAST of West Africa lie the spring-year-round cluster of islands and islets known as the Canaries. According to ancient myth these Spanish-ruled islands may well be the peaks of the lost continent of Atlantis (a position also claimed by the Portuguese-controlled Azores). Legends have also referred to the islands as the Elysian Fields and the Garden of Hesperides.

This outpost of Spanish civilization in the Atlantic is dubbed the "Islas Afortunadas," or the fortunate islands. The archipelago, 70 miles from Africa, consists of seven principal islands, the largest being Tenerife. Others include Gran Canaria, Lanzarote, Fuerteventura, La Palma, Gomera, and Hierro.

Geographically part of Africa, since 1927 the Canaries have been two provinces of Spain, Las Palmas and Santa Cruz de Tenerife. The islands are volcanic, and eruptions were frequent as late as the 19th century. At one time the archipelago was believed to have been a single land mass.

HISTORY: The first Canarians were the tall, fair-haired Guanches, who were cave-dwellers. Their origins remain an enigma, although some people believe they migrated from the southwest of France around 2000 B.C. After colonizing the islands, the Guanches appear to have lost their art of navigation and did not even travel among the islands. This accounts perhaps for the different characteristics of the denizens of each islet.

The Guanches worshipped the summits of the mountains which were considered the homes of their deities—Teide on Tenerife, Bentaiga on Gran Canaria. Their kings and nobles were embalmed, and many interesting relics remain from those days to be examined in the museums on the islands.

Colonizing Romans discovered and explored the islands in 30 B.C. The Romans charted the flora and fauna and took back with them two Canary dogs. In 1016 the Arabs came looking for slaves, particularly on Lanzarote, the island nearest to Africa.

Then in 1402, Jean de Bethencourt, a Norman, led his first expedition to the islands. After conquering Lanzarote and building a fortress at Fuerteventura, he returned to Spain. Henry III of Castile financed his next expedition. By 1483, after a five-year struggle, Gran Canaria fell to the Spaniards. Tenerife and La Palma succumbed by 1496 to attacks ordered by the Catholic monarchs, Isabella and Ferdinand. The islands were, at last, Spanish.

Dutch and English sorties in the 16th and 17th centuries rocked the islands. In 1797 Lord Nelson lost an arm which was shot off by a cannonball during an attack on Santa Cruz de Tenerife. That cannon is still shown in the town today.

GENERAL TIPS: Food prices tend to be higher on imported goods from Spain. Liquor is duty free and therefore cheap, with the exception of whisky. The local drink is rum, distilled throughout the islands. Wines are generally imported from the mainland, but there are some interesting local vintages as well. Ask for the Malvasia of Lanzarote and the mellow reds from Monte in Gran Canaria. Local wines range from 100 pesetas (96¢) to 200 pesetas ($1.92) a bottle if you buy in the vineyard bodegas.

In shopping, it's best to purchase luxury goods in the free port of Las Palmas. Store hours are from 9 a.m. to 1 p.m. and 4 to 7 p.m. Closings are usually on Saturday afternoon, all day on Sunday, and on feast days. Bazaars on the islands remain open as long as there is someone around to buy.

Outside the main towns, the local shops and bars are often unobtrusive in the extreme. Look for a half-open, green-painted door with a faded Coca-Cola sign. It may take some nerve to walk into the dark interiors of these bars, as strangers stick mainly to the well-trodden tourist paths. Once in, however, you'll be treated courteously; your drink will be enormous, and everyone will try to tell you where to go and what to see.

Water is plentiful in both Las Palmas and Tenerife. Outside big towns, reliance on rainwater is heavy. However, you'd better not drink it, unless you have a cast-iron stomach. Bottled water with or without gas can be purchased everywhere at a small cost. In Lanzarote there is a shortage of water, and most of it is supplied to outlying areas from the *potabilizadoras* which distill sea water. Unless you know the source of your water, it's best to avoid getting sick by sticking to the bottled variety.

As for food, the large hotels and tourist restaurants offer dishes tempered to the international palate. If you wish to sample the local delicacies, you must seek out the places where the Spaniards eat and join them. Fresh fish is the most recommended bill of fare. *Sama, vieja,* and *burro* are native to the area. Fish is usually grilled or boiled and served with *mojo picón,* a sauce made with olive oil, vinegar, salt, hot peppers, and such spices as coriander and cumin.

Puchero is the main meat dish, a stew of any and every vegetable with meat. Many thick soups are recommended. Sometimes these soups are difficult to tell from the main dish because of their virility and substance. The best known one is *potaje de berros y jaramagos* (made of watercress and herbs). Spanish omelets or tortillas are common. The celebrated wrinkled potatoes are *papas arrugadas,* potatoes boiled in their skins and served with a hot sauce. Something to try as well is *gofio.* It's a loaf made from ground toasted corn or wheat and used to sop up a gravy or sauce. It would make a health-food addict jump for joy, and is not unlike the couscous of North Africa. A favorite exotic local dish is *pollitos asados à la crème de platanos,* that is, roast chicken in a banana sauce. *Churros,* a sort of doughnut, very crisp and deep-fried, is served hot with your morning coffee.

Some good local cheeses are *Guia* in the Gran Canaria and a bland white goat's cheese served with wine, usually as a predinner bar snack on Lanzarote.

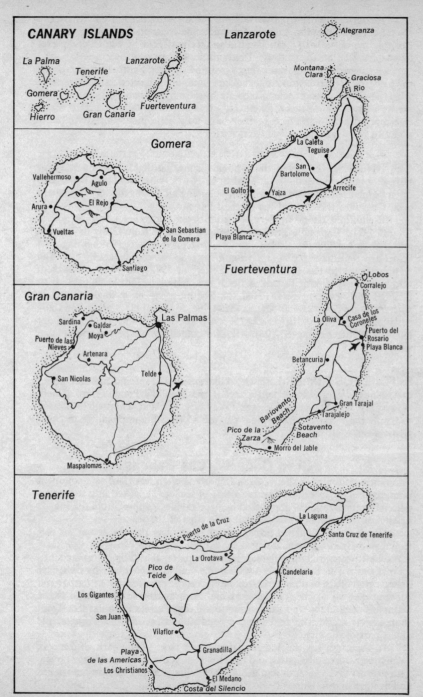

CANARY ISLANDS

La Palma
Tenerife
Lanzarote
Gomera
Hierro
Gran Canaria
Fuerteventura

Lanzarote

Alegranza
Montana Clara
Graciosa
El Rio
La Caleta Teguise
San Bartolome
El Golfo
Yaiza
Arrecife
Playa Blanca

Gomera

Vallehermoso
Agulo
Arura
El Rejo
Vueltas
San Sebastian de la Gomera
Santiago

Fuerteventura

Lobos
Corralejo
La Oliva
Casa de los Coroneles
Puerto del Rosario
Playa Blanca
Betancuria
Bariovento Beach
Gran Tarajal
Tarajalejo
Pico de la Zarza
Sotavento Beach
Morro del Jable

Gran Canaria

Sardina
Galdar
Moya
Puerto de las Nieves
Artenara
San Nicolas
Las Palmas
Telde
Maspalomas

Tenerife

Puerto de la Cruz
La Laguna
Santa Cruz de Tenerife
La Orotava
Candelaria
Pico de Teide
Los Gigantes
San Juan
Vilaflor
Playa de las Americas
Los Christianos
Granadilla
El Medano
Costa del Silencio

Of course, the main reason to go to the Canaries is sunshine. There is a saying in Las Palmas that there is sunshine somewhere on the island every day. For that reason in both Gran Canaria and Tenerife, the new hotel complexes have sprung up on the southern sandy dunes and beaches.

The average temperatures range from 64 degrees Fahrenheit in January to 76 degrees Fahrenheit in August. The islands are subjected to southwesterly winds across the Atlantic which account for the muggy atmosphere in the north of the islands where the wind has to cross the mountains. Lanzarote. and Fuerteventura are not affected—they have no central mountains and are exposed to the warm dry winds from Africa.

GETTING THERE: **Iberia,** the national airline, has flights from many European cities and connections via Madrid to North America. These flights can often be incorporated as a stopover into ongoing air tickets for very little extra cost. Consult a travel agent for the best bargain.

In addition, steamship services from Spain and other ports run to the Canaries. The **Compañía Transmediterránea** operates from Cádiz to Tenerife and then to Las Palmas and back to Cádiz. Departure is every other day. The vessel leaves Cádiz at 6 p.m., arriving in Tenerife two days later at 8 a.m. The ship continues to Las Palmas, arriving there at 3:30 p.m. Then it's back to Cádiz two days later at 11 a.m. A berth in a first-class, four-berth cabin with facilities costs 14,720 pesetas ($141.31). The most expensive single, first class with facilities, costs 21,350 pesetas ($204.96). A tourist-class berth in a four-berth cabin goes for 8010 pesetas ($76.90), and a berth in a double without facilities is 9610 pesetas ($92.26). All fares quoted are per person and are one way.

BEFORE YOU GO: For those who'd like answers to specific questions about the islands, write to Peter and Caryl Barnes, Willow Point, Friary Island, Wraysbury, near Staines, Middlesex TW19 5JR, England. They will be pleased to try to assist you. When writing, enclose $5 (U.S.), a nominal fee to cover postage and their time.

1. Gran Canaria (Las Palmas)

Almost circular in shape, Gran Canaria is often described as a continent in miniature, because such a wide variety of scenery is packed into so small a place. The topography is dominated by deep ravines, running from the rugged heights of the central massif down to the edge of the sea.

The dachshund-shaped provincial capital is **Las Palmas,** the major metropolis on Gran Canaria. It's also the largest port in Spain.

The town is roughly divided into two parts: the harbor area and Las Palmas town. The **Puerto de la Luz** is a free bunkering port used by passenger liners, cargo boats, and tankers. Adjoining it is the area behind the harbor and between the two beaches of **Canteras** and **Alcaravaneras,** where most of the big hotels, nightclubs, and bazaars are found. Las Palmas town has its elegant shopping street, **Mayor de Triana,** a residential area, and the **Vegueta,** the oldest part of the city.

To the south lies the **Parque Doramus,** a large public park with a zoo, swimming pool, tennis courts, and the Hotel Santa Catalina, built in the typical 18th-century style. In addition, the **Canary Village** is an exhibition of islands architecture and folklore.

Farther south in the Vegueta is the **Cathedral of Santa Ana,** still unfinished. Its style ranges from a lofty and spacious Gothic interior to a neoclassic facade. For 10 pesetas (10¢) you can see a fine collection of plate and vestments stored in the Treasury.

Opposite the cathedral is **Plaza de Santa Ana,** decorated with two beautiful bronze statues of Canary dogs, the fierce animals which gave the islands their name. At the other end of the square stands the Town Hall and the Bishop's Palace. Like all Spanish squares, this one is used as a meeting place for old men, a playground for children, and a place where women go for shopping. All day it rings to the sound of voices.

A short distance away is the **Plaza Espiritú Santo,** a tiny triangle of garden bordered by busy roads. There is a fountain and a small chapel used only during the feast of Corpus Christi, when the pavements are covered with flower designs. This is the oldest part of town. Many of the houses have typical carved wooden balconies and ornate and heavy front doors opening onto cool dark courtyards with palms and hanging baskets of flowers.

On the corner of Calle Dr. Chil and Dr. Verneau is the **Canary Museum** (tel. 31-56-00), a funny, musty place with a large collection of Guanche remains and exhibits of the geography and biology of the island. It is open from 10 a.m. to 1 p.m. and 3 to 6 p.m., Monday to Friday (from 10 a.m. to noon on Saturday). On Sunday and holidays, it is closed. Admission is 50 pesetas (48¢) per person.

Columbus lived here while he fitted out his ships for voyages across the Atlantic. The **Casa de Colón,** the former palace of the governors, is now a museum of fine arts, open from 9 a.m. to 3 p.m. daily except Saturday and Sunday. There is also a museum which contains maps and documents of his voyages and the small statue of Santa Ana to which he prayed for success in his journey. Admission is 5 pesetas (5¢).

Warning: Las Palmas can get very humid, particularly in autumn.

GETTING AROUND: Transportation is basic but adequate.

Car Rentals

Hertz and **Avis** are represented both at the airport and in Las Palmas. Hertz is at 27–29 Sagasta (tel. 26-45-76), and Avis is at José M. Duran (tel. 26-13-62). Both offer a compact car on an unlimited-mileage basis for 3000 pesetas ($28.80) a day. **Carop** operates through Autos Maroso, 22 Venegas, Las Palmas (tel. 36-30-22), at 1500 pesetas ($14.40) a day. Tax and insurance are extra. The availability of small cars is very limited, so it's wise to reserve one well in advance. Otherwise, you may be forced to pay for a more expensive car.

Motorcycles

This is a popular means of touring the island, especially for young people. Motorcycles are rented from **Puíg,** 4 Montevideo (tel. 27-49-01). A Suzuki costs 800 pesetas ($7.68) daily or 4800 pesetas ($46.08) weekly, with an additional 200 pesetas ($1.92) assessed for taxes and full insurance. Many of the hotels on the southern part of the island also have bicycles and tandems for rent.

Taxis

There are ranks throughout Las Palmas and the airport. Rates are inexpensive, and taxis are metered, although drivers charge extra for luggage. If you arrive by boat, it's best to ask for the price of a particular trip, as drivers are entitled to collect various surcharges for the transporting of bags and extra passengers. A charge ranging from 10 pesetas (10¢) to 40 pesetas (38¢) is levied, depending on the size of the baggage.

From the airport to Las Palmas, a taxi ride costs 800 pesetas ($7.68); from the airport to Maspalomas, 1250 pesetas ($12); and from the air terminal to the center of the city, 180 pesetas ($1.82). From the harbor to the city center depends on which jetty you take, as the rates range from 200 pesetas ($1.92) to 600 pesetas ($5.76).

Tariffs increase after dark. Always ask how much the fare is before you get in. Prices are posted at the airport, showing rates to various parts of the island. Taxi drivers also have a price list for out-of-town meter areas, and all tariffs are strictly controlled by the government. If you get cheated, it's your own fault.

For radio taxis, call 25-07-77 or 20-21-00.

Buses

There is a very efficient and frequent bus service throughout the island. The main bus station is on Calle Raphael Cabrera opposite the **Parque San Telmo.** Information on times and prices can be obtained by telephoning 36-86-31 or 36-01-79, but you'd better speak Spanish. Timetables and prices are also available at the Tourist Office, Parque Santa Catalina, Las Palmas.

The cost of a journey from Las Palmas to Maspalomas is 200 pesetas ($1.92), and the service goes on right through the night in both directions. Las Palmas to Agaete will run 150 pesetas ($1.44). Almost the longest trip on the island, from Las Palmas to Puerto Rico, is 280 pesetas ($2.69). The cost of a journey from the airport to the air terminal in Las Palmas is 90 pesetas (86¢). You can buy vouchers for use on the buses from various points in Las Palmas.

Besides regular bus service, a microbus system is operated by a cooperative on the island. These microbuses are known to everybody as *gua-guas* (pronounced "waa-waas"). Don't ask for a microbus, as no one will know what you're talking about. These small buses depart from various points in Las Palmas. Expect to pay about two-thirds of the big bus fare. But, be warned, gua-guas stop at almost every street corner and are a strictly local service. The minimum charge is 25 pesetas (24¢), rising according to the distance you travel. The best way to learn more about this economical service is to use the general information leaflet available at the Tourist Office.

Tartanas

These are horse-drawn carriages available on the Calle Simón Bolívar, oppoiste the Plaza Santa Catalina. Most routes are slow and gentle, following the Generalísimo Franco. Negotiate the price before you embark—around 300 pesetas ($2.88) per person for one hour or 700 pesetas ($6.72) for four persons. The one-hour drive includes the docks, market area, and seafront.

Excursions

Cyrasa, Intersol, and other companies operate excursions by coach with a guide to Bandama (half day), Tejeda (full day), and within the city itself. The trip for Tejeda, without lunch, is 725 pesetas ($6.96). A full-day trip to Maspalomas goes for 500 pesetas ($4.80), excluding lunch, and a full day's jaunt to Puerto Rico, including lunch, comes to 900 pesetas ($8.64). A trip to Puerto Rico and Sioux City (includes visit) costs 1250 pesetas ($12). A day trip by air to Lanzarote, including a tour of the island and lunch, costs 7800 pesetas ($74.88); to Tenerife by jetfoil, including a coach drive through the mountains and villages, is 6000 pesetas ($57.60); and a day in Marrakesh (including land arrangements and lunch), 14,500 pesetas ($139.20).

WHERE TO STAY: The **Tourist Office,** at the Parque Santa Catalina (tel. 26-46-23), is presided over by the helpful Arturo Tavío, a pure Canarian of many generations. He clearly loves the islands, and his affection is contagious. He has a list of available accommodations in all price ranges. His hours are from 9 a.m. to 1:30 p.m. and from 5 to 7 p.m. (Saturday 9 a.m. to 1:30 p.m.; closed Sunday and holidays).

Paradors, previously mentioned in the section on mainland Spain, are the most popular form of hotels in the Canaries. For those who wish to reserve in advance, just one letter or telephone call to Madrid will solve the problem. Address your request to **Paradors in Spain,** 36 Calle Almagro, Madrid 4 (tel. 41-01-607); Telex 46865RRPP. The office is open Monday to Friday 9 a.m. to 5:30 p.m., and from 9 a.m. to 1 p.m. on Saturday.

Hotel Faycan, 61 Nicholas Estevanez (tel. 27-06-50), stands just half a block from Canteras Beach. If you look sideways, you can see the sea from many of the rooms. You enter a typical dark, cool lobby, with a convenient bar patronized by locals and residents alike. The clean, simple rooms are equipped with private baths and toilets, renting for 1290 pesetas ($12.38) in a single, from 1690 pesetas ($16.22) in a double. If you're traveling with a child, ask about a three-bedded room, going for 2090 pesetas ($20.06).

These tariffs include a serve-yourself breakfast of juice, boiled eggs, cheese, fresh rolls, jam, and tea or coffee. The dining room (in the basement) is large and functional, brightened by a small walled garden with lush plants and a tiny pool. Dinner there goes for 450 pesetas ($4.32) for a choice of soup, salad, or an hors d'oeuvres, followed by a meat dish with vegetables, plus ice cream or flan. The main dishes are varied every day, but appetizers and desserts remain fairly constant. The Faycan is good value and convenient to the main life of the town, yet it's quiet.

Hotel Residencia Malomy, 61 Nicolas Estevanez (tel. 26-14-78), is next door to the Faycan (although the address is the same). It offers even better value, as its double rooms with private bath rent for 1500 pesetas ($14.40), including a continental breakfast. If you're alone, the staff will rent you a double room for only 1200 pesetas ($11.52). Units are simple and clean, and comfortable enough. There's no dining room, but you're in walking distance of many restaurants and bars.

Residencia Verol, 25 Sagasta (tel. 26-21-04), is one block from Canteras beach. The place at first looks like a bar, as the entrance is right on the corner. You climb steps to a bustling coffeeshop with an ever-flickering TV. Sandwiches and hamburgers are sold here, along with coffee and beer. The tiny reception to Verol is behind the bar, although it has a small entrance from the street on its own. Safe-deposit boxes are provided for residents—not so much as an indication of danger, but as a precaution against petty theft. Rooms are basic but adequate, nevertheless. Most units contain private baths or showers, and the prices are very reasonable: from 815 pesetas ($7.82) in a single, from 1000 pesetas ($9.60) to 1500 pesetas ($14.40) in a double. An additional 100 pesetas (96¢) is charged for a continental breakfast. An elevator leads to the upper floors.

Hotel Residencia Tigaday, 4 Ripoche (tel. 26-47-20), is another rawbone place, with single rooms renting for 1300 pesetas ($12.48), doubles for 1800 pesetas ($17.28), plus another 100 pesetas (96¢) charged for a continental breakfast. There is no restaurant, but you're close to Parque Santa Catalina and the beach, an easy walk to many bars and dining rooms, several of which are quite low cost. Tigaday is strictly for those desiring merely a room and who like to spend the days and part of the night in outside activities.

Hotel Gran Canaria, 38 Paseo Canteras (tel. 27-50-78), is grander than many of my choices, but not so friendly. It's right in the center of life, overlooking the beach, although many of its rooms don't have a sea view. It has plenty of lounges and a restaurant serving rather ordinary international dishes. Singles rent for 2015 pesetas ($19.34), with doubles going for 3150 pesetas ($30.24), each containing a private bath. A continental breakfast is an additional 200 pesetas ($1.92), and a main meal such as lunch or dinner is an extra 875 pesetas ($8.40). Gran Canaria is very well situated and quite comfortable without the colorful atmosphere of some of the smaller places.

The super-splurge place to stay in Las Palmas is surely the **Reina Isabel,** 40 Alfred L. Jones (tel. 26-01-00), right on Canteras beach. In fact, it's the only hotel which actually is on the water. Rooms go for 3250 pesetas ($31.20) in a single, from 5100 pesetas ($48.96) in a double. The facilities, for some, may be worth the difference in price. A four-course lunch or dinner in the Reina Garden costs 1400 pesetas ($13.44) or you can have a sandwich of cheese, roast beef, chicken, or veal Pepito—a sort of minute steak—for from 200 pesetas ($1.92) to 300 pesetas ($2.88). A club sandwich is 250 pesetas ($2.40).

The ground floor lounge, just off the hotel lobby, is elegant, with large, comfortable armchairs. The covered open terrace, the Reina Bar, is open from 10:30 a.m. to midnight, serving liquid refreshment. The terrace is filled with potted plants and bamboo furniture, a fountain splashes, and cool breezes come in from the sea across the sandy Canteras beach.

Opening onto the promenade is the Captain's Cabin pub. This is a replica of an English timbered pub. It's open during English pub hours—11 a.m. to 2:30 p.m. and 8 p.m. to midnight. Irish coffee goes for 200 pesetas ($1.92), and half a pint of draft beer is 80 pesetas (77¢). They also have toasted sandwiches. Reina Isabel has become what is undoubtedly the best five-star hotel in Las Palmas.

Hotel Los Frailes, Tafira (tel. 35-12-06). Some 17 years ago, Thomas Hutley, who had owned a pub near Henley, England, visited Las Palmas, liked what he saw, and bought Los Frailes. He has been there ever since. The hotel is reached along a tree-lined avenue. A monastery since before the Spaniards arrived on the island, the building still retains the cloisters. The dining room was the old chapel. Set in extensive gardens, the converted hotel surrounds a patio where you can sit and admire the view in peace, yet you are only 20 minutes from the center of Las Palmas. In the evening you can hear crickets chirping in the bushes. There is a large lounge with comfortable chairs and television (in Spanish), and the bar has been added to the old building with Canary-style furnishings. Rooms are comfortable; some have private baths, and rent for 700 pesetas ($6.72) in a single, 1100 pesetas ($10.56) in a double. A continental breakfast is an extra 150 pesetas ($1.44), and a lunch or dinner costs 650 pesetas ($6.24). Full board, added to the room rate, is yet another 1100 pesetas ($10.56). A bell rings to summon you to meals. This is a delightful retreat away from the bustle of the harbor area, and it's an ideal spot from which to tour the interior of the island. Yet a taxi to Las Palmas costs only 450 pesetas ($4.32); a bus, 75 pesetas (72¢).

The island's parador is the **Parador Nacional de Turismo,** Cruz de Tejeda (tel. 65-80-50), some 22 miles from Las Palmas. Right in the center of the island, it nestles against a hillside of pine and jagged rocks, in a col between the north and south of the island. A good road leads all the way from Las Palmas. But, on the other side, the roads to Maspalomas and Mogan pass the Roque Nublio and are steep—often little more than dirt tracks. It's a fascinating drive, but not a fast one.

The parador itself is an attractive building in the Spanish style, with a courtyard, designed by Nestor de la Torre. The lobby is cool with a polished floor; and from the lounge magnificent views open over the forest and the valleys of the south. You can drive out for lunch or dinner at a cost of 800 pesetas ($7.68). The typical Spanish menu makes few concessions to foreigners, other than printing the menu in English. If you're staying over, a spotless, shining wood and starched linen room will cost 2500 pesetas ($24) for two, with bath. Singles with bath cost 2000 pesetas ($19.20). The price of three meals a day is 1530 pesetas ($14.69) per person.

Hotel Don Gregory, San Agustín (tel. 76-26-58), is my super-splurge hotel for the south of the Gran Canaria. It's a beachside hotel that offers many free facilities in sunny San Agustín, a fast developing area. The Don Gregory manages to provide an oasis in the jungle of high-rise hotels and apartment blocks. A double goes for 5850 pesetas ($56.16); a single, 3800 pesetas ($36.48). Breakfast, a help-yourself affair from a wide choice, is 400 pesetas ($3.84), served on a covered patio by the pool. Lunch is a buffet with several hot dishes alongside the salads and vegetables, and you select as much as you want for 1400 pesetas ($13.44). Dinner is more formal, a four-course meal costing 1400 pesetas also. In this area of expensive tourist restaurants, it is good to note that full-board added to your room rate is 2635 pesetas ($25.30) per person per day.

Bedrooms all have balconies overlooking the sea, and are decorated in English nautical style, with much use of wood, brass, and tartan furnishings. Well-equipped bathrooms provide plenty of space for your bits and pieces. The built-in radios work, and there is a good telephone service for quick room service. Included in your room rate are a wind-sheltered, heated swimming pool, tennis courts, windsurfing boards and instruction, pedalos, catamaran sailing boats, and scuba-diving in the swimming pool. You can also borrow fishing rods if you wish to join the Spaniards fishing off the sandy beach. Golf is available free at Maspalomas, but you must get there yourself—it's not far. Moored out in the deeper water of the bay is a diving raft. There is a beach bar and restaurant if you don't want to go back up to the hotel for lunch.

Your evenings are occupied with cocktails, a well-cooked dinner, and then films in the lounge, or perhaps live band disco-dancing in the bar overlooking the pool, a fashion show, or other entertainment. The staff is most friendly and efficient, and it is obvious that Señor Muntadas, the director of the hotel, has considerable experience in running a smooth, efficient operation.

WHERE TO EAT: Las Palmas is divided into two main sections: the southern industrial, mercantile part, containing the cathedral and the oldest part of town; the northern, resort area with the Puerto de la Luz, the bazaars, the Canteras and Alcaravaneras beaches, plus the main hotels and restaurants. There are many places to eat, providing food from all countries at prices ranging from "give-away" to extravagant. My choices follow.

Kim's Steak House, 19 Alfredo Jones, Puerto de la Luz. You're assured of a welcome from Joan and Gordon Gray, as well as good food. Even the locals eat here, as the steakhouse has been established for many years now. The menu of the day, which changes every day, goes for 380 pesetas ($3.65). If you want to branch out, I'd recommend the chili con carne at 160 pesetas ($1.54); soup or salad, 150 pesetas ($1.44); followed by a kebab or half a chicken with a baked potato and vegetable or salad, 400 pesetas ($3.84). The Grays specialize in coffees—Irish, Jamaican, Mexican, Spanish, or American, from 200 pesetas ($1.92). The house wine is "Siglo," sold at 650 pesetas ($6.24) per bottle.

Mr. Gray was a film editor in England, and later he helped start independent television there. He has many interesting tales to relate about the beginnings of commercial television in England. The waiter, Manuel, will first produce your drink, and, if you wish, bring a portion of papas arrugadas with mojo picante (hot sauce) for 85 pesetas (82¢) as an appetizer.

Bar La Strada, 58 Tomás Miller (tel. 27-33-51), in Las Palmas, is on the ground floor. At the bar there is the best selection of tapas (hors d'oeuvres) in town, a tempting array including fish, meat, and vegetables dishes. Fifty different dishes are offered, ranging in price from 70 pesetas (67¢) up to 220 pesetas ($2.11), the latter the charge for a plate of Serrano ham. Portions are priced according to your selection and whether you request a half or full portion. Everything is on display, so selecting is easy—you simply point. The bar is traditional, with smoked hams hanging from the ceiling and a long wooden counter with high stools. It's open from 8 a.m. until late at night.

Upstairs is a self-service smörgåsbord where a meal costs 395 pesetas ($3.79). As you leave, the staff will present you with a card, granting 15 pesetas (14¢) off your next meal.

Le Cerdo que Rie (The Laughing Pig), 31 Paseo de Las Canteras, is open in the evening only. The menu of the day at 300 pesetas ($2.88) is served from 5 to 7 p.m. Otherwise, you make selections à la carte. These might include soup of the day, goulash, or hot pepper soup, 110 pesetas ($1.06); mixed or chef's salad, 175 pesetas ($1.68); avocado or asparagus vinaigrette, 250 pesetas ($2.40); shrimp cocktail or French snails, 300 pesetas ($2.88); fish or meat dishes, 250 pesetas ($2.40) to 500 pesetas ($4.80); and flamed specialties, 550 pesetas ($5.28). Desserts are in the 130-peseta ($1.25) to 225-peseta ($2.16) range. A glass of wine or local beer costs 90 pesetas (86¢). A bottle of wine goes for from 265 pesetas ($2.54).

Restaurant Buffet International, 67 Tomás Miller, Puerto de la Luz, offers as much as you can eat, costing from 400 pesetas ($3.84). Service is from noon to 11 p.m. The red cloth-covered tables are set for six or eight diners, so there is every chance that you'll share it with international company. Help yourself from the circular buffet to a variety of cold dishes, and you'll also find several hot selections, such as sardines or chicken with vegetables. The bright and rather commercial atmosphere is broken by potted plants.

Cafetería Piccadilly, 33 Alfredo Jones (tel. 27-95-35), is a clean bar, stretching back off the pavement into a dark interior. Here you can get a multitude of dishes from 11:30 a.m. to 11:30 p.m. Specialties include solomillo, potatoes, and salad, 375 pesetas ($3.60); pescado (fish), à la plancha with fried potatoes and greens, 275 pesetas ($2.64); and mixed cold meats, cheese, olives, and potato salad, 225 pesetas ($2.16). Ham sandwiches are 90 pesetas (86¢); a hamburger, 225 pesetas ($2.16). Earlier in the day the cafetería serves a breakfast of bacon, fried egg, toast, marmalade, fruit, and coffee for 150 pesetas ($1.44).

Part of the **Concorde Hotel** at 85 Tomás Miller, is the plate-glass-fronted Snack Bar with waitress service. Fresh flowers adorn the spotless tables, and it's open from 9:30 a.m. to midnight, serving breakfast and mainly Scandinavian and German dishes. Featured are marinated herring and vegetable salad at 150 pesetas ($1.44) or wienerschnitzel with french fries and salad, 300 pesetas ($2.88). A three-course meal with steak is between 600 pesetas ($5.76) and 700 pesetas ($6.72).

Mesón Vasco Kai-Alde, 35 Dr. Grau Bassas, is a typically Spanish restaurant with stone walls and metal-grilled windows. Its nice, cool, dark interior offers a haven from the heat and humidity of summertime Las Palmas. At a small bar in one corner you can order a drink before adjourning to one of the tables covered with cheerful blue-checked cloths. The menu offers a tomato and green salad; melon and ham; homemade soups such as fish soup; fish dishes from blackfish Romana to eel Aguinaga. Meat dishes include chicken stew, kidney in sherry sauce, lamb cutlets, and filet steak. Complete meals begin at 800 pesetas ($7.68), excluding wine. The tall, elegant Spaniard who serves behind the bar is the owner, and he keeps an eye on the service.

El Rayo, 3 Ripoche, Puerto de la Luz, stands behind the Bar Central on the Parque Santa Catalina, a spotless little restaurant a few steps down from street level. It offers food very like home-cooking, Spanish-style. The menu of the day goes for 350 pesetas ($3.36), with a choice of fish soup, noodle soup, or Russian salad, then a selection of veal or fish, followed by fresh fruit and ice cream. Bread and a half liter of wine or water (bottled) are included. For those who want a slightly wider choice, there is an à la carte menu from which you can select a three-course meal for around 800 pesetas ($7.68).

Restaurant Don Quijote, 74 Secretario Artiles (tel. 27-83-17), is a white arched place with typically Spanish upright, high-backed chairs set around wooden tables on a polished red-tiled floor. Service is from 1 p.m. to midnight except Monday. Background music is played during the day, and in the evening a live guitar player entertains. Terracotta-covered lights hang above the tables, giving a warm and friendly glow to the bare white walls. Specialties include gazpacho Andaluz, seafood cocktail Don Quijote, sole au champagne, fondue bourguignonne, steak tartare, and fried Camembert. Dining à la carte can cost more than 1200 pesetas ($11.52) per person, although a set menu is presented for 750 pesetas ($7.20).

Bar Restaurant Gourmet, 35 Las Canteras, is in an old stone building with high shuttered windows which are opened in the evenings so that diners can view the promenade and sea. Candles on the dark wooden tables flicker on the wooded arched ceiling, and settles divide the dining area into more intimate alcoves. Although the place is so very Spanish looking it is owned by Norman Smith, who has a firm hand over his staff.

Appetizers run from garlic bread with mixed salad, avocado with prawns, rose canapés (smoked salmon strips with caviar, boiled egg, and Rhode Island sauce), to chicken pâté with Cumberland sauce, at prices ranging from 60 pesetas (58¢) to 325 pesetas ($3.12). Main dishes are likely to feature chicken in wine (or else Mexican style), grilled lamb chops with garlic and parsley butter, Flemish-style beef stew, or chateaubriand with béarnaise sauce for two persons, at prices ranging from 375 pesetas ($3.60) to 525 pesetas ($5.04) a dish. Specialties are sole meunière at 400 pesetas ($3.84) and fondue bourguignonne for 2500 pesetas ($24). Desserts include the usual ice creams and flan, but also chocolate mousse, apple pie, crêpes suzette, and banana flambé, from 100 pesetas (96¢) to 285 pesetas ($2.74).

The cheapest way to dine here is to order the menu of the day at 472 pesetas ($4.53), a good meal—bread and consommé, chicken in wine, ice cream, and half a bottle of the house wine. The standard of cooking and the service is high.

In the **Lord Nelson,** 8 Las Canteras and 43 Sagasta, Puerta de la Luz, you'll encounter a nautical decor and cannons. The German-owned pub offers bar snacks, as well as complete meals, and allows you to sit and watch the world go by. A good medium-priced meal for two persons will cost around 1200 pesetas ($11.52), and you can order between 1 and 11 p.m. Spaghetti and pasta dishes are featured, along with the invariable seafood cocktail. Roast duck or chicken is alluring, as are the more expensively priced steaks. The dessert specialty—served only for two guests—is bananas flambé. You can eat inside or at tables on the promenade, right beside the beach.

Undoubtedly, the splurge meal in Las Palmas is to be had in the **Grill Room** of the Reina Isabel Hotel, P. de las Canteras. Take the elevator from the lobby to the top floor (tel. 26-01-00 for reservations). There is a club-style lobby with deep leather armchairs for your predinner drink. Then you go into an elegant dining room with mirrors and trellises separating the tables. Try to get a table by the window—high over the Canteras beach and the city.

Melon with Serrano ham is a good appetizer at 500 pesetas ($4.80), although there is a selection of soups at 325 pesetas ($3.12) which range from iced consommés to French onion to Andalusian gazpacho. Paella is 750 pesetas ($7.20) per person. The bass with fennel is 800 pesetas ($7.68). A T-bone steak will set you back 800 pesetas also, but there are many veal dishes at 650 pesetas ($6.24). All dishes are garnished, and service and tax are included. Incidentally, the portions are big. Wines are imported, although there are some half bottles at prices going from 350 pesetas ($3.36) up. The atmosphere is sophisticated and relaxed, and the service is good. Afterward you can join the disco dancing in the Fiesta Bar.

On the Parque Santa Catalina, the **Bar La Peña** does a very good menu of the day for 350 pesetas ($3.36), including an appetizer of soup or salad, then spaghetti bolognaise or fried fish accompanied by bread and a glass of wine. You might, however, prefer the red mullet at 390 pesetas ($3.74). Wine begins at 190 pesetas ($1.82) a half bottle.

Next door is the **Bar Marisquería la Guanche.** The bar and restaurant speads from its place along the side of the square into a roofed area of the parque. The entrance is decorated with a display of the day's fish and shellfish. Temptations include half a dozen oysters at 750 pesetas ($7.20); octopus Galicia, 290 pesetas ($2.78); and squid à la Roma, 325 pesetas ($3.12). Main dishes include such regulars in the Spanish repertoire as hake cooked Basque style, at 790 pesetas ($7.58). It's imported. The house wine goes for 350 pesetas ($3.36).

Both of these establishments open right onto the Plaza Santa Catalina, and tables are set out onto the square. You need not come here to eat, but you may prefer only a drink, as it's the sort of place where everyone rests after sightseeing or shopping.

In the old part of town, the best place for tapas and Canary Island specialties is **Bar Herreno,** 23 General Mola. It's behind the market, close to the cathedral. English is spoken, and it's well worth investigating.

Down in the south where San Agustín turns into Playa del Inglés and then into Maspalomas stands **Loopy's Tavern,** 31 Las Retamas, San Agustín (tel. 76-28-92). It looks thrown together, a complex of huts and shanties, decorated with wagon wheels, postcards, and Victoriana. Basically, it's a ranch-style building, with lots of wood and nails, with an outside barbecue grill for charcoal steaks. The tavern is open early until 2 a.m. In this cozy, intimate atmosphere the specialty is crêpes stuffed with chicken, ham, peppers, or mushrooms, at 200 pesetas ($1.92). A special feature is the king-size hamburger at 145 pesetas ($1.39). Chicken in the basket goes for 360 pesetas ($3.46). Everything is washed down with authentic Irish coffee. Lewis Turner, who runs the tavern, also has an authentic pizzería underneath, offering 17 different pizzas which range in price from 275 pesetas ($2.64) to 425 pesetas ($4.08).

This end of the island is artificial and of recent construction. Therefore, dining here tends to be expensive. There are many good bars, but a square meal at a reasonable price is hard to come by, unless you seek out some local Spanish place off the main road.

Just off the Parque Santa Catalina on the corner of Calle General Vives and Calle Ripoche is a genuine **Wimpy Bar**, where you'll come closest to finding the nearest thing to an American hamburger. The Wimpy special is 190 pesetas ($1.82), and if you order a salad to go with it, count on spending another 155 pesetas ($1.49). A regular Wimpy burger costs 95 pesetas (91¢); a king-size version, 175 pesetas ($1.68). You can also order fish and chips at 180 pesetas ($1.73), to be followed by apple pie and cream at 80 pesetas (77¢). The place is clean and cheerful, and is run on the same lines as a McDonald's. They also do take-away.

NIGHTLIFE: Cards advertising strip clubs, nightclubs, and discos are given out on the streets. It's wise to be cautious, although most places in Las Palmas are comparatively harmless for the person who's sensible. The police keep a pretty stern eye on most operations.

Nightclubs come and go in Las Palmas. Most are expensive and not of a very high standard, as befits a busy international port. Visitors seeking the high nightlife should inquire when they arrive on the island as to what is currently the rage.

The **Fiesta Bar** on the roof of the Reina Isabel Hotel, by the swimming pool and outside the Grill Room, offers disco dancing from 10 p.m. to 2 a.m. nightly. Admission is free to "respectably dressed" residents and nonresidents, but the management reserves the right to charge up to 500 pesetas ($4.80) admission to those wearing jeans, Hawaiian shirts, and other super-casual clothes. Ties are not obligatory but are preferred. Decor is blue and gold with bamboo tables and chairs, and potted plants give a touch of green to what is one of the city's most popular discos.

Lord Nelson, 8 Las Canteras, in Las Palmas, has a smashing disco in the cellars from 10 p.m. to 3 a.m. each night. Regular admission is 350 pesetas ($3.36), rising to 600 pesetas ($5.76) on weekends and holidays. You enter the disco past portholes behind which fish swim. Many guests like to take a meal here, ordering one of 13 platos combinados (meat and vegetable plates with salad garnish), ranging in price from 275 pesetas ($2.64) to 550 pesetas ($5.28), the latter the cost of a plate of grilled sole with two vegetables.

An innovation only recently permitted under Spanish law is the addition of the **Casino Gran Canaria,** in the Hotel Tamarindos with its own entrance from the road at Playa San Agustín (tel. 76-27-24). It is open from 8 p.m. to 3 a.m., except Saturday when its hours are from 9 p.m. to 4 a.m. An admission card is obtainable by presenting your passport or identity document and the payment of the appropriate fee. A one-day card is 300 pesetas ($2.88); a week's card, 1000 pesetas ($9.60). Games include French and American roulette (one zero), blackjack, chemin de fer, and punto y banco. Decor in the large gambling room is the usual dark wood and warm furnishings. The bar operates throughout opening hours, and the gambling is strictly controlled by a government representative on duty throughout the evening. The operators are not allowed to close down a table without his permission. At present the Casino does not have its own restaurant and uses the facilities of the Tamarindos Hotel, which offers a high standard of service and cuisine.

EXPLORING THE ISLAND: The north of the island is lush. Here are banana plantations and small fishing villages clustered around small rocky bays, with waves constantly breaking against the rugged shore. At **Galdar** and **Cenobio de Valerón** there is much evidence of the Guanches. The cliffs are honeycombed with caves; and at Galdar is a grave enclosure which may have been the burial place of the local Guanarteme (king) and his family. At **Arucas** an amazing Gothic church rises out of banana trees and orchards. At **Agaete** are found sugarcanes and the island's first sugar refinery. This part of the island is not often visited by tourists, and, perhaps because of that, retains much of its pristine character. It's well worth a day or two of exploration.

South of Las Palmas, a motorway runs to the airport of Gando. This is a more barren part of the island, with a wide coastal plain, sloping to small sandy beaches separated by rocky headlands. At **Cuatro Puertos,** a sacred cave was dug into the hillside. Its use by the Guanches is uncertain, but it may have been an embalming place or a sanctuary.

Running from Telde inland to Santa Brigida, the **Atalaya Valley** is a steep and narrow enclave where people still live in caves in the rocky hillsides. The silence is magical, broken only by the tinkle of a goat's bell or the bark of a dog.

Past the airport, the road continues south to **San Agustín, Playa del Inglés,** and **Maspalomas.** Once a quiet and deserted area of sand dunes and palm trees, this is the area of the new big hotels, discos, and tourists. Although it's a paradise of sun and sea, it is an entirely commercial area and anonymous.

Beyond the lighthouse on the southern tip of the island the road continues to **Puerto Rico,** an entirely artificial harbor and development of apartments and villas. Here it's possible to go deep-sea fishing or out on yachting trips.

Right in the center of the island is the **Cumbre,** the mountain. Its northern face is covered with thick pine forests. Its eastern side, with steep valleys, is dotted with tiny rough houses. However, to the south and west it is almost barren. The road from Las Palmas climbs up through rich agricultural land and villages of large houses and estates to **Cruz de Tejeda** where there is a parador. On a clear day the views of the island are fantastic, although sometimes obscured by clouds.

From here one can see the jagged peak of the **Rogue Nublio** and the other sacred mountain of the Guanches, **Bentaiga.** On a clear day, it's possible to view all the way to Teide on Tenerife, some 60 miles away. The descent from Tejeda to Maspalomas is unforgettable, a twisting track between peaks and valleys to **San Bartolomé,** a sudden oasis of a village gay with flowers and pleasant gardens.

If the weather is overcast in Las Palmas, one can nearly always be sure of sunshine in the south of the island.

About eight miles from the center of Las Palmas, the **Bandama Crater** is one kilometer across and about 600 feet deep. Its claim to fame: it is the only crater in the world where a small settlement of people lives all year. It also qualifies as having one of the world's most bizarre golf courses, an 18-holer laid out on the outer and lower slopes.

MISCELLANY: The **Pueblo Canario** (tel. 24-35-93) is the Canary Islands village in the Parque Doramas, which also contains the old Spanish-style Hotel

Santa Catalina. This was created by Nestor, who did much in the Gran Canaria to promote concern for traditional island architecture and customs.

The village includes a chapel, an inn, and other period buildings grouped around a central courtyard, on which folk dancing takes place on Thursday between 5:30 and 7 p.m., and on Sunday at 11:30 a.m. This is an attractive spectacle performed in the traditional style by local dancers. There is no charge, but if you sit at the bar, 65 pesetas (62¢) will be added to the cost of your drinks.

El Mercado Municipal is nicknamed "The Market of the Forty Thieves," because there are that number of stalls. Off León y Castillo, toward the harbor, most of these stalls sell leather goods and souvenirs. But you can also buy meat, vegetables, and other household goods—you name it, it's there. Bargain as you will or just walk around watching the people and the deals they conclude.

The **Nestor Museum** contains a collection of his works, and is open from 10 a.m. to noon and 4 to 7 p.m., Monday, Tuesday, Thursday, and Friday. On Saturday, hours are from 10 a.m. to noon only, and on Sunday and holidays, 10:30 a.m. to 1:30 p.m. Admission is 25 pesetas (24¢).

The **British Club,** 274 León y Castillo (tel. 24-54-51), is two doors down from the municipal offices overlooking the port. It boasts good home-cooking, a lunch or dinner costing around 500 pesetas ($4.80). The club is open Tuesday to Saturday from 10 a.m. to midnight and on Sunday for lunch (a traditional roast) from 10 a.m. to 4 p.m. It is closed Monday. You can enjoy bar snacks, English-language newspapers, a library, bridge, table tennis, and billiards. Bingo, films, and amateur dramatics and dances are arranged. In all, it's a jolly atmosphere, and you tend to be asked if "you've come for the panto rehearsal."

The honorary secretary is Mrs. Pat Pridgeon, who offers a temporary membership for 100 pesetas (96¢) daily, 200 pesetas ($1.92) for one week, and 500 pesetas ($4.80) per month. In all, it's a good place at which to catch up on world news, write letters, or simply relax, and it lies on the no. 1 bus route.

In winter, the **Teatro Perez Galdos,** on Lentini (tel. 21-54-69), just before you get to the Barranco, gives performances of plays, ballets, and concerts. Information on performances is available from the Tourist Office or from one of the daily newspapers. The fine building in which it's housed is another example of the work of Nestor. It was opened in 1927. The huge foyer is decorated with paintings of Canary fruits, the theme of the magnificent carved balustrade. Buses pass the theater, so it's quite easy to get back to the Puerto de la Luz end of town.

The **Parque Santa Catalina** is the hub of national and international life, in the Puerto de la Luz part of Las Palmas. It's a large tree-shaded patio bordered on three sides by streets and on the fourth by cafés and shops. The cafés spill onto the paved square (see "Where to Eat"), and you can while away many hours with a coffee or a beer. Here a bootblack, there a letter writer or reader of newspapers. Photographers, lottery-ticket sellers, and many others may seek you out. Moorish Africans have their stalls here, selling leather goods, kaftans, and sandals. The flamboyant Lolita, who sells chewing gum and matches, uses the profits to feed stray cats in her home down by the docks. Before the death of her husband, she was a dressmaker of international renown.

Chess tournaments often take place here. You can obtain a ticket for 100 pesetas (96¢) from the photographer who stands close by, and then you wait your turn to challenge the resident player. Local women walk between the people selling lacework. Expect to pay a half to a third of the asking price.

If you're offered gold or other jewelry, beware, for chances are it won't be entirely what it's claimed to be. For shoeshining while you drink your coffee, the price is 75 pesetas (72¢). Prices of refreshments tend to be higher here, a coffee and Spanish brandy going for around 175 pesetas ($1.68). For those who need them, there are clean toilets with an attendant at the old city end of the Parque. The attendant deserves the tip of 25 pesetas (24¢) which is customary.

Across the street, from which the Tartanas depart, lies the Tourist Office in another one of Nestor's buildings. Duty-free shops line the square and nearby streets. There is little, however, that is now a bargain for North Americans. Cuban cigars are available, a package of 25 costing 800 pesetas ($7.68), and a liter of J & B whisky goes for around 650 pesetas ($6.24).

The **British-American Clinic**, 5 Sagasta, Puerto de la Luz (tel. 26-45-38), is operated by the dapper Dr. Stanley S. Pavillard, who always sports a carnation in his buttonhole. The clinic offers 24-hour emergency service with two ambulances. It does not, however, have beds, although the staff will make all the necessary arrangements if you're really ill. It does offer an X-ray department and E.C.G. Subsidiary clinics are at the Playa del Inglés (Hotel Buenos Aires), 1 Avenida España (tel. 76-27-42), and at Puerto Rico (Center Cívico Comercial; tel. 74-57-47). These clinics are at the biggest tourist centers on this island, and may be of great help to readers who might need their services.

Canary Tourist Radio, 836 kHz, broadcasts at 3 p.m. daily except Sunday. You'll hear world news and tourist tips in several languages. Established in 1963, it is produced by Xavier Ingemar Palin.

On the beaches of **Las Cantera** and **Alcaravaneras**, chairs cost 100 pesetas (96¢) daily; umbrellas, 65 pesetas (62¢). Use of the changing rooms on Canteras beach is 30 pesetas (29¢). However, in the southern resorts expect to pay 20% more than in the north. On Las Canteras beach, a first-aid station is available.

On the main road to the south, just before San Agustín, on the right is **Cañón del Aguilar,** the home of the Sioux City (tel. San Agustín 73). Suddenly, you're transported to the Old West. Admission is 600 pesetas ($5.76); children, half price. Hours are from 10 a.m. to 8 p.m. daily except Sunday. A minibus takes you up to the "Cañón City," although you now drive your car up for 100 pesetas (96¢). Built originally as a film set, everything was imported from the U.S., including the cattle in the corral. There is a free bus from San Agustín to the cañón. Shows lasting 1½ hours take place at noon and again at 5:30 p.m.

At the **Western Inn Bar,** a beer is 90 pesetas (86¢). You can also buy a gunbelt or a cowboy hat from the Wells Fargo Company or the Miners' Union Shop. At the three-star saloon with its long bar a pork chop costs 250 pesetas ($2.40); chicken, 200 pesetas ($1.92). In summer you can enjoy an evening barbecue before the 6 p.m. performance. You can also gamble at the pinball machines. A ride on a well-trained horse is 270 pesetas ($2.59) for 30 minutes. The saddles are, of course, western. In the Indian Reserve the shops sell skins, beads, and Sioux City T-shirts.

At set intervals, an announcer lets you know the attractions, including a cattle drive and an Indian trick-rider. Naturally, you can expect a bank robbery, with bloody killings and a fight, not to mention a jailbreak. Handcuffs, "Wanted" notices, axeheads, and arrows are sold. At the inn, oldtime wrestling shows are staged. Madame Rosa runs a Turkish bath for gentlemen.

OUTDOOR ACTIVITIES: In a setting of sun and sea, the sporting life is practiced with much enthusiasm.

Waterskiing

In Puerto Rico, you can waterski in the small-boat harbor, where you'll be charged 1000 pesetas ($9.60) for ten minutes, 2300 pesetas ($22.08) for half an hour. You are only charged for the time you are actually on skis at sea—not for the time it takes to get out of the harbor. If you wish to book a boat and skis, write to **Nautical Holidays S.A.,** Bungalow Jamaica 76, Puerto Rico (tel. 74-51-16).

Nudist Beaches

There are now two nudist beaches, apparently accepted by the Catholic church in recognition of the tourists' dollars. One is at **La Cañada de la Pensa,** the other **Playa del Inglés.** There is also a naturist zone at **Playa de Maspalomas,** popular with the gay crowd, where you can manage to lose yourself in the sand dunes.

Big-Game Fishing

Puerto Rico is the center for nautical activities in the south of the island. Several man-made harbors combine around a recent development of holiday apartments, in an area which was once barren. The facilities have attracted a number of sailors as well as private yachtspeople.

Marítima Insular, S.A., 3 Alejandro Hidalgo, Las Palmas (tel. 23-31-95), with branches at Maspalomas and at Puerto Rico (tel. 74-50-18), will take reservations for big-game fishing. This is the only Gran Canaria operation for such fishing, with ocean-going sports fishing boats. The organization is only for the serious fisherman of high standards. The cost of the charter of the boat for a party of four is 22,000 pesetas ($211.20) for the day except when marlin and tuna are running. At that time, the boat's owners will do a split charter, one-quarter of the boat costing 5500 pesetas ($52.80) per person for the day.

For those who have only a short time to spare, the **M/Y Salmon** leaves Puerto Rico twice a day at 11 a.m. and 1 p.m. for a 1½-hour trip along the coast to Mogan, with only a short stop for bathing before returning to port. The cost is 400 pesetas ($3.84). There's a bar on board. The vessel operates daily except Wednesday and Thursday.

For the less serious mariner, I offer the following suggestions.

Punta Umbria II sails daily from Puerto Rico. From around 9:30 a.m. each morning, their buses collect participants from the various hotels of San Agustín, Playa de la Inglés, and Maspalomas. You can, of course, make your own way to the dock (and must if you are living in Las Palmas). The cruise starts at 11 a.m. when a breakfast of cheese and sausage is served as the boat leaves the harbor for the sharkfishing areas to the accompaniment of disco-music and a loudspeaker commentary.

Four sharkfishing lines are set, and you may be there on *the* day when a shark is caught. If not, you can lie on the sundeck or prop up the bar. Drinks are sold at normal prices. After the fishing trip, the boat turns toward the coast and a lunch of fish, papas arrugadas with mojo, salad, bread, and red wine, then coffee with cognac.

At the end of the afternoon, she moors in a bay at Mogan for those who wish to swim in the clear waters. Then it's back to Puerto Rico and the bus to your hotel. The cost is 1600 pesetas ($15.36) per person, including food. Tickets—you must be sure they are yellow ones—are obtainable from Punta Umbria's office, from hotel reception offices, and from travel agents.

For the more romantic, there are two sailing ships, the Windjammer **San Miguel,** Spanish owned and run, and the topsail schooner **Gefion,** owned by a Dutchman and sailed under a Spanish flag.

The San Miguel sails daily, except Monday, from the Pasíto Blanceo, Puerto Rico, at 10 a.m. For advance reservations, call 76-00-76. A day's cruise, including lunch and wine, is 1800 pesetas ($17.28). At the bar drinks are extra but sold at normal prices.

The *Gefion* is claimed to be the oldest topsail schooner still in action, built in 1894 in Sweden and used transatlantic to Newfoundland. In 1940 she was engined for the first time. After some years of neglect, she was restored in 1970 by her owner to her present glory—the only change from her original shape being the conversion of the hold into a comfortable salon. She's not fast but she's strong and powerful, and you can spend the day helping to sail her, sunbathing, or scuba-diving. You can also fish or just chat below decks to the background of romantic music. Lunch is included in the day's price of 1800 pesetas ($17.28), a cocktail followed by a cold buffet, wine, coffee, and brandy. The day starts from Puerto Rico at 10:30 a.m., returning at 4 p.m. Reservations can be made by calling 76-18-96.

Bullfights

These take place every Sunday from November to April at a portable bullring down at the Playa del Inglés. The Tourist Office will provide details of dates and the price of tickets (which varies). Posters placed throughout the town advertise these fights.

Hang Gliding

Escuela Tamaran, 244 León y Castillo (tel. 24-35-40), in Las Palmas, answers the phone in the evening only, from 7 to 9 p.m. Luís Hernandez offers weekend flying courses, including expert tuition, insurance, and transport to and from the gliding site. The school holds an international rating from the Spanish Federation of Air Sport. Clients travel to such places at Gomera and La Palma with experienced gliders for this fantastic sport. A weekend course costs 5750 pesetas ($55.20), inclusive.

Camping

This is not entirely looked upon favorably by the islanders, especially in the wake of invasions by young people in the past few years and several health hazards. Organized camping sites with facilities are available at **Tauro Beach,** near Puerto Rico. Pitching a tent costs 75 pesetas (72¢) to 125 pesetas ($1.20), depending on size, and a car or camper is an additional 75 pesetas (72¢). **Camping Caravaning de Temisas** (Aguimes), 20 miles from the airport and 7½ miles from the sea at Arinaga, also provides sites at the same price. A small cooking stove should be included in your equipment, together with proper tents. You may also be required to prove that you have made adequate sanitary arrangements in your camp.

Donkey Safaris

These operate daily from **Viajes Canyrama,** 49 Nicolas Estevañez in Las Palmas (tel. 27-65-53). Participants are taken by bus to Barranco de Guaya de Que to ride the donkeys to a Canary village for a lunch of paella and wine before returning to Las Palmas. The cost is 1750 pesetas ($16.80), including lunch.

Walking and Rock Climbing

An organization, **National Delegation of Youth,** operates from a head office in a bare building on a side of the Plaza del Cairasco (tel. 21-63-04) in

Las Palmas. This group is enthusiastic about the potential of the island, and this enthusiasm rubs off and you may want to head for the wilds.

The group has prepared many cross-country walks and rock climbs of varying difficulty. Most of them last from three to six hours. Many hikes lasting from two or three days are also offered in the central mountains.

There are two mountain refuges on the island, one at **Los Llanos de la Pez;** the other, the **Refugio San Bernardo,** at Pozo de la Nieves. Modest charges are made for overnight stays which must be arranged in advance. The cost is only 75 pesetas (72¢) per person, although you must bring along your own food.

Equipment can't be hired, but arrangements can sometimes be made to borrow ropes and other gear from members of the group. The president of the company is Eladio Pérez Alvarez, who directs a highly organized group of climbing instructors and a professional, although very young, membership.

In addition, the club has investigated potholing, particularly in Lanzarote, where it appears there are some very deep—perhaps the deepest in the world—potholes.

Greyhound Racing

This takes place nightly at 7 p.m. at the **Canodromo Gran Canaria,** Playa del Inglés (tel. 76-18-64). Most of the greyhounds come from Ireland, and the standard of racing is quite good. Tickets on the electronic betting system cost 100 pesetas (96¢) each. There is a complicated system of betting, but you get a paper in your own language explaining it and translating the various racing terms so that you can better participate in the evening's excitement.

Cock-Fighting

For those who have the stomach for it, or who are compulsive gamblers, cock-fighting takes place from December to May on Sunday at 11 a.m. in the **Polideportivo López Socas,** Escaleritas, Las Palmas. Admission is free and the meetings last about two hours. The Tourist Board has further information on this and on fights elsewhere in the island.

2. Tenerife

The largest of the Canary Islands, Tenerife is the capital island of the province that bears its name. The province consists of not only Tenerife itself, but La Gomera, La Palma, and Hierro. The last two islands are comparatively small and isolated. Overnight accommodations are scant, although La Palma boasts a beautiful parador, on the seafront at Santa Cruz, the main town. La Gomera is reached from Los Cristianos in the south of Tenerife and is worth at least a day's visit.

Tenerife's capital is **Santa Cruz de Tenerife,** which, with 150,000 inhabitants, is the second-largest port in the Canaries. Right in the center of the seafront lies the **Plaza de España,** with its memorial to the fallen in the Civil War. This square has a complicated traffic pattern, with many whistling policemen, shouted insults, streetside cafés, the Tourist Office, and a perpetual smell of oil and diesel. If you arrive by boat, this is your first view of the island. It's best to stop for a coffee to collect yourself before embarking upon further exploration.

Up from the front, run streets of shops. To the west of the plaza lies the **Plaza de la Candelaría,** with a statue of the Virgin of Candelaría atop an obelisk, and beneath three Guanche kings who were converted to Christianity. Here, too, is the **Church of the Conception,** with a tall, lantern-shaped tower once used by sailors as a landmark. Visit, too, the **Church of San Francisco,** a fine example of colonial architecture but with an elaborate interior and altars of gilded wood.

Up the hill from the port is the **Parque Municipal,** filled with subtropical plants and, at its entrance, a floral clock. There's also a small zoo here.

The **Municipal Museum,** on José Murphy, up from the port and opposite a tiny dusty square in the center of town, houses a fine collection of pictures by Spanish artists.

The nearest bathing beach is the man-made one at **Las Teresitas,** a few minutes outside town to the north and beyond the Nautical Club and the main harbor installations. It was built behind a breakwater, with a wide stretch of white sand. The water is clean, the bathing safe.

JET FOIL: Trasmediterránea now operates a jet foil between Las Palmas and Santa Cruz on Tenerife. The 1¾-hour journey is very popular with business people who can get between the islands with time for a full day's work in between. For the visitor, the service takes a lot of pain out of the ferry crossing, which can sometimes be quite rough. There's a maximum baggage allowance of 14 kilograms per person, and you'll have to negotiate to take much more with you. Heavy or bulky pieces are handed to the baggagemen at the gangway in exchange for a tag. Coffee and crackers are served free during the crossing, which costs 2520 pesetas ($24.19) for a one-way ticket. There are reductions for round trips and excursions. The best seats are at the front downstairs.

ABOUT YOUR ARRIVAL: There are two separate airports serving the island. The old one in the north of the island is **Los Rodeos;** the newer and more sophisticated one in the south is **Reina Sofía.** There is very little consistency over which airport planes will arrive at or depart from. You could, in fact, arrive at one airport, only to find that your inter-island flight was leaving from the other. So be sure to reconfirm your onward flight and double-check the departure airport.

If you happen to be staying in Puerto de la Cruz, you can take a taxi, which will cost about 3500 pesetas ($33.60), or use the cheaper method of a self-drive car, which even for one person goes for about 2500 pesetas ($24). There are no drop-off charges if you use Hertz or Avis, and you have the vehicle for 24 hours. This is not practical if you are leaving or arriving at Los Rodeos in the north. Otherwise, a bus from Reina Sofía to Santa Cruz costs 275 pesetas ($2.64) for the one-hour journey. A bus from Santa Cruz to Puerto, a 50-minute journey, via La Laguna and the Rodeos airport, goes for 180 pesetas ($1.73). If you're planning to use the bus between the two airports, be sure to allow plenty of time. One leaves roughly every half hour in both directions.

WHERE TO STAY: In the Tourist Office at Santa Cruz, on the Plaza de España, and at Puerto de la Cruz, Plaza de la Iglesia, you can obtain lists of accommodations of all types and prices. Around the corner from the Santa Cruz office, on José Antonio Primo de Riveira, is the **Patronato de Turismo de Tenerife,** which can also provide advice on hotels and restaurants throughout the island.

Santa Cruz

Hotel Residencia Pelinor, 8 Bethencourt Alfonso (tel. 24-68-75), is easily found just off the Plaza de España. In a modern block, it is surrounded by shops of all sorts as well as snackbars, making it ideal for business or pleasure. Run by Don Laureano Cruz, the hotel-residencia offers eight floors of small and simple rooms, all with baths. Accommodations are fresh smelling and well cleaned. Singles rent for 1150 pesetas ($11.04); doubles with bath, 1800 pesetas ($17.28). A continental breakfast costs 120 pesetas ($1.15). No other meals are served, but there are plenty of opportunities for dining right nearby. English is spoken at the hotel. There's a friendly, cheerful atmosphere, plus a rooftop solarium.

Hotel Anaga, 17 Imelda Seris (tel. 24-50-90), again, is just off the Plaza de España. A typical commercial overnight stop, it is unremarkable, but clean and convenient. The rooms are plainly furnished with telephones—but no radios or anything. The cupboard space is good, and shiny linoleum covers the floors. Many of the accommodations contain private baths, although there are adequate public facilities as well. Singles with bath range from 1100 pesetas ($10.56). Doubles with bath start at 1500 pesetas ($14.40). A continental breakfast is an extra 120 pesetas ($1.15). The restaurant on the first floor is light and clean, serving a set dinner for 450 pesetas ($4.32), and there is a terrace on the roof for sunbathing.

Hotel Diplomatico, 6 Antonio Nebrija (tel. 22-39-41), is a three-star hotel in a town where only two hotels have four stars and one five. It's up the hill from the bustle of the port, on a quiet street behind the market. All rooms contain private baths and tiny balconies overlooking the town to the sea. Spotlessly clean and comfortable, the accommodations rent as follows: 1550 pesetas ($14.88) in a single with bath, 2400 pesetas ($23.04) in a double with bath. There is a swimming pool and rooftop terrace, plus a bar and dining room boasting a quite good international menu. The Diplomatico offers good value and is a cut above the other places, although not so handily placed for the action.

Hotel Parque, 40 Mendez Nuñez (tel. 27-44-00), is one of the four-star hotels. More expensive than my previous recommendations, it still offers good value. The Parque stands up a hill high above the port at the corner of the Municipal Park, with views over the sea or the trees. Rooms are neat and clean, with rugs on the floor. All have private baths as well as refrigerators. Singles range from 1550 pesetas ($14.88); doubles, 2600 pesetas ($24.96). The restaurant, with its reasonable menu of international dishes, offers a set meal for 550 pesetas ($5.28).

Less expensive is the **Residencia Tamaide,** 118 Rambla Generalísimo Franco (tel. 27-71-00). The "rambla" is a wide two-way roadway running across the top of the town. The Tamaide is in the residential part of town— more elegant, where the air is fresher. Yet it's within walking distance of the port and commercial sector. All rooms have balconies and baths or showers, and are neatly and simply furnished. Singles cost from 1200 pesetas ($11.52); doubles, 1900 pesetas ($18.24). There is no restaurant, but many abound in the neighborhood, including a Chinese one. A swimming pool and sun terrace make the atmosphere even more pleasant.

Residencia Taburiente, 19 Dr. Guigou (tel. 27-60-00), is just around the corner from the Tamaide and of very much the same standard. The staff is helpful, although little English is spoken. The public area is pleasant with wood paneling; and the rooms are carpeted and well painted, containing plain furnishings, telephones, and good cupboards. All have private baths or showers.

Singles cost from 1500 pesetas ($14.40); doubles, 2000 pesetas ($19.20). The rooftop pool and solarium are popular. Under the residencia is a bar-restaurant with the usual price list displayed outside in many languages, although no one really speaks any of them.

Puerto de la Cruz

Hotel San Borondon, 4 Calle Puerto Viejo (tel. 37-16-47), is, as its name suggests, behind the old port, although still within easy reach of the tourist attractions. It's entered through a pretty flower-covered arch. The rooms are grouped around a grassy sunken garden and seawater swimming pool—a sun trap between high hedges. The rooms are reached along covered walkways. All have private baths or showers. Well furnished and comfortable, the doubles cost from 2200 pesetas ($21.12); singles, 1600 pesetas ($15.36). Lunch or dinner runs 550 pesetas ($5.28). It's a quiet and peaceful oasis, and English is spoken.

Residencia Bambi, El Lomito (tel. 37-12-90), stands on a small street, one block up from the Promenade. All rooms have tiny kitchenettes with freezer/ refrigerators, crockery, cutlery, but no cooker. All the accommodations have private baths, and the residencia has recently been redecorated. Doubles with bath cost from 1350 pesetas ($12.96); singles, 1000 pesetas ($9.60). An elevator services all floors. Off the large lobby downstairs is a dining room serving ample portions of wholesome food, a lunch or dinner costing from 550 pesetas ($5.28). The bar is pleasant, with wood beams. The Bambi is unremarkable, but the value is good. The hotel is used extensively by a tour group, and reservations are entirely on a person-by-person daily basis. No advance bookings are accepted.

Now for some very typically Spanish recommendations, although the clientele consists almost entirely of overseas visitors.

Hotel Marquesa, 11 Quintana (tel. 37-14-46), overlooks the gardens in front of the parish church. The oldest hotel in Puerto, it boasts more than 100 years of service. When you look at the attractive building, with its typical Spanish balconies and shuttered windows, you will know this is so. Family owned and run, the old building has been adapted somewhat to modern standards with the addition on a new wing at the back fronting the sea.

The central courtyard has been roofed in and made into a large and cheerful lounge, off of which run the bar and dining room. In the new part the accommodations contain neat wooden furniture, rugs, and modern baths. In the old part, reached off the gallery around the courtyard, the ceilings are high (some of the doorways are eight feet high). Bathrooms have been built into these lofty chambers. The old furniture, for the most part, has been retained, and many of the beds are huge. Some of these rooms have balconies overlooking the sea, others the square. The antique part is even furnished with heavy old Spanish pieces, including interesting pictures on the stairway and a beautiful old balustrade which must have felt a million hands.

Rates are surprisingly low: 1000 pesetas ($9.60) in singles, from 1600 pesetas ($15.36) in doubles. The half-board rate is 800 pesetas ($7.68) per person in addition to the room tariff.

The cool, paneled dining room offers a table d'hôte menu for 550 pesetas ($5.28), excluding wine. The cooking here is authentically Spanish, although some concession is made to the international palate. In all, I think the Marquesa is much more worthwhile for a stay than the anonymous international tourist operations in this characterless town.

If the hotel doesn't have a room, or if you prefer more isolation, then I recommend the annex:

Residencia Marquesol, 3 Calle Esquivel (tel. 37-18-48). All 23 rooms are serviced by an elevator, and contain private baths, radios, and balconies. Many of the accommodations are large, overlooking the beautiful tiled roofs of the old houses. On the roof is a solarium, and in the basement is a well-stocked bar. Alfonso, who acts as porter and general factotum, helps run the place with great pride and diligence. If you don't want to eat in the Marquesa, you can bring your own food and drink. But, of course, there are no cooking facilities. A single with bath costs from 600 pesetas ($5.76); a double with bath, 1300 pesetas ($12.48). A continental breakfast is an additional 125 pesetas ($1.20).

Hotel Monopol, 15 Quintana (tel. 37-13-46), is another Spanish-type building which has been added to. The enclosed courtyard has been filled with green plants and white seats, making it a peaceful resting place to escape the heat of the day. The newer part is reached through the courtyard toward the sea. A bar overlooks a small swimming pool and terrace and, in the distance, the Atlantic rollers. Bedrooms are neat and functional, some with flower-clad balconies overlooking the square, others in the modern part fronting the sea. All have private baths. Singles cost from 900 pesetas ($8.64) to 1350 pesetas ($12.96); doubles, 1650 pesetas ($15.84) to 2500 pesetas ($24). The menu of the day goes for 500 pesetas ($4.80). Picnic lunches are also provided, if desired. The hotel has undergone a careful restoration and is in good condition.

Hotel Los Príncipes, Calle Quintana (tel. 37-17-90), is a modern building, facing a charming plaza with flowers and palm trees. It's in the old part of town, near the fishing harbor and market, standing on the same street as the previously recommended Marquesa. At the hotel's coffeeshop, facing the square, you can order drinks, sandwiches, tapas, and light meals costing from 230 pesetas ($2.21) to 430 pesetas ($4.13) a dish. There is also a restaurant serving a set dinner for around 650 pesetas ($6.24). After passing through the cool, spacious lobby, you are shown to neatly furnished bedrooms, all of which have private baths and phones (some have balconies). Singles cost 1500 pesetas ($14.40) to 1800 pesetas ($17.28); doubles, 2640 pesetas ($25.34) to 3200 pesetas ($30.72), including a continental breakfast. On the roof is a heated swimming pool with wide sun terraces, although the beaches and public pools are only minutes away. The hotel is nice with a quiet situation and a cheerful atmosphere.

Hotel Martianez, 19 Avenida del Generalísimo (tel. 38-06-00), is a modern high-rise block just up from the beaches. It is best known for the flamenco show it offers. The lobby is pleasant, as are the lounges and bar. The bedrooms are decorated in a typical Spanish style, with good beds and flowery balconies. All contain private baths. A single goes for 2630 pesetas ($25.25); a double, 3800 pesetas ($36.48), which makes it a splurge, but good value for those readers wanting a bit of luxury. Meals run around 900 pesetas ($8.64).

The undoubted splurge hotel of the island is the **Hotel San Felipe,** Playa de Martianez, Puerto de la Cruz (tel. 37-11-40). It lies along the waterfront, a bit away from the Manrique complex but within easy walking distance of the shops and promenades of the resort. The hotel has been completely revamped and is a comfortable luxury establishment where the friendliness and helpfulness of the staff is one of the first things you notice. A high-rise building, it has bedrooms facing either the sea or the gardens and the banana plantation. Rooms are well furnished with good storage space, balconies, and private baths. Singles rent for 2530 pesetas ($24.29); doubles go for 4260 pesetas ($40.90).

Lunch is an informal buffet in the swimming-pool bar or a more formal meal in the bright, light dining room. In the gardens is an Olympic-size swimming pool with excellent diving boards, as well as tennis courts floodlit in the evenings. All sorts of other services are offered—yoga, keep-fit classes, billiards, bridge, a library, hair-dressing, massage, and gymnastics. The hotel has a seven-seater limousine used to transfer guests to the airports and harbor.

El Medano

El Medano is at the southern tip of the island where the great new complexes of hotels have been built. It's reached by a metalled road, then the usual dirt track toward the sea. The new airport, some three to four miles from the heart of town, has made this part of the island more accessible to visitors. However, it has not increased the noise at El Medano, because flight paths do not cross it.

Hotel El Medano, Playa de El Medano, Granadilla de Abona (tel. 70-40-00), lies at one side of a sandy bar, built on a pier so that it's possible at high tide to dive from the sun terrace straight into the sea. But don't try this stunt at low tide, as there's nothing but sand beneath. The lobby leads to a pleasant dining room, lounge, and bar. Beyond is a sun terrace, with loungers and chairs. The public rooms are furnished with comfortable chairs in pretty light colors. The rooms all look onto the sea, and most of them have private balconies. Some are very large, and all have fully equipped bathrooms. The furnishings are basic, as in the typical seaside hotel where little time is spent in your room. The floors are of stone. Beds are comfortable, and extra pillows and blankets are supplied very willingly. Singles cost 1585 pesetas ($15.22); doubles, 2675 pesetas ($25.68). Breakfast is 175 pesetas ($1.68). A lunch or dinner costs 780 pesetas ($7.49). The hotel is within easy reach of Santa Cruz, the Playa de las Américas, and Los Cristianos complexes. However, Teo López, who runs the hotel, gives film shows and other diversions in the evening for those who don't wish to join the locals in one of the many, many bars in the small town. Mrs. López, who is English, looks after the housekeeping.

Hostal Residencia Carel, El Medano, Granadilla de Abona (tel. Medano 17), is run by Don Manuel Ramos and his family. About 300 yards from the sea, their hotel lies a little above the beach right in the middle of this small town. A new building, it has a nice restaurant as one of its main features. Mama speaks English. Shrimps cost 200 pesetas ($1.92) for a big dishful, although you may prefer the prawns in garlic butter. The menu of the day goes for 350 pesetas ($3.36). On the à la carte menu, meat dishes begin at 185 pesetas ($1.78), going up to 450 pesetas ($4.32) for a sirloin steak. Rooms are pleasantly furnished and comfortable, a total of 24 in all, renting for 1350 pesetas ($12.96) in a double, 790 pesetas ($7.58) in a single. The management has installed a small disco with free admission and drinks at average hotel prices. However, the management reserves the right to require its guests to be tidily dressed and sober.

Hotel Playa Sur Tenerife, Playa de El Medano (tel. 70-41-50). At the far end of the sandy bay, this building which has been a hotel for many years has been refurbished and freshly decorated. German owned and run, it caters very much to holiday makers. If you want to get on here with your fellow guests, a knowledge of German is more important than Spanish.

There's a pleasant lounge and dining room with a wooden ceiling, along with ample tables and comfortable chairs. They boast an international cuisine with Spanish specialties, and vegetarians and other dieters will find special menus. By the sheltered swimming pool is a pleasant bar, and there's also a sauna and massage parlor in which you can relax after windsurfing or whatever.

Bedrooms are prettily furnished, and each has a balcony and a sea view. A double with shower, toilet, and phone costs 1280 pesetas ($12.29) per person daily, including a continental breakfast. A single goes for 1680 pesetas ($16.13), so it's not cheap, but there are reductions for stays of one week or more. Full board costs an additional 1200 pesetas ($11.52) per person daily. They have a minibus for transfers to the nearby Reina Sofia airport, the ten-minute journey costing 300 pesetas ($2.88). If ordered in advance, taxis are available to take you into the center of Medano.

A Parador in a Crater

Parador Nacional Canadas del Teide, Apartado 15 de la Orotava (tel. La Orotava 33-23-04), lies in the crater of the ancient volcano, which now forms a plateau at the highest part of the island from which the peak of Teide rises, 3700 yards from the sea. The parador was built to withstand differences in temperature, as it can be cold at night, and there is often snow on the peak. The building is like a chalet, with balconies and shutters. In the dark wooden interior, huge log fires burn in the lounge and bar. The food in the dining room is uncompromisingly Spanish. A lunch or dinner at 900 pesetas ($8.64) will fill the best trencherman. Local wine is served unless you ask for a bottle from the mainland. The bar also serves snacks. A double room costs from 3000 pesetas ($28.80), a single going for 2400 pesetas ($23.04). Tariffs are reduced off-season. There's a swimming pool for the many days when the temperature is in the 90s.

WHERE TO DINE: My survey of places to eat, snack, or drink will range around the island, beginning first in the capital of:

Santa Cruz

Restaurant La Estancia, 110 Mendez Nuñez (tel. 27-20-49), is just off the Rambla Generalísimo Franco. It's rather quixotic in decor—black and white with iron grills and wrought iron. The chef specializes in Creole cookery. The restaurant's expensive, although it offers good value. It is heavily patronized by the locals as well. You might begin with ceviche, or perhaps shark-wing soup, even oxtail. The omelets, in a variety of styles, are a good luncheon choice. Main dishes include baby eels (a local delicacy), grilled halibut, veal chops, steak tartare, and tournedos Rossini. If you partake of all these à la carte dishes, your tab is likely to climb beyond 1200 pesetas ($11.52). Otherwise, it's best to stick to the menu of the day for 850 pesetas ($8.16). In addition to the more mundane items, the menu offers parillada criollo, a charcoal steak cooked at your table, 1500 pesetas ($14.40) for two persons. The cheese selection is mainly local, and desserts feature chocolate mousse and flan. Service is good and efficient.

Restaurant Quo Vadis, Villalba Hervas, is a cheap and cheerful place, just off the Plaza de España, right among shops and stores. It offers good-tasting soups or such appetizers as egg mayonnaise or asparagus (hot with butter or cold with sauce). Pork chops, grilled grouper, Russian salad, steaks, and other such fare are featured daily. The menu of the day costs 425 pesetas ($4.08) for two courses, plus bread and a glass of wine. The platefuls are large.

Cafetería Olympio, Plaza de la Candelaría, is a modern complex right on the corner of the square, overlooking a war memorial and, beyond, the harbor and its ships. The first floor has a balcony of tables for those who wish to eat outside. Inside is a large dining room, ideal for a quick meal. Prices depend on where you sit, the bar being cheaper. Soups range from consommé to shellfish, and the salads are also tempting. A minute or ham steak is also offered, served with tomatoes, salad, and french fries. Desserts are standard. A combined dish of meat, fried potatoes, egg, tomatoes, and sausage costs 360 pesetas ($3.46) at a table, less at the bar. A good breakfast costs 140 pesetas ($1.34) at the bar, 175 pesetas ($1.68) at a table.

La Masia, Mendez Nuñez y San Fernando, just up the street from Estancia, is an expensive and luxurious retreat for a quiet, elegant meal. It is very much patronized by local people, so go early if you want a table. Grilled wooden portals lead to a dark dining room with wooden panels. You might begin with mushrooms with garlic, or perhaps Costa Brava anchovies. The fresh fish dishes range from 440 pesetas ($4.22) to 565 pesetas ($5.42), depending on what's running at the moment. Steaks, chops, and escalopes are fully garnished, ranging from 450 pesetas ($4.32) to 675 pesetas ($6.48). Wines are cheap—for example, a bottle of the house wine costs from 275 pesetas ($2.64) to 340 pesetas ($3.26).

La Caseta de Madera, Barrio de los Llanos (tel. 21-00-23), is just a shack right down among the outbuildings and warehouses, right beside the sea below the Zona Industrial at the end of Avenida José Antonio Prima de Rivera. The bar is half an old wooden boat, and the fish comes almost flapping from the sea. It's served with salad and french fries or papas arrugadas, washed down with local wines, although the bar is sophisticated enough to cater to stronger tastes. Your meal will cost you about 1000 pesetas ($9.60), including a typical dessert and coffee. However, the owner, Francisco González Poleo, will not open if there is no fish. La Caseta is a connoisseur's delight, but perhaps a little too basic for most visitors. To get there, follow the sea wall until you reach the red Coca-Cola sign. The place is very popular, especially on Saturday, although it is closed on Sunday.

Puerto de la Cruz

This town, contrived entirely for tourists, boasts many bar/cafés which sell *perros calientes,* hamburgers, french fries, soft drinks, wine (generally not local), and coffee. Among these, the **Cafetería Oasis,** 11 Avenida de Colón (tel. 38-16-07), is owned by Anna Welsch. She, along with the piano and organ music, is as popular as ever. Soups range from 75 pesetas (72¢) to 100 pesetas (96¢), and most main dishes are priced at 300 pesetas ($2.88). You can, however, go mad and order prawns in garlic butter, 600 pesetas ($5.76); steak baked in pastry, 500 pesetas ($4.80); and avocado with prawns, 600 pesetas ($5.76). Salads go for 250 pesetas ($2.40), and desserts cost from 100 pesetas (96¢) to 250 pesetas ($2.40).

Café de París, Avenida de Colón, is the coffeeshop of the popular Hotel Valle Mar. It's an attractive pavement café, with canopies and palms in the French tradition. Large and busy from morning till night, it's an ideal place to rest from sightseeing, as it is right on the main street. A coffee or drink can be spun out for as long as you like. A meat dish with a salad and potatoes will cost around 450 pesetas ($4.32); an omelet, 275 pesetas ($2.64). The café also specializes in exotic and fattening cakes and pastries—a chocolate gâteau, an enormous slice, going for 140 pesetas ($1.34), and strawberry flan with cream, also 140 pesetas. A wide variety of ice creams are in the 80-pesetas (77¢) to 170-pesetas ($1.63) range. A menu of the day, the cheapest way to eat here, goes for 400 pesetas ($3.84).

Restaurant Viking, Avenida Generalísimo Franco (tel. 38-29-57), is on one of the main streets of Puerto, beneath the Hotel Martina. Patrons find it a cool spot for just a drink or a coffee, although they can stay to order a set meal for 365 pesetas ($3.50). A meal on the à la carte menu is likely to run around 550 pesetas ($5.28), however. For that, your choices are likely to include matjes herring served with "long" potatoes, a tomato, onion, cucumber, and lettuce salad, filet mignon Viking, and dessert. Portions are large. The owner is Scandinavian, so you are going to get reasonably authentic dishes. The place is open daily except Monday from 11 a.m. to 11 p.m.

Restaurante El Pescado, 3B Avenida Venezuela (tel. 38-28-06). If you turn up from the sea by the Café de París, you come to the cul-de-sac Venezuela. At El Pescado there are two small dining rooms separated by a central kitchen and decorated with dark wood paneling and tables with upholstered bench seats. Hours are from 12:30 to 2:45 p.m. and 6:30 to 10:45 p.m. Live guitar music is presented in the evenings. Fishermen's soup with Pernod or garlic soup Catalán style await your selection. The chef obviously specializes in fresh fish, and the menu depends quite a lot on what fish is caught. When I was there squid, clams, halibut, cigalas, lobster, and langostinos were available at prices ranging from 750 pesetas ($7.20). A paella Valenciana for two costs 1100 pesetas ($10.56), and it overflows with shellfish and chicken. A Canarian puchero (the first time I have found it in a Puerto restaurant) is 2250 pesetas ($21.60) for four people. You must, however, wait some 45 minutes for paella or puchero to be prepared, so expect to sip the house wine at 400 pesetas ($3.84) a large carafe while you wait. Desserts are around 150 pesetas ($1.44), and the day's catch of fish is marked on a blackboard outside the restaurant in traditional style with weights and prices. Make sure you enter through the proper door, or you'll find yourself in the backyard in the midst of the trash cans.

For the best selection of budget restaurants, head for the Calle de San Felipe, which is fast becoming a street for good, inexpensive, international food establishments. At last count, there were nearly a dozen such restaurants. In a five-minute walk, you can have a selection of Spanish, French, German, Peruvian, or Italian dining spots. It's possible to eat a three-course meal at lunch, with bread and a quarter of a liter of wine, for 300 pesetas ($2.88) all day and late at night.

Restaurant El Inca, Calle de San Felipe, is in the old part of town, on a small street running off the Plaza General Franco. It is attractive, with iron grills and clean tables. The chef specializes in Peruvian dishes and fresh local foods. The menu includes such selections as melon with ham, cebiche mixto (marinated fish), and garlic soup Peruvian style. Main-course specialties include sole à la Inca, ox heart en brochette, duck with rice, and chicken with a special sauce. Desserts include the usual puddings, but also banana flambé. Complete meals begin at 800 pesetas ($7.68). The least expensive way to dine here is to order the menu of the house for 350 pesetas ($3.36), including, say, garlic soup, a Peruvian-style grilled halibut in a special sauce, plus wine, bread, and ice cream. The restaurant is open from noon to 4 p.m. and from 7 to 11 p.m. daily, except Wednesday.

Casa de la Paella, 31 Calle de San Felipe, is a small French bistro-type restaurant, with a small bar, and a simple decor. It offers a selection of homemade soups and salads. In the latter category, asparagus is the most expensive. Main dishes include lobster mayonnaise, also expensive, as are the snails. The chef's specialty is chicken Valiente, with various sauces, or you can order a pepper steak. All main dishes include three vegetables, and desserts consist mainly of crêpes which range from plain to Cointreau. A three-course meal here, without wine, begins at 600 pesetas ($5.76), although you can spend a lot more, of course.

Restaurante A' Roda Galega, 34 Galle de San Felipe (tel. 38-03-99), has an Italian chef so you can count on good pasta. Canary soup is especially good, as are calamares, veal stew Galician style, squid Galicia, and prawns in garlic. You might also try boiled pork à Roda, with cabbage and potatoes, or Canarian rabbit. The menu of the day is two plates at 80% of the list price, plus bread, wine, and dessert. You can eat well for about 600 pesetas ($5.76).

You can have, the chef assures me, a six-course meal that will satisfy the biggest appetite for 950 pesetas ($9.12) a person. A good bottle of wine will cost from 350 pesetas ($3.36). The place is open from 11 a.m. to 10:30 p.m. It is easily recognizable in this narrow street of small enterprises by the hams and smoked sausages hanging over the bar and the traditional dark furnishings beloved by Spaniards.

Rancho Grande, Calle San Telmo, is built in the typical Spanish style, with a wooden balcony overhanging the walkway and the sea in the old part of town. Try for a seat on the balcony where you can watch the world go by and see the water breaking on the rocks below. They serve food throughout the day, starting with breakfast at 290 pesetas ($2.78). Lunch can include an avocado pear at 450 pesetas ($4.32) or melon and ham at 250 pesetas ($2.40). Main courses, priced from 325 pesetas ($3.12) to 550 pesetas ($5.28), include lamb chops, spare ribs, skewered meat, and pepper steak. T-bone steaks are priced from 600 pesetas ($5.76) to 800 pesetas ($7.68), and diners usually order a salad at 195 pesetas ($1.87) to go with it. Beer is 50 pesetas (48¢) to 80 pesetas (77¢), and half a liter of wine begins at 150 pesetas ($1.44).

Afterward there's a large selection of mouthwatering cakes and pastries from which to select your dessert. These include apple pie and sponge cake with real strawberries topped with mounds of whipped cream. Make your selection at the buffet and wait for the waiter to bring it to your table.

La Papaya, 14 Calle del Lomo (tel. 38-28-11), occupies the converted ground floor of an old Canary house in the old town near San Felipe, the street of restaurants. Luís Gimenez, the owner, greets everyone with a glass of sherry, while diners make their selections from his typical Spanish menu. The simple house has doors with windows opening right onto the street. There are several rooms with small tables everywhere. Humming with life, it's very popular with local business people.

The menu changes often but always includes fresh fish, sama with Canary potatoes and mojo, a zarzuela (mixed fish and shellfish stew), and paella. Rabbit, roast beef, pepper steak, and pork chops are always available. Most of the fresh vegetables and salad greens come from Luís's own garden. The average cost for a meal which is almost more than you can eat ranges from 800 pesetas ($7.68) to 1000 pesetas ($9.60). You can sit out behind the house, enjoying an apéritif before you're called in to dinner.

In this area is the street, **Cruz Verde,** running from Lomo to the sea, where almost every house is a restaurant. Among them **La Parranda** and **Patio Canario** feature fresh fish, paella, and Canarian specialties.

Capitán Metro Steak House, 6 Calle Cologan (tel. 38-04-44). A cheerful nautical air permeates this spotless place, with its bright tables decorated with fresh flowers. The menu is international and very good. Appetizers include soups at 125 pesetas ($1.20), or else you may prefer a fresh salad at 175 pesetas ($1.68). Chicken dishes are priced around 325 pesetas ($3.12), and pork "Bombay" goes for 350 pesetas ($3.36). Two persons can order a pretty good paella at 900 pesetas ($8.64). If your budget will allow it, the chef does succulent steaks: pepper steak, filets, ranch house, and T-bones, at prices ranging from 450 pesetas ($4.32) to 675 pesetas ($6.48). Desserts start at 100 pesetas (96¢). There is a good house wine at 180 pesetas ($1.73) for half a liter. The service is quick and efficient.

Restaurant Buffet Tosca, 1 José Antonio, is a busy, self-service establishment in the nicest part of town, near the fishing harbor. You can eat as much as you like—or can—for only 450 pesetas ($4.32). That gets you a selection of hot and cold fish and meat dishes, along with salads, cold meats, desserts, and fresh fruit. The buffet is open daily from 12:30 p.m.

At Icod de los Vinos

Icod Agustín y Rosa, 15 San Sebastian, Icod de los Vinos (tel. 81-07-92), is on the north coast of the island, to the west of Puerto de la Cruz. The town of Icod is famous for its Dragon Tree, the oldest on the island. Visitors may like to slake their thirst and break their fast at this friendly place, run by Agustín and his wife, Rosa, with a little help from their friends. In the middle of town, a short walk from the dragon tree, you enter through the bar to a large, well-lit dining room overlooking Icod to the sea. Simple white cloths are placed on wooden tables, with a wide menu of Spanish food served to the accompaniment of much chatter and laughter. If you don't understand anything, you get a passable explanation in Spanish. Soups or hors d'oeuvres cost 75 pesetas (72¢) to 100 pesetas (96¢); a choice of seven omelets, from brain to pea, 150 pesetas ($1.44); octopus, 150 pesetas also; and baked fish, 300 pesetas ($2.88). Here you can sample the Canary Island dessert of "Bien-me-Sabe," a meringue with almonds and honey. Also I'd recommend trying the local Icod wine which has a distinctive bouquet. A bottle of the house wine costs about 200 pesetas ($1.92). A set meal goes for 450 pesetas ($4.32). If you'd like to spend the night, you'll find double rooms renting for 820 pesetas ($7.87).

Hostal del Drago is an old Spanish building on one corner of the square where the dragon tree stands. Although called a hostal, it does not have any accommodations, but you can get tapas in the bar where they have a large selection priced from 90 pesetas (86¢) to 130 pesetas ($1.25) a portion. In the restaurant or at one of the tables in the garden, you can have a meal from an extensive menu ranging from soups and asparagus, to grilled fish, steaks, and chicken to the ever-popular flan for dessert. A three-course meal will set you back 500 pesetas ($4.80) or more, according to your choice. There is also a large souvenir and postcard shop. If you go in at lunchtime, don't be surprised to find the family dining at their own table in a line watching color television. All is very Spanish, but there is an English menu which the waiter will understand only if you point to what you want.

Garachico

On the north side of the island, a few miles from Icod, this small town was completely engulfed in lava when Teide erupted in 1706. Surrounded by vineyards and banana plantations, it is now a busy little town with a pleasant square dominated by the Church of Santa Ana.

The local people certainly know how to eat, and there are two restaurants in town where you can dine like a lord for almost nothing. Remember that Spanish lunch does not start until around 2 p.m., and that the fish must be caught and prepared first—so don't go early.

La Perla de Garachico, Calle de 18 de Julio (tel. 83-02-86). There is the usual plain clean room with a bar offering drinks, coffee, and tapas. From the dining room, a spotless kitchen is visible. The owners will show you the fish you are going to eat before they prepare it, or else you can choose your own steak. Soup is about 90 pesetas (86¢); omelets, from 110 pesetas to 125 pesetas ($1.20), depending on the flavor. A steak with vegetables or salad costs 220 pesetas ($2.11). The fish of the day is grilled or boiled and served with mojo verde (flavored with coriander), salad, and potatoes for just 375 pesetas ($3.60).

On the Calle Esteban de Ponte, behind the church, is a tiny house, the **Casa Ramón**. The front room gleams with polished wood and bright red-and-white-checked tablecloths. While Ramón is out fishing, his smiling wife cleans and prepares the food. Then at 2 p.m. they serve a smashing set meal of soup or salad or beans followed by the fish you have just watched Ramón cook, either grilled or boiled in fresh water, and served with salad and potatoes. Served separately if you prefer is a spicy sauce, mojo. Dessert is flan or ice cream, and the whole repast costs about 300 pesetas ($2.88). The meal is washed down with local wine at about 150 pesetas ($1.44) for a large flagon. In keeping with the local custom, there is a washbasin in the restaurant in which you can wash your hands if you decide to eat with your fingers. A truly local experience. This totally unsophisticated and charming little place is popular, and you may have to go to a nearby bar while waiting for a seat.

If you're driving from Icod to Garachico to visit the crater of Teide, or the beaches of the south, you can climb up the mountain through banana trees to the **Mirador de Garachico** which has fine photographic views. There you can sit with the lava behind you, the sea beneath you, and eat sandwiches and smoked meats, buy provisions for a picnic, or else browse in the Bazar Típico which is full of unusual souvenirs of the island. Try for a snack, orejas de elefante (elephant's ears), sweet, crisp fritters with an apple center at 30 pesetas (29¢) each.

El Medano

Fishing boats are drawn up on the beach and on the wide promenade where at festivals there is dancing, but on any day the old men sit and smoke. **Casa Mario**, Calle Marcial (tel. Medano 29). Mario and his two brothers run the bar, and the women of the family do the cooking. It is a small spotless room opening onto the promenade, with three or four tables, plus the bar. A few tables are placed outside on the pavement. On Wednesday at lunchtime they do a special Canary meal, making so much food there is plenty left over for the evening as well. In huge pots in the spotless kitchen simmers a fish stew to be eaten with a sauce made of garlic, lemon, oil, and coriander, or else a *punchero,* a typical stew of meat with a vast array of vegetables in a luscious herb-flavored juice. A Canary soup with chick peas or a fish soup jostles for position on the stove. You're invited to inspect the pots and choose what you'll have as your meal. When you've finished one helping, you can go back for more. A glass of wine completes the meal, and you'll rise replete for the small cost of about 350 pesetas ($3.36) per person. The bar is the meeting place for the locals, who congregate to listen to *fútbol* on the radio—played loud—or else to argue violently in Spanish. The bar is very popular in the evenings when tables are set out on the tiled patio for drinking.

Bar Familiar has a large bar downstairs where tapas are served at around 50 pesetas (48¢) to 225 pesetas ($2.16) a portion. Selections include prawns, potato salad, or octopus in mojo. Upstairs is a restaurant where the menu of the day goes for 410 pesetas ($3.94), including three courses with wine. Otherwise, on the à la carte menu, the fish soup at 95 pesetas (91¢) is preferred as an appetizer. Fish is sold by weight, and you can make your selection before it is cooked. Sole and langostinos are the usual orders, although many guests prefer the calamares. A chateaubriand for two costs 900 pesetas ($8.64). The house specialty is rabbit, Canary style, much less expensive at 325 pesetas ($3.12). Complete à la carte meals average about 800 pesetas ($7.68).

Across the square, the **Casa Bernardo** (tel. Medano 33), has a large poster on the walls, with pictures and the names of the local fish in five lanugages.

Father does the fishing, the son runs the gleaming chrome and plastic bar, and mama is always busy in the kitchen. Fish is so fresh it's served almost alive, actually grilled or fried. A specialty is *vieja,* a parrotfish with mojo picon, the red hot sauce of the island. Langostinos, crayfish, and prawns vary in price, according to size, but an adult-size portion will cost from 120 pesetas ($1.15) to 250 pesetas ($2.40).

The **Bar Avencio** is narrow and dark, the entrance almost covered by bushes. It's well recommended for its prawns fried in garlic butter, costing 120 pesetas ($1.15) for a small portion or 325 pesetas ($3.12) for a large plateful with bread and a glass of wine. The onion soup is very substantial, costing 110 pesetas ($1.06), and the house wine can be recommended. The place has a friendly atmosphere, and Canary artifacts and fishing gear hang from the walls. This is a magnificent repast for the aficionado.

Bar/Restaurante FeFo must have an address, but you can't miss it. It's right down by the edge of the beach, its wide windows opening the bar out to the pavement with its colorful tables and umbrellas. Inside, FeFo and his family dispense the usual drinks from a long curved bar. For lunch they serve large portions of fresh fish from the day's catch, along with a salad and potatoes, for 300 pesetas ($2.88). If they've got them, do order the fresh grilled sardines at 250 pesetas ($2.40). Calamares at 200 pesetas ($1.92) are also popular. Pork chops and a meat stew are featured at 225 pesetas ($2.16). Local beer is 50 pesetas (48¢); a carafe of wine, 100 pesetas (96¢).

Los Cristianos

Restaurante Casa del Mar, Esplanade Muelle de los Cristianos (tel. 79-11-23), stands down by the harbor. This restaurant is on the third floor of the Instituto Social de la Marina, a modern building on the quayside by the car park. It has a fine view over the harbor and out to sea, and is open daily for lunch and dinner. Although it has an English menu, only Spanish is spoken. In fine weather you can eat on the balcony. The menu consists of paella for two at 900 pesetas ($8.64) including salad and french fries. Other fish dishes go for around 600 pesetas ($5.76), each, with chicken and other meats costing from 300 pesetas ($3.88).

Playa de las Americas

This is, as yet, an incomplete development where there are few places which caught my interest. It has been held back by the world recession. Although a considerable number of hotels have been completed, their prices are fairly high, and the surrounding area suffers from not having been taken over by the municipality, and are therefore covered with litter and rubbish.

The beachside restaurants evoke Coney Island, and the entertainment is mostly disco. I don't feel I can recommend any particular establishment as of this writing. However, if you're touring in the area, know that **O'Casey's Pub,** in the Veronica II complex, is still there, although other establishments come and go. At the pub you'll find many beers and the usual alcoholic and soft drinks available.

San Juan

This small fishing village lies on the west coast of the island, beyond the modern complexes of the south. It is between the banana plantations and the sea on the old coast road. It is minus the sophistication of Los Cristianos, and that forms part of its charm.

The restaurant, **Brisas del Mar,** Playa San Juan (tel. 86-79-54), overlooks the sea and fishing boats that bring in the catch. It's so popular with the locals that it's often difficult, especially on weekends, to find a table. But it's well worth trying if you're in the area. Appetizers from soups to prawns range in price from 85 pesetas (82¢) to 225 pesetas ($2.16). Main fish dishes cost from 175 pesetas ($1.68) to 600 pesetas ($5.76). The available fish dishes are written up on a blackboard, and you'll be invited to go in the kitchen to select the catch you want prepared for you. A salad comes with the fish plate. Depending on the filling, omelets go from 125 pesetas ($1.20) to 280 pesetas ($2.69). Local wine is 100 pesetas (69¢) a carafe. At a wash basin you can clean up after you've eaten your prawns with your fingers, as the locals do. Eating begins at noon, finishing at 10 p.m.

NIGHTLIFE: It's spread out among the various resorts. My favorite spots follow.

Puerto de la Cruz

Nightclub Plaza de Toros La Rueda, Las Cabezas (tel. 38-29-10), is open every night for an hour's dancing at 9 before the show begins at 10. Offered are a good comedian, flamenco dancing, and a mini-bullfight where you can join in if you wish. The entrance is 900 pesetas ($8.64). For that, you can drink all you want until 1 a.m., from a range of beers, sangría, wines, and Spanish champagne. In all, it offers good clean entertainment and puts on quite a show.

The best place for flamenco is probably the **Hotel Martianez.** You enter the nightclub from the Calle Valois entrance into a spacious typical Andalusian room, with grills, plants, wooden tables, and rush chairs. It is air-conditioned. A big band plays for dancing, and a superb flamenco troupe performs at 10:30 and again at 11:45 p.m. The first drink costs 1000 pesetas ($9.60). For reservations telephone 38-06-00.

Between the Avenida de Colón in Puerto de la Cruz and the sea, Cesar Manrique has devised a fabulous complex. There are several swimming pools here bordered by sun terraces. Those who do not want to risk the black sand and dangerous undertow of Martianez Beach can swim and sun among the palms. Loungers are available. Admission to the pools is 100 pesetas (69¢)—50 pesetas (48¢) for children—rising to 150 pesetas ($1.44) and 75 pesetas (72¢) in high season. A sun-bed costs 75 pesetas (72¢); an umbrella, 100 pesetas (69¢). Beyond the pools is a "Willow Pattern" bridge leading to the **Isla del Lago** (island in the lake), a unique architectural and landscaping masterpiece. By day it's an upstairs terrace, cafetería, and restaurant. But at night the whole place is transformed, with lights dancing on the water. An incredible nightclub is built inside the island below sea level, and it offers disco dancing and a spectacular floor show. The dance floor is open to the sky, and it's like being in a cave. Entertainment is offered nightly, costing 1500 pesetas ($14.40) for the dance and show, with limitless drinks included. Those who don't feel like going in can stay above ground in the bar and listen to the music under the night sky.

In the Hotel Valle Mar, on Avenida de Colón, is the nightclub **Los Caprichos.** It's richly decorated in red plush with comfortable chairs grouped around small tables. There is dancing to a live band. Each night the show at 11:30 is different, ranging from flamenco to guitar music to Spanish dancing to international pop groups. Programs are posted in the lobby. The entrance is free, and drinks costs from 170 pesetas ($1.63) to 250 pesetas ($2.40) each.

La Cueva, La Longuera, Los Realejos (tel. 34-08-05), stands high on a cliff above Realejos, with wonderful views over the ocean. The nightclub is in a

Guanche cave, containing a restaurant and stage for the twice-nightly floor shows which take place there. It's mostly patronized by people who come on the set excursion, which includes transportation from Puerto, dinner, wine, and dancing to the live band in between shows. The trip costs 1800 pesetas ($17.28) per person. Without a meal, the bill is 1100 pesetas ($10.56). Evenings are lively. The entertainment might be South American, African, whatever. For the same price, there is a nightly Hawaiian show at the **Hotel Parque San Antonio** from 8:30 p.m., including dinner and dancing, followed by a spectacular show at 10:30 p.m. For details, phone 38-29-60.

If you're interested in gambling, the majestic old Taoro Hotel has been revamped in part to contain the **Casino Taoro,** Parque Taoro (tel. 38-05-50). There is a splendid restaurant where a good three-course meal costs 1200 pesetas ($11.52) per person, a bar with muted lights and trailing ferns and, of course, the gaming room, a sunken area beneath the bar and restaurant where blackjack, roulette, baccarat, and slot machines are played. Admission for one day is 400 pesetas ($3.84), and other charges and conditions are as for the Casino in Gran Canaria. The management reserves the right to refuse entry to minors under 21 years old and prefers male guests to wear a jacket and tie.

Los Cristianos

The **Sala Plaza Toró El Torito** (tel. 38-38-52) is just off the main freeway. There is a modern disco with a small dance floor, and flamenco shows are staged every evening from Wednesday through Sunday. In a bullring you can pit your wits against a very small cow. Open from 9 p.m., the club is active till 1 a.m. The price of the dinner show is 1600 pesetas ($15.36), but only 1000 pesetas ($9.60) if you come for drinks. With bus transportation included, the dinner show goes for 2000 pesetas ($19.20), and drinks only cost 1500 pesetas ($14.40). Reservations should be made in advance, and tickets are available from travel agents, hotel porters, and at the door. The location is 4½ miles from Playa de las Américas.

EXPLORING THE ISLAND: To the northeast of Santa Cruz lies a rugged pine-covered area, the **Montanas de Anaga** and the **Forest of Las Mercedes.** It's well worth a visit, as it's an area of great beauty and contrasting scenery.

To the south and north of Santa Cruz, *autopistas* (motorways) run to the beaches of Los Cristianos and Las Américas and to the airport and Puerto de la Cruz.

The northern motorway also brings you to **La Laguna,** the first capital of Tenerife and the seat of the only university on the island. This is a lovely old town in which to walk, visiting the **Nava Palace** owned by the father of the man who later founded the Botanical Gardens, the **Convent of Santa Catalina,** and the **Church and Monastery of Santo Domingo.** Also to be seen are many old seigneurial houses, with their coats-of-arms and sculptured lava facades; the **cathedral,** a modern building dating from 1913, and the **bishop's palace,** plus a mass of other beautiful churches and buildings in the traditional style.

After La Laguna, the motorway bears west and descends to **Puerto de la Cruz.** Once only a tiny fishing port, it was taken over first by the wintering wealthy, then developed as a broader-based all-year-round holiday resort. There is a wide promenade, with swimming pools, amusement parks, and gardens, as the beaches are rocky or made of black pebbly sand. Hotels tower in all directions, and it is only by searching that you find any traces of the old town. The **Church of Nuestra Senora de la Peña,** on the Plaza de la Iglesia, is early 17th century, and has a particularly fine baroque altarpiece in the usual gilded wood.

A market near the fishing port is open from 9 a.m. to 1 p.m. and 4 to 7 p.m. daily except Sunday.

Also right on the seafront is the tiny **Chapel of San Telmo,** built in 1626 by local fishermen and dedicated to their patron saint. It is now used by Catholic visitors, and masses are said in many European languages each Sunday.

The former **Royal Customs House,** 1 Calle Las Lonjas (tel. 37-30-61), in Puerto de la Cruz, lies between the Town Hall and the fishing harbor. Originally built in 1620 as a private residence, it is the oldest house in Puerto. It offers a 22-minute audio-visual presentation of the history of the island—from the time of the ancient inhabitants to the arrival of the Spanish conquerors in 1496 and up to the present day. Shows are given every half hour from 10 a.m. except Saturday afternoon and Sunday. Admission is 50 pesetas (48¢). A shop selling real Canary crafts, South American artisan work, and Spectra Star kites from California is also found here.

On the road down from the motorway to Puerto, on the right, lie the **Botanical Gardens.** These merit exploration even if you're not interested in gardening, as some of the trees and flowers are exotic and fantastic. A guide is available at the gate to identify the more extraordinary ones.

The gardens are open all day from 9 a.m. to 7 p.m. in summer, to 6 p.m. off-season, charging an admission of 70 pesetas (67¢) per person. They were founded in 1788 for the purpose of acclimatizing exotic plants brought back by the Spanish Conquistadores. Bromeliads and aroids can be seen on the trunks and branches of trees, and morning glory covers the stone walls. There are palm trees and giant rubber-tree plants from South America, as well as the delicate strelitzia which is now entirely adapted to the islands.

Behind Puerto, in a deep valley leading upward to the slopes of Teide, lies the town of **La Orotava.** One of the earliest to be established on the island by the Spanish, it was built on the site of the old Guanche kingdom of Bencomo and still retains much of its original splendor. Even today, it is the home of noble and well-to-do families, with lovely old houses and interior staircases and balconies of carved wood. Many flowers decorate the streets. The **Casa de los Balcones** now displays a collection of local arts and crafts which are for sale.

Along the north coast of the island, to the west of Puerto, lie many small villages, nestled between the foothills of Teide and the sea. Among these, **Icod de los Vinos** is probably the best known, because of its dragon tree, reputed to be 3000 years old. The town lies in a fertile wine-growing area, and its local wines are rather special. Above the dragon tree lies a small tree-shaded square surrounded by pretty Spanish houses. It's the most charming place in town, with views out over the sea and the countryside.

On the west side of the island are the massive cliffs of Los Gigantes, then a series of attractive little fishing ports lying between the sea and the banana plantations. These are passed before you arrive at the southern tip of the island and the urbanizations of **Las Américas, Los Cristianos,** and **Ten Bel.**

From here, the Autopista del Sur leads all the way to Santa Cruz, a journey of some 50 minutes. You'll pass **El Medano** which still seems to remain unchanged despite the proximity of the big hotels and the proposed plan for a new airport inland.

In the center of the island, the peak of **Teide** is the focal point. It is set in a wide crater of barren rocks, **Las Cañadas,** and rises far above the pine-covered slopes which descend to the coastal plain, wide in the south, narrow in the north.

As you climb up and enter the Cañadas, you'll be amazed at the wide barren crater stretching in all directions. The rocks are of fantastic colors, and there is a great silence. Beneath the peak is a parador, and on the side of the peak, within walking distance of the summit, a refuge.

For the lazy, a cable car runs to the upper station. From there, it's just a short walk to the edge of the cone. The altitude is high, however, and many visitors experience difficulty breathing. The cable cars run from 10 a.m. to 4 p.m. and the last one leaves the upper station at 5 p.m. A return trip costs 300 pesetas ($2.88).

From the Cañadas there is an excellent road running along the spine of the island to the airport at Los Rodeos. Beautiful views unfold on both sides. At some points you can see the sea on both sides of the island at once. It's lovely if the weather is good, rather mysterious if the clouds descend and isolate you.

ODDS AND ENDS: In Puerto de la Cruz, close to the tiny fishing harbor where you wonder how they get their boats in and out, is **La Fregata,** Edificio Bahía (tel. 37-10-33), the frigate pub. It's surrounded by fishermen mending their nets, selling fish, and talking. For several years it's been run by Tony Pestaille, and it's entirely like an English pub with a long bar, polished tables, beer mats, and bar billiards in the basement. A half pint of real English beer costs 75 pesetas (72¢). Toasted sandwiches go for 100 pesetas (96¢). Tony knows the island and is willing to help tourists with local information. The atmosphere and the talk is so cosmopolitan that it's almost a shock to walk out and be back in Spain again.

Another English pub at Puerto de la Cruz is **Dick Turpin Tavern,** 24 Calvo Sotelo. This one has music every night from a real old piano. There's a lively atmosphere with singing until far into the night. A half pint of draft beer costs 70 pesetas (67¢). It's open from 11 a.m. to 2 p.m. and 5 p.m. to 1 a.m.

Casa Iriarte, 21 Calle San Juan (tel. 37-15-93), in Puerto de la Cruz, is a 300-year-old house with galleries surrounding a patio now devoted entirely to crafts people from the islands. You can watch them embroidering, fashioning filigree silver and gold, hand-tooling leather, carving wood and ivory. The artisans sell their produce, and prices are lower than in the stores. Casa Iriarte is considered a National Historic Monument and is the only old Canary mansion left that is open entirely free to the public. Built before 1790, it is one of the few real Spanish houses containing a courtyard left in Puerto that you can enter.

A part of Casa Iriarte houses the only Nautical Museum in the Canary Islands, with a huge exhibition of maps and perfect scale model boats, including all the Tall Ships which participated in the American Bicentennial Atlantic crossing. This museum is unique in that it shows the history of Tenerife as it relates to the sea, from its ancient discovery, as a stepping stone to the New World, and throughout history to the present. The entrance charge is 150 pesetas ($1.44), and the visitor receives a free bottle of wine similar to that sent by the governor of Santa Cruz to Nelson after the latter lost his right arm in an unsuccessful attempt to take Santa Cruz.

A visit to **Loro Parque,** Punta Brava, just outside Puerto de la Cruz, attracts the family trade. Reached by free bus service from the Café Columbus on the Martianez Beach every 20 minutes, it is a tropical garden where exotic birds and animals fly or play free among the branches. During the day special exhibitions are staged. For the price of your coffee and cakes, whisky or Coca-Cola, you can watch parrots play ball or ride a bicycle. But if you don't wish to stay, you can walk through the gardens past flocks of flamingos and an exotic jungle, returning to Puerto by bus, all for the 325-peseta ($3.12) admission charge. There's also a very expensive restaurant in the park, offering a French cuisine. Hours of the park are from 10 a.m. to 6 p.m.

Above Puerto at Las Arenas, the pottery shop, **La Calera** (tel. 37-02-26), sells all sorts of local products made on the premises. They range from ashtrays to gigantic Ali Baba vases.

Back in Santa Cruz, **Artespaña** is a big chain of stores created by the government to offer and sell representative Spanish handicrafts. Artespaña has two of these shops in Tenerife, one downtown in Santa Cruz at 8 Plaza de la Candelaría, just off the Plaza de España (tel. 24-62-75), and the other one in a 17th-century balcony house in La Orotava, 5 Calle de San Francisco (tel. 33-03-42). These shops give you the opportunity to acquire the most interesting examples of the country's popular arts, such as ceramics, Canary Islands embroideries and lace, Toledo swords, shields, and jewelry.

A five-minute walk from the Plaza de España, at the end of Puente Serrador, takes you to the **Market.** On the Calle José Manuel Guimera and Hernández Alfonso, fruit, vegetables, clothes and shoes, flowers, pottery, earthenware—everything—is for sale. It's the Petticoat Lane or flea market of Santa Cruz. The street is wide, tree-lined and cool on a hot day. On Sunday, the market is devoted to stamps and stamp-collecting, a popular Spanish hobby.

Next door is the **Mercado de Nuestra Señora de Africa,** a two-story building housing many open-sided shops in cloisters around a central courtyard with a fountain. Flower sellers in big straw hats are grouped around. Outside the market, record sellers play their wares, seemingly oblivious of each other, making a cacophany worth experiencing.

Also at Santa Cruz, a **Safari Park Kudu,** Carretera de la Esperanza, shelters all sorts of ferocious animals. It's open from 10 a.m. to 7 p.m. in summer, 9 a.m. to 6 p.m. in winter. Entrance is 300 pesetas ($2.88) per person, including transportation to and from Puerto or Santa Cruz. Buses leave the Café Columbus in Puerto de la Cruz at 10 a.m. and 4 p.m. daily, heading for the park. Inside the bar is a restaurant as well as a snackbar.

Daily at 10 a.m., the cruiser **"Jumbo"** leaves the Pier at Los Cristianos for an excursion around the southwest coast of the island. At noon, the boat anchors in a quiet, clear bay so that you can swim and snorkel, then eat a fish luncheon washed down with sangría. Before you leave the ship at the end of the day, the crew serves champagne to send you on your way. The day costs 2000 pesetas ($19.20) per person. Reservations can be made through Nauti Sport S.A., 2 Avenida Generalísimo, Puerto de la Cruz (tel. 37-15-88) or at Caseta Muelle, Los Cristianos (tel. 79-04-11). Don't forget that the drive from Puerto will take two hours.

El Barco, Tenerife Pottery, 87 Las Arenas (tel. 37-16-23), in Puerto de la Cruz. Everything here is made in the pottery from Mount Teide clay and painted by hand. You can watch the craftsmen at work and order tiles to take home as a souvenir. Also made in the pottery and for sale there is ceramic jewelry. The Canary Craft Corner has a wide selection of local handiwork, lace and embroidery, along with hand-tooled tin and leatherwork. Refreshments are available on the terrace, and a free bus leaves from the Café Columbus in Puerto de la Cruz several times a day. The pottery lies high above the town. It's open daily except Sunday and holidays.

Safari Shangri-La, Finca el Patio (tel. 86-31-72), is a donkey trek into the heart of the Tinerfeño countryside. At 2000 feet below rugged cliffs lies the village of Masca. Until recently, this village could only be approached by mule-train. Now there is a road, but the Safari still follows the old tracks past native houses where it seems time has stood still. You will pass 400-year-old fincas (farmhouses) still using the traditional methods of cultivation and see the inhabitants still wearing, as everyday clothing, the costume now usually only associated with the folklore of the country.

The owners and breeders of the donkeys provide their own interesting story. Hank and Diane Young visited Tenerife during a world cruise in their own yacht, after having sold out in their home state of California. They fell in love with the island, particularly the area around Santiago del Teide, and sold their boat and bought a delapidated finca. They set about restoring the house and revitalizing the farm, building stables and a large paved corral. Then they acquired the first of their present herd of donkeys—which now number some 34—and, on my visit, had an additional six baby donkeys.

The Youngs imported roping saddles from the States and started out in business, taking people on a three-hour ride through the mountains to Masca and back. Hank and Diane escort the party with a stable lad, and a truck follows as escort in case someone tires of riding. During your visit, you break for a lunch, which is accompanied by guitar music. The cost of the day, including transport, lunch, wine, and your donkey is 2500 pesetas ($24) per person.

Bananera el Guanche, La Orotava (tel. 33-18-53), is a banana plantation, open daily from 8 a.m. to 7 p.m. Every 15 minutes the bus leaves from the Café Columbus on the promenade in Puerto, so the plantation is within easy reach. The whole process of banana growing is explained in a simple fashion, and you are given a drink of banana liqueur and a Canary banana. In the shop all sorts of souvenirs are available, and you can buy seeds, rum, rum honey, flowers, and avocados. On its journey back to Puerto, the bus stops at **La Calera,** a fascinating pottery on Las Arenas, Puerto de la Cruz (tel. 37-02-26). It's well worth a visit to see the pots being thrown, baked, and painted. They are very beautiful and a charming souvenir of the island.

GETTING AROUND: By car or coach, ferry or bus, the island enjoys a respectable system of transport.

Car Rentals

Hertz and **Avis** are represented at the airport and in Puerto de la Cruz. Hertz in Puerto is at Plaza de Augustín de Betancourt (tel. 38-45-60). In addition, it has two other offices—one at Playa de Las Américas, Grupo Urbania (tel. 79-08-61), and at Aeropuerto Reina Sofia (tel. 77-10-03). Avis is in the Edificio Iberia, Puerto de la Cruz (tel. 37-20-57), at the airport (tel. 77-13-69), and at Playa de las Américas. The Avis address at Playa de las Américas is Urbanisación Paraíso del Sol (tel. 79-13-02). Both charge about 2500 pesetas ($24) a day for a Seat Panda with unlimited mileage, although tax and insurance are extra. There are several smaller local car-rental companies which offer good service.

Among them, I'd recommend **Occa Rentacar,** at the airports and at Avenida Generalísimo Franco, Puerto de la Cruz (tel. 38-47-13), and at Hotel Gran Tinerfe, Playa de las Américas (tel. 38-39-88). This company charges 2300 pesetas ($22.08) per day on an unlimited mileage basis for a Seat Panda, plus tax and insurance. If you rent a car for a week or more, it costs only 14,200 pesetas ($136.32).

Care should always be taken in reading the insurance clauses, however.

Motorcycles

Very few scooters are now available on the island, but many of the smaller car-hire companies also rent out Suzuki motorbikes (125 cc, 185 cc, and 250 cc). If you're interested in such a rental, you might try **Motos Rueda,** 26 Calle la Verdad, Puerto de la Cruz (tel. 38-29-02), or **Rent-a-Bike,** 59 Calle Calvo Sotelo, Puerto de la Cruz (tel. 38-33-70). Charges range from around 1100 pesetas ($10.56) per day for a Honda 1000. Insurance and tax are extra. Helmets are rented for 100 pesetas (96¢), and a deposit of 4000 pesetas ($38.40) to 5000 pesetas ($48) is required, according to the size and power of the machine.

Taxis

These are quite inexpensive and available from ranks at the airport and in Santa Cruz and at Puerto de la Cruz. Make sure they work on the meter, and know that they're entitled to charge you for each case or bundle. If you want to rent one for the day, agree on the price first, of course. If you go to a remote part of the island, ask the driver to wait while you sightsee. Waiting time is 600 pesetas ($5.76) an hour. Typical fares are as follows: from Puerto to Los Rodeos Airport, 1100 pesetas ($10.56); to Reina Sofía Airport, 3800 pesetas ($36.48); to La Laguna, 1200 pesetas ($11.52); to Santa Cruz, 1600 pesetas ($15.36); and to Medano, 3700 pesetas ($35.52).

Buses

There is a good network of bus routes, with the main depot in Santa Cruz at Bravo Murillo (tel. 24-30-23). From various points in Santa Cruz, buses run to Puerto, La Laguna, and to the south of the island. But it is always well to check that you'll be able to catch another bus back if you travel any distance from town. It is often not possible to travel from the south to the north of the island without changing buses. The south is served from Santa Cruz, the north from Puerto de la Cruz. Buses leave from Calle Tomé Cano and from Heliodoro Rodríguez López in Santa Cruz and from Avenida Carrero Blanco in Puerto de la Cruz. Fares are low and it is possible to cover the island and all the tourist attractions far more cheaply than by taking the organized excursions. Inquire at the Tourist Office for times and prices. For example, the round-trip fare to Cañadas del Teide is 325 pesetas ($3.12).

A day return to Las Américas, or Los Cristianos, leaving Puerto at 8:30 a.m. and returning there at 7:30 p.m., costs 525 pesetas ($5.04).

In addition to the regular buses, there's a microbus service on many routes. It's quite possible, given time, to tour the whole island this way, stopping at villages you didn't know existed. The Tourist Office will provide information on the various departure points and fares.

Excursions by Coach

Viajes Marsans, 1 San José (tel. 24-26-18), Santa Cruz; **Meliá,** 9 Pilar (tel. 24-41-50), Santa Cruz; and **Wagons-Lits/Cook,** 9 Pilar (tel. 24-67-36), operate coach tours from Santa Cruz.

A day's drive up the spine of the island, through the Cañadas to Teide, returning via La Orotava and Puerto de la Cruz, costs 1100 pesetas ($10.56), excluding lunch. A trip to the Mercedes pine forests of the north on a Saturday afternoon goes for 775 pesetas ($7.44); and a day's tour around the beaches of the island costs 975 pesetas ($9.36), excluding lunch.

From Puerto de la Cruz, **Cyrasa,** Avenida Cristóbal Colón (in the Hotel Belgica; tel. 37-17-39), operates a half-day jaunt that takes in the northwest coast. That tour goes to Icod to see the dragon tree, then to Garachico, a small fishing village, which was almost entirely engulfed by a volcano. This costs 650 pesetas ($6.24). Cyrasa also offers a full-day tour of the island, which includes a visit to La Laguna, going for 1500 pesetas ($14.40), including lunch.

FERRY TO GOMERA: This is a motorway over the sea. In the south of Tenerife, almost hidden among the high-rise hotels, the car-ferry, Benchijigua, runs several trips daily from the old port of Los Cristianos to the port of San Sebastián on the island of Gomera. The cost of a round trip is 900 pesetas ($8.64) for adults, 450 pesetas ($4.32) for children. The cost of taking a small car over is 1820 pesetas ($17.47); a motorcycle, 1300 pesetas ($12.48)—both are round-trip fares. (There is bus service from Santa Cruz to Cristianos, 1¾ hours before the boat sails.)

The ferry is much used by local business people in the general course of their day's work. I'd recommend it for visitors as well, as a day on Gomera is a particularly worthwhile excursion.

The **Parador Nacional** (tel. 87-11-00) is really the only place to eat. A taxi from the harbor costs 200 pesetas ($1.92). It is a beautiful low building erected around a shady courtyard with much antique furniture. There is a delightful formal drawing room and a cool dining room with a polished floor and sparkling tables. The menu of the day costs 950 pesetas ($9.12), consisting of a lunch of three substantial courses and a bottle of Gomera wine (mostly white) which is an additional 175 pesetas ($1.68). If you wish to spend the night, a double with bath will cost 4000 pesetas ($38.40); a single, 3100 pesetas ($29.76). However, just for lunch the parador is good value. It also has a swimming pool set in gardens high above the sea.

For a low-cost overnight stay, try **Hotel Garajonay,** 17 Ruíz de Padron, San Sebastián de la Gomera (tel. 87-05-50), which lies in the small harbor town. At this simple place, a single without bath costs 600 pesetas ($5.76), rising to 900 pesetas ($8.64) in a double. If you want a private bath, expect to pay an extra 200 pesetas ($1.92) per room.

A taxi ride of about 3½ hours to Vallehermoso and back to the parador costs about 3500 pesetas ($33.60), or a drive around to Vallehermoso and on to Valle Gran Rey and Playa Santiago costs about 5000 pesetas ($48) by taxi. Although these rates are high, the cost can be divided among four passengers. The roads are tortuous, the progress slow.

At Hermigua, a typical house, **Los Telares,** has been restored and is worth a visit to see how workers wove cloth and ground corn. Souvenirs are available.

Around Agulo in the north is a rich region of vines and fruit trees. High above the town is the **Restaurant Las Rosas,** with a daily menu offered at lunch for 500 pesetas ($4.80). From here, you can look across at neighboring Tenerife with magnificent views of Teide.

Self-drive cars are available from the harbor, but it is well to book in advance if you want to be sure of a car.

Excursions to Gomera are available from Puerto de la Cruz and Santa Cruz, covering the drive to Los Cristianos, the ferry, and a coach drive around the island, including lunch. The cost is 4250 pesetas ($40.80), and you must start out at 6:15 a.m. You won't be home until around 9 p.m., making it a long, tiring day.

The *Benchijugua* has two large lounges with a bar and snacks as well, plus a restaurant, to while away the 1½-hour journey.

OUTDOOR FUN: This is a marvelous island for walking, as one is rewarded with such beautiful views. It's possible from the top of Teide at dawn to see every island in the archipelago.

Walking and Climbing

Mr. Talg, owner and manager of the **Hotel Tigaiga** at Puerto de la Cruz, knows the island well, and has especially prepared several walks of varying duration and difficulty for visitors. These are printed on easily carried sheets. Armed with a picnic lunch, one can spend a day entirely alone among the pines or in the lush coastal area. Time permitting, Mr. Talg will accompany the serious hiker with an enthusiasm beyond belief. His knowledge of the flora and fauna of the island makes the experience doubly interesting. By the way, don't forget to help yourself from the large bunch of bananas hanging at the front entrance to the hotel.

High up in the Cañadas, on the side of the Peak of Teide, is the **Refugio de Altavista**, a modern cabin simply furnished with dormitories, a kitchen, lounge, and bar. It is open only when required by hikers, who bring their own food and drink. The refugio is staffed by one or two of the local men who keep it clean and warm. It's an ideal overnight place from which to walk to the summit of Teide to see the dawn break, an unforgettable experience.

Reservations must be made through the Patronato de Turismo in Santa Cruz (tel. 24-20-90), or at La Orotava (tel. 33-02-00). To stay overnight costs 175 pesetas ($1.68) per person.

Flamenco

Every Sunday at 11 a.m. in Puerto de la Cruz at Mr. Talg's **Hotel Tigaiga**, there is an exhibition of Canary folk dancing and singing as well as Canary wrestling. The gardens are beautiful, incidentally, and are planted with rare trees and shrubs, each with its name carefully visible. The entrance is 100 pesetas (96¢).

Golf

At El Penon, Tacoronte, 14 kilometers from Santa Cruz, 22 kilometers from Puerto de la Cruz, is an 18-hole course (tel. Guamasa 4). Greens fees are about 600 pesetas ($5.76) Monday to Friday, rising to 800 pesetas ($7.68) on weekends and holidays. Rental of clubs is 175 pesetas ($1.68), and caddies are available at a cost of 150 pesetas ($1.44) per hour. There is also a snackbar and restaurant on the grounds. A beer in the clubhouse will cost you 90 pesetas (86¢). For more information, telephone 25-02-40.

Fishing

To practice surf casting, you can get in touch with **Club de Pesca Neptuno,** 21 Calle Pérez Galdos (tel. 28-13-21), where you will get information as to the best places for this sport.

Bullfights

This takes place in the bullring on the Rambla de Generalísimo Franco in Santa Cruz. It's not a regular event, although times of bullfights are posted throughout the island.

Wrestling

There are several places where wrestling takes place on the island. But for the visitor, the ever-enthusiastic Mr. Talg, at the Hotel Tigaiga, in the **Parque Taoro,** above Puerto de la Cruz (tel. 37-11-90), often runs exhibitions on Sunday morning at 11. Admission is 125 pesetas ($1.20), and the entire event will be explained to you so that you can understand the finer points. Lunch, including such specialties as paella and fondue bourguignonne, is available at the Café Tinguaro.

Since the sport is not held every Sunday, it's best to call for further information (tel. 25-72-55). The address is Federación Tinerfeña de Lucha, 39 San Juan, La Laguna.

Outdoor Fun

There are not many opportunities for sailing trips from Puerto de la Cruz. This can be remedied by a day aboard the *Marino Riquer,* a sailing ship more than 100 years old. During the day's coastal voyage you can bathe or fish or just lie on deck, watching the other passengers hard at work. Departure by coach is from Café Columbus in Puerto de la Cruz at 9 a.m., the return at 5:30 p.m. The cost, including transport and food, is 2000 pesetas ($19.20) per person.

3. Lanzarote

Lanzarote is the most easterly of the Canary Islands and the closest to Africa. Like the other islands in the archipelago, the south is bare, dry, and sandy, the north lusher and more cultivated. But on Lanzarote you don't have the marked difference in temperature and climate found on the sister islands. No central mountain creates rainfall in the north, leaving Lanzarote exposed to the hot airs from Africa.

The island is still unspoiled by tourism. Roads have been paved leading in from the airport, so visitors no longer disappear in a cloud of dust.

The capital is **Arrecife,** a busy town with a fish-canning factory, salt pans, and a thriving harbor where the large fleet of fishing boats unload their catches and where ocean-going vessels call. On the main street, León y. Castillo, very few people speak English. But don't let that put you off, as the island people are generally very kind, from the policeman to the attendant in the chemist shop.

On the reef from which the town takes its name is the **Castillo de San Gabriel,** a squat fortress housing a museum of archeology and anthropology. It's usually open from 9 a.m. to 1 p.m. and 3 to 7 p.m. The custodian has studied his subject with care and will willingly tell you—in Spanish—about the collection of relics from the island's past.

In the big-ship harbor is the **Castillo de San José,** another fortress skillfully adapted by Cesar Manrique, the island's favorite son. It contains a very good exhibition of modern painting and sculpture. Its restaurant is expensive—the cheapest items on the menu are fruit juice at 45 pesetas (43¢) and spaghetti at 275 pesetas ($2.64). However, it's pleasant to have a drink at the black leather bar, or a coffee. The tiny rocky garden jutting right over the harbor is tranquil, too. At night the harbor is floodlit.

In town stands the **Church of San Gines,** named after the patron saint of the island, whose festival on August 24 and 29 is an occasion for frantic celebrations and processions.

WHERE TO STAY: I'll begin my hotel recommendations on Lanzarote at:

Arrecife

Hotel Residencia Lancelot Playa, Avenida Mancomunidad (tel. 81-14-00), is just opposite the other Protucasa hotel on the island, the high-rise Arrecife Grand, on the main seafront promenade. Across the road is the Reducto Beach, where the locals swim, and there's a big sign warning against playing football. The hotel is within strolling distance of many of the more internationally geared restaurants and nightspots. It's typically Spanish, with shiny floors and cheerful furnishings. Facilities include a small lounge, bar, coffeeshop, and dining room, and on the roof a swimming pool and solarium served by a second bar.

The simple, pleasant rooms all have baths or showers and most offer sea views as well. Singles cost 1800 pesetas ($17.28); doubles, from 2500 pesetas ($24). Most rooms have space for extra beds, and cots can be provided. Breakfast is included, and a table d'hôte menu—standard fare—goes for 800 pesetas ($7.68). This hotel is a good bet for someone coming off the ship and not desiring to drive for miles trying to find a room.

Hostal Miramar, 2 Calle Coll (tel. 81-04-38), overlooks the Puento de las Bolas and the Castillo de San Gabriel on the Arrecife seafront. An unobtrusive facade leads to a small lobby with a tiny lounge overlooking the castle. Rooms are simple but clean, renting for 1200 pesetas ($11.52) in a single with bath, 2200 pesetas ($21.12) in a double with bath, plus an additional 130 pesetas ($1.25) for a continental breakfast. The Miramar is good to know about, as pleasant, modest accommodations are scarce in Arrecife. The hostal doesn't have a restaurant, but you are only five minutes from the center of town and the Arrecife Gran where there are many restaurants. The establishment is also handy if you arrive by ship, as it lies on the docks side of town.

Rooms and Meals at Playa Blanca

Hostal Playa del Sol, Playa Blanca, Yaiza, is closed as of this writing, pending a change of management. However, it's the best located hotel on the island, offering a simple but adequate accommodation at a reasonable price. Visitors should definitely investigate to see if it has reopened when they arrive in Lanzarote.

This square concrete building has nothing but its terrace between it and the golden sand of the tiny bay. Fishing boats are drawn up on the sand. A peaceful, sleepy atmosphere prevails—still unspoiled even though there are two supermarkets in the village.

The rooms contain two beds, a mirror and dressing table, and large cupboards, and you can be comfortable at a low cost. Each room has a shower plus water basin and toilet. Two have large shuttered windows and tiny balconies overlooking the sea, but others either front the road or the inner court.

Breakfast is served on the terrace with your feet practically in the sand, as you watch the fishermen and their women pulling in nets full of jumping silver fish. There's a wide menu for lunch and dinner. Emphasis is on fresh fish—vieja, lenguado, mero, calamares, parrotfish, served with mojo canario, a red sauce of oil, garlic, herbs, and chilis. Papas arrugadas, potatoes cooked for ages in heavily salted water, complete the feast. Somehow the salt doesn't spoil the taste of the white part inside. Paella is also available, and langostinos are a specialty. They're caught in the waters between the island and the African coast.

The atmosphere is international, with residents coming from all over the world to sit on the terrace, swap stories, and drink the local wine and beer.

This place is acknowledged to be one of the cheaper establishments and is considered the best spot on the island for ordering fish. To stay here you need to be content with talking, drinking, swimming, and walking, as there isn't much else to do. It takes about an hour to get into Arrecife. For those who wish to sun themselves all over, there's a 12-bed solarium on the roof.

Less than 100 yards from the Playa del Sol is the **Restaurant Casa Salvador,** where everyone goes to drink in the evenings. The tiny bar is full of tourists and locals alike, and conversation jumps from topic to topic and language to language. The large restaurant looks out over the sea. The menu of the day at 450 pesetas ($4.32) includes half a liter of wine. On the à la carte menu, fish soup is 135 pesetas ($1.30); omelets, 160 pesetas ($1.54) to 230 pesetas ($2.21); paella, 250 pesetas ($2.40). You can also order langostinos, the price depending on availability, or half a roast chicken at 235 pesetas ($2.26).

Salvador and his family also own and run the **Hostal Playa Blanca** (tel. 83-00-46), a few yards up the road, built on rocks overlooking the bay. Only ten rooms are available, and they are well kept and simply furnished. The cost of a double room is 1400 pesetas ($13.44) per day. Write for an accommodation, or else ask at the bar when you arrive. A continental breakfast at 125 pesetas ($1.20) is served down in the bar.

Puerto del Carmen

Hotel los Fariones, at Puerto del Carmen (tel. 82-51-75), is a long-established hotel with a long palm-lined terrace leading to tropical gardens where exotic birds sing and down to a sandy cove, also palm lined, where the sea laps gently against the protecting rocks. There are two swimming pools, mini-golf, tennis, and indoor games for the energetic. For the less active, a large lounge and busy bar open onto the terrace. At night the boîte, La Cueva, hums with life—at a peaceful distance from the hotel. Rooms are well furnished, having sea views and balconies. Singles, including a continental breakfast, rent for 2900 pesetas ($27.84); doubles, 2225 pesetas ($21.36) per person. For half board, add an additional 1250 pesetas ($12) per person daily.

Playa de los Pocillos

For those who can afford it, the **Hotel San Antonio,** Playa de los Pocillos (tel. 82-50-50) is right on the sea between long sandy beaches south of the airport. All rooms overlook the water and subtropical gardens full of lush vegetation planted in volcanic ash. The hotel has its own desalinization plant so the water is safe to drink. There is an excellent quick laundry and drycleaning service as well. Try to slump into one of the soft sinky chairs in the lounges and bar with your favorite cocktail. There is live music for dancing every night, as well as a popular disco. Other facilities include a super swimming pool, tennis courts, and game rooms. In the dining room, the chef offers a wide range of international dishes. There is a cold buffet by the pool every day for lunch and a barbecue every Sunday to the accompaniment of folk songs and dances by a local troupe.

In this island where water and amenities are scarce, the San Antonio is a haven at a cost of 2000 pesetas ($19.20) per person, based on double occupancy. A single rents for 2500 pesetas ($24). Full board is 4200 ($40.32) per person, but many guests don't want to obligate themselves to eating in a hotel when there are quite a number of places to explore and eat in. Oligario Tejada is the manager, and Ramón Perie is the public relations man to whom you should talk for information on the cultural activities of Lanzarote.

Your Own Villa

There are many privately owned villas and apartments on the island—mainly in the complexes around the Fariones Hotel. Many are rented out for short or long periods when not required by their owners. Although they vary in size, some accommodating up to ten persons, most of them shelter four adults with room for cots for small children. These villas or apartments are fully furnished, and a maid comes in daily except Sunday. Prearrival groceries can be provided upon request.

For further information, get in touch with **Property Managers S.L.,** Plaza San Antonio, Playa de los Pocillos, Lanzarote (tel. 82-60-20). A one-bedroom apartment for two persons will cost about 19,000 pesetas ($182.40) per week, the cost going up to about 26,000 pesetas ($249.60) per week for a two-bedroom apartment for four persons.

If you want to book a villa in advance, you should address your request to Arthur Grimshaw, **Lanzarote Villas,** 37 East St., Horsham, RH12 1HF, Sussex, England (tel. Horsham 51304). Mr. Grimshaw controls the renting of all the Lanzarote villas, and, incidentally, you can book a full package through him, including air flights and accommodations.

The Super-Splurge

Hotel Las Salinas–Sheraton, Costa Teguise (tel. 81-30-40), lies about eight miles to the north of Arrecife, toward Arieta and Jameos del Agua. The hotel stands like an oasis among lava fields, right on the coast, with a mere handful of apartments in what is to be a massive development. Las Salinas is set in gardens, contrasting with the black of the lava. It is a white cantilevered building, surrounded by palms, grass, and a mass of bougainvillea on every balcony. There is free bus service to and from Arrecife and the airport.

The cool, marble-floored lobby leads to a large water garden, open to the sky. Around this garden, rooms are grouped on three floors. There are interesting nooks full of comfortable armchairs, as well as a large lounge where, in the evenings, cabarets and piano entertainments are staged. The dining room is large and airy, overlooking the swimming pool and bay, and there is a grill room. There are three bars, in addition to the one at the pool.

The swimming pool is an architectural masterpiece, reflecting, as does the whole hotel, the hand of Cesar Manrique, who designed it. You can swim around islands, under bridges, in deep or shallow water. The bedrooms have large beds, baths, and separate toilets, color TV, video movies, radio, and direct-dial phones, plus minibars. Each has a terrace surrounded with flowers and ferns which is totally invisible from all other rooms, so you can let yourself go if you want to.

Breakfast is served in your room or at the buffet beside the pool. You can eat as much as you like from a variety of meats, eggs, bacon, sausage, breads, and cakes. Lunch is either table d'hôte in the dining room, or, again, you can eat from a poolside buffet with a choice of some 38 cold main dishes, two hot dishes, including a mix-your-own sauce for pasta to be made up from 20 different spices and relishes. Follow that with a choice from some 16 desserts—and you can eat as much as you like of anything.

Dinner is a four-course delight, even the table d'hôte offers three or four choices with each course. There is also an à la carte menu. The cuisine is of a high standard. Gabriel Felip, the general manager, is now assisted by Michael Boyer, the resident manager.

Rooms rent for 6000 pesetas ($57.60) in a single, 8200 pesetas ($78.72) in a double, with breakfast costing an additional 500 pesetas ($4.80); lunch or dinner, 1900 pesetas ($18.24). The full-board supplement comes to 3440 pesetas ($33.02) per person daily.

Activities included in the room rate are tennis, windsurfing, dinghy sailing, and fishing. Greens fees for the 18-hole golf course are 700 pesetas ($6.72), with use of the clubhouse included. The hotel charges 500 pesetas ($4.80) for water-skiing, and a scuba-diving course lasting seven days is priced at 9000 pesetas ($86.40).

WHERE TO EAT: My recommendations range throughout the island, beginning in:

Arrecife

Cafetería Avenida, Avenida Mancomunidad, is one of a row of cafés on the main promenade of town. Under a large awning, you can sit on the terrace and watch the world go by for the price of a sangría or beer at 55 pesetas (48¢). Tapas (bar snacks) are good at a cost of 90 pesetas (86¢) a portion. It caters more to those seeking snacks and sandwiches costing around 90 pesetas also. However, the cook will prepare pork chops and french fries, or steak with fries, for around 375 pesetas ($3.60). This place is used a lot by the locals which indicates that it's reliable. It's certainly a very pleasant place at which to write your postcards, as the atmosphere is nice and friendly. Incidentally, the Avenida also rents out some double rooms at 1600 pesetas ($15.36), which can be an ideal situation if you want to be in town.

La Marisquería del Molino, Muelle Pescador, Puerto de Naos, is presided over by Don Jacinto Duque Carabello. In the scruffy part of town, it's right on the fishing quay, surmounted by a tatty old windmill. Smart expensive cars are usually parked outside, as the restaurant attracts local business people drawn to its good food. You eat either in the small bar downstairs, jostled by waiters and hurried drinkers, or upstairs in the smartly decorated restaurant. The fish—calamares, mero, langostinos, cigales, viejas, or percebes—is delivered daily from the ships across the road. The price varies a little according to the catch of the day, but a dish costs around 320 pesetas ($3.07) to 550 pesetas ($5.28), including potatoes and a salad. Half portions of fresh fish go for half price, and one-quarter servings at the bar cost about 75 pesetas (72¢). Local wine is served. In the downstairs bar, tapas of octopus, rabbit (a very local specialty), vegetable, and fish salads are excellent.

Restaurant Martín, 11 Plaza Calvo Sotelo, is run by Señor Martín, who caters to local shopowners and dignitaries. The restaurant is a simple room, packed with tables. At the back is a bar where you can order half portions of many of the regular dishes at less than half price. The menu of the day costs 405 pesetas ($3.89) for two dishes, soup or salad, then meat or fish with vegetables, bread, a dessert, and a quarter liter of wine. On the à la carte menu your tab can easily climb to 800 pesetas ($7.68). Typical selections are prawns in garlic, calamares, tongue, ham with peas, and meatballs, followed by pineapple with kirsch. Local wines are cheap, a bottle of Mogaza going for 450 pesetas ($4.32). This wine is considered one of the best. You can also order Yaiza or Uga wine for 200 pesetas ($1.92) a bottle. The restaurant offers excellent value, as well as fascinating local color, but it's best to arrive early as it is very busy around 2 p.m. and you'll most likely have to wait for a table.

Marisqueria Abdon, 54 Calle Canalejas, lies on a back street behind the Café Avenida. At this restaurant you can select your own fish swimming in a tank. It's another owner-run place, where Señor Abdon Betencort presides behind the bar and cooks your meal as it's ordered. A substantial menu of the day costs 350 pesetas ($3.36). You can also order à la carte—selecting such dishes as seafood soup, asparagus in three sauces, paella with seafood, large boiled crawfish, squid (fried or grilled), and mussels marinara. Complete meals ordered this way begin at 800 pesetas ($7.68). Have the local wine by the carafe. The place is very popular with tourists, and its atmosphere is so nice and friendly it's like being part of a family.

Or if you're not in the mood for fish, try the **Restaurant Chino Taiwan,** next door. Local workers often gather here to try the usual Chinese dishes: prawn crackers at 180 pesetas ($1.73); chop suey, the special of the house, at 300 pesetas ($2.88); and most other set dishes ranging in price from 250 pesetas ($2.40) to 300 pesetas ($2.88). A three-course meal will cost from 350 pesetas ($3.36) to 900 pesetas ($8.64). They also do take-away meals, and are open from 11:30 a.m. to 11:30 p.m. seven days a week.

Bar Brasilia, 5 León y Castillo. When you go into town—to the bank or the pharmacy, for example—stop at the Brasilia for coffee and churros, those doughnut-like sticks, deep-fried and sweet, served in a pile wrapped in a napkin. Order one portion for two people, unless you're a good trencherman (or woman). This is the traditional morning snack of the local shopkeeper, banker, or passerby. The bar stretches far back from the street, a noisy passageway of tables flanking the long bar. A dull roar of chatter bounces off large black and white photos of old Lanzarote. There are clean, functional toilets, and in the Brasilia itself hurried, anonymous service. They also do such tapas as Russian salad, fish-and-potato pie, sandwiches, and stuffed rolls, at a cost ranging from 50 pesetas (48¢) to 85p (82¢). Coffee is 45p (43¢). But it is for the churros that I recommend this place.

Arrieta

Bar Arrieta Miguel lies on the edge of the sea, with tables on the terrace. The fish has only a few yards to travel from sea to pan. As with so many of the really good fish restaurants, Miguel's is a very simple place. It's really just some long lines of oilcloth-covered tables, plus a bar. At first glance it might look uninviting, but it's clean and the cookery is very good. The menu includes such delicacies as sancocho Canario, caldo de pescado, and escoldones de gofio, along with calamares à la Romana, plus pulpos en aceite y vinagre. There is always a mixed salad along with papas arrugadas or french fries served with the fish. Local cheese and ice cream make up the selection to end your meal. The fresh fish of the day is served fried, grilled, or breaded. Expect to pay around 600 pesetas ($5.75) per person for a meal, including some local wine. Closed Monday.

Teguise

The **Bar-Restaurant Acatife** is on the main square opposite the church and the Palace of Spinola, with the inevitable half-open green painted door. It opens onto a large bar and then a restaurant in which you can order soup at 85 pesetas (82¢); rabbit, 300 pesetas ($2.88); paella, 200 pesetas ($1.92); and desserts, from 75 pesetas (72¢). White wine is available at 160 pesetas ($1.54) per bottle.

Caleta de Famara

The village lies on the north coast of the island at the end of a long beach dominated by the cliffs on which perches the Mirador del Río. Across the water you can see Graciosa. To get there, drive past the Monumento toward Teguise, then turn off through the fields to Caleta de Famara.

Once there you'll discover the **Bar Restaurant Garcia.** A long, narrow room starts with a bar, running through to a large window overlooking the houses, then out to sea. Tables covered with oilcloth are laid with fresh paper-mats and napkins. The menu is impressively long, including a special fish soup, prawns and calamares, rabbit for two, paella for two, and chops.

I always ask for the fish of the day, and the cook will prepare it as you like it—grilled, fried, breaded, or in batter. You'll also receive a large dish of beautifully cooked mussels to be eaten with salad and potatoes. Look out for the homemade mojo verde, surely the strongest on the island. Your main dish will cost around 250 pesetas ($2.40), with a communal dish of salad and potatoes going for around 100 pesetas (96¢) a person. Drink the local wine or ask for an imported one at around 325 pesetas ($3.12) a bottle. Local beer is 45 pesetas (43¢). Closed Thursday.

Puerto del Carmen

The **Victoria Inn,** Puerto del Carmen, is run by Ted and Liv Martin. He is English and she Norwegian. He is found behind the bar from 6 p.m. till midnight except Thursday when it's shut all day. The kitchen keeps the same hours. Drinks are good measures at reasonable prices, with bottled English beer going for 80 pesetas (77¢). Liv helps with the waiting and serving, and Honorio reigns in the kitchen, turning out a very good pepper steak. Only ask for *muy fuerte* (very hot) if you mean it. There is no daily specialty, except on Sunday when it's likely to be roast pork with all the trimmings. Otherwise, the menu carries such items as soup, shrimp cocktail, scampi Provençale, the already-mentioned pepper steak, pork filet with cheese sauce, or grilled sole. Prices begin at 575 pesetas ($5.52) for one dish, going up to 800 pesetas ($7.68) for a three-course meal. All dishes are served with potatoes and a vegetable or salad, and the portions are ample. Apple pie with ice cream is good and popular as are the strawberry crêpes. Wines are fine value at 250 pesetas ($2.40) for three-quarters of a liter. The atmosphere is very cosmopolitan, with mainly English-speaking tourists, and the food really good.

Bar Maravista, Puerto del Carmen (tel. 82-50-10), is up the hill from the sea, among apartments. A cheerful lighted doorway leads into a courtyard where you can eat lunch or take your coffee and drink. You wait for your table in a small bar and lounge. Then you're shown into a bright, busy restaurant of bench seats, red and white tablecloths, and candles under an arched roof. You dine to music from strolling guitar players. Victoriano presides. The menu is international, but always there is fresh fish featured. The fish is cooked to your specifications. Several soups are featured, the favorite being seafood. Other openers might include melon and ham or shrimp with garlic. Main-dish selections include pork chops, spaghetti bolognese, grilled sole, and pepper steak. The chef also does an excellent kebab—pinchitos—with various meats. A plateful of giant prawns with sauce is almost too large. The least expensive way to dine here is to order the menu of the day at 460 pesetas ($4.42), including two dishes, bread, and one-quarter of a liter of wine. Otherwise, if you order à la carte, expect a final tab of 800 pesetas' ($7.68). The restaurant is popular with tourists, as it offers good value and more comfort and elegance than many of the local restaurants. It is also air-conditioned.

Bar Playa, Puerto del Carmen, is a good choice for a sunny lunch. Right on the old fishing quay, it's a place where everybody rushes outside if a boat comes in or a fish is caught from the jetty. You can sit outside, joining a cosmopolitan crowd talking at the top of their voices. A beer is 70 pesetas (67¢); a Cuba libre, 120 pesetas ($1.15); sangría, 220 pesetas ($2.11); and wine, 230 pesetas ($2.21) a liter. Sandwiches begin at 65 pesetas (62¢). Tapas of octopus with mojo verde, sardines, salad of egg, beans, tuna, and onions go for about 165 pesetas ($1.58) a portion. You can eat outside or go into the air-conditioned bar for a hot dog or Wimpy at 90 pesetas (86¢). The place is noisy and cheerful. You can visit in your swimming trunks or bikini—no one minds.

Restaurante Romantica I, Centro Olivin, is tucked away up a small alley beside the excellent fish and meat shops on the road leading down from the Fariones to the old town. This small grill and restaurant serves the best steaks on the island—by my tastes and those of many others. It is small, with only five tables, each seating six people, and a tiled floor and white walls. Service is good, and the menu is simple. Everything is cooked on a charcoal grill, served on a wooden platter, and dishes are accompanied by a baked potato and salad. Filet mignon costs 575 pesetas ($5.52); garlic bread, 90 pesetas (86¢) a portion. House wine is 375 pesetas ($3.60) a liter. If you do not want a steak, there is usually something else available—plaice, for example, at 475 pesetas ($4.56).

Restaurante El Toro, Carretera de Macher Bajo, entered by the Casa Heidi, is owned and run by Señor Alvarez, brother of the innkeeper of the Hostal del Sol. This must surely be the restaurant with a difference. It is just on the outskirts of Puerto del Carmen and has its own bullring—albeit, for miniature bulls (you would know them as calves). On Monday, Wednesday, and Friday there is a barbecue from 7:30 p.m. to midnight. During the evening, normally around 10 p.m., guests are offered the opportunity of facing the bulls and being the matador of the evening. The cost for the evening's entertainment, including a barbecue dinner, is 800 pesetas ($7.68) a person. Wine and other drinks are extra.

If you prefer to eat in the restaurant on these nights, or on any other evening from noon to 4 p.m. or from 6 p.m. to midnight, you can enjoy a meal in the lofty, cool, white barn-like dining room, off tiled stone tables surrounded by hanging ferns. The kitchen is open to view, and you can watch your T-bone or whatever is being cooked to your requirements on the large grill. There is no bar, and drinks are served at your table. One word of warning: Service is slow, mainly because of the desire of the chef to produce perfection with every dish. You may agree that the food is extremely good, and well worth the 1400 or more pesetas ($13.44) that your substantial meal with wine will cost. If you wish to settle for just a steak and salad, your bill will come to something like 500 pesetas ($4.80).

El Varadero, in Puerto del Carmen, is one set of "Green Doors" you'll want to venture behind. Revamped and altered, it is now a gourmet restaurant, owned and run by Caspar von Tangen-Jordan, a Norwegian who trained in the Swiss hotel school and has diplomas on the walls on view for all to see. He is so well known that his place is often called simply Caspar's.

Down below the Victoria pub by the boat slipway, the old fish warehouse has been attractively converted into a very pleasant restaurant, with high ceilings (much use of white and green paint), hanging plants, and fishing gear.

Some tables are downstairs; others are up among the rafters at the rear of the place.

The limited menu offers a choice of international dishes, including sole Walewska, pork with rice and pineapple, beef Stroganoff, all served with superb sauces. Prices are on the high side, a three-course meal for two costing around 3000 pesetas ($28.80), including wine.

Caspar has the efficient services of Karina, a German baroness who visited the island and liked it so much she decided to live here. She attends to table reservations and takes orders, and is well versed in the intricacies of the various dishes. Closed Tuesday.

Simpson's Pub is a bar in a complex of apartments in the center of the Fariones development, just below the Eldorado Apartments. Go up the hill past the supermarket, taking the first turn left. The pub is on the left. Down by the pool, it's a cool spot in which to pass the middle of the day with a light lunch.

It's run by a very English couple, Alan and Audrey Simpson, who in spite of having been on the island for many years, produce the most English of bar snacks to go with your drink. These include giant sausages, York ham, Alan's "favourite" cottage pie, Audrey's special veal, onion, and green peppers in a special sauce—topped with sliced potatoes. The prawn cocktail has a nice, crisp, fresh taste, and, to finish, try a piece of real American chocolate cake made by Anne, who helps at lunchtime. She is a Californian, and the cake is based on her grandmother's recipe.

Simpson's is very typically English, with its dark-green walls covered with military prints, some straight from Windsor Castle. The long bar is lined with high stools, and there are plenty of tables as well for diners. Sunday night is party night when they have a cold buffet and dancing until midnight. The buffet has cold beef and York ham, mashed potatoes, and fried onions, along with a mixed salad, followed by the famous chocolate cake, costing 450 pesetas ($4.32) a head.

Restaurant Romantica II, Centro Atlantico, on the Avenida de las Playas, between the Fariones and the San Antonio Hotels. This place is run by the same team as the cheaper Romantica I recommended in Puerto del Carmen. It's a first-floor restaurant, decorated in the Spanish style, with large or small tables. There's a bar where you can wait for your table or your friends. A pianist plays throughout the evening.

All steaks are cooked on the charcoal grill in full view of the diners. They come skewered on an alarming variety of swords, daggers, and spears, and are eaten with a salad and jacket potatoes. They also do a special Canary dish, a whole fish cooked in the oven, baked in a thick jacket of salt which has to be broken away by force, leaving the delicate fish ready to eat. Appetizers include garlic bread with tomatoes or ham, soups, and salads. A meal will cost around 1000 pesetas ($9.60) per person, including half a bottle of good wine.

Yaiza

In Yaiza, but unknown to coach trippers and hardly ever found by other tourists, is the **Restaurant El Volcan,** next door to one of the souvenir shops. Go here for Sunday lunch—at around 2 p.m. That's when the locals come in from the fields (yes, on Sunday they look after the family plot). They order *puchero,* the stew made from braised meat and vegetables and washed down with local wine from the barrel. Puchero for two, served only on Sunday, goes for 425 pesetas ($4.08). The menu of the day costs 460 pesetas ($4.42), and is quite filling. A bottle of the local wine goes for 325 pesetas ($3.12). The restaurant is open for lunch only. El Volcan lies just near the road up to the Fire Mountains and makes a good stopping place after a visit there.

La Era is one of the longest established restaurants on the island. It is expensive, but recommended, nevertheless, for its situation alone. The house is old, a farmhouse built around a courtyard with the grain stores and stables now serving as small dining rooms. Each is carefully decorated to enhance its allure, with ferns and ceramic pieces. You dine by candlelight. There is a standard set menu for 475 pesetas ($4.56). On the à la carte menu, you can order soup, melon, rabbit, pincho, a pork chop, mixed grill, and squid, a dinner averaging around 800 pesetas ($7.68). You drink your coffee sitting in the courtyard, or else you can wander into the garden, filled with palms and local plants along with bougainvillea and mimosa.

Playa Blanca

Restaurant Playa Blanca is a cool white structure with windows the whole length of the building, open and overlooking the shimmering sea and the waves lapping the sandy shore of the bay below. This must be one of the best located places on the island, about 100 feet back from the sea and protected from prevailing winds. You have a choice of a table outside and the free use of a lounger or a table inside surrounded by plants, with gentle background music.

The standard of cookery is high, with much use of the fresh fish landed just along the bay. Meals are served throughout the day—asparagus with mayonnaise, tunafish salad, calamares, prawns, sardines, fish soup, Canarian vegetable soup. Specialties include a mixed fish grill, a zarzuela, paella with shellfish, prawns in garlic, and chicken à la Cazadora. They do enormous steaks served with salad and potatoes, pork chops, beef burgers, and spaghetti. A meal will cost around 800 pesetas ($7.68), and a bottle of Vina Sol goes for an extra 450 pesetas ($4.32). You can order a light meal, an omelet perhaps, for 250 pesetas ($2.40). The place is run by the Robayna brothers, with Paco often behind the bar or waiting at the tables.

Haria

Los Helechos, above Haria in the north of the island, is perched on the edge of the Famara cliffs, offering fantastic views down to the sea at Arrieta and to Haria. The latter is an almost biblical-looking town of white houses and hundreds of lofty date palms. The restaurant takes its name from the delicate ferns which hang in baskets throughout the dining room. Try to get a table by the window. As soon as you arrive, order paella—it's the best on the island, prepared specially for you so you'll have to wait browsing in the souvenir shop or nibbling cold meats with your drink. For that nibble, I always prefer the Lanzarote goat cheese at 250 pesetas ($2.40), or else the fresh cooked ham or pork from the bone, 275 pesetas ($2.64). The paella then arrives, and it's beautifully decorated, bursting with shellfish and meats to be washed down with cold local white wine. The paella costs 800 pesetas ($7.68) for two people, an ample dish. There is also a full menu with main dishes ranging from 150 pesetas ($1.44) to 550 pesetas ($5.28). A menu of the day goes for 300 pesetas ($2.88), and local wine is sold at 200 pesetas ($1.92) a bottle. This a notable stopover on your way up to the Mirador del Río.

At Mirador del Río

Right in the north of the island, at the **Mirador del Río,** only tapas at the bar are served. But these are sometimes fresh fish and vegetable salads as well as succulent sponge cakes decorated with chocolate or fruits. Try queso blanco, a white goat cheese with a glass of either cold white or the red local wine.

NIGHTLIFE: My recommendations begin first in the town of Arrecife, then branch out to the beach resorts.

Arrecife

The red-light district is on the main Arrecife–Tahice road. You can't miss it, if that's what you're looking for.

Otherwise, the best nightclub is **Bambu Nightclub,** behind the Café de París on the Avenida Mancomunidad, next to the Café Avenida, almost opposite the Arrecife Grand Hotel. The club is open nightly from 8 p.m. until around 3 a.m. In this hot, dark atmosphere, mainly disco music is played, but occasional groups are featured. Admission is 250 pesetas ($2.40), which includes the price of your first drink, but tourists showing their passports get in free. Drinks are 150 pesetas ($1.44) for a gin or tonic, but only 70 pesetas (67¢) for the local brew.

At the **Bar Mexicana,** on the Avenida Mancomunidad between the Lancelot Playa and the Cafés Avenida and de París, the atmosphere becomes noisier and more informal as the evening progresses. The guitarist encourages people to sing with him. Before you know it, you're involved in a full-scale sing-along. Don't worry if you don't know the words. Drinks are at normal prices, and there is no admission charge, as this is a bar, not a club. You can also order fish, prepared Mexican style, at 320 pesetas ($3.07) or a steak at 420 pesetas ($4.03).

Playa de los Pocillos

The Hotel San Antonio has a good disco nightclub, the **Beach Club,** on the edge of the beach, with good parking above. The entrance fee of 600 pesetas ($5.76), which includes your first drink, is not charged to residents of the hotel. If you're tidily dressed and it's early in the evening, you'll probably get in free. The decor is plushy red, with deep settees and flashing lights, a throbbing beat pounding ceaselessly. The place is very lively and popular with young people. Go after 9:30 p.m. and drink sangría by the jug for 350 pesetas ($3.36). Other drinks cost from 200 pesetas ($1.92).

Puerto del Carmen

Let's face it, most of the tourists are here.

The **Tahiche Club** is attached to the Fariones Hotel, but is right on the beach. It's decorated in the Polynesian style, with palm fronds and thatch. There's an open area with tables and a small inside bar. It's open every evening with disco or live groups featured. Hours are from 10 p.m. to 2 a.m. Admission is free. You need pay only for your drinks, with a beer going for 75 pesetas (72¢). On Friday the club offers folk dancing at 11 p.m.

In the Fariones complex is the **Bierkeller,** run by Peter. It's what you'd expect: a stone floor, scrubbed wooden tables and stools. German beer is 100 pesetas (96¢) for a small stein, and lively songs are sung to the accordion and guitar.

Joker Discoteca on the Calle Reina Sofia is a lively and extremely popular place for holiday-making young people, and also used by a surprising number of middle-aged vacationers who happily rub shoulders with those of more tender years. The place is an inferno of flashing lights glancing off mirrors above the dance floor and the din of disco music. On odd corners are TV sets showing oldies such as Charlie Chaplin films. This is an alternative to watching your partner or the fellow dancers. Admission is 300 pesetas ($2.88), which includes your first drink; each subsequent drink is 200 pesetas ($1.92).

EXPLORING THE ISLAND: From Arrecife, the road to the north leads to **Teguise,** the ancient capital of the island, with a peaceful square bordered on one side by the 18th-century **Palace of Spinola,** a beautiful old house recently restored to its former glory. The palace is well worth a visit to see its elegant salons with old paintings and a lovely collection of polished seashells. The antique kitchen has been restored to show the old water purifiers. The water drips from one stone bowl in which lichens grow, into another and then through the stone into your cup. From the small walled garden there are steps to the roof for a very photogenic view of the steeple of San Miguel. The palace is open from 10 a.m. to 1 p.m. and 3 to 6 p.m. It is closed all day on Sunday and on Saturday afternoon. Admission is free, but it's nice to tip the custodian.

The palace is owned by Union Explosivos Río Tinto Mining Company of Spain, which promotes a vast tourist complex, Costa Teguise, where there is a nine-hole golf course. For the greens fee of 1400 pesetas ($13.44), you can go around twice.

Across the square is the **Church of San Miguel,** hiding beneath its simple exterior a spotless colorful interior with beautiful statues. The Virgin on the high altar is from the 16th century. The **Convents of Santo Domingo** and **San Francisco** are in the process of being restored, with carefully chosen materials, to their original states. The convents are not generally open to view, unless you can persuade someone to let you see inside. In the town there remains the local craft which has survived centuries—that is, the making of timples, the small guitar-like instrument played throughout the islands.

Near Teguise on the road north is the **Castle of Guanapay,** placed most strategically on a hill as a defense against the Moors. Perched on the edge of a volcanic crater and entered across a drawbridge, it must have been almost unassailable. There are magnificent views across the island, and the silence is almost deafening.

The road to the north passes through **Los Valles,** a beautifully kept area of cultivation, before coming out above the Arabic-looking village of **Haria.** It nestles among tall waving palm trees at the bottom of the valley. The white houses are covered with bougainvillea and geraniums. The village square is tree lined and paved with tiles, produced locally.

The road continues through increasingly barren land to the **Mirador del Río,** a lookout blasted into the rock of the cliff overlooking the island of **La Graciosa.** This is another creation of favorite son Manrique. Admission is 40 pesetas (38¢), and it's open from 11 a.m. to 7 p.m. (closes earlier in winter). At the previously recommended bar, the view is not only over Graciosa but of the Montana Clara and Allegranza. Far below, at the bottom of cliffs, are salt pans, glowing red at the edge of the río, the stretch of water separating the island from Lanzarote.

To get there, you must take a boat from the tiny little port of Orzola. Once on the island, you'll find a lovely bathing beach, although the accommodation is rawboned. Regular day excursions from Puerto del Carmen cost 3000 pesetas ($28.80), including lunch.

In the area of ancient volcanic activity in the north lie the **Cuevas de los Verdes,** an underground gallery running for nearly four miles, from the volcano which created it to the sea. A guided tour, 50 minutes, of the multicolored lava costs 110 pesetas ($1.06). Hours are 11 a.m. to 6 p.m.

Created by the same eruption, the **Grotto Jameos del Agua** has been transformed into a restaurant and nightclub. It's open during the day and on Tuesday and Saturday from 10:30 p.m. till 3 a.m. when men are required to wear a jacket and tie. During the day music is piped through the cavern. Even chattering tourists can't completely spoil the mysterious appearance of the cave, with its subterranean lake inhabited by thousands of tiny blind white crabs. Birds fly through from the restaurant to the gardens at the other end of the cavern, and turtles swim in the pool in the pretty garden—you can join them if you wish. Menuhin played in the cave, finding it acoustically superb. The entrance fee is 110 pesetas ($1.06) during the day, 500 pesetas ($4.80) on Tuesday and Friday night when there is a cabaret with dancing.

The Gent's, to misquote Noel Coward, is very definitely a loo with a view, a must for anyone who can visit it. It overlooks a subterranean grotto and is tastefully lit to show up the lava and rocks.

A road runs straight across the island from Arrecife. At the crossroads, right in the middle, is favorite son Manrique's **Monument to Lanzarote Man** or, some people say, fertility. Others claim it represents a man and his camel. At any rate, it's an incredible modern erection of metal towering above the fields and contrasting sharply with the life that goes on around it. Women still ride donkeys past it and till the fields with camel and wooden plowshares.

What used to be a humble farmer's cottage beneath the monument has been transformed into a restaurant and museum of island crafts. It's known as Manrique's **El Monumento.** An attractive courtyard contains yokes and farming implements, an old camel plow, and donkey and camel saddles. There is also a small bodega where you can taste the local wines—they vary a lot from village to village. The restaurant serves a fascinating variety of local foods—tortillas de carnival to be eaten in the fingers, juicy with honey and spices, sweet potatoes, papas arrugadas, dried fish, rabbit stew, and, if you have puchero, the staff will make specially for you gofio balls which are rolled in a piece of goatskin for shape before being fried and dunked into the soup. The entrance to the cottage is free. Tapas cost around 100 pesetas (96¢), and local wine is 60 pesetas (58¢) a glass. The monument is open from 10 a.m. to 5 p.m. weekdays, from 10 a.m. to 7 p.m. on Saturday and Sunday. Tapas are served beginning at noon.

To the south of Arrecife the road passes the airport and the wide beaches of the southeast coast before coming to an area known as **La Geria.** When the volcano erupted in 1730, this area was devastated. Casting about for a way to make a living, the local people realized that the lava pebbles retained moisture from the heavy night dew. They devised an incredible way of cultivating their vines. The result was to produce the famous Malvasia wines. The growers dig craters 10 to 20 feet wide down into the earth. These are then surrounded by loose stone walls. The vine is planted, and the whole pit covered with a layer of picon (lava granules). The vine flourishes in this soil, watered by the moisture in the picon in this otherwise arid land. Coming suddenly upon this region, you might think you've landed on the moon, as acre upon acre of walled-in pits look like the holes in cheese.

This part of the island is mostly lava, and it's possible to see the paths it took when the mountain erupted in 1730. Palm trees, standing tall against the sky, and the low whitewashed houses give the area an African look. **Yaiza,** the capital of the south, lies on the very edge of the lava flow. Beyond, the road forks, one direction leading to **Playa Blanca** in the south. The other heads to **El Golfo,** a crater right on the edge of the sea. On the sea side the wall has fallen away, leaving a semicircular lagoon of brilliant green water. No one knows how deep it is, or why it's green, perhaps because of a strange fungus growing there. It's a good picnic spot, and excellent bathing is possible in the salty water of the lake. Also on this road, at **Janubio,** are the largest salt pans on the island. There's a road down to the entrance, where you can see the various processes of extracting salt from seawater.

The **Montanas del Fuego** (Fire Mountains) are the most spectacular feature of the island. This is the region of the eruptions of 1730–1736, protected now as a tourist attraction. The entrance to the area costs 150 pesetas ($1.44) per car, and visiting hours are from 9 a.m. to 5 p.m. You drive your own car through in a convoy with a leader and an escort but no commentary. The road leads through the jagged lava fields past sinister craters to the **Islote del Hilario,** a circular restaurant and bar built on the site of the old hermit Hilario's hut to which he returned with his donkey after the devastation. He planted a fig tree, the only vegetation in the area, an ancestor perhaps of the one which now grows through the middle of the restaurant. In all directions the view is of lava and craters. The ground is so hot you can fry an egg on the natural barbecue, set fire to brushwood, and cause geysers by pouring water into readymade gushers.

Timanfaya is the biggest mountain. For the ardent explorer, it's possible to take a camel ride up Timanfaya from the station just before you enter the park. The cost is 500 pesetas ($4.80) per camel for two persons. It's an eerie sight to see the camels wind their way up the side of the mountain to the crater. The camels go home at lunchtime, as they have to work in the fields in the afternoon.

North of Fire Mountains, the lava stops suddenly just short of the tiny village of **Mancha Blanca.** There's a legend that Our Lady of the Sorrows appeared and commanded the lava to stop, thus saving the village from engulfment. A church was built in the village, and each year there's a festival in her honor.

The best bathing beaches in the island are those on the southeast coast and right in the south at **Punta Papagayo.** Here the sand is golden, the sea crystal clear, and the beaches almost deserted except on weekends.

ODDS AND ENDS: As part of your day's adventure, you might consider some of the following suggestions.

Smoked Salmon and Eels

On the road from Arrecife to Yaiza along the coast at Uga is the Ahumadería where Wolfgang and Erika Lündstedt run a thriving cottage industry, smoking imported salmon and local eels. Wolfgang, an electronics engineer, came to the island some time ago, liked it, and set about finding a way to stay. His fish is not cheap, but it's smoked to a secret recipe of special woods, some of it imported, and the taste is superb. His produce travels well and keeps for ages if chilled or frozen.

Introducing Paquita

At **Francesca,** Caleton del Barranquillo, just along from the San Antonio Hotel on the populated (tourist-wise) side of the island, you can introduce yourself to Paquita. Feel free to ask her anything about the island or its history. She has lived there for many years and is entirely under its spell. She provides fresh bread, canned foods, and liquor, as well as queso blanco, a white goat cheese which she gets fresh from Los Valles. Her place is open from 8 a.m. to 8:30 p.m. You can also discuss your laundry and dry-cleaning problems with her. Most of the big hotels require three days, but Paquita knows how to get service much quicker.

Handicrafts of the Island

Artisanía Lanzarote, 5 Alicante, in Arrecife (tel. 81-37-02). Pino has in her shop a wide selection of the handmade work of the island, embroidery and pottery. She will always explain, not only how, but where and when a particular piece was made. Prices are fair both to the buyer and the maker, Pino making only a small commission on each sale. If you wish to commission a particular piece, she will be available.

GETTING AROUND: You'll find the usual methods, as outlined below.

Car Rentals

Hertz and **Avis** are at the airport. Avis also has an office at Puerto del Carmen by the Fariones (tel. 82-52-54). Either charges 2400 pesetas ($23.04) per day for a Seat Panda. All rentals are based on unlimited mileage. If you rent a car for a week, they give you the car free one day in every seven.

Another car-rental agency, **Riverol** (at both the airport and Fariones complex) rents a Safari Suzuki (open Jeep-type four-seater) at a cost of 15,500 pesetas ($148.80) a week, plus tax and insurance. In addition, it's possible to rent Honda and Kawasaki motorcycles, costing from 900 pesetas ($8.64), plus tax and insurance. Riverol also rents out more sober, small motor cars as well.

Excursions

These are available from **Cyrasa,** 12 Avenida del Generalísimo Franco (tel. 81-03-13), or at one of the big hotels in the Fariones complex. A full day's jaunt to Fire Mountains, El Golfo, and the south, including lunch at Uga, costs 1800 pesetas ($17.28). A half day to the north and the Mirador del Río goes for 1000 pesetas ($9.60), including lunch. On Tuesday and Saturday there are evening excursions to the nightclub at Jameos del Agua, costing 1250 pesetas ($12).

At La Era, an attractive old Canary farmhouse in Yaiza, Canary wrestling is staged and a film on the island shown. The cost of transport from your hotel, including dinner and unlimited wine per person, is 1550 pesetas ($14.88) per person.

Taxis

There are ranks at all major hotels and at the airport. Usually it's better to ask your driver to wait at an agreed price if you use a taxi for a whole day's exploring. Prices are reasonable, but always agree in advance, of course. From the airport to Puerto del Carmen costs 400 pesetas ($3.84); from the airport to Arrecife, 275 pesetas ($2.64).

Many of the taxi drivers now speak a little bit of English. Most certainly they are knowledgeable about the island. You must arrange your price first. However, a tour of the north of the island should cost about 2200 pesetas ($21.12); to the south, 1950 pesetas ($18.72); or an evening visit to Jameos del Agua, 1500 pesetas ($14.40). Waiting time at 220 pesetas ($2.11) an hour is extra. These prices quoted are valid from Puerto del Carmen or from any of the urban developments and hotels on the southeast coast.

Buses

There are three bus routes—north, central, and south. On the whole they cater to working people who come into Arrecife in the morning and return to their villages at night. From Playa Blanca (Yaiza) to Arrecife costs 110 pesetas ($1.06); from Puerto del Carmen to Arrecife, 75 pesetas (72¢).

Information on both buses and taxis (which are all state controlled) can be obtained by calling 81-06-72. It's not difficult to use the system. Although no one will speak English, everyone will try to help see that you're going in the right direction.

OUTDOOR ACTIVITIES: From deep-sea fishing to windsurfing, there's plenty to do.

Beyond the Victoria Inn in Puerto del Carmen, Bob Wright, an Englishman who with his partner Dennis Wright also runs a school in Poole, Dorset, England, has started a highly professional and successful diving school, **Clubulanza,** in Puerto del Carmen. They have compressed-air facilities. If you are already proficient, each dive costs about 2000 pesetas ($19.20), including full use of all equipment. There is a terrace for relaxing on and a bar. A delightful, informal atmosphere prevails, yet a wonderful businesslike approach to a sport which can be dangerous if not approached sensibly is evident. Bob is ex-Royal Navy, quiet and friendly, as well as passionately interested in diving. Manolo, who comes from Tenerife, assists him.

Deep-Sea Fishing

It's possible to go deep-sea fishing if you head to Puerto del Carmen. Reservations are controlled through **Marítima Insular S.A.** in Las Palmas (tel. 23-31-95). Otherwise, you can stroll along the quay, and you'll probably find a skipper and can make your own arrangements. Most of the fishing boats tend to move with the fish from island to island. Don't be surprised if you're told, "Oh, he's over in Tenerife." Expect to pay around 5000 pesetas ($48) per person for a day's fishing with bait and all equipment provided.

In many of the small fishing villages, it's possible to persuade the local fishermen to take you out for the day, using their unique style of fishing by nets.

You can also take day trips to **Lobos,** the island in the strait between Lanzarote and Fuerteventura. The motorboat, M.V. *Alicia* sails from Puerto del Carmen to Lobos at 8:30 a.m. The cost of the day is 1800 pesetas ($17.28), including a paella cooked and served by the lonely lighthouse keeper, and the local wine. On Monday and Thursday, she sails past Lobos to Fuerteventura, leaving at 7 a.m.; and on Tuesday, Saturday, and Sunday she goes to Papagayo at 9 a.m. The day costs 1750 pesetas ($16.80), including a beach barbecue with wine.

Windsurfing

This is available at the **International Windsurfing School** at Los Alisios, near Las Rocas Apartments, Puerto del Carmen (tel. 82-53-20). José is the chief instructor. The day begins at 10 a.m. If there is no wind or too much swell, they take you to another of the island's beaches in their minibus, guaranteeing a day's windsurfing.

Windsurfing prices range from 1000 pesetas ($9.60) to 1500 pesetas ($14.40) per person daily, depending on your ability. José hails from San Sebastián on the mainland, but has been on the island since 1975 when he started this school. He has five different types of board—some slow for teaching, others streamlined for experts. Whenever boards are out, José or his assistant keep watch and are in radio contact with a rescue boat in case of trouble.

Golf

The golf course at **Costa Teguise** lies at the foot of a volcano, a unique links of Bermuda grass and black sandy bunkers. Only nine holes are in operation at present, but they offer an interesting challenge to the sportsperson on a holiday. Designed by an Englishman, John Harris, the course winds and twists through lava fields, past lush watered flowering bushes and stark palm trees. There's a pleasant clubhouse for a relaxing drink after your round. A beer there goes for 70 pesetas (67¢), a stiff vodka and tonic for 170 pesetas ($1.63). Greens fees, unless you're staying at the Salinas-Sheraton, are 1200 pesetas ($11.52) for 18 holes. Rental of a full set of clubs is 400 pesetas ($3.84). A trolley is 50 pesetas (48¢); an electric buggy, 1000 pesetas ($9.60). Par for the course is three. There is a pro available as well as a practice ground for beginners.

4. Fuerteventura

Separated from Lanzarote by a narrow channel, the island's capital, **Puerto del Rosario,** is a good base for excursions into the interior. Many unspoiled beaches dot the coastline.

GETTING THERE: From the brand-new harbor at Playa Blanca there is now a car-ferry service to Corralejo in the north of Fuerteventura. At present the service is on the *Alisur,* but she'll be joined by the *Vetancuria,* run by Transmediterránea, in the near future.

The *Alisur* runs daily except Tuesday in the morning, returning in the evening. The cost of a round trip is 1500 pesetas ($14.40) for adults, half price for children. The charge for automobiles varies with the length of the car, ranging from 2500 pesetas ($24) to 3500 pesetas ($33.60) for a round trip. Tickets are on sale at the harbor or at travel agencies in Arrecife and Puerto del Carmen.

An excursion is also run, costing 3000 pesetas ($28.80) per person, including the pickup at your hotel, the coach drive to Playa Blanca, the ferry trip, and a bus ride around Fuerteventura. After visiting Betancuria, the old capital of the island, as well as Lajares and La Oliva, lunch is at La Antigua; then the bus returns to the ferry and Lanzarote by way of the beautiful beaches of Corralejo. The ferry has a bar and a snackbar, serving hot and cold drinks, along with sandwiches and rolls.

LODGINGS: There is an attractive Moorish-style parador near the airport.

The **Parador Nacional de Fuerteventura,** Playa Blanca, Puerto Rosario (tel. 85-11-50), is entered through a high arch in the wall leading to a courtyard and then to a pleasant wooden-floored lobby. Wooden staircases and passages continue on to the rooms. These are simply furnished but comfortable, some with private terraces leading out into the garden. In the garden, right on the edge of the sea, is a swimming pool. Stretching away beside the hotel is a wide sandy beach, but currents make bathing dangerous.

A single is lodged here for 2160 pesetas ($20.75), the tariff going up in a double to 2700 pesetas ($25.92). A continental breakfast costs an extra 250 pesetas ($2.40) per person. A lunch or dinner goes for another 950 pesetas ($9.12). The parador is open only during the season these days.

You can also try **Las Gavias,** 3 Avenida R. Gonzales, Puerto del Rosario (tel. 85-12-00). The price in a double is 3750 pesetas ($36), which is more expensive than the parador and, therefore, can only be recommended in an emergency. Singles go for 2000 pesetas ($19.20). No main meals are offered.

Right in the north of the island, overlooking the island of Lobos and across to Lanzarote, is *the* splurge:

Ybarra Hotel Tres Islas, Playa de Corralejo, La Oliva (tel. 86-60-00), is set in splendid isolation on a marvelous stretch of golden beach, where barbecues are held. It is self-supporting in the way of entertainment, as there is nothing for miles around. Facilities include a large swimming pool, tennis courts, and bowling alley, plus a hairdressing salon, shops, and a chemist. In addition to a restaurant and grill room, a snackbar serves hamburgers, sausages, and other light meals. There are film shows, a pool bar, beach bar, sailing and windsurfing nearby, a disco, bowling alleys—you name it. Skin-diving and beach games occupy many a day. All in all, it's one of the most beautiful spots in the Canary Islands. But this retreat has a price tag. The single rate is 4670 pesetas ($44.83), although two persons get a better bargain, 8140 pesetas ($78.14). A continental breakfast costs 400 pesetas ($3.48) per person, and a set luncheon or dinner goes for 1200 pesetas ($11.52).

There are several hotels at the south of the island and some cheaper and charming local residencias in Corralejo in the north for whose who wish to explore the island.

Chapter XVI

MOROCCO ON $25 A DAY

1. The ABCs of Morocco
2. Tangier
3. Ceuta
4. Tetuan
5. Chaouen
6. Rabat
7. Meknes
8. Fez
9. Marrakesh
10. The Edge of the Sahara
11. Casablanca
12. Essaouira
13. Agadir
14. The Anti-Atlas

THE KINGDOM OF MOROCCO, the westernmost point of North Africa, has, since the dawn of travel, evoked an image of romance. Long before the present massive invasion, Morocco was known to film-goers—whether they went there with Marlene Dietrich in *Morocco*, Gary Cooper in *Beau Geste*, Humphrey Bogart and Ingrid Bergman in *Casablanca*, or Hope, Crosby, and Lamour in *Road to Morocco*.

Morocco is the most accessible of the far-off lands for those who live in Western Europe or the eastern U.S.

Geographically, Morocco is bounded on the east by not altogether friendly Algeria, on the west by the Atlantic, with its stretches of fine sands and pine forest, on the north by the Mediterranean, with its rugged coastline, and on the south by the forbidding Sahara. Because of its location in the temperate zone of the northwest corner of Africa, it boasts 300 days of guaranteed sunshine per year. In winter this comes as a welcome relief; in summer inland cities in particular can be stifling. However, Morocco's 1000 miles of beach keep the summer visitors pouring in.

The kingdom is used to the foreigner. The Phoenicians once came this way, as did the Carthaginians and the Romans, followed by the Portuguese, the French, the Spanish (who still have two enclaves in the north, Ceuta and Melilla). Historically, Morocco was the first African nation to sign a treaty (in 1787) of friendship with the United States.

If you speak French, even the la-plume-de-ma-tante variety, you'll fare better in Morocco than with English, although in the past years English has become more common. But it is the French presence—a holdover from colonial days—that lingers. Recently, King Hassan II has been trying to get rid of French influences, a policy reflected, for example, in the street names of the capital city of Rabat. The word *rue* is being replaced by the Arabic *zankat*.

Although the nation is Moslem, it tolerates religious freedom. For example, many Jews in the imperial city of Meknes fled to Israel after Morocco was granted independence in 1956; others stayed to live peacefully in the medina. The king ordered new housing on the outskirts of Casablanca and decreed that Jews and Arabs would live in the project on a communal basis, an experiment that so far has worked.

Note: A word of warning to serious sightseers. The greatest specimens of Moorish architecture, the mosques, cannot be visited by non-Moslems (an exception is the one in Meknes). If you want to see the inside of a mosque, head back to Córdoba, Spain (although, naturally, a cathedral has been placed inside the mosque).

All in all, whether you're planning a desert safari or want to go mountain skiing, you'll find a wide range of activities in Morocco. Truman Capote summed up Morocco's peculiar charm when he advised prospective visitors "to have yourself vaccinated against typhoid, liquidate your bank account, and say goodbye to your friends. Who knows when you will see them again?" (Capote means you'll be taken in by the charm, not the natives.)

1. The ABCs of Morocco

Regardless of where you've traveled in Europe, Morocco is an entirely different trip. Don't be deceived by the short boat trip from Spain. You've entered an entirely different world when you step on the shores of Africa, and because of that, these "facts of life" may assume even greater importance. Knowing how to cope in your "gateway" to Africa can help ease your adjustment into this always-fascinating, often-perplexing land.

AIRLINES/AIRPORTS: If you're in Europe, Paris is a good transfer point to Morocco, as both Royal Air Maroc and Air France fly from there to Tangier and Casablanca. Of course, you can also fly directly from New York to Morocco (see "Flights to Morocco" in the "Getting There" section of this guide, Chapter I).

Once in Morocco, you can travel to major destinations by plane, availing yourself, as mentioned, of Royal Air Inter's domestic routes. Fez, Meknes, Tetuan, Oujda, Quarzazate, Agadir, Marrakesh, and Rabat are just some of the cities connected by this airline.

Most international flights come into Casablanca (rather, the airport at Nouassar). Royal Air Maroc has connecting flights to Rabat (Salé). Another popular routing is to take a Royal Air Inter flight to Tangier, from which you can either fly to the already previewed sections of Gibraltar or else Málaga on Spain's Costa del Sol.

Mohammed V International Airport at Casablanca is about 12 miles south of the city. A C.T.M. bus will take you into the city terminal for a fare of 6

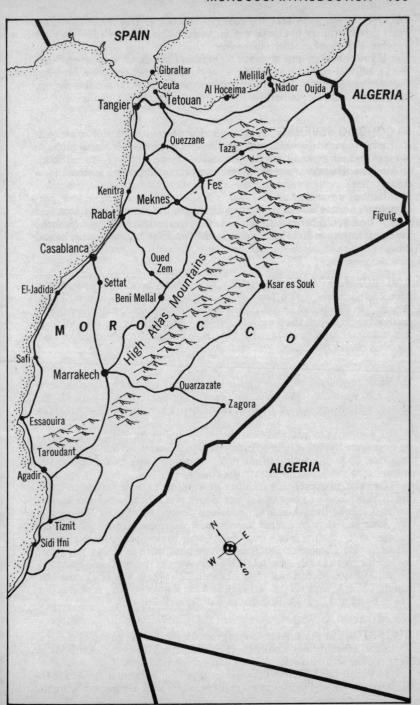

DH (98¢). If you go by taxi, the legal rate is about 45 DH ($7.38), although many drivers will try to charge you far more.

For airport information, telephone 797-93.

If you're booked on a domestic flight from Casablanca, you have to leave from a different airport, **Casa-Anfa,** some three miles out of town if I clocked the mileage accurately. Regrettably, there is no bus service from this airport, and you must throw yourself on the mercy of a Casablanca taxi driver.

ALCOHOLIC BEVERAGES: Moslems view the consumption of liquor quite differently from North Americans and Europeans. Many Moroccans prefer to get high on hash instead. In fact, it is illegal—at least in theory—to sell liquor to Moslems. Therefore, you should exercise caution in inviting someone for a drink.

Instead of traveling around with a bottle, it's best to confine your consumption of liquor to that regularly sold in bars, restaurants, nightclubs, and such. There you'll be on safer ground. Don't expect to be served alcoholic beverages in certain local restaurants in the "medinas" of various towns and cities.

AMERICAN EXPRESS: Regrettably, there is no American Express office in Morocco. However, you'll find other listings in this section under "Travel Agents." In Casablanca, the **I.T.O. Atwater** travel agent, 26 Boulevard Mohammed el-Hansali, is the American Express representative, but the staff there handles travel arrangements only. That is, you cannot receive mail or cash travelers checks there.

BANKS: In general, banks are open at 8:30 a.m., conducting business until 11:30 a.m. when they close for lunch. They're open again at 2:30 p.m., staying so until 4:30. Business days are from Monday to Friday, as in most American cities.

If you arrive by plane in Casablanca, you'll find the **Banque Marocaine du Commerce Extérieur** open to exchange foreign currencies into dirhams. It's important to keep a record of all your transactions with banks in case you encounter any difficulty in leaving the country.

Likewise, such exchange facilities are available to those passengers arriving by either boat or plane in Tangier. Sometimes exchange bureaus operate on boats leaving from Algeciras or Málaga (Spain), heading for Morocco.

Since you can't go around to your local American Express office to exchange money, it's important to have a reliable bank. I patronize the Banque Marocaine du Commerce Extérieur, whose head office is at 241 Boulevard Mohammed V in Casablanca (tel. 722-44); at Avenue Hassan II in Agadir (tel. 29-93); at Place Mohammed V in Fez (tel. 223-14); at 114 Boulevard Mohammed V in Marrakesh (tel. 319-48); at 4 rue Richard d'Ivrey in Rabat (tel. 217-98); and at 17 rue de Belgique in Tangier (tel. 310-44).

BOOKSTORES: For English-language books, magazines, guides, and maps, go to the **Librairie des Colonnes** at 54 Boulevard Pasteur (tel.169-55) in Tangier. The staff also sells etchings and art reproductions.

In Rabat, the **Librairie-Tabacs-Journaux** of the Rabat Hilton (tel. 341-41), carries a line of English-language books, along with newspapers, journals, and magazines, and also sells guides, maps, and postcards. It's open from 8 a.m. to 8 p.m.

BUSES: C.T.M. and L.N. are the major bus companies, both employing an older Greyhound-type bus that is moderately comfortable but not always spotless. It does get crowded at times, and occasionally somebody gets on with a chicken or two. Be warned that you'll have meager toilet facilities in some of the smaller villages—a squat toilet only, if that. Bus fares are low: 12 DH ($1.97) in a deluxe seat and 10 DH ($1.64) in a first-class seat per 100 kilometers.

In Rabat, the C.T.M. office is on Avenue Hassan II; in Casablanca, at 23 rue Léon d'Africain; and in Marrakesh at Djemaa el-Fna square.

CAMPING: There are at least 30 camping sites throughout Morocco, including grounds outside the major cities, where you'll find adequate shower and toilet facilities. The Moroccan tourist office will provide more information and details. Camping along the southern border of Morocco is to be avoided because of potential danger.

CAR RENTALS: You can get the most out of Morocco if you see it by car. When two or more travel together, renting a car becomes economical as well. Service stations are fairly frequent, highways are well marked, and explicit maps are available.

You can rent a car in Morocco at unlimited-mileage rates. In Morocco, **Avis** has a whole fleet of cars that are of recent vintage and are well overhauled in case you're contemplating a long trip. There are 14 Avis stations throughout the main cities and airports in the country, and it's possible to rent a car in any one of them, dropping it off in another place without any additional charge. All the stations remain open on holidays and weekends.

In Casablanca, the main office is at 71 Avenue de l'Armée Royale (tel. 31-44-51); in Tangier at 54 Boulevard Pasteur (tel. 09-330-31). Other offices are found in Marrakesh, Agadir, Fez, Oujda, and Rabat.

CLIMATE AND CLOTHING: Morocco experiences weather extremes, and what you wear will depend on the time of the year, where you go, etc. Remember that you can freeze to death in the sky-high Atlas and burn to a crisp in the Sahara. The mountain resorts around Marrakesh can require much protective wool, even light woolen attire at certain times in the summer.

In winter, when many North Americans favor Morocco (these are the so-called rainy months), cities such as Tangier, Casablanca, Fez, Rabat, and Meknes have a climate like Southern California. When the sun goes down, you'll need light coats or jackets; but during the sunny hours you can sunbathe with comfort in wind-protected areas. Swimming in heated pools is popular in winter, although ocean bathing is not, unless you're a Finn. Cold Atlantic winds can sweep through Tangier and Casablanca, yet light woolen clothing is generally adequate.

In summer, the entire picture changes. Although light summer apparel is suitable in Casablanca and Tangier, it gets unbearably hot the farther south you go, especially in Marrakesh and the Sahara. Moroccan residents learn to protect themselves from the stifling heat. Those who can afford to do so retreat to the mountains.

Records show that Marrakesh has the highest percentage of sunny days in Morocco, Casablanca the least, with Tangier and Agadir somewhere in between.

For more specific information, refer to "Temperatures," in this section.

CONSULATES AND EMBASSIES: In general it's best not to telephone. If you've got business to transact, go there in person during regular office hours Monday to Friday.

In **Rabat,** the American Consulate is at 6 Avenue de Marrakesh, the British at 28 bis Avenue Allal ben Abdallah.

In **Casablanca,** the American Consulate is at 8 Boulevard Moulay Youssef, the British at 60 Boulevard d'Anfa.

In **Tangier,** the American Consulate is at Chemin des Amoureux (tel. 359-04), the British at 52 rue d'Angleterre (tel. 358-95).

CRIME: Go to Tangier at your own risk! My own personal experience and mounting outcries from readers lead to the conclusion that Tangier is a very dangerous city unless you exercise extreme caution. Unless you're looking for trouble, don't go wandering around at night, particularly through the narrow streets of the Medina and the Casbah. Use only authorized guides arranged through the Tourist Office. Avoid shady characters who approach you as "guides" and try to recommend hotels (the rates will be doubled, because you'll immediately be taken as a sucker). You especially flirt with danger should you go into any dive accompanied by a man who accosts you on the street with a tempting tale of a "little hot spot." I'll let two readers tell you of their painful experiences, as they are typical of other complaints.

One man from Howard Beach, New York, writes: "After supper, I took a walk. A character accosted me, knew of a nice native club, pretty girls, drinks for nothing, wine only two dollars a bottle. So, I went. To be brief, after two bottles of 'champagne,' which he first said was wine, but still was only two dollars a bottle, and after I had given him a few dollars for his 'trouble,' plus drinks for him and a 'B' girl, I said to myself it was time to go, and asked for the check. I was there 20 minutes. So I got the bill for $85. When I protested violently, I was surrounded by half a dozen cutthroats. I had to empty my wallet of $50 in Spanish, American, and Moroccan money, and then sign over two $20 travelers checks. I didn't think these guys would hesitate to dump me in the ocean with a knife in my back."

Another reader from Richmond, California, writes: "In one week we have had our car ransacked, we have been assaulted, and we have been held up at knife point. All over Europe we parked our car on narrow, dark back streets, sometimes even leaving bags on the seat—and nothing ever happened. In Tangier, we parked on a main, well-lit street (the Avenue d'Espagne), and our car was broken into, even though we had carefully removed anything that was visible from the outside. Both robberies seemed to bore the police. They never looked at the car, and they weren't interested in the serial numbers on the cameras that were stolen. At the very best, I would suggest that any prospective traveler to Tangier acquire some very good insurance and come prepared for endless hassles and abuse and insults, regardless of how well intentioned and respectful he or she may be."

Tangier may be one of the most dangerous cities of Morocco, but the warning sounded there is still valid wherever you travel in the country.

About Hash

A band of young Americans and Canadians have "gone Moroccan" in Marrakesh—that is, they've bought jellabas and put a pair of babouches on their feet. You'll see them sitting around Djemaa el-Fna square at night, eating a typical Moroccan meal and smoking kif.

For many of these expatriates, the monetary title of this book represents a far more luxurious standard of living than they would want to indulge in. Many know how to live—or at least survive—in the Medina for a dollar or two a day. However, many of these unwanted visitors have largely disappeared from the scene following a crackdown by the police who weren't too happy about their hash-smoking ways.

Kif, a raw-leaf marijuana, is still sold openly. It is commonly smoked in public in a clay pipe. Despite this rather blatant display, note that the sale of kif, as mentioned, is *illegal* in Morocco. In one year alone, some 100 foreigners were arrested on drug counts.

New Moroccan laws make the buying, selling, and exporting of pot or hash a very risky business. The maximum penalty has been raised from five to ten years in jail, and the minimum from three months to five years for most types of offenses. Fines have been increased considerably, up to 500,000 dirhams ($82,000).

Moroccan authorities consider many foreigners an "evil influence" on local youth, and the national law makes it a "major crime" to corrupt minors by inciting them to take drugs.

CUISINE: If you think the Spanish are proud, wait till you get to Morocco. They're fierce. Some Moroccans claim their cuisine is the finest in the world. Others less chauvinistic rank it after France and China. What you'll usually find in the first-class and deluxe hotels is a cuisine that is mainly French and continental, although each establishment is likely to have a Moroccan room serving local specialties. To go truly native, you'll have to sit with robed Berbers and chew on fried locusts, as you watch the deadly, but defanged, cobra coil slowly upward from his basket to the music of a snake charmer.

The national soup is called **harrira** and is prepared in many different ways. It usually contains diced mutton and such spices as saffron and coriander. It's served piping hot, usually accompanied by dried dates as well as lemon slices and cinnamon sprinkled on top.

Couscous is the national dish. It is made with a base of steamed semolina, and its ingredients vary widely, depending on the chef or what was available at the market. Usually, mutton with vegetables is the order of the day. Couscous is most often served in a ceramic circular bowl, with a matching cover.

What North Americans refer to as shish-kebab in Morocco is called **brochette**, as in French. Brochettes are made with a number of meats, such as veal, beef, and lamb. A simple **kefta** is ground beef or lamb seasoned with herbs and skewered over a charcoal fire. **Tajine** (or tagine) is another common dish. It is a Moroccan stew made with almost anything, perhaps camel meat. A favorite version of this dish is with lamb and prunes.

While in Morocco, you'll want to try the classic **lemon chicken.** In fact, if you find yourself in a typical Moroccan restaurant and think you're going to lose your appetite, this is your safest bet, because it contains ingredients you can readily identify. It is also superb in flavor (the list of other dishes, including pigeons stuffed with almonds, seems endless).

Most visitors to Morocco worry about their health. A stroll through the markets, where meat hangs out in the open, often fly-covered in hot months, only forces concern. However, most Moroccan dishes are simmered for long periods of time in tight dishes or cauterized over a hot flame on an open-air brazier (only the toughest of microbes hold up under these inferno baptisms), so you can relax.

The Moroccans eat with the fingers of their right hands. However, spoons and forks will be provided. Don't worry about messy fingers. Warm water placed beside a basin is presented to each guest before and after the meal. The water is then poured over the hands which are held over the basin.

If you're being really native (or if you don't care for it) you won't drink wine—or anything—with your meal. However, you can get a glass of something when you feel like it. Moroccan wines are good and inexpensive, and should be better known. The few restaurants and hotels that offer imported French wines charge prices that are paralyzing. A good accompaniment to many a meal is mineral water from Sidi Harazem (said to cure kidney disorders, it also tastes good). A meal usually concludes with mint tea.

CURRENCY: Here's how the U.S. dollar translates into Moroccan currency. The basic unit of Moroccan currency is the **dirham** (abbreviated DH). This chart is based on the exchange rate of 6.10 dirhams to $1 U.S. One dirham is worth about $.1639 U.S. As we go to press, this rate appears fairly stable, but, with world economic conditions being what they are, it's always best to confirm the up-to-date official rate of exchange before you go to Morocco by checking with your bank at home.

The Moroccan dirham is divided into 100 centimes. Dirhams come in coins of 1 and 5; centimes in 5, 10, 20, and 50. In bills, you are issued denominations of 5, 10, 50, and 100 dirhams.

Dirhams	U.S.$	Dirhams	U.S.$
1	$ .16	30	$4.92
2	.33	35	5.74
3	.49	40	6.56
4	.66	45	7.38
5	.82	50	8.20
6	.98	60	9.83
7	1.15	70	11.47
8	1.31	80	13.11
9	1.48	90	14.75
10	1.69	100	16.39
15	2.46	125	20.49
20	3.28	150	24.59
25	4.10	200	32.78

CUSTOMS: The following items may be temporarily imported to Morocco duty free: still and movie cameras with two rolls of film for each; personal clothing and jewelry; binoculars; portable typewriters; camping material; and sports gear. Most foodstuff is allowed, but in "reasonable quantities." The visitor is allowed to bring in 400 grams of tobacco, or 200 cigarettes or 50 cigars and one bottle of wine or spirits. Firearms and cartridges may be imported subject to a license issued by the police department in Rabat (Direction de la Sureté Nationale).

Citizens of the United States who have been outside the country for 48 hours or more are allowed to bring back to their home country $300 worth of merchandise duty free—that is, if they have claimed no similar exemption within the past 30 days. Beyond this free allowance, the next $600 worth of merchandise is assessed at a flat rate of 10% duty. If you make purchases in Morocco, it is important to keep your records.

Warning: After a tour of Morocco, if you are returning to Spain by car, know that your vehicle will probably be searched thoroughly, as Spanish Customs look for hashish (*kif*). Sometimes it takes hours to gain clearance. And from what I hear, Spanish jails aren't the Hilton.

DOCUMENTS FOR ENTRY: Very liberal visitor regulations make it easy to enter Morocco. A valid individual or joint passport is necessary. For U.S., Canadian, and United Kingdom visitors, no visa is required, and tourists may stay in Morocco for three months. Those wishing to stay longer must apply to the local police department for an extension. No vaccination certificate is required to enter Morocco.

DRINKING WATER: It is generally safe, at least in the big cities and towns. I'd avoid it in some of the remoter places, and drink mineral water instead. As a matter of personal taste, I find the water of the south, although safe, much too salty. Perhaps you will, too. If so, stick to mineral water. One, called "Oulmes," is quite excellent.

DRIVING REQUIREMENTS: Vehicles, including motorcycles, can remain in Morocco for six months free of duty; after that, they are subject to the usual import restrictions. In general, your valid hometown driver's license should be sufficient, particularly if you're dealing with the big companies such as Hertz and Avis. However, I have found that some of the smaller car-rental agencies insist on an international driving permit.

You must have adequate insurance to drive in Morocco. The **Carte Verte** (green card), the international insurance certificate, is now recognized and valid in Morocco. Your car-rental agency will arrange insurance for you as part of the rental agreement. Otherwise, if you're bringing in that new car you just purchased in Europe, you can get local insurance at all ports of entry, such as Casablanca and Tangier. The cost is about 70 DH ($11.47) for ten days, 185 DH ($30.32) for one month.

Third-party insurance is compulsory in case a driver doesn't possess a green card. This third-party insurance may be obtained at Customs upon arrival in Morocco.

Traffic drives on the right, and the French highway code is used. Inside Moroccan cities and towns and on its national highways, signposts conform to international codes and standards.

DRUGS: My advice is to take whatever medication or drugs you'll need with you. I've experienced great difficulty in getting a prescription filled in certain parts of Morocco. American brands do not exist in certain places (the French seemed to have cornered the market here).

If you're in a dire emergency, ask the concierge at your hotel to direct you to the nearest pharmacy. Perhaps it would be wise to have him call ahead and explain your needs to the druggist there in case there's a language problem. Moroccan pharmacies operate in accordance with the French *Codex.*

For an all-night pharmacy in Casablanca, telephone 743-13. In Rabat, call 261-50; and in Fez, 220-62.

ELECTRIC CURRENT: Count on 110 or 120 volts, 50 cycles.

EMERGENCY: In **Tangier,** to telephone the police, call 360-70, and don't be surprised if they're indifferent, especially about thefts. The Red Cross Clinic in the same city is telephoned at 311-99.

In **Rabat,** phone the police at 19, an ambulance at 228-78, and report a fire by calling 15.

In **Casablanca,** some good numbers to know are as follows: police, 19; ambulance or fire, 15.

In **Fez,** reach the police at 19, an ambulance at 255-56.

In **Meknes,** call the police at 19, an ambulance at 228-05.

At **Taza,** the police number is 360 and an ambulance 127. In case you've had an accident on the road outside town, call the highway police at 50.

In and around **Agadir,** dialing 19 gets you the police (for the gendarmerie at Essaouira, call 142).

In **Marrakesh,** the emergency numbers are as follows: 19 for the police, 305-11 for the gendarmerie, and 15 to report a fire.

EXCHANGING MONEY: At the border, foreign visitors are obligated to declare to Customs the amount of foreign currencies and Moroccan money (dirhams) in their possession. The carrying of Moroccan banknotes into the country is officially forbidden. Those bringing in Moroccan dirhams risk having them confiscated upon entry.

You may convert foreign currencies or travelers checks at any exchange office throughout Morocco. Many exchange counters are in hotels, and at all ports of entry. To change foreign currencies outside official exchange offices is a considerably risky practice. Further, it is strictly prohibited to give foreign currency to a resident of Morocco in exchange for goods or services. Payment must be in dirhams only.

Foreign nonresidents upon leaving Morocco can reconvert dirhams up to 50% of the amount mentioned on their exchange statements if their stay exceeds 48 hours—and up to 100% if their stay does not exceed 48 hours. It is officially forbidden to export Moroccan banknotes.

GAS: Morocco is not one of the rich Arab oil countries, but gas or "petrol" is easily available there. You'll spot such familiar signs as Mobil, at least in the main cities and towns. I've discovered that prices vary; however, count on spending, as of this writing, about 3.75 DH (62¢) per liter for normal motor fuel, nearly 4 DH (66¢) for super. The farther south you go, the steeper the gasoline prices. Obviously, if you're planning a long stretch of travel into the remote countryside, make sure you have a full tank and know how far down the road the next filling station is.

GUIDES: The sights in the medinas of Morocco are usually covered by foot. This is unquestionably preferable, allowing you to savor everything at your own speed. If you do want some help rather than an organized tour, I recommend engaging an English-speaking guide for a half day of general orientation. Maps are usually inadequate, and many of the sights described simply can't be found on your own, unless you have unlimited time to do so.

City-licensed guides are available either through your hotel or by going to the **Syndicat d'Initiative.** Some of the best guides are enterprising local students who ply their trade without the consent of the local authorities. However, employing one can be risky. I urge you to avoid the dozens of men or boys who will approach you as you walk along the streets or in the narrow alleyways of the medinas, luring you with a few English words. Many of them, if so employed, will not only suffer disappearing English but will lead you to places where you don't want to go (usually shops where a high-pressure salesman is waiting), and may demand an exorbitant—and illegal—fee.

Hiring an official guide is less expensive than you think. Prices are regulated; but it's important to have a clear understanding of the rate and the hours he is to work. The cost is the same from city to city. For a half day it is 40 DH ($6.56), and for a full day 60 DH ($9.83).

HAIRDRESSERS: Of widely varying quality, these salons are found in all the major cities and towns (ask at your hotel for the most recommendable one nearest you). For a shampoo and set, women pay from 28 DH ($4.59) to no more than 55 DH ($9.02) in the most deluxe establishments; and for a haircut (not styling), men are charged from 18 DH ($2.95) in a simple barbershop to around 35 DH ($5.74) for a more first-class job.

Women in Tangier might want to patronize the British-run **Medusa** hairdressing salon, in the Passage Bestofo on the Boulevard Pasteur.

HITCHHIKING: Ever since I learned about two American girls who hitched a ride outside Marrakesh in the late 1960s, and were never heard from again, I have never recommended hitchhiking in Morocco. Hitchhiking, of course, can be extremely hazardous anywhere in the world, including America (remember Truman Capote's *In Cold Blood*?). You have to be adventurous indeed to set out with all your traveling possessions and an outstretched thumb into the far reaches of Morocco. If you must hitch a ride—and then the reason should be strictly financial necessity—fellow tourists are your best bet. And, then, I'd suggest great caution.

HOLIDAYS: Official holidays include March 3, the Fête de Trône, which is Moroccan independence day, marking the accession of King Hassan II. November 18, another holiday, commemorates the accession of King Mohammed V. Religious holidays vary according to the Moslem calendar. Aid-es-Seghir is celebrated as ending the fast of Ramadan; Aid el-Kebir commemorates Abraham's sacrifice; Mouloud honors the Prophet's birth; and Achoura, the tenth day of the Moslem year, celebrates the beginning of the Hegiran year.

All banks and shops are closed on these religious holidays. Check with the tourist office for actual dates in the year you plan to travel.

HORSE-DRAWN CARRIAGES: These are the greatest transportation treat in Morocco. These brightly colored carriages can transport you through narrow streets or along the major boulevards in style, giving you an unrivaled opportunity to see everything—easily and at your leisure. Most carriages seat four to five passengers (same price). Give your destination in advance and agree upon the price. In Marrakesh, for example, most horse-drawn carriages charge

15 DH ($2.46) to take you from the Medina to the New Town. The usual rate is 20 DH ($3.28) for an hour's ride within the city.

LANGUAGE: Arabic, of course, is the national language, but French and Spanish are widely used. Since the 1960s English has made great inroads, especially in hotels, restaurants, and nightclubs where you can almost count on its being spoken. And if you've got some dirhams in your purse, shopkeepers will speak any language you want them to.

LAUNDRY: Take along some drip-dry clothing, as laundry and dry-cleaning can be highly erratic in Morocco. It's best to stick to the services of your hotel. In an emergency I often tip the maid to launder and press a shirt. For the regular hotel laundry, expect to pay about 12 DH ($1.97) per shirt. To have a woman's dress dry-cleaned in Morocco costs about 22 DH ($3.61), and a man's two-piece suit can be serviced for about 28 DH ($4.59).

MEDICAL: The **Red Crescent** takes the place of the Red Cross in Morocco. If you're in need of a doctor or dentist, it's best to call your nearest embassy or consulate (refer to the list in this section). Otherwise, **IAMAT** (the International Association for Medical Assistance to Travelers) will provide you with a list of English-speaking doctors before you go to Morocco. In the United States, the IAMAT office is at Suite 5620, 350 Fifth Ave., New York, NY 10001. Otherwise, telephone them at 212/279-6465 for information.

METRIC MEASURES: Morocco uses the metric system of weights and measures (refer to the ABC section on Spain).

MOSQUES: Many North Americans and Europeans visit Morocco with the mistaken notion that they will get to go inside mosques or religious shrines, as part of that country's sightseeing attractions. It simply isn't possible, as frustrating as that revelation may be.

If you're not a Moslem, you'll be committing a grave offense in entering a mosque, and may get yourself in a lot of trouble. To enter certain holy shrines in the countryside is to court suicide. Remember, in this land, you're the "infidel."

Occasionally, you'll come across some old *medrassa* which are no longer in use as places of worship, and there you'll get a tantalizing preview of what a mosque looks like inside. When a functioning mosque is open, and Moroccans are at prayer inside, do not linger outside on the threshold peering in. It's considered very bad form, as few Moslems want infidels to view them at these personal, private moments.

NEWSPAPERS: From Paris, the *International Herald Tribune* is flown to Casablanca and Rabat. Chances are, you can enjoy it in the late afternoon. It's likely to arrive later in other cities in Morocco.

PETS: An international health and inoculation certificate is necessary for pets to be taken into Morocco.

PHOTOGRAPHY: Provincial Moroccans do not like to be photographed. It is considered very bad manners. Under no circumstance should you ever try to take a picture of a woman. Such cities as Marrakesh and Tangier are so used to tourists at this point that it often rarely matters, but exercise caution, nevertheless.

Most film sold in France is available in Morocco as well. Color slides and photographs can be developed here, but I've found the services unreliable and time-consuming; therefore, I'd suggest that you wait until you return home.

Because light in Morocco is often filtered through a veil of dust (or mist), a photoelectric exposure meter should be carried along if you plan to do much photography.

POLITICS: The present monarch is King Hassan II who is both head of the civil state and leader of the Moslem religion in his country. Morocco is a hereditary constitutional monarchy, and the sovereign has wide powers. For example, he must approve all legislation, and he may dissolve the House of Representatives. He can also declare a state of emergency and suspend parliamentary government, as has been done.

Otherwise, the parliament of Morocco is bicameral. The major legislative body is the House of Representatives, and there is also the House of Councillors. The king heads the Supreme Council of Justice, which is independent of the executive and legislative branches.

A word of advice: It is extremely unwise to criticize the king while you are a guest in his country. If you object to the manner in which the country is run, save your barbs until you're back in Europe or North America.

POST OFFICES: In the large cities of Morocco, including Casablanca, Rabat, and Tangier, post offices are open from 8:30 a.m. to 6:30 p.m. In smaller places, they are likely to shut down between noon and 3 p.m. The clerk at your hotel will direct you to the post office branch nearest you.

It costs 1.50 DH (25¢) to send an airmail postcard to Canada or the United States, 2 DH (33¢) to send a letter (up to 20 grams). These tariffs are subject to change, so check at the local post office before you mail.

Stamps can also be purchased at tobacconists, as in France.

RELIGIOUS SERVICES: In all towns with a European population, you'll find Catholic churches (not always Protestant). In the cities, however, there exist not only Catholic but Protestant and Orthodox as well.

Jewish worshippers in Casablanca can attend the synagogue, **Ein Habanim,** 14 rue Lusitania (tel. 26-69); in Fez, the **Ruben Sadoun** synagogue on rue Fréjus; in Marrakesh, the **Attias** synagogue at 3 rue Ign Tourmert; and in Tangier the **Temple Nahon,** rue des Synagogues (tel. 396-36).

In **Tangier** Protestant services are held at the Anglican church, **St. Andrew's,** 34 rue Léon l'Africain, on Sunday at 8 a.m. and again at 11 a.m.

In **Meknes** Catholic services are conducted at the **Church of Notre-Dame,** Avenue Mohammed V.

In **Casablanca,** there's a Roman Catholic church, the **Cathedral of Sacré-Coeur,** on Boulevard Rachidi, and an Anglican Church at rue Guedj. In addition, there's also a Protestant church at 33 rue Azilal.

REST ROOMS: All modern airports and rail and bus terminals have toilets, maintained more or less well. Public toilets in the major cities and towns are often cesspools, and I'd recommend that you avoid them unless it's a case of dire emergency. It's best to patronize the rest rooms of major hotels and restaurants. The squat toilet is still very much in evidence in Morocco. (See "Toiletries" for a further tip.)

SHOPPING: Shopping is another strong reason visitors go to Morocco, although they must learn to haggle for bargains in the *souks* of Meknes, Fez, and Marrakesh. Advised one Moroccan: "Never pay the third price asked." I've always been able to cut prices quoted by at least half and often two-thirds. Even then, I'm sure the shopkeeper has made a generous profit.

Moroccan handicrafts enjoy world renown. Even if you're not in the market for anything, sellers will seek you out. Everybody from the smallest child in the street to the clerks at the more modern stores will try to sell you something . . . anything! Brightly colored Rabat carpets, embroidered tablecloths and matching napkins (always too small), silver boxes, gem-studded slave bracelets, engraved daggers, silk brocade caftans (a graceful T-shaped garment sold in every known color, with every conceivable type of adornment), even antique rifles—the merchandise is here. If you detest haggling, you can go to certain outlets in every major city which feature fixed prices. You'll end up paying more, of course; but then you don't have to embarrass yourself.

STORE HOURS: Most shops and stores are open from 8:30 a.m. to noon, reopening at 2:30 p.m. and conducting business until around 7 p.m. (some stay open even later). Many shops are closed on Sunday, and, because of the special way the Moslem week works, can also be shut down on Friday.

TAXIS: They come in two sizes, the cheaper vehicle, called **petit taxis,** seat three passengers and are used in the bigger cities or towns. These taxis charge about half the price of the larger cabs which travel out-of-town. Most of the taxis in Moroccan cities (with the exception of Marrakesh) are metered. If a taxi isn't metered, agree on the price to be charged to avoid a scene later. Fares vary from city to city, but tend to be low. For example, in Marrakesh, you can go from the New Town to the Place Djemaa el-Fna for 5 DH (82¢) during the day, 7 DH ($1.15) at night.

To dial a taxi in Rabat, call 205-18; in Casablanca, 203-93; in Tangier, 355-17; in Fez, 225-97; and at Oujda, 21-21.

TELEGRAMS: Similar to many European countries, telegrams are sent from the post office.

TELEPHONE: In Morocco the telephone services operate through the post office. Calls within cities such as Tangier and Casablanca can be made at public phone booths, costing .50 DH (8¢). As of this writing, international phone calls are routed through the capital city of Rabat. Therefore, expect delays of 2½ to 3 hours (my latest call from Fez to New York took four hours).

The large cities are linked by automatic telephone. In these cases, all you have to do is simply dial the number after you've learned the area code. Consult the phone directories of the *Postes Chérifiennes.*

TELEX: Chances are your hotel will send one for you. However, smaller inns and hotels, most likely, won't be equipped to send a Telex.

TEMPERATURES: The chart below lists average temperatures in Fahrenheit.

	Jan.	Feb.	Mar.	Apr.	May	Jun.	Jul.	Aug.	Sep.	Oct.	Nov.	Dec.
Agadir	69	70	72	74	76	77	80	80	79	78	76	69
Casablanca	63	63	66	68	72	75	81	81	82	77	68	64
Essaouira	64	64	64	66	68	68	72	70	70	70	68	66
Fez	61	63	66	72	79	88	97	97	90	81	66	61
Marrakesh	66	66	73	79	84	91	102	101	91	82	70	66
Meknes	59	61	64	70	77	84	93	93	86	79	66	61
Ouarzazate	63	67	73	80	86	96	102	100	91	80	70	62
Rabat	63	64	66	70	73	77	82	82	81	77	68	64
Tangier	59	61	62	66	72	77	80	82	79	73	64	61
Taroudannt	72	73	79	81	86	90	99	100	95	90	77	72

TIME: Greenwich Mean Time (GMT) is in force all year in Morocco. The country is five hours ahead of Eastern Standard Time (six hours in summer).

TIPPING: A nightmare! Everyone seems to have a hand out; and one is tempted to draw a Moroccan veil and fade away without parting with a dirham. Nevertheless, certain tips are expected—and rightly so. Here are the guidelines. Take every opportunity to fill your pockets with dirham and .50 dirham pieces. They'll go quickly enough. Most restaurants and hotels include a service charge, usually 15%—but don't take that too seriously. The waiter expects something extra. Give 3 DH (49¢) per bag to the porter for taking your luggage to your room, 3 DH to the taxi driver unless the ride has been unusually long. Attendants who watch cars at the entrance to restaurants or sights expect at least 2 DH (33¢). Guides who show you through museums expect at least 3

DH (49¢). Train and boat porters also expect 3 DH (if they don't get it, they are likely to chase after you). If you've required the assistance of a hotel concierge for a stay of at least three days, then about 25 DH ($4.10) is adequate.

TOBACCO: American and British cigarettes are sold in the big cities. You can also purchase Moroccan brands. I find the Moroccan Gauloises cheap but atrocious. You can purchase tobacco not only in tobacco shops but in most food markets and cafés. A popular Moroccan brand of cigarettes is called "Casa Sports," made with black tobacco, costing from 1.80 DH (30¢) per package. A package of American cigarettes sells for around 7 DH ($1.15).

TOILETRIES: Take what you'll need, as you may not find your local product in Morocco. It is wise to travel with insect repellent if you're going to tour. Certainly if you're visiting some spots in the Sahara in the summer, it's also discreet to carry along a supply of salt tablets. Naturally, suntan lotion is essential. To be on the safe side, I'd also recommend to the smart traveler that he or she take along a "stash" of toilet and tissue paper. When you've visited certain Moroccan toilets, you'll understand why!

TOURIST INFORMATION: Before you go, you can obtain information and have many of your questions asked by writing or calling the **Moroccan Tourist Office** at 521 Fifth Ave., New York, NY 10017 (tel. 212/557-2520).

In Morocco, there are many national and city tourist offices dispensing information to the traveler. English is spoken in all these offices.

In **Rabat,** tourist information is given out at the **ONMT** (the Office National Marocain du Tourisme), at 22 Avenue d'Alger (tel. 212-52), and there's also a Syndicat d'Initiative on the corner of rue Lumumba and rue Van Vollenhoven (tel. 232-72), which is run by the city.

In **Casablanca** the national tourist office is at the ONMT office on the Place des Nations Unies, and the city information office at 98 Boulevard Mohammed (tel. 22-15-24).

In **Tangier,** the ONMT office is at 29 Boulevard Pasteur (tel. 329-96).

In **Fez,** national tourist information is presented at the ONMT office on Boulevard Hassan II (tel. 234-60), and city information at the bureau of the Syndicat d'Initiative on Place Mohammed V (tel. 247-69).

In **Meknes,** the national tourist office is at Place Administrative (tel. 212-86), and city information is given out on the Esplanade de la Foire (tel. 209-91).

In **Tetuan,** you can seek information at the ONMT office on 30 Avenue Mohammed V (tel. 44-07).

In **Agadir,** the national tourist office and the Syndicat d'Initiative are on Avenue du Prince Héritier and the Boulevard Mohammed V, respectively.

Finally, in **Marrakesh** go to the ONMT office at Place Abdelmoumen Ben Ali (tel. 302-58), or the Syndicat d'Initiative at 176 Boulevard Mohammed V.

TRAINS: Fares are moderate to low. Children 4 to 10 travel for half fare. The major cities—Tangier, Fez, Rabat, Meknes, Casablanca, and Marrakesh—are serviced by trains. A typical fare is a second-class ticket between Tangier and Casablanca—40 DH ($6.56). Note that there are occasional supplements for air conditioning and express trains. The air-conditioned trains, for example, cost 12 DH ($1.97) more.

In Casablanca, the Moroccan Railways, called **Chemins de Fer du Maroc** is at Boulevard Ba-Hammad (tel. 24-58-01).

TRAVEL AGENTS: Each city or town has many travel agents where you can pick up information and purchase tickets on buses, trains, and planes.

In Casablanca, I have always found the Anglo-Moroccan–owned **Olive Branch Tours,** 76 rue de Foucauld (tel. 203-54 or 614-16), especially helpful. They can also assist you with sightseeing tours and often cash travelers checks as well.

There's also a "branch" of Olive in Marrakesh at Palais El Badia; in Tangier, at 11 Admar Ibn Alhass.

Travelers to Rabat would be wise to patronize **Wagon Lits/Cook,** 1 Avenue Al Amir Moulay Abdallah. In Fez, Wagons/Lits Cook has a small office in the Grand Hotel building; in Meknes, at the rue du Ghana, and in Agadir at 28 Avenue des Forces Armées Royales.

TRAVELING AROUND MOROCCO: It's easier to travel through Morocco than you might imagine. Train connections, for example, between the major cities are good, and **Royal Air Inter** has domestic flights to most of the principal tourist zones. The best way to capture the magic of Morocco is to travel by road. For the most part, roads connecting the major cities and coastal towns are good, less so if you go to remote inland points. Except for the approaches to Casablanca, there is little bumper-to-bumper driving (in many places you won't see a car or truck for miles, although you'll have an occasional donkey and sheep herd to cope with). You can reach the sights recommended in this book by rented car or bus, not always by train or air. Generally, your point of entry into Morocco will be either Tangier or Casablanca. At either of these cities, you can rent cars, as well as make bus and train connections.

Our magic carpet ride begins in . . .

1. Tangier

By ferryboat from Algeciras, you can be in Tangier in 2½ hours. The ride from Spain is so short that it's hard to imagine you have entered a whole other way of life. The world is now Islam, and you can hear the special sounds that call the faithful to prayer. Catholic Spain is far, far away—even though you can look out across the strait and see it.

A white sandy beach—about 2½ miles long—stretches in front of Tangier, a potent attraction in summer to Americans and Europeans. Because of its hard-hit economy following the collapse of Tangier's status as an international city in 1956, the government is making a strong bid for tourism. It casts a lean and hungry eye on the hordes of people who descend on the less desirable beaches of the Costa del Sol, and wonders why the crowds don't get the message and come on over. The so-called Moroccan Riviera with its beautiful beaches is so uncrowded in summer that tourists can swim nude near one of the Caves of Hercules.

By all means, spend the night in Tangier. Too many visitors arrive on one of those one-day excursions, then rush through the city—and everything becomes a blur. There's enough to see and do to jam-pack many days. Now let's zero in and find out what it's like:

The dazzling white city of Tangier is fickle: it winks at the Mediterranean with one eye, while casting a flirtatious glance at the Atlantic with the other.

Tangier does not look dark and mysterious, but bright and airy, with palm-lined boulevards, comfortable, white-painted hotels. However, once you've docked, once you've penetrated deep into the city (the Medina and the Casbah), you'll surely change your mind.

Tangier is a city of contrasts. Women in white haiks who look like mummies walk down the old streets, the way their grandmothers did before them, and their grandmothers' grandmothers before them. The modern Moroccan woman, on the other hand, may wear a dark djellaba. Once virtually every Moroccan woman peered over a veil at her liberated European counterpart. Today increasing numbers are veil-less, and their new-found freedom is also reflected in high-heel shoes and nail polish. At night, too, in the cabarets, you'll find that modesty is not mandatory for Moroccan women. The belly dancers don't even wear diamonds in their navals.

The contrast is seen in the men, as well. Old bearded relics of another day hobble down the alley-like streets with their weary donkeys; they look as if they had stepped fresh out of Jerusalem before the birth of Christ. More modern men pay homage to their Moslem traditions by wearing camel-hair robes. In total disregard of their origins, some of the young men wear blue jeans and leather jackets (in the cooler months), and would fit comfortably into the Bronx.

Tangier is a city whose origins dip deep into antiquity; many conquerors have presided over the Casbah. From around the time of World War I until '56, Tangier was an international city. It had acquired associations then, particularly during World War II, which it has not lived down today. It is often considered a wicked city, a hot-bed of intrigue, prostitution, money changers, and narcotics. The government, in an attempt to remove some of the stigma of this reputation, has cracked down on houses of prostitution, forcing the women to take to the streets. The situation has been made tough for the money changers, but they blithely go on their way, offering you extra dirham if you'll convert your pesetas or dollars. The drug trade flourishes in Tangier; the odor of kif (a kind of marijuana) permeates the air in some parts. However, foreigners caught with drugs, particularly if they're on the dealing end, are not dealt with lightly in Morocco, as is attested to by the presence in Moroccan jails of several Americans. So take care!

Moroccans are quick to point out that Tangier is the most religious city around, since its three different sects—Jews, Christians, Muslims—celebrate their holy day on a different day of the week. In a sense, the city has three sabbaths.

How to describe it? Tangier is a city of mosques, modern hotels, white-and purple-washed houses, exotic markets, foreign and Moroccan restaurants —and there's even a place where you can ask a Yank to serve you a hamburger, light on the onions if you wish.

A warning: One thing that is very confusing in Tangier is that all roads have two names, one European, such as rue des Vignes, and one Moroccan, as rue Prince Héritier. You can never be sure which one you'll get when you ask for directions. Most of the road signs are obliterated anyway so it's often a hit-or-miss affair. However, with concentration and patience, you will soon find your way around.

GETTING THERE: As a gateway to the Mediterranean, Tangier is conveniently reached by a number of means: sea, air, or land (it's even accessible if you happen to be crossing over the Sahara Desert). First, let's consider the most popular means of arrival.

By Ferry from Algeciras and Málaga

The **Compañía Transmediterránea** and **Limadet** run ferry services between Algeciras and Tangier, and Málaga and Tangier, usually one a day in winter and four a day in summer. On the Algeciras–Tangier run, the cost of a one-way, first-class ticket (Tourist A) is 1000 pesetas ($9.60); 800 pesetas ($7.68) in second class (Tourist B). Book tickets in Algeciras at Recinto Puerto (Aptdo. 139; tel. 67-28-90). From Málaga, the one-way fare is 1200 pesetas ($11.52) in Tourist A, 1000 pesetas ($9.60) in Tourist B. Children 4 to 12 pay half fare. Cars, Málaga–Tangier, pay 3000 pesetas ($28.80), and Algeciras–Tangier, 2700 pesetas ($25.92). In Tangier, book at the Intercona S.A., 31 rue Quevedo (tel. 341-01). Motorists taking cars should book well in advance.

By Air

Both **Iberia** and **Royal Air Maroc** operate between Tangier and Madrid. Iberia also maintains connections between Tangier and Málaga. **Air France** hooks up with Paris, and **British Airways** maintains a London–Tangier run.

WHERE TO STAY: Tangier offers a number of modest hotels within our price range. Most of the hotels listed below lie somewhere between the **Boulevard Pasteur** (main shopping and business street of the international section), and the beach, and many are within easy walking distance of either area. Some are built on sloping streets, affording views of the bay.

I'll lead off with my top budget choices, then follow with a hotel in the Medina—the Arab commercial and residential district. At the latter, incidentally, you'll find plenty of "local color."

Hotel Miramar, Avenue des F.A.R. (tel. 389-07), is as close as you can get to the wide and long beach. The Miramar is modern, and has much to offer. All of its quite good rooms, kissed by sea breezes, have private baths or showers. From April 1 to October 31, half board is required. A single is 135 DH ($22.13), half board; a double, 105 DH ($17.21) per person, with service and taxes included. A typical dinner might include a fresh melon, followed by filet of swordfish, then a grilled entrecôte or roast chicken, topped by a fresh fruit salad. From most of the rooms, you can see high-rising Gibraltar and the southern tip of Spain.

Hotel Panoramic Massilia, 3 rue Marco Polo (tel. 212-39), midway between the beach and the Boulevard Pasteur, is built on a hillside, giving many of the bedrooms a view of the sea. The furnishings are relatively modern, and the beds quite comfortable. A double room with shower and toilet costs 75 DH ($12.29), with a continental breakfast, taxes, and service included. There are also other rooms without toilet at 65 DH ($10.65). Three-bedded rooms go for 95 DH ($15.57), including breakfast, and there are some for 88 DH ($14.42) with showers. In all, the Massilia offers modest amenities, good service, and one of the best and most scenic positions of the low-cost hotels in Tangier.

Hotel d'Anjou, 3 rue Ibn Albanna (tel. 342-44). English-speaking Boubekri Lahousène is a considerate host who welcomes you to his little hotel. He charges 42 DH ($6.88) in a single, the cost rising to 50 DH ($8.20) in a double. Doubles contain private baths with shower. The hotel has hot water and, in the cooler months, central heating. A continental breakfast, French style, is the only meal served, but the hotel is most central and Mr. Lahousène will direct you to the most recommended restaurants nearby. I consider the d'Anjou one of the best bargains in Tangier.

Staying in the Medina

Hotel Mamora, 19 rue des Postes (tel. 341-05), near the "Socco Chico," is for those who want the experience of living in the Medina—yet want to feel safe and secure. Comfortably furnished doubles with shower (no toilet) are a low 60 DH ($9.83). The best doubles, with private bath, rent for 70 DH ($11.47), and a single with shower costs only 52 DH ($8.52), rising to 57 DH ($9.34) with private bath. A continental breakfast is an additional 10 DH ($1.64). And if you wish, you can return to the hotel for lunch and join the sunbathers on the roof terrace, with its excellent views of the Medina and the Casbah. The Mamora has a rooftop restaurant, serving 40-DH ($6.56) meals.

Super-Splurge Hotels

Rif Hotel, Avenue d'Espagne (tel. 359-10), is the place for the visitor who requires comfort and elegance with total Moroccan style. A six-story, 27-year-old building, it faces the beach and the broad waters of Tangier Bay, with a welcoming, cool marbled lobby with deep, comfortable leather armchairs. The lounges and public rooms mainly overlook the sea and are decorated in extravagant Moorish style. The mosaics on the walls are handmade, and the carved wooden ceilings are carefully fashioned. Modern furnishings blend well with the traditional, and the fresh cool dining room and the leather-covered bar look out on to the sheltered patio and pool area. Cool green trees and shrubs climb behind and overhang the pool and grotto; loungers and chairs are dotted among the palms and creepers.

All rooms overlooking the bay are in the traditional style with Moorish filigree woodwork on the cupboards and friezes. Good beds and balconies are another plus, and bathrooms are efficient. At the back, overlooking the garden, the rooms are furnished in a contemporary style, and there are several duplex apartments designed and decorated by Patrick Frank, a French antiquarian who, like so many, has settled in Morocco. Again there is much adaption of the ancient styles with Moorish lanterns providing a soft light, lush carpets, and carved woodwork reflecting the glow.

Drinks in the bar can be expensive: expect to pay 18 DH ($2.95) for a gin or scotch, about 10 DH ($1.64) for a beer. Lunchtime salads and sandwiches are available around the pool if you do not wish a set meal in the dining room, costing 45 DH ($7.38). Rooms are 190 DH ($31.14) for two persons, 150 DH ($24.59) for singles. Duplexes are more expensive. Half board is obligatory from April to October.

The Rif maintains, as always, its position as the doyen of Tangier hotels. Its special feature is the excellence of the staff, who, without exception, are friendly and well trained. The barman remembers your usual order and has your drink lined up before you've asked for it. The headwaiters and the section leaders are eager to find out what fish arrived today, to squeeze fresh oranges for your breakfast juice, and to cater to your special requests. Mr. Seffati is very ably assisted and supported by Simon Cohen. Apart from some new young staff members, I recognized everyone from two years ago, and it was almost as if they recognized me.

Tennis with the pro costs 12 DH ($1.97), and there is a sauna for 16 DH ($2.62).

Rembrandt Hotel, Boulevard Mohammed V (tel. 378-70), is built on a hillside right on the main boulevard, as it climbs toward the Place de France. A cool lobby leads to a smart bar and neat dining room, and there are lounges with TV and air conditioning. You can take the stairs or else a somewhat erratic (but safe) elevator to the upper floors where many of the rooms look over the bay and harbor. Some units are simple, and others contain tiny balconies, plus sitting rooms with TV. All have private baths and toilets en suite. Overnight will cost from 98 DH ($16.06) to 150 DH ($24.59) per person, the latter charge for sole occupancy of a double room. Service and the local tax are included in these rates.

A continental breakfast is an extra 10 DH ($1.69) per person, and a lunch or dinner goes for 45 DH ($7.38). For that, you are likely to get a meal beginning with soup, salad, or juice, following with a meat and vegetable dish (or else a Moroccan specialty), plus dessert. A small à la carte menu offers grills, fresh fish (when available), and both international and Moroccan dishes.

Outside is a pleasant, private garden, with a small clean swimming pool. You are five minutes from the harbor and within easy walking distance of the main restaurants and shops. You'll probably still want to take a taxi to the Casbah, but the markets are not too far away.

READERS' HOTEL SELECTIONS: "Hotel Valencia, 72 Avenue d'Espagne (tel. 217-14). We walked from the boat down the Avenue d'Espagne and ran right into this hotel. The people are very helpful and friendly. It is clean, and we had a twin-bedded room with breakfast for 75 DH ($12.29). It is easy to get to the market area, and the train station is right across the street. Buses which run to other towns in Morocco, are also about a half a block away" (Frances Terrazas, Los Angeles, Calif.). . . . "We highly recommend the Bristol Hotel, 14 rue El Antaki (tel. 310-70). For 110 DH ($18.03), we had a room with private bath and shower, breakfast, and either lunch or dinner, served in a lovely antique room. There is an elevator, central heating, and a cool breeze, because it is about 100 yards from the beach. From the ferry, walk straight into the city, ignoring the beggars and guides. This is a real find" (Eileen and Peter Koenigsberg, Brooklyn, N.Y.).

WHERE TO EAT: Food in Tangier tends to be expensive, but moderately priced meals are available at places ranging from a French bistro to a Danish-owned café. The international cuisine generally represents French, Moroccan, and English cooking. Some of the more elaborate Moroccan restaurants charge high prices, but they provide entertainment and a sultan-posh decor, in addition to specially prepared meals. Here are the restaurant selections, by nationality:

French

L'Alhambra, 16 rue du Docteur Fumey (tel. 210-21), is about as close as you'll get to an authentic French bistro in Tangier. Excellently prepared French dishes, along with a few Moroccan specialties, are served inexpensively. A set meal is offered for 28 DH ($4.59), plus 12% service—a handsome repast that might skip from France (pâté de foie) to the national dish of Morocco, couscous, a semolina-based potpourri that is often made with lamb, raisins, almonds, whatever the chef has in mind or in the kitchen. An alternate choice would be beef bourguignon. The owner, the incomparable Mme Rey, is French to the core. She watches and evaluates everything with a disciplined eye, and is preening proud of the gleam on her pots and pans.

La Grenouille, 3 rue El Jabha El Quatania (tel. 390-42), although French in name, is run by Briton Frank Walker. On a small side street off the Boulevard Pasteur, it is one of the best gastronomic bargains in all of Morocco. The restaurant is on two levels, and decor includes soft lighting, rattan chairs, red upholstered divans along the walls, plus a cozy bar at one end. Courteous, efficient waiters will place bamboo placemats before you. On the walls are Moroccan metal plates. For 30 DH ($4.92), plus 15% tax, you have a wide choice of dishes. Begin with a salade niçoise or soup or raie au beurre noir, or baked macaroni and cheese, even snails or sardines. The second course might be a filet mignon or roast chicken or veal liver or wienerschnitzel, accompanied by potatoes, a salad, and vegetable: then a dessert of peach Melba, a special cake, or cheese. It all makes a memorable dining experience. The clientele is discriminating, mostly English and French residents.

Chez Larbi, 18 rue Samuel Pepys, near the Fez market (tel. 396-78), serves tasty French and English dishes. The cost of three full courses is 22 DH ($3.61), plus whatever wine you order. You can ask for wine by the bottle or glass. There is a wide selection for each course offered. The proprietors, Larbi and Mohammed, both serve and supervise, and are very courteous, speaking good English. They can also offer various suggestions about Tangier's attractions.

Scandinavian and English

The **Viking Restaurant,** 19 rue Balmès (tel. 370-44), offers fare from Denmark, England, and Morocco. Good home-cooked, belt-stretching food is served in this intimate dining spot. The British side is reflected in such dishes as shepherd's pie. One of the best main courses is sole meunière. However, owner Janette Lucas is best known for her very good steaks, particularly her pepper steak. A scalding-hot Moroccan dish that many of the restaurant's devotees prefer is shrimp pil-pil. What tips the economy scale is what you get with your main dish: a salad, potatoes, and rice, plus a green vegetable. Expect to spend from 32 DH ($5.25) to 50 DH ($8.20) for a complete meal. Guests are greeted with a wide smile, and you instantly feel at home at this restaurant. It is open weekdays from 11:30 a.m. to 2:30 p.m. and 7 to 11 p.m. Closed Sunday.

Spanish

Restaurant Romero, 12 Avenida Moulay Abdallah (tel. 322-77), is for those with nostalgia for a Spanish budget restaurant. *"Si en su casa se come bien, aquí también"* is the motto appearing over the door ("If you eat well at home, you will here, too"). The tourist menu costs 28 DH ($4.59) and includes vegetable soup, consommé, or hors d'oeuvres; hake, flounder, or fresh anchovies; ravioli, fried calf liver, or a breaded veal cutlet; and finally flan and fruit. Add on 12% for service. If you order from the à la carte menu, selecting such dishes as paella, couscous, or spaghetti, expect to spend around 45 DH ($7.38) to 50 DH ($8.20) for a complete meal. The decor is in the simple tavern style (once you get beyond the neon lights).

Splurge Restaurants

Le Detroit, Riad Sultan (tel. 380-80), at the old gate to the Casbah on the top of the hill, is a former palace that has been transformed into the most exciting restaurant in Tangier. The view is spectacular: the southern coast of Spain lies before you (on a clear day you can see Gibraltar). With taste, the best of traditional Moroccan architecture has been recreated. Native music is played, and belly dancing is featured. You can sit, sultan fashion, on low, cushioned seats, as the most typical Moroccan dishes are brought to your table. The couscous, with seven vegetables, costs 34 DH ($5.57), and if you're really a big spender, you can try a gourmet dish of Morocco, pastilla, 35 DH ($5.74). (If you thought old King Cole had it good, wait till you try this cinnamon and sugar-coated pigeon pie.) For an à la carte dinner, expect to spend from 55 DH ($9.02) and up.

The **Marhaba Palace,** nearby, on the Riad Sultan, is just outside the entrance to the Casbah. It is a real old Moroccan residence, with arches and tiling. In the afternoon, it's the best place to go for mint tea. The palace features an orchestra seated on a rostrum, plus at least one dancing boy who does the Rif tray dance.

The Parade, 35 rue Prince Héritier, is *the* gathering place for the international set, including both resident Americans and Britishers. Surrounded by high walls, it opens onto an enticing garden patio, which leads to a little combination bar-restaurant. Against one wall is a bar crowned with a red canopy. The owner, Lily Wickman, an Edith Piaf type who chain-smokes cheroots, presides over the bar. Handsome young bartenders are on hand as well as a delightful apple-cheeked old Moroccan woman who obviously adores Lily and makes sure she has her supper before the evening begins. A sequinned slipper which belonged to Eugenie Bankhead, Tallulah's sister, stands on a pedestal where it was placed after being passed around the crowd filled with champagne. It was taken down for a time, which evidently was bad luck—so many bad things happened that they put it back and there it has remained.

At the tables in the alcove and around the wall, fresh linen cloths and napkins are used. There's not much room so you are not expected to linger at your table, but you can return to the bar for your brandy.

Homemade soups include vichyssoise costing 8 DH ($1.31) and tomato 6 DH (98¢), each served with fresh bread. Fish dishes, including lotte en brochette with ratatouille and tiny potatoes, are from 20 DH ($3.28) to 26 DH ($4.26). Meat dishes, such as steak au poivre or an excellent filet, go for 16 DH ($2.62) to 24 DH ($3.93). Steak-and-kidney pie is 20 DH ($3.28). Desserts range from 6 DH (98¢) to 12 DH ($1.97).

The clientele consists mostly of regular expatriates from every country in the world, plus a few chosen locals and tourists who go early to get a table and to see the parrot before he calls for Halima to put him to bed before the main crowd comes in. The Parade, in the New Town, is open for lunch and for drinks and dinner around 8 p.m. Closed on Wednesday off-season.

Damascus, 2 bis rue Moulay Abdellah (tel. 347-30), is in the typical Moroccan style, offering specialties that represent some of the best of both the French and Moroccan kitchens. It is, in addition, a bar as well as a salon de thé. (tearoom). Unlike some of the country's so-called Moroccan restaurants, this serves a fine version of *la haute cuisine marocaine,* including pigeon pies, tajines, and kebabs, along with more familiar French dishes. Meals begin at 65 DH ($10.65).

READER'S RESTAURANT SUGGESTION: "The **Restaurant Económico** on rue de la Plage is a real budget type and very popular. It offers a small salad, main dish (fish, meat, couscous, beef stew) in substantial quantity, and dessert of orange slices with cinnamon, for 12 DH ($1.97) to 18 DH ($2.95). The proprietor is friendly and courteous. His sons speak English, and the menu is in English. You can send one of the boys out to get a large bottle of wine for 10 DH ($1.64)" (Joseph Montuore, Temple Hills, Md.).

The Social Center

The **Café de Paris,** 1 Place de France (tel. 384-44), is a kind of social center of the town, where all rumors are spread. Few visitors are in Tangier for more than 24 hours without paying at least one call on this centrally located café. It's a natural meeting ground for both Europeans and Arabs. Real-estate transactions take place here, as well as assignations of every conceivable type— and you can also have a cup of coffee or chilled drink. No one insists that you vacate your table. For around 6 DH (98¢) for sipping rights, you can sit and watch the passing parade. A simple meal is available for 30 DH ($4.92). Five of the principal streets of Tangier rendezvous on the Place de France, as do all the principal players.

READER'S CAFÉ SUGGESTION: "The **Zagora,** a restaurant/coffeehouse on Boulevard Pasteur, is also great for sidewalk coffee/mint tea sipping and viewing the scene. You get a larger glass of cafe con leche for 3.50 DH (57¢) than at the Café de Paris" (Joseph Montuore, Temple Hills, Md.).

Tea for Two

Madame Porte, corner of Avenue du Prince Moulay Abdallah and rue El Mouttanabi, is an institution, attracting those who wouldn't be caught sipping mint tea in the Medina. The tea, 5 DH (82¢), and the French pastries are good and proper. The British writer Alec Waugh reports that Porte serves "the best dry martinis I have ever tasted. They are lagoon-size, ice cold, served in a German-type wine glass with a long, thin sliver of lemon peel curving around the rim, and cost 18 DH ($2.95). One of them is as much as I can manage." Madame stays open till 9:30 p.m.

READER'S WINERY SUGGESTION: "Alongside the Hotel Chellah, on the former rue Jeanne d'Arc, now rue Allal Ben Abdallah, there is a winery where you can get a bottle of good wine for about 7 DH ($1.15) and up, and Star bottled water for 3 DH (49¢). The cost is reduced when the bottles are returned. The proprietor is French and very courteous" (Joseph Montuore, Temple Hills, Md.).

WHAT TO SEE AND DO: Here follows a potpourri of things to do and see in Tangier, including such adventures as a visit to the Casbah and excursions to the Caves of Hercules.

The Casbah

When Charles Boyer invited Hedy Lamarr to come with him to a Casbah, the request sparked a whole new meaning for romance, glamor, and intrigue. Foreigners who visit this part of the world can rarely resist Mr. Boyer's old invitation. Although a number of expatriates have moved in, the Casbah still is the old Arab residential quarter of the city. It sits proudly on a hill, looking down at the bay and the streets of the Medina, another residential and also commercial district. The best way to reach it is to continue north from the Grand Socco on the rue d'Italie, then turn right and pass through the old gate. It's quite a climb, so wear your walking shoes.

The major sight to be visited here is the former **Palace of the Sultans,** now a museum (free). Run by the government, this old palace shows the Moorish architecture, and contains a handsome display of Moroccan handicrafts. Its patio was once accustomed to the bare feet of dancing girls; its great treasure boxes, now empty, once held gold and jewels. The museum also shows archeological finds from the surrounding district.

After your visit here, you can begin your exploration of the narrow winding streets. Don't be surprised if you run into a snake charmer; give him 2 DH (33¢) if you'd like to see him make the snake rise.

The Soccos of the Medina

Both the **Big Socco** and the **Little Socco** (sometimes called *Petit* or *Chico*) make up the teeming life of old Tangier. A trip through the markets can be fascinating. Smell the exotic spices; drink the mint tea. Surely Tangier has the world's largest oranges. In and around the Soccos, you'll find the shops, the bazaars, and the vegetable markets for which the city is so well known.

The Big Market has been cleaned up considerably and "beautified," but not all the colorful Arab life has been chased away. Next to the Big Socco is the **Mendoubia,** a garden with an 800-year-old dragon tree (that's what the tourist people claim) and about three dozen cannons used during one of the sieges of Tangier.

The Little Socco is not a market, but a small plaza almost completely surrounded by cafés. It's the meeting place for foreigners and visitors—plus what one resident termed as "some rather doubtful locals."

The Old American Legation

The Tangier Legation building, now a museum and study center, 8 Zan-kat/rue d'Amérique, is the oldest diplomatic property of the United States to be continuously owned. In the Medina of Tangier, it is the first real estate the U.S. government (it is believed) ever acquired abroad. In 1821 Sultan Sidi Moulay Suliman gave it to the American people. The legation is maintained by the staff of the American consul-general through their voluntary efforts and through contributions. It offers one of the finest lithographic collections I've seen.

Long a seat of America's diplomatic representation to the sultans of Morocco, the building ended that role in 1961 with the construction of the new American consulate building. In later years, as it gradually fell into disrepair, it was used as an Arabic-language school for American diplomats and later as a Peace Corps training center. As a special Bicentennial project, it was restored to some of its former glory. The jewel of the additions is a Moorish pavilion overlooking a courtyard.

Note in particular the carved doors leading from the terrace into the pavilion, which are more than 400 years old. The antique doors, shutters, ceilings, and tiles within the pavilion were found in Fez and other parts of Morocco.

In the Environs

The environs of Tangier have some interesting Roman and Phoenician ruins, but the best two excursions from the city are to **Cape Spartel,** the most northwestern tip of Africa, and to the **Caves of Hercules.** For this, of course, you'll need some means of transportation, either a guide or a taxi (naturally, you'll cut down costs if you share).

On Cape Spartel is a lighthouse, built by an engineer about a century ago on the spot where the Mediterranean meets the Atlantic. It's some five miles from Tangier to the cape. The view from here is magnificent.

From Spartel, it's about a mile to the Caves of Hercules, where many prehistoric remains have been found. The caves have been greatly enlarged by workers carving out millstones.

The miles and miles of beach viewed from here point up an enormous potential tourist development for Morocco.

READER'S SHOPPING SUGGESTION: "Achmed, the proprietor of **Kaftan Dalila,** 54 Boulevard Pasteur, will make a caftan for the women, to fit, for about 200 DH ($32.78) within three days" (Joseph Montuore, Temple Hills, Md.).

TANGIER NIGHTLIFE: From belly dancers to discos, Tangier tries to please all tastes. Forget all those '40s movies about espionage or whatever. Bogart is long dead, and Hedy Lamarr is in retirement. The nightlife of Tangier has long surpassed its heyday in the '50s. Its bars and nightclubs today often attract very unsavory characters, such as pimps and thieves. You can risk your life going into the wrong places. At best, you risk your wallet. You'll be taken for whatever they think they can get from you in some places. It's not a pretty picture unless you pick and choose carefully among the offerings.

Belly Dancing

Morocco Palace, 11 Avenue Prince Moulay Abdellah (tel. 398-14), is about the best place to see belly dancing in Tangier. Count on spending around 60 DH ($9.83) for a drink and the show. The decor includes Moroccan inlaid tiles on walls and pillars, with small tables and settees. An orchestra usually plays at night, and one of the numbers consists of a girl dancing with a tray of drinks and lit candles balanced on her head.

Nightclubs

El Piano, 31 rue América del Sur (tel. 350-13), offers dancing and good music. At least three nights a week a floor show is staged, with the likes of snake charmers, tray dancers, folkloric groups, and singers. Entrance to the club on show nights costs around 60 DH ($9.83), but includes a half bottle of Moroccan champagne per person. Other nights there is no entrance charge, and drinks go for around 15 DH ($2.46). These prices, by the way, are considered the least expensive of any nightclub in Tangier (it's run by an Englishman, Richard Kemp). El Piano opens at 8 nightly; the show lasts from 11 p.m. till 12:30 a.m., with dancing sandwiched between the acts. After the show, dancing continues into the early hours of the morning.

Discos

The Ranch Discothèque, 17 rue Omar Ibn Al Hass (tel. 382-66), is considered one of the best discos of Africa. Sometimes there are spontaneous jam sessions with visiting musicians, and guests can always count on a reliable piano player. It's not only a place at which you can enjoy yourself, but meet friends from all over the world, as you listen to records from Gordon Lightfoot among others. The owner, Houceine Marzouki, directs an English-speaking staff. For 10 DH ($1.64), you're not only admitted but given a drink.

Gospel, rue Sanlucar, is another major disco. You walk down a flight of stairs, and there's a small dance floor, cozy nooks for whatever, plus the usual psychedelic lights. A drink, which you can nurse throughout the night, costs 15 DH ($2.46). The clientele is mixed, Moroccan and European.

READER'S TOURING SUGGESTION: "My brother and I 'stumbled' upon a small city, Asilah, that's absolutely perfect to see. It's some 30 to 40 kilometers outside Tangier, lying right on a beach. It's a small place, complete with a market (the usual bargaining) and camels. There are several hotels and campsites there, and it seems to attract many German and French visitors. This is an ideal place to visit if you want a taste of Morocco, but don't want to travel far into the country and don't want to deal with the hassles of Tangier" (Howard S. Smith, Kingston, N.Y.).

After leaving Tangier, the classic tour of Morocco is to visit the four Imperial Cities of Fez, Marrakesh, Rabat, and Meknes. However, your point of entry may be Ceuta. If so, you'll want to visit Tetuan on the way to Tangier. We'll do all of the above, leaving our caravan in Casablanca, where many people get the plane or boat for back home.

2. Ceuta

Ceuta is a Spanish enclave on the North African coast. When Morocco was given its independence in 1956, Spain held onto two military enclaves, Ceuta and Melilla. Ceuta is really an Andalusian-style town, characterized by gleaming white buildings and wrought-iron balconies filled with flowers.

The town sits on the promontory of Monte Acho, which is the southern tip of one of the two so-called Pillars of Hercules. The other one is Gibraltar. These two pillars formed the gateway to the ancient world. You can climb Monte Acho for a panoramic view of the Mediterranean that includes Gibraltar on a clear day. There's a military outpost, Fort Acho, which was a penal colony. You can only look at it from the outside.

WHAT TO SEE: The sights of Ceuta (Sebta in Arabic) are limited, but they include: the **Church of Our Lady in Africa** from the 18th century; the **San Felipe moat** from the days of the Portuguese occupation, plus a tiny **Archeological Museum,** a few pretty squares, and a main shopping street. Chances are you'll be moving on after a half day to Morocco proper.

HOW TO GET THERE: Car ferries run from Algeciras to Ceuta daily. The trip takes between 1 and 1½ hours, and departures from Algeciras are from 8 a.m. until 8:30 p.m. (about 13 sailings a day). In summer some extra ships are put on. There are two ship lines serving the route—Compañía Transmediterránea and ISNASA. The cost of a ticket is the same for both lines: 480 pesetas ($4.61) for adults, 300 pesetas ($2.88) for children from 2 to 7 on Transmediterránea, from 3 to 9 on ISNASA. Tickets may be purchased in Madrid for the Compañía Transmediterránea at 63 Alcalá (tel. 225-21-10 or 225-51-10), or from authorized travel agencies. In Algeciras tickets are available at the Maritime Station or travel agencies for both companies.

WHERE TO STAY: Biggest and best in Ceuta is **Gran Hotel La Muralla,** 15 Plaza de Africa (tel. 514-940), right in the heart of town on a pretty, palm-lined square, with the Church of Neustra Señora de Africa across the street. You can get a double room with bath for 4000 pesetas ($38.40), a single with bath for 2900 pesetas ($27.84). A continental breakfast is an additional 250 pesetas ($2.88). This four-star hotel has many amenities, including a swimming pool, bar, air conditioning, even a nightclub. The hotel has a somewhat secure parking lot between the hotel and army post. At the other hotels in town, you leave your vehicle on the street, an unwise situation.

Cheaper is the three-star **Africa,** Muelle Cañonero Dato (tel. 514-140), overlooking the ocean, a little bit out of town. Its doubles with bath rent for 2100 pesetas ($20.16); its singles with showers cost 1550 pesetas ($14.88). A continental breakfast is the only meal served, costing 150 pesetas ($1.44).

WHERE TO EAT: El Mesón de Serafín (tel. 514-003), is spectacularly situated on top of Monte Acho, providing sweeping views of the Mediterranean. In true mesón style, it has a rustic decor created by hanging hams and the like. Spanish regional dishes are featured. Figure on spending about 800 pesetas ($7.68) for the daily menu.

In town there's the simpler **La Terraza,** 4 Plaza de Abastos Vieja (tel. 514-029), a restaurant with a bar. Although the inside decor is modern, I prefer the sidewalk terrace with its al fresco dining. The tourist menu here costs 600 pesetas ($5.76).

Those on a shoestring should head to **Las Fuentecitas, Marcado,** inside the Ceuta market. There are no frills in this *económico,* just a half dozen tables, rotating fans in summer, and simple home-cooking. The tab for a four-course meal comes to 550 pesetas ($5.28).

Should you be overnighting in Ceuta and want to dance a bit, you can head for the **Whisky à Gogo,** a disco at 13 General Yague. Drinks average 400 pesetas ($3.56).

Once you've seen the little there is to see in Ceuta, you can take the bus to Tetuan. Buses leave every hour from the Paso de Colón, starting at 6 a.m. and running till 10 p.m. The cost is only 60 pesetas (58¢).

3. Tetuan

Until April of 1956, Tetuan was part of the Spanish Protectorate in North Africa. Thus, the Spanish influence, even today, is still stronger than the French. This is true not only as regards the language spoken, but also in respect to a more integrated city. For example, residents fairly well shun the "native" and "European" quarter concepts. Although there is a small medina, the two cultures blend easily in what might, in many respects, be called a Spanish city, characterized by fountains and balconied houses in the Andalusian style.

GETTING THERE: Tetuan lies 24 miles south of the Spanish enclave of Ceuta, a short drive by car or bus. Coming from Ceuta, the road to Tetuan skirts what has been called the Moroccan Costa del Sol, a long stretch of Mediterranean beach which, till now, has only been slightly built up. In the background you can see the Rif mountains.

The Moroccan buses leaving the Bab Sebta, the border station between Ceuta and Morocco, cost 8 DH ($1.31) per person. The CTM first-class buses leave Ceuta at 9:30 p.m. and get into Tetuan at 10:30 p.m. From Tetuan to Ceuta, they leave at 4:15 p.m. There are also numerous second-class buses.

THE SIGHTS: Tetuan is still a walled city for most of its perimeter, and numerous turrets and crenellated ramparts can be seen from its former fortifications as well as seven large gates.

The **Medina** is great for exploration. It is entered through the city gates and filled with 17 gleaming white mosques (entrance forbidden to foreigners). It's characterized by its *souks,* narrow, arched passageways, and little shops. Tinsmiths, silk merchants, tanners, and others ply their age-old trades. On market days, the Medina teems with the people from the Rif mountains, who wear red-striped *foutahs* and *esparto* hats with blue tassels.

Other main sights include the **Royal Palace,** open every morning from 10 a.m. to 1:30 p.m., charging a 5 DH (82¢) entrance fee. On the Place Hassan II, it dates from the 17th century, but was completely restored in 1948. It's an example of the Hispano-Moorish style of architecture, and its old walls witnessed the nightly rituals of the caliphs.

The **Archeological Museum** is also interesting. It's open daily, except Tuesday, from 9 a.m. to noon and from 3 to 6 p.m., charging 5 DH (82¢) for admission. It contains exhibits found at two ancient Roman cities of North Africa, Lixus and Tamuda. Bronzes, pottery, and mosaics make for good viewing. Of the latter, the most outstanding is the *Three Graces of Lixus*.

BEACHES: The closest beach to Tetuan is the one at **Martil** (formerly known as Rio Martin), eight miles away. By car, you can take the road toward Ceuta for less than a mile, then turn right to Martil, which is Tetuan's port. The beach is about 6½ miles long and has restaurants and cafés (the latter don't serve alcoholic beverages, however). There are also bus services. Check at your hotel or at the Tourist Office in Tetuan at 30 Calle Mohammed V.

LOW-COST HOTELS: About the best all-around economy hotel is the **National,** 8 Boulevard Mohammed Torrés (tel. 32-90). It has a restaurant and a bar, and is well kept. Most of its rooms contain private baths. Accommodations cost anywhere from 55 DH ($9.02) to 70 DH ($11.47) per person for the lodgings with bath. Half board for one person sharing a double room is 110 DH ($18.03).

Those on a tighter budget might try the **Régina,** 8 Calle Sidi Mandri (tel. 21-13). It has 86 rooms, only three of which contain complete private baths, but 17 of them offer showers. It provides only minimum comfort, and its rates are as follows: only 26 DH ($4.26) in a bathless single, 34 DH ($5.57) in a bathless double. Doubles with showers (no toilets) cost 40 DH ($6.56) and peak at 48 DH ($7.87) with a complete bath. A continental breakfast is included.

For those wanting to overnight in style, I'd suggest the **Dersa,** 8 Boulevard General Franco (tel. 34-90), which has 75 rooms, 50 of them with bath. All have phones, incidentally. Even though this is the best hotel in town, it is still modest. However, it has more facilities than the abovementioned choices, including a restaurant, bar, and nightclub. Half board in a room for two costs 185 DH ($30.32) per person.

BUDGET DINING: **Zarhun,** 7 Mohammed Torrés (tel. 66-61), is about your best bet if you want a typically Moroccan meal. Decorated in the traditional Moorish style, it offers a complete tourist meal for 38 DH ($6.23).

The **Italiano,** 8 Mohammed Torrés, is right next door and specializes in Italian and French dishes. English is spoken, and you can get a meal for about 28 DH ($4.59). At this Italian restaurant, owned by the National, you can get a tremendous bowl of soup, all you can eat, for 21 DH ($3.44), a complete meal in itself with lots of fresh crusty bread.

4. Chaouen

"The most idyllic spot we found in a week of traveling about Morocco (by rented car) was the town of Chaouen, nestled among the Rif mountains, about 160 kilometers (about two hours by excellent highway) from Tangier (about 85 kilometers from Tetuan). Chaouen is one of those beautiful white towns tucked right at the base of three magnificent mountain peaks. The air is clean and crystal clear, and the panoramas are spectacular.

"In town is a fine three-story establishment called **Hotel Chaouen,** Plaza del Maghzen (tel. 6324), formerly a government parador but now a part of the Maroc Tourist chain. We paid 80 DH ($13.11) for a fine double room with shower. Breakfast was 9 DH ($1.48) per person (the unusual wheaty croissants were still warm from the village baker's), while a four-course dinner was 42 DH ($6.88). When we awoke in the morning, we opened our shutters to find a mountain right outside our window and a terrace and swimming pool beneath.

"The ancient town fortress has been converted into a lovely, strollable Jardin Municipal—admission 2 DH (33¢)—with the omnipresent Rif as a striking backdrop to the palms and the brilliant tropical flowers. It was a joy to get up in the morning, stroll through the streets as the town gradually came to life, and then purchase the day's supply of fruits and Sidi Harazem for our journey. The finest moments, however, are in the evening, after dinner, when you can step out of the hotel and listen to the muezzin finish his call for evening prayer. Then, as the final tones of his voice are fading, a lone flute begins a serene melody. A second flute, then a third also begin, playing together or in counterpoint to each other. And as you walk through the streets, the shops now closing and the people going to prayer and then home to eat, and listen to the mournful sounds of the flutes before they drift off into the surrounding mountains, it is possible to feel closer to Morocco than during any other part of your trip" (Charles E. Colson, Oak Brook, Illinois).

5. Rabat

As the capital of Morocco, Rabat is the primary home of King Hassan II, who maintains elaborate palaces in the other Imperial Cities as well. Founded in the 12th century, and once known as the Camp of Victory, Rabat today is essentially a modern city of gardens and monumental gateways. The third-largest city in Morocco, it lies on the Atlantic coast, 57 miles northeast of Casablanca. It is separated by the Bou Regreg from its sister city, **Salé**, on the opposite bank.

THE SIGHTS: Most visits begin at the **Quadias Casbah.** The Casbah, surrounded by a wall with bastions, is reached by a splendid gateway (*bab*) constructed in the reign of Yacoub El Mansour (1185-1199). The gate leads to the inner garden, designed in 1915 and richly planted with orange trees. Bougainvillea drape the walls, and storks find places for their nests on the battlements. After a stroll through the gardens, the visitor can stop off at the **Moorish Café,** with its belvedere overlooking the city of Salé on the opposite side of the river. Coffee or the traditional mint tea are available, but you may find the pastries too sweet.

Installed in the gardens is the **Museum of Oudaïa** (tel. 261-64), housed in a small palace built in the 17th century during the reign of Moulay Ismail. Various Rabat carpets are exhibited in the old oratory chamber. After seeing them, you pass into a patio with a pond. Moroccan musical instruments are displayed in the loggia. One salon is devoted to jewelry, including gold pieces and silver filigree. Decorated in the traditional Moroccan style, another salon is complete with brocaded divans, antique Rabat carpets on the floor, a finely chiseled copper incense burner, as well as sculptured cedar chests and embroidered cushions. Perhaps the section devoted to costumes, such as Rif dress, is the most interesting. One tableau depicts a Berber wedding ceremony; others show the dress of the natives who live in the High Atlas. Hours are daily except Tuesday from 10 a.m. to 3 p.m.

The Tower of Hassan rises over the ruins of a large mosque; the 144-foot tower was originally its minaret. The minaret, incidentally, was built to rival the Giralda in Seville. Construction started in 1184 on orders from Yacoub El

Mansour, who wantéd a mosque big enough to shelter his entire army. Work stopped upon the death of the sultan. At many points in its sad decline, the mosque was used as a quarry for building materials. Finally, the 1755 earthquake that struck Lisbon did further damage. A ramp climbs to the pinnacle, from which you can look out over the rooftops of Salé. At the eastern end of the grounds is the constantly guarded memorial and mausoleum of Mohammed V, who died in 1961. He was the father of the present king, Hassan II, and was instrumental in liberating Morocco from Spanish and French rule.

The **Medina** has been likened to that of an Andalusian town. In fact, many Muslims driven from Spain did settle in the Medina, erecting the Andalusian wall in the 17th century. The Old Town was built between this wall and the Almohad walls from the 12th century. Here the life holds forth in *souk* after *souk*. You may want to purchase a Rabat carpet, the craftsmanship enjoying world fame. The Medina is mainly for strolling and shopping, as it holds few monuments of interest. At the old wool market, the Place Souq el Ghezel, you could, in the 16th century, purchase a Christian slave—real cheap! At one time foreign emissaries were obliged to live on the rue des Consuls; but that requirement has long ago been dispensed with. This street leads to the Place du Mellah. Branching off from here are the houses and shops of the **Mellah,** or Jewish quarter.

The **Mechouar** is the enclosure that contains the royal palace where King Hassan II and his family live. Nearby are the barracks of the "Black Guard," descendants of West African slaves. The best time to visit is on a Friday when it is announced that the king will pray at Ahl-Fes Mosque across the vast courtyard. The crowds form as early as 10 a.m., although the ceremony doesn't get under way until after 12 o'clock.

It begins with a parade by the Royal Guard in their brilliant scarlet uniforms (white in summer). Afterward, infantrymen station themselves at key positions along the route the king will follow. Then Hassan II appears, dressed entirely in white, and riding in a gilded coach. However, after he has said his prayers, he rides back to the palace mounted on a white horse with gold shoes on its feet. If the sun is hot, a parasol will shade the king from its rays. It is an impressive ceremony which seems strange because of Hassan II's reputation as a modern monarch. But tradition is respected.

The **Museum of Antiquities** (Musée Archéologique), on Zankat al Brihi, contains the celebrated Roman bronzes from the archeological diggings at Volubilis. The best known perhaps are the busts of Juba II and Cato of Utica, housed in a special oval-shaped rotunda, along with other finds which include the Ephebe Couronne (young man with ivy crown), the "barking dog of Volubilis," and minor bronzes. Other salons display a reproduction of a geometrical mosaic floor from Volubilis and the statue of Ptolemy, son of Juba II and Cleopatra Selenea. The main entrance and first floor contain many displays of Roman life and crafts of ancient Morocco, as well as artifacts from prehistoric periods. Admission is free; closed Tuesday.

Outside the city walls, **Chellah** was the last Roman city (Sala Colonia) to go up on the Atlantic coast. Next to Rabat on the Bou Regreg estuary, it lies in ruins today. Once non-Moslems weren't allowed through the gateway, but in this more democratic day they can pass. The gateway, richly decorated, was begun by Abou Said (1310–1331) and completed by his son, Abou El Hassan, in 1339. Inside the walls you can see the marble tombs of the former sultan and an inner courtyard of a sanctuary, as well as a mosaic-decorated minaret crowned by a stork's nest. The remains of a Roman bath and two ancient villas have been discovered. The rest of the former necropolis is planted with gardens; and a path leads down to a spring. It's a serene oasis on a hot afternoon.

WHERE TO STAY: Hôtel Shéhèrazade, 21 rue de Tunis (tel. 222-26), was built in 1972 in a modern architectural design, with vertical zigzag bay windows on the front, allowing extra bedroom space and views up and down the avenue. For such a superior hotel, the prices are moderate: 84 DH ($13.77) in a single with bath, 110 DH ($18.03) in a double with bath, these tariffs including a continental breakfast. A person can take half board for an extra 45 DH ($7.38) per day. The entire hotel is tastefully conceived and furnished; the lounge, bar, and dining room have a subtle Moroccan theme, and there is an attractive rear courtyard.

Hotel Balima, rue Jakarta (tel. 216-71), occupies the bull's-eye position on Rabat's major boulevard, with its better stores and airline agencies. The hotel is a seven-story, semi-modern building, with a lofty lounge containing an abundance of plastic furniture. The 80 bedrooms are comfortable, clean, and serviceable. All have their own bath or shower, toilet, telephone, and view. Singles are 75 DH ($12.29); doubles, 85 DH ($13.93). Add 11 DH ($1.80) for a continental breakfast.

Royal, at 1 rue Hamman (tel. 211-71), is a modernized 67-room hotel in a new section of Rabat. Trailing wisteria and what may be the tallest palm tree in Rabat greet you at the entrance. The rooms are immaculately kept and sensibly priced. Doubles with full bath are 90 DH ($14.75), 75 DH ($12.29) if occupied by one person. It's another 11 DH ($1.80) if you want a continental breakfast, which is the only meal served. The Royal is convenient—a block from the Boulevard Mohammed V, about four from the railway station.

Nouvel Hotel, 1 rue d'Asti (tel. 610-55), is one of the newest of the small hotels, just a block or so from the Boulevard Mohammed V. It is crisply clean, with a marble entry, a modest little lounge and reception area, and an elevator. The range of prices is based on the various types of plumbing in the room. A twin-bedded room with bath and toilet is 80 DH ($13.11); a double with shower, 70 DH ($11.47). A group of economy rooms, with hot and cold running water and shower (use of corridor toilet), rent for 55 DH ($9.02) for two persons, 45 DH ($7.38) for one. A continental breakfast is an additional 9 DH ($1.48).

Grand Hotel, 19 rue Patrice Lumumba (tel. 272-85), is a well-located little hotel (opposite the tourist bureau) in a good section of town. The elevator leads to 60 fair-size and comfortable bedrooms. Twin-bedded rooms with bath cost 60 DH ($9.83), 38 DH ($6.23) with hot and cold running water only. The Grand has central heating and a garage.

The Hotel Splendid, 8 rue/Zankat Ghazzah (tel. 232-83), lies two blocks east of the intersection of Avenue Hassan II and Boulevard Mohammed V. The hotel is often frequented by members of the American Peace Corps, and the staff speaks some English. A simple room with no toilet or bath, but with a wash basin, rents for 30 DH ($4.92) per person nightly. The rooms are clean and spacious, and there's a lovely garden where guests gather. Showers are an extra 3 DH (49¢).

Terminus, 388 Avenue Mohammed V (tel. 230-90), occupies the upper floors of an older, nonelevator hotel right next to the railway station. The lounge is modest, and so are the rooms—but all is safely clean. Three persons will pay 105 DH ($17.21) for a room with private bath, 92 DH ($15.08) with shower, and 72 DH ($11.80) with sink. Two persons pay 82 DH ($13.44) with shower, and 70 DH ($11.47) with sink. The tariff for one person, for a room with private bath and toilet, is 68 DH ($11.15). A continental breakfast and taxes are included.

Hotel Central, Al Basra (tel. 221-31), provides basic accommodations in an excellent section. The reception area is nil; but the rooms are fairly clean and comfortable, a good buy if you're really watching those dirhams. The price for two persons in a twin-bedded room with bath is only 70 DH ($11.47), 40 DH ($6.56) in a room with hot and cold running water only. You'll be charged an additional 5 DH (82¢) for use of a shower. A continental breakfast is another 10 DH ($1.64).

WHERE TO EAT: **Pizza Restaurant Italia,** Place Mohammed V, is a huge rotunda building, with a bar to the right as you enter. Across from the railway station, it is in the very bull's-eye center of Rabat. Pizzas begin at 10 DH ($1.64), and pasta specialties include cannelloni at 14 DH ($2.30) and spaghetti with fruits of the sea at 17 DH ($2.79). A popular main course is the osso bucco of Lombardy at 24 DH ($3.93). A good beginning is the onion soup, 10 DH ($1.64). Closed Monday.

The **Koutoubia,** 10 Zankat Pierre Parent (tel. 601-25), is for Moroccan specialties. It's in the traditional style, with colored glass and booths. The restaurant features such dishes as couscous and tajine with onions and raisins. A good opening is the Moroccan soup. Specialties include chiche kabbat in the Tunisian style and a brochette of lamb. The Koutoubia is among the finest in its field, yet reasonably priced. Expect to spend from 60 DH ($9.83) for a complete meal. Your host, Bennani-Ahmed, doesn't speak English but is most gracious and considerate.

Jour et Nuit, Place Bremond, is open day and night. Three dining rooms provide both table and counter service. Yet many visitors prefer a table in the courtyard, opposite the Jardins Triangle de Vue. If you're visiting for lunch, you may enjoy the ham omelet, preceded by a bowl of vegetable soup. For dessert, dare you try a Moroccan banana split? Featured throughout the day are such reliables as hamburgers, steak sandwiches, and spaghetti bolognese. Most of the plates here range in price from 12 DH ($1.97) to 20 DH ($3.28). If you want to order a complete meal, expect to pay from 25 DH ($4.10) to 40 DH ($6.56). The place attracts a clientele of well-heeled Europeanized Moroccans.

Those with a yen for Chinese cookery can try the **Hong Kong,** 361 Boulevard Mohammed V, where a sharkfin soup goes for 14 DH ($2.30), and most standard entrees are 15 DH ($2.46) to 30 DH ($4.92). After ascending a steep flight of stairs, you will be greeted by a simple Chinese decor. Some tables have a view of the street.

If you want to go really native, continue down Mohammed V, cross Hassan II, to the *souk* entrance where you will come upon the **Doghmi** at no. 313, with a tourist menu for only 20 DH ($3.28) that'll include harira, soup, or hors d'oeuvres, then steak, chicken, or couscous, plus rice, french fries, or spaghetti. Finish with fruit, flan, or yogurt. You can sit outdoors, where a half dozen tables have been placed on the sidewalk. Inside the place looks like a French café.

More fastidious native-goers will prefer **El Bahia,** Avenue Hassan II (tel. 345-05), around the corner from the Doghmi, which has a dozen gaily decorated tables along the sidewalk, up against the old walls of the Medina. A plate of the day goes for 20 DH ($3.28), and Moroccan specialties are featured beginning at 14 DH ($2.30). There is a pleasant patio with more tables and sunshades; a fountain in the center with goldfish; ivy-covered walls; plus more tables inside the buildings as well as upstairs. You enter the patio through two huge doors with great nails and a heavy knocker.

The **Café de la Paix,** 1 Avenue Moulay Youssef, opposite the railroad station, offers a tourist menu for 24 DH ($3.93) that might feature a soup, hors d'oeuvres, or a small pizza; then roast chicken, grilled lamb, or a steak. You finish with flan, yogurt, or a half grapefruit. This is a no-frills place, with a Parisian-type, glass-enclosed terrace, and a very simple restaurant upstairs, containing about 40 tables, a wooden-planked floor, wallpapered walls, and a view of the street below.

Competing is the adjacent **Restaurant Français**, Avenue Moulay Youssef, with a tourist menu for 28 DH ($4.59) offering similar fare. Nine tables are placed outdoors for al fresco dining. Other tables are reached by passing under a bower of trelliswork into a kind of cabaña, or you can go into the café section, where more tables and bentwood chairs accommodate hungry diners. Napkins are placed fan-like in the glasses, and a slowly turning ceiling fan provides some breezes for those torrid nights. The terrace in front of the café, by the way, is enclosed by potted bushes.

Even cheaper is the **Milk Bar**, 465 Mohammed V (tel. 208-15), also opposite the railroad station, with a menu for only 20 DH ($3.28), including hors d'oeuvres or tuna fish, rice salad, then hake with carrots, plus a fruit cup. You can have lamb instead of fish. If you don't order from the tourist menu here, expect to spend from 28 DH ($4.59) to 40 DH ($6.56) for a complete meal. A French-type terrace with ten tables is outside.

READER'S RESTAURANT SELECTION: "From the Grand Hotel, walk for two blocks in the general direction of Place Mohammed V. In an arcade at 23 bis Avenue Allal Ben Abdallah is the **Café Restaurant Saadi** (tel. 310-28). It is a small restaurant which offers a choice of some 18 different tajines, plus a selection of other dishes, including very good onion soup. Soup, tajines, and wine for two (leaving absolutely no space for dessert) costs 75 DH ($12.29). We dined there on three successive nights, and all the food was excellent" (Mrs. H. Chadim, Curtin, Australia).

AN EXCURSION TO SALÉ: Salé is the sister city of Rabat, lying on the opposite side of the Bou Regreg river. Once famed as a pirates' nest, in the 17th century it flourished as a center of the corsairs, much to the horror of the French and English fleets. Robinson Crusoe, you may recall, was captured by the "Salee rovers."

In the Middle Ages, it became known as a merchant port and entrepôt of the west coast of Africa. The town is believed to date from the 11th century, although the Merinides built the encircling ramparts in the centuries to follow. The Merinides were also responsible for the **Bab Mrisa,** the former entrance to the harbor. The 13th-century gateway leads to the **Mellah** or Jewish quarter.

The Merinides are further credited with the **Medersa of Abou Al Hassan,** a college built in 1341 by the "Black Sultan." It is across from the **Great Mosque,** which dates from the 12th century (you can observe it only from the outside). If you're traveling with a guide (highly recommended), ask him to point out the **Fondouk Askour,** a 14th-century hospice noted for its gateway, and the most prized monument of Salé, the **Tomb of Sidi Abdallah Ben Hassoun,** the city's patron saint. It is characterized by its curious dome and its galleries in many colors. These are but some of the monuments that have earned Salé the reputation as a "city of sanctuaries."

Of course, most of your time will be spent walking through the narrow streets and looking at the shops. Salé is known for its matting work, a specialty of the local craftsmen. On the rue Kechachine, you'll find carpenters and stone carvers, and on the rue Haddadine, blacksmiths and brass workers. Many Andalusian Moors, fleeing Spain after the reconquest, settled in Salé, and perhaps for that reason the appearance of the town is often compared to that of a Muslim town in Andalusia before the fall of Granada.

Allow at least half a day for exploring Salé. You'll need that or more. (The best way of reaching Salé is to take a ferry near the Casbah des Oudaïs.)

6. Meknes

Fourth of the Imperial Cities, Meknes is encircled by a triple enclosure of 28 miles of ramparts and bastions. Nine gates with their four-cornered towers pierce these ramparts; minarets stud the cityscape. In spite of its massive, sober look, Meknes is also a city of gardens.

The commercial life, including the hotels and restaurants, is found in the "Nouvelle Ville," but the sights are in the Medina and the **"Ville Imperiale."**

It was the Alaouite sultan, Moulay Ismail, who made Meknes "imperial." During his long 55-year reign, which began in 1672, his extensive building program, often carried out by slaves, earned for Meknes the title of the "Moroccan Versailles."

Traditionally, Meknes has been a bitter rival of Fez, 36 miles to the east. Meknes is serviced by the same train and bus connections from Rabat, some 70 miles away on the coast.

THE SIGHTS: Most tours start at **Bab Mansour,** the city's most interesting gate, begun during the reign of Moulay Ismail and completed by his son and successor, Moulay Abdullah, in 1752. The decorative gate is characterized by an ogival horseshoe-shaped archway. Opposite the gate sprawls the vast rectangular square (about 650 feet in length, 330 feet in width), the **Place El-Hedim.** It is bordered by the Bab Mansour gateway and one called **Bab Djama En-Nouar,** smaller and dating from the 18th century. If you're driving, incidentally, you can leave your car here (tip the attendant).

At the far end of the square stands **Dar Jamal,** a palace constructed by the vizier Djamai during the reign of Moulay Hassan (1873–1894). It has been turned into a museum of Moroccan handicrafts, although it has served many functions in its day—once a military hospital, also a harem. Passing through the handsome courtyard, you proceed through one ornamental salon after another, observing the handicrafts, including such items as antique Meknes embroidery and old Berber silver jewelry. The reception room is furnished in the classic Moroccan style. Copies of the Koran on display date from the 17th century. The admission is free, but you're expected to tip the guide, as always. Closed Tuesday.

From the Dar Jamal, walk down the rue Sekkakine, with its mélange of jewelry shops and hardware merchants, to the gateway of **Bab Berrima.** This leads to the **Mosque of Bab Berrima,** built during the reign of Sidi Mohammed Ben Abdullah (1757–1790). The mosque forms a corner of the Berrima quarter, which used to be the Casbah. The quarter is surrounded by a high four-cornered wall, and is separated from the **Mellah,** the former Jewish quarter, by another wall. The Mellah is inhabited mainly by Muslims today, following a mass exodus to Israel of most of its Jewish inhabitants after Morocco was granted independence in 1956.

The **Medina of Meknes** is not special, nothing like Fez. But it is, nevertheless, a bustling center of activity—especially in the Berbers' rug-making section. While in the Medina you may want to visit the **Medersa Bou Inania,** a college whose construction was launched during the reign of the Merinide sultan, Abou El-Hassan (1331–1350). Note especially the bronze door and intricate carving. If you stand in the courtyard, with its large ablution basin, and look up, you'll see where the students were lodged. Another medersa worth seeing is the **Filala,** which was built during the reign of Moulay Ismail near the Great Mosque.

The Imperial City

This quarter, entered through the Bab Mansour, was almost completely the work of Moulay Ismail. (It's best, by the way, to tour the city by car, getting out at specific points.) Much of what remains of the Ville Imperiale is in ruins, including the palace of the former sultan, **Dar Kebira.** Now hardly more than a shell, the palace, dating from 1697, at one time comprised nearly two dozen buildings. By passing through the Bab Filala, you reach the **Koubbet El-Khiyatine,** a pavilion where Moulay Ismail used to receive foreign ambassadors.

At the opposite side of the Place Lalla Aouda stands the **Mausoleum of Moulay Ismail.** This is the only mosque in Morocco that a non-Muslim can visit, and even then you can't go in to see the actual tomb. However, you enter a main courtyard and that in turn is followed by yet another smaller courtyard (it's imperative to remove your shoes in this one).

From the mausoleum, you can walk across the grounds to a music school. There a guide will take you down some steep steps nearby to an old **Christian prison**—severe, damp, spooky. Hopefully, you won't get lost in these catacombs and will emerge before the thick door at the top of the steps is locked.

Passing on through the **Bab Er-Rih** ("Gateway of the Wind"), you reach the **Dar el Makhzen,** the imperial palace where King Hassan II stays whenever he is in town. Nearby are the **Gardens of the Sultanas,** with ornamental ponds and fountains as well as an arboretum.

Other sights of the Imperial City include the **Borj El-Ma** ("The Bastion of Water"), the **Casbah of Hedrache** (formerly a barracks) and the **Heri** (storehouse). The latter monument was really a granary, with large vaulted underground silos (the storerooms were above). From the Heri, a lane leads to the **Dar el Beida,** an 18th-century fortress, now a military academy. Nearby is an **Ostrich Farm,** also dating from the 18th century.

Beyond, you arrive in the **Jbabra section** to visit the **Roua,** the great stables of Moulay Ismail, said to have sheltered 12,000 horses and mules at one time. In ruins and exposed to the sky, these vast chambers are foreboding in their immensity. The former stables are enclosed by walls and divided by arches. A palace, now gone, had been built over the stables, and contained nearly two dozen pavilions. The barracks of the king's Black Guard were here as well. The descendants of these former slaves are reputed to form King Hassan II's bodyguard today. Nearby, some 50,000 slaves once dug out a pleasure lake which serves as a reservoir and comprises nearly ten acres.

WHERE TO STAY: Hotel Rif, 10 Zankat Accra (tel. 225-91), is a leader in Meknes in the first-class field. The accommodations are excellent, with most opening onto the inner courtyard with its swimming pool. The bedrooms are well designed, with many built-ins. Singles go for 110 DH ($18.03); doubles, 125 DH ($20.49). A continental breakfast is an additional 12 DH ($1.97). The entire hotel has a sophisticated decor, the use of chalk white effectively offset by bold colors. There's one color to a floor. The graciously appointed dining room overlooks the courtyard, making meals pleasant. An afternoon sit-down mint tea is recommended in the Moroccan-style salon. In the evening, there's belly dancing and dancing to records in the lower-level nightclub, where drinks go for 30 DH ($4.92) and up. A recent improvement is a rooftop sunbathing terrace with a bar.

Hotel de Nice, 10 Zankat Accra (tel. 203-18), is a small, semi-modern hotel, which was refurbished in 1974 and now features a restaurant and a "New York" bar. Owned by the Rif, recommended above, it offers well-maintained and fairly comfortable bedrooms, 33 in all, 30 of which contain baths. Doubles with full bath cost 80 DH ($13.11) for two, 62 DH ($10.16) for one. Add 8 DH ($1.31) for a continental breakfast. Service and taxes are included. This hotel is excellent value.

Palace, rue du Ghana (tel. 223-88), is a fairly modern, three-floor (no elevator) hotel in "downtown" Meknes. You'll find neon lighting and plastic furnishings; however, the bedrooms are compact and scoured daily—and the rates are not bad. The cheapest room for two persons is 68 DH ($11.15); the same room is 55 DH ($9.02) for a single. These accommodations include a shower and hot and cold running water, but you have to use the corridor toilet. A double with a full bath at the Palace is 76 DH ($12.46) for two, 68 DH ($11.15) for one. The simple breakfast is 10 DH ($1.64), and rates include service and taxes.

Majestic, 19 Avenue Mohammed V (tel. 220-25), is owned and managed by a zealous collector of memorabilia and handicrafts from all parts of Morocco. His hobby is displayed on the walls and ceilings of the reception lounge and in the corridors. A traditional Moroccan-style tea salon has been installed, but the general decor leaves much to be desired. Some of the bathrooms are utterly simple, the showers merely showerheads and the drain in the corner of the bathroom. Doubles with bath and toilet are 68 DH ($11.15), 58 DH ($9.51) without toilet but with a shower. The cheapest bathless doubles are 50 DH ($8.20), and singles are 40 DH ($6.56). A continental breakfast costs 9 DH ($1.48). Not glamorous perhaps, but the Majestic is clean and cheap.

WHERE TO EAT: La Hacienda, Route des Fez-Meknes, is a country-style inn about two miles outside of Meknes on the road to Fez (signs point the way through a woodland). It's ideal for long, leisurely luncheons or dinners in a holiday atmosphere. A large rustic dining room and buildings are built hacienda-style around a swimming pool (use of the pool is 12 DH—$1.97). Inside it's more rustic—rough plaster walls, a beamed ceiling, straw lanterns, brass sheep horns and farm tools. The menu offers many French dishes, such as a dozen escargots or the potage du jour. Main dishes include entrecôte with anchovies and hamburger, the latter a fine luncheon choice on a hot day. Finish with a basket of fruit. Expect to spend from 35 DH ($5.74) to 55 DH ($9.02) for a complete meal.

Guillaume Tell, Avenue des F.A.R. in the New Town, is a big brasserie. Sidewalk café tables, enclosed behind glass, are out front. The cuisine is primarily French, with some Moroccan dishes. On the à la carte menu, where a complete meal costs from 28 DH ($4.59) to 50 DH ($8.20), you might begin with the soup of the day, then follow with roast chicken, or perhaps brochettes of kidney. The chef also prepares a special couscous, although the best bargain is one of the fresh fish plates. For dessert, I'd suggest the crème caramel. Taxes and service are included. Economy tip: Adjoining is a snack counter where you can get sandwiches to go and french fries. The sandwiches are made with french bread. This is one of the best bargain lunches in Meknes. The tourist menu, by the way, costs 28 DH ($4.59) and includes a vegetable soup, lamb chops, french fries, string beans, and a dessert.

Wimpy, 17 Avenue Mohammed V, is a snackbar that serves a mixed grill for 15 DH ($2.46), a cheeseburger for 10 DH ($1.64), a milkshake for 6.50 DH ($1.06), and a Coca-Cola for 4 DH (66¢).

A final choice for more adventurous readers is the **Novelty,** 12 rue de Marseille. It offers a meal for 28 DH ($4.59), which includes a choice of soup or hors d'oeuvres, followed by a main course and dessert. The chef's specialty, couscous, 18 DH ($2.95), is featured on Thursday. The restaurant is on the mezzanine. And there's a bar downstairs heavily patronized by Moroccans. It has a typical North African atmosphere.

READER'S RESTAURANT SUGGESTION: "We found an excellent place to eat, the restaurant called **Café Bar Restaurant Poker D'As,** 4 rue de Paris. The owner is Mohamed El Hamel, a really friendly man. The price for a meal with three courses—soup or salad, meat or fish, vegetables, french fries, bread, and dessert—is 28 DH ($4.59). It is excellent. You can also order a more expensive menu for 38 DH ($6.23) or à la carte. The price is reasonable, the service very good, and the waiters polite. The restaurant is two blocks from the Hotel Rif" (Mrs. Joel Kessler, Bad Windsheim, West Germany).

ONE-DAY EXCURSIONS FROM MEKNES:

Nineteen miles north of Meknes lie the finest Roman ruins in Morocco, **Volubilis,** one of the country's most ancient cities. It's on a windswept plain, reached after passing through some dramatic scenery. During the reign of Juba II (25 B.C.—A.D.23), it became a royal residence and the capital of Mauretania Tingitana. Eventually it was annexed to the Roman Empire. Rome abandoned the colony in 285, and the city drifted along until the appearance of Islam in 684. Again, in the course of time, Volubilis fell into decay. Serious excavations were begun in 1915.

Chances are you may have seen more dramatic ruins than these; but their scope is impressive, nevertheless. Volubilis sprawls over 100 acres encircled by a second-century rampart approximately 1½ miles long.

Guides at the entrance will offer to direct you through the ruins for a fee. You must buy a 3-DH (49¢) admission ticket.

The most notable buildings include the House of Orpheus (named for a large mosaic in the reception room depicting Orpheus at play with a group of animals); the Baths of Galius (the most important ones found in Morocco, although badly decayed); an Arch of Triumph ordered constructed by Silvius Aurelius Sebastianus; the Basilica with two good-size apses; the Forum, from the third century; the House of the Youth, typical of the private villas of that time in that it was built around a patio; the mosaics of the House of the Labors of Hercules; the House of the Beasts, noted for its mosaics of wild animals; and the colonnade of the Palace of Gordius, ranging upward to the Tangier Gate, from which there is a superb panorama of the archeological garden.

For dining in the area, try **Les Corbeilles Fleuries,** Moulay-Idriss Zere-houne (tel. 110-103). Assaid Ahmed El Mernissi offers a complete meal for 42 DH ($6.88). The repast is likely to include varied hors d'oeuvres, followed by "tajine marocain" and the vegetables of the season, plus fresh fruit. Drinks are extra, as is the 12% service charge. The restaurant is open nightly until 10 p.m.

Lying only a short ride from Volubilis is **Moulay-Idriss,** 21 miles from Meknes. It is one of the most venerated sites in Morocco. On two rocky spurs split by a deep gorge is this ancient city, considered sacred because it contains the *zawiya* of Moulay-Idriss, the founder of the Idrisside dynasty, the first Arab dynasty to rule over Morocco. His mausoleum, whose green-tile roof dominates the city, is the site of a colorful yearly pilgrimage—called a *moussem*—in August and September. If you are not of the Islamic world, then the entrance to the mosque is, of course, forbidden. In fact, foreigners at one time were not welcomed in Moulay-Idriss, but happily that state has changed.

Even if Moulay-Idriss were not a holy city, you might still want to visit it just for its dramatic scenery. You pull your car into the market square, where it's easy to secure the services of a guide. He will rarely speak English (except for a few words), but you should consider his services, nevertheless. The reason being that although a walk through the town is of interest, the most moving sights are in the surrounding hills. You'll need help to get you up and down the narrow streets and over the encircling roads (many of which lead to blind alleys). Outside the town, incidentally, are hot springs once used by the Romans.

You may want to conclude your tour by walking through the teeming *souks* of the Medina. The town hasn't quite arrived in the 20th century, although electricity has been installed in some places. As of yet, there is no recommendable hotel or restaurant. If you're hungry, and not fastidious, you can get lamb kebabs grilled over an open charcoal brazier in the marketplace. Regular bus service is run from Meknes.

7. Fez

Fez has been called "the most complete example of Oriental civilization." It is three cities in one: the pearl-gray rampart-enclosed ancient town, **Fes El Bali,** is on the right bank; the "New Fez," **Fes El Jedid,** is on the left. Then there is an even newer town, the European quarter founded in 1916 three miles west of the Medina. It is called **Fez Debibagh,** named after a mosque found there.

Fez is on the north-south caravan route between the Sahara and Tangier, 100 miles inland from the Atlantic. It stretches out between low hills, and is crowned by ruins of old fortresses. The most ancient of the Imperial Cities of Morocco, Fez was founded in 808 by Idriss II. It reached the apex of its fame and influence under the Merinides in the 14th century, and its reputation as a seat of learning was renowned throughout Europe.

After Granada fell to Isabella and Ferdinand, Fez became a center for refugees, who brought with them a spectacular knowledge of arts, science, and crafts. Those crafts are still practiced today. In fact, a walk through the Medina of Fes El Bali is like plunging back to the Middle Ages. Fez became known as a "city of mosques" (there are more than 300, including the world-famed Karaouyine, the largest in Africa).

On the banks of the Fez River, an affluent of the Sebou, Fez is best approached by a high road on a hilltop crowned by the Merinid tombs. From that vantage point, the minaret-studded city—best viewed at sunset—spreads before you.

WHERE TO STAY: Hotels are fairly inexpensive in Fez.

The Zalagh, 6 rue Mohammed Diouri (tel. 255-02), is classified as first class by the government, and it is one of the members of the prestigious O.M.C.F. chain that owns the celebrated La Mamounia in Marrakesh and Le Palais Jamai in the Medina at Fez. Yet the Zalagh charges reasonable prices. You pay 125 DH ($20.49) for a double room with complete bath, 85 DH ($13.93) in a single with bath. French windows open onto your own balcony, where you can enjoy the view and have a breakfast of coffee and croissants for an extra 15 DH ($2.46). All of the bedrooms contain private baths, but only the public rooms are air-conditioned. There is, however, a swimming pool surrounded by a flagstone terrace. Meals are a Moroccan event here, and the dining room decor is sumptuous.

Splendid, 9 Avenue Mohammed V, rue no. 2 (tel. 221-48). The intimate lounge is Scandinavian, with original artwork. White is used throughout the bedrooms, relieved by vibrant colors. The bedrooms have style, and open onto a tiny courtyard garden where you can order drinks at one of the patio tables. Prices depend on the plumbing you choose. Singles are 42 DH ($6.88) with hot and cold running water. Double rooms range from 68 DH ($11.15) to 80 DH ($13.11), the latter with twin beds and private bath. A continental breakfast is an extra 11 DH ($1.80). The Splendid is in the center of the New Town, overlooking a square. A French and Moroccan restaurant is on the premises.

Le Grand, Boulevard Chefchaouini (tel. 255-11), is contemporary and traditionally Moroccan at the same time. It offers 100 rooms with a wide range of plumbing. The best bargain is a double-bedded room with hot and cold running water and a shower for 70 DH ($11.47) for two, 60 DH ($9.83) for one. Doubles with complete baths, either tubs or showers, are 105 DH ($17.21). The more expensive singles, with complete bath, cost 75 DH ($12.29). The furnishings are comfortable, if not always new, and most of the rooms are spacious. All of the public rooms are air-conditioned, as are five of the bedrooms. A continental breakfast is an extra 12 DH ($1.97), and an English one—ham and eggs—is 21 DH ($3.44). If you stay a minimum of three days, you can get half board prices, but you must ask for these when registering. Le Grand's nightclub is previewed later.

Hotel Volubillis, Avenue Allal Ben Abdellah (tel. 230-97), is like a resort hotel in Palm Springs. Two floors of air-conditioned private units and public rooms open onto a large garden with swimming pool, palms, and flowering bushes. It's chic and at the same time informal living, with emphasis on the relaxed life. The room decor is severe, yet attractive, with warm wall colors and good modern furniture as well as picture-window doors leading out onto private terraces. All rooms have complete private baths. The rate is 140 DH ($22.95) in a double, 110 DH ($18.03) in a single. Both include breakfast. Most dining room tables have a view of the garden, and you can order a complete luncheon here for a high 48 DH ($7.87). The hotel also has a bar and snackbar. At night a disco opens and plays the latest international records. There's no cover charge, just the price of your drinks.

READER'S HOTEL SELECTION: "**Grand Hotel de la Paix,** 44 Avenue Hassan II (tel. 250-72), stands not far from the main post office. A double with bathroom and breakfast costs 65 DH ($10.65). Parking in front of the hotel is ample, but tip the attendant and he will guard your car well. The hotel's restaurant, Le Nautilus, is a pleasant, good place for eating, serving excellent Moroccan tajines, a dish not to be missed" (Mrs. H. Chadim, Curtin, Australia).

WHERE TO EAT: Fez is poor in restaurants, with some notable exceptions previewed below. Most visitors dine in their hotel, taking the half-board plan (a room with breakfast and one main meal, usually dinner).

The best all-around budget restaurant is **À La Tour d'Argent,** 30 Avenue Es-Slaoui, a far cry from its celebrated namesake in Paris, but fine in its own right. Its special attraction is its three-course menu for 42 DH ($6.88). Recently I enjoyed a selection of hors d'oeuvres, followed by sauteed rabbit with potatoes and string beans. The cooking is essentially French. You can dine outside at the sidewalk tables if the weather's right. A popular bar adjoins.

In this New Town section is **Es Saada,** 42 Avenue Es-Slaoui (tel. 236-81). A busy, bustling café is up front, the restaurant in back. It offers such Moroccan specialties as tajine, couscous, and steak for 24 DH ($3.93), each main dish served with a large choice of vegetables. The chef also prepares a mishoui, that is a whole roast animal, most often a sheep, and you're invited to have a big plate with accompaniments for 25 DH ($4.10). The owner is extremely nice and speaks some English.

Splurge Restaurants

Dar Saada, 21 rue Attarine (tel. 333-43), is an experience. First of all, it is a modest sightseeing event, a former private home with salons opening onto a small three-floor-high courtyard. As it's right in the Medina, it's hard to find, but worth the search. Guides will be only too willing to show you there. This petit palais is rich in architectural detail, with its tile mosaics, cedarwood carvings, arched doors, and niches (once it housed a harem). Dar Saada—whose English nickname is "The Happy House"—is now used as a showroom of locally produced carpets, both old and modern, large and small, which can be shipped, and antiques, including all sorts of unusual objects. The owner, M. Bousfiha, has installed a typical restaurant on the top floor, which serves regional dishes in true sultan fashion. Specialties priced from 32 DH ($5.25) to 40 DH ($6.56) are worth trying: chicken cooked with olives, lemons, or almonds; pastilla (pigeon pie); mechoui (oven-baken lamb); and kebab. A corbeille of fresh fruit finishes off the meal, or you may prefer the cornes de gazelles with mint tea. In fact, you can just drop in for tea and pastries during your shopping expedition through the Medina.

Pavillon el Anmbra, Laraichi, 27 bis Route d'Immouzer (tel. 251-77), is for super-splurgers only, but it's a totally Moroccan experience that's worth the price. It draws upon the styles of the 14th century and is richly decorated with many antiques and handicrafts. In spacious surroundings, you dine on low sofas, with all the Aladdin-lamp trappings. For a complete meal, including two Moroccan specialties, such as pigeon pie, figure about 70 DH ($11.47). Called bsteelah, the pie is the supreme glory of Moroccan cuisine: a crisp crusted pie cooked in butter with a filling of pigeon meat, eggs, almond paste, sugar, and cinnamon. I'm also fond of the chicken with olives, lemons, and almonds. This price includes mineral water, fresh fruit, ice cream and mint tea, as well as service. All dishes are à la carte. For a lighter meal you can order a specially prepared Moroccan main dish such as couscous for 28 DH ($4.59). The oven-baked lamb, the keftas (skewered meat), and tajine (meat and vegetables simmered in earthenware dishes) are recommended. The restaurant serves lunch daily from noon to 3 p.m., dinner from 7 to 10 p.m.

L'Adour Restaurant, 9 Avenue Mohammed V, rue no. 2 (tel. 221-48), part of the Splendid Hotel, is your best bet for French cooking in the New Town. However, you pay 40 DH ($6.56) for a complete meal, but that includes tax and service. I recently enjoyed some tempting hors d'oeuvres, followed by the Moroccan dish, tajine, and a selection of fruit for that price. At lunch try the spaghetti bolognese or an omelet. The sole meunière is also fine. Most Moroccan dishes, such as couscous, cost from 32 DH ($5.25). If you order à la carte, your order may go as high as 65 DH ($10.65). L'Adour is a good safe bet for those who've had too much local color.

READERS' RESTAURANT SUGGESTIONS: "Le Normandie, in Le Grand Hotel, Boulevard Chefchaouni (tel. 255-11), has got to be one of the finest French restaurants in all Morocco. A three-course meal costs 38 DH ($6.23), but far exceeds the quality of any other place we tried in town" (Nick Chickering, Nevada City, Calif.). . . . "A delightful, tiny restaurant 100 yards from the Hotel Splendid is the **Sandwich Rialto,** approximately 23 Boulevard Mohammed V, rue 2 (I could find no number on the building). You get generous portions. A two-dish meal costs 15 DH ($2.46), a four-courser 18 DH ($2.95), tax and service included. The waiter/cook permitted a substitution on the soup course, when I asked for harira since it was Ramadan, the time for fasting. It must have pleased him, because he not only gave me the harira but offered a complimentary tray of dates and confections. The food was nicely prepared. The menu has expanded to include couscous Fassi at 13 DH ($2.13) and a Moroccan tajine at 10 DH ($1.64). Couple this with friendly service and you have a hit. I would recommend this place highly even if the prices were doubled" (Bonnie Emrick, Elmhurst, Ill.).

FEZ NIGHTLIFE: Not much. Your best bet is **Night Club Oriental,** Le Grand Hotel, Boulevard Chefchaouni (tel. 255-11), which features a nightly cabaret—complete with Moroccan folkloric presentations and disco dancing—for 35 DH ($5.74), including your first drink. The show starts at 10:30 p.m.

EXPLORING FES EL BALI: In the ancient city, or Medina, you'll find the greatest collection of palaces, mosques, *souks,* national monuments, and *medrassa* (former schools or colleges, now relatively abandoned). If you venture deep into the Medina, you may never return. Not that you'll be so enraptured by it, although that's a likely possibility. Rather, you may never find your way out. A guide is absolutely essential, even for those who pride themselves on getting around Moroccan cities without hired help.

The streets, a labyrinthine maze of alleyways, are extremely narrow. The houses rise high, blocking sight of the sun. Inside, the buildings are often dark, musty, even gloomy, especially so in winter. Yet many of the buildings, in spite of their unprepossessing facades, conceal private courtyards and sumptuously decorated salons.

Aside from the historical monuments outlined below, take time to observe the everyday life—by far the most enduring attraction of the Medina. For example, women make the dough for their bread at home, then take it to the baker who pops it in his ancient oven. Except for the mosques and private homes, you can wander past almost any door and watch the craftsmen practice their age-old secrets.

Throughout the Medina is a maze-like serpentine collection of *souks,* with hustlers trying to lure you inside. The teeming crowds rub shoulders as they make their way through, giving way only to the heavily laden donkeys, the "taxis" of Fez, which stubbornly knock you down with the load jutting out from their backs if you don't get out of the way. Each craft has its section. Thus you'll find the weavers, the goldsmiths, the spice merchants, the dyers, the bookbinders, the coppersmiths, even the barbers, huddled near each other and, needless to say, madly competitive.

You won't need a guide to take you to the **Tanners' Quarter.** Just follow your nose. In one of the most serious recommendations in this guide, I suggest you buy a sprig of mint from one of the many vendors in the alleyways before venturing into this grotesquerie of medieval horror. You're taken first through the section of vats where the animal hides are treated by scantily clothed men, the stench from the slain beasts rising to greet you. You proceed to a terrace where you can look down at the many-hued dyes resting in vats in which the treated hides are submerged. Thrilling, most certainly. But you won't want to linger.

In the Andalusian Quarter, you'll find the **Quartier des Potiers** (potters). As you approach the sector, and if you don't already have a hired guide, you'll receive countless offers from young boys to show you through for a fee. The potters practice their craft with consummate skill, most of the workers trained by their fathers who in turn were trained by their fathers, ad infinitum.

The quarter takes its name from the **Mosque of the Andalusians** (no admission to non-Muslims) built for the refugees from Córdoba and dating from the ninth century, although the present structure is mainly from the 13th century. You can't go inside, but can admire the restored porch roof over the north doorway.

The Medina is traditionally entered through the **Bab Boujeloud,** actually two gates, the newer one built in 1913. You come first to the **Dar Batha,** a 19th-century palace turned into the **Museum of Moroccan Art and Handicrafts.** It is in the Hispano-Moorish style of architecture, and can be visited daily except Tuesday from 9 a.m. till sunset. There is no admission, but tip the guide.

Inside are collections of embroidery, tapestries, pottery, ceramics, manuscripts, wool carpets, funereal art, jewelry, leatherwork. The Moorish garden is especially attractive.

From the palace, you can make your way to the **Bou Inania Medersa,** a former college complex dating from the 14th century and a fine example of Merinid architecture. Note the mosaic-covered walls, the carved plaster, and the elaborate cedarwood friezes. Its pentroof is superbly decorated as well; and its courtyard is paved with onyx and pink and white marble. Upstairs are the rooms that housed the former students. The so-called clock, perhaps a former carillon, is a curiosity. Men only are admitted to the Hall of Ablutions. Finally, staircases lead to the Mosque of the Dead. It is open daily except Friday morning.

Another college to be visited is the **Attarine Medersa,** on the rue de Souq el-Attarine, which is even older than the Bou Inania. It is also a smaller complex and in some ways more graceful. It, too, dates from the 14th century, 1325 to be exact. If you climb to the terrace, you'll enjoy a view of the monumental **Karaouyine Mosque,** founded in the ninth century and still the largest in North Africa, with its 270 columns and 16 naves. It literally dominates the Medina. Of course, non-Muslims are forbidden to enter; but nobody stops you if you walk around, peering into the many doorways.

A short walk from the Karaouyine Mosque and you're at **Nejjarine Square,** one of the most delightful spots in the city. The plaza is known for its mosaic fountain. The much-photographed **Nejjarine Fondouk** has an entrance surmounted by a handsome pentroof. A *fondouk,* incidentally, was a caravansary or stable that also offered lodgings to men in its upstairs rooms. This one dates from the 18th century. From this point, you can venture into the Nejjarine *souk,* with its compelling odors of thuya and cedarwood worked by cabinetmakers. Continuing on, the ancient **Kissaria** just isn't what it used to be, as the fabric market was destroyed by fire. But the animation and the flamboyantly colored fabrics—many with gold embroidery—are still there. Hopefully, you'll get to see an auction.

Near the Nejjarine Fondouk is the **Zawiya of Moulay Idriss,** a sanctuary dedicated to the founder of Fez. It is a much revered sight, sacred to Moroccans, and visitors are asked to respect that. Wooden beams bar the streets leading to it, marking the limit of the so-called *horm* or holy asylum. You definitely cannot go inside the sanctuary. In fact, you're advised not to get too close to the *horm* limit.

In our final round-up of the sights of Fes el Bali, make sure your guide has taken you to the **Seffarin Medersa,** the oldest in Fez, dating from 1255. It is near the sector where the coppersmiths ply their trade, on the Place Seffarine.

The **Cherratine Medersa,** from 1670, is the largest in Fez. It does not have the interest that the Merinid medrassa possess; note the bronze-faced doors, however, on the rue Cherratine.

Incidentally, all of the medrassa, unless they are being restored, are open daily except Friday morning. Always tip the guide in charge.

Finally, the **Tetuani Fondouk** was named to commemorate its past function—a way station to serve the merchants and their camels who came down from Tetuan. See especially its delicately carved wood ceiling from the 14th century. The goods and camels were kept downstairs, the beds placed in cramped quarters above.

Crossing through the **Bou-Jeloud Gardens,** you leave Fes al Bali, and enter.

FES EL JEDID: Less colorful, but interesting nevertheless, the so-called New Town contains the **Dar el Makhzen,** the imperial palace complex where King Hassan II stays when he is in town. The palace, its grounds, and adjoining buildings occupy nearly 200 acres.

The **Mellah,** the old Jewish quarter, lies in this sector, enclosed behind its own walls. It dates from the early 14th century, and today this former ghetto has far fewer Jews than Muslims; however, some of the most fascinating shops are run by Jewish goldsmiths. In addition to a Jewish cemetery, there are a few synagogues in the Mellah as well. Unlike the mosques, the synagogues can be visited (see especially the Serfati and the Fassiin or Fasyne or Fasiyin—take your own choice of spelling).

Perhaps what will interest you most about Fes el Jedid is the **Old Mechaouar** courtyard, which is surrounded by high walls. On an afternoon, jugglers, fortune tellers, soothsayers, acrobats, and dancers entertain, although this spectacle has lost many adherents over the years and is a pale imitation of the show staged at the Place Djemaa El Fna at Marrakesh.

Also in this district is the Great Mosque, founded in 1276, and the **Mosque of Moulay Abdallah,** surrounded by an interesting quarter of the same name.

THE CORNICHE ROUTE: Before the sun sets, strike out by car for the **Route du Tour des Fes,** a corniche highway above the town which encircles Fez for about ten miles. If you stop for drinks on the terrace of the Merinides Hotel, you can enjoy a view not only of the Old Town but the Sebou River, Mount Senhadia, and east to the Atlas range as well.

You might also want to stop over at the badly deteriorated **Merinid necropolis,** on El Kolla hill. Most of the tombs of the sultans date from the 14th century.

Housed in a small fort nearby is an **Armory Museum** containing a collection of weapons from around the world, including Spain, Iran, Tunisia, Japan, France, Turkey, and Senegal. Even prehistoric weapons and American-made Colts and automatic pistols are displayed. Note especially the 16th-century Milanese armor and the 15th-century Moroccan cannons. Admission is free, but tip the guide.

EXCURSIONS FROM FEZ: Fez is the hub of an excursion wheel, its spokes branching out in all directions. The most popular day's jaunt—to the Roman ruins of **Volubilis** and the **Sanctuary of Moulay-Idriss**—is described in the Meknes section. But there are many other sights.

Heading east from Fez, on the road to Taza that ultimately leads to Algeria, after 11 miles you come to a turnoff on the right marked **Sidi Harazem**. Although it was known to the Romans, this resort oasis has only recently been developed, and is one of the leading spa centers of Morocco.

Once the storks perched on top of the mud houses and the Berbers had Sidi Harazem pretty much to themselves. Nowadays, an influx of spa-loving Germans and off-the-record Algerians is pouring in. Can other Europeans, and eventually Americans, be far behind?

The hot (93 degrees) artesian springs at the spa are said to cure everything from kidney stones to gout. The bottled Sidi Harazem natural mineral water remains the most popular drink with meals in Morocco. Incidentally, near the springs is a prehistoric stone circle of 26 monoliths, the Stonehenge of Morocco.

Those wanting to escape the stiffling heat of Fez in summer often book a room here at the following:

The **Hotel Sidi-Harazem,** in Sidi Harazem (tel. Sidi Harazem 455–22), is an ingeniously conceived resort hotel—part of the spa complex and centering on an array of mineral water swimming pools and baths, as well as spacious gardens. It's a combination of an up-to-date hotel and first-rate spa facility. Yet the price is quite reasonable: 95 DH ($15.57) for a single, 120 DH ($19.67) for a double, both with private baths. You pay another 20 DH ($3.28) for a continental breakfast and 45 DH ($7.38) for a complete, many-course luncheon or dinner.

Our final excursion from Fez is to **Azrou,** south of the city on the road to Marrakesh. Passing through interesting countryside, you arrive first at the Berber village of **Immouzer du-Khandar** (alt. 4400 feet; 21 miles from Fez). It sits on a rocky plateau overlooking the Sebou plain in a setting of mountains, pine forests, and several fine fishing lakes. It appears that sleepy Immouzer du-Khandar will one day become an improtant mountain resort.

Adjoining the hillside marketplace is a series of caves inhabited by Berbers. For a few dirhams the dwellers will show you the inside of their primitive homes.

Hotel Royal, Avenue Mohammed V, Immouzer du-Khandar (tel. 630-80), is a village inn, right in the town center. It's a third-class hotel, modest in scope, with a dining room opening onto a pond and garden. There is no lounge to speak of—only a large bar and a dining room, presided over by Madame Fontanive. Most visitors stop by for a meal of gargantuan portions. If you just "leave it to the chef," chances are you'll have everything from hors d'oeuvres to freshly caught fish fried in butter, followed by a meat course, cheese, dessert, and coffee, all for 58 DH ($9.51). You can dine for less, of course.

The upstairs bedrooms are immaculate. One person pays 52 DH ($8.52) for a room; two, 62 DH ($10.16); three, 72 DH ($11.80). Add 12 DH ($1.97) for a continental breakfast. Rooms contain showers and hot and cold running water, but no toilet. A double with complete bath costs 68 DH ($11.15).

The king maintains a handsome and stately chalet here, by the way (you can't miss seeing it, as well as the villa across the way where he houses overflow guests).

You next arrive at the fashionable little summer resort and winter sports center of **Ifrane,** 37 miles from Fez. At an altitude of 5250 feet, its setting is idyllic, in the center of a wooded plateau of oak and cedar. The climate, especially the air, is invigorating. Seven miles from Ifrane is the **Tizi-n-Tretten** pass, which is snowcovered for most of the year. Skiers are attracted to its slopes, especially to the sports resort of **Mischliffen,** with its ski lifts and marked courses.

But back to the main road. From Ifrane, the highway cuts across the cedar forest to our final destination, **Azrou,** "The Rock." (Bus connections are possible from Fez.) Azrou lies 11 miles from Ifrane. The town is at an altitude of some 4000 feet, and is noted for its handicrafts, especially its cedarwood carvings and Beni M'Guild carpets. In the center of Azrou is a handicrafts cooperative where on any day of the week, except Friday, you can see women at the looms making the carpets, as well as purchase a selection of the cedarwood carvings in an adjoining aisle. The 17th-century Casbah here, built by Moulay Ismael, is also interesting but run-down.

For food and/or lodgings, try the **Hotel du Panorama,** Azrou (tel. 20-10), an all-purpose mountain lodge, open all year to attract travelers who either want to escape the summer heat or ski in winter. In spring or fall, fishermen show up. It's in the center of town, set on the rise of a hill. Madame Duffal, a Frenchwoman, runs everything well, seeing to it that the large tavern bar, the dining room, and the bedrooms are well kept. Most of the accommodations contain private balconies opening onto the panoramic views—hence, the name of the hotel. The price of rooms for two with hot and cold running water is 55 DH ($9.02), 75 DH ($12.29) with a complete bath. A continental breakfast is an extra 11 DH ($1.80). An average meal, including service charge, costs 37 DH ($6.06). You pay extra for your wine. Pension is required on national holidays.

A convenient, inexpensive stopping-off place for those driving from Tangier to Fez is the pleasant, European-style town of **Souk el Arba,** where you'll find the **Grand Hotel** (tel. 20-20) renting out one of its ten very simple, but clean, rooms for 38 DH ($6.23) for a bathless double. A continental breakfast is an extra 9 DH ($1.48). The hotel also has a pleasant outdoor café where a 28-DH ($4.59) meal will provide you hors d'oeuvres, a fish dish, sauté of beef, french fries, and dessert.

8. Marrakesh

The red city of Marrakesh is a palm-treed oasis at the threshold of the Sahara. Second oldest of the imperial cities, Marrakesh (famed for its red ochre color) was founded by the Almoravids in the 11th century. Today it is the capital of Southern Morocco, and as such is a jewel of the Islamic world. Its chief monument is its Koutoubia Mosque, built by the Almohads with a characteristic minaret that dominates the cityscape.

Some have called Marrakesh the most mysterious town in all of Africa. Here you'll be far removed from the Mediterranean—Tangier and Casablanca may look toward Europe, but Marrakesh is deeply rooted in Africa.

It is at its best in winter, when snow covers the peaks of the Atlas Mountains in the background. For years, it was known as a winter playground of the rich (Winston Churchill used to be a frequent visitor, spending many hours painting the date palms and mountains). In winter, the temperature averages around 68 degrees Fahrenheit; but in July and August, midday temperatures of 110 degrees are frequent. Of course, the heat is dry, and the high temperatures seemingly don't deter the huge influx of visitors during the summer. Winter remains the best time to visit.

GETTING THERE: Royal Air Maroc and British Airways fly from London, and both Royal Air Maroc and Air France leave from Paris several times weekly. If you're visiting Gibraltar, you can fly BA to Marrakesh. Royal Air Inter Lines connects Marrakesh to most major Moroccan towns; and the air-conditioned Moroccan railways maintain daily service from Casablanca, 150 miles away. The least expensive and most uncomfortable way is to go by bus, which connects Marrakesh with Tangier, Fez, Rabat, and Casablanca.

WHERE TO STAY: Marrakesh offers some of the best hotel bargains in North Africa. Many of the hotels are new, complete with air conditioning and swimming pools. If you're willing to settle for fewer extras, you can live quite reasonably at a good standard in Marrakesh.

Hotel des Almoravides, Arset Djenan Lakhdar (tel. 251-42), gets a four-star A rating from the government. It was built in 1972. It has its own garden and swimming pool, with its pert umbrella tables where you can order poolside refreshments. More than half of the 105 modern, streamlined bedrooms overlook this garden, and also have a view of the minarets (you'll hear the wailing prayers five times a day). All of the rooms are air-conditioned, and have dressing rooms and full bath. Sliding glass doors open onto private balconies. Single travelers pay 105 DH ($17.21); couples, 135 DH ($22.13)—including tax and service. A continental breakfast is another 16 DH ($2.62). Half board is compulsory, a set lunch or dinner going for 51 DH ($8.36). The general atmosphere is plush, and you'll find an American bar which emphasizes comfort and style.

Hotel Toubkal, Zankar Haroun El Rachid (tel. 329-72), is an attractive, fully air-conditioned place near the ramparts of the Old Town. It boasts an inspiring view of the Atlas range. The Toubkal is built of local orchre-colored stone in a palm grove near the Casino, with enough space for a good-size garden and a handsome swimming pool. The rate is 120 DH ($19.67) for two persons, 95 DH ($15.57) for one, including tax and service. Bedrooms have private baths. For half board, the charge is 155 DH ($25.41) for one, 270 DH ($44.25) for two. Guests gather in the intimate bar or around the pool for drinks, and take their meals in a Scandinavian-inspired dining room. It's one of the best all-around bets for value in Marrakesh.

Hotel de la Menara, Avenue des Remparts (tel. 329-77), is a modern Moroccan-style hotel offering a surprising amount of style and comfort for your dirhams. Its bedrooms have good-size balconies overlooking a palm-studded garden and courtyard. Vines climb the balconies, water bubbles up in the sunken fountain, and guests splash in the swimming pool. Rooms are spacious, and all have baths. A double or twin-bedded room is 155 DH ($25.41), including a continental breakfast, service, and taxes. A set lunch or dinner costs 65 DH ($10.65). The hotel is a ten-minute stroll from the Old Town.

Chems, Avenue Homane el Fetouaki (tel. 238-70), is in a fashionable newer section of town, yet within an easy walk of the Medina and Djemaa El Fna. When you swim in the magnificent pool of the hotel garden, you can see the towers of the Koutoubia. This 140-room hotel was built in 1972 amid a grove of orange trees. For such good accommodations, the rates are low: 125 DH ($20.49) in a double with either private bath or shower, 94 DH ($15.41) in a single. On half board, two pay 215 DH ($35.24). Rates include taxes, service and a continental breakfast. Popular and enjoyable are the cocktail lounge, the garden, the solarium, and a disco.

El Maghreb, Avenue des Remparts (tel. 309-99), is an older Moroccan-style hotel in a residential section midway between the Medina and the New Town. It combines many architectural features characteristic of the country—in fact, its elaborately carved entry doorway is almost mosque-like. Two lounges are also decorated in the traditional manner, as is the main dining room and particularly the salon devoted to serving authentic Moroccan meals (on request). The bedrooms, each with private bath (some with showers), carry out the same Moroccan theme; regrettably, none is air-conditioned. The half-board charge is 120 DH ($19.67) in a single, 110 DH ($18.03) per person in a double. Emphasis is on the relaxed life in the garden, with its swimming pool.

Hotel de la Renaissance, Avenue Mohammed V (tel. 312-33), is like a small commercial hotel. It boasts no seductive garden nor swimming pool, but it does offer good-size rooms, more than adequate, but not air-conditioned. Including service and taxes, as well as a continental breakfast and fully equipped private baths, singles go from 85 DH ($13.93), doubles from 110 DH ($18.03) to 115 DH ($18.85). Half board is 125 DH ($20.49) per person. The hotel is noted for its bar-restaurant, "La Mirador," that has a fine terrace that provides a panoramic view of the Atlas range.

Grand Hotel Tazi, 2 Bab Agnaou (tel. 221-52), supplies good accommodations in a somewhat nondescript part of town, within walking distance of the Place Djemaa El Fna. It is a modest, two-story 50-room establishment, with public rooms decorated in Moorish style. The bar especially captures this atmosphere. Guests enjoy the sun around the swimming pool or else relax on garden furniture on the roof terrace. A single with private bath goes for 55 DH ($9.02) to 60 DH ($9.83), a double with bath for 85 DH ($13.93). Two persons pay 145 DH ($23.77) for half board.

l'Hotel Excelsior, rue Tarik Ibn Ziyad (tel. 317-33), is a home away from home for French expatriates. The 36-room hotel is run by the industrious and gracious Mme Kempf. Prices are charged according to plumbing; more expensive rooms have tub baths, others showers. Singles range from 57 DH ($9.34) to 60 DH ($9.83), doubles from 75 DH ($12.29) to 80 DH ($13.11). Taxes, service, and continental breakfast are included. Some triple rooms go from 97 DH ($15.90) to 105 DH ($17.21). The bedrooms are rather homelike, with coordinated fabric at the windows and on the beds, as well as Moroccan rugs and decorative artifacts. Breakfast is served in the Moorish-style lounge, nicely tiled and decorated.

Hotel des Ambassadeurs, 2 Avenue Mohammed V (tel. 300-07), is an oasis. It's the domain of a sweet-smiling, white-haired Frenchwoman, Martha Lamon. She has made her hotel homey, and it attracts many repeat guests. The bedrooms are simple and comfortable; many have small terraces with abundant green plants, a pleasant setting for breakfast. The bedrooms with terraces cost 75 DH ($12.29) to 95 DH ($15.57) for two, 62 DH ($10.16) to 75 DH ($12.29) for one. A few rooms with a bath or shower (hallway toilet) cost 85 DH ($13.93) for two and 78 DH ($12.78) for one person. The budget-stretching hot-and-cold-running-water rooms go for 55 DH ($9.02) for two, 45 DH ($7.38) for one. Service and taxes are included; a continental breakfast is an additional 11 DH ($1.80).

Hotel Koutoubia, 51 Boulevard El Mansour Eddahbi (tel. 309-21), in Gueliz, looks more like a private villa with its formal salmon-colored facade and entry. Although the bar is rather plastic, the dining room is Moroccan. At the side of the hotel is a swimming pool. The least expensive singles have showers but no toilets and cost 58 DH ($9.51). You'll pay 68 DH ($11.15) for a single with bath. Doubles range from 68 DH ($11.15) to 90 DH ($14.75), the latter with a complete bath. Service and taxes are included. A continental breakfast is 12 DH ($1.97). The half-board rate is 88 DH ($14.42) in a single, 150 DH ($24.59) for two.

For Low Budgets

Hotel du Haouz, Avenue Hassan II (tel. 319-89), is a respectable, neat hotel on a tree-lined street in the New Town where you can bed down for a few dirhams nightly. It is an immaculately kept walk-up hotel, offering central heating in winter, but no air conditioning in summer. The 30 bedrooms are fairly comfortable, roomy, and decently furnished. It's 75 DH ($12.29) in a double with private bath; singles with bath go for 52 DH ($8.52).

CTM Hotel, Place Djemaa El Fna (tel. 223-25), is a haven for backpackers who want a prime position on the main square. The CTM is on the second floor, and offers small rooms opening onto a courtyard. A few of the quite adequate rooms have private baths (these are preferable, as the corridor toilets are the squat type). A single with full bath rents for 50 DH ($8.20); with shower, for 47 DH ($7.70). Doubles are at 65 DH ($10.65) with private bath, 55 DH ($9.02) with shower, 48 DH ($7.87) with hot and cold running water. *Note:* There must be the tiniest single room in all the world here, with a sink and narrow bed, renting for only 28 DH ($4.59). The best bargains are the triples, with running water, at 80 DH ($13.11). A continental breakfast, costing 9 DH ($1.48), is served on the roof terrace where there's a view of the marketplace.

WHERE TO EAT: After dark, the most adventurous of our readers will head for the **Djemaa El Fna** for dinner. If you're interested in native food, you'll find it here . . . and how! You won't come across restaurants, but open-air stands where each chef is noted for a different specialty. At one, tiny fish will be deep-frying; at another a young boy will be cooking chunks of lamb on a charcoal brazier; then there are the large bowls of food, both salads and spicy dishes. You sit at benches and place your order with the main cook. Everything is accompanied by the round loaves of barley bread. Of course, you pay for what you eat, but you can get a big plate for a low 9 DH ($1.48). Frankly, many people are horrified at the sanitation conditions here; others have practically banqueted here and never felt better. If you're not fastidious, then plunge in.

If you like your restaurant with a roof over it, then try the curiously named **Iceberg,** Avenue El Mouahidine, near the Koutoubia (tel. 229-51), a café-restaurant proud of its "salle climatisée." Upstairs, the Iceberg is a small café with a few sidewalk tables; downstairs is the large basement restaurant. It specializes in Moroccan dishes and features mint tea with sweet pastries. Best bet is the five-course meal for 35 DH ($5.74). Considering its quality and scope, I consider this the best value in Marrakesh. For example, I recently enjoyed a selection of hors d'oeuvres, followed by an omelet, then leg of lamb, potatoes, and dessert (cheese, flan, or strawberries in season). Lemon chicken is a specialty. English is spoken by the affable, engaging owner, Aldoui My Driss. If you're planning to return to his restaurant, he'll often suggest a special dinner for you, which he insists you eat Moroccan style—that is, with your fingers. Perhaps it'll be his large and tasty tajine, a dish made with lamb and cooked with olives and fresh hearts of artichoke in a savory sauce.

The **Café Restaurant Oriental,** 33 rue Bab Agnaou, is a fairly safe bet in the Medina. And the price is right. For just 18 DH ($2.95) you can enjoy the traditional Moroccan chicken with lemon, along with a salad and dessert. It's about one block from the Djemaa El Fna, and offers two plain dining rooms. A specialty is couscous chicken at 18 DH ($2.95), but on a hot summer day you may prefer a simple omelet at 10 DH ($1.64). Tajine lamb at 15 DH ($2.46) is also popular. Incidentally, you can order at least ten kinds of fresh-fruit milkshakes at 6 DH (98¢), definitely not the type they make at Whelan's. Expect to spend from 18 DH ($2.95) to 35 DH ($5.74) for a complete meal.

Another little starvation oasis in the Medina is the **Restaurant Des Amis,** which translates itself as "The Friendly Restaurant." It also translates its menu into English, as most of its clientele are young Americans and Canadians. It lies right off the Djemaa El Fna, at 2 Riad Zitoun Kedim. (To reach Des Amis, go through the gate next to the bus station.) Provided you don't expect too much, you can get a three-course meal for 21 DH ($3.44). Roast chicken or couscous is usually the main dish.

Al Moutamid, Avenue Mohammed V, is another Gueliz possibility. For just 31 DH ($5.08), I recently enjoyed a four-course meal that began with hors d'oeuvres, followed with a Spanish omelet, then a pepper steak, and was topped off by a fruit salad. Not bad at all. Usually a dozen tables are placed outside; adjoining is a café where you can order an apéritif.

Splurge Restaurants

If you're willing to spend more dirhams, you can get your best fixed-price meal at **La Taverne,** a French restaurant in the New Town at 23 Boulevard Mohammed Zerktouni (tel. 310-35). Not only is it the most preferred of the French restaurants, far surpassing the quality of the more expensive Le Jacaranda nearby, but it features an attractive garden setting as well. The interior, however, is cold and impersonal. For 48 DH ($7.87), not including 12% service and tax, you'll be presented with a five-course meal. To begin with, you're given a salade niçoise, ravioli, or cold tongue, then steak or chicken, and dessert. If you don't want to eat so much, you can sample à la carte Moroccan specialties which begin at 18 DH ($2.95), and French dishes with prices starting at 14 DH ($2.30). The menu is large, the service good, and the cuisine well prepared.

A good place for splurgers to sample Moroccan specialties is at the **Restaurant de Foucauld,** next to a hotel of the same name at rue El Mouahidine, near the Koutoubia and Djemaa El Fna (tel. 254-99). Each day at either lunch or dinner, you're given a range of at least 14 typically Moroccan dishes, including pigeons stuffed with almonds or poulet with prunes. Should you prefer the set meal to the à la carte offerings, you'll be presented with a four-course dinner for 38 DH ($6.23). A good French dish in season is the roast rabbit (lapin) with mustard sauce. For an à la carte repast, expect to spend from 21 DH ($3.44) to 50 DH ($8.20). The restaurant, naturally, is Moroccan-style, a quiet and shady spot on a hot summer day.

For a really super-splurge meal in the Medina, head for **Gharnata,** 5 Derb El Arsa (tel. 252-16). In a palatial setting, seated on low sofas, you are entertained by folkloric groups while you dine on authentic Moroccan dishes. Have you hotel call to make sure you tie in your visit with one of the presentations. A local soup makes an excellent beginning, followed by one of the typical dishes, such as chicken with lemon, pigeon pie, and pigeon filled with almonds. Most of the local specialties range in price from 12 DH ($1.97) to 38 DH ($6.23). If featured, order milk of almonds, a nectar worthy of the gods. Moroccan pastries and a mint tea round out your repast. Service and tax are extra. A guide hired by the restaurant usually waits for visitors in a nearby square, and he'll direct you to the right restaurant. Otherwise, you'll never find it.

Le Zagora, La Palmeraie, Route de Casablanca, 5½ miles from Marrakesh (tel. Koudiat 1). This one's a flying carpet introduction to Moroccan folklore. A hacienda-style complex of buildings has been erected on a plot of ground in the Palm Grove. You can dine here in the true Moroccan fashion, or come out in the afternoon for mint tea and a swim in the pool. Most visitors, however, show up when one of the folklore shows is staged. You have your exotic meal under a large tent outside while watching a "fantasia" of a spectacle in which men in flowing robes with sabers perform on horseback. Belly dancing and traditional folk music follow. Call in advance; shows usually start at 7:30 p.m., sometimes at 2:30 p.m. There are six different Moroccan meals offered, ranging from 70 DH ($11.47) to 100 DH ($16.39). In the afternoon, mint tea and pastries are served. A small bus picks up guests from the major hotels (ask your concierge). Reservations are made through Zagora Voyages, 49 Avenue Mohammed V (tel. 322-70). This outfit, which owns the Zagora, also operates a similar establishment, the **Ksar El Hamra**, Riad Zitoun in Marrakesh, which charges 60 DH ($9.83) for a basic Moroccan meal and a folkloric show.

Sidewalk Cafés

One of the most popular pastimes in Marrakesh is sitting and sipping at a sidewalk café. The most interesting panorama unfolds at the pretentiously named **Café de France**, right on the heartbeat Djemaa El Fna. The café is utterly simple, but not the action taking place on the stage in front of it. A coffee costs only 3.50 DH (57¢), probably the cheapest entertainment in the city.

In Gueliz, seek out the **Brasserie des Negociants**, 11 Avenue Mohammed V, which is right in the hub. Should you wish to spread a rumor around Marrakesh quickly, then launch it here. As you sit sipping a coffee at 3 DH (49¢) or a Coke at 4 DH (66¢), at least ten boys will offer to shine your shoes. Often the same ones will approach you two or three times, just in case you should change your mind.

READER'S RESTAURANT SUGGESTION: "A few doors from the Café Oriental is the **Cafeteria Snack La Baraka**, 28 rue Bab Agnaou, in the Medina. It's nice looking, having about 18 tables with soft leather chairs. The tourist menu offered 16 choices for 24 DH ($3.93). We had a light meal of cheese omelet, and famous Moroccan lemon chicken. Both were cooked to perfection. Most dishes are priced from 10 DH ($1.64) to 20 DH ($3.28). The manager allowed us lots of time to relax over strong, delicious coffee while we talked to some native Berber college students" (Bonnie Emrick, Elmhurst, Ill.).

THE SIGHTS: The peculiar charm of Marrakesh certainly isn't reflected in the dull New Town, **Gueliz**, which was founded in 1913 about 1½ miles west of the Medina. Unlike the old town, Gueliz is characterized by wide boulevards. Despite its lack of charm, you'll spend much time in this quarter, as the majority of the hotels and restaurants are here. Life in Marrakesh really centers on . . .

Djemaa El Fna

The largest *souk* in Morocco is a world unto itself. Camera-carrying tourists from the Mamounia Hotel and kif-smoking young people rub shoulders with Berber men in town from the Atlas Mountains or wandering tribesmen from the Sahara in their indigo-blue robes. If you go at 2 o'clock on a winter afternoon (4 or 5 o'clock in summer), you'll meet the cast of characters, ranging from acrobats of Amizmiz, monkey trainers, soothsayers, palm readers, trick cyclists, pate-polishing barbers, magicians, jugglers, fellahs (small farmers), flame eaters, lottery sellers, acupuncturists, scribes.

The most characteristic star in this drama is the red-clad water seller, a goatskin sack draped across his back, a necklace of brass cups dangling from his throat. Tinkling his bell in your ear, he makes his way through this mass of humanity. Today he earns more money posing for tourists (give him at least

2 DH or 33¢) than he does selling water from the gold faucet of his goatskin sack.

Everybody in Djemaa El Fna has something to sell, and you are the prime target. The merchandise is varied, ranging from a gigantic brass ant to a live chicken (what the mountain man thinks you're going to do with a live chicken I don't know, unless he suspects Westerners of voodoo).

Snake charmers are here, too. With one eye on a defanged black cobra, another on you, the snake charmer will take the snake from its rush basket, his tongue darting out in rhythm with the snake's. Then he'll put the snake away and rush over to collect a dirham from you as entertainment tax. Only the most mercenary visitor walks away without paying his price. After all, the charmer earns his living from this exhibition—not to mention the money for snake food.

Don't think this square was conceived as a tourist attraction. Its origins lie deep in the traditions of Marrakesh, and if you look hard enough you'll find a circle of Arabs around an ancient man who spins tales straight from a *Thousand and One Nights*.

If Allah is smiling on you during your visit you'll get to see a performance by the black Muslims of Mauritania, who are known for their acrobatic feats and barefoot dancing. Scarlet-colored sashes are slung around their ivory-toned garb, a dramatic sight in movement to the tam-tam.

Although the drama peaks in the afternoon, the square is an experience at any time of the day or night. Many get up at sunrise to see it come alive, listening to the solitary sound of the fluteplayer.

Incidentally, the name of this square is translated roughly as "Rendezvous of the Dead." It must be the worst-named square in Morocco.

READER'S SIGHTSEEING TIP: At Djemaa El Fna, there is a staircase alongside Café de France where, if you buy a 3 DH (49¢) bottle of soda, you can view the entire marketplace from an unobstructed terrace. The panoramic view is great and one is able to see all the entertainment groups in action. I suggest a telephoto lens for good photographs and binoculars for better vision. There you can take all the snapshots you want without someone rushing over to you with the usual demand of 1 DH (16¢) for each entertainment group" (Joseph Montuore, Temple Hills, Md.).

Djemaa El Fna lies in the shadow of . . .

The Koutoubia

Dominating the city, this mosque is graced with a minaret 222 feet high. It was built in the 12th century from pink sandstone from the former quarries at Gueliz. Abd El Moumen started the mosque, and it is said to have been completed by Abdoul Yussef, the second ruler of the Almohad dynasty, who reigned until 1184. The tower is crowned by three decorative gilt balls which, according to legend, were presented by the wife of the sultan Yakout El Mansour, "The Victorious One." The Koutoubia, the "Mosque of the Scribes," is the sister of the Giralda Tower at Seville and the Tower of Hassan at Rabat—both frank imitations. The sides, each one different, are covered with beautiful decorative facing. The Koutoubia was erected on the site of the "Palace of Stone," in which the Almohads lived. All in all, this mosque makes Marrakesh one of the great cities of the Islamic world, and represents a triumph of Moorish architecture. Regrettably for sightseers, non-Muslims are forbidden to enter this most enduring and characteristic monument of Marrakesh.

The Djemaa El Fna provides an excellent gateway to the labyrinthine alleyways of . . .

The Souks of the Medina

After you've learned the ground rules of the market square, you'll be ready to venture into the nearby maze of *souks,* beginning at the northern edge at either the Bab er Robb or Bab Agnaou gateways. Some of the finest craftsmen in Morocco are found on these narrow streets.

Everybody heads for the dyers' *souk,* as it is, naturally, the most colorful (but not on Friday). Hanging on lines strung across the streets are silk and woolen skeins in every hue of the rainbow. Leather workers, bookbinders, shoemakers, brass and copper artisans ply their age-old crafts, the rules changing little from generation to generation. The aromas alone will lure you to the exotic spice section. Fabric is sold in the "Kissarias," and the bright sunlight only enhances the brilliance of the gold embroidery.

Some of the alleyways are covered with latticework, casting slanting shadows on the ground and making everybody and everything zebra-striped. Lopeared donkeys, heavily laden with goods, ply their way through the crowds of locals and foreigners. Merchants try to lure you into their *souks,* tempting you with all sorts of kettles and braziers, wrought-iron lanterns, daggers in silver, camel-hair blankets. Perhaps the rugs will catch your eye—especially those from Chichaoua, with their red backgrounds and geometric designs. Or those from Glaoua with black stripes splashed with color. During your tour of the Medina, you can visit . . .

Medersa Ibn Yussef

This monument was built in the reign of Aboul Hassan, a 14th-century Merinid sultan. The Saadian monarch, Moulay Abou Abdallah, rebuilt it in 1565. The style is traditional, with a quartet of ornately decorative inner facades surrounding a central courtyard. Look for the 11th-century marble basin with its heraldic birds. Until 1956, the medersa was used as a university, filled with medical students who lived in the cell-like rooms upstairs. The monument is open daily, except Friday morning. (Tip the guide.)

The Saadian Tombs

These tombs, built during the reign of the Saadian monarch Ahmed El Dehbi in the 16th century, are elaborately decorated. They contain the remains of all but five of the Saadian rulers. The royal burial ground, in back of the Casbah Mosque, wasn't discovered until 1917. All in all, the necropolis forms the most dramatic architecture in the city, and of the three halls, the most elegant is the Chamber of the 12 Columns. Many of the tombs contain the remains of children. The mausoleum may be visited daily, from 8:30 a.m. to noon and 2:30 to 6 p.m. (free, but tip the guide).

After visiting the tombs, ask your guide to show you the nearby **Mellah,** the old Jewish ghetto of Marrakesh. Jews were housed here ever since the 16th-century orders from the Saadian monarch Moulay Abdallah. Many jewelry shops are found here.

North of the old Mellah lies the . . .

Bahia Palace and Gardens

If King Hassan II isn't putting up a special VIP guest or one of his relatives isn't in town, you can visit this splendidly decorated palace, built between 1894 and 1900. Called "the Brilliant Palace," Bahia is noted for its decoration and its Moorish gardens. Incidentally, these gardens—imbued with the smell of sweet jasmine—are irrigated by water from an artificial lake. In the palace you proceed haphazardly through tiny courtyards and sumptuously decorated salons (the former harem has now given way to a reception room). The hours vary but in summer are from 8:30 a.m. to noon and 2:30 to 6 p.m. (but don't count on that).

Dar Si Said

Now an arts museum and school of handicrafts (tel. 224-64), this second palace was erected at the end of the 19th century by the brother of Ba Ahmed, grand vizier of King Moulay Hassan. You enter via a sweet-smelling patio garden, graced with the sound of chirping birds. The collection is interesting, especially the handicrafts from the High Atlas Mountains. The rugs and capes are exceptional, as is the jewelry. The room of engraved daggers, muskets, and powderhorns evoke old Buster Crabbe movies about the French Foreign Legion. Note also the waterbags of camel skin, the copper and brass work, the Safi and Zagora pottery, even the decorated doors to Berber houses. The admission-free museum (tip the guide) is open daily except Tuesday from 9 a.m. to 12:30 p.m. and 2:30 to 6 p.m.

The **Royal Palace,** where King Hassan II lives when he is in Marrakesh, cannot be visited, but visitors are fond of riding around it in a horsedrawn carriage. It's a huge place, the trip around its high walls about two miles. The palace is known as Dar el-Makhzen.

A Garland of Gardens

Marrakesh is famous for its gardens. The best known is the two-mile long **Aguedal,** a splendid imperial garden laid out by the Almohads in the 12th century. The garden, studded with olive trees, is irrigated by pools. At certain times of the year this oasis has an especially sweet scent. The sultan Moulay Abd Er Rahman is credited with giving Aguedal its present form in the 19th century.

Surrounded by an adobe enclosure, the **Menara Gardens** are about 1200 yards long and 800 yards wide. These gardens of olive trees were originally laid out by the Almohads. In the 19th century, Sultan Abd Er Rahman erected a pavilion which is surrounded by a 12-foot-wide parapet. Apparently, the sultan met his "favorites" here in this tranquil setting.

Yet a third garden is the **Mamounia,** the same gardens in which the deluxe hotel of the same name stands. It is cool and tranquil, dates from the Saadian era, and offers many a shady walk through its orange and olive trees.

Finally, no trip to Marrakesh is complete without a tour of the celebrated **Palm Grove** and a horse-drawn **carriage ride** around the ramparts. Frankly, the cost depends on your negotiations with the driver. But expect to pay from 12 DH ($1.97) to 30 DH ($4.92) for most short jaunts through the Grove, which stretches on for nearly 12 miles. The palm oasis embraces an area of about 30,000 acres; the number of trees is usually reported at 150,000. At some point, you may want to stop off and mount a camel—most short rides cost 4 DH (66¢). Before your visit to the Grove, you can circle the ramparts. Trips usually begin at the **Place de la Liberté,** and last for nearly five miles. This way you'll get to see the interesting gates of Marrakesh. The word for gateway is "Bab," and you'll pass by **Bab Doukkala,** of Almoravid origin, and the especially delightful **Bab Agnaou,** from the 12th century.

MARRAKESH NIGHTLIFE: For a big night on the town, head for the **Casino,** the chicest one in North Africa, set in gardens by the Mamounia Hotel.

You need both 24 DH ($3.93) and your passport before you enter the gaming rooms. Baccarat, blackjack, roulette, and craps get going at 9 every night of the week. Far more interesting—to me at least—is the show downstairs. The budget-bursting dinner costs 140 DH ($22.95), but you can go after dinner and pay 18 DH ($2.95) for a mint tea or 24 DH ($3.93) for milk of the almonds. If you don't order food, 30 DH ($4.92) is added to your bill "for the spectacle," plus tax and a 15% service charge. For that price, you'll be entertained by the usual array of snake charmers, acrobats, and belly dancers.

La Mamounia Discotheque, Mamounia Hotel, Avenue Bab Djedid (tel. 323-81), is the leading disco-nightclub in Marrakesh, providing a colorful backdrop for a sophisticated collection of travelers. Make your way through the sedate coffee drinkers in the lounge to the lower-level club, with its clusters of crystal rods hanging from the ceiling, cozy nooks, velvet-covered chairs, and circular dance floor. Both records and live groups are featured. The price for your first drink, 50 DH ($8.20), includes tax, service, and cover charge.

ONE-DAY EXCURSIONS FROM MARRAKESH: Separating Marrakesh from the Sahara Desert is the Great Atlas Mountain range. You can spend more than a week making excursions from Marrakesh into the Atlas, but few are blessed with such time or money. Unless you have your own car, tours to the Atlas tend to be super-expensive. Several agencies, such as **World Travel Service,** 78 Avenue Hassan II (tel. 312-30), offer infrequent tours to the ski resort of Oukaimeden (cost: 120 DH, or $19.67) or to the Ourika Valley (cost: 100 DH, or $16.39). Ask at your hotel, or call the agency directly.

The jaunt to the **Ourika Valley** is one of the most popular excursions. After leaving Marrakesh, the road is dull, but suddenly you're in the foothills of the Atlas—and the scenery improves.

One of the first Berber villages you come to is called **Dar Caid Ouriki,** noted for its painted minaret. Your final destination for the day is usually the village of **Setti Fatma,** at the end of the valley, a distance of 42 miles from Marrakesh. It is charming in a primitive way, with a nicely decorated earthen *zawiya.*

Of course, many will want to stop over at one of the inns or hotels in the valley for lunch. The first hotel you'll come to is the **Ourika,** Vallée de L'Ourika, Route S513, Arbalou (tel. 04), an unexpected island of sophistication in the foothills of the Atlas, 28 miles southeast of Marrakesh. It's lodged on a ledge above the road that splits the Ourika Valley, and from nearly every bedroom there's a view of the mountain range. A short winding driveway leads past the swimming pool and terrace. The hotel is designed for spacious living. On the lower level is a disco (dancing to records only), open only on Saturday night and holidays. The price of a room includes service and taxes; a single with bath is 90 DH ($14.75); a double, 140 DH ($22.95). A continental breakfast is an additional 15 DH ($2.46); half board (breakfast and lunch or dinner, plus the room) costs 140 DH ($22.95) per person. Even if you can't stay overnight here, you can stop in for a big-splurge lunch—58 DH ($9.51) for a set meal, plus 15% for service and taxes.

An alternate and much less expensive choice farther up the road is **Ramuntcho,** Vallée de L'Ourika, Route S513, Arbalou (tel. 118), a roadside inn on the lower portion of the winding road cutting through the Ourika Valley. The inn, owned by René Dufour, has, for decades, been known for its hearty food and pleasant rooms; its cluttered atmosphere has a peculiar fascination. Overlooking the river is the terrace dining room, partially shaded by orange trees; inside, the atmosphere is that of a country tavern, with rugged stone walls, a raised hearth, and large windows. In spite of his many years in Morocco, Monsieur Dufour is as French as a Parisian bistro. He offers a six-course meal for 50 DH ($8.20), including a wide choice of hors d'oeuvres, a fish or egg dish, followed by eight main choices, such as pastilla (pigeon pie) or tajine (lamb, veal, or chicken cooked with prunes or onions). Then a salad course, followed by a selection from the cheese board, and, finally dessert. Half-board rates are 125 DH ($20.49) per person.

Alternatively, you can branch off the Ourika Valley road to the winter resort of the Atlas, **Oukaimeden**, about 50 miles from Marrakesh. The road to it is paved, but likely to be dangerous for inexperienced drivers. The resort is perched high up at 7742 feet and boasts one of the highest ski lifts in the world (10,498 feet).

A good hotel has been built, the **Imlil** (tel. 591-13), offering 30 rooms with toilets and bidets, another 10 with complete bath, and even more facilities often rented to large families or groups. Room rates range from 135 DH ($22.13) to 149 ($24.42) for two persons per day and this includes full board. There's a 20-DH ($3.28) supplement for single occupancy. The hotel's chef serves a good, well-prepared cuisine, and in the bar guests enjoy a musical ambience. The resort also has a nightclub, Zin Zin, with its salle de cinéma. Ski instruction is available, and all equipment can be rented on the premises.

Another excursion south of Marrakesh is to the Berber village of **Asni**, noted for its Casbah. Many of the city people go there to escape the heat of summer as the town is at an altitude of 4000 feet, surrounded by the highest peaks of the Great Atlas (Mount Toubkal, 13,664 feet, looms behind the village). The view is impressive. Since Asni is 32 miles from Marrakesh, it is easily reached on a morning's excursion. If you're stopping over—either for a meal or overnight—then try:

Grand Hotel du Toubkal, Asni (tel. 03), lies just 30 miles south of Marrakesh on the road to Taroudannt. A resort-style hotel with recreational facilities such as a swimming pool and solarium, it enjoys an enviable position in a gentle valley at the foot of the snow-covered Atlas range. It is spread out, with terrace dining and wide verandas. It's worth the drive from Marrakesh just to sample the food, which includes some Berber specialties. A set meal costs 45 DH ($7.38). After lunch, you can go out back to look at the caged monkeys and wild boar. The lucky few will get to stay over in one of the bedrooms, which are simple, their mood enhanced by Moroccan fabrics and tiles. The half-board rate is 78 DH ($12.78) for one person, 130 DH ($21.31) for two, for rooms without bath. With complete bath, half board is 95 DH ($15.57) for one person, 150 DH ($24.59) for two.

From Asni you can continue southwest on the road to Taroudannt to **Tizi n'Test**, at 6890 feet, one of the most magnificent mountain panoramas in the Atlas, with the Valley of the Sous spread before your feet.

9. The Edge of the Sahara

If you'd like to go on the trail that Marlene Dietrich took when she followed Gary Cooper into the desert in the 1930 version of *Morocco*, then the deep south—south of the Atlas Mountains—is just the place to experience that Foreign Legion–type exotica. Rich in folklore and scenery, this is a land of sand and more sand, with an occasional quiet village surrounded oasis-like with olive groves and orchards. The sky is an incredible intense blue, lighting the red houses that stand baking in the sun.

A few comfortable government-built hotels that represent Saharan-style architecture are found along this trail, but you must always call ahead for a reservation. Names here evoke an *Arabian Nights* fantasy. The heat is dry, although in summer the mercury is likely to hit 107 degrees Fahrenheit.

Marrakesh is the major starting point for people who want to experience this mysterious land, much of which looks unchanged since biblical times (definitely Old Testament). From Marrakesh, you can take a southern route, going first to Ouarzazate and on to Zagora, then heading east to Tinerhir, Er Rachidia (with a detour to Erfoud), before turning north via Midelt and Azrou to Meknes. It's possible to travel by bus along this route, each stage of the journey, from Ouarzazate to Tinerhir, for example, costing 16 DH ($2.62).

After leaving Marrakesh, you come to the—

TIZI N'TICHKA PASS: It can be visited on a day trip. At a peak of 7415 feet, it offers a vast panoramic view of the Atlas. From December to April, the pass can be closed temporarily until snowplows clear it. The road was constructed before World War II. Before that, it took almost two weeks to cross the pass, and travelers were victimized by mountain bandits. From the pass, you can travel to—

TELOUET: This round-trip journey from Tizi n'Tichka is less than 35 miles. The road rises to 5900 feet. Once at Telouet, you'll find one of the most fascinating casbahs in Berber country. Here the Lords of the Atlas, the Glaoui family, reigned supreme until the early years of the 20th century. At the end of the road stands Dar Glaoui, the former residence of the caid. It lies on a hill looking down over the valley. After having a simple lunch in this large village on the south slope of the Atlas range, you can journey back to the pass and return to Marrakesh, having traveled a distance of about 180 miles. Or you can continue south to—

OUARZAZATE: This is a *Beau Geste*-looking town, reached in half a day's journey from Marrakesh. A distance of some 127 miles from "the red city," Ouarzazate is like an oasis of palm trees, appearing after the wasteland of the desert. At the head of two valleys, it lies on a river from which it takes its name. Ouzguita tribesmen can be seen on its hot streets, selling their carpets.

Established in 1928 as a military outpost, earthy-pink Ouarzazate has only a tiny population and is dominated by a fortress sheltering the royal army. About two buses leave every day, one heading north to Marrakesh, another east to Er Rachidia (formerly known as Ksar-es-Souk).

Guides who will immediately attach themselves to you will show you the few sights. One is a small museum of arts and crafts in regional government offices (on the right of the road to Taourirt). You will also be directed to a carpet weavers' cooperative shop where Berber jewelry and stone articles are for sale. About a mile east on the Boumalne road stands the Casbah of Taourirt, a fortress that is a typical example of the Saharan casbah style. Once the pasha of Marrakesh lived here.

The Diafa chain's **Hotel Azghor** (tel. 20-58) stands here, offering 106 beautifully furnished bedrooms, a luxurious swimming pool, and an umbrella-shaded sun terrace. The clay-built hotel was constructed on a hill, overhanging the village which is dominated by its casbahs. From the hotel's precincts you'll have panoramic views in many directions. The Azghor is mercifully air-conditioned, charging 120 DH ($19.67) in a single and 160 DH ($26.22) in a double. A tourist menu is offered for 48 DH ($7.87) in the hotel's elegant dining room which you may be ready to visit after a stopover in the bar. The service and amenities are first class.

In an emergency, serious economizers will consider **La Gazelle** (tel. 088-21-51), a minimum hotel of modest comfort, charging 43 DH ($7.05) in a double with shower and toilet, plus another 8 DH ($1.31) per person for a continental breakfast. You can also order dinner here for 35 DH ($5.74).

TIFOULTOUT: In this pre-Saharan world, you may want luxury if it's available—one last chance to splurge before the desert and those distant oases. If so, I'd recommend a visit to **Hotel Le Zat** (tel. 182), five miles away from Ouarzazate. This deluxe establishment was a nobleman's residence before its conversion into a hotel.

Twenty beautifully furnished rooms, decorated in a typical Moroccan style, are rented at rates that begin at 180 DH ($29.50) in a single, 235 DH ($38.52) in a double. If you can't afford to stay here, you might visit for a meal, a Moroccan dinner averaging around 85 DH ($13.93).

Peter O'Toole and the crew shooting desert sequences of *Lawrence of Arabia* stayed here.

ZAGORA: This is the last stop before the gazelle country and the desert. Zagora is a thriving village in the Draa Valley, lying 107 miles south from our last stopover at Quarzazate. From the top of Djebel Zagora, you can look out onto a panoramic view of the desert and valley. The town contains the remains of a fortress built in the 11th century by the Almoravides.

The most interesting excursion from Zagora is to **Tamgrout**, 14 miles to the south, where there is an ancient library with illustrated Korans written on gazelle skin. The oldest of these date from the 13th century. The antique Korans are displayed at the Zaouia Nasseria. In the village are several potteries, although the craft appears undistinguished.

Back in Zagora, weary travelers take delight as they approach **Hotel Tinsouline** (tel. 22), the southernmost I recommend in Morocco. It offers 100 pleasantly furnished rooms decorated in a stylized fashion, all with private bath or shower and air conditioning. A single costs 90 DH ($14.75); a double, 120 DH ($19.67). The swimming pool is a welcome sight after a trek through the desert. The overall setting of this clay-built structure is one of peace and serenity. The bar, decorated in the local style, the restful lounges, and the restaurant are appealing. The latter offers a tourist dinner for 50 DH ($8.20).

KELAA DES M'GOUNA: This oasis makes a stopover between Ouarzazate and Tinerhir. The hamlet sits on a Saharan plateau. Kelaa is a village of roses, and there is a festival every spring. Instead of the usual date palms, you'll see fruit and nut trees as well.

The **Hotel la Rose du Dades** (tel. 18) rises like a red fort over the village. Approached from a distance, it is imposing. Inside this four-star establishment, the tired visitor discovers 101 well-furnished bedrooms in the south Moroccan style. The rooms are tastefully coordinated in design, costing 120 DH ($19.67) in a single, 150 DH ($24.59) in a double. The hotel also has a large Moroccan room, as well as a modern bar, and a restaurant seating 150 guests. Typical Moroccan food is served, a tourist dinner costing 50 DH ($8.20). In addition, there is a nightclub decorated in the Saharan style. In all, it's an exotic oasis.

TINERHIR: This town—standing on a hill dominating an oasis—was once a garrison of the French Foreign Legion. The ksar of Tinerhir, a palace, can be visited; and numerous casbahs, also worth a visit, rise like tall silhouettes, looking out upon palm groves, an oasis of olive trees, and walnut trees. The flowers from the walnut trees are processed to extract the oil.

From Tinerhir you can take excursions to the **Dades or Todra Gorge.** The red ochre flanks of the mountains hem in the Todra Valley and its palm groves. The narrow Todra Gorge—some nine miles from Tinerhir—lies between steep rocky walls. The trail takes you to the top of some naked summits. From there, other trails branch off, going either to the Plateau of the Lakes (via the Tizi Tirhourghezine Pass) or over to the Upper Dades Valley, a rough journey in any direction.

From Tinerhir, it's also possible to visit the Dades Valley and **M'Semrir,** the road there passing several imposing *ksour,* ranging from palatial palaces to medieval fortresses which seem to emerge from palm groves and tamarisks. At a distance of some 14 miles you may want to turn back. The terrain the rest of the way is strictly for the most adventurous of explorers. The road is narrow and the bends are hairpins. However, the mountain scenery is of exceptional beauty, and the gorges are full of greenery. The rocks are red or mauve in color, depending on the time of day. You'll motor through the hamlet of Tinjdad, where a pastoral people make little bonnets and weave wood for djellabas. From Aremba Cliff, there is a panoramic view.

At Tinerhir, the **Hotel Sargho** (tel. 01) is a casbah-style hotel that appears so stern and imposing you'll think at first you've arrived at a red ochre fortress. Behind its thick walls, you'll enjoy comparative luxury, delighting in the coolness of some 70 comfortably furnished bedrooms, each of which has air conditioning, and contains either a private bath or shower. Rates are 120 DH ($19.67) in a double, dropping to 90 DH ($14.75) in a single. A continental breakfast costs 20 DH ($3.28). At this beautifully situated hotel, shaded galleries frame an ochre patio which is paved with bricks. In the middle is an inviting swimming pool. The hotel also has a bar and restaurant, serving a tourist menu for 50 DH ($8.20). From its terraces there is a view of the palm groves.

READER'S HOTEL SELECTION: "Although the Sargho is modern, it is expensive, catering especially to tour groups. Few individual European tourists travel through here. The **Hotel Todgha** (tel. 09) is clean, comfortable, friendly, and a double cost 67 DH ($10.98); a single, 60 DH ($9.83)—including a continental breakfast. A tourist menu is offered for 40 DH ($6.56)" (Frank L. Esterquest, Oxford, Ohio).

ERFOUD: This town of ox-blood red buildings—shaded by pepper trees and eucalyptus—is a gateway to the Sahara. At an altitude of 3051 feet, Erfoud stands near the Ziz River, at the foot of the Djebel. You can explore its *souks,* usually crowded with men in huge white turbans and veiled women. The local Jewesses are seen in their distinctive headdresses and vermilion skirts. At Erfoud you can enjoy beautiful desert sunsets over the palm groves. The best vantage point for seeing this is to take the steep trail up to the small **Bordj Est',** an old fortress.

South of Erfoud takes you to the charming oasis known as **Tafilalet,** which is kept green by the underground waters of the Ziz and Rheris. Here vegetation seems come to an end, but, before doing so, the effect of vegetation is glorious, with fruit trees, tamarisks, and date palms. The oasis, which is about 12 miles long, is noted for its dates.

You can drive south for 14 miles to **Rissani,** with its casbahs and barracks. While here, you can visit a fascinating *souk* on Tuesday or Thursday morning around 10 o'clock. If you go on Sunday, you'll get to see an authentic Saharan camel market. In the hamlet is a colorful mosque with a graceful minaret.

From Rissani, it is 1½ miles to the venerated and much restored **Mausoleum of Moulay Ali Cherif,** the ancient ancestor of the Alaouite dynasty. This bearded man was most pious, devoting (according to legend) one year to study, followed by an entire year of prayer.

Immediately west of Rissani lie the ruins of **Sijilmassa,** the famous "red town." Trans-desert caravans of long ago used to arrive here, bringing gold from the Sudan. Sijilmassa was the most westerly terminus across the Sahara. Its counterpart was Timbuctoo in the south.

Back in Erfoud, the **Si Jilmassa** (tel. 80) stands apart from the residential sector of town. At the doorway to the Sahara, it dominates a palm grove. Eighty air-conditioned rooms are rented to guests, each well furnished in a modern, functional style, and each equipped with private baths or showers. A single rents for 90 DH ($14.75), a double for 120 DH ($19.67), with a continental breakfast costing an extra 20 DH ($3.28) per person. The lounges are decorated in a characteristic Moroccan style, and there is a bar and a large restaurant, serving a tourist menu for 48 DH ($7.87). However, at certain times guests are permitted to dine under one of the huge Berber tents arranged for that purpose. The first-class superior hotel also has a swimming pool, always a welcome sight in this part of the country.

Most simple, but also possible, is the **Hotel du Ziz,** 94 Avenue Mohammed V (tel. 44), which charges 36 DH ($5.90) per person for half board, 53 DH ($8.69) for complete board. Furnishings and plumbing are minimal.

ER RACHIDIA: Once known as Ksar-es-Souk, this is a large palm grove, with a bustling market on the main square. If you're coming from Erfoud, our last stopover, you can visit the **Blue Springs**—noted for their limpid water—at Meski. Another excursion is to the **Cirque de Jaffar,** a natural amphitheater near Midelt, which is 75 miles from Er Rachidia.

Er Rachidia lies in the valley of the Ziz, at the crossing of two age-old routes, the road from Meknes to the oasis of Tafilalet and the Deep South Atlas highway to southern Algeria. From both Meknes and Erfoud, there is bus service to Er Rachidia.

The best hotel there is the **Ksar-es-Souk Motel** (tel. 184), which is modern, clean, and comfortable, with air-conditioned rooms and a pleasant restaurant, serving a tourist menu at 45 DH ($7.38). The singles here rent for 90 DH ($14.75), increasing to 120 DH ($19.67) in a double, plus 20 DH ($3.28) for a continental breakfast.

10. Casablanca

Casablanca is the gateway to North Africa. Morocco's commercial and industrial capital is essentially a modern city, and that means you won't be spending much time viewing historical monuments as you would in Fez and Marrakesh.

Big and bustling, "Casa," as it is affectionately known, charms many, but strikes others as cold and impersonal. Most travelers to Morocco eventually pass through the city, often staying over one or two nights to catch boats or make plane connections. That time can be well spent.

Casablanca, "white house" in Spanish, lies south of Rabat on the Atlantic coast. It grew haphazardly and dramatically in the 20th century. Its history before that has been confused; only in modern times has it begun to shake off its varied colonial overtones and emerge as a truly Moroccan city.

In the 18th century, Sultan Sidi Mohammed ben Abdallah rebuilt Casablanca. It had first been destroyed by the Portuguese in 1468 because it sheltered a den of pirates menacing Christian shipping on the Atlantic. The Portuguese occupied the city in 1575, staying there until 1755 when the earthquake struck Lisbon. The French occupied Casablanca in 1907.

Once all life in Casablanca was concentrated in the **Old Medina,** the original Arab settlement. Parts of it still lie behind ramparts. Like most such quarters in Morocco, the Medina is a maze of narrow streets and whitewashed buildings. Although it has a teeming center, and it's interesting to watch many craftsmen at work, and to visit the *souks,* I find the Medina here far less appealing than those in most other Moroccan cities, including Tangier. Lying northwest of the heartbeat Place Mohammed V, the Old Medina contains a Great Mosque erected under the rule of Sidi Mohammed ben Abdallah (1757–1790), but you have to appreciate it from the outside unless you're a Muslim. Three gateways—Bab Kedim, Bab El-Assa, and Bab El-Marsa—connect the Old Medina with the port.

THE SIGHTS: The **Harbor,** one of the largest in Africa, is an audacious engineering achievement. It paved the way for Casablanca's expansion and development. It is reached from the Place Mohammed V by going along the Boulevard El Hansali.

Many visitors find the **New Medina,** built by the French beginning in 1921, more intriguing than the old. It looks like a filmmaker's conception of what a medina should look like. It grew up around a palace built by a sultan after World War I and set in a high walled garden. Its chief architectural monument today is still this Royal Palace, where King Hassan II stays whenever he is in Casablanca. You can sit on the Mahkama (court of justice), built in 1941. More enticing is the *joutiya,* or handicrafts market, where you can bargain for copperware and Mediouna carpets.

The **United Nations Square** (Place des Nations Unies) is the most monumental square of Casablanca. Here you'll find the central Post Office, the Royal Automobile Club, the Municipal Theater, the Prefecture (City Hall). On this square is a branch of the Moroccan National Tourist office, corner of 2 rue Poggi. A better branch, however, is at 98 Boulevard Mohammed V (tel. 22-15-24).

Nearby is the magnificent rectangular park, **Arab League,** with its promenades and ornamental lakes.

Although you can't visit any mosques, there are two places of worship, both Catholic, worthy of being listed as sightseeing attractions. On the Boulevard Rachidi stands the gleaming white **Cathedral of Sacré-Coeur,** built in 1930 and named after the Sacred Heart church in Paris. Another European church, **Notre-Dame de Lourdes,** on the Boulevard Mohammed Zerktouni, is noted for its remarkable stained glass.

WHERE TO STAY: Transatlantique, 79 rue Colbert (tel. 26-07-61), leads all other hotels in its price category. It's a substantial, rather old-fashioned, 57-room hotel, offering abundant facilities and conveniences. On a quiet and narrow street in the heart of the city, it lies about three blocks from the Medina and is near many airline agencies, as well as the bus terminal. The salon is very Moorish; and in summer a small garden is put to use. The Transatlantique is part of a prestigious Moroccan hotel chain that includes the deluxe Mamounia in Marrakesh. You can get a double room for 130 DH ($21.31), a single for 100 DH ($16.39), plus an extra 20 DH ($3.28) for a continental breakfast.

Washington, 107 Boulevard Rahal El Meskini (tel. 26-97-77), is one of the best all-around hotel buys in Casablanca, now that it's been modernized and newly furnished. Visitors enjoy the French provincial dining room and the intimate wood-paneled bar. There are 87 bedrooms in all, each with its own fully equipped bath. Doubles are 120 DH ($19.67); singles, 85 DH ($13.93). Continental breakfast is an additional 12 DH ($1.97). The commercial area surrounding the hotel is nondescript, but comparatively safe.

Hotel Balmoral, 9 rue Reitzer (tel. 26-01-15), is a tiny, 34-room hotel in a block of modern apartments at the Parc de la Ligue Arabe. You won't get much in the way of a Moroccan atmosphere, but you will be fairly comfortable. The lounge is small, and there's an English-speaking receptionist. The cheapest accommodations have no private bath, only hot and cold running water, and these cost 60 DH ($9.83) double, 50 DH ($8.20) single. Several rooms contain showers but no toilets, and cost 65 DH ($10.65) double, 58 DH ($9.51) single. The best rooms, full baths and toilets, are 90 DH ($14.75) double, 75 DH ($12.29) single. Breakfast is another 10 DH ($1.64).

Hotel Georges V, 1 rue Sidi Belyout (tel. 22-24-48), sits impudently across from the most glamorous hotel in Casablanca, the deluxe El Mansour. Yet the Georges V maintains moderate prices. The small 34-room hotel is quite plain inside, with a "leather chair lobby," a two-passenger elevator, and painted furniture in the bedrooms. The most expensive rooms are the twins with bath, 80 DH ($13.11). Singles with bath go for 60 DH ($9.83). Bathless doubles—hot and cold running water only—are 70 DH ($11.47). Taxes and service are extra; continental breakfast is 10 DH ($1.64).

Hotel Trocadéro, 88 Boulevard Lahcen ou Ider (tel. 26-98-01), is a modern little hotel near the center of city life. The surrounding area is completely commercial, but the Trocadéro is its own oasis. The lounge and good-looking bar are paneled and stylish; there are 36 rather comfortable bedrooms. Doubles with bath cost 90 DH ($14.75); singles with bath, 70 DH ($11.47)—a continental breakfast included.

l'Hotel de Sully, 284 Boulevard Rahal El Meskini, across from the Place de la Victoire (tel. 27-95-35), is another one of those well-run little hotels that overcome their dull commercial surroundings. The de Sully is at a busy center, where major streets converge; the hotel is confined within a portion of an eight-story building. Most important, it's clean and cheap. Doubles with bath are 90 DH ($14.75); singles with bath, 70 DH ($11.47). A continental breakfast is included. There's an elevator, and a garage is nearby.

Hotel Guynemer, 2 rue Pegoud (tel. 27-57-64), is a tiny, rather undistinguished hotel hidden on a quiet and narrow street, right in the heart of the city. Yet its prices are impressive. Twin-bedded rooms with private baths go for 85 DH ($13.93), singles with bath for 65 DH ($10.65). Bathless rooms—hot and cold running water—cost 50 DH ($8.20) to 65 DH ($10.65) double, 40 DH ($6.56) single. Rooms are comfortable and immaculate. Adjoining the reception area is a sitting room where guests congregate. The rue Pegoud runs off the Avenue Lalla Yacoute which becomes the Boulevard de Paris.

Excelsior, 2 rue Noilly (tel. 26-22-81), has a "core of the apple" position, just off the Old Medina—right between the teeming life there and the fashionable promenade on Casablanca's major boulevard. It is old-fashioned, but it serves well. Doubles with private bath cost 105 DH ($17.21); singles with bath, 80 DH ($13.11). Rates include service, taxes, and continental breakfast.

Hotel Metropole, 89 rue Mohammed Smiha (tel. 30-12-13), occupies a section of an eight-floor commercial building, most convenient if you arrive or leave by bus for the airport (the shuttle stops about 400 yards from the hotel, and luggage can easily be carried). There is no lounge, but the 56 bedrooms are quite large. The doubles with private bath cost 105 DH ($17.21), and the singles with bath are 80 DH ($13.11), including a continental breakfast.

WHERE TO EAT: Al Mounia, 95 rue du Prince Moulay Abdallah (tel. 22-26-69), is the finest Moroccan restaurant in Casablanca, yet it is reasonably priced. The air-conditioned setting is palace-like; outdoor tables are placed in the front garden in summer. The traditional opener to any Moroccan meal is the local soup harrira, 13 DH ($2.13). Main-dish specialties include tajine with almonds, couscous, or pastilla, all 28 DH ($4.59) each. Moroccan pastries at 5 DH (82¢) and mint tea round out your dining adventure. Closed Sunday.

La Chaouia, 254 Boulevard Mohammed V, is a brasserie-restaurant run by Mme Gomez and M Leyrat. The restaurant is known for its oysters, one dozen costing from 38 DH ($6.23) to 60 DH ($9.83). You can dine here quite reasonably on other dishes. A fish soup makes a good appetizer, or else you may prefer the elaborate bouillabaisse marseillaise. The chef's specialty is loup (sea bass) flambé with fennel, which tastes as it does on the French Riviera. The best buy, if you're really hungry, is the sauerkraut from Alsace with pork products. A tarte maison is the final offering. For a complete meal, expect to pay from 38 DH ($6.23) to 70 DH ($11.47).

Le Petit Poucet, 90 Boulevard Mohammed V. In the old days, diners used to go here to devour lobsters. Nowadays, no one can afford this delicacy, although the sign still remains outside. The ambience is traditional; it's been a restaurant in Casablanca since 1920. Splurgers can sample half a dozen oysters from 25 DH ($4.10). The chef's specialty is grilled loup (sea bass) flambé with fennel, 37 DH ($6.06), or steak tartare at 35 DH ($5.74). The tarte maison finishes off the meal nicely at 7 DH ($1.15).

Calluaud, 10 rue Sidi Beliouth (tel. 26-99-68), across from the Hotel El Mansour, has a faithful following, and often attracts expatriate French people. You can order a set meal here for just 30 DH ($4.92), taxes and service included. On the à la carte menu, a typical beginning is the salade niçoise, followed by rouget grillé. The vin maison (wine of the house) is sold by the glass, and a plate of assorted cheeses rounds out the meal. An à la carte meal ranges in price from 35 DH ($5.74) to 60 DH ($9.83). The restaurant serves till midnight.

Le Chianti, 51–53 rue Claude Bernard, is a large, bustling trattoria on a small quiet street off the Boulevard de Paris. Run by a family and attracting families, it is decorated with a folkloric theme, complete with murals. A good beginning is the hors d'oeuvres of the house, followed by green lasagne or the risotto maison. A pizza with shellfish can also rest on your plate. A popular dessert is crème caramel. A complete meal will cost from 28 DH ($4.59) to 50 DH ($8.20).

Las Delicias, 168–170 Boulevard Mohammed V, is recommended for Spanish food. It invites with sidewalk tables and a large bar. The chef offers a daily meal for 35 DH ($5.74), including tax and service, but you pay extra for your wine. À la carte specialties include Valencian paella, tripe in the Andalusian style, and fried squid. À la carte meals range in price from 38 DH ($6.23) to 65 DH ($10.65).

Slavia, 152 Boulevard Mohammed V, is recommended only as a starvation oasis. You make your way through an arcade to reach this working person's restaurant. A set meal, in utterly basic surroundings, is offered for just 20 DH ($3.28). The cooking is simple, but all is clean and the ingredients used in the meal are fresh. Economy tip: You can buy ten meal tickets at 150 DH ($24.59) if you're waiting in Casablanca for that boat, plane, or money from home.

Saigon, 40 rue Colbert (tel. 27-60-07), is presided over graciously by its owner who still wears her native apparel—a brocaded gown and a slit skirt. This is a Vietnamese "home away from home" in far-off Casablanca, a second-floor restaurant decorated with Oriental objects of art. The entrance has become a tropical garden, with many birds and a little pond filled with fish. There is also an exhibition room for Oriental crafts. The cuisine combines both Chinese and Vietnamese specialties, with French overtones. Favorite dishes include duck with almonds and poulet sauté with bamboo shoots. Try also the well-flavored chicken soup, followed perhaps by the beef sauté. Most guests order jasmine tea to drink with their meals. Expect to spend from 28 DH ($4.59) to 60 DH ($9.83) for a complete meal here. Closed Tuesday.

À La Bonne Pizza, 65 rue Gay-Lussac (tel. 27-77-10), serves generous portions in a rustic decor. A three-course menu, including service, tax, and drink, is offered for just 30 DH ($4.92). A meal begins with minestrone or pâté, then follows with escalope milanese and spaghetti, and ends with a dessert. Specialties include cannelloni and onion tarts. A quarter carafe of wine is placed on your table as well. Pizzas are, of course, the draw in the evening.

Rôtisserie de la Reina Pedauque, 58 rue Allal Ben Abdallah, has been run by a Frenchwoman, Madame Ranzenigo, for many years. The decor is cozy, like an old French inn, with checkered tablecloths, a tiled floor, beamed ceiling, wood-paneled walls, antiques, and a spinning wheel. There's a tourist menu for 32 DH ($5.25), which entitles you to a choice of vegetable soup, hors d'oeuvres, or terrine du chef; then a leg of lamb, entrecôte, or chicken; plus a tarte maison. Taxes and service are included.

Equally pleasant is **La Lombardie,** 201 Boulevard Rahal El Meskini (tel. 26-56-85), with French and Italian specialties. The tables are placed in a row along the wall, and there are quaint arches and wood paneling. À la carte dishes include a salade niçoise for 8 DH ($1.31) or terrine de chef, 12 DH ($1.97). Osso bucco, that specialty of Lombardy, goes for 24 DH ($3.93); filet de merland doré, 20 DH ($3.28); spaghetti with tomato sauce, 5 DH (82¢); and ravioli à la carbonara, 11 DH ($1.80). There's a huge selection of other dishes, ranging from 10 DH ($1.64) to 30 DH ($4.92). Finish off with a huge almond tart for 7 DH ($1.15).

Fairly good kosher food can be obtained at **Les Archers,** 2 Boulevard Yacoute. The menu is rather limited and the decor aseptic, but you can eat well for about 35 DH ($5.74). Closed Friday night and Saturday noon.

CASABLANCA NIGHTLIFE: The most popular watering hole for Americans is **Basin Street,** 79 Boulevard de Paris, a bar/cocktail lounge/grill. American-owned Basin Street serves really fine drinks, including a dry martini at 20 DH ($3.28) and a screwdriver, also 20 DH. You can order food in these friendly surroundings—a big bowl of chili, a hamburger à la Basin Street, with lettuce and tomato. Another specialty is spaghetti à la napolitaine. Most of the snacks range in price from 16 DH ($2.62) to 35 DH ($5.74). Recorded music is played in the background.

If you're in the mood for Spanish food and entertainment, then seek out **La Corrida,** 59 rue Gay-Lussac (tel. 27-81-55). The restaurant, set in a Spanish garden, is in the center of town. Go here in the evening when you dine under palm trees by candlelight in summer. House specialties include the paella at 30 DH ($4.92) and zarzuela de pescados, a savory fish stew, at 27 DH ($4.43). At night you can watch a flamenco show, ordering a set dinner, including the cost of the entertainment, for about 55 DH ($9.02). The restaurant is closed Sunday. Otherwise, it is open from 11 a.m. to 2 p.m. and 7 to 11 p.m.

If the night is hot and the moon high, head out for the beach and **Tio Pepe,** Boulevard de la Corniche, in Ain-Diab, next to the Bellerive Hotel. The restaurant features a 45-DH ($7.38) set meal, including service. From the à la carte menu you can order paella at 30 DH ($4.92). Later you can go into the nightclub section where you'll be entertained (usually) by groups. Drinks start at 28 DH ($4.59), and the nightclub opens at 10 p.m.

ANFA AND AIN DIAB: The most beautiful residences, heavily Europeanized, lie in the suburb of **Anfa.** This quarter, reached from the Place Mohammed V, along Hassan I Boulevard, was the site of the world-famous Anfa Hotel (torn down in 1973), the meeting place of Churchill, Roosevelt, and De Gaulle for the Casablanca Conference of World War II. The conference, in January of 1943, planned the invasion of Sicily, and here Roosevelt announced that "unconditional surrender" was demanded of the Axis powers.

The coast road to **Aîn Diab** passes the **Municipal Swimming Pool** (admission 8 DH, or $1.31) and the **Casablanca Aquarium.** Facing the sea, the aquarium shelters much evidence of Moroccan underwater life, both freshwater and saltwater species. Land and sea reptiles are exhibited here, as well as sea turtles and crocodiles. Admission is only 3 DH (49¢), money well spent. After a stopover here, you can head on out along the Corniche for a day at the beach.

Should you like to overnight or dine in this sector, I recommend the **Hotel Bellerive,** Boulevard la Corniche, Aîn-Diab (tel. 36-71-92), fine during hot weather as it faces the ocean. It's on the outskirts of Casablanca, about a ten-minute drive from the heart of the city. Most bedrooms face the ocean and have private balconies; the rooms are furnished in a nondescript manner, but contain all the necessities, including armchairs, desk, reading lamps, and complete baths. You can stay here and have all three meals a day for 225 DH ($36.88) for two, 155 DH ($25.41) for one. Taxes and service are included in the rates. The lounge is homelike, the guests informal. The municipal swimming pool is three minutes away, and a bus will take you into Casablanca, although a car is preferable.

11. Essaouira

On the southern coast, this small Atlantic port, peopled with Berbers, is one of the best places to stop for a relaxing holiday along the sea for those wanting to avoid the commercialism of Agadir. On a rocky promontory, it looks out upon a bay with sandy beaches.

The white-walled town, founded in 1760 and once known as Mogador, has a certain beauty and harmony in design. The shutters and doors of its white-washed buildings are in a deep blue color. One of the boys of the town will probably attach himself to you and show you around, for a small fee, of course. There aren't many sights, other than the Great Mosque—just the town.

Its most intriguing feature is its busy, industrious inhabitants, many of whom are employed in fishing and woodworking. A specialty of the craftsmen of the town is furniture made of thuya wood. A purple dye from shellfish here was once used in the robes of patrician Romans (hence the expression, "born to the purple").

From the Skala, an 18th-century fort lined with cannons at the harbor, you'll have a panoramic view of the sea and the "Purple Islands." Allow time for a leisurely stroll along the waterfront, with its lovely gardens and mimosas and palm trees. The town's Medina is one of the most colorful along the Atlantic coast, and all visitors go shopping here. Seek out the **Société Cooperatives des Marqueteurs d'Essaouira,** the national crafts store at 6 rue Albert, which has a stunning collection of inlay work. From Essaouira, you can take a good road to Marrakesh, a distance of 106 miles. Buses run daily to Casablanca, Marrakesh, and Agadir.

HOTELS: Hotel des Iles, Boulevard Mohammed V (tel. 23-29), is the preferred choice if you can afford it. The well-run hotel faces the beach, offering about 75 pleasantly furnished rooms with private baths. Some of these accommodations are in bungalows opening onto a swimming pool. A single room rents fro 98 DH ($16.06), a double for 125 DH ($20.49). Frankly, this hotel outdistances every other choice by far. After it, we'll plunge down to the following choice which is presented for those who must keep costs bone-trimmed.

Hotel du Mechouar, Avenue Ohba Ibn Naffia (tel. 20-18), is adequate. Most of its 25 bedrooms contain private showers, and are well kept, but simple in furnishing and decor. The price is right—38 DH ($6.23) in a single, 60 DH ($9.83) in a double.

FOOD: For dining, everybody seems to head for **Chalet de la Plage,** Boulevard Mohammed V, which is a club-bistro across from the beach that has good specialties—none finer than its shellfish and well-seasoned whitefish dishes which are the pride of the chef. Both the service and the food are excellent, a meal costing around 42 DH ($6.88).

Café Restaurant Mogador stands on the seafront, overlooking the islands. A small restaurant, it enjoys a good reputation, both among locals and the foreigners who come here, for its seafood dishes. Service is polite and friendly, and the dishes of the sea are well prepared. A table d'hôte meal costs 28 DH ($4.59), although you can also order à la carte.

However, the most adventurous readers will stroll along the quayside of the port, having a lunch of freshly grilled sardines straight from the sea. Many vendors there will be happy to oblige. Just follow your nose along this scent trail. A big plate of these succulent sardines rarely costs more than 6 DH (98¢).

12. Agadir

The center of south Morocco's resort area, Agadir overlooks miles of exquisite sands and a sea where the climate permits swimming all year long. Along the Atlantic seaboard, the beach stretches for nine miles and is said to offer the safest bathing on the coast. In winter and early spring, expect daytime temperatures in the mid-70s. Summer temperatures climb to around 85; however, that is mild compared to the caldron, Marrakesh. Agadir is protected by the rugged High Atlas mountain range to the north and the Anti-Atlas range to the south. Rapidly becoming commercial, it will soon become a Moroccan Miami Beach.

It has rapidly bounced back from the disastrous earthquake of February 1960, whose violence almost completely destroyed Agadir. The old districts were demolished by the sudden devastation, a tale vividly recounted by Robin

Maugham, nephew of W. Somerset Maugham. Some 15,000 casualties were reported, and on the periphery of Agadir entire villages were wiped out.

But over the past two decades the recovery has been so rapid that Agadir has quickly regained its position as the chief tourist center of south Morocco, not that it has much competition for that title.

Seismologists predict that the chances that another such earthquake will return are slim indeed. New buildings incorporate antiseismic features. The earthquake did not entirely destroy the fishing port, which has been enlarged.

Some readers have found prices in the shops of Agadir higher than those charged at Marrakesh. Granted, the merchandise is often exquisite and much of it is geared to European and North American tastes. If you're planning day trips, hold off on serious purchases until you visit the *souks* of such places as Taroudant, where items are much more reasonably priced. In Agadir you might want to visit the municipal market on Avenue Hassan II, a two-story mall filled with shops selling every item from kaftans to silver jewelry. The air is scented with such spices as cumin and coriander.

WHERE TO STAY: Royal, Boulevard Mohammed V (tel. 224-75), is a three-star hotel, lying ten minutes from the beach and the heart of town in a tranquil residential sector of Agadir. Monsieur Georges Rignier, the friendly manager, speaks English and offers a gracious welcome. He has carefully selected a staff to provide fine hospitality and good service. The handsomely furnished rooms are with private baths and phones. If you can get one, ask for a bungalow set in a large exotic garden. Bungalows open onto a swimming pool. On top of the hotel is a bar offering a panoramic view, as the Royal is perched on a hill between the sea and the center of town. Most guests stay here on the half-board plan, which costs 150 DH ($24.59) per person, based on double occupancy. Without meals, a regular single rents for 150 DH ($24.59), going up to 200 DH ($32.78) in a double.

Another good bet is the **Hotel Salam,** Boulevard Mohammed V (tel. 221-20), which also offers bungalows, in addition to a block of 150 bedrooms. The bungalows are preferred by many, although they have different amenities and shapes. Some are quite spacious. A single rents for 160 DH ($26.22), that tariff going up to 210 DH ($34.42) in a double, including a continental breakfast. The hotel is nicely equipped, with many amenities and much comfort, everything enhanced by the cooperative staff. The swimming pool is a magnet all year, and on the premises are two restaurants, serving French and Moroccan dishes along with an assortment of international specialties. The hotel also has two comfortable bars as well, and offers a sauna and tennis courts. At certain times this hotel is likely to be overrun by tour groups.

Hotel Kamal, Avenue Hassan II (tel. 228-17), is one of the most preferred hotels of Agadir. It is not only centrally located, but offers nearly 65 bedrooms that are well furnished, clean, and most comfortable. For such a top-grade hotel, rates are 125 DH ($20.49) in a single, rising to 190 DH ($31.14) in a double. These tariffs represent good value for those seeking a "safe oasis" in Agadir. Twenty-five furnished apartments are also rented. In winter the swimming pool is heated. On the premises is a very good restaurant, serving reasonably priced meals.

Still on the major hotel boulevard, the small **Miramar,** Boulevard Mohammed V (tel. 226-73), is a real little bargain, a modern establishment containing at least a dozen rooms with private baths. Bathless singles go for 65 DH ($10.65); doubles, from 100 DH ($16.39) to 135 DH ($22.13), depending on the plumbing. The hotel is simple and functional in style, and is recommendable because of its central location and reasonable tariffs.

Less fastidious travelers who are hotel bargain shoppers may want to stroll along Avenue Kennedy. A vintage choice is the **Hotel de Paris,** Avenue Kennedy (tel. 226-94), which offers clean, cheap double rooms for just 85 DH ($13.93). Smaller singles rent for only 50 DH ($8.20). A continental breakfast is another 10 DH ($1.64).

For those on the most rawboned of budgets, I'd suggest two hotels on the Avenue Hassan II. Both are clean, but I don't want to sound more enthusiastic than that. They are completely basic, but are the super-bargains of the resort. I prefer the **Residence Mer et Soleil,** Avenue Hassan II (tel. 217-41), where singles rent for 51 DH ($8.36); doubles, 62 DH ($10.16).

Almost comparable is the cut-rate **Hotel Petite Suède,** Avenue Hassan II (tel. 228-79), a small family-run pension in the center of town. A single with a continental breakfast rents for 32 DH ($5.25); a double goes for 45 DH ($7.38). The clean, friendly hotel, where English is spoken, is the only place in the center of town to charge these low tariffs. It's also very close to the beach.

WHERE TO DINE: For just one night you may want to forget your budget and dine at **La Kasbah de Tafraout,** Avenue des F.A.R. (tel. 238-95), in the town center, opposite the Siesta. It is expensive and attracts a large number of tourists, as it serves the most carefully prepared Moroccan specialties in Agadir. Here you can sample some of the finest native dishes, including, if featured, pastilla, that rich pigeon pie. Of course, couscous, the cereal and vegetable dish with chicken and lamb, is inevitably presented. Other specialties include chicken with preserved lemon or olives and charcoal meats, served Moroccan style. The atmosphere is in the typical Moroccan idiom, with mosaic and arabesque plasterwork. Expect to pay from 80 DH ($13.11) to 100 DH ($16.39) for a Moroccan banquet.

Les Arcades, 1 Avenue Allal Ben Abdallah (tel. 234-67), is much cheaper, and it serves not only Moroccan but French specialties. The cookery is elegant, presented with elaborate style, and the fare includes well-prepared soups, native ragoûts made with lamb, pigeon, or chicken, stuffed savory pastries, and carefully chosen and recognizable main dishes from the French repertoire. Fish and meat are fresh. Expect to pay from 50 DH ($8.20) for a meal.

La Taverne, Avenue Hassan II, offers a goodly assortment of Moroccan specialties and seafood dishes. The fish from the Atlantic is often superb, especially when it's grilled. Helpings are large. On my most recent visit, the chef prepared a chicken stuffed with almonds, semolina, and raisins. The stuffing was golden and sweet, enough excitement to wake up jaded palates. Expect to pay from 50 DH ($8.20) for a meal.

La Guedra, Avenue Prince Héritier Sidi Mohammed (tel. 236-40), is your best choice if you're seeking crêpes, pasta dishes, or omelets with a variety of fillings. You'll pay from 25 DH ($4.10).

On Agadir Beach, **Jour et Nuit** (tel. 224-48) lives up to the promise of its name. It's a grill room and snackbar open all day and night, attracting a lively crowd that seems to grow more exotic the later the hour. Snacks are from 15 DH ($2.46).

LODGINGS AT INEZGANE: Visitors with cars who find Agadir too commercial for their tastes—or all the hotels booked by tour groups—may want to go to Inezgane, six miles southeast of Agadir. This is a walled village, and outside of it are several seaside hotels along the beach south from Agadir.

The French-run **Le Provençal,** Ben Sarga (tel. 31-208), is really a motel, lying ten kilometers from Inezgane on the road to Tiznit. If you'll settle for plain comfort, you'll find a single at 85 DH ($13.93), a double at 125 DH ($20.49), plus an extra 15 DH ($2.46) for a continental breakfast. In all, about 20 rooms with shower are offered. The hotel has a small pool.

13. The Anti-Atlas

If you have a taste for the exotic, often eerie landscape, then a trek through the Anti-Atlas mountains to the southwest of Agadir will prove a rewarding excursion. New and improved hotels, attracting an international clientele, have eased some of the burdens travelers of yore reported. The Anti-Atlas lie on the doorway of the vast Sahara, from which the famous "Blue Men" emerge to trade in such villages as Tiznit and Goulimine.

Roads have been greatly upgraded by the Moroccan government. Several travel agencies in Agadir run excursions in air-conditioned motorcoaches to these points. Other more adventurous readers strike out in a Landrover with a Berber tent.

The Anti-Atlas is a mountainous barrier which shields the Sous from the dry winds of the blistering Sahara. The Sous form a near rectangle. Agadir, Taroudant, Tafraoute, and Tiznit are the four points, although the desert outpost of Goulimine is also a lure.

However, a severe warning must be issued. If you venture into the Anti-Atlas in summer, especially July, you'd better be able to take the heat.

TIZNIT: Enclosed by towered walls, Tiznit is a charming sight. Its walls, four miles long, are red-washed, and machicolated gates lead to squares. Palm trees pierce the sky, and its garden oases attract the nomadic "Blue People" of the desert. In other words, Tiznit is something of a stage setting, except it is for real. Tiznit seems like a bit of greenery, surrounded by vast white sands.

On the road directly south from Agadir, Tiznit used to be a stopover point for excursionists heading for Goulimine. That desert outpost now has suitable accommodations itself (see below).

Founded in 1882, Tiznit lies some ten miles from the coast. Copper and silver-chased daggers are made and sold here. In addition, much interesting Berber jewelry of engraved silver is made here by craftspeople. A guide will be only too happy to show you through the *souk* of jewelers.

The town's accommodations range from fair to poor. The **Minzah,** 115 rue Tafoukt (tel. 139), is just adequate, but it does have a small swimming pool. Basic bedrooms with fair comfort are rented for 60 DH ($9.83) in a single, 85 DH ($13.93) in a double.

GOULIMINE: This westerly oasis could be a backdrop for *Lawrence of Arabia.* It's possible to reach it by a decent highway south from Agadir, but the run is 125 miles. It is known as a port, but only for camels, as it's surrounded by a sea of sand.

Try to go on a Saturday or Sunday at market time; otherwise, Goulimine can be a dull, desert outpost. Goulimine is famous for its so-called Blue People, who are actually nomads who wander the desert in their indigo cloaks. They emerge from the vast desert to enjoy a rest stop at Goulimine, then seem to disappear again into the vastness of the sandy sea. Many know the route all the way to Timbuctu.

You can see the Blue People in the evening at one of their camps, eating black date bread. On some times, usually Saturday or Sunday, you can watch the Guedra ritual, a provocative dance, almost erotic, by the campfire. The female dancer performs on her knees, and is almost entirely concealed by a midnight-blue robe. To guttural chants that sound like a heartbeat, she dances a spell-binding rhythm. The dancer's hands are most expressive, filled with gestures which were created and passed down by dancers through centuries. The intensity of the earthenware drums echoes through the camp.

The market begins at dawn on Saturday morning, as jellaba-clad Chleuh Berbers mix with nomadic camel drivers, each trying to work the best deal.

In this desert outpost, your best bet is the **Hotel Salam,** Route de Tan Tan (tel. 57), facing the camel market. Built in the casbah style, it offers nearly 30 rooms, about half a dozen with shower. The comfort is moderate, and the tariff is low—only 60 DH ($9.83) in a double room without bath, going up to 80 DH ($13.11) with shower, a continental breakfast included. The hotel has a bar and restaurant, serving fair food. Someone on the staff can arrange excursions into the desert.

TAFRAOUT: From Tiznit to Tafraout, a fair road cuts through 69 miles of stunning countryside and Anti-Atlas valleys to reach this town of jumbled rocks, lying under a ring of red boulders and granite cliffs. The houses here almost seem to huddle among the rocks, as they look out toward the Valley of the Cyclops. If you came here seeking an exotic landscape, you will surely have found it. Palms and gardens soften the austerity, and at almond-blossom time in mid-February the countryside is as stunning as Portugal's Algarve Coast. The best time to visit is on Wednesday, the market day.

Readers Hadley and Kate Phillips, of Lenoir, North Carolina, write: "At first we thought it was a mirage, but the four-star **Hotel des Amandiers** (tel. 08) actually existed. The bill was real, too—85 DH ($13.93) in a single, 120 DH ($19.67) in a double. In this remote desert oasis, we wanted all the comfort we could get, even though cheaper lodgings were available. A swimming pool is on the premises, and what a relief it was. Travel to blistering south Morocco in July and August at your own risk!"

TAROUDANT: From Tafraout, you can head north again along a mountain road to medieval Taroudant, a distance of some 120 miles. Taroudant is a town of stone carvers, and it's encircled by tawny-colored, well-preserved battlements and bastions. In 1520 it was the capital of the Saadian dynasty. The drive from Tafraout might be difficult, but Taroudant will prove worth the effort. It is set in beautiful gardens and olive groves in a sun-bathed landscape. Actually, if you're not taking the southern tour through the Anti-Atlas, you can reach Taroudant by daily bus service from Agadir, 50 miles away.

A tour of the walls is most popular. Frankly, I prefer it under moonlight, although others like to get up at sunrise for a trek. The journey is a distance of three miles. Later you can visit the *souks,* as Taroudant is famous for its craftsmen. Daggers, richly ornamented rifles, Berber jewelry, and hundreds of trinkets are for sale. The *souks* of local handicrafts are in the center of town.

Accommodations

Although Taroudant possesses one of the most exclusive and elegant hotels in Morocco, the **Gazelle d'Or,** those on a budget will come out a lot better at the following recommendations.

Hotel Salam, Les Remparts (tel. 130), is a converted pasha's palace, in the casbah style, with antique doors just inside the city wall. Most impressive, it offers an array of modern amenities and facilities, including two restaurants, a swimming pool, and two bars. Rooms—30 in all with private baths or showers—are attractively decorated and pleasantly equipped, costing 85 DH ($13.93) in a single, 120 DH ($19.67) in a double. The Salam has a beautiful garden as well through which peacocks wander freely. There is an abundance of fragrant flora. Horseback riding can be arranged.

A much better bargain is the **Taroudant Hotel,** Place Assarag (tel. 016). It is reached by heading down a busy little street, right in the heart of the *souk* district. To get to your room, you may have to conduct several negotiations for the purchase of jewelry. Rooms are clean and simply furnished, going for 30 DH ($4.92) in a single, 48 DH ($7.87) in a double, plus another 9 DH ($1.48) for a continental breakfast.

THE FOOD AND THE LANGUAGE

1. Menu Translations
2. Capsule Vocabulary

IF YOU FIND yourself gaping at a menu all in Spanish or at a loss for words—that's where this Appendix comes in.

1. Menu Translations

Spanish menus are a bit bewildering in that regional specialties, from Andalusia to Galicia, crop up regularly to confound the foreign visitor who has successfully learned that a *tortilla* is an omelet. If it's any comfort, vacationing Spaniards are often confused in their own country, particularly after each chef has asserted his individuality by tacking a flowery phrase on the end of such common fare as beans. Nevertheless, a basic knowledge of the essentials of the Spanish diet, from soup to specialties, from salads to salt, can save the foreign diner from the clutches of an octopus and unite him or her happily in the embrace of a lobster.

SOUPS (SOPAS)

sopa de ajo	garlic soup	**sopa de guisantes**	pea soup
sopa de cebolla	onion soup	**sopa de verduras**	vegetable soup
sopa clara	consommé		
sopa espesa	thick soup	**sopa de lentejas**	lentil soup
sopa de fideos	noodle soup	**sopa de pescado**	fish soup
caldo gallego	Galician broth	**sopa de tomate**	tomato soup
caldo de gallina	chicken soup		

EGGS (HUEVOS)

huevos escalfados	poached eggs	**huevos pasados por agua**	soft boiled eggs
huevos fritos	fried eggs	**huevos revueltos**	scrambled eggs
huevos duros	hard boiled eggs		

| huevos y "bacon" | bacon and eggs | tortilla | omelet |

FISH (PESCADO)

almejas	clams	langostinos	prawns
anchoas	anchovies	lenguado	sole
anguilas	eels	mejillones	mussels
arenque	herring	merluza	hake
atun	tuna	necoras	spider crabs
bacalao	cod	ostras	oysters
calamares	squid	rodaballo	turbot
cangrejo	crab	salmonete	mullet
caracoles	snails	sardinas	sardines
gambas	shrimp	trucha	trout
langosta	lobster	vieiras	scallops

SPECIALTIES

cochinillo asado	roast suckling pig		tomatoes, cucumbers, peppers, olive oil, vinegar, garlic
cordero lechal asado	roast lamb	jamon serrano	cured ham
entremeses	hors d'oeuvres	paella	saffron rice with chicken, seafood
gazpacho	a cold soup: raw		

MEAT (CARNE)

albondigas	meatballs	higado	liver
bistec	beefsteak	jamón	ham
callos	tripe	lengua	tongue
cerdo	pork	riñón	kidney
chuleta	cutlet	rosbif	roast beef
cocido	stew	solomillo	loin
conejo	rabbit	ternera	veal
cordero	lamb	tocino	bacon
costillas	chops	vaca	beef

POULTRY (AVES)

gallina	fowl	pavo	turkey
ganso	goose	perdiz	partridge
paloma	pigeon	pollo	chicken
pato	duck		

VEGETABLES (VERDURAS)

aceitunas	olives	guisantes	peas
alcachofa	artichoke	judias verdes	string beans
arroz	rice	nabo	turnip
berenjena	eggplant	patata	potato
cebolla	onion	pepino	cucumber
col	cabbage	remolachas	beets
coliflor	cauliflower	setas	mushrooms
esparragos	asparagus	tomate	tomato
espinacas	spinach	zanahorias	carrots

SALAD (ENSALADA)

ensalada verde	green salad	ensalada de pepinos	cucumber salad
lechuga	lettuce		
ensalada mixta	mixed salad		

DESSERTS (POSTRES)

bunuelos	fritters	helado	ice cream
compota	stewed fruit	pasteles	pastries
flan	caramel custard	queso	cheese
fruta	fruit	torta	cake
galletas	tea cakes		

FRUIT (FRUTAS)

albaricoque	apricot	limón	lemon
aquacate	avocado	manzana	apple
cerezas	cherries	melocoton	peach
ciruela	plum	naranja	orange
datil	date	pera	pear
frambuesa	raspberry	piña	pineapple
fresa	strawberry	platano	banana
granada	pomegranate	toronja	grapefruit
higo	fig	uvas	grapes

BEVERAGES

agua	water	jugo de naranjas	orange juice
agua mineral	mineral water	jugo de tomate	tomato juice
cafe	coffee	leche	milk
cerveza	beer	sangría	red wine, fruit juice, and soda
ginebra	gin		
jerez	sherry	sidra	cider

sifon	soda	**vino blanco**	white wine
te	tea	**vino tinto**	red wine

CONDIMENTS

aceite	oil	**pimienta**	pepper
ajo	garlic	**sal**	salt
azucar	sugar	**vinagre**	vinegar
mostaza	mustard		

MISCELLANEOUS

hielo	ice	**cocido**	broiled
mantequilla	butter	**frito**	fried
pan	bread	**poco hecho**	rare
panecillo	roll	**asado**	roast
tostada	toast	**muy hecho**	well done
empanado	breaded		

2. Capsule Vocabulary

		Pronounced
Hello	**Buenos dias**	bway-noss dee-ahss
How are you?	**Como está usted?**	koh-moh ess-tah oo-steth
Very well	**Muy bien**	mwee byen
Thank you	**Gracias**	grah-theeahss
Good-bye	**Adios**	ad-dyohss
Please	**Por favór**	pohr fah-bohr
Yes	**Si**	see
No	**No**	noh
Excuse me	**Perdoneme**	pehrdoh-neh-may
Give me	**Deme**	day-may
Where is?	**Donde está**	dohn-day ess-tah
the station	**la estación**	la ess-tah-thyohn
a hotel	**un hotel**	oon-oh-tel
a restaurant	**un restaurante**	oon res-tow-rahn-tay
the toilet	**el servicio**	el ser-vee-the-o

To the right	A la derecha	ah lah day-ray-chuh
To the left	A la izquierda	ah lah eeth-kyayr-duh
Straight ahead	Adelante	ah-day-lahn-tay
I would like	Quiero	kyehr-oh
to eat	comer	ko-mayr
a room	una habitación	oo-nah ah-bee-tah-thyo-n
How much is it?	Cuanto?	kwahn-toh
The check, please	La cuenta	lah kwen-tah
When	Cuando?	kwan-doh
Yesterday	Ayer	ah-yayr
Today	Hoy	oy
Tomorrow	Mañana	mahn-yah-nah
Breakfast	Desayuno	deh-sai-yoo-noh
Lunch	Comida	co-mee-dah
Dinner	Cena	thay-nah

1 uno (oo-noh)
2 dos (dose)
3 tres (trayss)
4 cuatro (kwah-troh)
5 cinco (theen-koh)
6 seis (sayss)
7 siete (syeh-tay)
8 ocho (oh-choh)
9 nueve (nway-bay)
10 diez (dyeth)
11 once (ohn-thay)
12 doce (doh-thay)
13 trece (tray-thay)
14 catorce (kah-tor-thay)
15 quince (keen-thay)
16 dieciseis (dyeth-ee-sayss)
17 diecisiete (dyeth-ee-sye-tay)
18 dieciocho (dyeth-ee-oh-choh)
19 diecinueve (dyeth-ee-nywaybay)
20 veinte (bayn-tay)
30 trienta (trayn-tah)
40 cuarenta (kwah-ren-tah)
50 cincuenta (theen-kween-tah)
60 sesenta (say-sen-tah)
70 setenta (say-ten-tah)
80 ochenta (oh-chen-tah)
90 noventa (noh-ben-tah)
100 cien (thyen)